Visual Basic 6 MTS
Programming

Matthew Bortniker
James M. Conard

Wrox Press Ltd. ®

Visual Basic 6 MTS Programming

wrox

Published by Wrox Press Ltd. Arden House, 1102 Warwick Rd, Birmingham, B27 6BH
Printed in USA
ISBN 1-861002-4-40

Trademark Acknowledgements

Credits

Authors
Matthew Bortniker
James M. Conard

Case Studies
Jason Bock
Donald Xie

Additional Material
Richard Anderson
Frank Miller
Rachelle Reese
Jake Sturm

Managing Editor
Dominic Shakeshaft

Editors
Craig A. Berry
Soheb Siddiqi
Lisa Stephenson

Development Editor
Dominic Lowe

Technical Reviewers
Mark Bell
Robert Chang
John Gomez
John Granade
Richard Grimes
Richard Harrison
Richard Lindauer
James Moore

Design/Layout
Mark Burdett
Jon McNulty
Chris Morris

Cover
Andrew Guillaume
Concept by Third Wave
Photo by Glen Graves'
Photography

Index
Catherine Alexander
Andrew Criddle

Acknowledgements

Now that I have written a book for Wrox Press, Ltd, I know why they consistently produce the best programming books on the market. It's because Wrox Press, Ltd. has the greatest editing staff in the world.

I want to thank Dominic Lowe for believing in my ideas. If it were not for Dominic, this book would never have been written. Special thanks also goes to Chris Hindley, who guided me along the initial writing process and an especially large thank you goes to Craig Berry, whom I greatly admire. I have previously worked with Craig as a technical reviewer and when I heard that he was going to be working with my book, I knew I was going to have several sleepless nights reworking my material to meet his standards. At the same time, I also knew that Craig would help me produce the best book possible; and he has – thank you Craig! Also, thanks go to Soheb Siddiqi and Lisa Stephenson who followed my progress. Both Soheb and Lisa left numerous signs along the way, letting me know they were never far away. I am also grateful for having Jason Bock, Donald Xie and all the technical reviewers, who each provided valuable advice; my thanks to each of you.

I also would like to thank my two mentors Tim Steele and Gene Stamper as well as my colleagues Cindy Kennedy, Lila Webb, Robert Boggs, and Joe Westover who covered for me while I took time off from the office to write this book.

--- Matthew Bortniker

I would like to thank everyone at Wrox for making this book come together so smoothly. A special thanks to Matt Bortniker, Dominic Shakeshaft and Dominic Lowe for allowing me to participate in this project and for helping me put my vision on paper. I hope I exceeded your expectations and I apologize for all of my delays. Thanks to Craig Berry and the rest of the technical editing team, Lisa and Soheb. You guys did a great job of taking this from a good book to an excellent book. Your ideas, input and direction were invaluable. Thanks to Richard Anderson and Richard Grimes for timely information on some of the complex details of MTS and COM+. I look forward to participating with all of you on future projects.

Thanks to everyone who has helped me over the years. Thanks to SCAN Corporation for giving me my first opportunity at age 16 when I was still in High School. Thanks to Barry Torman and the wonderful staff of developers at Progressive Business Solutions. It was at Progressive where I learned how to convey complex technology concepts to other developers. I would also like to thank Martin Gudgin, Don Box, Keith Brown, Chris Sells, Bill Vaughn and the many others who go out of their way to contribute to the DCOM and VB mailing lists. I have indirectly learned a lot from these talented individuals.

I also want to thank my loving wife Amanda for her patience over the last eight months. I promise we'll be taking a vacation soon. Thanks to my best friend Jeremy Cox for his kind words and wisdom. But most of all I want to thank the Lord Jesus Christ for his unbroken promises. It is Him, and only Him, who has given me the motivation to succeed within the true measurement of success. I'm frequently reminded of John 15:16 which places everything into perspective:

"Ye have not chosen me, but I have chosen you, and ordained you, that ye should go and bring forth fruit, and that your fruit should remain: that whatsoever ye shall ask of the Father in my name, he may give it you."

--- James M. Conard

The VB COM Series

The VB COM Series from Wrox Press is dedicated to teaching VB COM across all levels of the Visual Basic programming community - from learners to professional enterprise programmers. This series intentionally introduces VB COM to an audience that has hitherto been told that it doesn't need to know about VB COM. Our long-term aim is to ensure a mature and well-informed community of programmers who use Visual Basic.

Table of Contents

Table of Contents

A Simple Sales Order Application Case Study

Introduction

There are a great many myths and legends that have sprung up around Microsoft Transaction Server or MTS, many of which stem from the bad old days of version 1.0. However, the ugly duckling has become a swan. MTS is now an incredibly powerful method of easily building high performance, scalable applications.

Today, it's one of the foundations upon which any successful enterprise-wide application should be built. What's more, MTS isn't a completely new service that you need to spend a great deal of time learning before you can employ it efficiently. MTS is really an extension of the Component Object Model (COM), but at the same time, it's so much more. So you get the familiarity of COM programming, a great deal of which Visual Basic actually takes care of for you, combined with the significant advantages that the MTS run time confers. In fact, MTS helps out to such a degree that it actually allows you to concentrate more on the implementation of business rules rather than the complexities of programming for a distributed environment.

Therefore, the purpose of this book is to lead the Visual Basic programmer who wants to learn how to use MTS services in their own projects. If you take the time to work your way through this book, you'll not only fully understand what MTS is and how it works, but you'll soon be able to implement your own MTS applications that are secure, high-performance, scalable, and robust.

Who Should Read this Book

I've tried to write this book for anyone who has a working knowledge of Visual Basic and wants to learn about MTS. I believe that this book can be a great benefit to both the MTS beginner, and the advanced Visual Basic programmer who wants to create enterprise applications using n-tier architecture.

While it's not essential, you'll find that a basic knowledge of the COM will make your journey though this book a much more pleasant experience. Additionally, you'll find it helpful if you have some experience of HTML, ASP and Microsoft's SQL Server 7, but again, this is not mandatory.

The VB COM Series

The Wrox Press **VB COM Series** of books is dedicated to teaching VB COM across all levels of the Visual Basic programming community - from learners to professional enterprise programmers. This series intentionally introduces VB COM to an audience that has hitherto been told that it doesn't need to know about VB COM. Our long-term aim is to ensure a mature and well-informed community of programmers who use Visual Basic.

This book is the second in the series, and it builds upon the firm COM foundations of the first book, **VB COM - A Visual Basic Programmer's Introduction to COM**. However, it's not necessary to have read the previous book before reading this one.

What's Covered in This Book

The following is a brief synopsis of many of the things you'll learn over the course of this book. Keep in mind that there is much more for you to experience, including case studies and hands-on projects that give you practical experience of using MTS.

Chapter 1 begins with an introduction to Microsoft Transaction Server (MTS). We'll learn about what MTS is, its origins and why Visual Basic is a good language to use to build MTS components. Then I'll introduce you to distributed applications. We'll discuss the various types of tiered architectures, including Microsoft's vision for Distributed interNet Applications (DNA).

Chapter 2 will provide you with information and advice for installing and configuring the MTS management tool known as MTS Explorer. We'll then proceed with a walkthrough of MTS Explorer, where we'll see how to use this GUI management application.

In Chapter 3, we will review the Component Object Model (COM), including COM interfaces and creating COM objects; we'll even touch upon the Distributed Component Object Model (DCOM). We'll then move on to some deep theory about MTS architecture. Subjects such as Context Wrappers, Object Contexts, object lifecycles, processes, threads, apartments and creating MTS objects will all be covered.

Chapter 4 starts with a discussion on transactions and their four required elements, known as the ACID properties. Next, we'll learn how transactions are managed in distributed systems. We'll look at Microsoft's Distributed Transaction Coordinator (MS DTC), and see how it manages and processes distributed transactions. We'll also learn about resource managers and resource dispensers, and distinguish between them.

Chapter 5 is concerned with developing MTS components. We'll discuss, among other things, the insides of MTS components, various strategies for developing MTS components, MTS component interfaces and passing state.

Having learnt the theory of how to build MTS components, we'll actually go ahead and build some in Chapter 6. Here, we'll put together the basics of the `PasswordPersist` case study, which we'll continue to develop over the course of the next 5 chapters.

In Chapter 7, we'll see how to use MTS Explorer to manage the MTS components that we have written. To achieve that, you'll take a visual tour of MTS component and package management using MTS Explorer. First, we'll discuss what MTS packages are, and then we'll learn how to add and delete packages, as well as add and delete components from packages. Topics presented in this chapter include importing and exporting packages, and working with remote MTS servers.

Chapter 8 is all about security. We will learn about security from the ground up, starting with Windows NT security. We'll then move on to discuss COM and MTS security. We'll discover how MTS implements roles in its security model, as well as how MTS implements programmatic and declarative security.

Chapter 9 will help you solve problems with your MTS components and MTS applications. We'll discuss error handling, error messages, and how to raise meaningful errors to help us isolate problems within our MTS application. We'll also see various techniques for debugging your MTS components.

The purpose of Chapter 10 is to help you get the most out of your MTS applications, as well as the operating system on which they reside. The topics covered in this chapter include system performance, tracing and monitoring, creating alerts to let you know when something may be going wrong with your system and automating your MTS management functions with Visual Basic script.

Chapter 11 is about using MTS with data services. We'll learn database theory with projects using MS SQL Server, although the same concepts can be applied to other database management systems, including Oracle. We will also take a deeper look at MS DTC and distributed transactions.

Chapter 12 brings MTS to the Internet. In this chapter, we will learn about Active Server Pages (ASP) and Internet Information Services (IIS), and how MTS fits into the scheme of things.

Chapter 13 completes our journey through MTS with a discussion about the future of MTS and how it will be incorporated into COM+.

What You Need to Use this Book

To build the projects presented in this book, you should be using at least Windows NT 4.0 with Service Pack 4.0 as your operating system. Additionally, you'll need to install MTS services and IIS from the Windows NT Option Pack or by downloading it (for free) from Microsoft's web site. Chapter 11 is concerned with data services and uses SQL Server 7 in the examples. However the theory is fairly generic, so you can use just about any database management system, including Oracle.

Of course, you'll need a copy of Visual Basic 6. If you have Visual C++ or Visual Studio 6, you'll be able to learn to use some additional tools, not available with Visual Basic 6, which can help you debug MTS components written in Visual Basic. If you don't have access to Visual C++ or Visual Studio 6, don't worry! After all, this book is about Visual Basic and MTS, and that's where we will concentrate our efforts.

Conventions Used

I've used a number of different styles of text and layout in this book to help differentiate between different kinds of information. Here are some of the styles I've used and an explanation of what they mean:

> **These boxes hold important, not-to-be forgotten, mission-critical details, which are directly relevant to the surrounding text.**

Background information, asides and references appear in text like this.

- ❑ **Important words** are in a bold font
- ❑ Words that appear on the screen, such as menu options, are in a similar font to the one used on screen, for example, the File menu.
- ❑ Keys that you press on the keyboard, like *Ctrl* and *Enter*, are in italics.
- ❑ All filenames, function names and other code snippets are in this style: DblTxtBx

Code that is new or important is presented like this:

```
Private Sub Command1_Click

    MsgBox "The Command1 button has been clicked!"

End Sub
```

Whereas code that we've seen before, or has less to do with the matter being discussed, looks like this:

```
Private Sub Command1_Click

    MsgBox "The Command1 button has been clicked!"

End Sub
```

Source Code

All the projects that are given in this book can be downloaded from Wrox's web site at:

```
http://www.wrox.com
```

Tell Us What You Think

I hope that you'll find this book useful and enjoyable. You are the one that counts, and I would really appreciate your views and comments on this book. You can contact me either by email (feedback@wrox.com) or via the Wrox web site.

MTS and the Distributed Environment

Once you've read through this first chapter, you'll have an understanding of what MTS is and how it works within a distributed environment. I'll be introducing some other elements of the distributed environment along the way, so this is what we'll be looking at through the chapter:

- ❑ What Microsoft Transaction Server is
- ❑ What a Distributed Environment is
- ❑ Why use Visual Basic with MTS?
- ❑ What Distributed Applications are
- ❑ What tiered architectures are in a distributed environment
- ❑ The differences between 2-tier, 3-tier and n-tier architectures
- ❑ DNA – what it is, and how it impacts our vision of a distributed environment

What Is MTS?

A good place to start will be to ask ourselves: what exactly is MTS, or Microsoft Transaction Server? Here's a brief description to get things rolling:

> **MTS is a component-based model for developing, deploying, and managing secure, high performance, scalable, robust applications. Additionally, MTS is a runtime environment that supports the administration of COM components in an n-tiered environment.**

Don't worry if your mind is still trying to wrap itself around those last few sentences. After all, if you could explain MTS in one paragraph, there wouldn't be much need for an entire book on the topic!

Although this book is all about using MTS, it's important to recognize that MTS is actually just an extension of the **Component Object Model (COM)**. As a matter of fact, with the release of Windows 2000, MTS will disappear and become an integral part of COM+.

So does that mean that with COM+ we'll be able to forget everything we've ever learned about MTS? Quite the reverse: learning about MTS and using it today will not only give us powerful solutions right now, but will also prepare us for the key issues and technologies that we'll need to understand about distributed environments when COM+ is released. So now is the right time to master MTS.

As you work your way though this chapter (and indeed the whole book), you'll discover that MTS is a lot of things. Instead of trying to comprehend everything about MTS at once, begin by thinking of MTS as a set of COM services working together in a component-based application.

> **A component-based application is simply an application built from smaller specialized working parts – hence the word 'component'. For example, a Customer-Invoicing program may consist of a component that is responsible for retrieving customer information based on inputting the customer's phone number. Meanwhile, another component may provide a data grid for displaying that customer information.**

Now you know that a component-based application is built from smaller specialized working parts called components, we'll spend the rest of this chapter conducting an overview of MTS - by breaking it down into smaller parts itself.

An Overview of MTS

By the time you've worked your way through this book, you will be able to implement your own cost effective, high performance, scalable and robust applications using MTS!

Originally codenamed VIPER in 1996 Microsoft released a BackOffice component called **Microsoft Transaction Server (MTS)**, selling for approximately $2000.00. Today, MTS is an integral part of Windows NT and it is free. With NT4.0, MTS services can be installed from NT Option Pack or downloaded from Microsoft's web site. With Windows 2000 (NT5) the COM and MTS services will already be integrated into the operating system.

> **A scaled down version of MTS is available for Windows95/98. Although you can do quite a lot with this scaled down version, it's missing some key functionality – so I will be assuming that you're using the full Windows NT version in this book.**

Because MTS supports component-based applications, it allows for the separation of business logic that can be implemented into ActiveX components. Changes in business logic can easily be made without major and wide spread changes to the application. In addition, ActiveX components allow for software reuse. When developing applications, you can use components that you create, use components from a third party, or even use components that can be shared from other Microsoft BackOffice components and applications.

In addition, MTS delivers numerous features that are transparent to the developer that eliminate complex low-level programming. This allows the developer to focus primarily on the business logic for the application. As a result, the programmer is faced with less complex programming, which results in shorter development time. What's more, MTS also provides easier management, deployment, and integration for your completed components.

Any good developer will tell you that in order for an application to be successful it must provide high performance, be robust, be scalable and be secure. MTS makes it easy and cost effective to build such applications.

If all this sounds too good to believe, then read on.

What Does MTS Do? (A Brief Statement)

MTS allows developers to create these multi-user, feature-rich components – pretty much as we currently create single-user COM components.

> **Microsoft Transaction Server makes multi-user component-based development easier, period.**

How Does MTS Do That?

MTS handles all the low-level complexity of distributed application development, so we can concentrate on the actual functionality and features of our application. How does it do this?

Well, MTS provides a programmable infrastructure of its own, implemented as a dynamic link library (DLL) that hosts other in-process DLL components. It can then expose these DLLs to out-of-process clients - or even remote clients.

We'll cover the details of the MTS architecture in Chapter 3, so we'll get a chance to explore these details later on.

MTS is based entirely on COM. This way, MTS leverages a mature technology and a well-known methodology, something that's very important when you're developing enterprise level applications. Because MTS is based entirely on COM, it requires no additional run-time environment on client machines (beyond what's provided by COM). This is also why we can instantiate and invoke methods on MTS components in the same way that we usually work with any single-user component.

When Microsoft Transaction Server was first released, Microsoft estimated it would save developers 30% to 40% of the development time and cost by providing infrastructure features. I would probably have to disagree with Microsoft's initial projections: I believe MTS saves upward of 50% to 60% of the development time to create a distributed application. That's assuming, of course, that you could actually create an infrastructure nearly as scalable and robust as MTS provides. (I'm sure I'll get some emails on that statement!)

What Complex Issues Does MTS Handle?

Take your pick. MTS supports such features as:

- ❑   Transactions
- ❑   Static load balancing
- ❑   Multi-threading and resource pooling
- ❑   Fault-tolerance
- ❑   Multi-user concurrency
- ❑   Role-based security

Have you ever tried to implement efficient resource pooling or concurrency techniques without MTS? It's not fun. Each of the features I've listed here are tough to handle, but MTS looks after them for us. So I ask you: what do you plan on doing with your free time after your next distributed application project that uses MTS?

MTS is an Object Broker and a Transaction Processor

Microsoft Transaction Server is really two products rolled into one:

- ❑   An **Object Request Broker (ORB)**. MTS manages component instances and services for these objects in a configurable run-time environment.

- ❑   A **Transaction Processor**. MTS works with the Microsoft Distributed Transaction Coordinator (MS DTC) service to coordinate transactions across any number of different types of data sources.

Don't worry if some of these details are unfamiliar. We'll be examining all of the subjects mentioned above in great depth throughout the book.

It's important to remember that there are two types of equally important components that execute in MTS: **transactional components** and **non-transactional components**. Both types can benefit from the run-time services provided by MTS.

Despite its name, Microsoft Transaction Server, some consider the transaction processing capabilities to be the least important features of MTS. However, transactions play a much more vital role in *n*-tier applications dealing with distributed data, distributed users and distributed components than a typical 2-tier client-server system.

If you're not up to speed on transactions, don't worry: we'll discuss them in detail in Chapter 4.

Why Use Visual Basic with MTS?

I would venture to say that MTS is as revolutionary to distributed application development as Visual Basic was to Windows programming. Why? Because just as Visual Basic sheltered us from complex windows programming issues such as message pumps, device contexts, and memory allocation, MTS shelters us from complex distributed application issues such as multi-user concurrency, multi-threading and resource pooling.

> The question "Why VB?" can be answered with another simple answer. Visual Basic is an excellent environment for developing MTS COM components because it transparently takes care of the necessary low-level programming (often referred to as software plumbing) that COM components require.

By using Visual Basic, we don't have to worry about threading and locking issues or writing custom marshalling code. These details are an essential pre-requisite for creating MTS components, as MTS is a COM-based transaction server. So, it saves you a lot of time which you can invest more wisely by concentrating exclusively on writing components that address business problems in your problem domain. Really, the relationship of COM to MTS and Windows Programming to VB are very similar.

Both MTS and VB are about abstracting us from the details and complexities of developing software by implementing redundant infrastructure code for us.

As you work though this book, you'll learn to appreciate how efficient and time saving Visual Basic really is when developing MTS/COM components for your enterprise applications.

Visual Basic 6.0 and MTS

It's clear, then, that Visual Basic is extremely suitable for developing MTS components; but the latest version of VB, Version 6, is currently the best choice of all.

With the release of Visual Basic 6.0, MTS component development was integrated in the VB development environment. You can use the new MTSTransactionMode property of class modules to specify how your component handles transactions. Also, with Service Pack 4.0 comes the ability to debug MTS components using the standard VB debugger, rather than having to rely on other arcane methods.

Now you have some idea of what MTS is, I would like to take a quick but important detour into distributed programming, so that you have an idea where MTS fits into the larger picture of the distributed environment.

Distributed Applications

A distributed application utilizes the resources of multiple machines, by separating the application processing and functionality into more manageable portions that can be deployed in a wide variety of physical configurations. There are a number of benefits to dividing applications up into pieces, including reusability, scalability, and manageability.

The major reason for the popularity of distributed applications is the explosive growth of the Internet. Companies are finally starting to see the value of the Internet as an application platform rather than just a new advertising tool. Internet applications can be distributed out of the box, without any additional modifications required. Distributed applications are composed of:

- Distributed components
- Distributed data
- Distributed users

Once we've understood these elements of the distributed environment, we'll move on to consider:

- ❑ Enterprise applications
- ❑ Distributed architectures

Let's now look at each of these elements in turn, and gradually build up our understanding of a distributed environment.

Distributed Components

Distributed components are what make up a distributed application. These components have the ability to be located anywhere on the network, totally transparent to the application that needs to utilize them. The **Distributed Component Object Model (DCOM)** handles this transparent communication across both process boundaries and physical machine boundaries.

What does transparent communication provide us with, besides easier setup and configuration? Well, it provides an unbelievable amount of flexibility to move components from network servers to database servers or web servers to client workstations. This movement of components is the key to true scalability of distributed applications. Distributed components can be built using any COM compliant programming language such as Visual Basic, Visual C++, Visual J++, and Visual InterDev.

Distributed Data

Almost all of today's business applications are **data-centric**. Their sole reason for existence is to display, modify, delete and add data. Without the need to process data in these ways, there would be no need for 90% of today's applications.

Distributed applications not only need to deal with components in several different locations, but also with **distributed data** or data sources located in several different locations. Usually these data sources are not the same type and sometimes they aren't even relational, which is the case with email and file systems.

For example, a large Order-Entry system on the web could be responsible for managing an inventory of products in a Microsoft SQL Server database at the United States warehouse, updating an Oracle accounting database located in Germany, and storing customer information in a public folder on the corporate Microsoft Exchange Server.

Distributed Users (Disconnected Environment)

More than 40% of the personal computers sold to corporations today are laptops, intended for use in a disconnected environment. Disconnected environments add a number of other complexities to an application.

Usually these complexities are related to the transfer and management of data in a multi-user, connectionless environment. In this type of environment, users usually need to bring sets of data down locally for disconnected viewing, modification, addition or deletion of data and then merge their changes to the network database system once they connect to the network again.

> The Microsoft Data Access Components, part of Microsoft's Universal Data Access Strategy, provide this functionality, known as data-remoting. Additionally, Microsoft SQL Server 7.0 provides enhanced support for data replication to any type of data source and support for heterogeneous joins to other data sources.

Distributed Applications also have to handle international users in a modular way, so that a minimal amount of code is required to provide your applications in many different languages.

Enterprise Applications

An enterprise application can be, and usually is, just used as another term for a distributed application – but not always.

Enterprise applications are just large-scale, complex business applications. However, enterprise applications are not necessarily separated into logical pieces to make it easier to solve their requirements.

Distributed Architecture

The key word here is clearly *distributed*. Although you could run all the components of a distributed application on a single server, this would defeat the point. You therefore need to physically distribute the application across two or more tiers.

Traditional Client-Server (2-Tier) Architecture

Before we discuss any more details about distributed applications, let's review the commonly used **client-server** or **2-tier architecture**. Development applications such as Visual Basic help endorse 2-tier architectures. Take a look at VB's common data controls. No doubt, the ease of data controls allows for rapid application development. Binding a GUI client to a data source has never been easier. However, there are prices to pay for this simple architecture.

Let's look briefly at the 2-tier client-server. Typically, we have a user's PC for the client (front-end) and a network server that contains the database (back-end). Logic is divided between these two physical locations. Usually the client contains most of the business logic, although with the advent of stored procedures, SQL language routines allow business logic to be stored and executed on the database server:

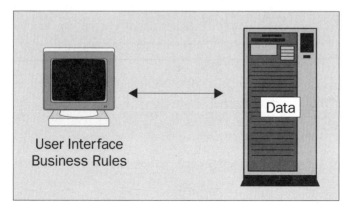

The 2-tier scenario works very well when you have a small business that only uses or needs a single data source. However, the goal of most businesses is to grow. As the business grows, so will the database and its requirements.

Business rules will also change. Whenever this happens, the application must be rebuilt and redistributed to each PC. Having to rebuild and redistribute applications make for a high cost of maintenance. As you can see, using stored procedures is the best method, as you'll only need to make these changes on the server. Of course, you need to keep the stored procedure name(s) the same.

But what if your business merges with another company that has a 2-tier system similar to yours? Suppose the other company is using a different database system such as Oracle. MS SQL server does have remote stored procedures but they are proprietary. In other words, Microsoft's remote stored procedures only work with Microsoft's SQL server. Thus, Microsoft's remote stored procedures are useless when you need information from the Oracle database.

> *Of course, you can implement another set of stored procedures on the Oracle server, but now you have two different sets of stored procedures at two different locations. By the way, don't forget that you need an ODBC driver on each client machine for each database system.*

As you can see, the 2-tier client-server is not easily scalable, thus it begins to break down as the company starts to grow.

3-tier and n-tier Architecture

Due to the limitations of the 2-tier client-server architecture, distributed applications are often divided up into three or more logical tiers or sections. Components in each of these tiers perform a specific type of processing – there's a **User Services** (Presentation) tier, a **Business Services** tier, and a **Data Services** tier in a 3-tier application.

The main distinction between this 3-tier architecture and your traditional 2-tier client-server architecture is that, with a 3-tier architecture, the evolving business logic is separated from the user interface and the data source.

Breaking up monolithic applications into these separate tiers or sections can reduce the complexity of the overall application, and results in applications that can meet the growing needs of today's businesses. Developers can specialize in designing and developing a specific tier or tiers. Applications can utilize several development tools in an application and take advantage of their best features without dealing with the shortcomings of any one specific development tool.

N-tier applications are just 3-tier applications that further sub-divide the standard User Services, Business Services, or Data Services tiers. So, for example, you might divide the Business Services into data-centric and user-centric tiers.

The Distributed Component Object Model (DCOM) is the behind the scenes coordinator that allows any number of these separate tiers or sections, implemented as groups of components, to communicate and come together to create a complete distributed application.

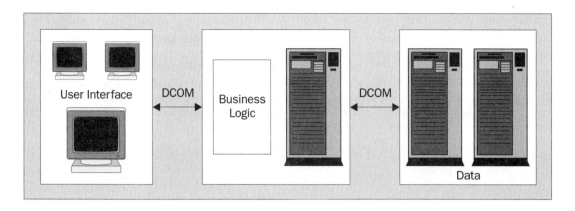

When speaking in terms of tiers, we do not necessarily mean that we have three separate machines. All it means is you have separated partitions for client, business, and data services. Of course putting all partitions on a sole machine defeats the purpose of distributed computing. However, using only two separate machines (one machine for the presentation services and another for the business and data services) is not uncommon.

Let's discuss each of these three tiers in more detail.

User Services - Presentation Tier

The **Presentation Tier**, often referred to as **User Services**, is the client or front-end that the user works with. Usually systems implement user services with a Win32 type interface, although many user services are now being developed using Internet technologies. We'll discuss the Internet in detail in a later chapter.

Visually, the front-end may not appear any different from the client for a 2-tier system. However, all business logic is completely removed from the client. Furthermore, if business components are moved to a middle or central MTS machine, ODBC only needs to be configured at the MTS machine(s) and can be eliminated from each workstation. It would be correct to say that user services are now the *client* of business services.

Because we can move business components away from the client machine, we can shift the processing load to a server. At the same time, we don't always want to ignore the potential for work to be done at the client. These days, client desktops are highly powered machines, and it's illogical to transfer all the processing to the server when we could utilize the client. This means there are two kinds of clients we can develop: **fat clients** and **thin clients**.

The difference should be fairly obvious. The 'thickness' of the client refers to how much processing goes on at the Presentation tier. A thin client would more likely be entirely web-based, so it may only be a simple browser. By comparison, a Win32 client would more normally be considered a thick client and might even carry out some rudimentary business processing.

Ultimately, the type and mechanism that the client uses should be immaterial to your business components, allowing you to deploy your application in whatever way you see fit.

Business Services - Middle Tier

Business Services are often referred to as the second or middle tier. This is where MTS and business components reside. MTS eliminates the need to write complicated low-level code so the programmer can spend more time designing the business rules for the application. Because business rules have the highest likelihood of changing, it makes sense to encapsulate business rules into components, thus separating the logic from the client. This way, when you need to make a change to a business rule, you only need to make a change to a shared component as opposed to making changes to every client application.

Needless to say, this is a time and cost efficient way to do things. In the chapters that follow, you'll learn how MTS runs the show.

> *The Object Request Broker aspect of MTS means that distributed objects can run in the MTS environment regardless of whether they have anything to do with transactions.*

Data Services - Data Tier

The Data Services in an n-tiered system operate the same way as in a 2-tiered model. Although most of, if not all of, the business logic is separated in the business partition, some use of stored procedures, triggers, and other functions may be used.

It's important for an application to have free passage to its data sources. **Universal Data Access (UDA)** is Microsoft's solution to accessing various types of data sources such as relational and non-relational databases. Of course, Universal Data Access is a COM-based infrastructure that is based on open industry standards. Specifically, UDA is a set of system-level (COM) interfaces known as **OLE DB**.

Furthermore, UDA denotes an interface at the application level called **ActiveX Data Objects (ADO)**. ADO is a programming alternative that relies on OLE DB to access data. What other programming alternatives for data access are there? Microsoft provides several less efficient technologies such as Data Access Objects (DAO) and Remote Data Objects to name but a few.

Requirements of Distributed Applications

Designing and developing large-scale, distributed applications usually means satisfying hundreds or thousands of different business requirements. What makes it even more difficult is that every design or development decision you make to satisfy each business requirement can directly affect many other business requirements. However, all distributed applications share six common **functionality requirements**:

- ❑ High performance
- ❑ Scalable
- ❑ Extensible
- ❑ Maintainable
- ❑ Secure
- ❑ Reusable

Each of these functionality requirements needs to be considered together in *every step* of the design and development processes to create a truly successful distributed application. These six functionality requirements should also be used as a checklist during the design of a distributed application's physical architecture.

High Performance

There are two general aspects when creating distributed applications that impact performance. These aspects are:

- ❑ The application design or architecture
- ❑ The coding techniques or methodologies utilized

Everyone wants a high performance application and components, however if there is no documented or planned technique of performing tasks such as database access and business rules logic, these items can often be implemented incorrectly in a distributed application.

Out of the two, the application architecture can affect the performance of distributed applications the most, and is the harder to correct after the performance problems are noticed. In fact, I would estimate that 80% of performance problems in distributed applications are directly caused by the physical architecture of the application, as opposed to the coding techniques. Physical architectures are usually flawed due to an incomplete or undocumented application design. These flaws in distributed application architectures are often due to:

- ❑ Re-execution of time-consuming logic
- ❑ Location of components
- ❑ Database access techniques.

Performance problems are also attributed to the increase in the number of users and the scalability of a distributed application. Because there are so many different ways to architect a distributed application, it's very important to always consider the impact on performance when you are designing a distributed application.

When it comes to high-level languages such as Visual Basic, they're great in the fact that there are many different ways to accomplish the same task. This is the reason VB is such a good rapid application development (RAD) tool. However, these many methodologies or techniques for solving a problem accommodate poorly written code that results in lousy performance.

There isn't much we can do in a design phase to positively impact performance in distributed applications, except clearly define and document standard techniques in certain key programming areas, and always consider performance impacts throughout the development process of any application.

Scalable

Scalability works hand-in-hand with performance. Contrary to what most developers think, scalability is not just another Microsoft buzzword. Scalability actually is the process of an application meeting the growing needs of a business. As a business grows, more-and-more users need to utilize your distributed application. Your distributed application has to **scale** or meet this need of additional users with little or no modification. I've often heard the question, "I'm developing an application for a small group of users, why do I have to worry about scalability?"

> **What's interesting about scalability is that if you don't want to concern yourself about it now, you don't have to. However, if you don't concern yourself about scalability now, by the time you're forced to it won't be just a concern, but instead a major problem.**

Many developers mistakenly believe that distributed applications developed using this 3-tier model are all scalable. Although a distributed architecture is key to scalability, consideration must be given when developing the distributed components. As I mentioned before, the tiers in the 3-tier model are logical not physical. That is, the tiers in the 3-tier model can exist all on one machine, each on a separate machine or any configuration in-between. However, scalability deals directly with the physical architecture rather than the logical architecture.

Making a distributed application scalable usually involves spreading application processing across multiple machines. These machines are not always additional database or application servers, but also client workstations. In fact, the more application logic you can put on a client workstation the easier your application will scale with more users. Think about it: every time you add an additional client, an additional processing overhead must be incurred somewhere.

Why not have it on that additional client workstation that you're adding already, instead of creating an additional burden on the already overworked server(s)? Ironically, when you look at today's typical client workstation, most of them are often under-worked. They have more processing power than they know what to do with.

Well, that all sounds great, we'll put our business logic, database access, and user interface on the client machine - and just used a shared data storage system. We've done that already: it is called client-server architecture and that has two main problems.

Database connection(s) per client

In a client-server architecture, the client was responsible for the application logic, user interface and storage system access. The client application would create a connection (if you were lucky, although it usually ended up being several connections) to the database or data storage system. It would hold on to this connection for the life of the application.

This works fine for a few users, but imagine what happens when you want to create a web front-end for this client-server system that must support thousands of sustained users. Thousands of users, each holding expensive database connection(s) will quickly kill your database server(s). So the client-server architecture did not easily support Internet front-ends because of the usual high number of users associated with them.

No easy way to share and maintain changing business logic

In a client-server architecture, it was often desirable for the server to store shared business logic because it was easier to maintain centrally located code, especially when this code usually changes as a business' needs change. This business logic code was often exposed through stored procedures stored in the database system itself. However, this required knowledge of a specific vendor's SQL dialect, and could only be used when accessing a relational database system.

The only real solution to providing a scalable architecture is not at either extreme, but rather somewhere in the middle. By sharing application processing between shared servers and client workstations, you can create scalable and easily maintainable distributed applications.

Easily Maintainable

Without proper planning and documentation before a product goes into a development phase, several programmers can be assured a job for several years. Any of you who have ever had to maintain someone else's undocumented code knows it's not a fun task. A design document, that describes the details and inner workings of an application, can accommodate for a lazy programmer's lack of in-line and procedural comments, and thereby create a maintainable distributed application.

However, maintainability is not just limited to a few lines of code. In distributed application development the architecture of the application must also be maintainable. Distributed applications are composed of many dependent components, utilizing different types of technologies and often spanning several machines. Therefore, deployment of new and updated versions of software must also be considered in the design process to determine the application architecture that will be used.

> An application's maintainability doesn't matter as much with the desktop and small client-server implementations. But when you're creating enterprise level applications, expected to be used over the next decade with hundreds to hundreds of thousands of users, your distributed application better be easy to manage.

Your distributed application should provide a set of tools for managing users, storage system backups/restores, and deployment.

Extensible (Open Architecture)

This goal of a distributed application is the most influenced by having or not having a well-documented design. Without any documentation or blueprints of a distributed application, it's very hard to go back to that application a year, or even 6 months, after development, and add enhancements or features without breaking the rest of the application. It isn't impossible to create an extensible or open-architecture distributed application without a design, it's just painful in the long run.

In distributed applications, extensibility begins with well-defined COM components. When I refer to the definition of COM components, I'm referring to the interface(s) of the component. If an application is modeled after Microsoft DNA strategy it will be a modular, open-architecture system that easily integrates with existing database, message queuing and web-server systems now and in the future.

Remember that your application must not only support an extensible or open architecture right now, but also for the lifetime of the application.

Secure

In distributed applications, the security can be divided into two categories:

❑   Data Security
❑   Application Security

Let's take a look at these two categories now.

Data Security

Data security deals with securing a system's resources (any types of data) from unauthorized access. With 2-tier applications, the database or data sources are responsible for authenticating users' requests for data. But with distributed applications, the clients never access resources directly. Instead, all data source operations are routed through business service and data service components.

We must protect data sources from access by unauthorized clients, but still allow access to components executing on the behalf of clients. Data security also includes ensuring data is securely transferred across a network or the Internet.

Application Security

Application security involves restricting unauthorized users from accessing processes, components and interfaces that perform operations to resources on the behalf of a client. With all data source operations being routed through components, we can take a proactive approach to security and authenticate users when they call components instead of when they reach the data source.

Reusable

With the cost and time involved in creating today's enterprise applications and the increasing requirements of these enterprise applications, both corporation and developers want to base their distributed applications on sets of reusable components.

Component-based development has been popular for several years now in desktop and client-server applications, and distributed application development couldn't exist without it. Binary, reusable components save time/money every time they're reused, also providing one code-set for bug fixes and enhancements.

Distributed interNet Architecture (DNA)

> "The Windows DNA architecture consists of a set of rich system services and component based application services that support open technology standards, all exposed in a unified way through the Component Object Model (COM)."

Yeah, sure: that explains everything. The Windows Distributed interNet Architecture (DNA) is one of those concepts that's difficult to shorten into one sentence, draw four lines around and position neatly in a box. However, don't let the long acronyms and terms scare you. DNA is not a new technology, it's not even a new object library.

The Windows DNA framework is simply a model for efficiently designing and developing distributed applications that meet our six common goals, by utilizing a comprehensive set of existing application and operating system services. This framework defines dozens of the services available and the products that provide these services to create 3-tier or n-tier distributed applications that can run on any network from your local LAN to the Internet.

> **What's great about DNA, is that it's an** open **model. You don't have to learn about every service and product that provides the service to utilize and understand the DNA model.**

Products that are not built into the operating system provide **Application Services**. Application services are usually targeted at providing a set of functionality for one specific tier. However, they can be utilized on any tier(s) in a logical 3-tier or n-tier model. Application Services are not built into the operating system, so their execution has to be managed through a configuration application or the services applet in the Control Panel.

Operating System Services, by contrast, are built into the operating system and execute totally transparent to the users. An example of an Operating System service is DCOM. It doesn't need to be started or stopped like other Application services, because it is always running.

When we talk about Operating Systems services, we are referring to Windows NT 4.0 or Windows 2000 as being the operating system required for most Windows DNA services.

DNA is about Infrastructure

DNA actually makes developing distributed applications easier, because it's all about using these application and operating system services to minimize the amount of infrastructure code required to create a distributed application.

Just think about all the times that you wrote hundreds of lines of code to provide transaction processing, message queuing, security, or custom database access in your applications. Now imagine all of these distributed application requirements being lifted off your shoulders. Instead Microsoft will take care of these details for you, by providing you with a set of efficient and programmable services, leaving you to concentrate on the business requirements of the application.

> **The bottom line is developing distributed applications by the Windows DNA model will result in higher performance, more reliable, and scalable distributed applications, delivered faster than every before, at a lower cost.**

Before DNA, usually only large-scale or enterprise applications distributed application processes. However, because of the application infrastructure, Microsoft continues to build and enhance its applications, to make it easier to develop distributed applications. Soon many of your smaller network applications will be using the DNA model instead of your traditional client-server model.

DNA is about Interoperability

DNA can interoperate, or use what's already there, with existing legacy systems, so that you can leverage and extend current technology investments. Try telling the Chief Information Officer of a medium-size manufacturing company that you want to scrap all of their existing software and hardware so you can develop new distributed applications based on the DNA model.
It won't happen – just like converting all companies that use Oracle database systems to Microsoft SQL Server 7.0 database systems.

Microsoft has finally realized that not everyone will or can afford to convert every legacy system to run on the newest Microsoft platform. The evidence of this discovery can be found in the DNA model, with its interoperability and support for industry standards. For example, the Windows DNA model supports the open Internet standards for HTML and XML.

DCOM allows applications to communicate across processes and across machine boundaries to compiled components that provide services. It allows developers to create service-based applications while using component-based development methodologies.

While DCOM is mainly a Windows platform service (I say mainly because DCOM has been ported over to some versions of Unix) the open Internet standards supported by the Windows DNA model ensure that you can create cross platform distributed applications.

Universal Data Access (UDA) also affects interoperability. Just think about it. Most of the time you need to work with existing legacy systems because they store legacy data.

UDA is implemented by several sets of technologies all sharing the same methodology: providing data access to all types of data from all different sources, both relational and non-relational, using the same data access library. UDA allows you to use the same data access library to run queries against your SQL Server database and your legacy AS400 databases.

DNA is about the Internet

When Microsoft introduced the DNA architecture in September 1997, they introduced a framework for creating new Internet applications as well as integrating the web with already existing client-server and desktop systems. The Internet is a great application platform for two main reasons:

❑ The Internet allows developers to create applications that are platform independent without making developers learn a new proprietary language
❑ The Internet provides a flexible mechanism for deploying applications

Deployment is a major problem for lots of organizations, especially when you're talking about deploying a large-scale, enterprise application to several separated locations. We divide applications that integrate web technologies defined in the Windows DNA framework into four separate categories:

Browser-Neutral

Browser-Neutral applications support current HTML. Although nothing fancy, this technology is designed to work regardless of the type of Internet browser being used. Because browser-neutral applications are not as flashy as many multimedia enhanced sites, this technology tends to be practical for generic online documentation such as published by libraries and schools.

Browser-Enhanced

Browser-Enhanced applications tend to be browser specific. In other words, Microsoft's browser supports different enhancements than Netscape's browser offers. Because of the lack of cross platform abilities of these browsers, browser-enhanced applications work best with intranets. This allows intranet applications to take full advantage of a browser's enhanced capabilities. As an example, Microsoft browsers take advantage of ActiveX Controls, VB Script, and Microsoft enhanced DHTML.

Internet-Reliant

Internet-Reliant applications are clients that must be connected to the Internet in order to operate. These are fully-fledged applications located on the client machine, as opposed to web-based applications that are run within a browser. An example is a stock-ticker application that must constantly be connected to the Internet in order to receive data.

Internet-Enhanced

Internet-Enhanced applications offer the most functionality. They are written using the Win32 API, and are designed to work as stand-alone applications that are also equipped to take advantage of the Internet. Most Microsoft products such as Visual Basic, Visual Studio, Microsoft Office, and Microsoft Money are Internet-enhanced as they support Internet technologies.

> **Microsoft Money is an excellent example. As a stand-alone application, you enter your financial information and run basic reports. As an Internet enhanced application, you can pay your bills online while browsing the latest financial review without having to leave the application.**

Because DNA supports Internet applications, the distinction between Windows (Win32) applications and web applications is fading. Many Win32 applications are currently Internet-enhanced, and as users become more accustomed to Internet applications, they will demand what we refer to as Internet-Dependant applications. And with the new support for developing web applications in Visual Studio 6.0 we, as developers, will be ready for the demand and probably encourage it a little.

We'll discuss Internet Applications more in Chapter 11, but it's important to know the major benefits of using the Internet as an application platform, so we can more easily analyze our application designs, have a clear perspective of optional architectures and understand what DNA contributes to Internet development.

If you plan to use the web in any way to build distributed applications, the Windows DNA architecture will help you, because it describes how to take advantage of an existing infrastructure on the Windows platform for web applications.

Why Visual Basic and DNA?

Choosing the right development tool is essential to implementing any successful distributed application. To create scalable and high performance distributed applications, no one tool can do it all. As an enterprise developer, knowing how to leverage the best qualities from each development tool can provide extraordinary benefits.

Some of you may be flipping back to the title page by now, double-checking that this is a Visual Basic book – and wondering why we're discussing different development tools...

Well, as experienced Visual Basic developers, we all know that Visual Basic is a great development tool for creating Windows and now web-based applications. However, we also all have to admit that there are some things that Visual Basic just can't do quite as well as other tools, like that other product named Visual C++. We've all been in the same boat, defending Visual Basic to those Visual C++ gurus, as the best tool for developing Windows applications.

What's great is that with the release of Visual Basic 6.0 Enterprise Edition, the Visual C++ developers are losing their bragging rights. Visual Basic 6.0 brings improved native code compilation, faster string handling capabilities, and advanced debugging capabilities directly from the Visual Basic IDE. In addition the Enterprise Edition provides:

❑ Integrated Visual Database Tools for defining database structure and creating stored procedures on Enterprise Database systems such as SQL Server 7.0, Oracle 8, and AS/400 databases.

❑ Access to the Microsoft Repository through the Visual Component Manager 2.0 interface, for storing code, objects, and compiled components so they are available for reuse by other developers within your team or organization.

❑ Integration with Visual Modeler 2.0 for designing and implementing multi-tier applications through the use of modeling and round-trip engineering.

❑ Profiling and analysis of compiled Visual Basic multi-tier applications through the use of Visual Studio Analyzer.

❑ Easier deployment of components and applications through the totally revised Packaging and Deployment Wizard, formerly know as the Application Setup Wizard.

With these new features and capabilities Visual Basic is definitely the best tool for *rapidly* developing distributed applications. It's still true that Visual C++ creates the fastest and smallest components when developed using Active Template Library (ATL). However, these performance gains can be negligible or non-existent, especially if most of the component's execution time is just utilizing other COM components.

DNA Services

Let's now get a quick introduction to some of the services that DNA defines, as we'll be seeing them again throughout the book.

MTS

We have learned that distributed applications share six common functionality requirements. Because MTS and DNA go hand in hand, lets look at each functionality requirement and see how they apply to MTS.

High Performance

MTS provides and manages numerous high performance services such as security, transaction processing, and the sharing of resources. Because these high performance services are already provided with MTS, developers don't need to worry about how to incorporate these services into their applications. As a result developers can spend more time developing business logic while MTS provides high performance services.

Maintainable

Integrated with MTS is a graphic user interface (GUI) management system referred to as the MTS Explorer. The MTS Explorer provides an easy way of deploying and managing distributed MTS applications with a simple point and click of the mouse.

The MTS Explorer also allows you to administer remote MTS machines. You can even import and export MTS components to and from other MTS machines.

Extensible

MTS systems are flexible in that they allow you to take legacy systems and integrate them with today's technology, and grow into future technologies as they come into existence. For example, an MTS application can easily be incorporated to work with other technologies such as databases, message queuing, and web services without major changes being made to the original MTS application.

Scalable

MTS provides numerous features that provide scalability. For example, MTS closely works with services that can manage database connections. As more users require information from a database, MTS can dynamically increase the amount of database connections to meet the demand. Furthermore, MTS can dynamically release database connections as the demand for database access decreases.

MTS also has the ability to run multiple servers. As more simultaneous demands are made on a MTS server, additional MTS servers can be added, thus providing scalability to the overall MTS system.

Secure

MTS provides distributed security services that build upon Windows NT security model. As a result, MTS makes it easy to prevent unauthorized access to MTS applications.

Reusable

The component object model (COM) is a specification based on a binary standard for reuse through interfaces. This means that a COM component can be reused without any dependency from the language it was written in. Because MTS is an extension of COM, and thus component-based, MTS allows for software reuse. For example, Business rules that are implemented as a MTS component can be shared among numerous clients. Furthermore, you can develop MTS applications from components that you created or obtained from third-party sources. You can even share components from other applications.

COM

Before we start working with MTS, you should have an understanding of COM. COM is the acronym for **Component Object Model** and is an outgrowth of the object-oriented paradigm. COM is a specification that is based on a binary standard for reuse through interfaces.

This means that components written for COM can be reused without any dependencies from the language it was written in. It doesn't matter, for example, if an application contains components written in Visual Basic, C++, Java, or even COBOL – as long as these components follow the COM specification. We'll be discussing COM in more detail in Chapter 3.

DCOM

The **Distributed Component Object Model** (DCOM) is probably the most important product of Windows DNA. DCOM is actually an infrastructure unto itself, based on extensible and highly supported COM.

However, contrary to what most developers think, DCOM is not a separate service: it's just an extension to COM or, as it is most often called, "COM with a longer wire". We'll also be covering DCOM in more detail in Chapter 3.

MSMQ

Microsoft Message Queue (MSMQ) is designed to allow DNA applications to undertake one-way (asynchronous) communication. Through message queuing, messages can be guaranteed that they will eventually be delivered even if receiving application(s) are down.

Another attractive feature of MSMQ is it furnishes an OLE Transactions resource manager. Through this resource manager, message queues can be treated as transactional resources. In other words, you can make the delivery of a message to the message queue transactional. Simply, if the message fails to be created or delivered, the transaction will abort. You'll learn about transactions in detail later in this book.

IIS

Internet Information Server (IIS) brings to Windows DNA powerful web features such as Active Server Pages (ASP). The beauty of IIS is that it's integrated with MTS. This means that web applications can make use of COM components and utilize MTS services such as transaction management and connection pooling.

IIS is administered through the Microsoft Management Console (MMC) using the IIS snap-in. You'll learn about the MMC and IIS administration in later chapters.

SQL Server

Windows DNA would not be complete without free passage to data sources. A sound choice for your data source is Microsoft SQL – a high performance and scalable relational database management system (RDBMS). MS SQL Server provides enhanced performance with scalability. It has the ability to utilize multi-processor technology without the need for complex server reconfigurations. The benefits of executing a single transaction across multiple processors not only adds to SQL Server's scalability, it can greatly enhance performance and throughput.

Perhaps the best reason to use MS SQL Server is that the MS Distributed Transaction Coordinator (MS DTC) seamlessly integrates with MTS. This is a very powerful feature that allows an application developer to concentrate on developing business logic as opposed to being concerned with how to deal with transaction management.

Summary

We've learned a lot in this first chapter. Here's what we covered:

- ❑ What MTS is
- ❑ Why it's a good idea to use VB with MTS
- ❑ The Distributed Environment
- ❑ Microsoft DNA

We discovered that MTS is a component-based model for deploying, developing, and managing secure high performance, scalable and robust applications. We also discussed why Visual Basic is an excellent choice for developing MTS COM components.

Then we moved on to consider the distributed environment; including the functionality requirements for distributed applications and the different types of distributed architecture, from basic client-server to n-tiers. Finally, we had a quick introduction to Distributed interNet Architecture (DNA).

You should now have a basic idea of how MTS fits in with the distributed environment, and some of the other players in the game. We'll be developing many of the threads introduced here through the rest of the book.

Our first stop will be to take a quick look at MTS in action and familiarize ourselves with the MTS Explorer. Then we'll dive in under the hood and examine the underlying architecture of MTS. So what are we waiting for?

2

Introducing the MTS Explorer

Now that you've been introduced to the concept of MTS, we're going to get a bit more practical and explore its GUI interface. This chapter will introduce you to MTS Explorer. However, instead of reading about the different features MTS Explorer has to offer, you will take command of MTS Explorer in a hands-on exercise. In other words, if you really want to learn how to configure and maneuver around using MTS Explorer, you'll want to be in the driver's seat.

The first part of this chapter will provide you with a visual and practical tour of MTS Explorer using Microsoft Management Console. Taking this tour will allow you to become familiar with many features that MTS Explorer has to offer. Then in the second part, you'll get the opportunity to see a small VB project running in MTS so that you have some idea of MTS in action.

After completing this chapter, you should know:

- ❏   The hardware and software requirements for MTS
- ❏   How to configure the Microsoft Manager Console
- ❏   How to navigate around the MTS Explorer
- ❏   How to import a package into the MTS Explorer.

MTS Installation

MTS 2.0 can be installed from the Windows NT 4.0 Option Pack or from the Visual Studio 6 Enterprise installation disks. MTS can also be downloaded from Microsoft's web site.

MTS can be used with Windows95/98 using DCOM support. Remember, MTS for Windows95/98 is scaled down, thus it does not provide complete functionality.

Before you start to install MTS, make sure that your machine meets the minimum requirements as stated below:

- ❑ Any Windows NT computer with an NT supported display, and a suitable pointing device
- ❑ A minimum of 30 megabytes of free disk space
- ❑ Although Microsoft states you only need 32 megabytes of memory, you really should have a minimum of 64 megabytes of RAM
- ❑ A CD drive if installing from a CD-ROM, although you can download MTS from Microsoft's web site

In addition to hardware requirements, you should be aware of a few software requirements before installing MTS:

- ❑ If you're using Windows NT 4.0 Server, you should have Service Pack 4 or greater installed. Microsoft has released Service Pack 5 for Windows NT.
- ❑ If you plan to use SQL Server 6.5 (all versions), you must install it before installing MTS. This is because SQL Server 6.5 writes over the registry setting for MS DTC. This inconvenience has been eliminated with SQL Server 7.0. However, to play it safe, take an extra five minutes and reinstall MTS as well. Also, be sure to use the latest service pack available for SQL Server. Service packs can be downloaded from Microsoft's FTP site.
- ❑ If you plan to use an Oracle 7.3.3 or greater database, contact Oracle Technical Support for an available patch.

Keep in mind that if you need to reinstall SQL Server, you'll need to reinstall MTS as well. This is because SQL Server has a tendency to overwrite registry settings that MTS needs.

It's time that you configure your own machine for developing MTS applications. Because SQL Server is a vital part of MTS, now's the time to install it as well (although we won't actually be using it until Chapter 10). As soon as you have installed both items, you're ready to learn to move around in the Transaction Server Explorer.

The MTS Explorer

The **MTS Explorer**, or **Transaction Server Explorer**, is a GUI administration tool that looks similar to the Windows NT Explorer and is primarily used to administrate MTS. Through the MTS Explorer, the administrator can work with components on any machine that is a part of the enterprise.

Microsoft Management Console

The **Microsoft Management Console (MMC)** is a new feature that installs from the Windows NT 4.0 Option Pack.

The MMC can also be downloaded from Microsoft's web site.

The MMC provides a common management environment for **snap-ins**. Snap-ins are administration components that can be integrated into a common environment, such as the MMC. Just such an example of a snap-in (administrative component) is the MTS Explorer. The goal of the MMC is to allow management applications to be accessed from a single user interface.

> *The MMC is nothing more than a host that contains management snap-ins. MMC does not have any management properties of its own.*

If you installed MTS from the NT 4.0 Option Pack, MMC will already be installed. Let's take a look at the console. Go to the Programs menu and find the folder Windows NT4.0 Option Pack. Find and click Transaction Server Explorer under Microsoft Transaction Server. This will launch the MMC (you should see the splash screen) with the MTS Explorer snap-in already set up:

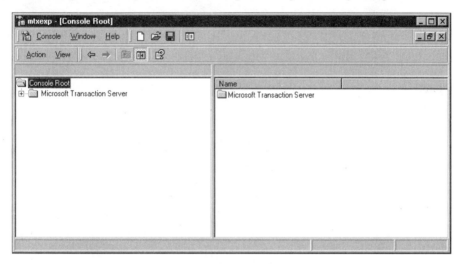

Now that you've opened the MTS Explorer and seen that it's a part of the MMC, go ahead and close it! This time, go to the Run command prompt and type in MMC. Microsoft Manager Console again opens, but notice that this time the MTS Explorer snap-in is not currently loaded:

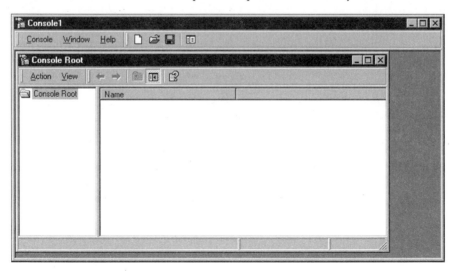

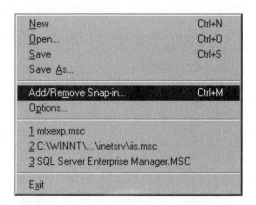

From the top tool bar, click <u>C</u>onsole and then
click Add/Re<u>m</u>ove Snap-in:

*MMC lists the most recent Microsoft Console files that have been opened. This is similar to the
recent Word files listed at the bottom of the <u>F</u>ile menu in MS Word. Notice that just above E<u>x</u>it
on the dropdown menu, you see <u>1</u> mtxexp. This is the previous instance of the MMC we just
opened for the MTS Explorer. The second item, <u>2</u> C:\WINNT\..\inetsrv\iis was created when I
installed IIS.*

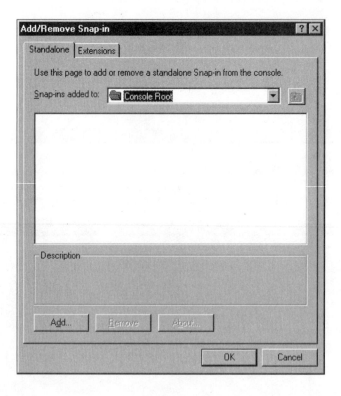

Click the Ad<u>d</u> button at the lower left and the Add Standalone Snap-in dialog will appear:

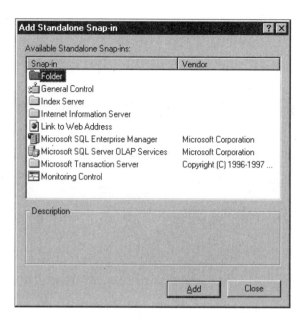

Highlight Microsoft Transaction Server and click A<u>d</u>d. Now highlight Microsoft SQL Enterprise Manager and click A<u>d</u>d.

> *If you've not installed Microsoft SQL Server 7.0, Microsoft SQL Enterprise Manager will not be listed in the Add Standalone Snap-in dialog.*

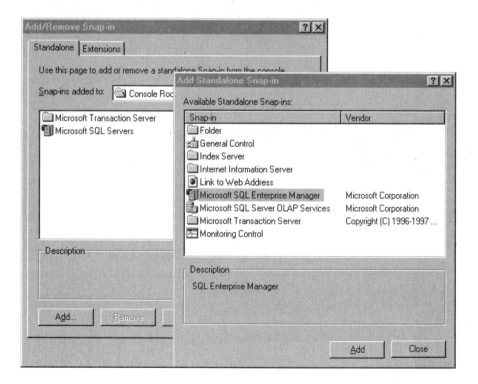

Notice when you click the Add button each selected snap-in is put into the list area on the Add/Remove Snap-in dialog. Click Close from the Add Standalone Snap-in dialog and then click OK from the Add/Remove Snap-in menu. You should now see both MTS and SQL Server as branches of the Console Root node:

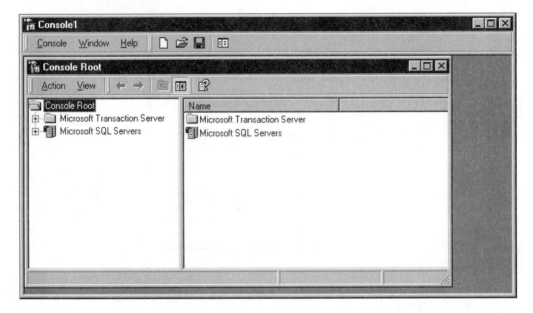

From the Console menu on the Console1 bar, select Save As... and enter a meaningful description such as MTS and SQL Server in the File name text box. Notice the file type msc in the text box labeled Save as type. This means that the file you're creating is a Microsoft Management Console file (MSC). MSC files are referred to as 'tools'.

Notice that you've created a dynamic menu entry in the Console menu. Remember MMC loads the most recent Microsoft Console files that have been opened. This can be handy for quickly opening your recent configurations:

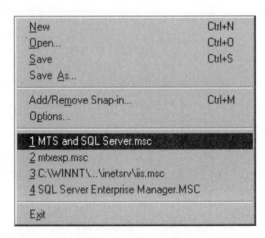

Be sure to look in your folder My Administrative Tools from the Programs menu in Start.
Open My Administrative Tools and you should see that a reference has been created called
MTS and SQL Server.

As you can see, with this particular configuration, you can manage both Microsoft SQL Servers and
Microsoft Transaction Server:

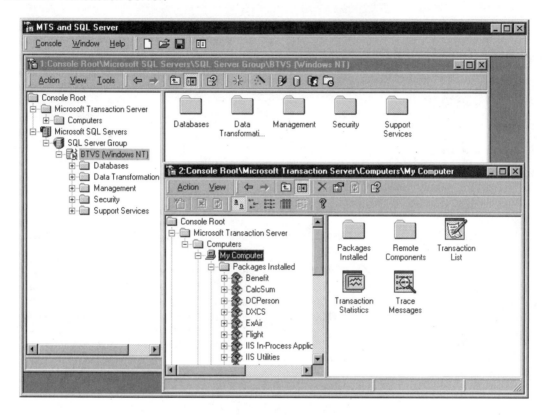

By clicking Window from the main menu bar you can run a different snap-in in each window.

For now, we want to concentrate on the MTS Explorer. Click on Console from the main menu bar
and this time select the menu option for MTS only. Remember that MTS Explorer is a snap-in, so it
will be in the MMC environment.

From the MTS Explorer, highlight the Console Root folder in the left-pane and then press the
asterisk key to open all the folders in the left-pane:

By highlighting the root folder and pressing the asterisk key, you can quickly open the folders and
sub-folders. This is an efficient way to see what's available. Consequently, highlighting any folder
will display all sub-folders.

Once you've had a play opening the various branches available, close the folders to match the screen shot below:

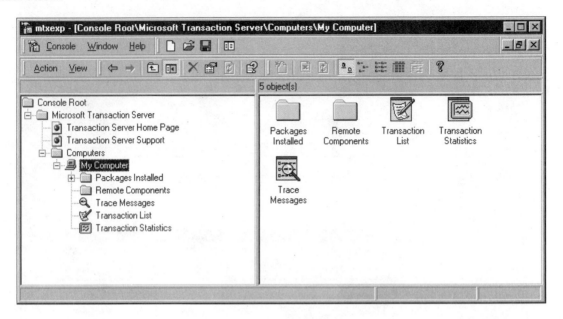

Before you go clicking around in the explorer again, highlight My Computer. First, notice the color of the My Computer icon in the left-pane. If the icon has a bright-green glow, it indicates that the MS DTC services are running. Conversely, if the icon has a dull-gray color, it means that the MS DTC services are not running. When the MS DTC services are starting you may be lucky enough to briefly notice the icon turn yellow.

Now I want you to click the Action menu:

The Action menu shows different options depending on what icon you highlight. You can also highlight an icon and then click the right mouse button. By highlighting My Computer and right-clicking your mouse, a pop-up menu appears that's almost identical to the one above.

Now go back to the items in the left-pane. Directly under My Computer is a folder called Packages Installed. Open the Packages Installed folder:

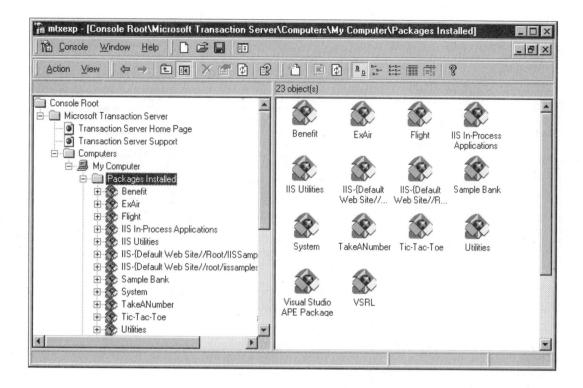

In this example, you see a list of packages that are installed on my local machine. These packages are not necessarily the same as the default packages that will automatically be installed on your machine.

The first object you should see is called Benefit. This is referred to as a **Package Object**. A package is made up of a group of components that execute in the same server process. Typically a package contains components that are closely related.

Packages can be added by highlighting the Packages Installed folder in the left-pane and right-clicking with your mouse (or using the Action menu, but the right-click option is usually the easiest). Clicking New and then Package will launch a wizard. Deleting a package is as easy as highlighting the package, either in the left- or right-pane, and hitting the delete key. You can also highlight the package and right-click your mouse. A pop-up menu with a Delete option is displayed.

Deleting a package from the MTS Explorer does not delete the actual component from disk; it only removes it from the MTS package. Furthermore, you can easily reinstall the component back into the same package or a different package. You will work with package management in Chapter 7.

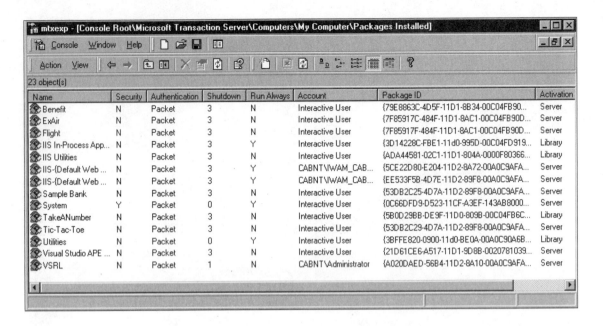

The above view is of the right-pane only. To see this information, highlight and then right-click the
Packages folder in the left-pane. Select View from the pop-up menu and then select Property View.
This screen shows each package that is installed on the selected server.

Starting from the left, the Name of the package is presented. The next two columns, Security and
Authentication, are security related – you'll learn about authorization checking and authentication in
Chapter 8. The column Shutdown tells you how long an inactive process will exist before
terminating. Run Always indicates whether a process should always be available. The Account
column displays what user the package will run under. The default is set for Interactive User, which
means that you're assigning privileges to components based on the privileges that are available to the
calling client. In simple terms, this means a client cannot access component resources that are not
permitted by Windows NT. The Package ID should already look familiar to you: it's simply a GUID
for the particular package. Yes, the package ID is a unique number, although the same GUID is used
if the same identical package is installed on another machine. Finally, the last column, Activation,
shows the package activation type where components will either be activated in the creator's process
(Library packages) or in a dedicated server process (Server packages).

> *Don't worry if these columns don't seem to make much sense. After you complete this book, you'll
> be well versed with the information displayed here. We'll be taking a more in depth look at them
> in Chapter 7.*

You can take a look at the properties for each package by highlighting a particular package such as
Benefit and then clicking your right mouse button. A five-tabbed pop-up form will display each
property listed:

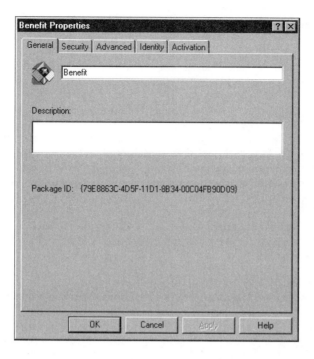

Go back to the left-pane view. Highlight the Benefit package and press the * key to expand the next few levels. The first item you'll see is the Components folder. This folder contains all the components for a particular package:

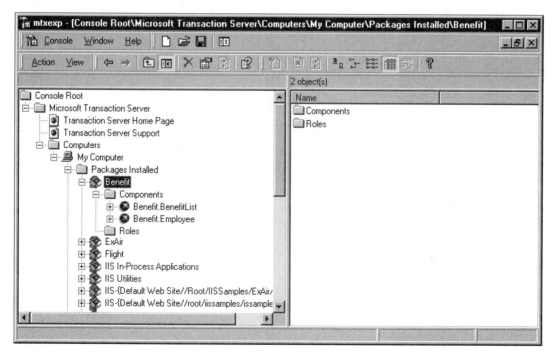

The two green black balls with a green cross represent components within the package. Each component can be configured to run with different settings – we'll be examining this in great detail throughout the book.

The Benefit package contains two components, BenefitList and Employee. Notice that both components have Benefit over the component name. This added information tells you what package the component belongs to.

Components can be added and deleted by highlighting the Components folder in the left-pane and right-clicking with your mouse. Clicking New and then Component will take you to a menu screen. Installing, deleting, and importing components is similar to working with packages. Additionally you can export components to other machines as well as manage general and security properties. You'll learn about component management in Chapter 7.

If you expand the BenefitList component, you'll find two more sub-folders. Clicking open the Interfaces folder lists the interfaces implemented by the component:

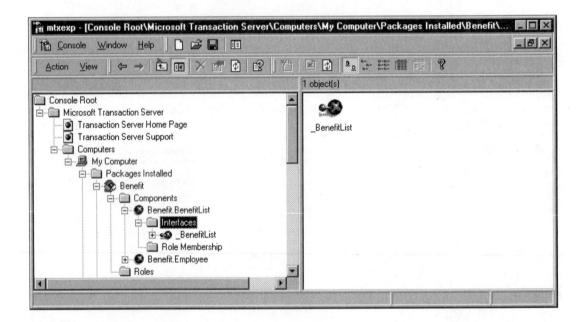

Double click the icon in the right-pane called _BenefitList.

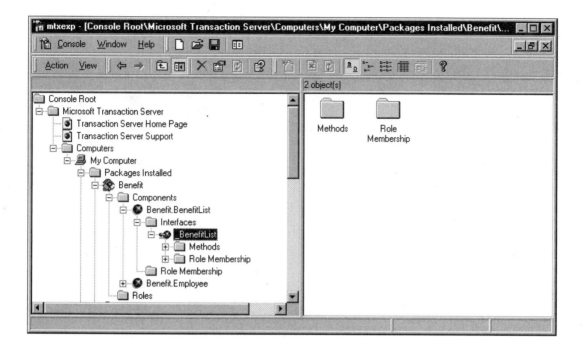

Believe it or not, there are two more folders! The Methods folder contains the methods for this interface. The Role Membership folder contains a list of roles supported at the interface level. Roles are symbolic representations of a user's access privileges. You'll learn about roles and role management in Chapter 8.

In this example, this folder is empty: click it open if you want to see for yourself! If a list were present, it would allow you to go down another level to a Role object that signifies a specific role. And yes, it's possible to go even deeper with a Users folder that houses specific users.

Go back to the Methods folder and open it. The right-pane displays each method that is used with the Benefit.List component:

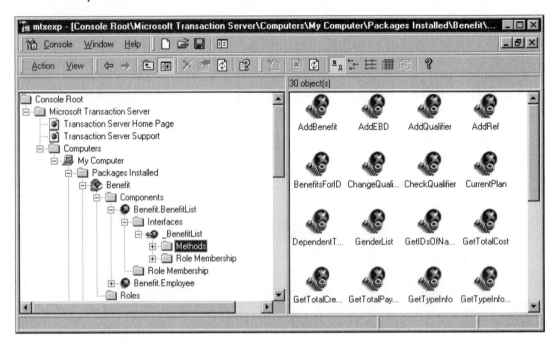

If you work your way down through the Employee component, you should see the same structure of sub-folders.

You have just toured the Packages Installed folder. There are a few more areas of the Explorer that I will quickly describe. As you work through this book, you'll have the opportunity to work with all these items:

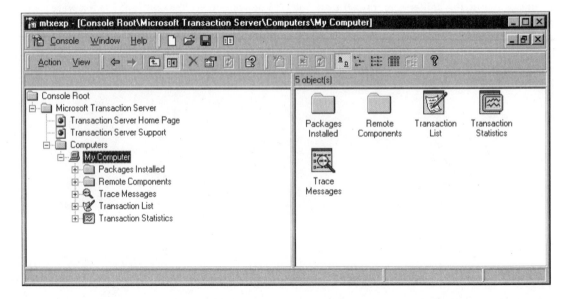

The folder below Packages Installed is Remote Components. In simple words, components in the Remote Components folder are selected to run on another server/machine. In order to use remote components, you'll need to add the remote server (computer/machine name) to the computer folder. The components that are added into the Remote Components folder are components that are under the current machine (in this case, My Compute) that can run on another server. This can become complicated if you have several servers each using components from other machines.

Trace Messages are next. Highlighting Trace Messages in the left-pane, or double-clicking the Trace Massages icon in the right-pane, allows you to monitor messages and logs for MS DTC. These messages can come from three locations: MS DTC service, MS DTC logs, or from the network connection manager. We'll look at how to use this in Chapter 11.

Either highlighting Transaction List in the left-pane, or double-clicking the Transaction List icon in the right pane, allows you to view active transactions for components on the server selected to be monitored. In this example, selecting the Transaction List would allow you to monitor transactions for My Compute .

You have finally made it to Transaction Statistics! Highlight Transaction Statistics in the left-pane or double-click the Transaction Statistics icon in the right-pane to display MS DTC information:

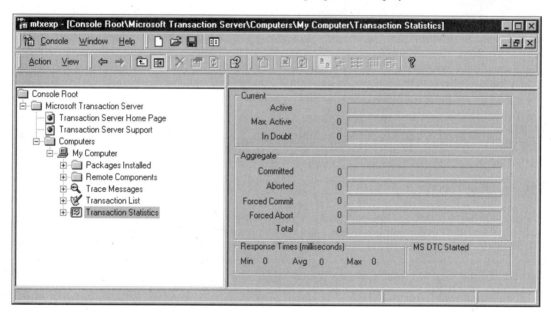

At the moment, this view is rather unexciting. However, when you're executing transactions through the MS DTC, you'll see all kinds of activity that provides statistics for MS DTC, such as current, aggregate, and status information:

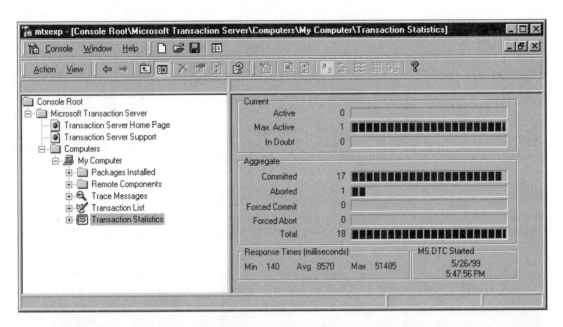

You have just completed a fairly brief visual tour of the MTS Explorer snap-in running in the MMC console. Yet there is still more on offer. Now that you're familiar with the MTS Explorer, try clicking around using both left and right mouse buttons and pay attention to the different types of menus and features that are offered. Remember that deleting a package or a component from MTS Explorer does not actually delete the item from the system. You can easily reinstall the package or component.

I saved perhaps the most fun part of MTS Explorer for last. You remember all those ball shaped icons for packages and components? They spin when in use!

MTS in Action

Let's visit The Grog Company, as we'll be hearing from them throughout this book. The Grog Company decides to write a program that will take two numbers and add them together.

The managers at The Grog Company are very interested in this particular calculator because it can only add. Off the record, I think the managers of the company plan to add bonuses to their regular paychecks.

This calculator will be built based on the COM specification. The client will be a GUI application that will be installed on each manager's PC. The server component will contain the business logic and will be installed on the main business server.

One nice thing about COM is that it is not based on monolithic coding. Because The Grog Company has two programmers, one programmer can write code for the client while the other programmer can write code for the server. Of course, both programmers need to plan together before writing any code!

Another beauty of COM is both programmers can work on their own PC and use any programming language they prefer. Because both programmers are connected to a network, they can test the client-server project from their own PCs.

Installing the Server Component

As my purpose here is simply to give you the opportunity to see MTS up and running, I don't want to get dragged into a discussion on the intricacies of coding a COM component for MTS. Therefore, I'm simply going to provide you with a DLL that we'll insert into a package in MTS, then we'll build the GUI and see it all running.

You can find the DLL (and the project information if you would rather compile it yourself) in the source code download for this book - available from the Wrox Press website.

The code in the DLL is actually very simple. It mainly just contains this basic function:

```
Public Function SumOfNumbers(lngSum1 As Long, lngSum2 As Long) As Long

   SumOfNumbers = (lngSum1 + lngSum2)

End Function
```

This is not a transaction component, i.e. we'll be seeing MTS being used as just an ORB in this instance.

Now we need to register this DLL to be used by MTS. To do this we need to place the DLL as a component in a package. Again, to simplify matters there is a pre-created package in the source code – it's the file with the extension PAK, called CalcProjectExport.PAK. All you have to do is import it into the MTS Explorer.

Open the MTS Explorer and browse to the Packages Installed folder. Highlight the folder and click your right mouse button. From the pop-up menu, select New and then click Package. This opens the Package Wizard:

The Package Wizard offers the two options Install pre-built packages and Create an empty package. Select the first option, Install pre-built packages.

From the Select Package Files dialog, click the Add… and locate the CalcProjectExport.PAK file from the directory where you stored your source code:

The Set Package Identity dialog deals with security. Keep the default set to Interactive user – the current logged on user and click Next>.

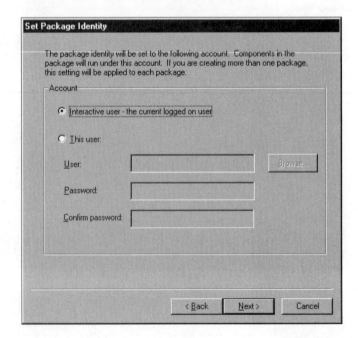

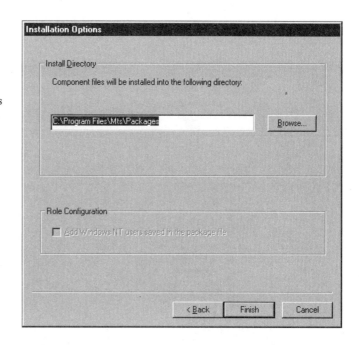

The Installation Options dialog asks where to install component files. In most cases, you can leave `C:\Program Files\Mts\Packages` as the default path. Click Finish.

Notice that both left- and right-panes show the newly installed package for MTSCalcSum:

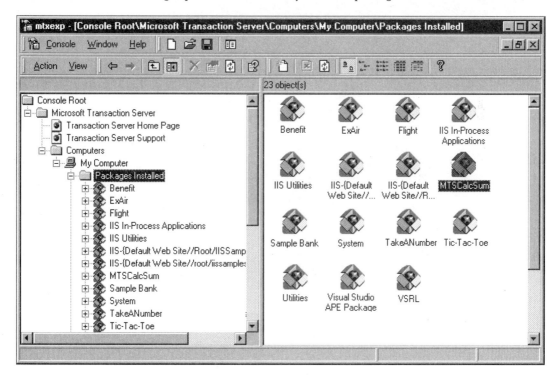

If you expand the package and the installed component to the Methods folder, you should see the `SumOfNumbers` function:

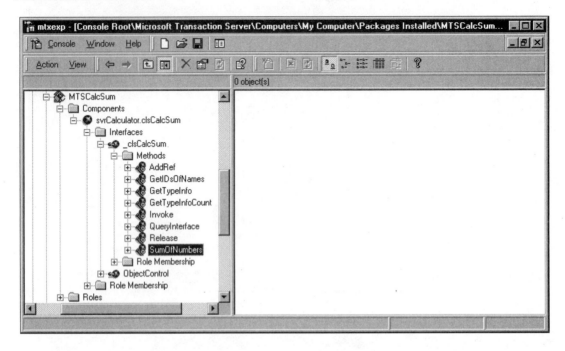

You'll notice there are more methods than the single SumOfNumbers function. This is because Visual Basic implements these other COM required interfaces for us. We'll be taking a look at this in the next chapter.

Your component is now ready to be run. All that needs to be done is to build it a client.

Building the Client

Start Visual Basic and select Standard EXE from the New Project box. Before we go any further, open the References dialog. Locate svrCalculator and select it:

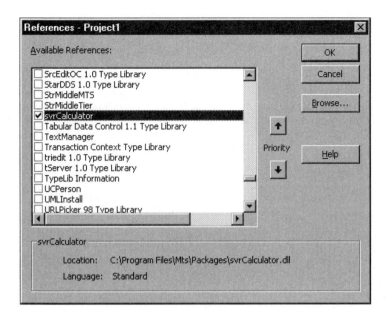

Notice that the Location is the svrCalculator DLL in the \ Program Files\MTS\Packages directory.

Let's name the client project `SumCalcClient`. Name the form `frmCalc` and set the form's caption to: I Can Add!

Place two command buttons on the form. One button should be larger than the other. Name the large command button `cmdCalcSum` with the caption <u>C</u>alculate Sum and name the small command button `cmdExit` with the caption E<u>x</u>it:

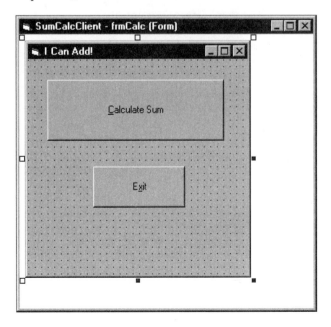

Enter the following code for the `Click` event of `cmdCalcSum`:

```
Private Sub cmdCalcSum_Click()

  Dim strReturn1 As String
  Dim strReturn2 As String

  Dim objCalcSum As svrCalculator.clsCalcSum
  Set objCalcSum = CreateObject("svrCalculator.clsCalcSum")

  strReturn1 = InputBox$("Enter a number: ")
  strReturn2 = InputBox$("Enter another number: ")

  If strReturn1 = "" Or strReturn2 = "" Then
    Set objCalcSum = Nothing
    Exit Sub
  End If

  MsgBox "The total = " & objCalcSum.SumOfNumbers _
    (CLng(strReturn1), CLng(strReturn2))

  Set objCalcSum = Nothing

End Sub
```

We can deduce that the total is derived from two numbers entered by the user. However, we don't know how these numbers are being added as the formula has been encapsulated into our server component. Although this demonstration is using both client and server on the same machine, you can see how business logic can be separated from the client.

Let's go ahead and put the following code in for the Exit command button:

```
Private Sub cmdExit_Click()

  Unload Me
  SetfrmCalc = Nothing

End Sub
```

Make sure that you save your project before continuing.

This example is all designed to run on the same machine. However, it's not very difficult to place the component DLL on another machine from the client. We'll cover the details of how to do that later in this book.

Run the client project and press the Calculate Sum button. After a short wait, you should be presented with two input boxes asking for the two numbers to sum, and then you'll be presented with a message box with your result:

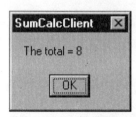

If you have the MTS Explorer open, then you can highlight the Components folder for MTSCalcSum package and watch your clsCalcSum spinning. The wait is caused by MTS performing some background processing, preparing your MTS component for use. If you press the button again you should find it now responds a lot faster. We'll be taking a look at what's going on here in the next chapter.

Summary

Congratulations, you have successfully configured your MTS development machine and learned to maneuver around MTS Explorer using the MMC.

Before moving on to another exciting chapter, pause a minute and think about what you learned in this chapter.

First, you verified that your development machine meets the minimum requirements for using MTS services. Next you actually installed MTS Services onto your development machine, either from the Windows NT Option Pack or by downloading MTS services from Microsoft's web site.

As if you already weren't having fun, you took a visual and hands-on tour of MTS Explorer using the Microsoft Management Console (MMC). You learned about snap-ins and how you can manage various applications by selecting current Microsoft Console (MSC) files and creating new MSC files. The last part of your tour quickly introduced you to many of the administrative tools MTS Explorer provides you with.

I'll admit it, this was a pretty easy chapter really, but that was because I know what's up ahead. I wanted to make sure you were familiar with the MTS Explorer and are all set up to go. From now on things will get a lot harder. In fact, just to make sure you're paying attention, in the next chapter we're going to dive deep down into the bowels of MTS and examine the underlying architecture and mechanics. I suggest you take a deep breath...

3

COM and MTS Architecture

In Chapter 1, we started discussing MTS, the powerful component-based system layered on top of COM. Then in Chapter 2, we took a quick waltz through the GUI for MTS, the MTS Explorer. Now we're going to go from one extreme to the other, by diving deep behind the scenes of MTS.

In this chapter, we'll first review the basics of COM and DCOM. Then we'll discuss the details of the MTS architecture, including the component instantiation process, the MTS Executive, an MTS object's life cycle and the MTS's simplistic concurrency model called activities. We will learn the correct way to instantiate components and use MTS object references.

To fully take advantage of MTS as a run time environment for your COM components, it's essential to have a detailed understanding of MTS's architecture. In particular, we're going to focus on several key areas:

- ❑ The MTS component instantiation process
- ❑ How MTS components interact with MTS
- ❑ How MTS interacts with MTS components
- ❑ Understanding MTS concurrency model
- ❑ Creating instances of MTS components

COM Architecture

Before we start working with MTS, you should have an understanding of the internals of COM.

COM is the acronym for Component Object Model.

COM is an outgrowth of the object-oriented paradigm and is a specification that is based on a binary standard for reuse through interfaces. This means that a component written for COM can be reused without any dependencies on the language it was written in. It doesn't matter if an application contains components written in Visual Basic, C++, Java, or even COBOL, just as long as these components follow the COM specification.

I don't really want to get into a heavy discussion of Visual Basic and COM here, so what I will do is simply give you a quick run through of the key ideas and concepts you need to understand. If you have not done so already, I recommend you read the first book in this VB COM series: A Visual Basic Programmer's Introduction to COM, by Thomas Lewis, published by Wrox Press (ISBN 1-861002-13-0). The entire purpose of that book is to give VB programmers all the knowledge they need to get a good grounding in the major concepts of COM.

COM Objects and Components

A COM object is an instance of a COM component, which should be thought of as a compiled piece of code that can provide a service to the system, not just to a single application. There are generally hundreds of components in the system that can potentially be used in thousands of different applications. A different software house could write each component, and each software house could use a different programming language. The possibilities are limitless.

The phrases COM object and COM component are frequently used interchangeably, and while this is not always correct, it's unlikely that you will be misunderstood if you find yourself making this mistake. Strictly, though, they are *different things: a COM object is an instance of a COM component.*

The COM Interface

Many of the advantages COM provides for distributed application development are delivered through the concept of interfaces. The COM interface is the mechanism by which a consumer or client interacts with a component. An interface is actually a very simple concept to understand:

> **An interface is a contract between a consumer and a component that describes the component's *functionality* to the consumer without describing the *implementation* at all.**

You can think of an interface as a class that has no implementation. In other words, an interface is simply a list of properties and methods that a COM component supports. When we define an interface, we just outline a set of properties and methods, without providing any programmatic details of how they should work.

Interfaces are definitely the key to the abstraction COM provides when utilizing components. Whenever we call methods on an object provided in a COM component, we are communicating with the interface instead of the actual object.

We, as VB developers, often forget that we need to think of interfaces as separate items from the classes they describe. VB kindly hides the details of interfaces from us when we create or use components, so we forget about the separation between the interfaces and implementation. However, there are some advantages to forcing this separation of interfaces and implementation in Visual Basic components

The COM Interface Contract

I have described an interface as a **contract** between a consumer and a component. Basically, this means that provided we never change the interfaces we create (that is, as long as we don't break the contract), the consumer doesn't have to worry about the implementation of our components.

Interface Architecture

Now we come to the crux of the matter. Essentially, a COM interface is a binary description of the layout of a block of memory containing an array of function pointers. The array has a fixed structure, and is known as a virtual method table (**vtable**). The pointers in the array point to the functions of a COM object that can be called by a consumer of the interface:

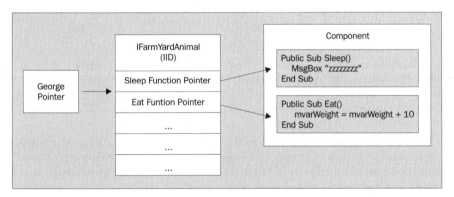

When a consumer wants to use the services of a COM object, it obtains the vtable for the appropriate interface, and looks up the method it wants to call. It then uses the function pointer to invoke the method. Each interface has its own vtable layout, and a COM object can expose any number of interfaces.

A Binary Contract

The order of the functions in the vtable, the parameters for each function, the name of the interface, and the amount of memory needed physically to store the pointers is known as the **interface signature**. Once a COM interface has been published, this signature must not change: it is **absolutely immutable**. If you alter any aspect of an interface signature once you've published it, you run the very real risk of breaking all the applications that are using it.

To illustrate why this arrangement requires absolute immutability, consider the following two cases. First, imagine that we update a well-known interface by removing an obsolete method, or even just change the parameter types of an existing method. A client written for the old version of the interface will try to call a method that doesn't exist, or pass the wrong kind of argument to one that does. Either will result in failure.

Second, think what would happen if a client written to use the new version of the interface came across a component that was still implementing the old one. It would either find that the vtable contained an extra entry it knew nothing about, or else once again a method would be called with the wrong arguments.

> **Through this reasoning, you can see how an interface is a lifetime binary contract with its consumers. Changing an interface is practically guaranteed to cause the failure of both old and new clients.**

The IUnknown Interface

Every COM object must implement an interface called **IUnknown**. This interface can be used to hold a pointer to any other interface. `IUnknown` is aptly named, because it enables interfaces to be used without actually knowing anything else about them. It contains three functions:

- ❏ `QueryInterface`
- ❏ `AddRef`
- ❏ `Release`

You can't actually call any of these functions directly from Visual Basic, despite the fact that VB implements the interface on our behalf. However, every time you create, destroy or make a function call on an object, you are using this interface.

QueryInterface

`QueryInterface` is the mechanism that a client uses to discover and navigate the interfaces of a component dynamically. `QueryInterface` is probably *the* most significant method of all COM interfaces, as it allows run time inspection of all the interfaces that a component supports. We've already seen that COM objects can implement many interfaces. Without the `QueryInterface` method, it would be difficult for a client to navigate around them, and impossible to provide true 'dynamic' discovery of a component's capabilities.

AddRef and Release

The `AddRef` and `Release` methods of the `IUnknown` interface manage an object's lifetime, using a mechanism called **reference counting**. When a component is first created by the COM runtime, its 'life' begins, and `AddRef` is implicitly called by the component itself. `AddRef` is a simple function that increases the reference count of the component by one. The count starts at zero, and so after a component has been created, its reference count will be equal to one.

Every time the `QueryInterface` function hands out an interface pointer to a consumer, it calls `AddRef` to increase the reference count by one. Conversely, when a consumer has finished using the interface, the `Release` method is called, decrementing the count by one. If this count reaches zero, the object knows that no more consumers are using it, and so it destroys itself.

The IDispatch Interface

The `IDispatch` interface provides information about the methods that an object supports and can execute them if required. The `IDispatch` interface has a number of methods, including, `GetIDsOfNames` and `Invoke`.

GetIDsOfNames

The `GetIDsOfNames` method reads the name of a method and returns its **dispatch identifier** (commonly known as **DISPID**). A DISPID is an identification value for each method that can be called by the `Invoke` method.

Invoke

The `Invoke` method provides access to the properties and methods exposed by an object. Our Automation controller can pass the DISPID returned by `GetIDsOfNames` to `Invoke` to execute the required method of our object.

Default Interfaces

Whenever you declare a class in Visual Basic, you're actually declaring a COM interface and providing the implementation in one go. This **default interface** is constructed from the public members of the class. As usual, Visual Basic is hiding the awkward details and making the process easier for you. This implicitly defined interface has the same name as the class itself, prefixed with an underscore.

> **All interfaces in Visual Basic are implicitly prefixed with an underscore. If you hadn't already guessed, most interfaces (excluding the default interface) also start with an `I` for interface.**

Creating Objects

You should be familiar with the concept that objects are created from classes - well, it's no different in COM. Every COM object is created from a COM class called a **coclass** (component object **class**). These are directly equivalent to the VB classes we all know and love, so when we tell COM that we want our VB objects to be COM-enabled, a new 'COM-ified' version of our class is created. Now when we create a new instance of the object, COM uses this coclass to create a new COM object for us to use.

The creation process is a bit more complex than that though. COM still needs to use two major services of the COM runtime: **location** (finding the component to work with) and **creation** (creating an instance of it to use).

Location

The COM runtime locates servers using the system registry, which includes, amid the vast quantity of information it contains, a list of all COM components within the system.

The mechanism used for locating a component works like an address book. The location of a component can be found by looking up the component under the `HKEY_CLASSES_ROOT\CLSID` key, and this then provides information about the location of the DLL, etc. We'll find out more about how COM uses this key in just a moment.

Creation

Once the COM runtime has located a server, it will ensure that it is running (loading it if necessary) before creating an instance of the requested component. The process is quite complex, and really beyond the scope of this book. For now, all you need to know is that the process of locating the server is handled by the **Service Control Manager (SCM)** of the COM runtime. In simple terms, the SCM is a system-wide service, residing in RPCSS.EXE, that is responsible for instantiating a component and binding it to the requesting client.

As part of the component creation process, we have to specify which of the component's interfaces we are interested in using first. Usually with VB it will be the default interface.

Type Libraries

A **type library** is the mechanism by which components within a COM server are described to the consumers of that server. It's simply a database that contains a list of what components, interfaces, enumerations and structures are available inside a COM server.

Visual Basic will generate the type library for you when a COM project is compiled. We need a type library when building a client application against a COM server, to provide the information that Visual Basic uses at compile time to create the client side vtable.

To tell your application how to find the type library that you want to use, you'll need to set a reference to the type library using the References dialog within Visual Basic. We saw how to do this in Chapter 2: simply select References from the Project menu and then select the type library you want.

The file name of a type library can have any one of several extensions: .tlb, .dll, .exe, .olb and .ocx are all possibilities. Any type libraries that you create yourself using Visual Basic will be either .exe or .dll.

Type libraries are recorded in the registry under HKEY_CLASSES_ROOT\TypeLib.

COM and the Registry

The registry is very important to the functioning of COM. It is here that COM stores all the information regarding the components that it can create, including location, process type, interface identifiers and much more.

In a moment we'll take a look at the registry entries that Visual Basic makes on our behalf for our DLLs, but first we need to take a quick detour into unique identifiers.

Identifiers: GUIDs, UUIDs, IIDs and CLSIDs

You've now come across interface identifiers (IIDs) and class identifiers (CLSIDs). Both of these are types of **GUID**, which stands for **Globally Unique Identifier**. This acronym is also synonymous with **UUID**, or **Universally Unique Identifier**. A GUID is a 128-bit number (16 bytes) that can be expressed in string format. For example, the identifier for the IUnknown interface is:

```
{00000000-0000-0000-C000-000000000046}
```

Visual Basic generates GUIDs for your COM classes and interfaces when you compile your component. It generates these numbers using the services of the COM runtime - more specifically, a COM API call to `CoCreateGuid`.

A GUID is created with a complex algorithm that uses the system clock and the network card's MAC address. (If you don't have a network card in your machine, other variables such as hard disk space and time since last reboot are used. In that case, though, the ID generated is only guaranteed to be unique on your computer.) The algorithm for generating GUIDs could generate 10 million a second until the year 5770 AD, and each one would be unique (source: Professional DCOM Programming by Dr Richard Grimes)

Basically, as I explained in the specific case of coclasses, COM uses a GUID as a key for accessing information in the system registry, in much the same way that you would use a primary key for accessing a specific row in a database. After all, in the final analysis, the registry is little more than a database, albeit a very important one.

COM Registry Entries

When you register, or compile, a `.DLL` Visual Basic automatically generates a CLSID for each class in the project. In addition to creating a CLSID, Visual Basic creates type information to support the exposed interface for the class. It registers the `.DLL` file with the operating system, making our newly created server available for external clients to use.

COM uses only one branch of the registry: `HKEY_CLASSES_ROOT`. Under `HKEY_CLASSES_ROOT` there are two main keys that are used by COM and one additional key that is used by DCOM.

Directly under `HKEY_CLASSES_ROOT`, below the file extensions you'll find several recognizable names: `ADODB.Recordset`, `MSComDlg.CommonDialog`, and `Word.Document.8`, just to name a few. These names are known as programmatic identifiers or ProgIDs. ProgIDs are used to map a friendly name for an object to its guaranteed unique CLSID:

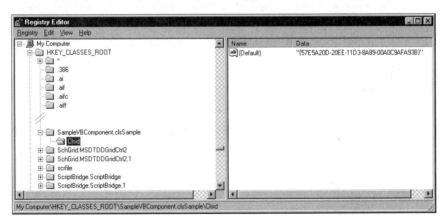

In the above example, our `SampleVBComponent.dll` has one class named `clsSample`. As you can see, Visual Basic kindly creates ProgIDs by combining the project name and class name, so in this case the ProgID is `SampleVBComponent.clsSample`. The ProgID naming is another one of the details VB hides from us.

CLSIDs are guaranteed to be unique. However, ProgIDs are not guaranteed to be unique, so you have to be very careful what names you use.

ProgIDs are really just programmer-friendly strings used in the registry to retrieve the unique CLSID. This lookup, using the ProgID to retrieve the CLSID for an object, is exactly what VB does for you when you create an instance of an object using the `CreateObject` or `GetObject` functions. So we would code:

```
Set objCalc = CreateObject("SampleVBComponent.clsSample")
```

But when we ran it, COM would look up the registry entry for this ProgID to find out the CLSID.

Once we have the CLSID for our object, we move to the other main key used by COM: `HKEY_CLASSES_ROOT\CLSID`. Under this key, we find hundreds of sub-keys using cryptic CLSIDs for their name:

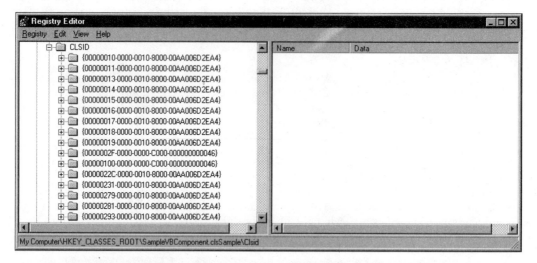

If we look up the sub-key using the same value as the CLSID of our `SampleVBComponent.clsSample` object, we find the following registry entries:

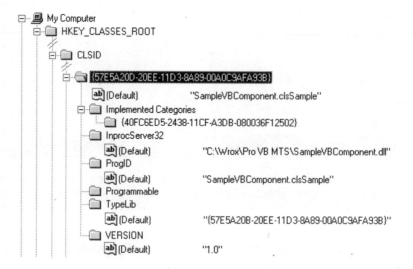

The sub-keys under the object's CLSID key vary depending on the type of components and their location. In this case, we're dealing with an in-process DLL component, so there is an InprocServer32 sub-key and a default value for that sub-key containing the location where the DLL can be found.

Out-of-process components running on the local machine have the sub-key LocalServer32 instead of InprocServer32. The LocalServer32 sub-key also has a default value specifying the path to the out-of-process EXE component.

What's interesting is that by adding a string value under the CLSID registry entry for our in-process DLL component, we can make it run out-of-process. We'll look at that when we discuss Microsoft Transaction Server.

DCOM

The **Distributed Component Object Model (DCOM)** is probably the most important product of Windows DNA. Originally referred to as Network OLE, Microsoft changed over to Distributed Component Object Model to describe applications that work together and are not limited to the same machine. In reality, DCOM is a mere extension to the Component Object Model: in fact, it's often called 'COM with a longer wire'.

Typically, COM is thought of as being implemented on the same machine, while DCOM can communicate across multiple network transport protocols, different operating systems and various computer makes. Just think, you can have an application written in several languages such as VB, C++, and COBOL, and distribute it across several networks such as Windows NT, various flavors of Unix and even Sun Solaris, using different protocols such as TCP/IP, IPX/SPX, and HTTP (with Windows NT 4, Service Pack 4)!

Just as exciting, these components don't appear to the client to be located on different machines: it is totally transparent. Imagine a monster-sized application that is spread across several networks and produces enormous processing power!

Location Transparency

DCOM allows applications to communicate with components in exactly the same way, irrespective of whether they are remote or running on the local computer. DCOM handles the communication details transparently, which allows applications to work with a component without any knowledge of the component's location. This transparency applies to the creator. However, the component's transparency doesn't apply to the creator's machine: it is stored in the registry.

When DCOM was released, it had to work with the existing COM registration system. What's great about DCOM is that existing out-of-process components can be distributed components, and execute on a remote server with no changes to the client's or server's code.

We could use the DCOM Configuration utility (DCOMCNFG.EXE) to make our out-of-process EXE component execute on a remote server, but that's not quite as much fun as modifying the registry directly. Besides, first we want to know the details of what's going on behind the scenes: then we'll use the easy way out.

COM and DCOM share the two main keys in the registry we just covered, and DCOM components also use one additional key. DCOM adds a sub-key under `HKEY_CLASSES_ROOT\AppID` for each server object that will be executed remotely. This additional key is very similar to the `HKEY_CLASSES_ROOT\CLSID` key in the fact that they have many sub-keys with GUIDs for names:

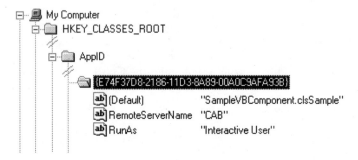

Suppose we rebuilt our sample component as an out-of-process EXE component. To enable it to execute remotely, we would first add a sub-key under the `AppID` key. This sub-key should have a GUID for a name: most commonly, it uses the same value as the CLSID, but it doesn't have to. Under this sub-key, there are different value entries that store information about the machine the component will execute on and security information, etc.

But how does DCOM know where to find the other information about the component, such as the threading model, location, and version? A string value named `AppID` is added to the object's CLSID sub-key. This `AppID` string value acts as a pointer to the sub-key for this object under `HKEY_CLASSES_ROOT\AppID`:

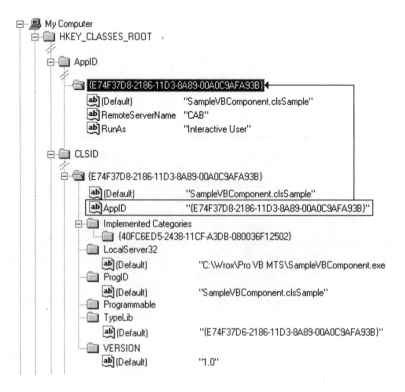

Proxies and Stubs

So how does DCOM do all this? If a client and an object are located on different machines, **proxies** and **stubs** are used to facilitate the communications between the two.

The proxy and stub are responsible for intercepting function calls between the client and component, and passing them back and forth across the network transparently. A proxy is created for the client, whilst a stub is created for the server:

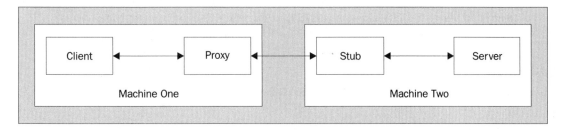

The proxy and stub shown above are COM objects. As far as the client is concerned, the proxy is the original COM object that it asked to be created. It doesn't know that it's talking to an imposter. This is possible because the proxy implements an identical interface to the original component. Because COM enforces encapsulation, the component doesn't know about the lack of implementation.

The server component doesn't care that a stub, and not the original client, is using it. It makes no assumptions on who consumes its services.

Remote Object Creation

So what is happening when an object is created remotely? First, the client requests that the COM Library create an instance of the server. The COM library uses its SCM (Service Control Manager) to determine the location of the component, using the CLSID passed to it by the client. If the component lives on a remote machine, the SCM on the client machine converses with the SCM on the server machine to actually request the services to create the component. Once the server object is running, an object reference is passed back through the COM Library. The client is given the object reference so that it may call upon the services of the component object:

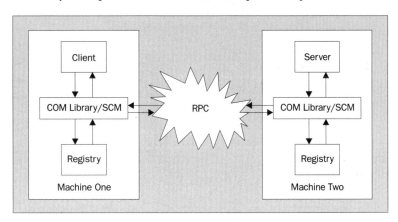

Because COM enables a client to use a component in an identical fashion whether it's created locally or remotely, it's possible for a developer to focus purely upon implementing business solutions. However, if a component is going to be used remotely, it is **essential** to consider network traffic and performance. We'll be seeing how MTS helps to solve these problems.

RPC

DCOM uses RPC as one of its foundation building blocks for enabling remote component communications. RPC basically enables function calls to be remoted in a standard fashion from one machine to another. Given that this is the main goal of DCOM, and that Microsoft has implemented RPC on nearly all versions of Windows, using RPC as the foundation for remote components' interoperation makes a lot of sense.

Process Space

I mentioned in-process and out-of-process components earlier. I want to make sure that you have a firm understanding of processes and threads, as MTS throws a new element into the mix.

When you start an application under Windows, such as Notepad, the operating system will create a **process** in which the application executes. This process will have its own address space. It will be isolated from other processes, such that if the application goes seriously wrong, the integrity of others in the system is maintained.

In-Process Servers

An in-process server is an object that runs within the same **process space** as the client application that is calling it. An ActiveX DLL is an example of an in-process server:

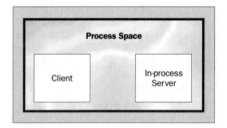

Process space is the allocated memory and resources that are assigned to an application (EXE server) within which our components are housed.

Out-of-Process Servers

An out-of-process server is an object that runs in its own process space.

If an out-of-process server crashes for some reason, it doesn't take the client application down with it. An ActiveX EXE is an example of an out-of-process server.

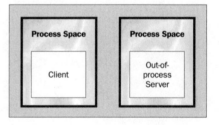

Surrogate Process for DLLs

When a client creates a component on a remote machine, the component must execute within the process of an application.

Out-of-process components can simply run within their own process space, which makes them ideal for remotely executing. If, however, our remote component were an in-process component, whose process space would the component be hosted in?

Because a DLL can only be loaded and used within an EXE (that is, it doesn't have its own process), we need a surrogate EXE to perform this role.

Threading Models

Put simply, you can think of a thread as a lightweight process. Unlike a process though, threads don't actually own system resources. Inside of a process you always have at least one **thread**, known as the main thread. A thread is the basic entity to which the operating system allocates CPU time. So, if we have 10 processes, each with a thread that's doing some intensive work, the operating system will give each thread 10% of the overall available CPU time.

A process can contain multiple threads that run **concurrently**. Each thread shares the system resources owned by the process, such as its virtual address space. This means that threads can execute the application's code, access global memory and other resources such as files, whilst not consuming too many additional resources.

Apartments

Apartments are a way of further subdividing process space whilst maintaining thread integrity. What this means is that you can divide up the same process space into apartments in which threads can run. From the perspective of the thread, other apartments appear to be in a separate process when in fact they are in the same process space:

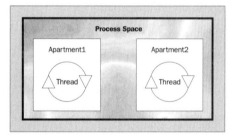

Single-Threaded Apartments

A **Single-Threaded Apartment (STA)**, or **Apartment-Threaded** model, basically just allows only a single thread to run within each apartment. A process can contain any number of STAs to provide multi-threading for components that are thread-unaware. The diagram above is an example of this.

This is the only threading option that Visual Basic components currently support. Therefore, the only multi-threading capability that VB is capable of is the multi-STA setup. If you want to support this threading model you must select the Apartment Threaded threading model in the Project Properties dialog:

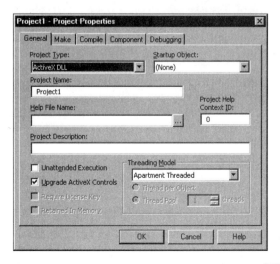

Selecting the Single Threaded model is something completely different. This has nothing to do with apartments and consequently you can only run a single thread within each process.

Multi-Threaded Apartments

By contrast, a **Multi-Threaded Apartment (MTA)**, or **Free-Threading model**, allows multiple threads to execute within the same apartment. However, each process can only support a single MTA:

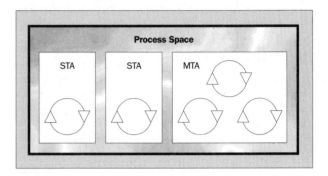

An MTA can run any number of threads so there is little use for more than one MTA per apartment. Visual Basic isn't yet capable of creating components that can run in an MTA environment.

I think that's enough background and revision for the moment. Let's now move on to looking at how MTS fits into the picture.

MTS Architecture

By now, you've heard that Microsoft Transaction Server provides a scalable and robust programming infrastructure without requiring any additional code. Hiding implementations of routine and complex operations from developers in a programmable infrastructure technology is great. However, as with COM, OLE DB, MSMQ or any other infrastructure technology, the more you understand about what's happening within the MTS environment behind-the-scenes, the better you'll be able to utilize Microsoft Transaction Server.

Component Instantiation under MTS

Microsoft Transaction Server is not a replacement for COM, but rather a service that hosts in-process components and provides extended features to COM. An MTS component requires no additional run time to be utilized by a client, other than what's already provided by DCOM. But how does this work?

> **MTS uses registry redirection to load an in-process DLL component into a MTS process on the local or a remote machine, instead of loading the component into the process of the creator.**

To see how this **registry redirection** works, let's compare the registry settings for an MTS component, to the registry settings for a standard DLL component:

Notice that this in-process DLL component has an entry under both the HKEY_CLASSES_ROOT\AppID key and the HKEY_CLASSES_ROOT\CLSID key. It also has both LocalServer32 and InprocServer32 sub-keys under the CLSID key. Strange for an in-process component isn't it? But notice that there's no value for the InprocServer32 sub-key. Instead, there's a reference to MTX.EXE with a GUID as a parameter under the LocalServer32 sub-key.

In summary, three things must happen to the registry entries for our DLL component for it to execute in the MTS environment:

❏ A LocalServer32 key is created.
   In the CLSID key for the component class, a LocalServer32 sub-key was created, even though this is an in-process DLL component. This sub-key contains for it's default value the path to the MTS executable (mtx.exe) with the GUID of the component's package as a parameter.

❏ The InprocServer32 key is modified.
   The default value for the InprocServer32 sub-key is cleared so that it no longer points to the location of the DLL. This value is no longer necessary since the MTS executable will load the DLL.

❑ An `AppID` key for this component is added.
MTS also creates a new sub-key for this component under the key
`HKEY_CLASSES_ROOT\AppID`, and an `AppID` string value under the component's CLSID key to
point to this new sub-key. Just as with out-of-process EXE components, this section of the registry
is used to store information about the security and identity of our MTS components. We'll cover
more about security in the next section.

Let's examine how this registry redirection fits into the component instantiation process. When a base
client (a client outside of MTS's direct control) invokes the `CreateObject` function or the `New`
keyword to create an instance of an MTS component, the request is sent through the VB run time and
eventually down to COM's Service Control Manager (SCM).

*If MTS is running on another machine, the base client's SCM forwards the creation requests to
the remote machine's SCM.*

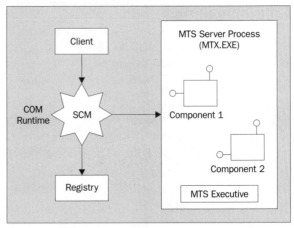

The server's SCM then searches through the
registry for the requested component by it's
CLSID. Until this point, the instantiation
process for MTS components is the same as
for any other COM component:

This is where the registry redirection comes into play. Instead of being routed to the location of the
DLL that implements the requested component, the server's SCM is redirected to the location of the
MTS executable (`MTX.EXE`) with a GUID as a command line parameter. This GUID is an identifier
that specifies which configured group of MTS components (package), the requested MTS component
belongs to.

If an instance of the MTS executable for the specified package is running, the server's SCM calls into
the process, requesting a new instance of the specified MTS component. If an instance of the MTS
executable is not running, the server's SCM launches a new one and then requests a new instance of
the specified component. Either way, the server's SCM gets a reference to a new MTS object and
establishes a connection between the object and the base client. Finally, a proxy/stub layer between
the base client and object is established to marshal data back and forth on method calls, just like with
any other cross-process component instantiation.

Since creating a **surrogate process** by loading a copy of `MTX.EXE` is very time consuming, MTS will
keep it in memory in case other calls are made to the component. You can use the MTS Explorer to
specify the amount of time in minutes a surrogate process should remain loaded without any activity
before it's destroyed. You can even specify that a surrogate process should never be destroyed. Only
one surrogate process (instance of `MTX.EXE`) for each package or group of components can be loaded
at a time.

The only responsibility of the MTS executable (**MTX.EXE**) is to provide a **dumb surrogate process** to host instances of MTS components and the **MTS Executive** (MTXEX.DLL). The MTS Executive is responsible for providing all the run time services for MTS components. Some of these run time services include:

- ❏ Thread Pooling
- ❏ Transaction Management
- ❏ Concurrency Management
- ❏ Authorization Checking
- ❏ Transaction Management

Only one copy of the MTS Executive can be loaded into each process hosting MTS components. It's important to note that the MTS Executive and instances of MTS components can be loaded into the same process as the client, instead of the surrogate process provided by the MTS executable. This isn't very common and it's usually not recommended.

The Context Wrapper

In order to provide extensive run time features and integrate with the existing version of COM, the MTS Executive uses the object-oriented technique of **interception** to intercept all requests and oversee object creation.

When a base client creates an instance of a component that runs under MTS's control, MTS intercepts the component creation request. Instead of instantiating the requested object, MTS creates a transparent layer called a **Context Wrapper** that sits between the client (actually the stub) and the object.

After an instance is created, the client thinks it's holding a reference to the actual object, but it's really only holding a reference to the Context Wrapper. The standard MTS behavior is for the client to never communicate with the object directly, but instead only communicate through this Context Wrapper. As far as the client is concerned, the Context Wrapper *is* the new object.

Of course, if the client and the object are in separate processes (a very common scenario), method calls will be routed through a proxy/stub layer before reaching the Context Wrapper:

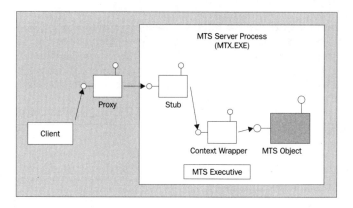

It's important to know that MTS creates a Context Wrapper for each class instantiated. It doesn't share Context Wrappers for multiple components, even if they're created by the same base client.

The previous illustration above shows the proxy and stub which would be located between the client application and Context Wrapper. They are usually omitted from illustrations for sake of space.

When the client invokes a method on the object, it is actually invoking a method on the Context Wrapper. The Context Wrapper forwards the call to the equivalent method on the actual object. When the object finishes processing the call, the control of execution passes back through the Context Wrapper before it's returned to the base client.

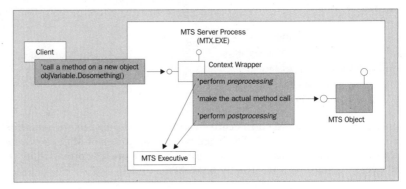

By routing all method invocations through the Context Wrapper, MTS can perform **pre-processing**, or processing before forwarding the call to the actual object, and **post-processing**, or processing after forwarding the call to the actual object. Although we can't modify the code to perform tasks in the pre-processing or post-processing stages, MTS exposes some configuration settings or attributes that allow us to change the behavior of the Context Wrapper in these stages.

However, if you're not careful in the way you handle component references, a client could gain a reference to the actual object instead of the Context Wrapper, in effect, by-passing the MTS interception scheme. If there's no interception, MTS can't control the object and no pre-processing or post-processing can take place.

A common area of confusion when discussing the Context Wrapper and interception is what happens when an MTS component has multiple interfaces. When an MTS object is created by a base client using `CreateObject` or the `New` keyword, Visual Basic makes the creation request to the SCM and requests that the reference returned is to the default interface.

So what happens if the client then requests a reference to another interface for the same MTS object? Behind the scenes, Visual Basic asks the Context Wrapper for a reference to the requested interface by calling the `QueryInterface` method of the `IUnknown` interface implemented by the Context Wrapper. Since the `QueryInterface` call is made against the Context Wrapper, if the requested interface is implemented by the object, the Context Wrapper dynamically creates the new interface on itself.

The actual MTS object is never involved with any calls to the `QueryInterface`, `AddRef` or `Release` functions of the `IUnknown` interface. This is possible because MTS reads your component's type library and learns the details about your component's interface(s) when you install them in MTS Explorer:

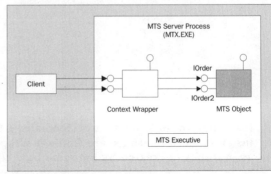

The Context Wrapper will remain in memory as long as the client holds a reference to it. But don't worry about this extra interception layer taking up a large amount of valuable system resources, because each Context Wrapper only consumes about 600 to 700 bytes of memory. Based on the estimate of 700 bytes each, 1497 Context Wrappers would only take up 1 MB of memory.

Just as interfaces are layered on top of objects, the Context Wrapper is an additional layer on top of the interface(s) of objects created under MTS's control. The best part about this additional level of abstraction is that it is **completely transparent** to the client. The client is totally unaware that it's talking to the Context Wrapper instead of the object's interface(s). In fact, the client can't tell the difference between an MTS object and any other COM object. This allows MTS to be a *pluggable* architecture as well. Existing COM components can execute in the MTS run time environment without any code changes required to the clients that use the components.

That's not the end of it though. The Context Wrapper and the abstraction it provides to the client of a component have another great feature.

The MTS object can actually be destroyed while the client continues to hold a reference to the Context Wrapper. We'll discuss more about this important feature called **Just-in-Time Activation** later in this chapter. But, as you can see, MTS uses the object-oriented techniques of interception and abstraction through the Context Wrapper to create a powerful run time environment for COM components.

You can create in-process DLL components as you always have, install them into MTS and they'll execute fine. However, in order to leverage the MTS as a sophisticated run time environment for COM components, you must learn how to interact with the MTS Executive through the Object Context and Object Control interfaces.

Object Context

For each object created within MTS, the MTS Executive also creates an instance of an object called the **Object Context**. The Object Context provides your MTS object with a vehicle to communicate with the MTS Executive and to retrieve run time information about the **context** in which the object is running. Through the Object Context, you can request the MTS Executive to perform specific tasks or check the state of the current object.

For example, you can control transaction outcome, instantiate other MTS components, and check the security of the caller. It's important not to confuse the Object Context and the Context Wrapper.

❏   The Object Context doesn't always exist during the lifetime of an MTS object, whereas the Context Wrapper lives until the client releases the reference to what it thinks is the object.

❏   The Object Context provides information to the MTS object about the context in which it executes. The Context Wrapper's responsibility is to intercept method invocations so the MTS Executive can perform pre-processing and post-processing work:

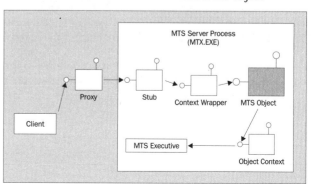

There is a one-to-one correlation between MTS objects and Object Contexts. The Object Context is only provided for the MTS object to communicate with the MTS Executive and it's not intended for the client to use in any way.

You can communicate with the Object Context through the Object Context class. The Object Context class is defined in the **Microsoft Transaction Server Type Library**, so first you'll need to add a reference to this DLL in Visual Basic:

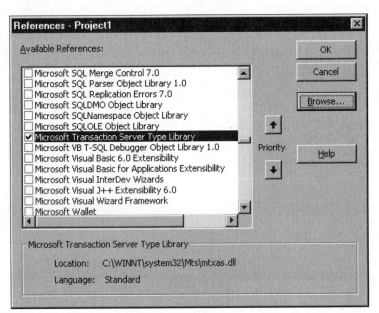

The Microsoft Transaction Server Type Library defines an enum that contains constants for common errors, and 4 objects:

- ❑ AppServer
- ❑ ObjectContext
- ❑ ObjectControl
- ❑ SecurityProperty

Don't worry, we will cover the rest of the MTS Type Library, but for now our focus will be on the **AppServer** class. AppServer defines two methods:

- ❑ GetObjectContext
- ❑ SafeRef

GetObjectContext returns a reference to the Object Context for an MTS object. SafeRef returns a reference to the Context Wrapper for an object. These two equally important functions return references to our MTS object from two different perspectives.

The reference returned from SafeRef is a reference to the Context Wrapper for an object, or the **outside** perspective of an object. This is the only view any code outside of our MTS component should see. We'll discuss SafeRef in more detail later in this chapter.

GetObjectContext returns a reference to the Object Context for an MTS component. Only the MTS component itself should ever have this **internal** perspective.

When I refer to internal and external perspectives, I'm referring to the perspectives from being inside the MTS Executive.

These global functions can be invoked without first creating an instance of the AppServer class, because the AppServer class is defined as Global Multiuse. As you can see in the example below, I prefer to hold a reference to the Object Context in a variable to avoid multiple calls to GetObjectContext:

```
'define a variable so we can hold an early-bound reference to the
'Object Context

Dim objContext As MTxAS.ObjectContext

'Get a reference to the Object Context for this object
Set objContext = GetObjectContext

'Release our reference to the Object Context
Set objContext = Nothing
```

This can provide a performance benefit if you're planning on invoking multiple methods or properties on the Object Context. However, when you only need to perform one operation, such as checking if security is enabled using the IsSecurityEnabled function, you can use the Object Context without maintaining a separate object variable:

```
'Check if Security is Enabled using the Object Context
If GetObjectContext.IsSecurityEnabled = True Then

  Debug.Print "Security is Enabled!"

End If
```

If you do elect to hold the reference to the Object Context in a local variable, make sure that you explicitly release every reference to it. Don't rely on Visual Basic to release your object references for you. Even though VB should release your object references as the method goes out of scope, it's good programming practice to clean up after yourself.

Once you have called the GetObjectContext function to return a reference to the Object Context for our MTS object, you can ask the MTS Executive for information about the run time environment, control transaction outcome, check the security of the caller, or create instances of other MTS components. We'll demonstrate the use of the Object Context object to provide this functionality throughout the rest of this chapter.

You should never pass a reference to the Context object outside the MTS object. There is a separate Object Context for each object created by MTS, and the Object Context obtained by calling the GetObjectContext function is intended for use *only* by *that* MTS object within the object's process. To prove this, I'll define a Public function named ReturnObjectContext in an MTS component that returns a reference to the Object Context:

```
'Function in an MTS component named ObjCtxExample.clsObjCtxExample
Public Function ReturnObjectContext() As MTxAS.ObjectContext

' Return the ObjectContext for our MTS object
' to the calling procedure.
    Set ReturnObjectContext = GetObjectContext

End Function
```

After the clsObjCtxExample component is registered in MTS, the base client creates an instance of it and calls methods on the Object Context returned by the MTS component:

```
'Base Client's Sub Main procedure
Public Sub Main()

    Dim objCtxExmplCls As ObjCtxExample.clsObjCtxExample

' Create an instance of the ObjCtxExample.clsObjCtxExample coclass
    Set objCtxExmplCls = CreateObject("ObjCtxExample.clsObjCtxExample")

' Check if security is enabled for
' the clsObjCtxExample MTS component
    If objCtxExmplCls.ReturnObjectContext.IsSecurityEnabled = True Then
        Debug.Print "Security is Enabled for our " _
                    & "instance of the clsObjCtxExample class!"
    End If
```

```
' Call the DisableCommit method to disable any transaction this
' MTS object's involved in from committing to a Data Source
  objCtxExmplCls.ReturnObjectContext.DisableCommit

' Release our reference to the clsObjCtxExample default interface
  Set objCtxExmplCls = Nothing

End Sub
```

Amazingly, the `IsSecurityEnabled` function executes fine, but when the `DisableCommit` function is invoked, Visual Basic returns this error. This error is returned when you execute any property or function, except for `IsSecurityEnabled` or `IsInTransaction`:

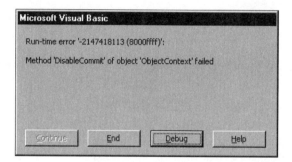

> **Just don't pass references to the Object Context around outside of the method where you obtained the reference. Period. The Object Context is for an MTS object to have access to the MTS Executive, not for a client or another MTS object to manipulate your MTS object's behavior in the run time environment.**

The Object Context is only available at certain times within an MTS object's lifetime. Specifically, the Object Context is not available during the component's creation (`Class_Initialize`) or a component's destruction (`Class_Terminate`). If the Object Context is not available, for this or any other reason, calls to `GetObjectContext` will not fail, but instead simply return a null reference or nothing.

MTS Object References

Whereas the `GetObjectContext` function returns a reference to the Object Context that describes the environment in which the object runs, the `SafeRef` function returns the external perspective of an MTS object. This external perspective is actually just a reference to the Context Wrapper for an MTS object, also called a **safe reference**.

If the client uses a reference to the actual MTS object's interface(s) instead of the Context Wrapper, MTS will not be able to intercept method calls made by the client. As we discussed before, if the Context Wrapper is bypassed, MTS can't perform pre-processing or post-processing on method calls.

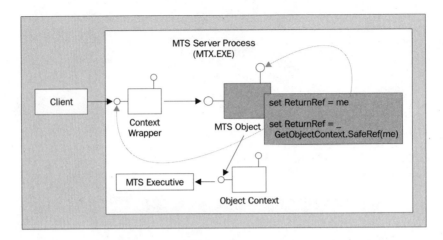

SafeRef should only be called when you want code external to your MTS object to have a reference to your object. So how should you know when to call SafeRef? There are three common scenarios in which you need to call SafeRef:

❑ When returning an MTS object's Me reference as a return value
❑ When returning an MTS object's Me reference as a ByRef parameter
❑ When passing an MTS object's Me reference to another object

When Returning an MTS Object's Me Reference as a Return Value

Very commonly, MTS objects will return a reference to themselves when a method or property procedure is invoked. In this case, you must use the SafeRef function to return a reference to the Context Wrapper and not the MTS object itself. This example shows an MTS object returning a reference to itself when the SafeRefReturnVal function is called:

```
'Public function defined in the clsSafeRefTests class
Public Function SafeRefReturnVal() As clsSafeRefTests

' Return a reference to this instance as a return value, but don't forget to
' SafeRef it first

  Set SafeRefReturnVal = SafeRef(Me)

End Function
```

When Returning an MTS Object's Me Reference as a ByRef Parameter

Just as commonly, MTS objects will pass a reference to themselves in a ByRef parameter instead of a return value. Of course ByRef parameters result in lower performance than a return value, because ByRef parameters are marshaled twice (both from the client to the object and back to the client) while return values are only marshaled once (from the object to the client), but we only have one return value to work with. In this example, we return the reference to the Context Wrapper (provided by SafeRef) into the passed variable when the SafeRefByRefParameter method is called:

```
'Public function defined in the clsSafeRefTests class
Public Sub SafeRefByRefParameter(ByRef objSafeRefTests _
                              As SafeRefTests.clsSafeRefTests)

' Return a reference to this instance in the byref parameter
' objSafeRefTests, but don't forget to SafeRef it first

    Set objSafeRefTests = SafeRef(Me)

End Sub
```

When Passing an MTS Object's Me Reference to Another Object

Sometimes you'll need to call another MTS or standard COM object to perform processing, but it needs a reference to the calling object for some reason. In this situation, you should call the `SafeRef` function before you pass the reference to the other object. The next example passes a reference to the Context Wrapper for our MTS object to a new instance of the `clsSecondObject`'s `ReceiveObjectParameter` method when our `SafeRefParameter` method is called:

```
'Public function defined in the clsSafeRefTests class
Public Sub SafeRefParameter()

' Create an instance of the clsSecondObject class and pass a reference
' to this instance in a parameter but don't forget to SafeRef it first

    Dim objSecondObject As SafeRefTests.clsSecondObject

' Create an instance of the clsSecondObject component
    Set objSecondObject = CreateObject("SafeRefTests.clsSecondObject")

' Call the ReceiveObjectParameter method an pass it a reference to this object
    objSecondObject.ReceiveObjectParameter SafeRef(Me)

' Release our reference to the default interface for the instance of
' SafeRefTests.clsSecondObject we created
    Set objSecondObject = Nothing

End Sub
```

In all of the above scenarios, if we didn't call `SafeRef` and instead just passed a reference using the `Me` keyword, any method calls on the object reference by the client would be made directly on the object's default interface instead of on the Context Wrapper. We wouldn't necessarily receive errors if we bypassed the Context Wrapper, but we would have inconsistent and unexpected behavior from our MTS objects.

It's not necessary to call `SafeRef` on a reference to an MTS object that actually points to a Context Wrapper. This includes references returned from creating an MTS object using the `New` keyword, the `CreateObject` function or the `CreateInstance` function of the Object Context.

The following example calls the `GetSubObject` function on a new instance of an MTS component. The `GetSubObject` function returns a reference to new instance of the `SafeRefTests.clsSubObject` MTS component. Notice that it's not necessary to call the `SafeRef` function when returning this new instance back to the base client: the instance of the `clsSubObject` component was created using the `CreateObject` function and the reference already points to the object's Context Wrapper.

```
'Public function defined in the clsSafeRefTests class
Public Function GetSubObject() As SafeRefTests.clsSubObject

' Create an instance of the clsSubObject class and return a reference to this
' new instance to the client

' NOTE: Calling SafeRef is not necessary because MTS intercepts
' component creation and returns a reference to the Context Wrapper instead
' of the raw object's interface. We *never* have a reference to the raw object's
' interface.

    Dim objSubObject As SafeRefTests.clsSubObject

' Create an instance of the SafeRefTests.clsSubObject component
    Set objSubObject = CreateObject("SafeRefTests.clsSubObject")

' Return a reference to the default interface for the instance of
' SafeRefTest.clsSubObject we created
' NOTICE:  IT IS NOT NECESSARY TO CALL SafeRef
    Set GetSubObject = objSubObject

' Now release our variable reference to the default interface for the instance
' of SafeRefTests.clsSubObject
    Set objSubObject = Nothing

End Function
```

The idea behind SafeRef is actually really simple. SafeRef just returns a reference to the existing Context Wrapper for our MTS object's default interface. Nothing more, nothing less. It's actually one of the simplest concepts in MTS. (You'll agree with that statement after reading the next section.) It's also simple to understand exactly when to call SafeRef or not. There are two simple rules:

❑ Only pass references to your own object (i.e. Me keyword) to SafeRef
❑ Don't pass references to your own object to anyone else without using SafeRef

If you follow these simple rules, you'll be fine. If you don't - well, happy debugging. Tracking whether or not clients are going through the interception mechanism provided by the Context Wrapper is very difficult, and you won't receive any errors to indicate that not calling SafeRef is the culprit of the problem. So be careful out there - it's not a safe world.

An MTS Object's Life Cycle

An MTS object has a very different life cycle to a standard COM object. A standard COM object has two stages in its lifetime: **creation** and **destruction**. In between these stages, methods and/or property procedures are called to invoke functions or change attributes about the object. When a COM object executes under the control of MTS, the MTS Executive manages **four** stages in the object's lifetime:

❑ Creation
❑ Activation
❑ Deactivation
❑ Destruction

The two additional stages between creation and destruction are a direct result of MTS's interception mechanism, and are a contributing factor to MTS providing scalability for n-tier applications. We'll discuss how these two additional stages contribute to scalability later in this chapter. First let's understand when these stages or events occur and the state of our MTS object at that time.

Activation

When MTS receives a component instantiation request, it creates and returns a reference to the Context Wrapper. MTS also instantiates the requested component. However, MTS does not put the object in an **activated** state. When an MTS object is activated, it has been associated with a Context Wrapper and the object's context has been created. Because the Object Context is not created until our MTS object is activated, calls to the function `GetObjectContext` fail and return `Nothing`.

An MTS object is only activated when the first method is invoked by the client. For example, in the following code sample, the instance of the `clsMTSLifeCycle` component is not activated until the `DoSomething` method is called:

```
Dim objMTSLifeCycle As MTSLifeCycle.clsMTSLifeCycle

'Create an instance of the clsMTSLifeCycle Component
Set objMTSLifeCycle = CreateObject("MTSLifeCycle.clsMTSLifeCycle")

'Now when the DoSomething is invoked on our instance of the
'clsMTSLifeCycle Component, the object will be activated
objMTSLifeCycle.DoSomething

'Release our instance of the clsMTSLifeCycle component
Set objMTSLifeCycle = Nothing
```

> **However, there is one exception to this rule. When the methods of the IUnknown interface (`QueryInterface`, `AddRef`, or `Release`) are invoked by the client, the MTS object will not be activated.**

This is because the Context Wrapper provides the implementation for these methods and doesn't forward calls to them on to the actual MTS object. Of course VB restricts us from calling the methods of the `IUnknown` interface directly anyway, because they're defined as restricted. However, this exception to the MTS activation rule also applies to any assignments with object variable references that force VB to call the methods `QueryInterface`, `AddRef` or `Release` behind the scenes.

For example, in the following code sample, the client forces VB to call the `AddRef`, `Release` and `QueryInterface` methods on an instance of the `clsMTSLifeCycle` component, but these method calls *will not* activate the object:

```
Dim objMTSLifeCycle As MTSLifeCycle.clsMTSLifeCycle
Dim objMTSLifeCycle2 As MTSLifeCycle.clsMTSLifeCycle

Dim objMTSLifeCycle_Interface2 As MTSLifeCycle.clsMTSLifeCycle

'Create an instance of the clsMTSLifeCycle Component
Set objMTSLifeCycle = CreateObject("MTSLifeCycle.clsMTSLifeCycle")
```

```
'Put a reference to our new instance in another variable also
'(This forces VB to call AddRef)
'The object will not be activated.
Set objMTSLifeCycle2 = objMTSLifeCycle

'Release our second reference (This forces VB to call Release)
'The object will not be activated.
Set objMTSLifeCycle2 = Nothing

'Get a reference to another interface
'(This forces VB to call QueryInterface)
'The object will not be activated.
Set objMTSLifeCycle_Interface2 = objMTSLifeCycle

'Release our instance of the clsMTSLifeCycle component
'by releasing the last reference (forces Release to be called)
Set objMTSLifeCycle = Nothing
```

Deactivation

Once an MTS object has been activated, it remains activated and in memory until it is placed in the **deactivated** state. When an MTS object is deactivated, it is no longer tied to the same Context Wrapper and the Object Context is not available. MTS can then reclaim and reuse any resources that were previously associated with the object.

There are two events that can cause an MTS object to be deactivated:

The MTS Object Requests Deactivation

An object can request deactivation by calling methods of the Object Context. These methods indicate one of the following:

- ❑ The object has successfully completed its work and is ready to be deactivated
- ❑ The object cannot successfully complete its work and it wants to be deactivated.

These methods are the only way an MTS object itself can cause deactivation.

> *For components that participate in transactions, calling these methods also affects the outcome of the current transaction. We'll discuss the role of these methods with transactional objects later in this chapter.*

The Client Releases the Last Reference.

When the client releases the last reference to the MTS object's interface(s), the MTS object is deactivated and destroyed. The Context Wrapper(s) are then destroyed also.

When either of these events occur, MTS deactivates and destroys the object by releasing all of its references to the object's interface(s). Remember from our discussion about the Context Wrapper that the MTS Executive creates and holds a reference to the object. The Context Wrapper simply gets a reference to the MTS object from the MTS Executive. This way the Context Wrapper is just a dumb interception layer. It doesn't have to worry about managing component references.

COM reference counting rules state that when all references to an object's interface(s) are released and the internal reference count is 0, the object is destroyed. MTS Executive respects these COM rules and allows the object to be destroyed just like any other COM object.

Just In Time (JIT) Activation

When an MTS object is deactivated and destroyed the client can continue to hold references to what it thinks is an MTS object, but is actually the MTS Object's Context Wrapper. When the client makes another method call, the MTS object is automatically activated again. If the MTS object has been destroyed, the Context Wrapper will make a request to the MTS Executive to create another instance. This ability for an object to be deactivated and reactivated while clients hold references to it is known as **Just-In-Time (JIT) Activation** or **deferred activation**.

> *MTS objects also exhibit the reverse of JIT:* **As Soon As Possible (ASAP) Deactivation.**

JIT Activation currently provides two important benefits:

- ❑ Resources are only accumulated when they are needed and are released as soon as they're no longer in use.
- ❑ Clients can use MTS just like normal COM components.

JIT Activation Uses Resources As Needed

One way to improve performance and scalability of applications is to only use objects when they are needed. To achieve this before JIT was available, clients were required to manually create, use, and release an object whenever they needed any functionality provided by the component. While this reduces resource consumption, the constant creation and destruction of objects by the client increases the complexity of the application, reduces performance and requires two additional round trips across the network (creation and destruction) each time an object is used.

MTS's JIT Activation model provides the best of both worlds, by abstracting the client from the physical object. Resources are not consumed until they are needed, and after they're utilized, these resources are destroyed.

An object that is never activated can never be deactivated. Thus, if a client creates an MTS object and then releases it without calling a method, the MTS object will never be activated or deactivated. After an MTS object has been destroyed, the next time a call is made by the client, a new instance of the component is seamlessly created by MTS without requiring any extra work on the client's side. That brings us to the next point.

JIT Activation allows clients to use MTS just like normal COM components

With a regular COM component, it may not be a great idea for a client to create an instance and hold onto the object's interface pointers if it has no intention of using the object for a while. A traditional COM server would consume resources as long as the client held a reference to one of the object's interface pointers, even though the object might not be performing any processing.

But with MTS, holding onto references to a stateless object is free – MTS destroys the object anyway as soon as it has no state to maintain. While acquiring interface pointers to objects is still a relatively expensive operation, holding onto them is not.

The SetComplete and SetAbort Methods

Earlier in this section, I mentioned the existence of methods that could deactivate an MTS object. These methods are **SetComplete** and **SetAbort**. We can easily add support to our MTS objects to force deactivation after every method call by calling these `SetComplete` or `SetAbort` methods on the Object Context, without requiring any additional changes to the consumers of our components.

In the following example, we tell MTS that everything looks good and it can deactivate our object when the `Retrieve` method has completed:

```
Public Function Retrieve() As ADODB.Recordset

' Procedure Description: This function retireves all of the Orders
'                        and returns them in a disconnected ADOR/ADODB recodset.

    Dim objContext As MTxAS.ObjectContext

' Get a reference to the ObjectContext for this object
    Set objContext = GetObjectContext

' ******Do some work*****

' Check and see if we have an ObjectContext
    If objObjectContext Is Nothing = False Then
    '..We do, tell it we are done
        objContext.SetComplete

    ' Release our reference to the ObjectContext
        Set objContext = Nothing
    End If

End Function
```

Calling `SetComplete` or `SetAbort` not only causes the MTS object to be placed in the deactivation state, but it does so by deactivating and destroying the current object. This behavior is to ensure the consistency of the current transaction, because the methods `SetComplete` and `SetAbort` also affect transaction outcome. Specifically, MTS does not allow an object to maintain private state that it acquired during a transaction.

When an MTS object calls `SetComplete` or `SetAbort`, any state or data it has stored in member variables will be lost. This is because currently any object will be destroyed after calling `SetComplete` or `SetAbort`.

> *With COM+,* `SetComplete` *and* `SetAbort` *will probably just deactivate the object for non-transactional components, and will function as they currently do for transactional components so that the integrity of the transaction is ensured.*

Consider the scenario illustrated in the diagram opposite:

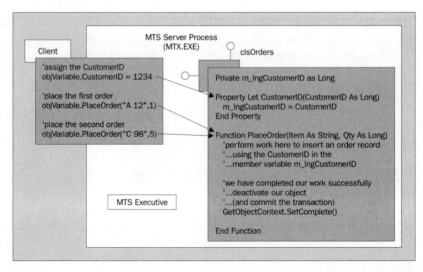

After creating an instance of our `clsOrders` MTS component, the client calls a property procedure named `CustomerID` to set the ID for the Customer placing the order. The `CustomerID` property stores the passed `CustomerID` parameter in a member variable named `m_lngCustomerID`.

The client then calls the `PlaceOrder` function twice to create two order records for the same customer. The first call to the `PlaceOrder` function will complete successfully, and call the `SetComplete` method of the Object Context to indicate to MTS that the object can be deactivated. However, on the second call to the `PlaceOrder` function, there won't be a value in the `m_lngCustomerID` member variable, because the object's state was reset when it was deactivated after the first call to the `PlaceOrder` function.

As you can see, this imposes a potential problem, because the client might expect state to be maintained by the object between method or property calls. After all, that's the behavior of typical COM components, and remember, the client can't differentiate a COM component from an MTS component.

So in this respect, the client must know about the implementation of the object and whether or not state will be maintained across method invocations. If you change which methods force deactivation, even though this is an implementation change, you should break compatibility with previous versions of the component because you are changing the behavior of the component.

Considering these facts, you shouldn't make the choice of calling `SetComplete` or `SetAbort` for non-transactional objects lightly. Transactional objects should always call `SetComplete` or `SetAbort` to dictate the outcome of the transaction to MTS, but non-transactional objects have a choice. MTS enforces statelessness or maintains no state in our components when `SetComplete` or `SetAbort` is called.

So should your non-transactional MTS components call `SetComplete` or `SetAbort` to enforce stateless MTS objects? That's your call. But don't decide yet - make sure you understand all the implications of stateless MTS objects and transactions. We'll cover these topics later in the remainder of this chapter and in Chapters 4 and 5.

To take advantage of JIT Activation in your MTS components, just use the methods `SetComplete` and `SetAbort` to deactivate your MTS objects as quickly as possible, and don't maintain any state (data in member variables) across method calls in your MTS objects.

> *Please note, I'm not saying in any way that all MTS components have to be stateless, I'm just saying, if you want to take advantage of JIT Activation, you must build stateless components. That's because once your object is deactivated, all state will be lost as a result of object destruction.*

The major question on most everyone's minds at this point is: How do you know when an MTS object is activated or deactivated? Well, I'm glad you asked, because that brings us to our next topic, the `IObjectControl` interface.

ObjectControl

We already know that the Object Context provides a way for an MTS component to communicate with the MTS Executive at run time, via calling `GetObjectContext` and calling methods or properties on the reference returned. But how does the MTS Executive communicate with the MTS objects it's hosting at run time? The answer is through the **ObjectControl interface** that is also defined in the Microsoft Transaction Server Type Library.

When an MTS object is created, the MTS Executive calls the `QueryInterface` method of the `IUnknown` interfaces on the new object, to determine whether or not it supports the `ObjectControl` interface. If the object does implement the `ObjectControl` interface, the MTS Executive calls methods on this interface to notify the object when certain stages of its lifetime occur, and to request run time information from the object.

The methods that are defined in the ObjectControl interface and called by the MTS Executive are:

- ❑   `Activate`
- ❑   `Deactivate`
- ❑   `CanBePooled`

Activate

The `Activate` method is called by the MTS Executive after the MTS object has been associated with a Context Wrapper and the object's context is created, but just before the first method call is executed.

This method is very important, because it provides an opportunity for an MTS object to perform initialization that requires the Object Context. Initialization performed in the component's `Class_Initialize` event cannot execute any methods of the Object Context, because even the Object Context is not created until the MTS object is activated.

> *An additional use applies if the MTS object supports pooling. When object pooling becomes available, all initialization must occur when the* `Activate` *method is called, since the object will be reused by several Context Wrappers without being destroyed. The* `Activate` *method will be called each time it is attached to another Context Wrapper.*

Deactivate

The `Deactivate` method is called by the MTS Executive just before the object is deactivated and disconnected from the Context Wrapper. As with the `Class_Initialize` event, code executing in the `Class_Terminate` event cannot use the Object Context. The `Deactivate` method provides an opportunity for an MTS object to perform a last-minute clean-up using the Object Context, before the object is deactivated.

For MTS components that have long activation periods, it's generally a good idea not to wait until the `Deactivate` method is called to release resources.

> **Microsoft Transaction Server yields many performance benefits by simply releasing resources as soon as possible.**

CanBePooled

The `CanBePooled` method is called by the MTS Executive after the object is deactivated. This method was intended for an MTS object to able to return `True` to indicate that it supported pooling or `False` to indicate that it didn't want to be pooled. However, don't let this method confuse you.

> **MTS 2.0 or 2.1 does not support object pooling.**

Currently, the value returned by your objects when the `CanBePooled` method is called is ignored, and after this method is called the MTS object is destroyed.

Components can take advantage of the ObjectControl interface in Visual Basic through the use of the `Implements` keyword, the same way a component would provide support for any other interface.

Remember, the COM rules state that whenever a component uses the `Implements` keyword, it must provide support for every method of the implemented interface, regardless of whether or not you want to perform processing when a particular method is called.

It's not a requirement for an MTS component to implement the ObjectControl interface. However, if a component does not implement this interface, instances of the MTS component will never know when they're being activated or deactivated, and will therefore be unable to perform initialization or destruction code that requires the Object Context. They will also not be able to take advantage of object pooling in the future, when it's provided with COM+.

```
'Provide support for the MTxAS.ObjectControl interface
Implements MTxAS.ObjectControl

Private Sub ObjectControl_Activate()

' Log that the object is being Activated
  Debug.Print "Activation" & vbCrLf & "Time: " & Now

End Sub

Private Function ObjectControl_CanBePooled() As Boolean

' The MTS Executive is asking our object if it wants to be pooled
  Debug.Print "CanBePooled?" & vbCrLf & "Time: " & Now

End Function

Private Sub ObjectControl_Deactivate()

' Log that the object is being Deactivated
  Debug.Print "Deactivation" & vbCrLf & "Time: " & Now

End Sub
```

MTS Explorer also provides a status view that allows an administrator to observe the lifecycle of MTS objects through the use of three different counters:

- ❑ **Objects**: This counter indicates the total number of MTS objects that have been created for a particular component.
- ❑ **Activated**: This counter indicates the total number of objects that are currently activated.
- ❑ **In Call**: This counter indicates the total number of objects that are currently executing a method call.

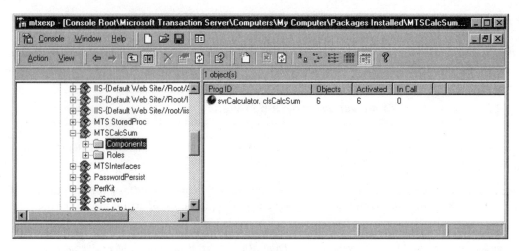

These counters are dependent on one another in a hierarchy. An MTS object must be created (listed in the Object counter) to be activated, and an MTS object must be activated (listed in the Activated counter) to execute a method call (listed in the In Call counter).

Using MTS Explorer to watch the status of your MTS components can be very helpful, especially when debugging. However, sometimes method execution, activation or object creation occurs so fast that you may not actually see this sequence appear. In these situations, you must resort to some of the more elaborate debugging measures that we will discuss in Chapter 9.

Activities

When a distributed application provides services to multiple users, it can receive simultaneous calls from clients. As a result, distributed applications must be concerned about issues such as **concurrency** and **thread management**. MTS shields you from these issues and allows you to create components that execute in a multi-user distributed environment, just as you would create a component that services a single user.

MTS accomplishes this amazing task through the use of **activities**. An activity is nothing more than a group of objects executing on the behalf of a single client. By grouping a single client's objects together into an activity, they're isolated from all other activities and objects. One client's work can't interfere with another's. This simple concept is very important in OLTP systems, to ensure the integrity of data and prevent deadlock situations. But MTS provides more than just multi-user concurrency through activities:

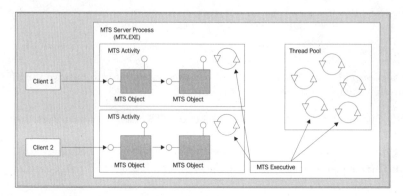

Activities also ensure that no two objects servicing the same client can execute at the same time. Objects within an activity are **serialized** to prevent parallel execution within the same activity. An activity can be composed of multiple objects executing in separate processes or on separate machines. For these reasons, an activity is sometimes referred to as a single logical thread of execution.

But why is serialization of objects so important? Think about a scenario in which two objects executing on behalf of the same user are trying to access the same resources at the exact same time. Each object could potentially block the other object from completing its operation. This situation is known as a **deadlock**. Activities help prevent deadlocks from occurring by only allowing one object to execute at a time on the behalf of a single user.

MTS enforces serialization of objects within an activity by linking an activity to a single physical thread of execution or a Single-Threaded Apartment (STA). Objects within an activity cannot execute concurrently because there's only one physical thread per activity. MTS manages a thread pool that can hold up to 100 of these single-threaded apartments.

The MTS Executive creates a new STA for each new activity until the pool reaches this limit. When the number of activities exceeds the maximum number of STAs, the MTS Executive begins to assign multiple activities to each STA. If two activities share the same STA, the MTS run time manages **multiplexing** STAs (physical threads) in and out of activities (logical threads). This is why activities are referred to as logical threads of execution instead of physical threads.

When multiplexing occurs, code executing on behalf of one user can potentially block the call of another client. So what's the performance impact when multiple activities share the same physical thread? You shouldn't notice an impact on performance due to multiplexing until you have well over 100 concurrent activities. Most objects only process method calls 10% of their lifetime. The other 90% of the time, they're waiting for additional requests until they're deactivated - and of course, a deactivated object is not performing any processing.

> By using a physical thread *per-activity* instead of a physical thread *per-object*, MTS can scale to support many objects without consuming too many resources.

Let's consider the alternative approach of a thread per object. Imagine 1,000 concurrent objects, each assigned to their own thread - the thread switching alone would kill the performance of the overall system. With an average of only 10% of those objects concurrently processing method calls, approximately 100 threads are concurrently executing but 900 are allocated and taking up resources. So attaching a single STA per-activity not only accomplishes the main goal of serializing object execution across an activity, but it also makes MTS a much more scalable run time environment for your objects.

Currently, the maximum number of threads in the thread pool is 100 per package and, unfortunately, this limit is hard-coded within the MTS Executive. If you must overcome this limitation, one workaround is to separate your components into separate packages. Packages can be configured to execute in their own process (MTX.EXE instance) and the process will be assigned its own thread pool. MTS also provides thread pooling when objects are loaded into the client's process.

One last item you should note about MTS's thread pooling is that once the MTS Executive creates a thread and adds it to the pool, the thread will not be destroyed until the process that owns the thread is destroyed. MTS's thread pooling is not a typical type of resource pooling, where the pool size varies based on performance algorithms. It's just a dump pool that will have a thread added to it as needed up to a maximum of 100.

An activity is created when a client creates an MTS object using the `CreateObject` function or the `New` keyword. This new object is called the **root** of the activity, because its creation caused a new activity to be created as well. The MTS Executive assigns the new activity a GUID value, called the **ActivityID**, and stores it in the Object Context for the root of the activity.

> **All objects created in the same activity share the same ActivityID.**

The ActivityID can't be changed and an object in an activity can't be moved to another activity. The activity is finally destroyed when the client releases that object.

The best thing about activities is that they're totally implemented by the MTS Executive behind the scenes. Your components aren't required to perform any additional work for MTS to provide them with these concurrency and threading services. Your only responsibility is to follow two simple rules to ensure that you use activities correctly.

Don't share object references across clients

There's only one minor problem with MTS using a single STA per activity to serialize objects within the activity - the MTS Executive doesn't serialize an activity's objects if the objects execute in *different* processes or on *different* machines. This behavior is probably because cross process and/or cross machine synchronization would severely degrade performance.

Consider a situation that could occur when multiple clients share the same object references. When MTS object references are shared across threads (including across processes or machines), there's the potential for multiple threads to concurrently call into the same activity.

This is not a problem if the objects within the activity all execute in the same process - MTS simply performs one request at a time and serializes the objects within the activity. However, if two threads (clients) were to concurrently call separate objects in the same activity, and these separate objects executed in different processes, MTS will not serialize the objects and the calls would execute concurrently.

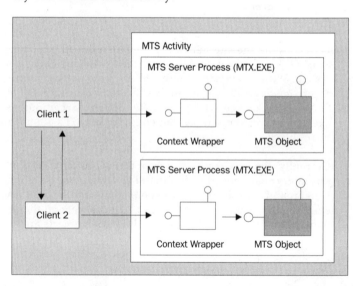

As we discussed before, concurrent execution of objects within an activity can cause unexpected results: it's possible for one thread to issue a request that would attempt to commit the current transaction while another thread is in the middle of doing work in the same transaction. The best solution to this problem is very simple.

> **Avoid designs that share object references between threads. Use local or module level variables within your applications and don't pass your references to any other objects or applications.**

Whenever another thread (or process) needs an MTS object, it calls the `CreateObject` function or uses the `New` keyword and creates the object along with a new activity. Because of JIT Activation, you don't have to worry about the performance impact of having many objects instead of sharing one.

Avoid creating objects in different activities when they belong to the same thread

Since activities begin sharing physical threads (STAs) when there are more activities than the maximum amount of threads in the thread pool (currently 100), you should minimize the number of activities for each client. The solution is for multiple objects to execute in the same activity and share the same STA.

But how do we get additional objects into an existing activity? We certainly can't move existing objects into an activity. However, existing MTS objects can create additional objects within their activity by making the creation request to the MTS Executive instead of COM's SCM. The **CreateInstance** function of the Object Context object is designed for exactly this purpose.

At first glance, the `CreateInstance` function looks very similar to the `CreateObject` function. Both functions take a ProgID as a parameter to indicate which object to create and both return a reference to a new instance in a variant. However, the `CreateInstance` function serves a very different and important purpose.

We'll discuss more about the `CreateInstance` function and its role with activities in the following section. At this point, just understand that MTS objects created using the `CreateInstance` function of an existing MTS object's Object Context will belong to the same activity as their creator.

Creating Instances of Components

With the introduction of the `CreateInstance` function on the Object Context, there are now three common ways to instantiate MTS components from Visual Basic:

- ❑ The `CreateObject` function
- ❑ The `New` keyword
- ❑ The `CreateInstance` function of the Object Context

But why does VB need yet another way to create an object? The `CreateObject` function, the `New` keyword and now the `CreateInstance` function - don't we have enough ways create an object already?

It's important to understand that the `CreateInstance` function is not a total replacement for the `CreateObject` function, or even the `New` keyword. Each of these techniques serve a very different purpose for creating MTS objects, depending upon the perspective of the creator. The important (and slightly difficult) task is to understand *when* and *when no*t to use which component instantiation technique, and why.

In this section, we are going to resolve this common area of confusion, and leave you with three simple rules to follow when creating instances of MTS components.

The CreateObject Function

When an object is created with the `CreateObject` function, a new activity is also created and the object executes within this new activity. The `CreateObject` function works fine for the base client to create the root of an activity, but it offers no technique for MTS objects to be created in an existing activity. This is because the creation request is always made through COM (the SCM) instead of MTS, and COM has no concept of Context Wrappers, Object Contexts or activities:

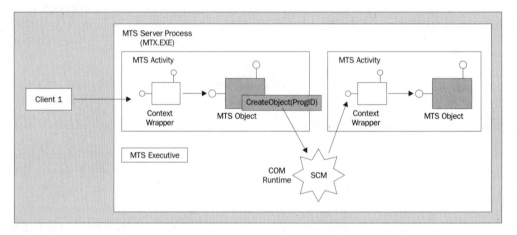

Besides the problems with concurrent execution within an activity, not creating MTS objects that perform work on the behalf of the same client represents other major problems.

The Object Context for the new object will not be inherited from the creator

When MTS objects are created in an existing activity, they inherit the Object Context's information about security and transactions from the creator. Without this information, objects executing in separate activities cannot enlist in the same transaction, and security information will be inaccurate. (I realize we've not had a full discussion about transactions or security yet, but we'll cover these important topics in detail in later chapters.)

The two objects will most likely execute in separate STAs

Recall from our discussion about activities, the only way two activities share an STA is when the number of activities exceeds the maximum number of STAs in the thread pool. You have no control over which activates are sharing STAs. So the activity of the root object and the activity of any objects created by the root using the `CreateObject` function are most likely *not* sharing the same STA.

Standard COM apartment rules state that when an object in one STA calls an object in another STA, a proxy/stub layer is used to marshal data across apartments, even if the threads are in the same process. Marshalling will also be performed if objects within the same activity execute in separate processes or on separate machines. The effect of marshalling can significantly reduce performance, especially with objects that make very many cross-apartment or cross-process method calls.

Performance can also suffer because work performed on the behalf of one base client is now consuming more than one STA and reducing the number of available STAs for other activities. If multiplexing is performed, because the number of activities exceeds the maximum number of STAs in the thread pool, it causes one activity to block the work of another.

> **In other words, when multiplexing is performed, one client can be blocked until the work performed on behalf of another client is completed.**

The MTS environment doesn't support the use of `Friend` property procedures or methods. This is because `Friend` properties or methods can only be called on objects created with the `New` keyword, and of course we can't use the `New` keyword to create other MTS objects in the same activity. Any attempt to call a `Friend` property or method on an object created with the `CreateObject` or `CreateInstance` functions will result in an error.

Currently there's no workaround. Neither of the three component instantiation techniques supports `Friend` scoped properties or methods with objects executing in the MTS environment. The only solution is to raise the scope of the property or method to `Public`, or better yet, define the properties and methods as a separate interface and just implement an additional interface in your component.

The New Keyword

MTS objects created with the `New` keyword are also created in a new activity. So for creating MTS objects from an existing MTS object, the `New` keyword also shares the same problem as the `CreateObject` function. However, the `New` keyword has an additional problem you should watch out for.

When instances of components are created using the `New` keyword and the component resides in the same DLL server as the creator, the Visual Basic run time will create the instance instead of COM's SCM or the MTS Executive. COM and MTS will be uninvolved with the object creation and totally unaware of the new object. As a result, the new object won't have its own Context Wrapper, Object Context or activity, nor will it be enlisted in the creators activity.

This problem can be very hard to track down, because your code won't necessarily crash, but it will exhibit unexpected behavior. Calls to the `GetObjectContext` function within this new object will be given a reference to the Object Context of its creator.

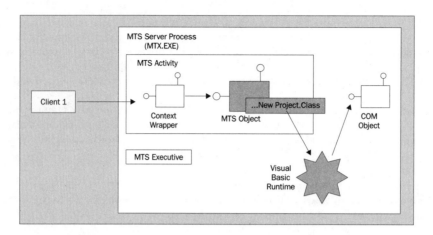

However, even with the problems with the New keyword, there are several situations when it should be used. The following are some of these situations.

Private or PublicNotCreatable classes cannot be created outside of their own project

The New keyword *must* be used to create objects from classes with Instancing properties of Private or PublicNotCreatable. These types of classes cannot be instantiated external to the project they're defined in.

Non-MTS Components

You can use the New keyword (or CreateObject) to create instances of non-MTS components such as ADO, CDO or many of the other COM components that don't need a Context Wrapper and that don't use the Object Context.

Root of the Activity

The New keyword (and CreateObject) can be used to create an MTS object that is the root of a new activity. The New keyword does offer a slight performance increase over the CreateObject function. This is partly because CreateObject returns an object reference in a variant, and it has to perform a ProgID to CLSID lookup in the registry, whereas the New keyword doesn't. But when using the New keyword instead of the CreateObject function, you give up the ability to dynamically instantiate a component on a remote machine.

> *You should totally avoid using the* Dim As New *syntax to create any type of object. Although this saves a line of code, Visual Basic will not create the object until it's used. This syntax causes Visual Basic to insert checks inside your code, to determine if the object is created yet and to create it when it's first used. The result is less efficient code, because the checks to determine if the object is created are performed every time you invoke a method or property using the object variable.*

The CreateInstance Function

The CreateInstance function of the Object Context makes object creation requests to the MTS Executive instead of to COM. As a result, objects created using the CreateInstance function by an existing MTS object will execute in the *same* activity as the creator. The new object will inherit the Object Context information (including security and transaction information) from the creator, and the MTS objects will be serialized within the activity - assuming, of course, that they execute in the same process.

There will also be better performance, because with the MTS objects executing within the same activity there's no need for a proxy/stub layer to perform marshalling of data across STAs. Again, this is assuming that the objects are executing within the same process.

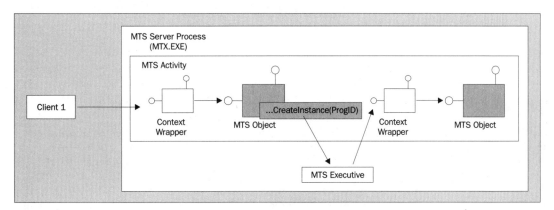

Even though an MTS object created by another using the `CreateInstance` function will execute in the same activity as its creator, MTS will still place a Context Wrapper between the creator and the new object. In other words, just because objects run in the same activity, that doesn't mean that MTS doesn't intercept method calls using a Context Wrapper for each MTS object during inter-activity communication. For this reason, objects created with the `CreateInstance` function can be returned to the base client without the need to call `SafeRef` on the new object first:

```
Dim objContext As MTxAS.ObjectContext
Dim objOrders as Northwind_BusSrv.clsOrders

'Get a reference to the Object Context for this object
Set objContext = GetObjectContext

'create an instance of the clsOrders component
Set objOrders = ojbContext.CreateInstance("Northwind_BusSrv.clsOrders")

'Release our reference to the Object Context
Set objContext = Nothing
```

Object Creation Summary

How you instantiate MTS components depends on the perspective of the creator. Follow these simple rules when creating instances of MTS components to ensure predictable results in the MTS run time environment:

- ❑ Use the `CreateObject` function or the `New` keyword when creating instances of MTS components *from the base client.*
- ❑ Only use the `New` keyword when creating instances of Private or PublicNotCreatable classes, when creating instances of non-MTS components or creating an instance of the root of an activity.
- ❑ Use the `CreateInstance` function of the Object Context when creating instances of other MTS components *from an MTS object.* This will ensure that the child or sub objects are always created in the same activity, and in turn they will inherit the transactional and security information from the Object Context of the creator.

My recommendation for developers who hate to remember all of these exceptions and rules to component instantiation is to just:

❑ Always use the `CreateObject` function for creating instances of non-MTS components and the root of the activity

❑ Always use the `CreateInstance` function when creating instances of MTS components from within an MTS object.

Summary

Phew! I bet you're glad that chapter's over. I realize that it might have been hard going at times, but a firm understanding of this material will help you through the rest of the book. We'll be revisiting many of the concepts covered here again and again. When we do, you may want to return to this chapter and possibly do some further reading.

We started out with a quick grounding in the fundamentals of COM and DCOM. If you haven't had much experience with them then I'd recommend you go and pick up another book on the subject. A firm understanding of COM is essential for far more than just this book. Again, I recommend VB COM: A Visual Basic Programmer's Introduction to COM as a good place to start.

From there, we went on to see how MTS builds on COM to provide the run time features that make MTS such a powerful tool. We learned

❑ How MTS components are instantiated
❑ How the Context Wrapper works
❑ How MTS components can use the Object Context to interact with MTS
❑ How to obtain and pass references to MTS objects
❑ How MTS interacts with MTS components through the ObjectControl interface
❑ How MTS uses activities to deal with multiple users
❑ How to create instances of MTS components, and which method is best in which situation

Next, we're going to continue on with our largely theoretical exploration of MTS by looking at the 'T' in MTS: Transactions.

Transaction Processing

In the last chapter, we took a rather detailed look at COM and MTS and saw what was going on behind those spinning balls. This chapter will be less intensive but no less important.

Up until this point, our focus has been on the Object Request Broker (ORB) features of MTS. But now it's time to turn our attention to the center of MTS, transactions. Transaction processing systems are nothing new. They have been around for decades. However, before the release of MTS, transaction processing had never been combined with object management, a very powerful combination for developing distributed, component-based, software systems.

After completing this chapter, you should be able to answer the following questions:

- ❑ What is a transaction?
- ❑ What does ACID have to do with transactions?
- ❑ How can I change data in multiple databases and still meet the requirements of the ACID test?
- ❑ How is MS DTC a part of MTS?
- ❑ What is the difference between database transactions and MTS transactions?
- ❑ What are Resource Dispensers and how do they work?
- ❑ How does database connection pooling work?
- ❑ What are the different stages in the life of an MTS transaction?

Introduction to Transactions

The first recorded use for the word **transaction** occurred in Roman civil law around 1460, which was used to define an adjustment for a dispute. Transaction was borrowed directly from the Latin word transactionem, meaning an agreement or accomplishment. It was not until another 200 years or so, the word transaction evolved to reflect a sense of business.

Actually transactions have existed since man has roamed the earth. To better understand transactions, let's go back in time some 2 million years ago and visit the original founder of the fictional Grog Company. Grog's first business transaction was with a local clansman named Borg. Grog admired Borg's collection of seashells. At the same time, Borg admired Grog's collection of beads. Grog offered to trade Borg five seashells for five beads. Borg accepted, and the trade was made. This is a transaction. Actually, being new at this transaction business, a few alternatives were tried first.

Grog in good faith first gave Borg five seashells. However, Borg decided to see what would happen by with-holding the delivery of beads to Grog and not keeping his end of the bargain. Grog beat Borg on the head with a woolly mammoth tusk and then took his seashells back.

Although Borg had a hard head, he was a quick learner and apologized to Grog. This time, Borg gave Grog the five beads in return for five seashells and the transaction was completed.

I don't have to tell you, but you know that software systems are not completely bulletproof. Functionality errors within the software, as well as errors that are beyond the control of the developer, such as hardware or network failures, *will* eventually occur. Distributed component-based systems are even more prone to failure because of their increased complexity. With remote components, executing on the behalf of clients, which are modifying data stored in different data sources, many pieces of complex software and hardware must work together seamlessly. When an error does occur, data cannot be left in an inconsistent state. An entire set of operations or changes performed on one or more data sources must *all* succeed (**commit**) or *all* fail (**roll back**).

To accomplish this all-or-nothing work management that ensures data consistency and integrity, we use transactions.

> **A transaction is an operation or a series of operations that change data from one consistent state to another.**

In other words, a transaction simply treats multiple operations as one unit of work. To better understand this, consider the famous banking transaction scenario:

An individual walks up to an ATM machine and proceeds to transfer $500 from their savings account to their checking account. Two operations are actually being performed with this transfer. $500 is being withdrawn from the savings account and the same $500 is being deposited into the checking account. These two operations must be performed as one unit of work or as a transaction.

Either *both* of these operations must succeed or *both* must fail. If either individual operation fails, the transaction as a whole is not successful and any work that was already performed must be rolled back or undone in order to maintain the integrity of the accounts. Imagine if the withdrawal of $500 from the savings account succeeded but the deposit of $500 dollars into the checking account failed for whatever reason. Not only would the balances of the accounts not be correct, but the bank also would not have a very happy customer.

While most of the time a transaction is composed of multiple operations or units of work, the general term transaction is used for just about any operation that modifies data. For this reason you'll sometimes hear a single operation being referred to as a transaction. Don't be confused.

A transaction can be composed of one or more operations, although most of the time a transaction is composed of multiple operations.

ACID Properties

A transaction is an action, or series of actions, that transform a system from one consistent state to another. Every transaction must meet the following four essential requirements, known collectively as the **ACID properties**:

- ❑ Atomicity
- ❑ Consistency
- ❑ Isolation
- ❑ Durability

Atomicity

Atomicity refers to the all-or-nothing proposition of a transaction that we mentioned earlier. Once a transaction is started, it will either *commit* or *abort*.

If *all* of a transaction's operations complete successfully, the transaction can commit and the changes made by *all* of the transaction's operations will remain. If *any* of the operations fail, the transaction will abort and *any* of the changes already made by its operations will be undone. There is no chance that some operations in a transaction complete and some operations will fail. For example, when Borg withheld his beads from Grog, Grog took back his seashells. This transaction was completely aborted. However, when Grog and Borg traded as agreed, the transaction was executed completely.

To provide the ability to rollback or undo uncommitted changes, many data sources implement a logging mechanism. For example, SQL Server uses a write-ahead transaction log where changes are written to the log before they are applied or committed to the actual data pages. However, other data sources, which are not relational database management systems (RDBMS), manage uncommitted transactions completely differently. As long as the data source is able to undo any uncommitted changes, if a transaction is rolled back, the technique used by a data source for managing transactions doesn't really matter.

Although the all-or-nothing behavior is the first thing that comes to mind in a discussion about transaction processing, it is important to remember that the atomicity property is only one of the four ACID properties. A transaction must also meet the other three ACID properties.

Consistency

A transaction also must be **consistent**.

> **This means that every process that makes up a transaction cannot break any business rules or semantics specified by the environment.**

In simpler terms, business logic for Grog's transaction needs to be consistent with every transaction Grog executes. When Grog agreed to trade five beads for five seashells, Grog did in fact receive five seashells. At the same time, he gave Borg five beads. The business logic in Grog's time is very simple: "x something" for "y something". Yet it shows that even 2 million years ago, transactions maintained consistency.

Consistency ensures that changes made as a result of a transaction do not violate the integrity of the data. For example, in our ATM banking transaction scenario, after the transfer of $500 from an individual's savings account to their checking account both accounts have to reflect the transfer. Individual operations within a transaction may leave the data in an inconsistent state because a transaction is about transforming data from one consistent state to another, however once a transaction is committed, a transaction must guarantee the consistency and integrity of the data in all the data sources affected.

Again, in our ATM banking scenario, both accounts are in a consistent state before the transfer. During the transfer, money is first withdrawn from the savings account. At this point the data is in an inconsistent state. $500 dollars has been withdrawn as part of a transfer and has not been accounted for in another account. However, the transaction is not yet complete. The same $500 is then deposited into the checking account. This operation effectively completes the transaction and both accounts are returned to a consistent state.

Data sources such as SQL Server, and other RDBMS, enforce data consistency and integrity through the use of **constraints**.

> *Applications or business components can also enforce data consistency and integrity, although it is usually recommended to implement this functionality at the data source level. This is to ensure that data consistency is enforced even when changes to the data are made outside of your application's or component's control.*

Remember, a transaction is not responsible for enforcing data integrity, but instead a transaction is only responsible for ensuring that data is returned to a *consistent* state after the transaction is either committed or aborted. The burden of understanding data integrity rules and possibly writing code to enforce them usually falls on the shoulders of the developer who is creating business components, so be prepared.

Transactions must also maintain data consistency and integrity when multiple concurrent users are accessing and modifying the same data, a concept that goes hand in hand with the next ACID property, **isolation**.

Isolation

> **All of the operations performed in a transaction must be isolated from operations performed by other transactions.**

This property is sometimes referred to as **serializability** because in order to prevent one transaction's operations for interfering with another's, requests must be serialized or sequenced so that only one request for the same data is serviced at a time.

Let's consider isolation in our ATM banking transaction scenario. At the exact time an individual is transferring $500 from the savings account to the checking account, his significant other, standing at another ATM machine, decides to withdraw $100 from their checking account. If one transaction is performed before the other, and the transactions are serialized, there will not be a problem. However, if the withdrawal of $100 from the checking account occurs during the $500 transfer, the balance of the checking will appear inconsistent. To the individual transferring the $500 from the savings to the checking account, it would appear that the checking account was short $100, but to the other person withdrawing $100 from the checking account the balance would appear as though it had gained $400. If concurrent transactions could modify the same data at the same time, rollbacks would produce inconsistent results.

Isolation not only guarantees that multiple transactions cannot modify the same data at the same time, but isolation also guarantees that changes caused by one transaction's operations will not be seen by another transaction until the changes are either committed or aborted. Concurrent transactions will be unaware of each other's partial and inconsistent changes. This means that all requests to modify or read data that is already involved in a transaction are blocked until the transaction completes. Most data sources such as SQL Server and other RDBMS implement isolation through the use of **locks**. Individual data items or sets of data are locked from concurrent access if it is involved in a transaction.

Durability

> **Durability simply ensures that once a transaction is committed, the results of the transaction will be persisted even if there is any type of system failure immediately following the transaction's completion.**

All data has been written to permanent storage and can be recovered. In our ATM banking transaction scenario, what if there is a power outage for the ATM machine in which the individual is performing the $500 transfer? If the $500 had already been deposited back into the checking account to complete the transaction, the power outage at the same ATM machine would not affect the resulting account balances. On the other hand, if the power outage happened during the transfer, any operations already performed would be rolled back, as part of the transactions atomicity property.

Data sources such as SQL Server and other RDBMS also use transaction logging to re-apply or recover any changes to data should an unforeseeable problem occur after a transaction has been committed.

All of these somewhat inter-related properties of a transaction are simply about ensuring that data involved in the transaction is managed correctly from the time a transaction begins until after a transaction is either committed or aborted.

Overall, transactions are pretty simplistic when all data modifications are performed against a single data source. However, distributed transactions, that modify data stored in multiple numbers and types of data sources possibly spread across any number of machines, are much more complex. The commit and abort behavior of a transaction can no longer be handled by the data source itself, but instead must be coordinated across these different data sources for each transaction. Even though MTS hides the details of distributed transactions from us, it is worthwhile to study and understand the "behind-the-scenes" architecture of distributed transactions. It's also important to remember that these ACID properties apply to all types of transactions no matter what types or numbers of data sources are involved in the transaction.

Database Transactions

Let's travel back to the future and apply Grog's transaction to a modern database transaction. When Grog first gave Borg the five seashells, the transaction was said to have begun. In SQL, transaction management uses the command, BEGIN TRANSACTION to mark the beginning of the transaction. If the transaction successfully completes, the COMMIT TRANSACTION command makes all actions in the transaction permanent. However, in the event that the transaction fails, such as when Borg decided to renege on his side of the deal, a ROLLBACK TRANSACTION is used to return everything back to the original state. A transaction that has been rolled back appears as if nothing ever happened.

The following SQL code segment is an example of Grog's transaction in terms of a database:

```
BEGIN TRANSACTION

  INSERT TradeSeashells (TransactionNo, CustName, Quantity)
    VALUES (01, "Borg", 5)

  IF @@error ! = 0
  BEGIN
    ROLLBACK TRANSACTION
    RETURN
  END

  UPDATE TradeSeashellsQuantity
    SET ShellsInStock = ShellsInStock - 5
    WHERE TransactionNo = 01

  IF @@error !=0
  BEGIN
    ROLLBACK TRANSACTION
    RETURN
  END

  INSERT AcquireBeads (TransactionNo, CustName, Quantity)
    VALUES (01,"Grog", 5)
```

```
IF @@error ! = 0
  BEGIN
    ROLLBACK TRANSACTION
    RETURN
  END

  UPDATE AcquireBeadsQuantity
    SET BeadsInStock = BeadsInStock + 5
    WHERE TransactionNo = 01

  IF @@error ! = 0
  BEGIN
    ROLLBACK TRANSACTION
    RETURN
  END

COMMIT TRANSACTION
```

We'll be taking a much more detailed look at database transasctions and SQL in Chapter 11.

The Architecture of Distributed Transactions

As business requirements increase and applications become more complex, it is becoming increasingly common for the need to access multiple databases, often at different locations. Suppose we have a transaction that requires data changes to occur in two separate databases and still require that all the properties of the ACID test be met. Basic transaction management using SQL Server will not suffice. There is no way to ensure that if one database server fails, the other has not already committed and become permanent. In other words, there is no way to guarantee atomicity without a way to coordinate multiple transaction processes occurring at multiple locations.

> **This coordination is carried out by transaction managers. The transaction manager assigns identifiers to transactions, monitors their progress, and takes responsibility for transaction completion and failure.**

Two-Phase Commit with MS DTC

Take another look at the SQL code for Grog's transaction. Recall that two parts of this transaction must complete for a commit to occur – an `INSERT` and `UPDATE` is required for changes to Grog's seashell inventory and another `INSERT` and `UPDATE` is required for Grog's bead inventory. Suppose Grog used MS SQL Server to record changes to his seashell inventory and Oracle to record changes to his bead inventory. What if the server where Oracle resides goes down? How can we guarantee atomicity? The solution comes from a protocol called **two-phase commit** and is coordinated by the **Microsoft Distributed Transaction Coordinator (MS DTC)**.

> **MS DTC is integrated into SQL Server and is a vital part of MTS. By adding another factor into the transaction process, MS DTC verifies all processes are ready and able to commit.**

Let's explore MS DTC a little closer and see how it works. In order for the two-phase commit protocol to be coordinated, each data source in the transaction must have MS DTC installed. From these installations, the main coordinator is always going to be where the transaction originates. This main coordinator is referred to as the **Commit Coordinator** and is responsible for ensuring that the transaction either commits or aborts on all servers that are involved with the transaction. It is also the responsibility of the commit coordinator to report back to the client application whether it has successfully committed or rolled back the transaction.

Grog's transaction requires changing data in one database to reflect his inventory for seashells. His transaction also, requires changing data in another database to reflect his inventory for beads:

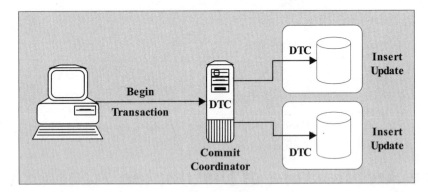

The commit coordinator is notified about the transaction's status:

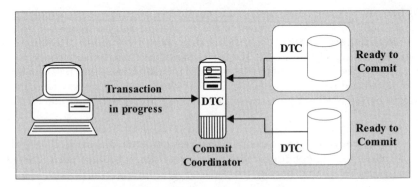

If the commit coordinator receives a "ready to commit" from each data source, the transaction is committed:

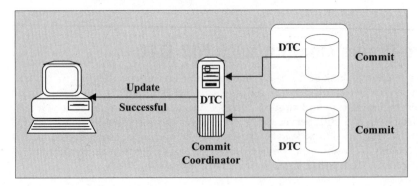

However, if one "failure" is received from any data source that is to be affected, the commit coordinator will issue a roll back and notify the client application:

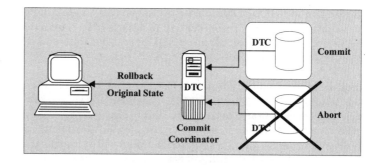

OLE Transactions and the XA Standard

OLE Transactions is Microsoft's protocol definition that allows applications to communicate with MS DTC. Microsoft originally designed the OLE Transactions interfaces (`ITransaction`, `ITransactionDispenser`, `ITransactionOptions`, and `ITransactionOutcomeEvents`), and then implemented those four interfaces in DTC.

> **In simpler terms, OLE Transactions is an object-oriented protocol based on COM that is used for transaction management.**

XA is a different two-phase protocol that is common in the Unix database world. The **XA standard** has been defined by the X/Open Distributed Transaction Processing (DTP) group. Although similar to OLE Transactions, the XA standard allows applications and resource managers to communicate with a transaction manager. However, XA is not object-oriented or COM based.

MS DTC supports both OLE Transactions and XA protocols. XA compliant resource managers, such as the ones found in Oracle, Sybase, Informix, and DB/2, can participate in MTS transactions.

You will learn more about MS DTC in Chapter 11. For now, let's move on and learn about transactions in MTS.

MTS Transactions

Microsoft Transaction Server provides a transaction model that eliminates the complex transaction-processing code required for distributed transactions coordinated by MS DTC. This transactional model *transparently* merges distributed transactions with COM components.

MTS transactions are implemented through the use of **declarative attributes** that are specified *external* to a component's implementation. All you have to do is configure your component's **transaction support** using the MTS Explorer and modify the components to vote on the transaction outcome.

MTS automatically handles the rest of the complex and redundant details of beginning and committing or aborting transactions by interacting with the MS DTC on the behalf of your component, based on the component's transaction support. Any operations your component performs against resources will automatically be performed within a distributed transaction. Components can optionally control the transaction's lifetime through the use of four methods provided by the ObjectContext object.

Since MTS relies on MS DTC to coordinate transactions, a single component can perform operations against several different types of resources within a *single* MTS transaction. For example, an MTS object could perform an operation against a SQL Server database and send an MSMQ message within the same MTS Transaction.

But that's not all! MTS extends transactions beyond what's possible with the simplistic SQL BEGIN TRANSACTION and COMMIT TRANSACTION statements. MTS allows transactions to seamlessly span multiple objects in the same activity. By simply changing a component's transaction support level, an MTS object can execute in its own transaction or it can be composed or combined with other MTS objects as part of a larger transaction. MTS will automatically synchronize commit/abort behavior across multiple objects. Multi-object transactions allow MTS components to be utilized much more flexibly, and it enhances MTS component reuse without requiring code changes.

Let's learn how to effectively use this declarative transaction model and what MTS is doing under the surface.

Transaction Support Levels

When the MTS Executive creates a new object on behalf of a client, the MTS Executive determines if the creator is executing under the context of a transaction, and it also checks the requested component's transaction support setting. These two pieces of information determine how the new object participates in transactions.

The only time the creator will be executing under the context of a transaction is when the creator is another MTS component. Base clients will *never* have a transaction.

> **Every MTS object is created either inside a transaction or without one.**

You can't add an object to a transaction after the object has been created or disassociate an object from the transaction in which it was created. A transactional object spends its entire life inside the transaction it was created in.

When an MTS transaction is committed or aborted, MTS destroys all the objects that were involved in the transaction. This behavior is required to enforce the consistency requirement of the ACID transaction properties.

There are four possible settings for a component's transaction support attribute:

- ❑ Requires a transaction
- ❑ Requires a new transaction
- ❑ Supports transactions
- ❑ Does not support transactions

Requires a transaction

When the transaction support is set to Requires a transaction, a component will *always* be instantiated inside the context of an existing transaction. The MTS Executive will enlist the new object in the creator's transaction if one exists, otherwise the MTS Executive will create a new transaction. Either way, the new component instance will execute within a transaction.

Requires a new transaction

When the transaction support is set to Requires a new transaction, a component will *always* be instantiated inside of a *new* transaction created specially for this object, regardless of whether it is was created by an object within an existing transaction or not. This setting is designed for components that must perform work within a transaction, but who's work must be kept separate from all other transactions. When you use this setting, the MTS object never runs inside the scope of the creator's transaction. The new transaction is completely independent of the creator's transaction. The creator's transaction may commit while this object aborts or visa versa.

Supports transactions

When the transaction support is set to Supports transactions, a component can be instantiated inside the creator's transaction but it doesn't require a transaction and can execute without one. This setting is different from Requires a transaction because the MTS Executive won't automatically create a transaction if the creator is not executing in one.

Does not support transactions

When the transaction support is set to Does not support transactions, a component will *never* be instantiated inside the context of a transaction. This setting is designed for components that are unaware of transactions and the requirements that go along with transactions, such as the requirement that an object must be destroyed to enforce the consistency requirement of the ACID properties.

This is the default transaction support level.

Setting the Transaction Support

As I've already mentioned, a component's transaction support can be configured using MTS Explorer. Simply right-click on a component in MTS Explorer and select Properties from the pop-up menu. From the Transaction tab in the Properties window, select one of the four possible transaction support settings:

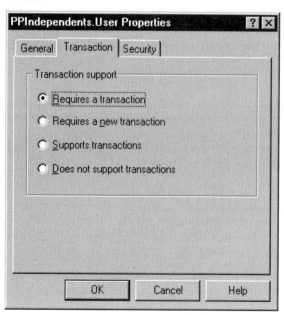

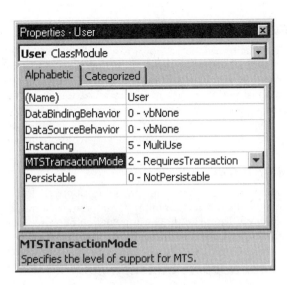

Visual Basic 6.0 also allows you to specify a default value for a component's transaction support setting by changing a class module's MTSTransactionMode property:

Notice that the terminology used in Visual Basic for the MTSTransactionMode values is not exactly the same as what's used in MTS Explorer. Don't let this bother you. Every Transaction Support level has a corresponding MTSTransactionMode setting. The following chart maps the possible MTSTransactionMode values to their equivalent transaction support attribute.

MTSTransactionMode Property	MTS Transaction Support Attribute
0 – NotAnMTSObject	N/A
1 – NoTransactions	Does not support transactions
2 – RequiresTransaction	Requires a transaction
3 – UsesTransaction	Supports transactions
4 – RequiresNewTransaction	Requires a new transaction

When you compile the project, Visual Basic will place a constant value for the transaction support setting in the component's type library. When the component is added to an MTS package, MTS reads the type library and automatically uses the transaction support setting stored in the type library as the default value.

> Since MTS does not read the type library when components are added from the registered component list, the transaction support setting stored in a component's type library is applied only if the component is added to a Package with the **Add File** dialog. In this case, you will need to use the **Properties** dialog to manually set the transaction support.

MTS Transaction Lifetime

An MTS Transaction goes through a complex four stage lifetime. These stages are:

- ❑ Starting a transaction
- ❑ Establishing and enlisting connections to resource managers
- ❑ Performing operations within the transaction
- ❑ Transaction outcome and completion

However, it is important to remember that the only requirements of MTS components to participate in MTS transactions is that they have a transaction support level of something other than Does not support Transactions and that they vote on the transaction outcome. For MTS to seamlessly integrate components and distributed transactions, MTS implements the complex requirements of MS DTC behind the scenes. Let's take a detailed look at what's happening in each phase of a transaction's lifetime and discuss how you can control a transaction's lifetime for both single component and multiple component MTS transactions.

Stage 1 – Starting a Transaction

Since MTS Transactions are based on a declarative model, an MTS component does not explicitly start an MTS Transaction. Instead, the MTS Executive automatically creates a new MTS Transaction when the base client instantiates an MTS component that has its transaction support set to Requires a Transaction, or when *any* client, including the base client and other MTS objects, instantiates an MTS component that has its transaction support set to Requires a New Transaction. This new object is known as the **root** of the transaction, because it is the first object created inside the MTS transaction. MTS stores information about the transaction in the Context object associated with the root object:

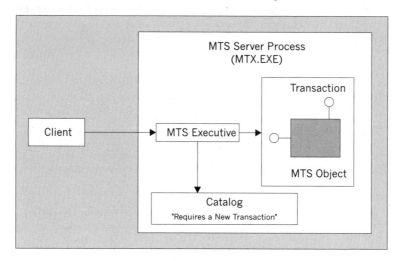

The root of the transaction, can then optionally enlist other MTS objects in the same transaction by instantiating MTS components that have a transaction support of either Requires a Transaction or Supports Transactions using the CreateInstance function. When an object is created in the same transaction, MTS automatically replicates the transaction information from the root object's Object Context to the new object's Object Context, so MTS can maintain the association between all objects in the transaction.

For these new objects to be enlisted in the creator's MTS transaction they must also be created in the same activity. An MTS transaction can never span activities, however the relationship of activities to MTS transactions is not always one-to-one. A single activity can possibly have several MTS transactions. If an MTS object instantiates an MTS component with a transaction support setting of Requires A New Transaction by using the `CreateInstance` function, this new object will be in the same activity but in a different MTS transaction that is completely independent of the creator's transaction.

An MTS transaction can be thought of as a logical transaction that abstracts or hides the details of an underlying MS DTC (physical) transaction. While this logical transaction is created when MTS creates the root object, it is not until the root object is activated that MTS creates a physical MS DTC transaction. The physical transaction is created with the highest level of isolation (serializable) and the timeout interval specified in MTS Explorer. Once it is created, MTS waits until we perform operations against resources that can participate in MS DTC transactions.

In this chapter I will use the terminology physical transaction *when referring to the underlying MS DTC transaction. Any other time the term transaction is used, you can assume we are discussing the MTS transaction or the logical transaction that MTS objects work with.*

Stage 2 – Enlisting Connections to Resource Managers

After both the MTS (logical) transaction and the underlying MS DTC (physical) transaction have been created, connections must be established to the data source before an MTS object can retrieve or manipulate data. But to ensure that all data modification operations performed by the MTS object against the data source are carried out within the MS DTC transaction, the connection to the data source must be **enlisted** or registered with the MS DTC transaction.

Once this happens, all operations through the connection are performed within the transaction and are monitored by the MS DTC. Although the entire enlistment process is performed by MTS behind the scenes for each connection, it's imperative to understand the details of how this important step in a transaction's lifetime is accomplished.

Transactional applications (in this case MTS objects) read and write to data through **Resource Managers (RM)**. A connection to a particular data source is actually just a connection to a Resource Manager. But the MTS transactional model adds an additional layer of software to the distributed transaction architecture called a **Resource Dispenser (RD)**.

It's important not to confuse Resource Managers and Resource Dispensers. They are two different software components in the MTS transactional model that serve different purposes.

> **A Resource Manager is a system service that manages durable resources.**

MS DTC coordinates transaction commitment and rollback with Resource Managers using the two-phase commit protocol. Examples of Resource Managers include: SQL Server, Oracle, and MSMQ.

> **A Resource Dispenser, on the other hand, is an in-process DLL that manages non-durable or temporary resources that reside in the Resource Dispenser's memory such as threads, objects, or memory blocks. These shared resources do not need to be protected from a system failure.**

Resource Dispensers can manage pools of reusable resources, automatically enlist or register them in transactions and provide an MTS object with methods and interfaces to perform operations against these resources. One of the most common non-durable resources managed by a Resource Dispenser are connections to an underlying Resource Manager that controls persistent storage.

There are currently five software components that also play the role of an MTS Resource Dispenser:

- ❑ **Shared Property Manager** (SPM, pronounced "spam") – allows multiple objects to share data within a server process. Even though the SPM is a Resource Dispenser, it does not participate in transactions. For this reason, we'll discuss the SPM in further detail when we discuss designing and developing MTS components in Chapter 5.
- ❑ **Microsoft Message Queue Server** (MSMQ) – includes a Resource Dispenser for enlisting MSMQ queues in MTS transactions.
- ❑ **COM Transaction Integrator** (COMTI) for CICS & IMS – includes a Resource Dispenser for managing SNA connections to IBM CICS and IMS. Cedar is used to access CICS and IMS transaction monitor mainframes.
- ❑ **ODBC Driver Manager** – a Resource Dispenser for managing ODBC database connections
- ❑ **OLE DB Service Component** – a Resource Dispenser for ADO connections.

If you need a component that can efficiently manage a custom, non-durable resource for your MTS components you might want to consider developing a custom MTS Resource Dispenser. However, you should be warned that developing a Resource Dispenser is much more difficult than developing MTS components because a Resource Dispenser must be multi-threaded and thread safe. Due to these requirements, we cannot develop custom MTS Resource Dispensers in Visual Basic.

However, with COM+ we can implement Compensating Resource Managers (CRMs) from any COM-compliant language. CRMs provide the ability for transactional objects to access custom resources (durable or non-durable) within a transaction without the need for a complex Resource Dispenser and Resource Manager pair. We'll discuss more about this exciting new feature of COM+ in Chapter 13.

Notice that these Resource Dispensers are the same components that are always used to access resources. For example, the OLE DB Service Component always resides between a client application or object using ADO or OLE DB and the OLE DB Provider and Data Source. MTS assigns the OLE DB Service Component the role of the Resource Dispenser and the Data Source is the Resource Manager:

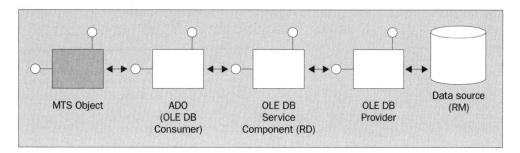

The ODBC Driver Manager also always resides between a client application or an object using a data access library to access a data source. But within the MTS environment the ODBC Driver Manager plays the role of the Resource Dispenser and the data source is the Resource Manager. The MSMQ Resource Dispenser and COMTI are based on a similar architecture:

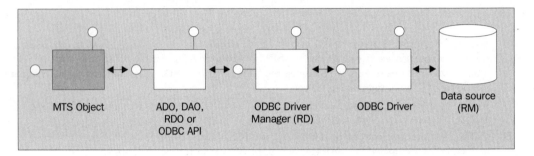

It is important to understand that not all Resource Dispensers have a corresponding Data Source that acts as a Resource Manager. Specifically, since the SPM manages a data source (memory) that does not participate in transactions, the data source is not considered a Resource Manager. The SPM is also unique, when compared to other Resource Dispensers, in the fact that it is an MTS component that MTS objects can access directly through its COM interfaces:

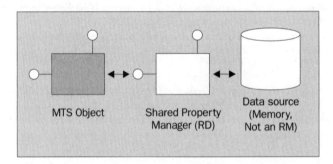

The point is that a Resource Dispenser is simply a role that is assigned to software components that are positioned between an MTS object and a resource. A Resource Dispenser can be accessed directly by MTS objects, as is the case with the SPM, or indirectly by another component layer, like with the OLE DB Service Component and the ODBC Driver Manager. While most Resource Dispensers have an associated Resource Manager, it is not required.

Under this Resource Dispenser role, as we mentioned, these software components are responsible for managing non-durable resources. But they can optionally also provide two important services:

❑ Resource pooling
❑ Transaction enlistment.

Resource Pooling

Resource pooling provides an efficient way of dispensing non-durable resources by providing an MTS object with a *recycled* resource instead of creating a new one. After a resource is used, it is made available for reuse by the same or another MTS object. This reusing or recycling of resources is completely transparent to the MTS object consuming the resource. Resource pooling can significantly improve performance in two ways:

1. **Resources can be reused from a pool faster than they can be created**

This is the most obvious way that resource pooling increases performance and most evident for objects that repeatedly use and release resources. Most applications allocate and hold onto resources for their entire lifetime to reduce resource creation overhead.

However, MTS objects cannot hold onto resources or state after they are deactivated, which usually occurs after each method call. Resource pooling eliminates any possible performance loss that would have occurred because of the repeated allocation of resources every time an MTS object is activated.

2. **Memory usage is reduced because multiple objects can share the same resource**

If each MTS object allocated its own resource, the objects would consume too much memory and CPU cycles. MTS objects would also have the risk that there's not enough of the resource available. Resource pooling allows hundreds or thousands of MTS objects to share only a handful of resources.

Of course, the performance enhancements provided by resource pooling are the most evident when the resources that are being pooled are expensive to create. In fact, pooling resources that are not expensive to create can actually have a negative impact on overall system performance because the pool itself is consuming resources that could be used by other resources. For example, network connections and data source connections can usually benefit from resource pooling because they are expensive resources, but objects usually don't benefit from resource pooling.

Resource pooling is managed by the Resource Dispenser and by a separate in-process DLL called the **Resource Dispenser Manager (DispMan)**. After a Resource Dispenser registers itself with the DispMan, the latter creates an instance of a component called a **Holder** and assigns the new object to the Resource Dispenser. The Holder object is responsible for maintaining the list of the resources and their status for its Resource Dispenser.

When the Resource Dispenser receives a request for a resource, the Resource Dispenser forwards the request to its Holder object. The Holder object examines the resource pool and determines whether to ask the Resource Dispenser for a new resource or reuse an existing one from the pool. If an unused resource is available in the pool that meets the requested criteria, the Holder object will simply assign this resource to the request. However, if there is not an adequate resource available, the Holder object will ask the Resource Dispenser to create a new one.

This Holder object and Resource Dispenser architecture has a clearly defined separation of resource access and management. The Holder object never communicates with the MTS object directly, but instead it always relies on the Resource Dispenser to hand out the resources to the requesting objects. The Holder is simply a dump pool manager that has no knowledge about the non-durable resource it is pooling including the details of how the resource is created, destroyed or used. The Resource Dispenser, on the other hand, is the important link between the MTS object and the Resource Manager that has detailed knowledge about the non-durable resource it manages but does not know anything about the resource pool:

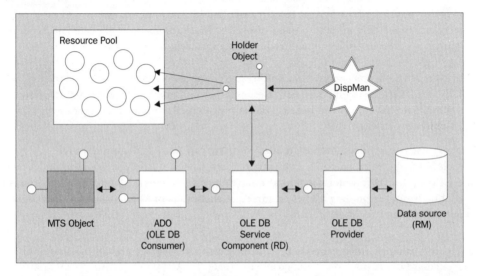

When an MTS object is finished with a resource, because the object is deactivated, the MTS transaction completes or the MTS object simply releases the resource, the resource is placed back into the pool of available resources, instead of being destroyed. Consequently, to maximize the performance and scalability benefits of resource pooling, when using resources that are pooled:

> **MTS objects should not request resources until they absolutely need them and release them as soon as possible.**

When your MTS objects use resources that are pooled, you should think of multiple objects sharing resources amongst each other instead of each object approach having its own dedicated resource(s).

It is important to remember that resource pools are created and used on a per-process basis. Pools cannot be shared or accessed across processes, so each process has its own pool for each Resource Dispenser. You should consider this limitation when designing and packaging MTS components so you can take advantage of resource pooling to maximize performance and scalability.

Connections to Data Sources (Resource Managers) are one of the most commonly used non-durable resource. Creating and destroying a connection to a Resource Manager is an expensive process. To efficiently provide MTS objects with data source connections, both the ODBC Driver Manager and the OLE DB Service Component are Resource Dispensers that provide resource pooling of Resource Manager connections.

The ODBC Driver Manager pools ODBC database connections for any ODBC Data Source that provides a multi-threaded ODBC Driver. While the OLE DB Service Component pools OLE DB Sessions to any data source that provides an OLE DB Provider.

If your not familiar with the OLE DB architecture, OLE DB Sessions are the underlying objects of an ADO connection.

So no matter what data access route you take, your MTS objects can take advantage of resource pooling of Resource Manager connections.

Within the MTS environment these Resource Dispensers utilize the general resource pooling architecture with the DispMan's Holder object as the pool manager. However, Resource Dispensers are also required to function properly outside of MTS without requiring code changes by the client. Both the ODBC Driver Manager and the OLE DB Service Component provide their own pool management systems when they execute outside of the MTS environment and the DispMan is not available.

Transaction Enlistment and Propagation

When a Resource Dispenser receives a request for a resource, the DispMan either reuses an existing resource or makes a request to the Resource Dispenser to create a new one. After the DispMan has allocated a resource from either of these scenarios, it attempts to obtain the current transaction information (MS DTC Transaction ID) for the calling MTS object from the MTS Executive. Remember, transactional MTS objects store this information in their Object Context. If no transaction information is available, the DispMan assumes that the object is non-transactional and it simply returns the resource back to the Resource Dispenser, which in-turn gives the resource to the MTS object. However, if the DispMan does obtain the transaction information it passes the information to the Resource Dispenser. The Resource Dispenser then performs two very important tasks:

1. **Enlists the resource with the MS DTC Transaction**
   The Resource Dispenser automatically passes the transaction information and the resource to the MS DTC to enlist or register the connection with the MS DTC transaction. This process is called transaction enlistment and it plays a significant role in MTS providing declarative transactions. By associating the connection to the Resource Manager with the MS DTC transaction, all operations through the connection are performed within the transaction and are monitored by MS DTC. When this transaction completes MS DTC can then execute the two-phase commit protocol with all the enlisted resource managers.

2. **Propagates the Transaction to the Resource Manager**
   If the Resource Manager supports OLE Transactions, the Resource Dispenser automatically passes or *propagates* the transaction information directly to the Resource Manager. However, if the Resource Manager supports XA, then the Resource Dispenser first converts the OLE transaction identifier into an XA Transaction Identifier (XID) with the help of MS DTC and then passes the XID to the Resource Manager using the XA protocol.

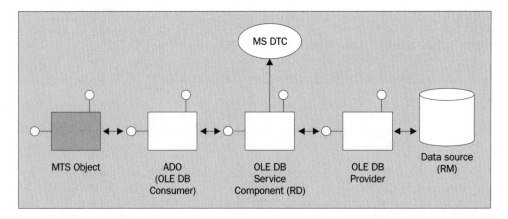

Finally, the resource is returned to the Resource Dispenser, which then returns it to the calling MTS object.

Once the connection to the Resource Manager is enlisted in the MS DTC transaction and the transaction is propagated to the Resource Manager, all work performed by the MTS object through the connection against the Resource Manager will be under the protection of a distributed transaction. All operations will be performed as a single unit of work and the transaction as a whole will be required to conform to the ACID properties (atomicity, consistency, isolation and durability).

It is important to understand that the transaction enlistment is totally optional. It is the Resource Dispenser's decision whether or not to enlist the resource in the current transaction. Both the ODBC Driver Manager and the OLE DB Service Component support transaction enlistment. With the OLE DB Service Component, transaction enlistment support is enabled by default, but it can be disabled by either:

❑ Setting the OLE DB Services key in the connection string to "-4", "-8" or "0"
❑ Modifying the default value of the OLEDB_SERVICES registry entry for the OLE DB provider you are using

Thankfully, MTS does an excellent job of isolating MTS components from these complex details of distributed transactions. In fact, our only responsibility in this stage of a transaction's lifetime is to open a connection to a data source. The MTS Executive, the dispenser manager, and the Resource Dispensers perform the complex tasks of resource pooling, transaction enlistment and transaction propagation.

However, the more you understand about the behind the scenes processing, the better you'll be able to diagnose problems and build scalable and high-performance MTS components.

Stage 3 – Performing Operations within the Transaction

Once each Resource Manager connection is enlisted in the physical MS DTC transaction and the MS DTC transaction is propagated to each Resource Manager involved, our MTS object can begin performing operations against Resource Managers. These operations are automatically part of a distributed transaction and can be performed using any data access technology that has a corresponding Resource Dispenser that provides connection enlistment, including ADO, DAO, RDO or the ODBC API.

For example, the following code sample shows how to perform a typical operation against a Resource Manager:

```
'Create an instance of an ADO Connection
Set conDataSource = New ADODB.Connection

'Open a connection to our Data Source
'this will cause Resource Dispenser to enlist the connection and
'propagate the transaction to the Resource Manager
conDataSource.Open ConnectionString:= _
  "UID=sa; PWD=; DATABASE=Northwind; Server=JConard; PROVIDER=SQLOLEDB"

'Delete the order record specified by the passed OrderID
conDataSource.Execute "DELETE Orders WHERE OrderID = " & OrderID

'Close the connection to the data source
'so it goes back in the Resource Pool
conDataSource.Close

'Release the instance of the ADO Connection
Set conDataSource = Nothing
```

As you can see, the code for connecting to and performing operations against the resource manager is the same as it would be for a non-transactional MTS object. This simplicity is only possible because an MTS Resource Dispenser *transparently* and *automatically* enlists the Resource Manager connection with the transaction and passes or propagates the transaction to the Resource Manager.

When the Resource Manager receives and processes operations against its data, it takes certain measures to ensure that the transaction meets the ACID requirements. Many resource managers implement a logging mechanism to provide the ability to rollback uncommitted changes to fulfill the atomicity requirement.

Logging mechanisms also allow a Resource Manager to ensure the durability of a transaction by being able to reapply or recover changes should an unforeseen problem occur. Locks are used to isolate a transaction's changes from affecting other transactions against the same Resource Manager. To ensure consistency, Resource Managers usually define special mechanisms or rules to protect the integrity of data.

Stage 4 – Transaction Outcome and Completion

After MTS objects perform changes to a data source and the MTS transaction ends, MTS must determine the transaction outcome and if the transaction should be committed or aborted. So how does MTS know when to commit or abort a transaction?

There are a number of internal Boolean flags in an MTS transaction that tells MTS whether it should allow the transaction to commit or abort. Each transaction maintains an overall value of True or False. For simplicity, let's refer to them as Abort, Continue and Complete. By default each transaction starts out with the Abort flag set to False. As long as this value is maintained, the transaction is free to continue its work. The other two flags are part of the Context Wrapper which is also a part of every transaction object:

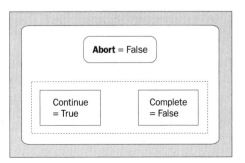

Each MTS object that participates in the transaction is responsible for casting votes on the transaction outcome. The decision to commit a transaction is a unanimous decision. If *all* objects in the transaction vote to commit the transaction then all operations performed within the transaction are permanently committed. If *any* object within the transaction votes to abort the transaction then all operations performed within the transaction will be rolled back.

An MTS object votes on the transaction outcome by calling one of four methods of the `IObjectContext` interface which is implemented by the Context object associated with every object running in the MTS environment:

- ❑ `SetComplete`
- ❑ `SetAbort`
- ❑ `EnableCommit`
- ❑ `DisableCommit`

This interface is automatically associated with every object's context object, allowing the developer a great deal of control over the behavior of MTS by using it to control when MTS will deactivate an object.

The SetComplete Method

The `SetComplete` method notifies the MTS Executive that the MTS object has completed its work successfully, that it can now be deactivated and its transactional updates are ready to be committed. The entire transaction may not commit after `SetComplete` is called because the object calling the method could be a sub object and the caller of this object may do other work in the transaction. However, if the caller of the `SetComplete` method is the root object, MTS will attempt to commit the transaction.

The following code example shows how to call the `SetComplete` method:

```
Dim objContext As MTxAS.ObjectContext

'Get a reference to the Object Context for this object
Set objContext = GetObjectContext

'******Do some work*****

'Check and see if we have an Object Context
If objContext Is Nothing = False Then
' We do, force MTS to allow the transactions to commit
   objContext.SetComplete

' Release our reference to the Object Context
   Set objContext = Nothing

End If
```

The SetAbort Method

The `SetAbort` method notifies the MTS Executive that the MTS object was unsuccessful in completing its work and it wants to prevent the transaction from being committed. If one or more MTS object in the transaction calls the `SetAbort` method, then the entire transaction will not commit. The following code example shows how to call the `SetAbort` method:

```
Dim objContext As MTxAS.ObjectContext

'Get a reference to the Object Context for this object
Set objContext = GetObjectContext

'******Do some work*****

'Check and see if we have an Object Context
If objContext Is Nothing = False Then
' We do, force MTS to abort the transaction
  objContext.SetAbort

' Release our reference to the Object Context
  Set objContext = Nothing

End If
```

The EnableCommit Method

The `EnableCommit` method notifies the MTS Executive that the transaction updates are consistent and the transaction can be committed at anytime. It's important to understand that `EnableCommit` does not force a transaction to commit. By calling this method, an object simply tells MTS, "I'm able to commit". `EnableCommit` is the default state when an object is first activated, so this method is called if you want the object's internal state to be maintained for whatever reason, otherwise `SetComplete` should be called. The following code example shows how to call the `EnableCommit` method:

```
Dim objContext As MTxAS.ObjectContext

'Get a reference to the Object Context for this object
Set objContext = GetObjectContext

'******Do some work*****

'Check and see if we have an Object Context
If objObjectContext Is Nothing = False Then
'  We do, tell MTS that we can commit at any time
  objContext.EnableCommit

' Release our reference to the Object Context
  Set objContext = Nothing

End If
```

The DisableCommit Method

The `DisableCommit` method is exactly the opposite of the `EnableCommit` method. The `DisableCommit` method notifies the MTS Executive that the object's work is not finished and the transaction cannot currently be committed. When an object finishes servicing a method call it may not be ready to commit its work. By calling `DisableCommit`, an object simply tells MTS, "I'm not able to commit" and MTS will not automatically commit the transaction. As a result, the object's state will be maintained across method calls until the transaction is committed or aborted. The following code example shows how to call the `DisableCommit` method:

```
Dim objContext As MTxAS.ObjectContext

'Get a reference to the Object Context for this object
Set objContext = GetObjectContext

'******Do some work*****

'Check and see if we have an Object Context
If objObjectContext Is Nothing = False Then
' We do, tell MTS that we are not ready to commit
  objContext.DisableCommit

' Release our reference to the Object Context
  Set objContext = Nothing

End If
```

Having established the outcome of the transaction, we can now set it to complete. There are actually three different ways a transaction can complete:

1. **The root object calls SetComplete or SetAbort**

   When the root object calls either `SetComplete` or `SetAbort` the transaction will end immediately.

   Only the root object can end a transaction this way. If any other object in the transaction calls the `SetComplete` or `SetAbort` methods they are only voting on the outcome of the transaction and they have no control over when it ends.

2. **Transaction times out**

   A transaction can end if there is no activity within the transaction for more than the configured transaction timeout value. When a transaction times out it will automatically abort. The default timeout value is 60 seconds.

   This value can be changed from the Options tab of the Computer Properties dialog window in MTS Explorer. If you are debugging transactional MTS objects, you will definitely want to increase the transaction timeout from the 60 second default so that you will have enough time to step through a method call on an MTS object without the transaction automatically aborting. We'll thoroughly discuss MTS object debugging in Chapter 9.

3. **The client releases the root object**

   MTS tries to commit the transaction when the root object is deactivated when the client releases all of its references to the object's Context Wrapper. When the client releases the root object's Context Wrapper MTS *implicitly* attempts to commit the transaction. Implicit commitments should always be avoided.

One problem with implicit commitments is that the client cannot be notified of the transaction outcome. When a root object calls `SetComplete`, MTS attempts to commit the transaction prior to returning control to the caller. If an error occurred while committing the transaction, MTS simply raises an error message to the client. This allows the client application to gracefully deal with the problem and possibly try the transaction again. However with implicit commitment the client is no longer connected to the root object's Context Wrapper and it consequently cannot receive error messages if the transaction cannot be committed. The client is totally unaware of the transaction outcome.

Implicit commitments also leave a transaction alive longer than necessary. While a transaction is alive it is holding precious locks to resources to ensure the isolation requirement of the ACID properties. Consequently, an open, inactive transaction could be blocking other transactions from performing operations on the same resource. This could create a performance bottleneck and severely limit an application's scalability. A much better approach is to explicitly commit or abort the transaction by calling the SetComplete or SetAbort methods which will cause the transaction to complete as soon as possible.

The Transaction Context Object

Although it is usually not a good solution, it is possible for the client to actually explicitly control a transasction. It can do this by creating a **Transaction Context object**. MTS will associate a context with this object and the client can then combine several other MTS objects into a single transaction.

The transaction context object is marked as Requires new transaction and so must be used as the root for a transaction.

Once the client has a reference to the transaction context object, it can call the CreateInstance method on the object to create a new transasction component within the same transaction and return a reference to the new object back to the client:

In order to use the transaction context object you will need to add a reference to the Transaction Context Type Library.

```
Dim objTxContext As TransactionContext
Dim objPat As Head.Pat
Dim objRub As Stomach.Rub

' Create Transaction Context Object
Set objTxContext = CreateObject("TxCtx.TransactionContext")

' Create Instances of Order component within transaction
Set objPat = objTxContext.CreateInstance("Head.Pat")
Set objRub = objTxContext.CreateInstance("Stomach.Rub")
```

The transaction context object has an additional two methods that can be called that allow the client to either commit or abort the transaction:

```
' Commit transaction
objTxContext.Commit
```

```
' Abort transaction
objTxContext.Abort
```

However tempting it might seem to use a transaction context object to roll up several transactions under one umberella, you are really better off developing an additional component of your own to achieve the same purpose because there are several significant draw backs with using a transaction context object:

❑ **The transaction context object runs in-process**
Because the transaction context is created within the same process space of the client that created it, it must reside on the same machine as the client. This may not be a problem is the client is really an ASP page running on the server but in other distributed environments it can be less stable and may significantly increase the network overhead.

❑ **The business logic that organizes the transaction is restricted to the client**
This goes against the principles of distributed computing whereby you collect all your business rules in one central location, allowing them to be easily changed and updated.

❑ **Calling Commit doesn't guarantee that a transaction will commit**
If any of the MTS object that the client creates to form part of the tranasction calls `SetAbort` or `DisableCommit`, without then calling `EnableCommit` or `SetComplete`, the transaction will actually be aborted. It is much better to allow MTS to automatically control transaction outcome than to try and do it explicitly yourself.

❑ **The base client doesn't have context**
Transactional coordination by the base client can only be done indirectly through the reference to the transaction context object. So the base client is unable to enlist Resource Dispensers in the transaction.

Summary

By now, you should really be getting a good idea of the scope of the advantages that MTS lends to your components for the distributed environement. In this chapter, we considered one of the central features of MTS – its transaction management.

We started off with a fairly basic discussion of transactions, where we learnt the four defining properties of a transaction: Atomicity, Consistency, Isolation and Durability. Then we moved on to consider the different levels or support our components could get with transactions before we took a rather detailed look at the lifetime of a transaction.

We're not quite finished with the topic of transactions as we'll be revisiting both them and the MS DTC in Chapter 11, when you consider how MTS transactions work with the data tier.

We've spent a good bit of time filling in a lot of background theory. In the next chapter we can begin to refocus our attention back towards the development of components for MTS.

Designing MTS Components and Interfaces

By now you should fully understand that the distributed architecture model (n-tier) has changed the way that we look at our applications. You shouldn't consider an application to be a single large monolithic executable, but rather a number of components that dynamically interact to embody an enterprise solution, providing clients with scalable and flexible solutions.

There's an undeniable connection between good application design and well-written software. The bottom line is that we have to carefully design our applications, taking into consideration not only our business problems, but also the way technologies like COM, DCOM, DBMS and MTS work. An ill-conceived design, that doesn't consider the basic principles of these technologies, will result in a poorly written application with poor performance, that defeats the very point of using these technologies in the first place.

In this chapter, we'll look at how to efficiently design and develop MTS components that scale to meet the demands of an enterprise application.

By the end of this chapter you will know:

- ❑ How to design and implement your own interfaces
- ❑ What level of granularity to choose for your MTS components
- ❑ The different ways to manage state in your components
- ❑ The different ways to pass state around your distributed application
- ❑ Some key pointers for coding MTS components

Application Perfomance Issues

Application performance is something that each and every developer should be concerned about. No matter how sophisticated and clever the code is, if it runs slow, that will be what's focussed on. Application performance and usability are almost the same thing. To make matters worse, distributed applications magnify the problem even more. However, performance is not always a function of our code. There are several other factors that will determine the overall performance of our application and should always be examined.

For this reason, when you start to design your application you should keep some important factors in mind:

- ❑ An increase in the number of application users will have a direct impact on the performance of your application. This increase will cause higher network traffic and increased component use. This in turn causes a heavier CPU workload and increased database access. In general, more users means an increase of everything.
- ❑ Databases should never be considered *static*. They will always continue to grow in size, complexity and usage for the lifetime of our applications.
- ❑ Over time, applications and their transactions tend to become more complex. This means an increase in the number of interfaces and transactional coordination. These little changes can create unnoticed resource consumption and process blocking.
- ❑ On demand component allocation can cause extreme uses of resources for short periods of time. If components are not properly shut down, they may run unnecessarily.
- ❑ Distributed applications are becoming easier and cheaper to build, which allows companies to use their computer systems and networks in new ways. This includes everything from spreadsheets to Internet usage. However, the result is an increased load on existing databases, servers, networks and of course administrators, who have to maintain the system and monitor it for potential security violations etc.

The workload that our application will experience is somewhat predicable over time. Typically, during the initial design phase we're able to determine an accurate number of expected users. However, once an application is deployed, it is essential to determine some baseline performance parameters. This is actually a fairly easy thing to do. SQL Server provides a series of tools that allow this. Additionally, there are several third party tools available that can provide this information on a regular basis.

Hardware Use

As the workload of our application increases, this will directly affect the performance of our application by increasing hardware usage. I realize this is often an area that we tend to forget about. After all, we are software gurus and not hardware junkies. Unfortunately, no amount of code optimization will overcome overworked hardware components.

Hardware factors that we should consider for our application include:

- ❑ An overworked network limits throughput of our components
- ❑ Inadequate memory causes slow paging to disk
- ❑ Disk thrashing caused by inadequate disk access causes slow application performance
- ❑ A high percentage of CPU usage causes excessive application wait states that can directly affect the performance of our application

If we're lucky, most companies will update their enterprise hardware environments every couple of years. This means that by the time a new piece of faster hardware is implemented, it will be time to rewrite our applications. What this really means is that our applications will typically reside under the same hardware infrastructure for most of their useful life. In order to ensure that hardware resources don't become a performance issue, they should be monitored every so often. This monitoring will help to create trend analysis that can be used to realistically determine percentage of usage over time. We'll come back to this in Chapter 10.

Architecture Strategies

Although, hardware is not something that we may have direct control over, the overall application architecture is another performance issue that we do have control over. There are a lot of architectural decisions that we can make that will directly affect the performance of our application.

The foundation of a good multi-tier, MTS application includes good logical packaging. Logical packaging is the process of grouping application services into common components. Deciding how to group logical and physical components for physical deployment is not an easy task.

Distributed applications can use various logical and physical design configurations. It's often difficult to determine how to optimize your application design to fit the workload characteristics of your run-time environment. You can use tools such as the Application Performance Explorer, that ships with the Enterprise Edition of Visual Studio, to provide a way to test your application design assumptions. This will help you to determine which design options work best in certain scenarios and identify tradeoffs between design options.

> *The Application Performance Explorer (APE) tests the run-time performance and resource load characteristics of the distributed application design scenarios you're considering. With APE, you can run automated "what-if" tests to demonstrate the resource consumption implications of architectural choices you might make.*

Let's start off by examining the effect of component granularity.

Designing And Implementing Interfaces

As we discussed in Chapter 3, an interface is really nothing more than a list of methods and property prototypes that define how something *could* be manipulated, if somebody wrote the code to implement the functionality it describes. When you write a component in VB, behind the scenes VB is creating its **default interface**, which contains each of the public methods and properties you added to your component.

To fully exploit COM, you need to understand interfaces. To do this, you need to understand how VB deals with COM behind the scenes, and how you can have greater control over what it does.

Basics of IDL – The Interface Definition Language

All COM interfaces are defined using the **Microsoft Interface Definition Language (MIDL)**. This is a variant of the Open Software Foundation **IDL**, designed for enabling remote procedure calls (RPC) in distributed computing. MIDL extends IDL by adding attributes and features are needed when dealing with objects rather than just functions.

IDL is important because it's the way in which abstract definitions for components and interfaces are put together in a language neutral syntax. When writing class modules, IDL for our components and interfaces is generated behind the scenes for us by VB. Let's nip backstage and see what VB actually does when we put together a simple component.

To create some IDL, you need to create an ActiveX project. For this small introduction to IDL follow these steps:

Start Visual Basic and create a new ActiveX DLL project called `IDLDemo`. Change the class module name to `IDemo`, then add the following code to the class module:

```
Public Sub AddItem(ByVal strName As String, ByRef lngQuantity As Long)

End Sub
```

Now compile it to a DLL.

Using OLE Viewer to View the Generated IDL

To view the IDL VB has created for the component and its default interface, we need to use the OLE Viewer application.

Run OLE Viewer, making sure you're in **Expert Mode**. Expand the **Object Classes** item and its child item **All Objects**. Beneath the **All Objects** item, search for an item with the name **IDLDemo.IDemo** (the programmatic identifier for the component we just compiled).

Expand the item. The OLE Viewer will query the interface for *every single* interface that is defined in the registry, located under the key `HKEY_CLASSES_ROOT/Interface`. It will list the interfaces supported by our component:

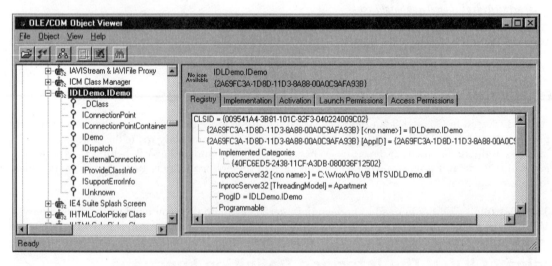

The default interface is listed at the bottom, simply because of the sorting used. All the interfaces above it are implemented by VB to provide the basic plumbing a typical COM component might require.

Right-click on the IDLDemo.IDemo item and select the View Type Information…. option. This will bring up a new window that shows the contents of the project's type library de-compiled to IDL:

```
ITypeLib Viewer                                                    _ □ ×
File  View

□ ⌐ IDLDemo                          // Generated .IDL file (by the OLE/COM Object Viewer)
  ⌐ dispinterface _IDemo             //
    ⊞ m Methods                      // typelib filename: IDLDemo.dll
    ⊞ ? Inherited Interfaces         [
  ⌐ ? interface _IDemo                   uuid(2A69FC38-1D8D-11D3-8A88-00A0C9AFA93B),
    m AddItem                            version(1.0)
    ⊞ ? Inherited Interfaces         ]
  ⌐ coclass IDemo                    library IDLDemo
    ⊞ _IDemo                         {
                                         // TLib :       // TLib : OLE Automation : {00020430-0000-
                                     0000-C000-000000000046}
                                         importlib("STDOLE2.TLB");

                                         // Forward declare all types defined in this typelib
                                         interface _IDemo;

                                         [
                                             odl,
                                             uuid(2A69FC39-1D8D-11D3-8A88-00A0C9AFA93B),
                                             version(1.0),
                                             hidden,
                                             dual,
                                             nonextensible,
Ready
```

If you look at the IDL, you can see it's fairly understandable, but there are lots of attributes and keywords that are completely new. I won't discuss them here as you can find a good description of them in the on-line help.

About halfway down the screen we can see the IDL VB has created for our default interface (called _IDemo) and its various attributes.

At the end of the IDL, you can see the coclass for the class module (component). This describes a creatable COM object, and lists the interfaces the class supports. The only interface supported is _IDemo, so why did OLE View show us more? The reason is that the IDL is giving us an abstract definition for a class that somebody has implemented. When creating IDL, the list of interfaces doesn't actually have to be complete. You just list the interface that the outside world will generally use.

Within the interface definition for _IDemo you can see how the method we added to our class module earlier, AddItem, is defined in IDL:

```
[id(0x60030000)]
HRESULT AddItem([in] BSTR strName,
                [in, out] long* lngQuantity);
```

The mapping is fairly easy to understand. BSTR (basic string) is the IDL equivalent of a string, [in] is the equivalent of ByVal, and [in,out] is the equivalent of ByRef.

Points to Note about IDL

Here are a couple of points to note about this IDL and IDL in general:

- ❑ There are no VB specifics anywhere - it's language neutral.
- ❑ The default interface for our class module has the same logical name as our class prefixed with an underscore.
- ❑ All interfaces created for us derive from the interface `IDispatch`. This enables the functionality of the interfaces to be accessed by those languages/tools that discover functionality at runtime (late-bound clients), whilst those who determine functionality at compile time (early-bound) can use the derived interface.
- ❑ The interface is assigned a physical name (IID/GUID) using the UUID keyword which is different to the physical name (CLSID) assigned to the class module (CLSID/GUID).
- ❑ Each method is assigned a unique ID that is used by late bound clients to identify it.
- ❑ Each method has a return type of `HRESULT`. This enables errors to be reported in a consistent way.
- ❑ Parameters have attributes to describe in generic form if they are `ByRef [in, out]` or `ByVal [in]`.
- ❑ When IDL is compiled, it can generate a type library. This is a mini-database that describes components and interfaces to languages like VB. The Object Browser in VB is basically a type library browser.

Al Major (Author of COM IDL & Interface Design ISBN 1861002254 published by Wrox Press) provides a useful IDL resource site : `www.boxspoon.com`

Schematic of IDL, Type Libraries and Components

You might find this diagram useful in understanding the relationship between IDL, type libraries and some components of IDE:

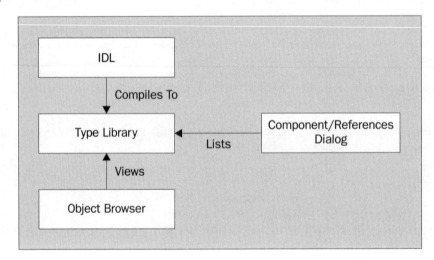

Beyond Default Interfaces

We've looked at how VB creates a default interface. Now let's consider how we can define our own interfaces in VB using abstract class modules, and write components that support multiple interfaces, providing us with better interface granularity.

Abstract Class Modules

To define an interface in VB, we create a class module, add the function prototypes (no code), and set the Instancing property of the class to 2 - PublicNotCreatable:

Because this class can never be created and has no implementation, we call it an **abstract class module**. Its sole purpose in life is to define an interface that can be implemented by other class modules using the Implements keyword.

Using an ActiveX DLL To Contain Interface Definitions

A good tip when designing interfaces in VB is to use a separate ActiveX project to contain the interface definitions. These interfaces can then be imported into other projects by using the References dialog. This has a number of advantages:

❑ The interface designer can put the interfaces together and then distribute them easily to one or more developers

❑ You have complete control over the interface definitions

❑ Nobody can change the interface definitions

❑ It improves project compatibility (discussed later), so that when the project using them is recompiled, the GUIDs of the interfaces do not change.

When designing and distributing interfaces using an ActiveX DLL as a container, you should always change the project properties to Binary Compatibility once you've published them, as they should become immutable:

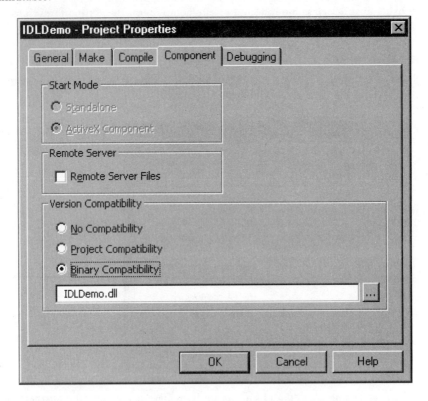

Binary Compatibility ensures that the GUIDs assigned to interfaces do not change when the project is compiled again. Also, remember that to be a good COM player, you should add a new interface rather than changing an old one once they're published.

> **Only change an existing interface if all of your clients can be recompiled, or if all of your clients are late bound (even then it's not really recommended).**

Using Our Own Interfaces

In this example, we'll demonstrate how to implement a component that supports multiple interfaces. We'll use an ActiveX DLL component to contain our definitions as we've discussed, and create another ActiveX DLL that will run inside of MTS and support three interfaces :

- ❏ IComplexOrder
- ❏ ICreateSimpleOrder
- ❏ Order (the default interface)

An ActiveX DLL to Hold Interface Definitions

First off, let's create the ActiveX DLL that contains the interfaces by following these steps:

Create a new ActiveX DLL project called `InterfacesDemo`. Leave the existing class module (you can't compile the project unless there is a publically creatable element in it, but you may want to rename it to something like `DummyClass`), and create two more class modules – one called `IComplexOrder` the other called `ISimpleOrder`. Change the Instancing property of the two new classes to PublicNotCreatable.

Add the following to the `ISimpleOrder` class module:

```
' Purpose: Create a simple order that consists of one part.
Public Sub CreateOneProductOrder(strFrom As String, _
                                 strTo As String, _
                                 strPartNumber As String, _
                                 lngQuantity As Long)

End Sub

' Purpose: Create a simple order where two parts are being ordered.
Public Sub CreateTwoProductOrder(strFrom As String, _
                                 strTo As String, _
                                 strPartNumber As String, _
                                 lngQuantity As Long, _
                                 strPartNumber2 As String, _
                                 lngQuantity2 As Long)

End Sub
```

Add the following to the `IComplexOrder`:

```
' Purpose: Begin the creation of a new order.
Public Sub BeginNewOrder(strFrom As String, _
                         strTo As String)

End Sub

' Purpose: Add an order line
Public Sub AddOrderLine(strPartNumber As String, _
                        lngQuantity As Long)

End Sub

' Purpose: Delete an order line
Public Sub DeleteOrderLine(strPartNumber As String)

End Sub

' Purpose: Commit the order
Public Sub CommitOrder()

End Sub

' Purpose: Don't process the order.
Public Sub AbortOrder()

End Sub
```

Save and compile the project.

These two interfaces are just something I've created from my imagination. The idea behind them is that some clients may want to place a simple order via a simple user interface, whilst others may want to place a complex order over a period of time. Neither is necessarily good, but they hopefully bring home the point.

Implementing the Interfaces

Now that we've defined our interfaces, we'll create a component that implements them.

Create a new ActiveX DLL project; call it `OrderEntry` and name the class `Order`.

Bring up the project References dialog and locate the ActiveX DLL containing the interface definitions, which should be called InterfacesDemo:

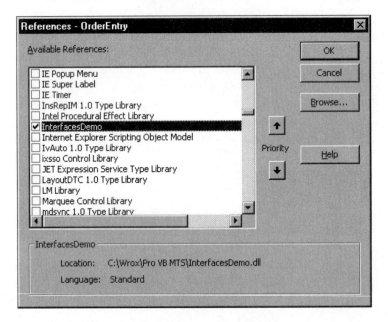

Click OK. To ensure that the interfaces have been added correctly, press *F2* to bring up the Object Browser, and select the InterfacesDemo project. We should then be able to see our interfaces:

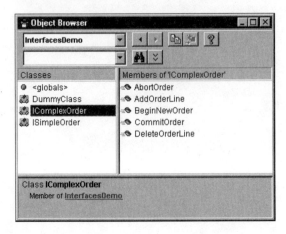

Bring up the class module and add the following lines to the Declarations section:

```
Option Explicit

Implements IComplexOrder
Implements ISimpleOrder
```

> **The Implements keyword in VB is how a class module implements an interface.**

After you've added the two Implements lines to the class module, clicking on the **Object box** (the left-hand combo box, which really should be called the interface box) shows the two new interfaces:

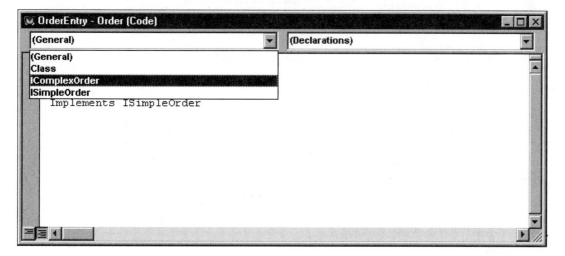

Select the IComplexOrder interface, and then click the **Procedures/Events Box** (the right-hand side combo) to see the methods and properties for the interface:

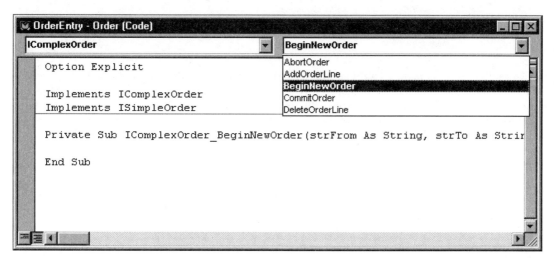

Click each method in turn and add an empty implementation. Then select the ISimpleOrder interface in the object box and do the same.

Your class module code should now look something like this:

```
Option Explicit

Implements IComplexOrder
Implements ICreateSimpleOrder

Private Sub IComplexOrder_AbortOrder()

End Sub

Private Sub IComplexOrder_AddOrderLine(strPartNumber As String, _
                                lngQuantity As Long)

End Sub

Private Sub IComplexOrder_BeginNewOrder(strFrom As String, _
                                strTo As String)

End Sub

Private Sub IComplexOrder_CommitOrder()

End Sub

Private Sub IComplexOrder_DeleteOrderLine(strPartNumber As String)

End Sub

Private Sub ICreateSimpleOrder_CreateOneProductOrder( _
        strFrom As String, strTo As String, strPartNumber As String, _
        lngQuantity As Long)

End Sub

Private Sub ICreateSimpleOrder_CreateTwoProductOrder( _
        strFrom As String, strTo As String, strPartNumber As String, _
        lngQuantity As Long, strPartNumber2 As String, _
        lngQuantity2 As Long)

End Sub
```

What we've done is implement a COM component (the class module) that implements three interfaces – the default interface (which currently has no methods), the IComplexOrder interface and the ISimpleOrder interface. You should note that each of the interface methods we've created uses the Private keyword. This ensures that the method does not appear in the default interface of the component implementing the interface.

Viewing the Interface in MTS

Compile the project, then create a new package called **MTSInterfaces** and add the `OrderEntry` component to it.

Looking in the MTS Explorer, we can view the component and the three interfaces:

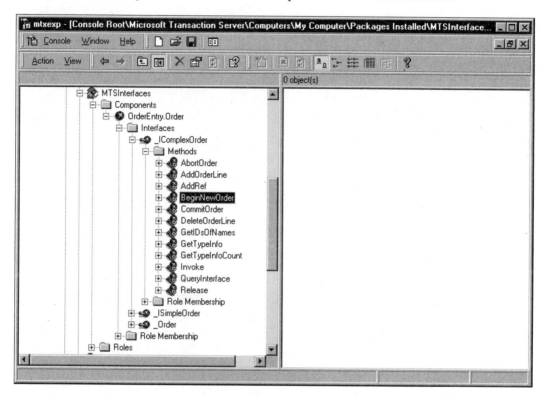

AddRef, QueryInterface and Release shown for each interface are inherited via the IUnknown interface. The functions GetIDsOfNames, GetTypeInfo, GetTypeInfoCount and Invoke are inherited from the IDispatch interface.

If you look at the properties from an interface inside of MTS, using the MTS Explorer, you'll see two property pages. The first page (General tab) shows the interface logical name (_IComplexOrder), a description and the physical name (IID):

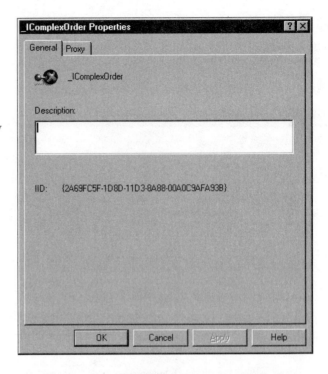

The second page (Proxy tab) shows information about how the interface is marshaled, in this case using the universal marshaler (we'll come back to marshalling later in the chapter). It also tells us where the type library for the interface lives, which is the ActiveX DLL we defined earlier to contain our interface definitions:

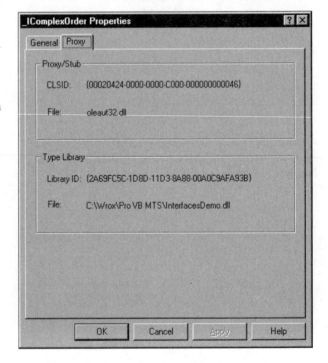

Factoring Functionality into Interfaces

Now that we've discussed the basics of interfaces and how they can be implemented in VB, let's take a step back and consider some basic design questions and issues with interfaces and MTS:

- ❑ Do you really need multiple interfaces or would multiple components do?
- ❑ How many interfaces should a component have?
- ❑ What functionality should be exposed by what interfaces?
- ❑ What happens if you need to update an interface once a component or application is deployed?
- ❑ What type client applications will be using your interfaces?

Do We Really Need Multiple Interfaces?

At the end of the day, you'll find that whether you have multiple interfaces on a component or whether you use several smaller components with one interface, your choice really doesn't make a big difference as to whether or not your components run well inside of MTS. The same code will be implemented behind the scenes, so technically speaking, it won't make any difference to the performance or scalability of your applications.

The key motivation behind multiple interfaces is to enable an object to expose functionality dynamically at run time. Inside of MTS, a successful and scalable object is destroyed after every method call. So the benefit of multiple interfaces is smaller, because the functionality they expose is process-oriented rather than object-oriented.

Consider our earlier example, where the order component supported two interfaces: the simple and complex order interfaces. The motivation here was to give our clients a degree of flexibility, and it showed that factoring related methods into smaller groups would be advantageous depending upon the client type. If we had just placed all of the methods into one big interface, some clients could have mixed the method calls violating the semantics of our object by mistake. By factoring the related methods into a separate interface, the semantics and relationships of the methods were clearly expressed. However, this example could just as easily be changed, and could achieve the same results by having two components, each supporting one interface, with each type of client using either a complex or simple order component.

If the component wasn't inside of MTS, we might have implemented another interface to expose some of the state that was modifed when the order was added to the database – maybe the time it took to add the order to the database, which we could have exposed via the `IOrderProcessingTime` interface:

```
Dim objOrder As IComplexOrder
Dim objTiming As IOrderProcessingTime

Set objOrder = New Order
objOrder.CreateNewOrder

Set objTiming = objOrder

MsgBox "The order was processed in " & CStr(objTiming.GetAddTime) & _
       "milliseconds"
```

In MTS, the `Order` object would have been destroyed when the `CreateNewOrder` method returned. Requesting the `IOrderProcessingTime` interface and asking for the time taken would just return zero, because the object state we're interested in accessing has long gone. To achieve this type of processing inside of MTS, we would have to know the unique identifer of the order added, and change the `IOrderProcessingTime` interface to accept the order ID. Because of the additional context that is required to overcome the statelessness, we might as well expose the interface and functionality via another component:

```
Dim objOrder As IComplexOrder
Dim objTiming As IOrderProcessingTime

Set objOrder = New Order
objOrder.CreateNewOrder

Set objTiming = New LastOrderProcessed

MsgBox "The order was processed in " & CStr(objTiming.GetAddTime) & _
       "milliseconds"
```

This code would obviously only work if no other client added another order.

So when are multiple interfaces *really* useful inside of MTS? And when to do they provide us with an advantage, rather than an alternative design option? The answer is version control.

Version Control - ISimpleOrder2

Once a COM interface is published, it's considered immutable. If you've got a few hundred clients using an existing interface, changing it is likely to break them. The correct way to change to an existing component is to introduce a new interface.

Let's says we've implemented the `Order` component from earlier that supported the `ISimpleOrder` interface. After it's been in use for a few months, we decide we want to add some new functionality to enable a priority order to be placed. We've got a couple of choices:

- ❑ Create a new component with an all new interface
- ❑ Implement a new interface on an existing component
- ❑ Change an existing interface and add a new method

When you want to add functionality to an existing interface, you should create a new interface appended with a version number. So `ISimpleOrder` would become `ISimpleOrder2` etc. A class module should then implement both interfaces to support both the old and new clients.

If you don't role your interfaces by hand you'll find that version control with COM objects and VB soon becomes a real nightmare. VB attempts to help you overcome this with the project compatibilty settings discussed later, but believe me, it's much less painful in the long run to role your own interfaces.

Always Consider Round Trips

When you're designing an interface, you should always consider that a method call could result in a roundtrip across the network or between processes. If you're designing a stateful MTS component, try and keep the number of method calls down to a minimum by increasing the complexity of each method call. We'll be taking a closer look at the considerations of state shortly.

Consider Your Clients Carefully

When you are designing an MTS component your should carefully consider the restriction of the client types you'll be using. If you clients are late-bound (such as VBScript or JavaScript) and discover functionality at run time *do not* use multiple interfaces. Late-bound clients can only access the properties and methods of the default interface.

> *This restriction applies because a component can only expose one* IDispatch *interface.*

Interface Granularity

Finally, when designing interfaces you should try and stick to these basic rules:

- ❑ Factor related methods and properties into their own interfaces
- ❑ Put transactional and non-transactional methods in different interfaces, which should ideally be exposed by different components that have non-transactional and transactional attributes set accordingly
- ❑ If you are supporting early- and late-bound clients, factor functionality into client-compatible interfaces. (Remember that late-bound clients can only access the default interface.)

MTS Component Granularity

Distributed applications split functionality into separate business components that can be deployed in a variety of physical configurations. Therefore, it's important to understand these configurations and how they'll impact the performance of our applications. Tuning our application code for optimum performance is only one of the ways to maintain application performance.

The first question that we have to ask about any component is whether or not it really needs to be executed remotely. This means that we have to be willing to accept any overhead caused by remote execution, such as network roundtrips and additional server resource consumption. If you decide that you are willing to accept such overheads, you then have to determine the appropriate component granularity and physical deployment.

Deployment is really concerned with where we should place each component for maximum performance. On the other hand, granularity is concerned with how logical services are organized into physical components. There are several questions that we should consider when thinking about the performance benefits of deployment and granularity:

- ❑ Will we get better performance when they're part of a single component or when they're broken into several smaller components?
- ❑ Does it make more sense to deploy a resource intensive component on a remote server (it can take advantage of server based resources) or on a local machine (reduce network traffic)?
- ❑ Where will performance bottlenecks for our components occur?
- ❑ How will the performance of our components be affected as we add more users to the application?
- ❑ Would it make more sense to use a queuing model like Microsoft Message Queue to control and help relieve the strain on back end resources?

It's important to understand that there's no best answer to any of these questions. I can't tell you how you should deploy a component under all circumstances. Each installation and application has its own unique business and infrastructure requirements. These are the things that make building distributed applications challenging. However, you should take advantage of the APE to help answer these questions. It can help to provide some really good insights and measurable answers that can help to answer your deployment and performance questions.

The granularity of our component is important in helping to determine the physical deployment of our components. The number of tasks that a given MTS component has to perform determines **component granularity**. This will have a direct impact on the performance, scalability, and reusability of our MTS components.

Let's examine a Customer Order component taken from an Order-Entry application:

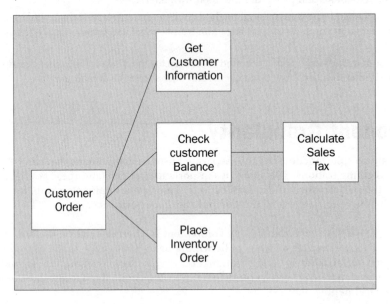

Fine-Grained Components

These are components that perform a single task. In our Order-Entry application `Get Customer Information` is an example of a fine-grained component. The sole purpose of this component is to return a customer's shipping address. This component will consume and release system resources quickly because it only has a single task to complete.

Fine-grained components have the following characteristics:

- ❑ Perform a single task
- ❑ Consume and release resources quickly after completing a task
- ❑ Enact a single business rule
- ❑ Isolate tasks in a single function which makes it easier to test and debug
- ❑ Easily reused in other packages with similar functionality
- ❑ Use system resources quickly and efficiently
- ❑ Easier to debug because they perform a single function

For example:

```
Public Sub GetCustomerInformation(ByVal CustomerAddress As String, _
                                  ByVal CustomerPhone As String)

  On Error GoTo GetCustomerInformation_Error

  Dim objContext As ObjectContext
  Set objContext = GetObjectContext()

' Place code to get customer record here

  objContext.SetComplete
  Set objContext = Nothing
  Exit Sub

GetCustomerInformation_Error:
  objContext.SetAbort
  Err.Raise Number:=vbObjectError + 1, _
            Description:="Unable to get record", _
            Source:=Err.Source

End Sub
```

If you take a look at this component closely, you can see that the entire component is dedicated to the single task of getting the customer's record.

We could use multiple VB subroutines or functions to achieve the task, but that's just a matter of programming preference.

Coarse-Grained Components

These are components that perform multiple tasks. As you can guess they're usually made up of multiple fine-grained components. Look again at our sample Order-Entry application. When we want to place an order we call the `Customer Order` component. This in turn calls several other components that are necessary to complete the transaction. This component will consume more resources and persist longer than a fine-grained component. Before the `Customer-Order` component can complete the order process it has to instantiate and then release each of the fine-grained components. Each of these components has to complete its own individual function before the `Customer Order` component can complete. These types of components are necessary to model the more complicated process of business. However, they can be difficult to use and even more difficult to debug.

Coarse-grained components have the following characteristics:

- ❑ Perform multiple tasks
- ❑ Consume resources longer because of the additional functionality
- ❑ Enact multiple business rules
- ❑ Tasks aren't isolated, which makes testing and debugging more difficult
- ❑ Use the services of other fine-grained components

For example:

```
Public Sub PlaceOrder(AccountNo As Long, OrderQuantity As Integer, _
                    ItemNumber As String)

    On Error GoTo PlaceOrder_Error

    Dim objContext As ContextObject
    Set objContext = GetObjectContext

' Call Get Customer Information component

' Call Check Customer Balance component

' Call Place Inventory Order Component

    objContext.SetComplete
    Set objContext = Nothing
    Exit Sub

PlaceOrder_Error
    objContext.SetAbort
    Err.Raise Number:=vbObjectError + 2, _
            Description:="Unable to place order", _
            Source:=Err.Source

End Sub
```

You can see that we have quite a bit of stuff going on in this component model. We have to call several other components, and each of these components must successfully complete in order for the entire transaction to be considered complete. It's important to understand that, unlike the fine-grained component, this component has a series of complex business rules that must be satisfied before acceptance of the order. The business rules have dictated that a course-grained component must be used.

Mixed Components

Fine-grained and coarse-grained components are important concepts that we have to discuss before we can begin to understand component development. However, we really don't sit down and say that we're going to write our application with only course- or fine-grained components. What we want to define is a methodology that allows the best performance based on the types of components that we have to write. This means that, before we write any code for our components, we need to answer some basic questions:

- ❑ How can we organize our components to get the maximum performance benefits?
- ❑ How can we write our components to get the most flexibility?
- ❑ How can we write our components to provide an easier deployment strategy?
- ❑ How do we write our components to take the best advantage of MTS?

As with anything that we have discussed, there's no best way to do this. Each project offers its own unique problems and requirements. However, we can define a general method that allows us to get the best of both the coarse- and fine-grained components. In order to get this advantage, we first have to organize our components into a logical grouping. For example, in our Order-Entry application, we might consider breaking our components into functional groupings like:

- ❏ Order taking components
- ❏ Order processing components
- ❏ Inventory management functions

Each of the components represents a specific business process or grouping that may occur. Of course, depending on the specific requirements of your application, you may decide to break the components into a different component structure. However, once we have the general physical structure down, we can start writing our application:

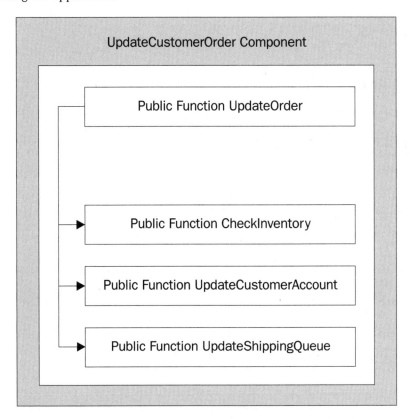

The component diagrammed above is an example of a mixed component. This is a more realistic example of the type of component that we would develop. Typically, this is a combination of both the coarse- and fine-grained components.

Transactional Attribute Considerations

One point that you should consider early on when designing coarse-grained or mixed components for MTS is the effect of the transactional attributes assigned in the MTS catalog. These attributes can seriously degrade the scalability of your applications if used incorrectly. They can also affect the re-use of your components when forming more sophisticated transactions that you may not have initially considered.

Resource Locks

When you mark a component as transactional (Requires New Transaction or Supports Transactions), you're giving resource managers an indication that any access to durable data (such as rows in a table) provided by resource managers (databases etc.) should be locked, thus isolating potential updates from other transactions. This means that your component, if transactional, should not access any durable resources that aren't going to be updated. If you did, it would mark those durable resources with a **read-lock**, preventing any other transactions from updating them, although other transactions could still read such data.

Therefore, any data your component is not going to update should be accessed via a non-transactional component, to ensure that data it is not marked with a read-lock, allowing updates to occur within other transactions.

Considerations of Requires New Transaction Attribute

If you mark a component with the attribute Requires New Transaction, you are effectively saying it can never form part of another transaction – it always has to be the root object in the transaction. During your initial design and implementation stage, this makes sense for many components. However, you may find yourself in the position where two such components need to run within one transaction. In that case, there are two solutions to the problem.

You can try an alternative approach, using the **Transactional Context object**. This object is marked with the Requires New Transaction attribute and can be used as the root object in a transaction, with sub-objects being created by the `CreateInstance` method of the `TransactionContext` object. This method works, but has a couple of limitations:

❑ The Transactional Context object is hosted in a library package so MTS has to be installed on the client machine

❑ The client has the responsibility for creating the sub-objects and committing the transaction

This might seem OK, but it means that the business logic is partially moved into the client-tier (not a good thing), and multiple base-clients may do the same thing, resulting in code duplications (not something you really want).

The better solution is to simply create a **Utility component** (a form of coarse-gained component) that is marked with the Requires New Transaction attribute, whose sole responsibility is to create the two components and encompass the transaction.

Managing State in MTS

Another implication for application performance is the methods you employ to handle data in your components. In a classic object-oriented design, objects are created and kept around for as long as they're needed. Their lifetime may last for the completion of one call or for the duration of the application. It really doesn't matter. As long as the object is needed, a reference is maintained to keep the object alive. These objects are said to **maintain state**, because their properties retain their values between function calls.

If an object does not maintain the values of its properties between function calls (because it is deactivated and reactivated) it is said to be **stateless**.

Stateful objects are not necessarily bad things to have around, but they're definitely something that you want to consider carefully when using them within MTS. Such objects are created early, kept around for the duration of the processing, and released only when their parent process says they are complete. This is definitely a potential problem for an application that's designed to be scalable.

Servers generally contain a finite amount of precious resources. Included under this label are things like database connections and, to a lesser degree these days, memory. Traditionally designed objects that maintain state also tend to maintain precious resources for a prolonged period of time. Depending upon the number of users, this means an exponential amount of resources will be consumed. Thus, stateful objects (components) are characterized by their higher use of system resources, potentially for long periods of time depending upon their controlling process.

Stateless components are better suited to MTS, and hence to scalable applications. This is not to say that these components don't consume resources like a stateful component. However, because their lifetime is shorter, their resources are requested, used and then returned to the server (MTS) more quickly than their stateful counterparts. If you're looking for scalability within your application then you should design stateless components – they help police the consumption of resources, a very important aspect of any online transaction processing (OLTP) system.

The link between stateless objects and JIT activation and ASAP deactivation should now become clearer to you. They enable and enforce the stateless object concept. After all, there is really no such thing as a stateless object, just objects that hold on to their state for a very short period of time – only long enough to complete a transaction. What JIT activation and ASAP deactivation ensure is the semantics of this concept, by destroying and recreating the object.

> Stateless objects are commonly described as process oriented objects. Their role in life is to ensure that a process is carried out, rather than to model real entities.

Holding State

In the real world, stateless MTS components are often not practical for certain tasks. There are times when it may be more efficient from a coding standpoint to develop a component that holds state. MTS can host any COM object, so the myth that *all* MTS components must be stateless is false.

Object state is where all the confusion comes into play. Traditional COM objects are generally designed to handle state for a long period of time. Now MTS comes into the picture and says object state should be kept for a very short period of time. Note that I said "object state". For an MTS component to remain stateful there are some trade-offs that we have to accept. MTS gains a degree of efficiency from being able to automatically activate and then quickly deactivate objects. However, when an object becomes deactivated it losses all state. This contradicts the very definition of a stateful object, so in order for an object to be considered stateful it cannot be deactivated.

When an object is stateful, MTS no longer has the ability to use its resources for any other object. Technically, an object becomes stateful if it doesn't call either `SetComplete` or `SetAbort` when it completes processing. In such cases, the stateful object has in effect locked a portion of the resources that MTS has to work with. MTS relies on its ability to dynamically manage resources in order to allow applications to effectively scale. Therefore, if a system were using a large number of stateful objects, it would be much less scalable. However, provided these stateful objects release previous resources (database connections) between method calls, the problem is less likely to cause dramatic problems provided a server has enough memory.

So how do you maintain object state? An object becomes deactivated when it calls either the `SetComplete` or `SetAbort` method of the Object Context. The object then becomes reactivated the next time the base-client invokes a method.

> **A stateful object can protect itself from a premature commit operation by calling the `DisableCommit` method before returning to the client.**

This method can guarantee that the current transaction cannot be successfully committed without the object doing its remaining work and then calling the `EnableCommit` method. What this means is that a component can extend its stateful duration, allowing multiple calls from the base-client to form part of a single transaction. However, the longer a transaction runs, the more resources it locks, and the less the server scales. The `Bank` sample provided with MTS clearly demonstrates this point, and shows a 50% decrease in scalability when this approach is used:

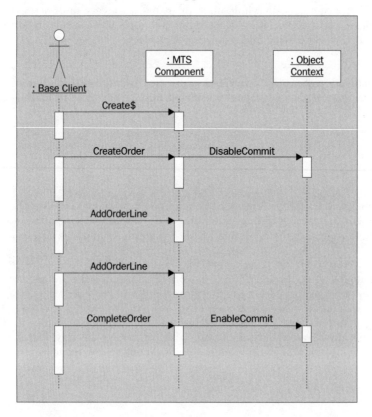

In the above diagram, we could have called `SetComplete` after the `CreateOrder` method call has been committed. However, by calling `DisableCommit` we've held on to resources until we call `EnableCommit` at the end. Thus, as the number of clients increases, it will take longer for the transaction to complete.

I recommend that you try to design your MTS components without maintaining state. But if you don't keep object state alive, what else can you do? You can maintain state somewhere else. Read on, and I'll explain.

Client State

You can make your transactional objects stateless by storing state at the client application. Client state is achieved by having the object pass its state to the client after completing each method in the object. What makes client state work is that, between calls, the MTS object is indeed stateless. Although this method can work well, it's important to realize that this method is only practical when you don't need to maintain large amounts of state. The reason is purely a bandwidth consideration. Sending information from the client to the object and back to the client can cause a heavy toll on system resources. Multiply this with 100 clients and your system may grind to a halt.

The Shared Property Manager

The **Shared Property Manager (SPM** or "spam") is a resource dispenser available in MTS. Its purpose is to maintain state in memory and allow the sharing of non-durable resources across objects in an MTS application (package).

With the Shared Property Manager, you can share global data or maintain state for additional or future references. Without synchronization, accessing global data can lead to concurrency problems as well as data corruption.

You can think of the SPM as a three-tier hierarchy, as described in the next diagram:

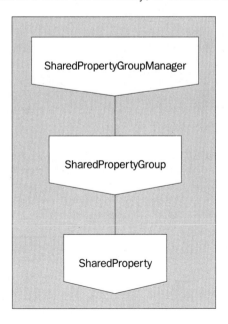

At the top of the hierarchy is the **SharedPropertyGroupManager**. Each running activity is allowed to contain only one instance of the SharedPropertyGroupManager. However, the SharedPropertyGroupManager can contain a group or collection of **SharedPropertyGroups**.

Each SharedPropertyGroup also has a collection of objects known as the **SharedProperty**. The SharedProperty object itself is used to create and access values. Each shared property contains a variant data type.

The SPM provides two important services:

❑ One is to provide lock-type synchronization so two objects cannot access the same SharedProperty (third-tier) at the same time.

❑ The other is the prevention of naming conflicts from properties that are created by other components. This is handled through the second-tier, where shared property groups provide shared properties.

Suppose you want to generate new customer sales invoice numbers in a sequential order. You could save the current invoice number to a database and retrieve it when you're ready to increment the invoice number. However, if you're processing numerous customer transactions, you create an additional resource burden to the server. Continually making numerous calls back-and-forth from the client to the database and back to the client every time you request the previous invoice number, or send the current invoice number for database storage, is not a recommended technique.

An alternative method is to keep the current customer invoice number in memory. Using the SPM is a good way to do this. Let's take a look at the following code to see how SPM actually works.

When using SPM, you need to add the reference for the Shared Property Manager Type Library (MTxSPM.dll).

```
Public Function GenCusInvNum() As Long

  On Error GoTo RaiseError

  Dim objSpmGpMgr As MTxSpm.SharedPropertyGroupManager
  Dim objSpmPropGrp As MTxSpm.SharedPropertyGroup
  Dim objSpmShdProp As MTxSpm.SharedProperty
  Dim blnBoolean As Boolean

  Set objSpmGpMgr = CreateObject("MTxSpm.SharedPropertyGroupManager.1")
  Set objSpmPropGrp = objSpmGpMgr.CreatePropertyGroup("CustSalesInvNoGroup", _
                  LockSetGet, Process, blnBoolean)

  Set objSpmShdProp = objSpmPropGrp.CreateProperty("CusSalesInvNo", blnBoolean)

  If blnBoolean = False Then
    objSpmShdProp.Value = 0
  End If

  objSpmShdProp.Value = objSpmShdProp.Value + 1
  CusSalesInvNo = objSpmShdProp.Value

  GetObjectContext.SetComplete
  Exit Function

RaiseError:
  GetObjectContext.SetAbort

End Function
```

For objects to share state, they all must be running in the same server process with the Shared Property Manager.

This code example is designed to create a new customer sales invoice number and increment it by maintaining state in memory. The first thing to do is create an object for the Shared Property Manager. This is the top level of the SPM three-tier hierarchy and is used to manage property groups. This includes allowing existing property groups to be accessed, as well as the creation of new property groups:

```
Set objSpmGpMgr = CreateObject("MTxSpm.SharedPropertyGroupManager.1")
```

The 1 at the end of this progID identifies a specific version of the object. ProgIds can contain an additional key called `CurVer` which allows you to specify a version.

Next, we need to create a shared property group. In the event a group already exists with the same name (in this case CusSalesInvNoGroup), the Boolean value for blnBoolean is changed from False to True. This is important, as this value determines whether a new property will be initialized.

Notice that LockSetGet follows the group name. This is used for locking a property while the value is being accessed. You could use LockMethod in place of LockSetGet if you want the property to remain locked until the entire method completes its task:

```
Set objSpmPropGrp = objSpmPropGrp.CreatePropertyGroup("CusSalesInvNoGroup", _
                    LockSetGet, Process, blnBoolean)
```

Now you need to either create a new CusSalesInvNo property or retrieve a reference to the current one in memory:

```
Set objSpmShdProp = objSpmPropGrp.CreateProperty("CusSalesInvNo", blnBoolean)
```

The following lines of code are used to initialize the property in the event that it did not exist. This is determined by the value returned when you created a group and assigned it a name. Note that the value of zero is being used. In other words, if the property is initialized it will have a value of zero:

```
If blnBoolean = False Then
  objSpmShdProp.Value = 0
End If
```

The value of the shared property (customer invoice number) is incremented by one:

```
objSpmShdProp.Value = objSpmShdProp.Value + 1
CusSalesInvNo = objSpmShdProp.Value
```

After successfully completing, we can call SetComplete and end the function:

```
GetObjectContext.SetComplete
```

However, in the event something goes wrong, we can raise an error and call SetAbort:

```
RaiseError:
  GetObjectContext.SetAbort
```

To maintain location transparency, it's a good idea to limit the use of a shared property group to objects created by the same component, or to objects created by components implemented within the same DLL. When components provided by different DLLs use the same shared property group, you run the risk of an administrator moving one or more of those components into a different package. Because components in different packages generally run in different processes, objects created by those components would no longer be able to share properties.

Persistent State

One important thing to understand about object state, client state, and shared state is that all state will be lost in the event of a system failure. Persistent state is different in that it is stored in some type of durable data store. When a transaction commits, state is made permanent in some type of storage such as a database. You may ask how can persistent state be used instead of maintaining state in MTS objects? You can use a database to store temporary state. Perhaps the appropriate question to ask is whether you should? The answer is, probably not.

The previous example about storing and retrieving invoice numbers is an example of using persistent state. As a rule databases are heavily utilized. Adding more than the regular demands to a database by storing temporary state can degrade the database's performance drastically. Nevertheless, you must make a decision how you want to deal with state in the event of a system failure. It's possible that this method may be a necessary decision in your systems environment.

Don't confuse the wording of persistent state with state that is persistent. Persistent state is durable. In other words, state is not maintained in memory. If the machine fails, persistent state will not be lost because it is durable.

> So keeping state *persistent* (transient) means that state is *maintained* but does not necessarily mean it is *durable*.

For example, you learned that the SPM allows state to persist (be kept in memory) but in the event of a system failure, state is lost.

Object Communication

COM provides the ability for our components to communicate through the different tiers of our application. Visual Basic allows us to easily and quickly capitalize on this benefit and build it into our application. The question we have to ask at this point is how we can take advantage of this capability? To answer this, we have to create an architecture that allows our components to communicate across the application tiers (and even across physical boundaries) in a practical way that meets the following objectives:

- ❑ Communication should be transparent to the users of the application
- ❑ Communication should be standardized across the entire application (this should be tempered with any unique business requirements)
- ❑ Communication should allow for developers of all skill levels to take advantage of architecture to implement their components quickly and efficiently
- ❑ Communication should use the minimum amount of network resources

Object Marshalling

Normally, a client and an in-process component are able to share the same address space. Therefore, any calls the client makes to the methods of an in-process component are able to share the same **address space**.

The total virtual memory allocation for an application/process is known as its address space.

Unfortunately, the components that we deal with when using MTS are often out-of-process. So instead, all method arguments must be moved across the boundary between the two processes. This process is called **marshalling**.

As discussed in Chapter 3, a client and an out-of-process component communicate through a proxy-stub relationship. The proxy and stub handle the marshalling and un-marshalling of arguments passed to methods of components. This is completely transparent to the client.

Marshalling is slower than passing parameters within a process. This is especially true when parameters are passed by reference. It's not possible to pass a pointer to another address space, so a copy must be marshaled to the components address space. When the method is finished, the data must be copied back.

Choosing Between ByVal And ByRef

When declaring methods for objects provided by an out-of-process component, always use `ByVal` to declare arguments that will contain object references. The reason for this is that cross-process marshalling by object references requires significantly less overhead if it's one way.

> **When passing a variable `ByVal`, only a copy of the variable is passed. If the procedure changes the value, the change affects only the local copy and not the variable itself.**

Declaring an argument `ByRef` means that the object reference must be marshaled to your component, and then back to the client when the method is finished.

> **When passing a variable `ByRef`, the procedure is given access to the actual variable contents in its memory address location. As a result, the variable value can be permanently changed by the procedure to which it is passed.**

There's only one reason to use `ByRef` in the declaration of an argument that's going to contain an object reference. That's when the method will replace the client's object reference with a reference from another object.

It's common practice to declare parameters in Visual Basic procedures `ByRef`, if they will be used to pass large strings or variant arrays, even if the procedure doesn't make any changes to the parameter. This is because it's much faster to pass a four-byte pointer to the data than make a copy of the entire string or array and pass a pointer to the copy.

This practice works well within the address space of your process. This means within your own program or with an in-process component, because the methods to which you're passing the parameter can use the pointer to access the data directly. Cross-process marshalling reverses this practice. Data sent `ByRef` is copied directly into the component's address space, and the method is passed a pointer to the local copy of the data. The method uses the pointer to modify the copy. When the method ends, the data for any `ByRef` parameters is copied back into the client's address space. Thus, a parameter declared `ByRef` would be passed cross-process twice per method call.

If you expect to pass a large amount of data in a string or variant array to a method of a component, and the method does not modify the value, declare the parameter `ByVal` for an out-of-process component and `ByRef` for an in-process component.

> *If you declare a parameter of a method `ByRef` in an out-of-process component, developers using the component cannot avoid the effects of marshalling by putting parenthesis around the parameter, or using the `ByVal` keyword when the method is called. Visual Basic does care. It will create a copy of the data in this situation, but since OLE automation has no way of knowing the data is just a copy, will marshall the copy back and forth between the process. The net result is that your data is copied a total of three times.*

Passing State

In addition to how you marshall the data, performance can be affected by the data type used to pass the data around. As we're developing components that communicate across processes, and often across the network, we need to make every effort to minimize the number of calls between objects. The cost of passing data out-of-process is far greater than passing it in-process. Therefore, instead of designing methods which require a series of parameters, we should design them with a single parameter that contains all the data we need to send. Fortunately for us there are several approaches we can use to pass complex data around in a single call.

User Defined Types

There are two ways that we can pass a user defined type (UDT) between objects.

> *A UDT is structured data that can combine variables of a variety of different data types.*

With Visual Basic 6.0, it's now possible to directly pass UDTs as parameters between objects:

```
Option Explicit

Public Enum SourceType
   Parameter1 As String * 10
   Parameter2 As Integer
End Type

Private mudtSource as SourceType

Public Function GetData() As SourceType

   mudtSource.Parameter1 = "This is a string"
   mudtSource.Parameter2 = 100

   GetData = mudtSource

End Function
```

In order for this to work in out-of-process components or across threads in a multi-threaded component, you will need an updated version of DCOM for Windows 9x, or Service Pack 4 for Windows NT 4.0.

However, there are some drawbacks with this approach. Firstly you need to declare the UDT as `Public`, which, although not a serious drawback for an MTS DLL component, prevents you from using this feature if they're not part of an ActiveX server. More importantly, public UDTs cannot be passed as parameters using the `ByVal` keyword. Being unable to pass UDTs by value means that the data must perform an extra round-trip, thus creating more network traffic. As if this wasn't enough, the COM marshalling that must take place to pass a complex data structure hits performance. Having said all this, there's a mechanism that gets around all these problems and still allows you to use UDTs.

You can use the `LSet` command to convert the data into a simple byte stream (String) which allows you to do a very fast memory copy from one UDT to the other, thus effectively converting a detailed UDT into a String, or a String into a detailed UDT:

```
Option Explicit

Private Type SourceType
    Parameter1 As String * 10
    Parameter2 As Integer
End Type

Private Type DestinationType
    Buffer As String * 11
End Type

Private Sub CopyType()

    Dim udtSource As SourceType
    Dim udtDest As DestinationType

    mudtSource.Parameter1 = "This is a string"
    mudtSource.Parameter2 = 100

    LSet udtDest = udtSource

End Sub
```

This method is probably the fastest and gives the best performance, but there is a trade-off in that it's considerably more fiddly to use.

Variant Arrays

A `Variant` data type can contain virtually any value of any data type – so you would think that an array of them would be a pretty useful method of passing data:

```
Dim vntArray(3) As Variant

vntArray(0) = "Hello"
vntArray(1) = 100
vntArray(2) = 99.99
vntArray(3) = "11/11/76"
```

However, a variant data type is highly inefficient when compared to the more basic data types such as String, Integer etc. This is because every time we use a variant variable, Visual Basic needs to check to find out what type of data it actually contains. If it isn't the right type of data then Visual Basic will attempt to convert it to a type we can use. All this adds up to a lot of overhead and our performance will suffer. Every time we use data in a variant array we will incur an overhead. Given that we're likely to require the data a lot, there's good chance that we may end up with poorly performing objects.

PropertyBag Objects

A **PropertyBag** object is an object that stores values provided to it using a key-value pair. In essence, you place values in with a name attached, then retrieve those values later by using the same name.

You enter data into the PropertyBag using the `WriteProperty` method and retrieve it using the `ReadProperty` method. There is also a `Contents` property, which provides us with access to the entire contents of the object as a byte stream:

```
Public Function GetObjectData() As String

   Dim pbData As PropertyBag
   Set pbData = New PropertyBag

   pbData.WriteProperty "Name", mstrName
   pbData.WriteProperty "BirthDate", mdtmBirthDate

   GetObjectData = pbData.Contents

End Function
```

```
Public Sub LoadObject(StringBuffer As String)

   Dim arData() As Byte
   Dim pbData As PropertyBag

   Set pbData = New PropertyBag

   arData = StringBuffer
   pbData.Contents = arData

   mstrName = pbData.ReadProperty("Name")
   mdtmBirthDate = pbData.ReadProperty("BirthDate")

End Sub
```

Disconnected Recordsets

The disconnected recordset is new with the release of Visual Basic 6 and ADO 2.0. This type of recordset is disassociated from its original source. The recordset can then be efficiently marshaled between components without maintaining a connection. However, the methods available to a recordset are available to the components. Additionally, the recordset can be sent back and then reattached to it source.

One of the real benefits of this method is that the database is then able to handle marshalling. This functionality is useful when passing data between different layers. However, be aware that this method has more overhead and is limited to the ability of shaping your data through SQL statements. Additionally, formatting of your data can become an issue.

If we wanted to create a generic component that returned a disconnected recordset to client application, we could enter the following code in a component:

```
Public Function GetData(strCn As String, strSQL As String) As Object

    Dim cnData As New ADODB.Connection
    Dim recData As New ADODB.Recordset

    cnData.Open strCn

' The ADODB.Recordset should generate Recordset
' objects that can be disconnected and later
' reconnected to process batch updates.

    recData.CursorLocation = adUseClientBatch

' Using the Unspecified parameters, an ADO/R
' recordset is returned.

    recData.Open strSQL, cnData, adOpenUnspecified, adLockUnspecified, _
            adCmdUnspecified

    Set GetData = recData

    cnData.Close
    Set cnData = Nothing
    Set recData = Nothing

End Function
```

Here are some tips to keep in mind when designing a component to use a disconnected recordset:

❑   Always place one simple method in your server component to test for minimum functionality before attempting to pass a recordset object back. This will help isolate any possible errors that may exist.

❑   Always try to build a simple client application to test your component before deploying it. If you're writing an Internet component, make sure that you test your component with Internet Explorer.

❑   It's easier to develop your application on a local test web server. This is because you will need to copy and register the DLL on the test server after each compile.

❑   The DSN passed to your business object will need to be a System DSN on your server. If it doesn't exist, or is set up wrong, your component will fail. It's always good to test the DSN with another application like Microsoft Access to ensure that it's set up properly.

❑   Method names on your custom business objects cannot exceed 255 characters. This allows compatibility across all RDS supported protocols (this includes HTTP, DCOM and in process components).

❑   If you used Visual Basic and a version of ADOR prior to 2.0 then you should rebuild your object to use the ADOR 2.0 type library.

XML

No doubt you've heard about the eXtensible Markup Langauge (**XML**). Since its official ratification in February 1998, it is fast becoming the *de-facto* way of exchanging and representing structured documents for many reasons – ease of use, availability of tools, media coverage etc. For these reasons, it has a viable use in our enterprise applications, and is ideal for passing information between tiers, especially business and presentation (user services).

Whilst a full discussion of XML is beyond the scope of this book, I'll introduce the basic concepts of XML and discuss its use in conjunction with MTS. If you would like to learn more about XML check out XML Applications ISBN 1861001525, from Wrox Press.

Using XML Documents for Business Transactions

Consider an MTS component that is responsible for processing a client order. An order is by no means a simple data structure. It contains header information (such as who the order is from, who it is to, delivery address etc.) and order lines (what the customer wants to buy). Each order line may have lots of associated information, such as a quantity ordered, part number, delivery conditions etc.

We know MTS achieves better scalability by keeping transactions short. To process orders (add them to our database) efficiently, we should capture the information that comprises them on the presentation tier (on the clients machine), before passing all the information in one go to the business tier for processing. Ideally, we want the order to be processed by invoking one method of a business object that keeps the transaction time short and calls `SetComplete` when done.

XML enables a complex data structure to be represented by using hierarchically arranged elements (nodes). These elements, interspersed with text, represent information that has an explicit relationship due to the structure of an XML document.

For our order-processing scenario, the client could gather the order information via its user interface over a period of time, and then create an XML document to represent it. That document could be structured like this:

```xml
<?xml version="1.0" ?>
<Order Date="06/03/1999">
    <From>Joe Bloggs</Order>
    <To>Wrox Press</To>
    <Items>
        <Item>
            <Description>Professional ASP Programming</Description>
            <Code>1234</Code>
            <Quantity>1</Quantity>
        </Item>
        <Item>
            <Description>Professional VBMTS Programming</Description>
            <Code>2345</Code>
            <Quantity>2</Quantity>
        </Item>
    </Items>
</Order>
```

The first thing that's obvious about this document is that you and I can both read it. We can also see that its hierarchy clearly represents the relationship between the data elements.

The first line of the document is called the XML declaration - a processing instruction (out-of-band information/metadata) that indicates the document confirms to version 1.0 of the W3C XML standard.

The next line is called the root element. An XML document has one of these, in this case called the `Order`. All subsequent elements are children of this element. The `Order` has the child elements `From`, `To`, `DeliveryAddress` and `Items`.

The Items element (which is simply a way of grouping the order lines) has two child elements both called Item. Each Item element details the order line and has three child elements - Description, Code and Quantity.

It generally helps to picture XML documents as a tree structure. So for our order, think of it like this:

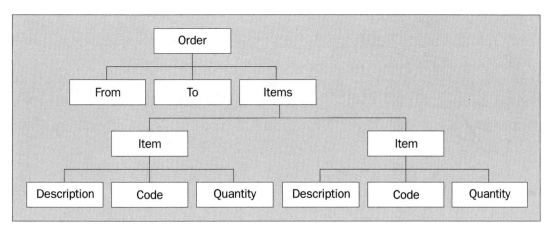

The tree structure clearly reinforces the relationships between the elements.

Using DOM to Create and Manipulate XML Documents

The **Document Object Model (DOM)** is a W3C standard that defines a number of interfaces for creating and manipulating XML documents. The API is very simple, and is based upon the concept of a tree with nodes (like the diagram above).

Each node in the tree can have a parent, a previous sibling, a next sibling and one or more children. In diagram above, the Items element has a parent element Orders, two children; Item and Item, and no next sibling.

A detailed description of the DOM interfaces can be found on the W3C web site. Rather than discuss the DOM API in any more detail, I'll show you the code used to create the XML document shown earlier. This, to an extent, explains how these interfaces are structured:

```
Private Sub CreateOrder()

    Dim XMLDocument As New DOMDocument
    Dim objOrder As IXMLDOMElement
    Dim objFrom As IXMLDOMElement
    Dim objDest As IXMLDOMElement
    Dim objItems As IXMLDOMElement

' Create the XML document
    Set objOrder = XMLDocument.createElement("Order")
    objOrder.setAttribute "Date", Now()

' Add the root element to the XML document
    XMLDocument.appendChild objOrder
```

```
    ' Create the From & To elements
      Set objFrom = XMLDocument.createElement("From")
      Set objDest = XMLDocument.createElement("To")

    ' Set the From Text
      objOrder.appendChild objFrom
      AppendText objFrom, "Joe Bloggs"

    ' Set the To Text
      objOrder.appendChild objDest
      AppendText objDest, "Wrox Press"

    ' Create the Items element
      Set objItems = XMLDocument.createElement("Items")
      objOrder.appendChild objItems

    ' Create a couple of items
      CreateItem objItems, "1234", "Professional ASP Programming", 1
      CreateItem objItems, "2345", "Professional VBMTS Programming", 2

    ' Display the XML document
      MsgBox XMLDocument.xml

End Sub


' Purpose: This routine creates the elements for an order line.
Public Sub CreateItem(objParent As IXMLDOMNode, strCode As String, _
                      strDescription As String, lngQuantity As Long)

    Dim objItem As IXMLDOMElement
    Dim objCode As IXMLDOMElement
    Dim objDesc As IXMLDOMElement
    Dim objQuantity As IXMLDOMElement

    Set objItem = objParent.ownerDocument.createElement("Item")
    objParent.appendChild objItem

    Set objCode = objParent.ownerDocument.createElement("Code")
    AppendText objCode, strCode
    objItem.appendChild objCode

    Set objDesc = objParent.ownerDocument.createElement("Description")
    AppendText objDesc, strDescription
    objItem.appendChild objDesc

    Set objQuantity = objParent.ownerDocument.createElement("Quantity")
    AppendText objQuantity, CStr(lngQuantity)
    objItem.appendChild objQuantity

End Sub


Public Sub AppendText(Node As IXMLDOMNode, strText As String)

    Dim objTextNode As IXMLDOMText
    Set objTxtNode = Node.ownerDocument.createTextNode(strText)

    Node.appendChild objTextNode

End Sub
```

In this code, the `CreateItem` method creates the XML elements to represent an order line. It adds these nodes to a parent node, which is the `Items` element.

Here is the output from this sample code parsed appropriately.

You won't actually get a message box looking quite like this with the above code.

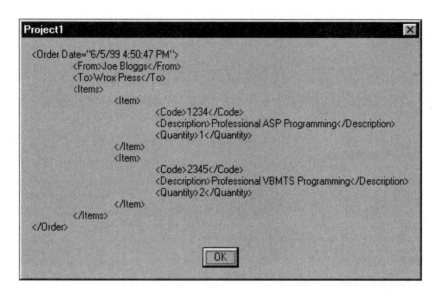

```
<Order Date="6/5/99 4:50:47 PM">
        <From>Joe Bloggs</From>
        <To>Wrox Press</To>
        <Items>
                <Item>
                        <Code>1234</Code>
                        <Description>Professional ASP Programming</Description>
                        <Quantity>1</Quantity>
                </Item>
                <Item>
                        <Code>2345</Code>
                        <Description>Professional VBMTS Programming</Description>
                        <Quantity>2</Quantity>
                </Item>
        </Items>
</Order>
```

Passing an XML Document between Tiers

As shown in the sample code for creating an order, it's possible to ask the DOM to save an XML document to a string:

```
Dim objDocument As DOMDocument
Dim strMyDocument As String

strMyDocument = objDocument.xml
```

This means it's possible to pass an XML document as a parameter to a method of an MTS component, as you would any other string parameter. An MTS object can access an XML document passed from another tier, by using the DOM API to rebuild and access the tree structure.

This code shows how a method could be written to display the Order Date:

```
Public Sub ProcessOrder(strOrderData as string )

   Dim objDocument As new DOMDocument
   objDocument.LoadXML strOrderData

' Display the order date - NOT a good idea for an MTS component
'                          but it demonstrates the point.

   MsgBox objDocument.FirstChild.Attributes.GetNamedItem("Date")

End Sub
```

That's all I'm going to tell you about XML in this chapter. So to recap, the advantages of using XML are:

❑ It's simple and easy to use

❑ Tools for creating and manipulating XML documents are widely available

❑ Information is hierarchical and allows complex relationships between data elements to be expressed

And using XML with MTS means:

❑ An XML document can be built over a prolonged period of time on the presentation tier, and then transferred for processing to the business tier in one go.

❑ An XML document can be passed as a string parameter, reducing the number of parameters needed for a complex method.

The Mixed Metaphor

Up to this point, we have discussed a variety of different methods for moving data across the tiers of our application. Of course, each of these methods offers some obvious benefits. However, each of these methods also has some limitations. If we were to do a reality check, we'd see that we could create a mixed metaphor that meets all of our needs. The mixed metaphor certainly doesn't mean that we can't use any of the other methods discussed. However, using this method allows the best of all possibilities.

This metaphor is based around the concept of the proxy-stub relationship that is the basis of COM. There are two separate pieces that we develop and use.

The **State object** contains a business relationship. This object is based around a relationship that the business defines. When creating this object, it should be based not on the database structure, but the relationships that are needed for the business and, as such, the front-end. Obviously, if we created a separate state object for each and every relationship, this could conceivably become hundreds of objects. With this mind, you may want to consider developing a set of generic objects. For example a generic set of objects may include a collection based on String and Integers. These objects are class collections that contain two unique methods to load and unload the collections into a variant array. Once the object is imploded into a variant array, the object can be transported easily across the network in one pass.

The **Server object** contains the actual business processes. These are the Public functions that are called by the user services and are used to load and unload the state objects. These functions are where you open and close your database connections.

MTS Component Strategies

COM DLLs can easily be used with MTS by simply installing them into packages. Both MTS DLLs and non-MTS DLLs can take advantage of database connection pooling which eliminates the high overhead costs associated from opening and closing a database connection.

In addition, MTS can provide several added benefits and performance enhancements to a standard COM DLL by adding only a few extra lines of MTS specific code. In order to achieve the maximum performance from MTS components, let me introduce you to a few design principles:

- ❑   Acquire resources as late as possible and release resources as soon as possible
- ❑   Call `SetComplete` and `SetAbort` methods often if the object is transactional
- ❑   Obtain object references early

Let's go over each of these three design principles in a bit more detail.

Holding on to Resources

You have learned that database connections take time to connect, tie-up system resources, and offer finite connections. You also learned that a resource dispenser for connection pooling is used to solve this problem. In order to enhance connection pooling, be sure to design applications so that they connect to the database as late as possible and released the connection immediately upon completion of a task.

Keeping the same username and password in a connection string will allow greater reuse in the database connection pool.

```
Public Function Example()

  Dime cnADOConnection As ADODB.Connection
  Set cnADOConnection = New ADODB.Connection

  cnADOconnection.ConnectionString = "Data Source=data source name here;" & _
                                     "uid=userid goes here;" & _
                                     "pwd=password here;" & _
                                     "server=server name goes here;" & _
                                     "database=name of database"

  cnADOConnection.Open

' WORK GOES HERE - Example: Insert and Update Database

  cnADOConnection.Close
  Set cnADOConnection = Nothing

End Function
```

Notice that as soon as the work has completed, we immediately close the connection and remove the connection instance.

Obtain Reference Pointers Early

Don't be afraid; grab a hold of those object references early as you like! Even if your component takes up a lot of system resources, obtaining a reference to it won't inhibit component or system performance. Remember that MTS is only holding a reference to a Context Wrapper. Just-In-Time activation ensures that the object will be created precisely when needed and, at the same time, ensures that objects are not created unnecessarily:

```
Dim MyTxObject As MyTxObject
Set MyTxObject = New MyTxObject        ' Object not created, just Context Wrapper

' lots of code goes here

myTxObject DoSomething                 ' Real object is created by JIT and then
                                       ' deactivated

' lots of code goes here

myTxObject DoSomethingElse             ' Another instance of the object is created
                                       ' then deactivated
```

Call SetComplete and SetAbort Methods Often

Just-In-Time Activation and As Soon As Possible Deactivation can be vastly enhanced with the
SetComplete and SetAbort methods. The SetComplete method declares when an object has
successfully completed its task and can be deactivated. If the object is part of a transaction,
SetComplete is used to indicate that the object has successfully completed its transactional work and
is ready to commit. The transaction will commit only if all other components bound by the
transaction successfully complete their transactional tasks.

The SetAbort method is used to notify MTS that the object has failed to complete its task and that it
can be deactivated. When dealing with transactions, a call to SetAbort should be used to ensure
that a transaction is not committed and thus rolled back.

```
Public Function Example(Return As Long)

   Dim objContext As ObjectContext
   Set objContext = GetObjectContext

   On Error GoTo RaiseError

' Code for Work or Transaction

   objContext.SetComplete        ' Work or Transaction Completed Successfully

   Exit Function

RaiseError:  ' Work or Transaction Failed

' Other error handling routines
   objContext.SetAbort

End Function
```

Summary

You have covered a lot of material in this chapter. You learned about:

❑ Application performance issues – Performance is not always a function of our code: other external factors, such as an increase in the number of users and hardware issues, can determine the overall performance of our applications.

❑ MTS component granularity – We introduced the differences between fine-grained and course-grained components and, to make things interesting, we also learned about mixed components.

❑ State - You discovered what state is and how to deal with it in your MTS applications.

❑ Strategies for developing your MTS components.

In the next chapter, we'll take a more practical look at managing components and packages.

6

Building MTS Components

In the last chapter, we looked at many of the design considerations when developing MTS components. It was largely theoretical in nature, so in this chapter we're going to see some of those prinicples in action.

We'll be developing a sample application called **PasswordPersist** that we'll continue to develop and extend through the remaining chapters of the book. In this chapter, we'll primarily be concerned with developing the MTS components themselves, although we'll also need to build the back-end (Access database) and front-end (VB form). In later chapters, these will be extended to include a SQL database and an ASP interface.

The Project Properties for an MTS Component

Before we move on to look at some code, let's take a brief moment think about how we want to set the project up for running in MTS. Create a new ActiveX DLL project and open its Project Properties dialog:

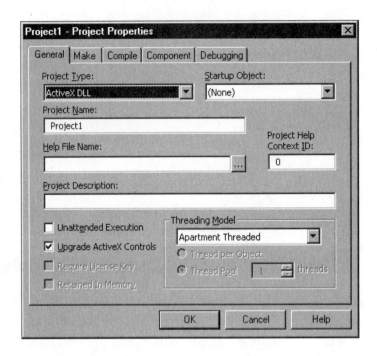

The General Tab

On the General tab, there are a few options we need to consider:

Threading Model

For ActiveX DLLs, we have a choice of two threading models: Apartment and Single Threaded. You may want to refer back to the discussion in Chapter 3 at this point.

The threading model that is used by the components of the application is an important issue that the developer of MTS applications needs to consider. The threading model of a component determines how the methods of the component are assigned to threads in order to be executed. The MTS environment itself manages all of the threads associated with its applications. A component should never create any threads on its own. This is primarily of concern to J++ and C++ developers, who have the ability to create threads directly. Developers creating objects in Visual Basic do not need to worry about this, as there is no way for them to explicitly create a thread.

Single Threaded

If a component is marked as Single Threaded, then all methods of that component will execute on the main thread. There is one main thread for each MTS application. Since there is only one thread, it means that only one method can execute at any given time. If there are multiple Single Threaded components that are being accessed my multiple clients simultaneously, then it is easy to see why a bottleneck will occur. Since only one method can execute at a time, all of the other methods will be sitting around waiting their turn. This can essentially grind a system to a halt.

> **A good rule of thumb to remember is Single Threading = BAD!**

Apartment Threaded

In a component that is marked as Apartment Threaded, each method of that component will execute on a thread that is associated with that component. Since each component running inside MTS has its own thread, this separates the methods into their own 'apartments', with each instance of a component corresponding to one apartment. While there is only one thread inside of a component, each instance of that component will have its own thread apartment. This will alleviate a great number of the problems that a single threaded component has. Since multiple components can be executing methods in their own apartments simultaneously, the scalability constraints that the single threaded components have are greatly relaxed.

> **When developing MTS components with VB make sure that you select this option.**

UnAttended Execution

The Unattended Execution check box is used to indicate that your component won't try to interact with the user directly. It prevents you from displaying a message box from your program and it makes sure you haven't included any forms or controls with your project. Elements which expect user input are not suitable for an MTS component, as we would expect the component to be running on a server or servers with no immediate observer. Our component would simply hang or pause until someone provided the necessary user input. Therefore, we want to tick this check box.

If you really need to provide some form of feedback, then write to a log or text file.

The Component Tab

Now switch to the Component tab, as there are several options we need to consider here as well:

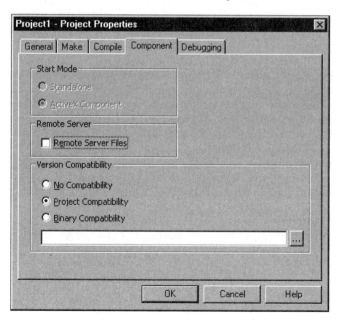

Compatibility Options

Suppose you created an application for the Grog Company. The users love the friendly client application that you designed and everything seems to be going great. Along comes the CEO of the company and informs you that he wants to double the current payroll bonus for the company owners.

You learned earlier that keeping business rules separate from the client application allows you to quickly make small changes to your business components without having to update every machine that has the client application. Within minutes the change has been made and you recompile the component. Before you have a chance to pat yourself on the back, the users start screaming that their application is no longer working. Suddenly you remember that you skipped this section of my book.

Let's think about what happened. Recall that when an ActiveX component is compiled, a GUID is created for each component and for each interface to the component. If you modify your component, it's possible that one or more interfaces can change, in which case a new GUID is created. However, the client doesn't know that the GUID has changed: it still thinks it can access the component through the old GUID. So what happens? The application fails unless we take proper precautions.

What went wrong at the Grog Company? You didn't select the appropriate compatibility setting when you recompiled your code.

When developing ActiveX components in Visual Basic, you can select one of three types of compatibility settings for your project:

- ❑ <u>N</u>o Compatibility
- ❑ <u>P</u>roject Compatibility
- ❑ <u>B</u>inary Compatibility

Project Compatibility

Let's start with Project Compatibility. This is the default selection when you first create an ActiveX EXE or ActiveX DLL. This setting is used to maintain compatibility during testing, and it's just what you want to use during the development phase of your component. New type library information is still created each time you recompile. However, the type library identifier will be maintained, thus enabling continued testing.

So, the reason project compatibility exists is to allow the developer to make modifications to the components during the testing phase. As an example, the developer may find that a new method needs to be added to the objects interface. However, adding a method actually changes the interface and this is not allowed with COM. Remember interfaces are immutable once they're published. However, during the development phase, changing an interface is OK, but only because you have no production clients that depend on the interface.

With all this said, I want you to read this next sentence carefully! As soon as you distribute the component, you must not change the interface, regardless of the compatibility setting you choose.

> **After you distribute your component, you cannot change the interface.**
> **However you can change the implementation of the interface.**

Binary Compatiblity

Binary Compatibility can be your safety net. Instead of creating new GUIDs during each compile, using binary compatibility will only create new GUIDs when necessary. Changing a business rule has nothing to do with interfaces, so there's no reason for a new interface GUID to be generated. The same goes for the class itself, no new features were added.

At the same time, by using Binary Compatibility, an alert will be generated in the event something was changed in the component that may result in an incompatible version.

No Compatibility

When compiling with No Compatibility, new GUIDs are created for each class and interface. This means that there is no backward compatibility. The only things that will work with these components are applications that have been created to work with the specific version of the compiled component.

Remote Server Files

Ticking this box will cause the compiler to generate a remote server file (with the extension `.vbr`) and a type library file (extension `.tlb`). These additional files can be important when you want to distribute your components across multiple machines. By including these files in the set-up for your application, you can register components as being remote on client workstations. We'll be finding out a bit more about this is the Simple Order Case Study after Chapter 13.

An MTS Class Template

In order to make our lives a bit easier developing MTS components, we're going to create ourselves a class template that we can as a base for any objects that we plan to use that support MTS. Create a new ActiveX DLL project, and change the name of the default class module to MTSTemplate. As an initial setting set the MTSTransactionMode of the class to 3 - Uses Transactions. We'll put a comment in the module to remind ourselves that this might need changing.

Add the following code to the class module:

```
Option Explicit

'****************************************************************
'* You will need to add a reference to the Microsoft Transaction Server   *
'* Type Library for this project                                *
'*                                                              *
'* The MTSTransactionMode Property is currently set at 3-Uses Transactions *
'* You may need to change this as appropriate for your project   *
'****************************************************************

Implements ObjectControl

Private mobjContext As ObjectContext

Public Function NameOfSub()

   On Error GoTo RaiseError

' code for work goes here
```

```
      mobjContext.SetComplete
      Exit Function

 RaiseError:

   mobjContext.SetAbort

 End Function
```

```
 Private Function ObjectControl_CanBePooled() As Boolean

 ' Uncomment one choice:
 ' ObjectControl_CanBePooled = True      'It's OK to recycle the object
 ' ObjectControl_CanBePooled = False     'It's not OK to recycle the object

 End Function
```

```
 Private Sub ObjectControl_Activate()

   Set mobjContext = GetObjectContext

 End Sub
```

```
 Private Sub ObjectControl_Deactivate()

   Set mobjContext = Nothing

 End Sub
```

Save your work in the `Templates\Classes` directory of Visual Basic. Now, whenever you add a new class you now have a new template option:

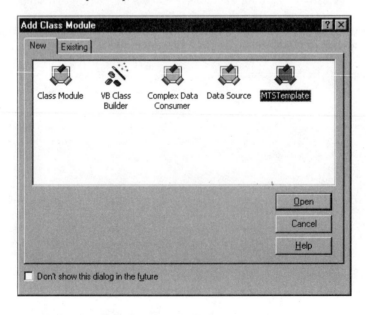

You could just as easily add other elements to this template, such as an ADO connection variable, but I'll leave that up to you.

The Password Persist Case Study

Throughout this book, we'll be developing an application, called `PasswordPersist`, to get some hands-on experience with MTS and how it relates to other layers of the system. But before we jump into the code, let's take a high level, informal look at `PasswordPersist` and see why such a system may be useful for the general Internet population. We'll also cover some of the risks and problems that are inherent in such a system.

The Burden of the Internet

If you used the Internet before it started to take off early in the 1990's, you may remember that you usually visited a site without any concerns for security. Most of the web sites were either educational or personal, and very few had anything to do with purchasing products online. However, with the rapid growth of e-commerce, more and more people are using the Internet to fulfill their shopping needs. This has a lot of advantages, one of the biggest being private consumerism (who doesn't want to avoid those huge shopping lines at Christmas?). However, one problem that will always plague e-commerce is security.

Concerns over misappropriation of credit card numbers has sparked web site developers to find secure ways of transferring customer information. We'll take a look at some of those solutions later, but one of the results of these secure web sites is the Username/Password (hence called U/P) combination. This makes sense. By making sure that the client has the correct U/P, the web-server has a pretty good idea as to who is on the other end. Of course, if your U/P is leaked to anyone, they can use it for their own purposes (some of which may not be desirable as far as you're concerned).

However, more and more web sites these days seem to require a U/P to access their information and use their services. This is getting to be quite a burden for the average user. Granted, you could limit the U/P combinations to just one, but if one hacker finds out what it is, they now have access to any web site you use that combination at. The problem with maintaining all of these combinations is that you'll probably end up storing all of the U/Ps into an Access database or a text file. If somebody stumbles upon that file, you'd probably scramble to cancel your credit cards.

An Online Solution

In this example, we're going to design the `PasswordPersist` system, and see how MTS fits into the picture as well. This system has one very simple goal in mind: allow anybody to store all of their U/Ps via a web site, which can be retrieved at any time. The **user** can store a list of **systems**, e.g. "Wrox Press" and "MySecureBank") along with any U/Ps that are associated with these systems, e.g. "MyUserName" and "MyPassword" for the Wrox Press system. This doesn't eliminate the persistence storage problem completely (the web site has that responsibility) but now the security issue is removed somewhat from the user. Another nice advantage is that the user doesn't need to keep a file or a piece of paper lying around for someone else to read. They can simply go to the `PasswordPersist` web site, look up the desired U/P for a given system, and go from there. All of the information is stored in one location (at least logically).

Of course, we don't have to limit the customer to just a U/P combination. Maybe the user has to remember a bank number for their online banking web site. Some sites have discount codes, which you may need if you want a reduced rate on a magazine subscription. If we're clever enough, we can make `PasswordPersist` flexible such that users can submit a slew of **attribute** combinations for a given system.

Potential Risks

As nice as this approach sounds, there are some risks involved in using this system, such as:

- ❑ **Service Dependency**: What happens if the server goes down, and you can't access your bank U/P? `PasswordPersist` better be up 24 hours a day, 7 days a week if we want customer satisfaction with our data delivery.

- ❑ **Secure Data**: By far, this is the biggest issue. Although `PasswordPersist` isn't responsible for the one U/P that users will have to remember to access the system, it should not allow anyone to see data from other users. We have to make sure that our system is as secure as we can possibly make it.

Although our discussions of security will not be limited to MTS, we can use some of the services that MTS has to make sure somebody (either external to the system or internal) doesn't use our components for unauthorized purposes.

The Use Cases and Requirements

Before we start to dive into the details of this system, let's go over how a typical client would use the system so we can anticipate usage behaviors before component design begins. We'll also create a preliminary list of requirements for the system, and we'll cover which ones this case study will address in detail.

Use Cases

As far as what a user can do with `PasswordPersist`, there are three basic use cases that we should be concerned with:

- ❑ Creating a New Account
- ❑ Modifying the Systems List
- ❑ Modifying the Attributes List

Let's go through the definition of each use case.

Create a New Account

The client will access the `PasswordPersist` web site, which will prompt them to create a new user account. The client will type in a U/P combination along with any other pertinent client information needed by the system. If the U/P combination is unique, a new account is created. Otherwise, the client is asked to try again until the combination is unique.

Modifying the System List

The client will log into `PasswordPersist`, and access the Modify System List screen. The client can either add new systems to their list, or delete systems that they have associated with their account.

Modifying the Attributes List

The client will log into `PasswordPersist`, select a system from a list, and access the Modify Attributes List screen. The client can either add new attributes to their list for a system, or delete attributes that they have associated with the selected system.

The Data Store

Let's start with the database that will be used to store user, system, and attribute information. We'll be using five tables that look like the following:

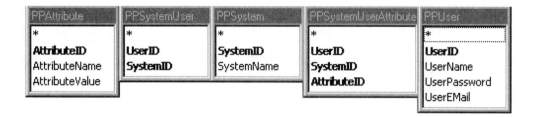

The PPUser, PPSystem, and PPAttribute tables are all independent - they don't rely upon any others for information. The U/P combination on the PPUser table must be unique. Also, we'd like to store the e-mail address of the client if it's given to us (we'll see why later on). The PPSystemUser table creates associations between a user and a system, and the PPSystemUserAttribute table creates associations between a user, a system, and an attribute. There's a reason why the database is designed this way - let's go through an example to demonstrate.

Suppose Joe Smith is the first client of PasswordPersist. He creates a user account with "jsmith" as the username and "5htyb" as the password. He then proceeds to create two systems, "Wrox Press" and "SuperHuge Bank". After he's done, we'd have the following entries in the PPUser, PPSystem, and PPSystemUser tables:

PPUser Table:

UserID	UserName	UserPassword	UserEMail
1	jsmith	5htyb	

PPSystem Table:

SystemID	SystemName
1	Wrox Press
2	SuperHuge Bank

PPSystemUser Table:

SystemID	UserID
1	1
2	1

We'll ignore any attributes for these two systems right now, since the same principle applies for systems and attributes. Now a second user, Jane Doe, creates a new account with "jdoe" as the username and "thg756e" as the password. She also creates the system, "Wrox Press". As we know, this entry already exists in the PPSystem table. Therefore, all we need to do is create a new record in the PPUser table and an entry in the PPSystemUser table like this:

PPUser Table:

UserID	UserName	UserPassword	UserEMail
1	jsmith	5htyb	
2	jdoe	thg756e	

PPSystemUser Table:

SystemID	UserID
1	1
2	1
1	2

This model allows us to reuse the entries in the PPSystem and PPAttribute tables. It's probably a good bet that systems will be repeated, like banks and computer companies. In our database, we can use associations to relate users to systems and attributes.

Case Sensitivity

There's one problem with this system. Some systems require that U/Ps are case sensitive, which means that if my username is "MyName" and my password is "MyPassword", I can't enter "myname" and "mypassword" as the U/P to gain access to the system. Therefore, we have to ensure that we add records to the PPSystem and PPAttribute table if and only if the textural fields within these tables are unique at the binary level. This may seem like a small problem, but let's go through a quick example to illustrate this fact.

Suppose Jane Doe comes back to our system and adds a U/P combination for the "Wrox Press" system. She chooses "Max" as the username (the name of her boyfriend's dog), and "TheYear1998" (the year she met her boyfriend). In this case, our PPSystemUserAttribute table now has an entry like this:

PPAttribute Table:

AttributeID	AttributeName	AttributeValue
1	Max	TheYear1998

`PPSystemUserAttribute` Table:

SystemID	UserID	AttributeID
1	2	1

Now Joe Smith comes in and decides to add a U/P to the "Wrox Press" system. He chooses "max" as his username (the name of his dog) and "theyear1998" (the year he met his girlfriend). If we don't have an index on the `PPAttribute` table that's case-sensitive, we'd end up with a new entry in the `PPSystemUserAttribute` table like this:

`PPSystemUserAttribute` Table:

SystemID	UserID	AttributeID
1	1	1

Even though Joe and Jane are (theoretically) oblivious to the fact that they're "sharing" the same U/P, Joe would be disappointed if "Wrox Press's" U/Ps are case-sensitive.

Therefore, we need to make sure that our indexes are case-sensitive. Unfortunately, this is something that has to be handled at the persistence layer; we can't do anything in our objects to circumvent how a database handles case-sensitivity. However, don't let that deter you from trying this example out. If SQL-Server isn't configured to handle case-sensitivity on your system, that's OK - the system will still work.

> *For future reference, SQL Server 7.0 supports this, but it must be configured during the installation of the product. For our purposes, we can assume that SQL Server has been configured correctly, but if you run the examples presented in this chapter, remember that your server may not be configured in the same manner. This can be changed after installation, but it is not recommended, because you have to rebuild all of the databases.*

Creating the Access Database

With the database design in place, we can create the Access database. We'll eventually move up to SQL Server, but for now, let's use Access for testing purposes.

You can find a copy of the database in the source code download for this chapter, or if you would prefer to build the database yourself, I'll provide you with a routine that you can run to create all the relevant tables and associations.

Create a new blank database called `PPAccessDB`. Add a new module to the database and then enter the following code:

> *You will need to change the path to your database in the code.*

```
Public Sub RunScript()

'  Starting Access Basic DAO Session...

   Dim ScriptWorkspace As Workspace
   Dim ScriptDatabase As Database
   Dim ScriptTableDef As TableDef
   Dim ScriptQueryDef As QueryDef
   Dim ScriptIndex As Index
   Dim ScriptField As Field
   Dim ScriptRelation As Relation

   Set ScriptWorkspace = DBEngine.Workspaces(0)

' Enter in the correct database path here.
   Set ScriptDatabase = ScriptWorkspace.OpenDatabase("C:\Wrox\VB MTS\PP.mdb")

' CREATE TABLE "PPAttribute"
   Set ScriptTableDef = ScriptDatabase.CreateTableDef("PPAttribute")
   Set ScriptField = ScriptTableDef.CreateField("AttributeID", DB_LONG)
   ScriptField.Attributes = ScriptField.Attributes + DB_AUTOINCRFIELD
   ScriptTableDef.Fields.Append ScriptField
   Set ScriptField = ScriptTableDef.CreateField("AttributeName", DB_TEXT, 50)
   ScriptField.Required = True
   ScriptTableDef.Fields.Append ScriptField
   Set ScriptField = ScriptTableDef.CreateField("AttributeValue", DB_TEXT, 50)
   ScriptTableDef.Fields.Append ScriptField
   ScriptDatabase.TableDefs.Append ScriptTableDef

' CREATE INDEX "PrimaryKey"
   Set ScriptTableDef = ScriptDatabase.TableDefs("PPAttribute")
   Set ScriptIndex = ScriptTableDef.CreateIndex("PrimaryKey")
   Set ScriptField = ScriptIndex.CreateField("AttributeID")
   ScriptIndex.Fields.Append ScriptField
   ScriptIndex.Primary = True
   ScriptIndex.Clustered = True
   ScriptTableDef.Indexes.Append ScriptIndex

' CREATE INDEX "AlternateKey"
   Set ScriptTableDef = ScriptDatabase.TableDefs("PPAttribute")
   Set ScriptIndex = ScriptTableDef.CreateIndex("AlternateKey")
   Set ScriptField = ScriptIndex.CreateField("AttributeName")
   ScriptIndex.Fields.Append ScriptField
   Set ScriptField = ScriptIndex.CreateField("AttributeValue")
   ScriptIndex.Fields.Append ScriptField
   ScriptIndex.Unique = True
   ScriptTableDef.Indexes.Append ScriptIndex

' CREATE TABLE "PPSystem"
   Set ScriptTableDef = ScriptDatabase.CreateTableDef("PPSystem")
   Set ScriptField = ScriptTableDef.CreateField("SystemID", DB_LONG)
   ScriptField.Attributes = ScriptField.Attributes + DB_AUTOINCRFIELD
   ScriptTableDef.Fields.Append ScriptField
   Set ScriptField = ScriptTableDef.CreateField("SystemName", DB_TEXT, 50)
   ScriptField.Required = True
   ScriptTableDef.Fields.Append ScriptField
   ScriptDatabase.TableDefs.Append ScriptTableDef

' CREATE INDEX "PrimaryKey"
   Set ScriptTableDef = ScriptDatabase.TableDefs("PPSystem")
   Set ScriptIndex = ScriptTableDef.CreateIndex("PrimaryKey")
   Set ScriptField = ScriptIndex.CreateField("SystemID")
```

```
    ScriptIndex.Fields.Append ScriptField
    ScriptIndex.Primary = True
    ScriptIndex.Clustered = True
    ScriptTableDef.Indexes.Append ScriptIndex

' CREATE INDEX "Name"

    Set ScriptTableDef = ScriptDatabase.TableDefs("PPSystem")
    Set ScriptIndex = ScriptTableDef.CreateIndex("Name")
    Set ScriptField = ScriptIndex.CreateField("SystemName")
    ScriptIndex.Fields.Append ScriptField
    ScriptIndex.Unique = True
    ScriptTableDef.Indexes.Append ScriptIndex

' CREATE TABLE "PPUser"
    Set ScriptTableDef = ScriptDatabase.CreateTableDef("PPUser")
    Set ScriptField = ScriptTableDef.CreateField("UserID", DB_LONG)
    ScriptField.Attributes = ScriptField.Attributes + DB_AUTOINCRFIELD
    ScriptTableDef.Fields.Append ScriptField
    Set ScriptField = ScriptTableDef.CreateField("UserName", DB_TEXT, 50)
    ScriptField.Required = True
    ScriptTableDef.Fields.Append ScriptField
    Set ScriptField = ScriptTableDef.CreateField("UserPassword", DB_TEXT, 50)
    ScriptField.Required = True
    ScriptTableDef.Fields.Append ScriptField
    Set ScriptField = ScriptTableDef.CreateField("UserEMail", DB_TEXT, 50)
    ScriptField.AllowZeroLength = True
    ScriptTableDef.Fields.Append ScriptField
    ScriptDatabase.TableDefs.Append ScriptTableDef

' CREATE INDEX "PrimaryKey"

    Set ScriptTableDef = ScriptDatabase.TableDefs("PPUser")
    Set ScriptIndex = ScriptTableDef.CreateIndex("PrimaryKey")
    Set ScriptField = ScriptIndex.CreateField("UserID")
    ScriptIndex.Fields.Append ScriptField
    ScriptIndex.Primary = True
    ScriptIndex.Clustered = True
    ScriptTableDef.Indexes.Append ScriptIndex

' CREATE INDEX "AlternateKey"
    Set ScriptTableDef = ScriptDatabase.TableDefs("PPUser")
    Set ScriptIndex = ScriptTableDef.CreateIndex("AlternateKey")
    Set ScriptField = ScriptIndex.CreateField("UserName")
    ScriptIndex.Fields.Append ScriptField
    Set ScriptField = ScriptIndex.CreateField("UserPassword")
    ScriptIndex.Fields.Append ScriptField
    ScriptIndex.Unique = True
    ScriptTableDef.Indexes.Append ScriptIndex

' CREATE TABLE "PPSystemUser"
    Set ScriptTableDef = ScriptDatabase.CreateTableDef("PPSystemUser")
    Set ScriptField = ScriptTableDef.CreateField("UserID", DB_LONG)
    ScriptField.Required = True
    ScriptTableDef.Fields.Append ScriptField
    Set ScriptField = ScriptTableDef.CreateField("SystemID", DB_LONG)
    ScriptField.Required = True
    ScriptTableDef.Fields.Append ScriptField
    ScriptDatabase.TableDefs.Append ScriptTableDef

' CREATE INDEX "PrimaryKey"
    Set ScriptTableDef = ScriptDatabase.TableDefs("PPSystemUser")
```

```
      Set ScriptIndex = ScriptTableDef.CreateIndex("PrimaryKey")
      Set ScriptField = ScriptIndex.CreateField("UserID")
      ScriptIndex.Fields.Append ScriptField
      Set ScriptField = ScriptIndex.CreateField("SystemID")
      ScriptIndex.Fields.Append ScriptField
      ScriptIndex.Primary = True
      ScriptIndex.Clustered = True
      ScriptTableDef.Indexes.Append ScriptIndex

    ' CREATE TABLE "PPSystemUserAttribute"
      Set ScriptTableDef = ScriptDatabase.CreateTableDef("PPSystemUserAttribute")
      Set ScriptField = ScriptTableDef.CreateField("UserID", DB_LONG)
      ScriptField.Required = True
      ScriptTableDef.Fields.Append ScriptField
      Set ScriptField = ScriptTableDef.CreateField("SystemID", DB_LONG)
      ScriptField.Required = True
      ScriptTableDef.Fields.Append ScriptField
      Set ScriptField = ScriptTableDef.CreateField("AttributeID", DB_LONG)
      ScriptField.Required = True
      ScriptTableDef.Fields.Append ScriptField
      ScriptDatabase.TableDefs.Append ScriptTableDef

    ' CREATE INDEX "PrimaryKey"
      Set ScriptTableDef = ScriptDatabase.TableDefs("PPSystemUserAttribute")
      Set ScriptIndex = ScriptTableDef.CreateIndex("PrimaryKey")
      Set ScriptField = ScriptIndex.CreateField("UserID")
      ScriptIndex.Fields.Append ScriptField
      Set ScriptField = ScriptIndex.CreateField("SystemID")
      ScriptIndex.Fields.Append ScriptField
      Set ScriptField = ScriptIndex.CreateField("AttributeID")
      ScriptIndex.Fields.Append ScriptField
      ScriptIndex.Primary = True
      ScriptIndex.Clustered = True
      ScriptTableDef.Indexes.Append ScriptIndex

    ' CREATE RELATIONSHIP "R/3"
      Set ScriptRelation = ScriptDatabase.CreateRelation("R/3", "PPUser", _
                                                  "PPSystemUser")
      Set ScriptField = ScriptRelation.CreateField("UserID")
      ScriptField.ForeignName = "UserID"
      ScriptRelation.Fields.Append ScriptField
      ScriptDatabase.Relations.Append ScriptRelation

    '  CREATE RELATIONSHIP "R/4"
      Set ScriptRelation = ScriptDatabase.CreateRelation("R/4", "PPSystem", _
                                                  "PPSystemUser")
      Set ScriptField = ScriptRelation.CreateField("SystemID")
      ScriptField.ForeignName = "SystemID"
      ScriptRelation.Fields.Append ScriptField
      ScriptDatabase.Relations.Append ScriptRelation

    ' CREATE RELATIONSHIP "PPSystemUserPPSystemUserAttribute"
      Set ScriptRelation = _
          ScriptDatabase.CreateRelation("PPSystemUserPPSystemUserAttribute", _
                              "PPSystemUser", "PPSystemUserAttribute")
      Set ScriptField = ScriptRelation.CreateField("UserID")
      ScriptField.ForeignName = "UserID"
      ScriptRelation.Fields.Append ScriptField
      Set ScriptField = ScriptRelation.CreateField("SystemID")
      ScriptField.ForeignName = "SystemID"
      ScriptRelation.Fields.Append ScriptField
      ScriptRelation.Attributes = ScriptRelation.Attributes + DB_RELATIONDELETECASCADE
```

```
    ScriptDatabase.Relations.Append ScriptRelation

' CREATE RELATIONSHIP "R/18"
    Set ScriptRelation = ScriptDatabase.CreateRelation("R/18", "PPAttribute", _
                                            "PPSystemUserAttribute")
    Set ScriptField = ScriptRelation.CreateField("AttributeID")
    ScriptField.ForeignName = "AttributeID"
    ScriptRelation.Fields.Append ScriptField
    ScriptDatabase.Relations.Append ScriptRelation
    ScriptDatabase.Close
    ScriptWorkspace.Close

' Terminating Access Basic DAO Session...

    MsgBox "Table creation complete!"

End Sub
```

Now simply run the routine and the 5 necesssary tables will be created for you.

In order for the above routine to run in Access 2000, you'll need to reference the DAO Object library and un-reference the ADO Object Library.

Creating the Data Source

Eventually, we'll need to access our database from our components, so let's set up an ODBC Data Source to make this connection easy. There are a lot of ways to connect to a data source, but I've chosen an ODBC Data Source for simplicity's sake during our testing.

> **Please note that the version of ODBC on my machine is 3.510.3711. If your version is different, the data source setup may be different from what I describe in this section.**

From the **Control Panel** window, double-click on the **ODBC Data Sources** icon. This should bring up the following screen:

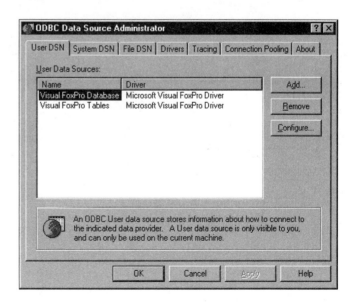

Select the System DSN tab and click the Add... button:

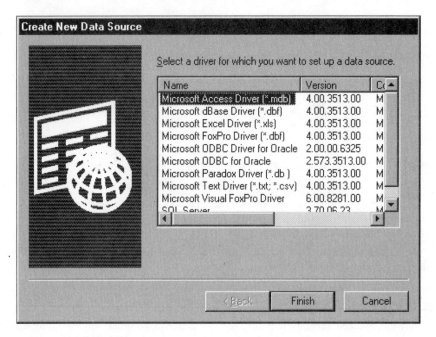

Make sure the Microsoft Access Driver is selected, and press the Finish button. On the screen that follows, name the data source PPAccessDB, and press the Select... button to choose our Access database.

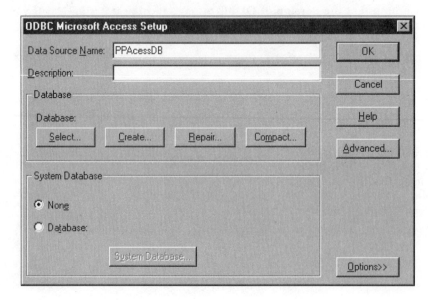

You have now set up the ODBC data source. We'll see in the next section how we can connect to our database.

The Component Design

Now that we have created the Access database, we'll look at how our components will be designed. We have to make sure our components can load and save the user, system, and attribute information correctly.

For starters, let's begin with the classes that we'll use in our components. We'll group these classes into packages later, which will eventually turn into COM DLLs, but for now we'll concentrate on what each class does and what they're responsible for.

The User Class

This class can retrieve information about a user and save a new user account if it's unique. There are two methods that are used to retrieve information, the difference between them being the search parameter passed into the method. Here's the class diagram:

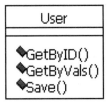

The System Class

This class can retrieve information about a system and save a new system if it's unique. Again, there are two methods for retrieving the information. Here's the class diagram:

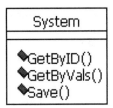

The Attribute Class

This class can retrieve information about an attribute and save a new attribute if it's unique. Once again, retrieval can be by two different methods. This is the class diagram:

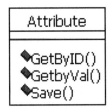

The SystemUser Class

This class can retrieve a list of system IDs currently associated for a user, create new system associations for a user, and delete systems associated with a user. The client can use the `System` class to retrieve more information about the system (like its name) if needed.

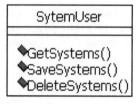

The SystemUserAttribute Class

This class can retrieve a list of attribute IDs currently associated for a user, create new attribute associations for a system, and delete attributes associated with a system. The client can use the `Attribute` class to retrieve more information about the attribute.

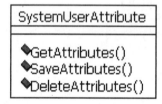

Components Design

As you can readily see, each class maps directly to a database table. That's not necessarily good or bad, but there's one interesting aspect that occurs by doing this. The `User`, `System`, and `Attribute` classes are all **independent** - that is, they don't have any dependencies to other classes. However, the `SystemUser` and `SystemUserAttribute` classes depend upon the information stored by the other three classes. For example, you can't call `Save` on a `SystemUser` object unless the system has already been created via a `System` object. The `SystemUser` class isn't responsible for creating the systems; that's delegated to the `System` class. Therefore, we'll group the three independent classes into one component (which we'll call `PPIndependents`), and put the other two into another component (called `PPAssociations`). From a logical perspective, this keeps the classes separated from a dependency standpoint.

Components and MTS

However, let's consider how transactions are going to come into play with these components. If a user decides to add three new systems, we would perform the following operations:

- ❑ Create a `System` object
- ❑ Call the `Save` method with each new system name
- ❑ Create a `SystemUser` object
- ❑ For each ID returned by `Save` from the `System` object, call the `Save` method on the `SystemUser` object

Now what would happen if one of the `Save` operations from the `SystemUser` object fails? Do we want the systems that were added by the `System` object to be rolled back? Remember, systems are independent - they don't rely upon a system-user association to exist. Therefore, one could argue that even if the `SystemUser`'s `Save` method fails, the `System`'s `Save` operation is atomic and does not have to be part of the `SystemUser`'s transaction. Even though we may have an 'orphaned' system record, that's OK. The client will probably come back and try to create the system again, and since we already have it stored, we'll simply make the association.

However, one could also make the argument that when systems are created and associated to users, that whole operation needs to be transactional - either it all works or it doesn't. Even though that orphaned record will probably be reused by a client, we have no guarantees that it will. We want reuse to occur with records from the `PPSystem` and `PPAttribute` tables that are already associated.

From an MTS perspective, there's a big difference between the two. If we choose the first approach, each object should exist in its own transaction. If we choose the second approach, the objects need to exist within one transaction.

I've decided to use the second approach. My decision doesn't stem from a transactional perspective *per se*; it's more from a logical approach. Although it's possible that unassociated records from the `PPSystem` and `PPAttribute` tables will eventually be associated, there's no guarantee that they will. Therefore, when records are added to the `PPSystem` and `PPAttribute` tables, they must also be associated through the `PPSystemUser` and `PPSystemUserAttribute` tables, respectively.

To accomplish this, each class will have its MTSTransactionMode set to 2 - RequiresTransactions. This means that the component will run within a transaction if it exists; otherwise it creates a new one.

Component Implementation

Now that we've gone through our class and component design, let's take a look at their implementations. We'll go through each component and the classes that the component contains, and see how the MTS environment will be used in these components.

Creating the PPIndependents Component

Let's go through the `PPIndependents` component first, which will contain our `User`, `System`, and `Attribute` classes. Create a new project in VB, specifying it as an **ActiveX DLL**, and change the name of the project to `PPIndependents`.

Next, add references to the Microsoft Transaction Server Type Library and the Microsoft ActiveX Data Objects 2.x Library:

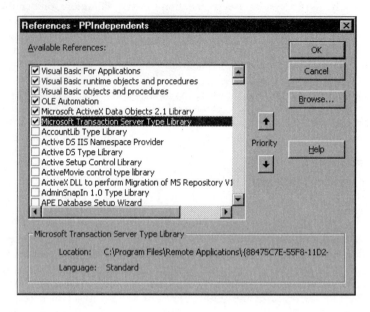

Once that's done, we need to create three classes, User, System, and Attribute. Add three instances of our MTSTemplate class module and make sure all three have their Instancing property set to 5 - Multiuse and their MTSTransactionMode set to 2 - RequiresTransaction. Now let's go through the User class and see how that class is implemented.

The User Class

Our Context object variable has already been declared and the Object Control interface implemented. We'll go and uncomment one of the lines for the CanBePooled method, so that we disable object pooling:

```
Private Function ObjectControl_CanBePooled() As Boolean

' Uncomment one choice:
' ObjectControl_CanBePooled = True     'It's OK to recycle the object
  ObjectControl_CanBePooled = False    'It's not OK to recycle the object

End Function
```

From our class definition, we need to implement three methods: GetByID, GetByVals, and Save. Let's start with the GetByID method, which will return the username and the password for a given user identified by the ID. When I first designed this function, I started by creating a UDT like this:

```
Public Type UserInfo

   UserName As String
   Password As String

End Type
```

Then, I would return this UDT from the `GetByID`unction:

```
Public Function GetByID(UserID As Long) As UserInfo

End Function
```

This is valid code in VB6. However, we know that (eventually) our main user interface is going to be a web page. VBScript doesn't know how to handle a UDT, so this approach won't work. Therefore, we'll change the return type to a `Boolean`, and we'll add two `Variant` arguments to the function. It isn't as clean as the UDT solution, but we really don't have a choice in this case.

> *Keep this tip in mind for future component design. Even though VB6 allows you to pass UDTs as arguments as well as the return value to procedures, some other environments won't know what to do with a UDT return type. We also could have set up stateful objects, like a `UserInfo` class, to pass information to and from our `User` object. This would work for scripting clients. This is perfectly valid design, but I've decided to use a leaner class design for this project simply to keep the discussions focused on MTS.*

Here's the code for `GetByID`:

```
Public Function GetByID(ByVal UserID As Variant, _
                        ByRef UserName As Variant, _
                        ByRef Password As Variant, _
                        ByRef EMail As Variant) As Variant

  On Error GoTo Error_GetByID

  Dim objConn As ADODB.Connection
  Dim objRS As ADODB.Recordset
  Dim strSQL As String

  GetByID = False

  Set objConn = CreateObject("ADODB.Connection")
  Set objRS = CreateObject("ADODB.Recordset")

  objConn.Open DB_CONN

  strSQL = "SELECT UserName, UserPassword, UserEMail " & _
           "FROM PPUser " & _
           "WHERE UserID = '" & Trim$(CStr(UserID)) & "'"

  objRS.Open strSQL, objConn, adOpenStatic

  If Not objRS Is Nothing Then
    If objRS.EOF = False Then
      UserName = Trim$("" & objRS("UserName"))
      Password = Trim$("" & objRS("UserPassword"))
      EMail = Trim$("" & objRS("UserEMail"))
      GetByID = True
    End If
    objRS.Close
    Set objRS = Nothing
  End If

  objConn.Close
  Set objConn = Nothing
```

```
        mobjContext.SetComplete

    Exit Function

Error_GetByID:

    GetByID = False

    If Not objRS Is Nothing Then
        Set objRS = Nothing
    End If

    If Not objConn Is Nothing Then
        Set objConn = Nothing
    End If

    mobjContext.SetAbort

End Function
```

I'd like to note first why some of the arguments are `ByVal` and others are `ByRef`. For example, the `UserID` is `ByVal` because we don't care what the function does to this value when it executes. However, we need to get the user's information out, which is why the other arguments are passed `ByRef`. That way, the information can be altered by the method and the client will receive the changes.

Let's move on to the method's implementation. First, we create a connection to the database using the `DB_CONN String` constant. This is a constant that contains connection information to the correct database. To include this constant in our component, add a standard module to `PPIndependents` and call it `PPLib`. The String constant can now be declared in the module as follows:

```
Public Const DB_CONN As String = "PPAccessDB"
```

Note that `PPAccessDB` is the name of the data source we created in the ODBC Data Sources configuration window. When we move the database to SQL-Server, we can update the connection string with the new information without changing any other code.

Then, we look up the user's information from the `PPUser` table and populate the arguments if we get a match. This is what the SQL `SELECT` statement is for. For those readers that are unfamiliar with SQL syntax, this statement says that the database engine should get the `UserName`, `UserPassword`, and `UserEMail` fields for each record in `PPUser` where the `UserID` field is equal to the one given.

If you want more information on SQL syntax, I recommend getting "Instant SQL Programming", by Joe Celko, published by Wrox Press, ISBN 1874416508.

The `GetByVals` method is virtually identical to `GetByID`:

```
Public Function GetByVals(ByRef UserID As Variant, _
                          ByVal UserName As Variant, _
                          ByVal Password As Variant) As Variant

    On Error GoTo Error_GetByVals
```

```
   Dim objConn As ADODB.Connection
   Dim objRS As ADODB.Recordset
   Dim strSQL As String

   GetByVals = False

   Set objConn = CreateObject("ADODB.Connection")
   Set objRS = CreateObject("ADODB.Recordset")

   objConn.Open DB_CONN

   strSQL = "SELECT UserID FROM PPUser " & _
            "WHERE UserName = '" & Trim$(CStr(UserName)) & "' " & _
            "AND UserPassword = '" & Trim$(CStr(Password)) & "'"

   objRS.Open strSQL, objConn, adOpenStatic

   If Not objRS Is Nothing Then
     If objRS.EOF = False Then
       UserID = CLng(objRS("UserID"))
       GetByVals = True
     End If
     objRS.Close
     Set objRS = Nothing
   End If

   objConn.Close

   Set objConn = Nothing

   mobjContext.SetComplete

   Exit Function

Error_GetByVals:

   GetByVals = False

   If Not objRS Is Nothing Then
     Set objRS = Nothing
   End If

   If Not objConn Is Nothing Then
     Set objConn = Nothing
   End If

   mobjContext.SetAbort

End Function
```

The only differences are that there is no `UserEMail` argument and the `UserID` argument is populated on a match of the `UserName` and `UserPassword`. Note that we call `SetComplete` when the method completes, and `SetAbort` if the method runs into an error.

The `Save` function is also pretty straightforward:

```
Public Function Save(ByVal UserName As Variant, _
                     ByVal UserPassword As Variant, _
                     ByVal UserEMail As Variant) As Variant

  On Error GoTo Error_Save

  Dim objConn As ADODB.Connection
  Dim strSQL As String
  Dim blnRet As Boolean
  Dim lngNewID As Long

  Save = 0

  Set objConn = CreateObject("ADODB.Connection")

  objConn.Open DB_CONN

  On Error Resume Next

  strSQL = "INSERT INTO PPUser " & _
           "(UserName, UserPassword, UserEMail) " & _
           "VALUES (" & _
           "'" & Trim$(Replace(UserName, "'", "''")) & "', '" & _
           Trim$(Replace(UserPassword, "'", "''")) & "', '" & _
           Trim$(Replace(UserEMail, "'", "''")) & "')"

  objConn.Execute strSQL

  On Error GoTo Error_Save

  If objConn.Errors.Count > 0 Then
    If objConn.Errors(0).NativeError = DUPLICATE_RECORD Then
    '  Duplicate error — it's OK to continue.
      Err.Clear
      objConn.Errors.Clear
    Else
      Err.Raise DUPLICATE_RECORD
    End If
  End If

  objConn.Close
  Set objConn = Nothing

' Return the new user ID.
  blnRet = GetByVals(lngNewID, UserName, UserPassword)

  If blnRet = True Then
    Save = lngNewID
  End If

  mobjContext.SetComplete

  Exit Function

Error_Save:

  If Not objConn Is Nothing Then
    objConn.Close
    Set objConn = Nothing
  End If
```

```
    Save = 0

    mobjContext.SetAbort

End Function
```

We take the arguments and try to save them to the PPUser table. Note that we use the Replace function to change any embedded single quotes to double quotes. This prevents any errors from occuring with our INSERT SQL statement. For example, if we were given the following information in the Save arguments:

- ❑ UserName: Joe
- ❑ UserPassword: Joe'sPassword
- ❑ UserEMail:

The resulting SQL statement would be without the Replace functions:

```
INSERT INTO PPUser (UserName, UserPassword, UserEMail) VALUES ('Joe',
              'Joe'sPassword', '')
```

The apostrophe in "Joe'sPassword" would confuse the database engine. By replacing the single quotes with two single quotes, we get the following SQL statement:

```
INSERT INTO PPUser (UserName, UserPassword, UserEMail) VALUES ('Joe',
              'Joe''sPassword', '')
```

The database engine now interprets the two single quotes as a literal single quote and will save it correctly.

Since the database enforces the uniqueness of the username and password for us, we'll get an error if the given combination isn't unique. It's OK if this occurs - we just need to make sure that we catch that error and continue only if we encountered the duplicate record error. That's what the DUPLICATE_RECORD constant is for, which is defined in the constants module PPLib.bas, as follows:

```
Public Const DUPLICATE_RECORD As Long = -1605
```

> *This value is specific for Access; once we move to SQL-Server, we'll need to change this value to correspond to SQL-Server's duplicate record error code.*

One other interesting thing to note in the Save function is that we close the connection to our database. Recall that we should get rid of our resource as soon as possible in MTS. By closing the connection before we call GetByVals, we'll ensure that we have only one connection open at a time.

The methodology used for the System and Attributes classes is identical to that used in the above User class. The only difference is the parameters used. Therefore, I'm just going to present you with the complete code for these class modules without any more discussion.

The System Class

```
Public Function GetByID(ByVal SystemID As Variant, _
                        ByRef SystemName As Variant) As Variant

    On Error GoTo Error_GetByID

    Dim objConn As ADODB.Connection
    Dim objRS As ADODB.Recordset
    Dim strSQL As String

    GetByID = False

    Set objConn = CreateObject("ADODB.Connection")
    Set objRS = CreateObject("ADODB.Recordset")

    objConn.Open DB_CONN

    strSQL = "SELECT SystemName " & _
             "FROM PPSystem " & _
             "WHERE SystemID = '" & Trim$(CStr(SystemID)) & "'"

    objRS.Open strSQL, objConn, adOpenStatic

    If Not objRS Is Nothing Then
        If objRS.RecordCount <> 0 Then
            SystemName = Trim$("" & objRS("SystemName"))
            GetByID = True
        End If
        objRS.Close
        Set objRS = Nothing
    End If

    objConn.Close
    Set objConn = Nothing

    mobjContext.SetComplete

    Exit Function

Error_GetByID:

    GetByID = False

    If Not objRS Is Nothing Then
        Set objRS = Nothing
    End If

    If Not objConn Is Nothing Then
        Set objConn = Nothing
    End If

    mobjContext.SetAbort
    Err.Raise Err.Number, Err.Source, Err.Description

End Function

Public Function GetByVals(ByRef SystemID As Variant, _
                          ByVal SystemName As Variant) As Variant

    On Error GoTo Error_GetByVals
```

```vb
    Dim objConn As ADODB.Connection
    Dim objRS As ADODB.Recordset
    Dim strSQL As String

    GetByVals = False

    Set objConn = CreateObject("ADODB.Connection")
    Set objRS = CreateObject("ADODB.Recordset")

    objConn.Open DB_CONN

    strSQL = "SELECT SystemID FROM PPSystem " & _
             "WHERE SystemName = '" & Trim$(CStr(SystemName)) & "'"

    objRS.Open strSQL, objConn, adOpenStatic

    If Not objRS Is Nothing Then
        If objRS.RecordCount <> 0 Then
            SystemID = CLng(objRS("SystemID"))
            GetByVals = True
        End If
        objRS.Close
        Set objRS = Nothing
    End If

    objConn.Close
    Set objConn = Nothing

    mobjContext.SetComplete

    Exit Function

Error_GetByVals:

    GetByVals = False

    If Not objRS Is Nothing Then
        Set objRS = Nothing
    End If

    If Not objConn Is Nothing Then
        Set objConn = Nothing
    End If

    mobjContext.SetAbort
    Err.Raise Err.Number, Err.Source, Err.Description

End Function

Public Function Save(ByVal SystemName As Variant) As Variant

    On Error GoTo Error_Save

    Dim blnRet As Boolean
    Dim lngNewID As Long
    Dim objConn As ADODB.Connection
    Dim strSQL As String

    Save = 0
```

```
Set objConn = CreateObject("ADODB.Connection")

objConn.Open DB_CONN

On Error Resume Next

strSQL = "INSERT INTO PPSystem " & _
         "(SystemName) " & _
         "VALUES (" & _
         "'" & Trim$(Replace(SystemName, "'", "''")) & "')"

objConn.Execute strSQL

On Error GoTo Error_Save

If objConn.Errors.Count > 0 Then
   If objConn.Errors(0).NativeError = DUPLICATE_RECORD Then
   ' Duplicate error - it's OK to continue.
     Err.Clear
     objConn.Errors.Clear
   Else
     Err.Raise DUPLICATE_RECORD
   End If
End If

objConn.Close
Set objConn = Nothing

' Return the new user ID.
blnRet = GetByVals(lngNewID, SystemName)

If blnRet = True Then
   Save = lngNewID
End If

mobjContext.SetComplete

Exit Function

Error_Save:

 If Not objConn Is Nothing Then
   objConn.Close
   Set objConn = Nothing
 End If

 Save = 0

 mobjContext.SetAbort
 Err.Raise Err.Number, Err.Source, Err.Description

End Function
```

The Attribute Class

```
Public Function GetByID(ByVal AttributeID As Variant, _
                        ByRef AttributeName As Variant, _
                        ByRef AttributeValue As Variant) As Variant

  On Error GoTo Error_GetByID
```

```
    Dim objConn As ADODB.Connection
    Dim objRS As ADODB.Recordset
    Dim strSQL As String

    GetByID = False

    Set objConn = CreateObject("ADODB.Connection")
    Set objRS = CreateObject("ADODB.Recordset")

    objConn.Open DB_CONN

    strSQL = "SELECT AttributeName, AttributeValue " & _
             "FROM PPAttribute " & _
             "WHERE AttributeID = '" & Trim$(CStr(AttributeID)) & "'"

    objRS.Open strSQL, objConn, adOpenStatic

    If Not objRS Is Nothing Then
       If objRS.RecordCount <> 0 Then
          AttributeName = Trim$("" & objRS("AttributeName"))
          AttributeValue = Trim$("" & objRS("AttributeValue"))
          GetByID = True
       End If
       objRS.Close
       Set objRS = Nothing
    End If

    objConn.Close
    Set objConn = Nothing

    mobjContext.SetComplete

    Exit Function

Error_GetByID:

    GetByID = False

    If Not objRS Is Nothing Then
       Set objRS = Nothing
    End If

    If Not objConn Is Nothing Then
       Set objConn = Nothing
    End If

    mobjContext.SetAbort
    Err.Raise Err.Number, Err.Source, Err.Description

End Function

Public Function GetByVals(ByRef AttributeID As Variant, _
                    ByVal AttributeName As Variant, _
                    ByVal AttributeValue As Variant) As Variant

    On Error GoTo Error_GetByVals

    Dim objConn As ADODB.Connection
    Dim objRS As ADODB.Recordset
    Dim strSQL As String
```

```
    GetByVals = False

    Set objConn = CreateObject("ADODB.Connection")
    Set objRS = CreateObject("ADODB.Recordset")

    objConn.Open DB_CONN

    strSQL = "SELECT AttributeID FROM PPAttribute " & _
             "WHERE AttributeName = '" & Trim$(CStr(AttributeName)) & "' " & _
             "AND AttributeValue = '" & Trim$(CStr(AttributeValue)) & "'"

    objRS.Open strSQL, objConn, adOpenStatic

    If Not objRS Is Nothing Then
       If objRS.RecordCount <> 0 Then
          AttributeID = CLng(objRS("AttributeID"))
          GetByVals = True
       End If
       objRS.Close
       Set objRS = Nothing
    End If

    objConn.Close
    Set objConn = Nothing

    mobjContext.SetComplete

    Exit Function

Error_GetByVals:

    GetByVals = False

    If Not objRS Is Nothing Then
      Set objRS = Nothing
    End If

    If Not objConn Is Nothing Then
      Set objConn = Nothing
    End If

    mobjContext.SetAbort
    Err.Raise Err.Number, Err.Source, Err.Description

End Function


Public Function Save(ByVal AttributeName As Variant, _
                 ByVal AttributeValue As Variant) As Variant

    On Error GoTo Error_Save

    Dim blnRet As Boolean
    Dim lngNewID As Long
    Dim objConn As ADODB.Connection
    Dim strSQL As String

    Save = 0

    Set objConn = CreateObject("ADODB.Connection")

    objConn.Open DB_CONN
```

```
   On Error Resume Next

   strSQL = "INSERT INTO PPAttribute " & _
            "(AttributeName, AttributeValue) " & _
            "VALUES (" & _
            "'" & Trim$(Replace(AttributeName, "'", "''")) & "', '" & _
            Trim$(Replace(AttributeValue, "'", "''")) & "') "

   objConn.Execute strSQL

   On Error GoTo Error_Save

   If objConn.Errors.Count > 0 Then
      If objConn.Errors(0).NativeError = DUPLICATE_RECORD Then
      ' Duplicate error - it's OK to continue.
         Err.Clear
         objConn.Errors.Clear
      Else
         Err.Raise DUPLICATE_RECORD
      End If
   End If

' Return the new attribute ID.
   objConn.Close
   Set objConn = Nothing

   blnRet = GetByVals(lngNewID, AttributeName, AttributeValue)

   If blnRet = True Then
      Save = lngNewID
   End If

   mobjContext.SetComplete

   Exit Function

Error_Save:

   If Not objConn Is Nothing Then
     objConn.Close
     Set objConn = Nothing
   End If

   Save = 0

   mobjContext.SetAbort
   Err.Raise Err.Number, Err.Source, Err.Description

End Function
```

Creating the PPAssociations Component

The PPAssociations component is identical in setup to the PPIndependents component. It is
an ActiveX DLL that has references to the ADO and MTS components. It contains two multiuse
classes, SystemUser and SystemUserAttribute, both of which have the
MTSTransactionMode set to 2 - **RequiresTransaction**. You'll also need to add the PPLib.bas file
for the PPIndependents project. We'll start with the SystemUser's code:

The SystemUser class

To start, let's take a look at `GetSystems`:

```
Public Function GetSystems(ByVal UserID As Variant, _
                           ByRef Systems As Variant) As Variant

  On Error GoTo Error_GetSystems

  Dim lngC As Long
  Dim objConn As ADODB.Connection
  Dim objRS As ADODB.Recordset
  Dim strSQL As String
  Dim vntSystems() As Variant

  GetSystems = False

  Set objConn = CreateObject("ADODB.Connection")

  Set objRS = CreateObject("ADODB.Recordset")

  objConn.Open DB_CONN

  strSQL = "SELECT SystemID " & _
           "FROM PPSystemUser " & _
           "WHERE UserID = '" & Trim$(CStr(UserID)) & "'"

  objRS.Open strSQL, objConn, adOpenStatic

  If objRS.RecordCount <> 0 Then
    ReDim vntSystems(0 To (objRS.RecordCount - 1)) As Variant
    For lngC = 0 To (objRS.RecordCount - 1)
      vntSystems(lngC) = CLng(objRS("SystemID"))
      objRS.MoveNext
    Next lngC
    Systems = vntSystems
    GetSystems = True
  End If

  objRS.Close
  Set objRS = Nothing
  objConn.Close
  Set objConn = Nothing

  mobjContext.SetComplete

  Exit Function

Error_GetSystems:

  GetSystems = False

  If Not objRS Is Nothing Then
    Set objRS = Nothing
  End If

  If Not objConn Is Nothing Then
    Set objConn = Nothing
  End If

  mobjContext.SetAbort

End Function
```

We query the `PPSystemUser` table to see if any systems have been associated with this user. If there are, we stuff the `SystemID` values into an array and pass that back to the client. The client could use the `GetByID` method on a `System` object to obtain the system names if they so chose.

The next function is `SaveSystems`:

```
Public Function SaveSystems(ByVal UserID As Variant, _
                            ByRef Systems As Variant) As Variant

    On Error GoTo Error_SaveSystems

    Dim lngC As Long
    Dim objConn As ADODB.Connection
    Dim strSQL As String

    SaveSystems = False

    Set objConn = CreateObject("ADODB.Connection")

    objConn.Open DB_CONN

    For lngC = LBound(Systems) To UBound(Systems)
      On Error Resume Next
      strSQL = "INSERT INTO PPSystemUser " & _
              "(SystemID, UserID) VALUES (" & _
              Trim$(CStr(Systems(lngC))) & ", " & _
              UserID & ")"
      objConn.Execute strSQL
      On Error GoTo Error_SaveSystems
      If objConn.Errors.Count > 0 Then
        If objConn.Errors(0).NativeError = DUPLICATE_RECORD Then
          ' Duplicate error — it's OK to continue.
          Err.Clear
          objConn.Errors.Clear
        Else
          Err.Raise DUPLICATE_RECORD
        End If
      End If
    Next lngC

    SaveSystems = True
    objConn.Close
    Set objConn = Nothing

    mobjContext.SetComplete

    Exit Function

Error_SaveSystems:

    SaveSystems = False

    If Not objConn Is Nothing Then
      Set objConn = Nothing
    End If

    mobjContext.SetAbort

End Function
```

This is virtually identical to the Save function we saw in the User class. Finally, we have the DeleteSystems method:

```
Public Function DeleteSystems(ByVal UserID As Variant, _
                              ByRef Systems As Variant) As Variant

    On Error GoTo Error_DeleteSystems

    Dim lngC As Long
    Dim objConn As ADODB.Connection
    Dim objRS As ADODB.Recordset
    Dim strSQL As String

    DeleteSystems = False

    Set objConn = CreateObject("ADODB.Connection")

    objConn.Open DB_CONN

    For lngC = LBound(Systems) To UBound(Systems)
        strSQL = "DELETE FROM PPSystemUser WHERE " & _
                "(SystemID = '" & _
                Trim$(CStr(Systems(lngC))) & "' " & _
                "AND UserID = '" & _
                Trim$(CStr(UserID)) & "')"
        objConn.Execute strSQL
    Next lngC

    DeleteSystems = True
    objConn.Close
    Set objConn = Nothing
    mobjContext.SetComplete

    Exit Function

Error_DeleteSystems:

    DeleteSystems = False

    If Not objConn Is Nothing Then
        Set objConn = Nothing
    End If

    mobjContext.SetAbort

End Function
```

We take each SystemID given to us in the array, and delete any system/user associations.

The classes in the PPIndependents component are pretty much the same as the ones in PPAssociations in terms of functionality. The only differences this time is that we needed to handle a group of associated items to get and save, and we also needed to allow for the deletion of associations.

The SystemUserAttribute Class

As with the classes in the PPIndependents project the methodology used is not significantly different, so I'm just going to present you with the code again:

```vb
Public Function GetAttributes(ByVal UserID As Variant, _
                              ByVal SystemID As Variant, _
                              ByRef Attributes As Variant) As Variant

    On Error GoTo Error_GetAttributes

    Dim lngC As Long
    Dim objConn As ADODB.Connection
    Dim objRS As ADODB.Recordset
    Dim strSQL As String
    Dim vntAttributes() As Variant

    GetAttributes = False

    Set objConn = CreateObject("ADODB.Connection")
    Set objRS = CreateObject("ADODB.Recordset")

    If Not objConn Is Nothing Then
        objConn.Open DB_CONN
        strSQL = "SELECT AttributeID " & _
                 "FROM PPSystemUserAttribute " & _
                 "WHERE UserID = '" & Trim$(CStr(UserID)) & "' " & _
                 "AND SystemID = '" & Trim$(CStr(SystemID)) & "'"
        objRS.Open strSQL, objConn, adOpenStatic

        If Not objRS Is Nothing Then
            If objRS.RecordCount <> 0 Then
                ReDim vntAttributes(0 To (objRS.RecordCount - 1)) As Variant

                For lngC = 0 To (objRS.RecordCount - 1)
                    vntAttributes(lngC) = CLng(objRS("AttributeID"))
                    objRS.MoveNext
                Next lngC

                Attributes = vntAttributes
                GetAttributes = True
            End If
            objRS.Close
            Set objRS = Nothing
        End If
        objConn.Close
        Set objConn = Nothing
    End If

    mobjContext.SetComplete

    Exit Function

Error_GetAttributes:

    GetAttributes = False

    If Not objRS Is Nothing Then
        Set objRS = Nothing
    End If

    If Not objConn Is Nothing Then
        Set objConn = Nothing
    End If

    mobjContext.SetAbort
```

```
        Err.Raise Err.Number, Err.Source, Err.Description

End Function

Public Function SaveAttributes(ByVal UserID As Variant, _
                              ByVal SystemID As Variant, _
                              ByRef Attributes As Variant) As Variant

    On Error GoTo Error_SaveAttributes

    Dim lngC As Long
    Dim objConn As ADODB.Connection
    Dim strSQL As String

    SaveAttributes = False

    Set objConn = CreateObject("ADODB.Connection")

    If Not objConn Is Nothing Then
        objConn.Open DB_CONN

        For lngC = LBound(Attributes) To UBound(Attributes)
            strSQL = "INSERT INTO PPSystemUserAttribute " & _
                "(SystemID, UserID, AttributeID) VALUES (" & _
                Trim$(CStr(SystemID)) & ", " & _
                Trim$(CStr(UserID)) & ", " & _
                Trim$(CStr(Attributes(lngC))) & ")"

            On Error Resume Next

            objConn.Execute strSQL

            On Error GoTo Error_SaveAttributes

            If objConn.Errors.Count > 0 Then
                If objConn.Errors(0).NativeError = DUPLICATE_RECORD Then
                ' Duplicate error - it's OK to continue.
                    Err.Clear
                    objConn.Errors.Clear
                Else
                    Err.Raise DUPLICATE_RECORD
                End If
            End If

        Next lngC

        SaveAttributes = True
        objConn.Close
        Set objConn = Nothing

    End If

    mobjContext.SetComplete

    Exit Function

Error_SaveAttributes:

    SaveAttributes = False
```

```
   If Not objRS Is Nothing Then
     Set objRS = Nothing
   End If

   If Not objConn Is Nothing Then
     Set objConn = Nothing
   End If

   mobjContext.SetAbort

   Err.Raise Err.Number, Err.Source, Err.Description

End Function

Public Function DeleteAttributes(ByVal UserID As Variant, _
                                 ByVal SystemID As Variant, _
                                 ByRef Attributes As Variant) As Variant

   On Error GoTo Error_DeleteAttributes

   Dim lngC As Long
   Dim objConn As ADODB.Connection
   Dim strSQL As String

   DeleteAttributes = False

   Set objConn = CreateObject("ADODB.Connection")

   If Not objConn Is Nothing Then
     objConn.Open DB_CONN

     For lngC = LBound(Attributes) To UBound(Attributes)
         strSQL = "DELETE FROM PPSystemUserAttribute WHERE " & _
                 "(SystemID = " & _
                 Trim$(CStr(SystemID)) & " " & _
                 "AND UserID = " & _
                 Trim$(CStr(UserID)) & " " & _
                 "AND AttributeID = " & _
                 Trim$(CStr(Attributes(lngC))) & ")"
         objConn.Execute strSQL
     Next lngC

     DeleteAttributes = True
     objConn.Close
     Set objConn = Nothing
   End If

   mobjContext.SetComplete

   Exit Function

Error_DeleteAttributes:

   DeleteAttributes = False

   If Not objRS Is Nothing Then
     Set objRS = Nothing
   End If
```

```
    If Not objConn Is Nothing Then
       Set objConn = Nothing
    End If

    mobjContext.SetAbort

    Err.Raise Err.Number, Err.Source, Err.Description

End Function
```

All that remains is to compile your two DLLs. In the next chapter, we'll add the components into an MTS package Now we need to create a VB client to test our components.

The Visual Basic Client

Although we will eventually be moving to a web-based user interface, for testing purposes it's easier for us to throw togother a Win32 based front-end. Let's use VB to create a simple Windows application that interacts with the PPAssociations and PPIndependents components.

Form Design

Here's what the one and only form looks like:

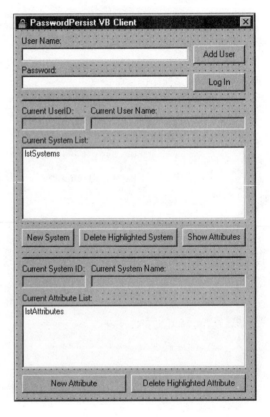

The top third of the form is where a user can either log into the system or add a new account. If either activity is successful, the system list for that user is shown. The user can either add new systems or delete associated systems. The user can also show any attributes for a selected system in the list. New attributes can be added and current ones can be deleted.

Here's a description of the significant controls needed for this application:

Control	Name
Form	frmMain
Add User Command Button	cmdAddUser
Log In Command Button	cmdLogin
User Name Text Box	txtUserName
Password Text Box	txtPassword
Current UserID Label	lblCurrentUserID
Current User Name Label	lblCurrentUserName
Current System List Box	lstSystems
New System Command Button	cmdNewSystem
Delete System Command Button	cmdDeleteSystem
Show Attributes Command Button	cmdShowAttrib
Current SystemID Label	lblCurrentSystemID
Current System Name Label	lblCurrentSystemName
Current Attribute List Box	lstAttributes
New Attribute Command Button	cmdNewAttribute
Delete Attribute Command Button	cmdDeleteAttribute

You will also need to add a reference to our PPIndependents and PPAssociations DLLs that we just compiled.

Logging on to PasswordPersist

When the user clicks on the **Log In** button, the Login method is called from the Click event of cmdLogin. Here's what Login looks like:

```
Private Sub Login()

    On Error GoTo Error_Login

    Dim blnRet As Boolean
    Dim lngID As Long
    Dim objUser As PPIndependents.User

    ClearForm

    Set objUser = CreateObject("PPIndependents.User")

    blnRet = objUser.GetByVals(lngID, txtUserName.Text, txtPassword.Text)
```

```
    If blnRet = True Then
        lblCurrentUserID.Caption = lngID
        lblCurrentUserName.Caption = txtUserName.Text
       ListSystems
    Else
        MsgBox "This U/P does not exist in the system. Please try again.", _
                vbOKOnly + vbInformation, _
                "Invalid U/P"
    End If

    Set objUser = Nothing

    Exit Sub

Error_Login:

    MsgBox "An unanticipated error occurred in Login: " & Err.Number & _
            " - " & Err.Description

    On Error Resume Next

    If Not objUser Is Nothing Then
        Set objUser = Nothing
    End If

End Sub
```

The first thing that Login does is reset the form by calling ClearForm. This is a method that clears out list and text boxes along with any pertinent labels. Here's what ClearForm looks like:

```
Private Sub ClearForm()

    On Error Resume Next

    lblCurrentUserID.Caption = ""
    lblCurrentUserName.Caption = ""
    lstSystems.Clear
    lblCurrentSystemID.Caption = ""
    lblCurrentSystemName.Caption = ""
    lstAttributes.Clear

End Sub
```

Once the form is reset, the user is checked by calling GetByVals on a User object. If the user is invalid, the program lets the user know. Otherwise, a list of systems is gathered and displayed via the ListSystems method. Here's what ListSystems looks like:

```
Private Sub ListSystems()

    On Error GoTo Error_ListSystems

    Dim blnRet As Boolean
    Dim lngC As Long
    Dim strSysName As String
    Dim objPPSystems As PPAssociations.SystemUser
    Dim objSystem As PPIndependents.System
    Dim vntSystems As Variant
```

```
        Set objPPSystems = CreateObject("PPAssociations.SystemUser")

        blnRet = objPPSystems.GetSystems(lblCurrentUserID, vntSystems)

        If blnRet = True Then
          Set objSystem = CreateObject("PPIndependents.System")
          If Not objSystem Is Nothing Then
            For lngC = LBound(vntSystems) To UBound(vntSystems)
              blnRet = objSystem.GetByID(vntSystems(lngC), strSysName)
              If blnRet = True Then
                With lstSystems
                  .AddItem strSysName
                  .ItemData(.NewIndex) = vntSystems(lngC)
                End With
              End If
            Next
          End If
        Else
          MsgBox "No systems currently exist for this user.", _
                vbOKOnly + vbInformation, _
                "No Systems"
        End If

        Set objPPSystems = Nothing

        Exit Sub

      Error_ListSystems:

        MsgBox "An unanticipated error occurred in ListSystems: " _
              & Err.Number & " - " & Err.Description

        On Error Resume Next

        If Not objPPSystems Is Nothing Then
          Set objPPSystems = Nothing
        End If

      End Sub
```

This method uses the `GetSystems` method on a `SystemUser` object. If there are any systems currently associated with this user, a `System` object is used to get the system names via a call to `GetByID`. The resulting system IDs and names are subsequently stored in the list box `lstSystems`.

Adding a New Account

If the user doesn't have an account in the system, s/he can create one via the **Add User** button, which calls the `AddUser` method:

```
      Private Sub AddUser()

        On Error GoTo Error_AddUser

        Dim blnRet As Boolean
        Dim lngID As Long
        Dim objUser As PPIndependents.User

        ClearForm
```

```
    Set objUser = CreateObject("PPIndependents.User")

    blnRet = objUser.GetByVals(lngID, txtUserName.Text, txtPassword.Text)

    If blnRet = True Then
    ' This user is a valid user already.
      MsgBox "This U/P already exists in the system", _
             vbOKOnly + vbInformation, _
             "Existing U/P"
    Else
      lngID = objUser.Save(txtUserName.Text, txtPassword.Text, "")
      If lngID > 0 Then
        lblCurrentUserID.Caption = lngID
        lblCurrentUserName.Caption = txtUserName.Text
        ListSystems
      End If
    End If

    Set objUser = Nothing

    Exit Sub

Error_AddUser:

    MsgBox "An unanticipated error occurred in AddUser: " & Err.Number & _
           " - " & Err.Description

    On Error Resume Next

    If Not objUser Is Nothing Then
      Set objUser = Nothing
    End If

End Sub
```

This function is similar to `Login`, except in this case we make sure that the given U/P doesn't exist in the system before we add it. If this is a new U/P, we add it to the system via a `Save` call on a `User` object.

Adding and Deleting Systems

If a user wants to add a system to his/her list, s/he can press the **New System** button, which calls the `AddNewSystem` method from the `Click` event:

```
Private Sub AddNewSystem()

  On Error GoTo Error_AddNewSystem

  Dim blnRet As Boolean
  Dim lngSystemID As Long
  Dim objSystem As PPAssociations.SystemUser
  Dim objPPSystem As PPIndependents.System
  Dim strNewSystem As String
  Dim vntSystems(0) As Variant

  strNewSystem = Trim$(InputBox("Please enter the new system name.", _
                                "New System Name"))
```

```
      If IsSystemInList(strNewSystem) = False Then
        Set objPPSystem = CreateObject("PPIndependents.System")
        lngSystemID = objPPSystem.Save(strNewSystem)

        If lngSystemID <> 0 Then
          vntSystems(0) = lngSystemID
          Set objSystem = CreateObject("PPAssociations.SystemUser")
          blnRet = objSystem.SaveSystems(lblCurrentUserID.Caption, vntSystems)

          If blnRet = True Then
            lstSystems.AddItem strNewSystem
            lstSystems.ItemData(lstSystems.NewIndex) = lngSystemID
          End If

          Set objSystem = Nothing
        End If

        Set objPPSystem = Nothing

      Else
        MsgBox "This system already exists for this user.", _
               vbOKOnly + vbInformation, _
               "Existing System"

      End If

      Exit Sub

Error_AddNewSystem:

      MsgBox "An unanticipated error occurred in AddNewSystem: " & _
             Err.Number & " - " & Err.Description

      On Error Resume Next

      If Not objSystem Is Nothing Then
        Set objSystem = Nothing
      End If

      If Not objPPSystem Is Nothing Then
        Set objPPSystem = Nothing
      End If

End Sub
```

We first check to see if the given system is in the system list via a call to `IsSystemInList`:

```
Private Function IsSystemInList(NewSystemName As String) As Boolean

   On Error Resume Next

   Dim lngC As Long

   For lngC = 0 To (lstSystems.ListCount - 1)
     If lstSystems.List(lngC) = NewSystemName Then
       IsSystemInList = True
       Exit For
     End If
   Next lngC

End Function
```

It's a brute-force check, but it's sufficient for our purposes. We really don't need to do this since our database won't allow a duplicate entry on the `PPSystem` table, but it's good defensive programming. If the system isn't in the list, it's added through a call to `Save` via a `System` object and a call to `SaveSystems` via a `SystemUser` object.

If the user wants to delete a system from their list, they can press the **Delete Highlighted System**, which calls the `DeleteSystem` method:

```
Private Sub DeleteSystem()

On Error GoTo Error_DeleteSystem

Dim blnRet As Boolean
Dim lngRet As Long
Dim objSystemUser As PPAssociations.SystemUser
Dim vntSystems(0) As Variant

If lstSystems.SelCount > 0 Then
  lngRet = MsgBox("Are you sure you want to delete " & _
          lstSystems.List(lstSystems.ListIndex) & _
          " from the current system list?", vbYesNo + vbQuestion, _
          "Delete System")

  If lngRet = vbYes Then
    vntSystems(0) = lstSystems.ItemData(lstSystems.ListIndex)
    Set objSystemUser = CreateObject("PPAssociations.SystemUser")
    blnRet = objSystemUser.DeleteSystems(lblCurrentUserID.Caption, _
                               vntSystems)

    If blnRet = True Then
      lstSystems.RemoveItem lstSystems.ListIndex
    End If

    Set objSystemUser = Nothing
  End If

Else
  MsgBox "Please select a system to delete.", _
         vbOKOnly + vbInformation, _
         "Delete System"
End If

Exit Sub

Error_DeleteSystem:

MsgBox "An unanticipated error occurred in DeleteSystem: " & _
       Err.Number & " - " & Err.Description

End Sub
```

Once the program makes sure that a system was deleted and verifies that the user really wants to delete the system, it calls `DeleteSystem` on a `SystemUser` object and removes the system from the list on success.

Retrieving, Adding and Deleting Attributes

Manipulating attributes is very similar to what we did with the system calls. To get an attribute list, the user presses the **ShowAttributes** button, which calls `ListAttributes`:

```
Private Sub ListAttributes()

  On Error GoTo Error_ListAttributes

  Dim blnRet As Boolean
  Dim lngC As Long
  Dim objAttrib As PPIndependents.Attribute
  Dim objPPAttribs As PPAssociations.SystemUserAttribute
  Dim strAttribName As String
  Dim strAttribValue As String
  Dim vntAttribs As Variant

  ClearAttributes

  If lstSystems.SelCount > 0 Then
    lblCurrentSystemID.Caption = lstSystems.ItemData(lstSystems.ListIndex)
    lblCurrentSystemName.Caption = lstSystems.List(lstSystems.ListIndex)
    Set objPPAttribs = CreateObject("PPAssociations.SystemUserAttribute")
    blnRet = objPPAttribs.GetAttributes(lblCurrentUserID.Caption, _
              lstSystems.ItemData(lstSystems.ListIndex), vntAttribs)

    If blnRet = True Then
      Set objAttrib = CreateObject("PPIndependents.Attribute")
      For lngC = LBound(vntAttribs) To UBound(vntAttribs)
        blnRet = objAttrib.GetByID(vntAttribs(lngC), strAttribName, _
                              strAttribValue)

        If blnRet Then
          With lstAttributes
            .AddItem strAttribName & " - " & strAttribValue
            .ItemData(.NewIndex) = vntAttribs(lngC)
          End With
        End If

      Next
    End If

    Set objPPAttribs = Nothing
    Set objAttrib = Nothing

  Else
    MsgBox "Please select a system to get attributes for.", _
          vbOKOnly + vbInformation, _
          "System Attributes"
  End If

  Exit Sub

Error_ListAttributes:

  MsgBox "An unanticipated error occurred in ListAttributes: " & _
        Err.Number & " - " & Err.Description

  On Error Resume Next

  If Not objPPAttribs Is Nothing Then
    Set objPPAttribs = Nothing
  End If

  If Not objAttrib Is Nothing Then
    Set objAttrib = Nothing
  End If

End Sub
```

The first task on our list is to clear out our attribute information, which is done in `ClearAttributes`:

```
Private Sub ClearAttributes()

   On Error Resume Next

   lblCurrentSystemID.Caption = ""
   lblCurrentSystemName.Caption = ""
   lstAttributes.Clear

End Sub
```

Then we see if there are any attributes associated for this user via the `GetAttributes` method on a `SystemUserAttribute` object. If there are, we add them to the attributes list.

Adding and deleting an attribute is identical to the system calls we just saw, so I'll just list them here for completeness sake:

```
Private Sub AddNewAttribute()

   On Error GoTo Error_AddNewAttribute

   Dim blnRet As Boolean
   Dim lngAttributeID As Long
   Dim objPPAttrib As PPAssociations.SystemUserAttribute
   Dim objAttrib As PPIndependents.Attribute
   Dim strNewAttributeName As String
   Dim strNewAttributeValue As String
   Dim vntAttribs(0) As Variant

   strNewAttributeName = Trim$(InputBox( _
                   "Please enter the new attibute name.", _
                   "New Attribute Name"))

   strNewAttributeValue = Trim$(InputBox( _
                       "Please enter the new attibute value.", _
                       "New Attribute Value"))

   If IsAttributeInList _
          (strNewAttributeName & " - " & strNewAttributeValue) = False Then
      Set objAttrib = CreateObject("PPIndependents.Attribute")
      lngAttributeID = objAttrib.Save(strNewAttributeName, _
                           strNewAttributeValue)

      If lngAttributeID <> 0 Then
         vntAttribs(0) = lngAttributeID
         Set objPPAttrib = CreateObject("PPAssociations.SystemUserAttribute")
         blnRet = objPPAttrib.SaveAttributes(lblCurrentUserID.Caption, _
                                    lblCurrentSystemID.Caption, _
                                    vntAttribs)
         If blnRet = True Then
            lstAttributes.AddItem strNewAttributeName & " - " & _
                           strNewAttributeValue
            lstAttributes.ItemData(lstAttributes.NewIndex) = lngAttributeID
         End If

      Set objPPAttrib = Nothing
   End If
```

```
      Set objAttrib = Nothing

  Else
    MsgBox "This attribute already exists for this system/user.", _
           vbOKOnly + vbInformation, _
           "Existing Attribute"
  End If

  Exit Sub

Error_AddNewAttribute:

  MsgBox "An unanticipated error occurred in AddNewAttribute: " & _
         Err.Number & " - " & Err.Description

  On Error Resume Next

  If Not objPPAttrib Is Nothing Then
    Set objPPAttrib = Nothing
  End If

  If Not objAttrib Is Nothing Then
    Set objAttrib = Nothing
  End If

End Sub

Private Sub DeleteAttribtue()

  On Error GoTo Error_DeleteAttribtue

  Dim blnRet As Boolean
  Dim lngRet As Long
  Dim objSystemUserAttribute As PPAssociations.SystemUserAttribute
  Dim vntAttribute(0) As Variant

  If lstAttributes.SelCount > 0 Then
    lngRet = MsgBox("Are you sure you want to delete " & _
                    lstAttributes.List(lstAttributes.ListIndex) & _
                    " from the current attribute list?", vbYesNo + _
                    vbQuestion, "Delete Attribute")

    If lngRet = vbYes Then
      vntAttribute(0) = lstAttributes.ItemData(lstAttributes.ListIndex)
      Set objSystemUserAttribute = CreateObject( _
                                 "PPAssociations.SystemUserAttribute")
      blnRet = objSystemUserAttribute.DeleteAttributes _
             (lblCurrentUserID.Caption, lblCurrentSystemID.Caption, _
              vntAttribute)

      If blnRet = True Then
        lstAttributes.RemoveItem lstAttributes.ListIndex
      End If

      Set objSystemUserAttribute = Nothing
    End If

  Else
    MsgBox "Please select an attribute to delete.", _
           vbOKOnly + vbInformation, _
           "Delete Attribute"
```

```
    End If

    Exit Sub

Error_DeleteAttribtue:

    MsgBox "An unanticipated error occurred in DeleteAttribtue: " & _
           Err.Number & " - " & Err.Description

End Sub
```

Although we will be moving the components into an MTS package in the next chapter, we have coded the objects is such a way so that they can act as a basic COM object. You can therefore run the client and experiment with the functionality of PasswordPersist. In fact, it's probably a good idea to do so in order to get some data into the database for later.

Summary

In comparison to the last three chapters or so, this chapter has been hands on all the way. We spent the majority of the chapter building the PasswordPersist application, so that we might see the theory we've so far only seen on paper in action. Over the next few chapters, we'll be expanding on this initial design in order to prepare the application for the purpose it was designed for.

In the next chapter, we'll look at how to place the components in an MTS package. Then we'll look at how to add several layers of security to our components, both programmatically and through the MTS Explorer. The next step will be to look at how we can administer our components when in action and how to automate the setup of the package. In Chapter 11, we'll move the back-end from Access to the more suitable SQL Server and then finally in Chapter 12, we'll change the front-end so that we can access the application from anywhere across the Internet.

7

Managing Components and Packages

Way back in Chapter 2, you were taken on a whirlwind tour of the MTS Explorer. At the time, I wasn't able to go into too much detail about the various elements that compose the Explorer because we had yet to cover the background knowledge of what is really going on. Now that we've spent the last 3-4 chapters covering the theory it is time once again to examine the MTS Explorer. This time we'll take out time to consider all the tasks we can perform.

This chapter focuses on packages and is mostly hands-on exercises where you will learn to create, import, export, modify, and delete packages using MTS Explorer. We'll be using the MTS components that we built for the `PasswordPersist` application from the last chapter.

After completing this chapter, you should be able to answer the following questions:

- ❑ What is a package?
- ❑ What are empty packages used for?
- ❑ How do I create packages and how do I add components to existing packages?
- ❑ How do I remove components from packages and how can I delete an entire package?
- ❑ Can I export my packages to other machines?
- ❑ What does the file extension `PAK` indicate?
- ❑ How do I import pre-built packages?
- ❑ Can I import other COM components?
- ❑ How do I tell the base-client that MTS components exist?
- ❑ What properties can I set for packages and components?

Packages and Components

Packages are a group of components, with their associated type libraries, that run in the same process, forming a single application unit. When a package is created, a GUID for the package is also created. This package GUID is how MTS identifies it. Aside from housing components, packages also dictate component properties and security features collectively as a group. Although not mandatory, each package should contain a group of components that perform related tasks within an application. By configuring components at the *package* level instead of *individually*, administration is much faster and simpler, just as administration of a group of users under Windows NT is faster and simpler than individual user accounts.

Each component that runs under MTS must belong to a package, but a component can only belong to one package on a single machine. However, a package can have many components belonging to the same or different DLLs. In addition, a single machine can have several different packages running at the same time, each with its own copy of the MTS Executive. Using the the MTS Explorer, you can manage all of MTS's configuration, including packages, components, and security settings, collectively known as the **MTS Catalog**. With MTS 2.0, the MTS Catalog is currently stored in the Windows registry.

> *Although the easiest and most straightforward way to manage the MTS Catalog is through the MTS Explorer, MTS also provides a programmable interface called Scriptable Administration Objects that allow you to perform administrative operations using code instead of through the MTS Explorer. Because Scriptable Administration Objects are dual interface COM components, you can use them from any tool or language that supports COM, including VBScript and JScript. Using Scriptable Administration Objects you can easily write scripts or applications to automate a routine task or create an enhanced version of the MTS Explorer. In Chapter 10, we'll take a look at how to script these administrative functions.*

You can either install pre-built packages or create an empty package and then add components to it. As a developer you will be using both methods. MTS components need to be registered into the Windows registry before they are recognized by MTS. Understand that a COM component already has a GUID and is registered with the Windows registry. However, when a component is added to an MTS package, the Windows registry must be updated to reflect the new configuration. Registration occurs when you install new or existing components or packages through MTS Explorer.

Conversely, registry settings are removed when a component or package is removed. As you develop your components, you can add them to existing packages. Additionally, you can install components that are already registered.

Types of Package

Packages come in two flavors: **Library** packages and **Server** packages. The main distinction between these two package types (also called **activation types**) is whose process the components are loaded in: a Library package runs in the same process as the client that called it, while a Server package runs in its own dedicated process on the local machine.

Server Package

> A Server package executes its components in a separate surrogate process.
> This process is a package-specific instance of the DLL surrogate MTX.EXE.

When a package is executed in a separate process, *all* the components within the package are isolated from components in another package. This type of *Fault Isolation* makes MTS a much more stable run-time environment for COM components, because if one component fails, it only causes the process (Server package) and all the components in the process to fail instead of all the packages on the system. Server packages also provide security checking for their components, whereas Library packages cannot unless they are loaded into the process of a Server package. We'll discuss security later, but for now you should know that MTS does not perform security checking on calls within a package (actually a process), so you should only group components that trust each other in the same package.

There is usually a considerable delay when creating the first object in a Server package. This is due to the fact that MTS doesn't create a new process for your Server package by executing MTX.EXE until a new instance of a component in the package is requested. However, when the process is loaded, MTS doesn't just load the DLL containing the requested component into this new process. Instead, MTS loads *all* of the DLLs for *all* of the components in the package. As you can see, this can considerably delay the instantiation of the first component.

A Server package can also timeout, as we'll discuss later in this chapter, and as a result destroy the process dedicated to the Server package. When the next instantiation request is serviced, the process will have to be recreated and all the associated DLLs will have to be loaded again. To avoid delays when creating the first object in a Server package, since its process has been started, you can preload the process by executing MTX.EXE with the parameter of /p:{package-guid}, where {package-guid} is the package identifier or the package name in quotes:

```
MTX.EXE /p:"Benefit"
```

Library Package

All objects created from a Library package execute in the address space of the client application that created them. For a client application to use a component in a Library package, MTS and the Library package *must* be installed on the *same* machine as the client application. No security checking or process isolation will be provided with Library packages, since components are loaded into the process of the creator and not an MTS controlled process.

A Library package can also be loaded into the process of one or more server packages. In this situation, the Server package would be referred to as the client application from the Library package's perspective. Library packages allow you to overcome the limitation of a component only belonging to one package on a machine. Both Library and Server packages rely on the MTS Executive. In the case of Library packages, in addition to the MTS objects, a copy of the MTS Executive will also be loaded into the client's process.

Choosing a Package Type

When determining what type of package your components should belong to, consider whether fault isolation and security are important (Server package) and consider if the client application has MTS installed on the same machine (Library package).

Most resource dispensers in MTS pool resources on a *per-process* basis. If a Library package is loaded into several separate client processes, each client process would have its own resource pool. As a result, Server packages usually benefit more from resource pooling, which is a major contributor to scalability in the MTS environment.

We'll see later in the chapter that you can use MTS Explorer to easily change the type of a package after it has been created, by changing the Package Activation Type property in your package's Properties dialog:

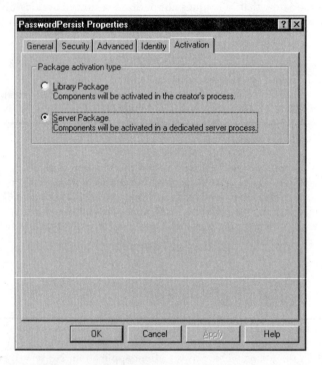

Also, using the MTS Explorer, an administrator or developer can easily partition components within the same DLL across multiple packages or have them all execute in a single package. However, this makes distribution and updates more error prone and complicated than it should be. I recommend keeping your packages very simple and designing your components and DLLs so that all components in a DLL belong to the same package.

> *You cannot have components with different threading models (Apartment, Single-Threaded) in the same package. This is because components with different threading models cannot be part of the same activity or transaction within a single process. To work around this issue, you can simply place all single threaded components in one package and all apartment-thread aware components in another package. However, it might be best to completely avoid single-threaded components altogether, because they are prone to deadlocks and they can severely reduce performance.*

Working with Packages and Components

In the following sections, you will create and edit a new package, You will also be working with the MTS component that you created in the last chapter. At the end of this chapter, you will execute the client application (also from the last chapter) and observe from the MTS Explorer the activation and termination of your MTS components object.

Creating an Empty Package

As mentioned earlier, you must first have a package before you can add a component. Because you are in the process of developing a new application, you need a place to install your component. It's important to keep in mind when designing applications that all components residing in the same package will run in the same process.

> **Components in a DLL do not have to be placed into the same package; they can be distributed into separate packages although this practice is not encouraged.**

Begin by opening the MTS Explorer. Expand the folder until you can highlight the Packages Installed folder and then right-click the folder, selecting New and then Package from the pop-up menu:

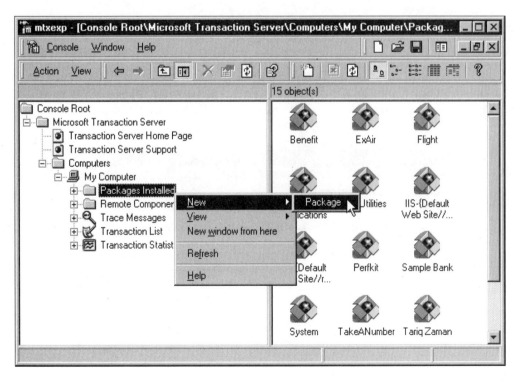

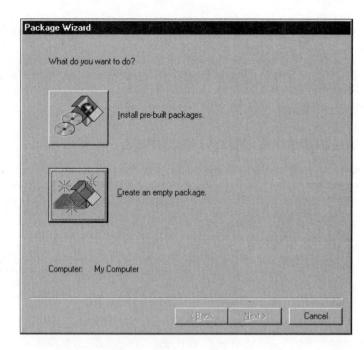

Completing this step opens the
Package Wizard:

The Package Wizard offers two options: Install pre-built packages and Create an empty package.

We used the first selection, Install pre-built packages, in Chapter 2 for importing a pre-built package and all of its related components. The package is saved in an INI formatted text file with the extension .PAK, that you can then use to recreate your package on any machine. We'll come back to this later in the chapter.

Select the second option, Create an empty package. In the Create Empty Package dialog, type PasswordPersist in the textbox under the label Enter a name for the new package: and then click Next>:

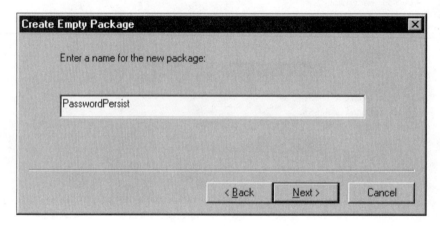

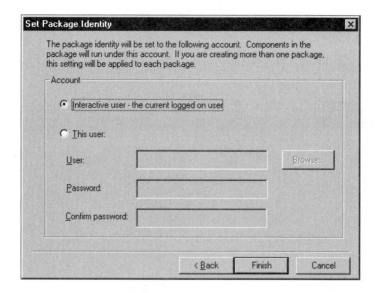

The Set Package Identity dialog deals with security. For now, keep the default setting, Interactive user – the current logged on user and click Finish. If no user is logged in, instantiation requests for components in this package would fail. Therefore it is usually recommended that you specify a user account to run under instead of relying on a user always being logged in. You will learn more about security in the next chapter.

MTS will create the new empty package called `PasswordPersist` and display it in MTS Explorer:

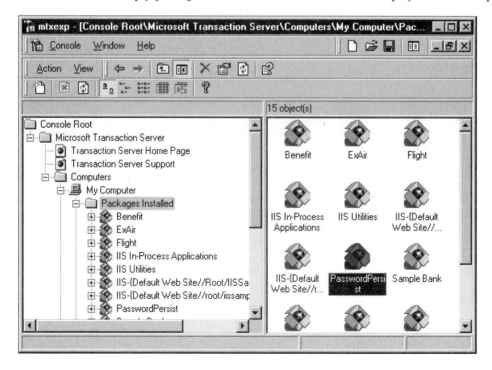

Behind the scenes, MTS will also create a new GUID to identify the package, called the **PackageID**, and create a new key in the registry with the name of the PackageID under:

```
HKEY_LOCAL_MACHINE\Software\Microsoft\Transaction Server\Packages\.
```

MTS stores all the information related to your package under its key in the registry:

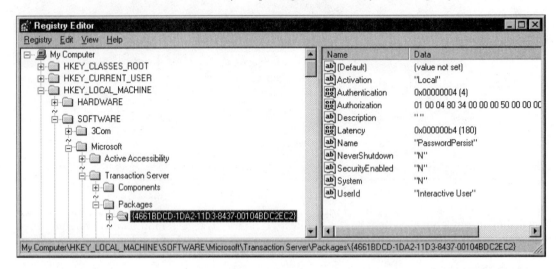

Recall from our discussion about MTS's architecture that it redirects COM to the MTS Executable `MTX.EXE` in the `LocalServer` registry key for your components. The PackageID is the parameter following `MTX.EXE` in the `LocalServer` registry key's default value for your component. `MTX.EXE` uses the PackageID to perform a lookup in the registry, so it knows how it should configure the server process.

In the next section, we will deal with adding components to the package we created.

Adding New Components

Once a package is created, regardless of whether it is empty or not, you can easily add and remove components as needed.

From the left-pane, make sure the folder Packages Installed is expanded, listing all the packages installed on the local machine.

Double-click the folder for the PasswordPersist package you just created. Again from the left-pane, highlight the folder Components and right-click your mouse button. From the pop-up menu, select New and then Component. Completing this step will launch the Component Wizard:

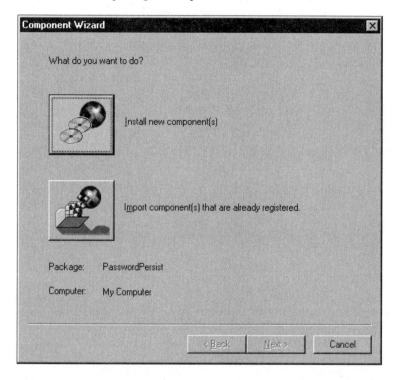

The Component Wizard looks very similar to the Package Wizard. It offers two options for installing components: Install new component(s) and Import component(s) that are already registered.

The first option, Install new components, is used for adding components that have not been registered on the local machine. These are components that do not currently exist in a package. If you have downloaded the PasswordPersist components from the Wrox website, your PPIndependents.dll and PPAssociations.dll will be non-registered components, so select this option now.

The second selection, Import component(s) that are already registered is used for components that are already registered as in-process servers in the Windows registry. Use this option if you were developing these components yourself as you worked through the book, on the same machine that MTS resides on. For more information about this option, see the section Adding Registered Components later in this chapter.

You can install as many components to reside in the same package as needed. Looking at the Install Components dialog, notice that two list boxes are displayed. The lower list box, labeled Components found, displays all components in the directory you specify to view. The list box at the top, labeled Files to install, are the files you select for your package from the Components found list box.

From the Install Components dialog, click Add files..., and locate the two library files containing our components - PPIndependents.dll and PPAssociations.dll - from the directory you previously stored your project. Select these files and click Finish.

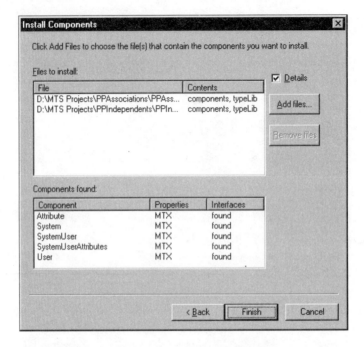

You now have all the components installed into the package PasswordPersist.

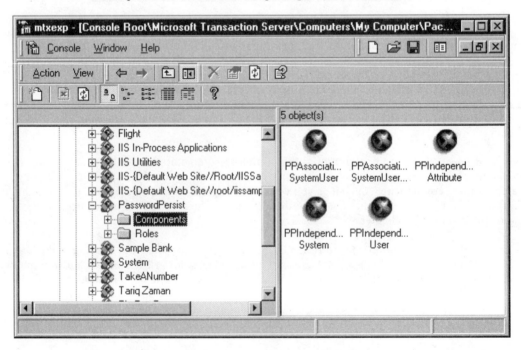

When a component is installed into the MTS Catalog, MTS changes the component's registry settings to redirect creation requests to MTS, and also adds another registry key and several string values for each component. This new registry key is the same as the component's CLSID, and is located under `HKEY_LOCAL_MACHINE\SOFTWARE\Microsoft\Transaction Server\Components`. Under this registry key, MTS creates several string values that are used to store the configuration values for the component in the MTS Environment:

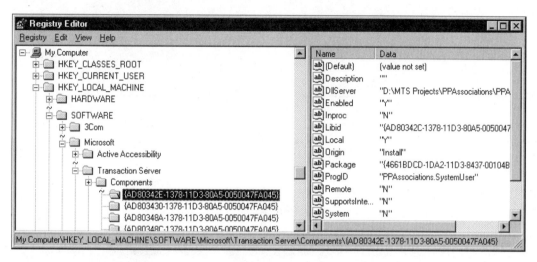

An Alternative Way to Add New Components

Now that you have learned how to install components into a package by using the Component Wizard, let's look at another way to add your components.

If you try to install a component that is already registered in an existing package, you will be notified with an error message:

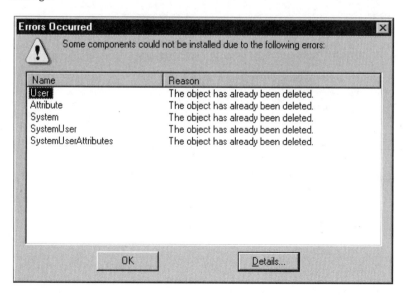

The error message is fairly straightforward but there may be times when you will need more information about a problem. By clicking Details..., a message box will give you added details:

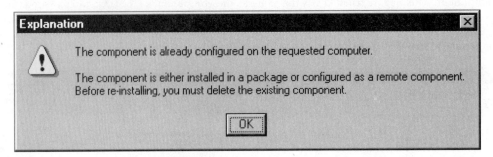

Therefore, if you just installed the PasswordPersist components using the Component Wizard in the previous section, you will not be able to use this alternate method without first removing the components from the package. For information about removing components, see the section Deleting Components later in this chapter.

Locate the package PasswordPersist in the Packages Installed folder. From the right-pane, double-click the Components folder for the package PasswordPersist:

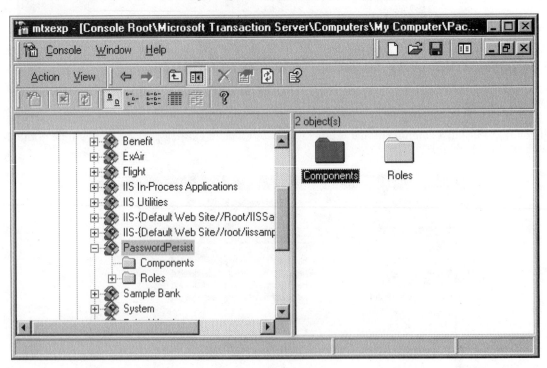

Open NT Explorer and size it as necessary so you can see both the NT and MTS Explorers on your desktop. Locate and highlight the component PPIndependents.dll in NT Explorer, and drag it with your mouse over to the right-pane in MTS Explorer:

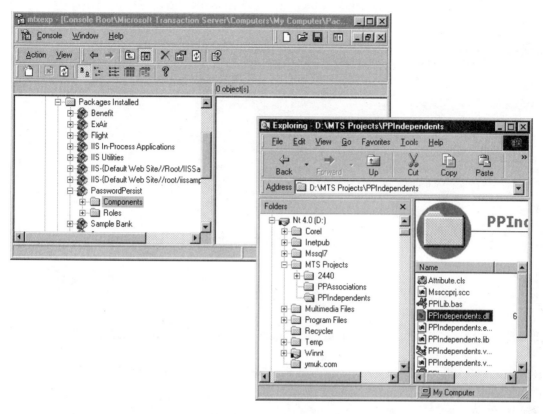

The three components of PPIndependents.dll are now installed in the package PasswordPersist. Repeat the exercise for PPAssociations.dll to install the remaining two components for PasswordPersist.

Moving Components

As you develop an application, you may find that you have a component in one package and want to move it to another package. Instead of deleting the component and then installing it to another package, you can easily move it.

Before you can move a component, you need to have another package to move it to. For this exercise, create an empty package from MTS Explorer called OhMy. See Creating an Empty Package at the beginning of this chapter.

Now that you have an empty package called `OhMy`, let's move the component `PPIndependents.User` from the package `PasswordPersist` to the package `OhMy`. From the MTS Explorer, open the package `PasswordPersist` and then open the **Components** folder. Highlight the component **PPIndependents.User** and click your right mouse button. Select <u>M</u>ove from the pop-up menu:

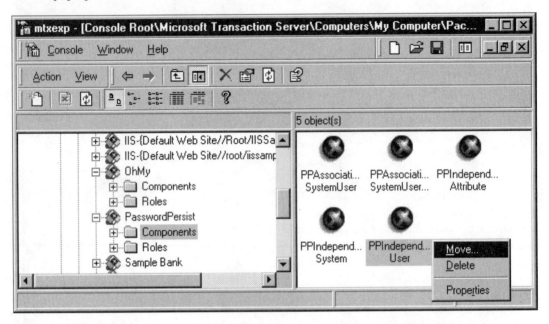

From the **Move component(s)** dialog, select the package where you want the component to reside:

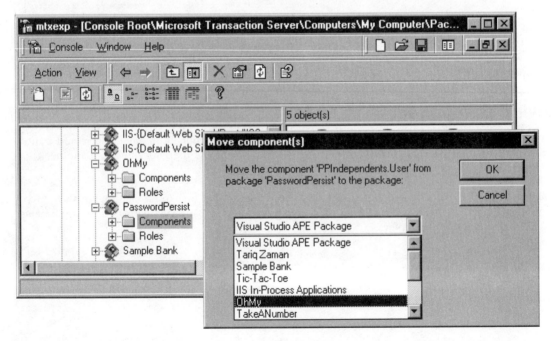

We have now moved the component PPIndependents.User from the package PasswordPersist to the new package location OhMy:

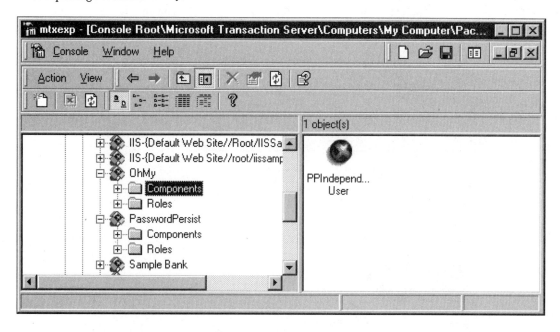

Since this was just a demonstrative exercise, move the `PPIndependents.User` component back to the `PasswordPersist` package.

Adding Registered Components

If you have a COM component that is already registered with the Windows registry to run as an in-process server, you can import the component through the **Component Wizard** using the MTS Explorer. Where are these COM components? You will have to be familiar with your OS environment. For example, Windows NT Server and Windows Workstation have numerous COM components that you may be able to use in an MTS application. You will see some of them in this exercise.

> **When planning your application, you should always try to add your components as new (Install New Components) because you cannot set component attributes for methods and interfaces in components that have been imported.**

Launch the Component Wizard again but this time select Import component(s). If you were developing your components on the same machine that MTS resides on (like I was), you can select the Import components that are already registered button. In this list, you should see the `PPIndependents` and the `PPAssociations` components:

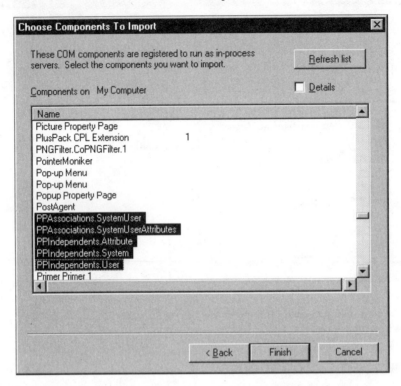

The Choose Component To Import dialog lists all the COM components on your system that are registered to run as in-process servers. Selecting the Details checkbox will display the DLL path and CLSID for the COM component. Locate and highlight the five components for `PasswordPersist` from the Name column, and select Finish.

Notice that the components are not properly identified. This is one example why it is preferable to install components as new whenever possible.

> **You may want to jump ahead to the section Deleting Components and remove the `System Clock` component before continuing to the Exporting Packages and Components section. However, leaving this component installed in this package will not adversely affect your application.**

Differences between New and Registered Components

By choosing the Install New Component option, we can browse for each DLL; MTS will register the DLL and add each component from the DLL into the package. Unfortunately, when adding components to a package using this option, there is no way to only add individual components from a DLL. However, you can easily delete them after they are added.

By adding components that are already registered, MTS allows you to select individual components instead of adding all of the components defined in the DLL. However, the disadvantage with this approach is that MTS will not read the type library for the components you are adding and consequently, it will not display information about your component's interfaces or methods belonging to those interfaces. Therefore, interface security, a topic we will discuss in the Security chapter, is not available when importing components that are already registered. For this reason, you are recommended to add components to packages by reference to the DLLs instead of importing components that are already registered.

Exporting Packages and Components

Now that you have successfully created an empty package and installed your components into it, it is time to discuss how to package your files so you can easily distribute them to other machines. Incidentally, this technique for distributing your components is the same for distributing MTS applications obtained or purchased from other sources.

Exporting is actually a two-step process. First, you need to export existing packages into packages that can be distributed to other machines. When exporting through MTS Explorer you are creating pre-built packages. These packages consist of a file with the extension .PAK and all associated components including type libraries and DLLs. Additionally, an EXE file is created for base client machines. This EXE file is used to place information about the package and components into the Windows registry (see the section MTS Base Clients). This leads to the second step. After you create a package for distribution, you need to install it onto another machine by using MTS Explorer's feature for installing pre-built packages.

> **You can create pre-built applications to a directory on your local machine or you can export your packages directly to another machine on your network through the MTS Explorer.**

For this part of the exercise, you will only export your packages into pre-built packages onto your local machine. After you learn to delete components and packages, you will return and complete the second step in the section called Importing Packages and Components.

From MTS Explorer, open the folder Packages Installed and highlight PasswordPersist. Then select Export from the Action menu. The Export Package dialog appears. Click Browse and locate the path where you want to save your package:

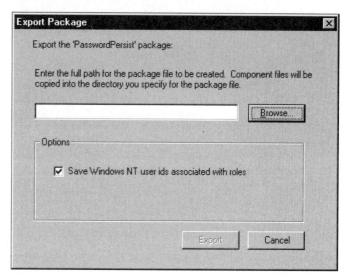

Notice that you have an option to Save Windows NT user ids associated with roles. The check box is selected by default. Under normal operations, you will want this option enabled. You will learn about roles in detail in the next chapter. For now, keep the default setting although it does not matter whether the Options checkbox is selected.

Enter a meaningful package name in the textbox labeled File name. For this example, enter PPExport, then select Save:

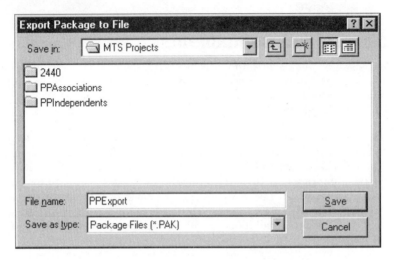

Click Export. Unless you have existing files with the same name at this location, you should get a message box telling you that The package was successfully exported. Also notice that the extension .PAK was added at the end of the path name.

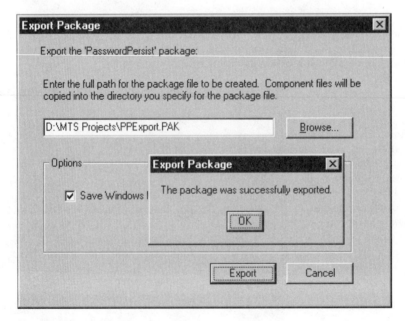

Open NT Explorer to the location you specified your files to be exported to. You should see a folder called clients. Inside the clients folder is an .EXE that supplies a DCOM configuration so the base client will know where to find these MTS components. The other files include PPIndependents.dll and the file PPExport.PAK. This is the file name you specified from the Export dialog, and the file contains all the information about the components and roles of a package.

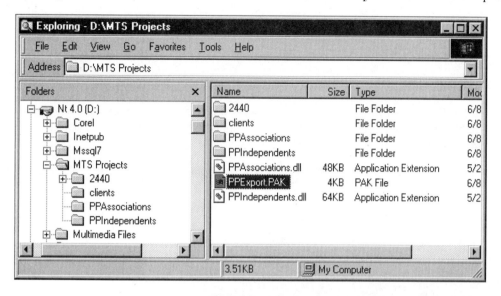

You may be interested at looking at the .PAK file that you just created. It is nothing more than a text file that can be opened with NotePad or WordPad. The following screen shot represents only a portion of the .PAK file for PPExport:

Deleting Components

You may be wondering what happens to a component when you delete it from an MTS package using the MTS Explorer. Rest assured that the component itself is not destroyed or deleted from existence. Simply, the component is removed from the GUI representation in MTS Explorer and the Windows registry is altered to reflect the removal of a component from an MTS package. The component itself still retains its GUID originally assigned when it was first created as a COM component. You can even reinstall the same component into the same package you just deleted it from with no adverse effects.

You can easily delete an individual component or a group of components using MTS Explorer.

Let's first delete the component inside the package PasswordPersist. From MTS Explorer, browse to the Components folder of the PasswordPersist package, and from either the left- or right-pane, highlight the component labeled PPIndependents.User:

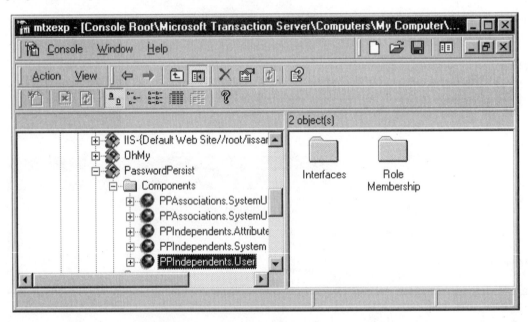

While the component is highlighted, click your right-mouse button and select Delete from the pop-up menu. The component is now deleted from MTS Explorer. After completing this step, the component is removed from the package. The Windows registry is also altered to reflect that the component has been removed by deleting the appropriate entry under:

HKEY_LOCAL_MACHINE\SOFTWARE\Microsoft\Transaction Server\Components.

Deleting Multiple Components

Suppose you had six components in this package and you wanted to remove three of them. For demonstration purposes, I have selected the package called Sample Bank.

> **Caution! I am using the package Sample Bank for demonstration purposes only. You will need to reinstall them if you wish to use this sample application.**

Holding down the *Control* key on your keyboard, you can selectively highlight as many components as you choose. When you have made your choices, right-click your mouse button. From the pop-up menu, select <u>D</u>elete:

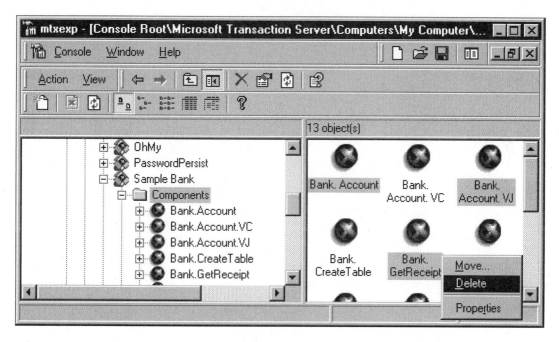

> **You can simultaneously remove multiple components from a package, but you cannot simultaneously remove multiple packages.**

You may now delete the entire `PasswordPersist` package by right-clicking on the package folder and selecting delete from the pop-up menu. Move on to the next section and learn how to import packages.

Importing Packages with Components

Pre-built packages are the packages you created during exporting. Typically they are used to install components to other MTS servers. Using pre-built packages, you can physically move the package files to another MTS server. If you have other MTS servers on your network, you can register them through your MTS Explorer and then import the package to the other MTS server(s). You will learn about working with other MTS servers later in this chapter.

From the MTS Explorer, open the **Packages Installed** folder. Remember you deleted the package for `PasswordPersist` so you will not see a package for it. Bring up the Package Wizard by following the steps described in the section on Creating an Empty Package.

The Package Wizard offers the two options Install pre-built packages and Create an empty package. This time, select the first option, Install pre-built packages:

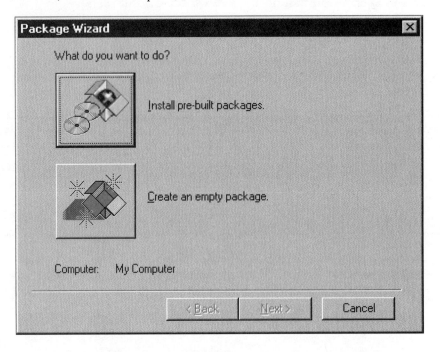

From the Select Package Files dialog, click the Add... button and locate PPExport.PAK from the directory where you previously stored your project:

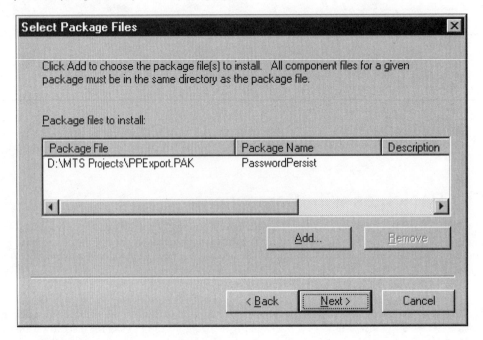

The Set Package Identity dialog deals with security. Keep the default set to Interactive user – the current logged on user and click Next>:

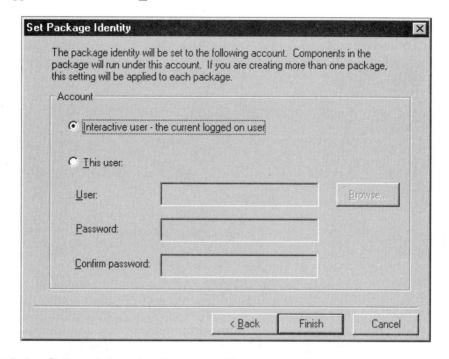

The Installation Options dialog asks where to install component files. In most cases, you can leave `C:\Program Files\Mts\Packages` as the default path. Click Finish:

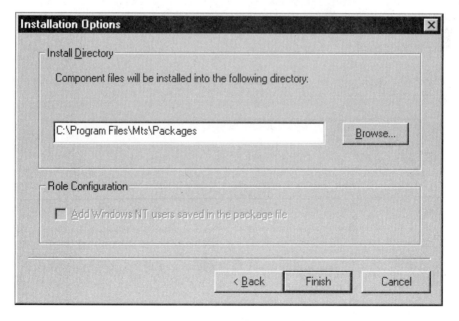

Refreshing the Registry

You learned when a component is added to an MTS package, its associated registry entries are added so MTS can recognize the components in the package. However, anytime a registry setting is modified for an MTS component, such as recompiling a component in Visual Basic, you need to update the registry. This is often referred to as refreshing the registry. The reason you need to refresh the registry is Visual Basic overwrites the previous MTS registry entries. By refreshing the registry, the associated MTS registry entries are recreated in the Windows registry.

You can refresh your components by highlighting MyComputer and right-clicking your mouse button. Select Refresh All Components:

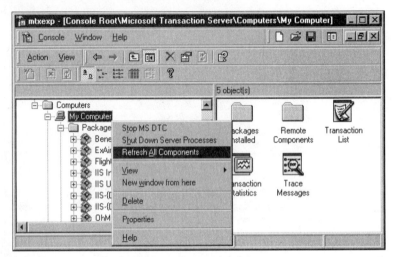

Package Administration

There is so much more to MTS Explorer than adding and deleting packages and components. MTS Explorer also allows you to modify package properties as well as modify some component properties.

Component Properties

Let's take a tour of the component properties using the MTS Explorer. Open the Components folder for PasswordPersist. Highlight the component PPIndependents.User and click your right mouse button. Select Properties from the pop-up menu:

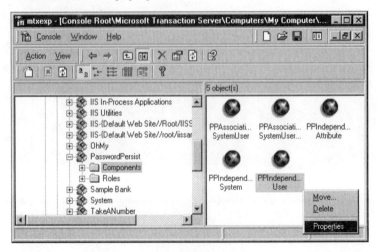

The Properties dialog for components has three tabs: General, Transaction, and Security.

The General tab provides basic information about the selected component. Additionally, it allows the programmer to enter a text description for the component. As you design more and more MTS components, you will find that entering a detailed description will be invaluable. Entering a description not only helps you remember component information, but it helps other programmers, who may be working on the same project, to identify it.

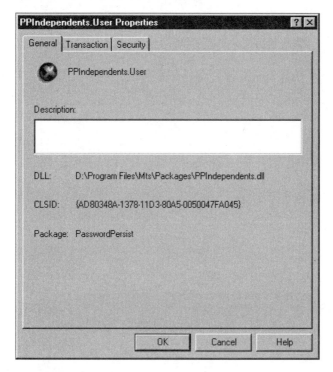

You may recall that when you created your component in Visual Basic, you used the new property setting for transactions called MTSTransactionMode. Using the Transaction tab for the selected component will override your original settings. This is a great way of modifying transaction properties without recompiling your DLL.

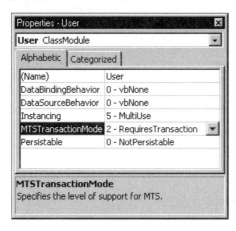

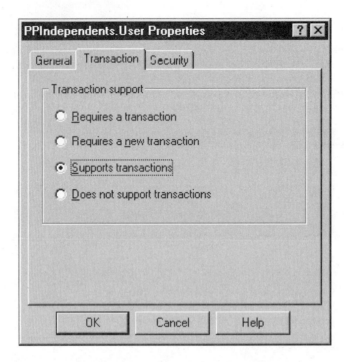

The Security tab is used to enable security for the selected component. You will learn about component security in the next chapter.

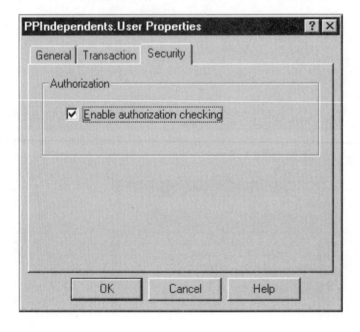

Package Properties

Still using MTS Explorer, highlight the Packages Installed folder in the left pane for PasswordPersist. Select Properties from the pop-up menu when you right-click:

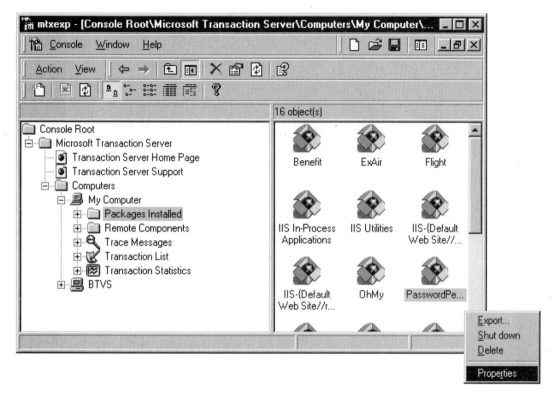

The properties dialog for packages has five tabs:

- ❑ General
- ❑ Security
- ❑ Advanced
- ❑ Identity
- ❑ Activation

General

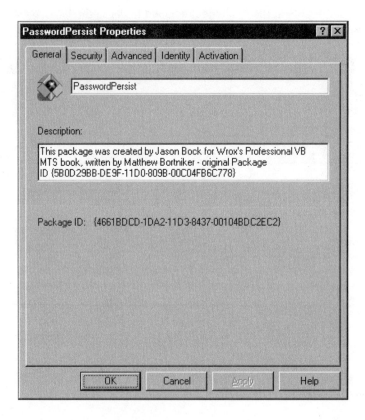

The General tab for package properties is used for a detailed description. Additionally, this dialog provides the `PackageID`. Remember, every time you create a package, a unique ID is created and written to the registry.

> **Aside from using a text description to describe the package version, you can use the PackageID to identify different versions by recording it. Additionally, you can do the same for component versions in the component property dialog by recording the CLSID.**

Incidentally, you can rename the package by changing the name in the first text box on the General tab. This will not affect your application.

Security

The Security tab is used to enable security for the selected package. The check box for Enable authorization checking is selected by default. When package security is enabled, security credentials of all client calls to the package are verified.

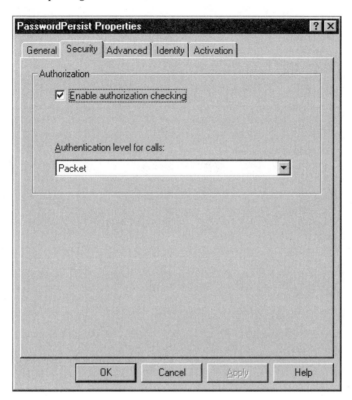

Advanced

The first frame on the Advanced tab displays shutdown options for the server process. Selecting the first of the two option buttons will keep the server process that is associated with the selected package constantly running. In other words, if you want the server process to be available at all times, you should use this setting. This setting can improve performance for component instantiation requests because MTS does not need to create a process and load all of the DLLs for the components included in the package:

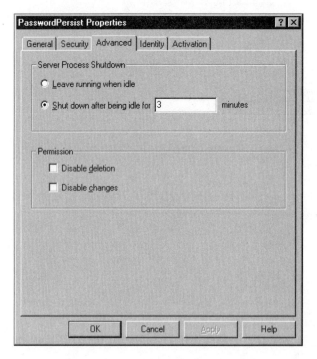

Selecting the second option button allows you to specify a time (in minutes) before a selected package automatically shuts down after being inactive. The default setting is 3 minutes, and the maximum is 1440 minutes = 24 hours. This allows a package-specific instance of MTX.EXE to be destroyed after all objects in the package have been released for the specified number of minutes.

The second frame on the Advanced tab is used to safeguard against accidental changes to the package. Disable changes prevents all changes to any of the package's configuration and Disable deletion prevents anyone from deleting the package. Both checkboxes are unchecked by default, and are used to keep users from accidentally deleting packages without first opening the Advanced tab and disabling this option.

When you have created and configured your package and its components, you should lock your package to prevent accidental changes using these options. If you want to delete the package or change it in any way, you must go back into the package's properties dialog and adjust these settings accordingly.

> The permission setting on the Advanced tab is used only for preventing accidental changes. It is not meant to guarantee that changes cannot be made by other users.

Identity

Although security access to packages are defined by roles (discussed in Chapter 8), MTS provides an additional tool to set privileges. The Identity tab is a security feature that allows the administrator to decide under which account the components in the selected package will run. There are several reasons for this feature (but we will not discuss them in this book) but basically every process on NT must run with a security account. When you create a process by double-clicking on an .exe name in Explorer or via the Start Menu, NT uses the interactive account to create and run the process. Since COM creates the process that runs the package (i.e. MTX.com) you have the problem of deciding who the user is. With the Identity tab you let the administrator decide, and the options are either to choose an account or have the account that is currently logged on.

Interactive User is the default setting. By selecting Interactive User, you are assigning privileges to components based on the privileges that are available to the calling client. What this means is a client cannot access component resources that are not permitted by Windows NT:

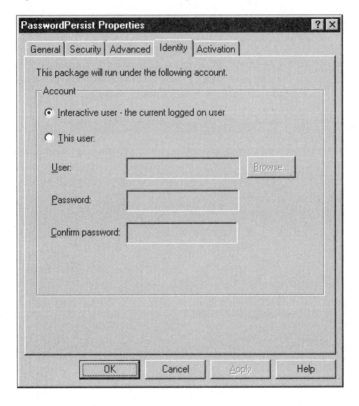

If you want to give access to another user account, you can specify it selecting the option button labeled This user and entering a password. You may find that security administration becomes easier to manage by assigning a user ID such as MTS Users for MTS use.

> **Caution: If you change the account password without updating the password in MTS Explorer, the package will fail to run and a run-time error will be generated.**

Activation

The Activation tab allows you to select how components in the package will be activated. You can select one of two options: the Library Package and the Server Package.

Selecting the option button labeled Library Package will run the package in the process of the client that called it. In other words, when a client requests the services of the package, it is loaded into the process space (in-process) of the client application.

The advantage of running in-process is greater performance. However, you can only use this option if the client and the component reside on the same machine. Furthermore, because components run in the same memory space as the client, a component that fails is likely to crash the client. It should also be noted that declarative security is not supported when using Library Packages.

The option button labeled Server Package is selected by default. When this option is selected, the package will run as a server package in its own dedicated process on the local machine. This scenario is referred to as a **surrogate process**.

Although performance may not be as efficient as running in process, it is usually preferable to run your components in their own dedicated process. Because components run in an isolated memory location separate from the client, the application achieves more stability in the event a component fails. Additionally, declarative security is supported with Server packages:

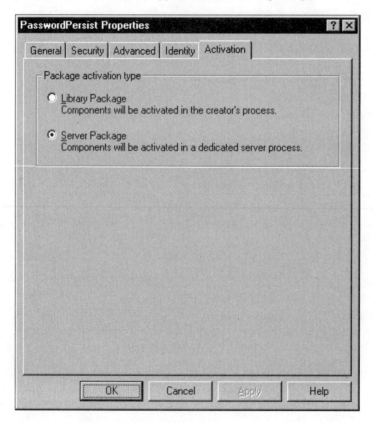

MTS Base Clients

Now that you have set up your middle-tier MTS packages and components, you need to let the base client know they exist. This is easily accomplished by running a specially created executable file on the base client machine.

When you exported the package `PasswordPersist`, you saw that a `.PAK` file and a copy of `PPIndependents.dll` and `PPAssociations.dll` were created in the folder you specified. Previously, I briefly mentioned that a subdirectory called `clients` is also created during the exporting process. The `clients` folder contains an executable file which has the same name as the `.PAK`, except that `.PAK` is replaced with `.EXE`. When this file is run on the base client machine, it places information about the package and its components into the Windows registry.

> **You will need to run an executable for each package that is required by the base client.**

Let's take a look at the `.EXE` that was created when you exported the `PasswordPersist` package.

Open NT Explorer and view the directory where you instructed your export files to be created. In my example below, the path is `D:\MTSProjects`. Open the `clients` folder and notice that a file named `PPExport.EXE` was created. (The `.PAK` file has a name of `PPExport.PAK`.)

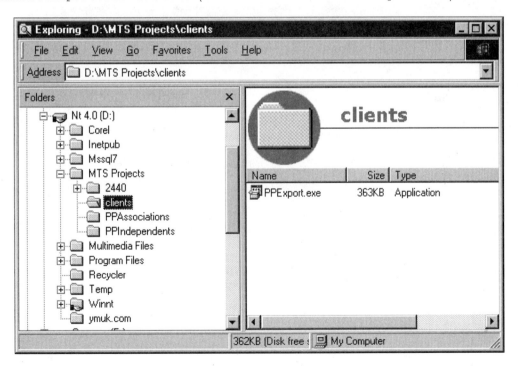

You can copy the executable file to any machine, typically a client machine. If you have several machines and you want to distribute the `.EXE` file, you may want to install the `.EXE` into a shared location on the network so it can easily be distributed to other machines.

Chapter 7

Running Your Component with MTS

You have arrived at the big moment. You will now run the client application that you created in the last chapter, and monitor the creation and termination of an object instance through MTS Explorer. Of course, the object instance will come from the components that you also created in Chapter 6.

Run the client program called `PPClient.exe`. Do not click any of the command buttons yet. With the client application running, start MTS Explorer. Size both windows as necessary, so you can see both on your desktop at the same time.

From MTS Explorer, open the Components folder for the package `PasswordPersist`. Make sure the dark colored balls with a big green "X" are visible in the right-pane. Also be sure that you have the right component folder open:

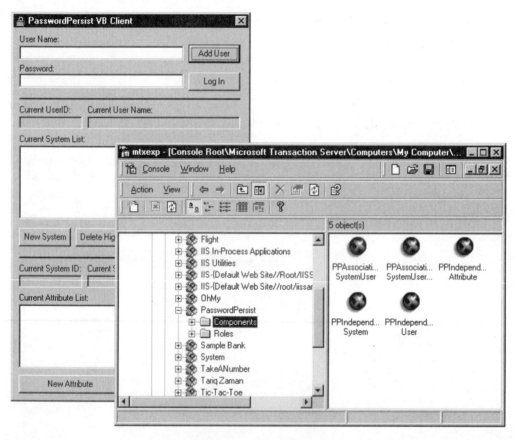

Go ahead and click the command button labeled Add User. As soon as the input box from the client opens, observe the component in the right-pane. If you followed these directions correctly, the ball icon of `PPIndependents.User` should be spinning. When this ball spins, it indicates that an object instance for this particular component has been created. Additionally, it indicates that it is running through MTS:

> **If the ball fails to spin, try refreshing the registry from MTS Explorer.**

The following code for this component is responsible for the creation of an object reference to the Context object:

```
Private Sub ObjectControl_Activate()

  Set mobjContext = GetObjectContext

End Sub
```

Keep your eye on the rotating ball – once the operation is complete, you should notice that the ball stops spinning. It is at this point that the instance of the object `PPIndependents.User` is terminated.

The following code is used to clean up after the object has completed its task:

```
Private Sub ObjectControl_Deactivate()

  Set mobjContext = Nothing

End Sub
```

Rebuilding Components and Packages

Once you've built and installed your components in the MTS Catalog, you should place your project(s) in Binary Compatibility mode to ensure that the type library identifier, CLSIDs and IIDs don't change during rebuilds.

If you try to rebuild a DLL on the same machine as MTS while any server package that contains one of the DLLs components is loaded, you will receive a **Permission denied** error from Visual Basic. This error also occurs if your components are installed in a Library package and any client processes that used your components are still loaded. You can get around this problem by right-clicking on the server package in MTS explorer and selecting the **Shut Down** option from the pop-up menu. If you want to shut down all of the packages on a machine, you can right-click on the computer name in MTS Explorer and select **Shut Down Server Processes** from the pop-up menu. The command line application `MTXSTOP.EXE` can also shut down all the server processes on the machine. While, Library packages will also allow you to select **Shut Down**, it has no effect. Instead you must destroy all the processes that loaded any MTS components you are trying to rebuild.

After a rebuild, if all the GUID values are the same (Binary compatibility is enabled and it worked), you can simply right-click on a package's components folder and select **Refresh** to force MTS to update the registry settings for each component in the package. You can also update the registry settings for all components on a machine regardless of the package they belong to by simply right-clicking on the machine and selecting the **Refresh all Components** option.

If any of the type library identifiers, CLSIDs, or IIDs do change for any reason, MTS will not be able to simply refresh the registry settings for the components. Instead, you must remove your components from the MTS package and then add them back to the package.

Since Visual Basic automatically registers a component when VB performs a build, you must update the MTS catalog, whether GUID value(s) change or not, after you perform a rebuild to ensure that the registry entries are changed for the component(s) and registry redirection will take place. If you do not update the MTS catalog after a rebuild, instances of your components will not execute in the MTS runtime environment. Visual Basic does provide an add-in that automatically refreshes the components for you after a rebuild, but it will only work if none of the GUID values for your components have changed.

Working with Remote Servers

You have learned about the classic three-tier architecture. Actually three-tier is often referred to as *n*-tier because machines can be added or even removed as necessary. Being able to add and remove machines makes *n*-tier architecture highly scalable. The point to understand is that the middle tier does not have to be a single machine. Likewise, you can have more than one MTS machine in the middle tier.

The ability to run multiple MTS machines also provides scalability. As more simultaneous demands are made, more MTS machines can be added to the middle tier.

Physically adding machines is referred to as **static load balancing**. This means that human interaction is necessary when demands on the system are increased. In the near future, **dynamic load balancing** will automatically juggle the load by spreading them to other machines.

The beauty of MTS is that it provides the ability to manage other MTS servers remotely from a single machine. This way an administrator can manage components and packages on other machines, eliminating a physical trip to each machine in order to work with them.

Adding a Computer

In order to manage remote servers from a central server, you need to add the appropriate computers to MTS Explorer on the central server. You will then need to add the components to the Remote Components folder of the newly installed remote computers.

From MTS Explorer, highlight My Computer (local computer). From the pop-up menu, select New and then Computer:

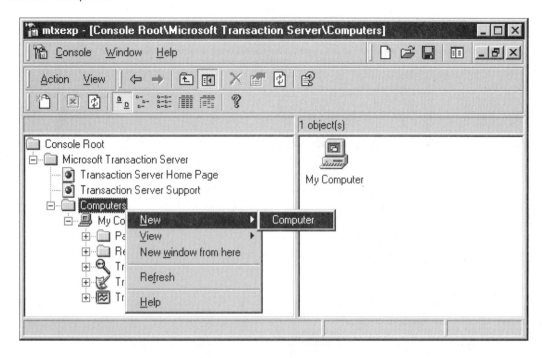

The Add Computer dialog does not recognize backslashes, so all you need to do is type in the name of the computer you want to connect to. You can also select Browse to search for the desired computer. After you have selected the remote computer, click OK:

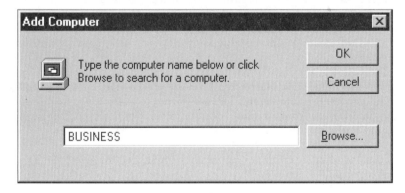

In this example, the computer Business has been added. From MTS Explorer, you can manage packages and components just as if you were physically at the other computer. The next screen shot shows that Business has only two packages installed: System and Utilities. In the next section, you will learn the steps necessary to set up components in remote machines:

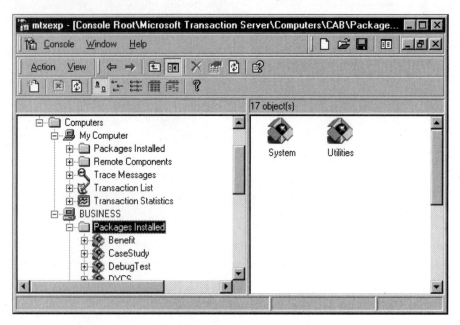

Pushing and Pulling Components

Load balancing with MTS is a static procedure. In other words, human interaction is required when bottlenecks begin due to increased demand at an MTS machine. Although dynamic load balancing is just around the corner where MTS can automatically distribute bottlenecks due to heavy workloads to other machines with less workload, it is practical to know how you can manually distribute server workload quickly and easily.

An administrator can copy component information from the source machine to a remote machine to allow other machines to access the component. This is referred to as **Pushing**. An administrator can also copy component information from a remote location to his own machine. Not surprisingly, this method is referred to as **Pulling.**

Distributing MTS workload to other machines can easily be managed through MTS Explorer. When components are pushed, or pulled, between servers, components are not removed from their current location but rather copies of their type libraries and proxy/stub DLLs are sent from one machine to another. In addition, the system registries of the remote computers are updated with the information held in the source machine. Therefore, only the information that is needed for other machines to access the component is copied. The actual component and package is not copied to the other machine, but remains resident on the machine where they are originally installed. With this in mind, realize that pushing and pulling components from machine to machine does not change the instantiation of components. The components execute on the machine where they are installed into packages. What all this boils down to is, pushing and pulling components simply allows additional machines to access the component without having to make a physical trip to the new machine and configure it to be a part of the MTS application.

Pushing Components

Before pushing components, make sure that you have share privileges on the source machine to include the folders where the components are located. Because you are pushing information away from your machine (My Computer), you need to make sure that you have read and write privileges at the destination machine (Business). In other words, the destination machine must grant both Read and Write privileges to the source machine. Furthermore, you will want an Administrator role for full access set up in the System package on each machine.

In the following example, components are copied from one MTS server to another MTS server. Here, component information is being pushed from My Computer to Business:

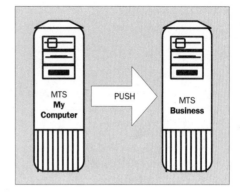

Expand the Remote Computer (in this example it is Business) and highlight the Remote Components folder. Right-click your mouse. From the pop-up menu, select New and then Remote Component.

From the Remote Components dialog, select the destination computer (in this example it is My Computer) from the drop-down list labeled Remote Computer. To the right is a list box labeled Package. This will list all available components in the selected package on My Computer. Highlight the component(s) you want to configure for remote access:

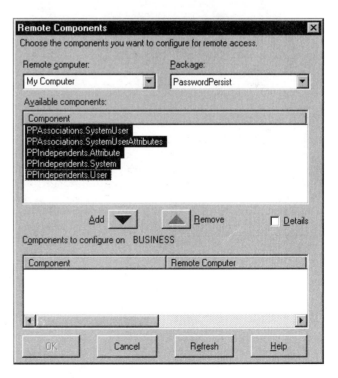

After you have selected your components, click the Add button. This will move all selected component listings to the list box (at the bottom of the Remote Components dialog) labeled Components to configure on BUSINESS. The last step is to click OK.

You can open the folder Remote Components of the remote machine (in this example it is called BUSINESS) to view components that have been pulled over from the source machine to be used for remote access.

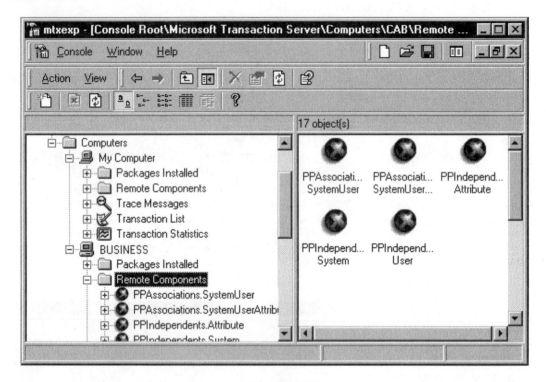

Pulling Components

Before pulling components, make sure that you have share privileges on the source machine to include the folders where components are located. Because you are pulling information to your machine, you only need to read information at the destination machine. Thus make sure the destination machine grants Read privileges to the source machine. Furthermore, you will want an Administrator role for full access set up in the System package on each machine.

In the following example, components are copied from another MTS server to another MTS machine. In this example we are pulling component information from the BUSINESS machine to the local machine called My Computer. In actuality, you probably will be at a new machine and will pull component information from another machine so it can access components on other machines:

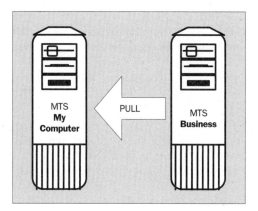

Expand My Computer and highlight the Remote Components folder. Right-click your mouse. From the pop-up menu, select New and then Remote Component.

From the Remote Components dialog, select the BUSINESS computer from the drop down list labeled Remote computer. To the right is a list box labeled Package. This will list all available components in the selected package. Highlight the component(s) that you want to configure for remote access.

After you have selected your components, click the Add button. This will move all selected component listings to the list box (at the bottom of the Remote Components dialog) labeled Components to configure on My Computer. The last step is to click OK:

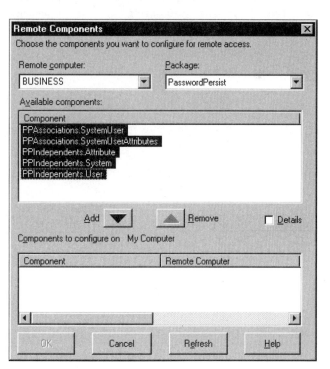

You can open the folder Remote Components from My Computer to view components that have been pulled over from the source machine.

Understand that you can push and pull components from one machine to the other using MTS Explorer from a dedicated administration machine. Often an NT Workstation connected to the network with MTS installed is used for MTS administration purposes. However you must make sure that appropriate share privileges (for the administrator) are enabled on each machine before you can distribute components remotely. Share points must be set for each folder that contains components you wish to distribute.

Summary

You have just completed a tour of package and component management using MTS Explorer. You began by learning what a package is and how to create them. Next you learned two ways of installing components into packages and then moved on to the next exercise where you discovered how to add registered components.

After creating your packages and installing your components, you covered how to create pre-built packages so you can distribute them to other machines.

You practiced deleting components and packages, and then reinstalling them by importing the pre-built packages you had created earlier. You learned what a .PAK file is and how it is used to import pre-built packages to other machines.

You also found that you need to let the base client know about new packages. You need to execute a special .EXE file that is created during exporting of packages on each machine where a base client resides.

During your tour you investigated each property setting for components and packages. Then you had a chance to run your component using MTS.

Finally, you learned how to add and work with remote machines through MTS Explorer. You can easily move components from the primary MTS server to another MTS server using the **Push** method, and you can easily bring over an MTS component from one MTS machine to the local MTS machine using the **Pull** method.

In the next chapter you will see how to add security options to your components and packages.

Implementing Security

Before the Internet, entering a remote computer system was usually done through the direct use of modems. At the same time, a new breed of vandals has emerged with one goal in mind – to break into computer systems without authorization. With the explosion of today's networking (and the Internet), digital break-ins have grown ever increasingly and continue to be on the rise. From what used to be isolated interest stories about computer break-ins, digital vandalism has evolved into a daily threat. Today, your system may be the next victim.

Aside from digital vandalism, security is necessary for general software management. Consider an application that accesses sensitive data about your company. Do you want everyone in your company to be able to access this data? Perhaps your computer system is not connected to a modem or network; should you still be concerned? Consider your applications; did you develop them yourself? How would you feel if someone accidentally changed a program setting and your system stopped working?

It's obvious that every system needs to have some level of security. In this chapter, you will learn how to secure access to your middle-tier components by implementing security to your MTS components. Additionally, you will learn how you can audit user access through programmatic security, and how to secure the MTS Explorer itself from unauthorized use. Along the way you will learn basic security fundamentals in the Windows NT and COM environments.

After completing this chapter, you should be able to answer the following questions:

- ❑ How does Windows NT security authenticate a user?
- ❑ How does the MTS security model differ from the COM security model?
- ❑ What is the difference between programmatic and declarative security?
- ❑ What are roles and how do they affect security?
- ❑ What is the difference between NT user accounts and MTS roles?
- ❑ How do I enable declarative security for my MTS packages?
- ❑ I locked myself out of MTS Explorer, what do I do?

Security in Distributed Applications

Distributed applications differ from traditional client-server applications in the way they must manage security. This type of security is known as **Authorization Security**, also called **Access Security**. As always, access to resources such as files and data sources must be secured from unauthorized users. All requests for these resources are routed through business service and data service components, instead of each user directly connecting to the data source. So how should security to resources be managed by distributed applications? If components are responsible for all access to resources on the behalf of clients, how is the access to these components restricted? These questions can be answered by dividing distributed application authorization security into two different sections:

❑ **Application Security** – involves authenticating user requests for processes, components and interfaces that execute on the behalf of the client. Security management is provided at the Application Security section, which leads to a more pro-active and scalable model because users are authenticated before they attempt to access resources.

❑ **Resource Security** or **Data Security** – involves allowing components to access resources on the behalf of clients. Security management is no longer performed at the resource level, something that was complex, error-prone and usually difficult to do.

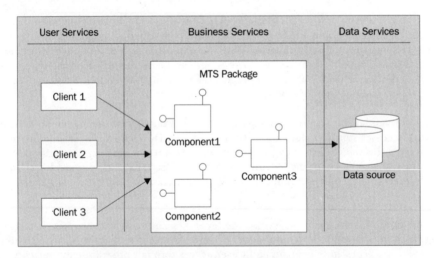

As we'll discuss later in this section, focusing on authorization security from these two different perspectives makes it much easier to design and implement secure, component based systems.

In addition to authorization security, distributed applications must also verify the credentials of the calling user. In other words, the user must prove to MTS who they are. This aspect of security, called **Authentication Security**, is believed by some to be one of the most important aspects of creating a secure distributed application. Authentication security is a very complex topic, and a full discussion about the underlying details of the authentication process is out of the scope of this book. Instead, we will discuss how COM and MTS hide the details of the actual authentication process to make it easier to develop secure distributed applications.

The Windows NT Security Model

Before learning about the MTS security model, I want to briefly go over Windows NT security. This will help you understand how MTS security builds upon the Windows NT and COM security models.

Windows NT security may be best referred to as client-server oriented. Whenever a client needs to access an object such as a file, a drive mapping, or even another server, the object request must go through an NT kernel component on the server. The server must be able to manage these requests by verifying whether the client is allowed to access the object.

Interestingly the Windows NT operating system doesn't maintain access verification tables. Nor does it directly verify access privileges. Instead, NT servers *impersonate* the identity of the calling client, so that verification comes from the operating system itself. This does not necessarily mean that each machine has its own set of security information stored locally. Read on and I'll explain further.

> **Impersonation is when a process takes on the security attributes of a user or another process.**

In a business environment, stand-alone computers need to be able to share information, by accessing other machines. Networking has evolved to today's standards in order to meet this need. Windows NT uses what is referred to as a **domain** to manage a group of networked machines. A domain is nothing more than a group of NT machines that share a common centralized directory database, also referred to as a **user account database**. The fact that all NT server machines in a domain share this database makes administration simpler, because it's not necessary to set up user accounts on each individual machine:

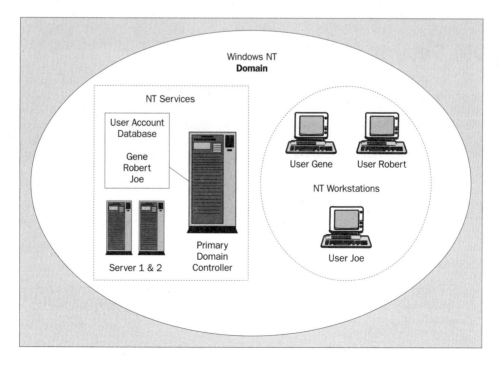

Windows NT Workgroups are based on a peer-to-peer orientation, which doesn't require a central server. This type of architecture is used in small environments, taking the place of a low-cost networking solution. However, security is difficult to implement on Windows NT Workgroup machines. Also this architecture cannot utilize global users in the way that Windows NT Domains can. As a result, it is necessary to create user accounts on every NT machine in the peer-to-peer network that a particular user wants to be able to log in to. Furthermore, if the user wishes to change his/her password, the password needs to be changed on each machine that the user wants to access.

Without going into great detail, the user account database is stored on a **domain controller**, and is replicated to a **backup domain controller**. Because the domain controller machine has the user database, user authentication for the domain takes place here (or at the backup domain controller).

When a new user account is created, a **Security Identification** (SID) is created. SIDs are similar to GUIDs, in that no two identical SIDs can exist. SIDs are generated by an algorithm in the same way as GUIDs in order to guarantee uniqueness. Here's an example.

Suppose you have a user with the user ID Shakespeare. This user decides to leave the company and, as a good administrator, you promptly delete him from the system. Then the user decides to stay, so you quickly recreate a new user ID called Shakespeare and give him back all his access rights. Everything may seem exactly as it was before. However, Shakespeare now has a new SID. As far as the system is concerned, the new user ID for Shakespeare represents another person.

Don't confuse user account with a user. The user account is a representation of the user, not the actual user. It is not unusual to have a user account that reflects the name of the user (for example, the user Jane Doe may have a user account of jdoe22).

The COM Security Model

Building upon NT security, COM security is broad in scope and relies on two types of permissions: **launch** and **access**. Launch permissions allow a user to start an application process, while access permissions allow a user to access an application where application processes have already been started. You can set permissions on a component basis but it does not give you control down to the individual interface. Simply, COM's security model is all or none at the component level. This can cause a serious breach of security because once a user gains access, security for all practical purposes is over.

You will learn about declarative and programmatic security in the next section. For now, realize that COM is capable of utilizing both.

When a user wants to activate an object across the network (DCOM), COM security authenticates the user's ID via a remote procedure call (RPC) and a **Security Support Provider** (SSP).

A security support provider is a DLL library that manages a security scheme. With Windows NT 4.0, NT LAN Manager Security Support Provider (NTLM) is the only default security provider that is easily used.

NTLM SSP

So how does NTLM SSP work? When a user logs into the system, the client NTLM sends the domain name, the user ID, and machine information to the server NTLM. The server NTLM takes this information and passes it to the **Primary Domain Controller (PDC)**. The PDC then generates a binary sequence that is sent back to the client NTLM. This binary sequence is referred to as a **challenge**.

The client NTLM encrypts the binary sequence by taking the user's password and handles it as a security key. This process is referred to as a **response**. The NTLM client sends the encrypted response back to the NTLM server. Realize that the password is not sent to the server NTLM.

At this point, the NTLM server contacts the user's domain by providing the name of the user's domain, the user's ID, and the challenge and response sequence. The user's domain must decipher the challenge and verify it against the response before finally authenticating the process the user wants to access.

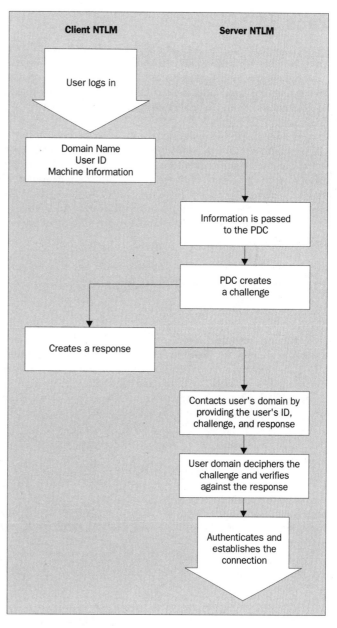

In this scenario, a server has to obtain the user credentials and then re-authenticate the user through the Domain Controller as part of establishing the connection. Once authentication is verified, the NTLM server will impersonate the client user.

> **The key concept to understand about NTLM is that the user's password is not transmitted across the network during authentication.**

Kerberos SSP

Windows 2000 will replace **NTLM** SSP with a **Kerberos** SSP as its default authentication scheme although NTLM will be available for legacy reasons. Kerberos is based on a public, industry-standard that was developed by Massachusetts Institute of Technology (MIT). Kerberos provides extended features, including faster authentication by eliminating the need for the application server to connect to the domain controller for client authentication.

Another enhancement is the authentication process in an n-tier environment. Servers can pass client user information across machines for use by other servers in an n-tier environment and allowing for mutual client-server authentication. You learned that when a client connects to a server, the server will impersonate the client. However, in an n-tier environment, the server may need to connect to another server in order to complete the client's request. What Kerberos does is allow the first server to connect to another server on behalf of the client. Additionally, the second server can go on to the third if needed. The second server (and so on) will also impersonate the client; this is known as delegation.

Finally, Kerberos allows users in a Windows NT security environment to access remote non-Windows NT services that also use a standard Kerberos SSP.

So how does a Kerberos SSP work?

When a user logs into the system, Windows NT will acquire one or more Kerberos **session tickets** and store them in a cache for possible reuse. Session tickets represent the user's network credentials, including the domain name, the user name, and an encrypted password that meets the Kerberos specification. Windows NT will manage the cache of Kerberos session tickets and use them appropriately for all connections to network services. These tickets are given a time expiration, thus requiring them to be occasionally renewed.

In summary, the client logs in to NT Domain Controller and receives a session ticket:

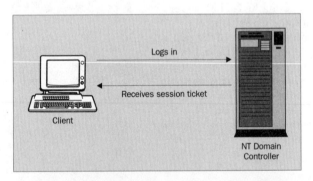

The client then presents the session ticket to the application server, where it will be verified.

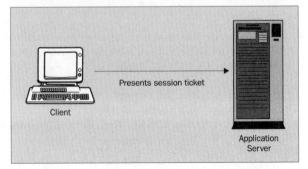

Application Security

Anyone who has worked with COM security agrees that it's much more difficult than it should be. COM security is too closely tied to the physical implementation of components and it's much to difficult to explain to your average system administrator. Very few system administrators understand what a CLSID is or how to use the DCOM Configuration tool (`dcomcnfg.exe`). Consequently, developers are often left with the remedial task of managing authorization permissions.

By only allowing authorization permissions to be defined at the process level, DCOM also lacks the ability to define authorization permissions down to the component, interface or method level. This opens a huge security hole or a design issue, whichever way you want to look at it. Either you sacrifice security to all the users that need to access any component in a COM server, or you implement one component per COM server, not a scalable solution by any means. Alternatively, you could implement code to handle security down to the method level by restricting access based on user name or SID (associated security ID with a user or group account), but this is a nontrivial and problematic task, and again too closely tied to the physical implementation of a component.

The MTS Security Model

The MTS security model is very flexible, and it offers several ways of handling security. You don't have to use MTS security if you don't want to, and how much security you do want to implement will depend on the type of your applications.

You can take advantage of two types of security, referred to as **Declarative Security** and **Programmatic Security**. Declarative security is implemented with the MTS Explorer and is based on using roles and Windows NT user accounts. Programmatic security is enabled directly though the source code of your MTS components.

One very attractive reason to use MTS security is to replace conventional client-server security. Let's look into this in detail.

With Windows NT, user accounts are set up to control individual user access. Through Windows NT user manager, you create separate user accounts and user groups. Suppose you have three databases; one for research data, one for library publications, and one for office administration. Ernest needs access to the research database, Shirley needs access to the publications database, and Dori needs access to the administration database. Using standard client-server security, the network administrator needs to create a user ID for Ernest, Shirley, and Dori. Additionally, permission to access the correct database is required for each user. Typically, the database will maintain its own access authorization, thus it is necessary to add these users and passwords as well.

Along comes a new employee named Jeff who needs access to the research database and the publications database. At the same time, Dori leaves the company. The network administrator needs to create a new user and grant access privileges to the two databases, and remove the user ID for Dori, as well as her permissions to the Administration database.

This is a small example that involves only four people. Imagine the administration challenges if 10 users were involved, a 100 users, even 1000 users or more.

You may be thinking that this is why NT allows for groups, and you're right. However, one very important point is being overlooked, and that is database connections. Recall that database connections are costly to system resources, and a database server can only handle a finite number of connections. If you have a small database server with 100 users, having all 100 users connect can bring the system to a crawl. To complicate matters, when a user is granted access to a database under the traditional client-server security model, the connection is first validated through the user's SID. In other words, the connection carries the user's SID. Since each connection relies on the users SID, the database connection becomes unique.

You learned earlier that MTS offers connection pooling through the use of the ODBC Resource Dispenser. As a quick review, when a client requests a database connection, the ODBC driver manager will search the connection pool for an available connection. If a suitable connection is available the connection is given to the client without having to establish a new connection. However, if each connection is unique to a SID, database pooling will be of little use. Only the original user can reuse its own connection.

As you have seen throughout this book, MTS is usually the hero. Using the security model for MTS, user accounts and user groups are hidden in the background. How does MTS do this? MTS authenticates through the use of **roles** instead.

MTS Security – Roles

> **Roles are symbolic names with predefined permissions for accessing component interfaces for a user or group of users.**

Roles allow for easier administration. Now you don't need to create a user ID and password for every user accessing the SQL Server. Don't misunderstand, you still need a user ID and a password for Windows NT, but you don't need to create a user and password on SQL Server for security. As you will soon see, roles will take care of this. Additionally, by eliminating the need for SIDs in a database connection, MTS, which is tightly integrated with the ODBC Resource Dispenser, can better utilize a database connection pool.

By introducing the concept of roles, MTS security builds on top of the security infrastructure already provided by Windows NT and COM. Roles are symbolic representations of users' access privileges, or in other words, a logical group of Windows NT user and group accounts defined within a server package.

Roles provide an abstraction layer for components from physical Windows NT user and group accounts, which are prone to change and offer no flexibility. They are used to define a single user or group of users that can access the components in a package. This is very similar to the way Windows NT defines a group of users, except that MTS uses roles at the package level while Windows NT uses groups at the systems level.

These roles are designed to allow the programmer and administrator to develop secure components. Roles can actually be set to control access to specific MTS components and interfaces. If a user tries to access a component or interface that is not specified in the package roles, the user will be denied permission to use the component.

> Although similar to groups, roles are unique to MTS. Roles extend COM's
> security model by providing security access down to the interface level.

Rather than checking whether the caller is a particular SID, all security checks for authorization are based on whether or not a caller is in a particular role. During development, developers can define roles and determine what security permission the roles are granted. At deployment time, an administrator can simply map specific Windows NT user and group accounts to these same roles. This eliminates the decision making required by the system administrator and makes the development and deployment of secure, component-based system much easier.

One important aspect of MTS security is that roles isolate components from actual users. Users are not stable in nature. As new users join the company, others move to different departments, and some leave the company altogether. Suppose that the user "Robert" was hard-coded into the component where he could only access a partial salary listing as opposed to seeing salaries for every employee. Robert gets promoted and now is required to work with salaries for everyone in the company. The only way to handle this would be to rewrite the code for the component, recompile it, and install it into a package. Additionally, you need to notify the base client of this new revision.

As you can see, it is essential that the component does not have to undergo these consequences as users come and go. Additionally, other vendors would have a difficult time making and selling MTS components if they constantly needed to be modified. Roles solve this problem. If you are using programmatic security, all you need to do is write code for a specific role. When a user gets promoted, leaves or joins the company, all the administrator has to worry about is creating, changing, and deleting the user. Depending how roles are set up, it may not be necessary to make any changes at all.

Roles also offer a much more natural way of administering security. Instead of thinking about which components a particular user or group should have permission to, you can think about security in terms of the role(s) that an individual plays within the organization. Consider the following scenario that classifies users by their roles and defines the operations each role can perform.

A typical organization has the need to manage information about employees. Access to employee data and modifications to employee data is restricted based on the type of employee. There are types of employees or roles that will be working with the employee data:

- ❑ **Everyone** – Everyone within the organization has the ability to view basic information about all employees. This information includes: First Name, Last Name, Phone Number, Pager Number, Address, City, State, Zip Code and Department.

- ❑ **Managers** – Managers have the ability to view all the employee information the Everyone role has access to and extended information about all employees including: Salary History, Promotions, and Performance Evaluation information.

- ❑ **Human Resource Personnel** – Human Resource Personnel are responsible for managing information about employees. So they not only have access to view information about all employees, but they also have the ability to add new employees, modify an existing employee's information and remove an employee (logical employee from the data source, don't worry, HR doesn't have the power to fire anyone in this organization).

As you can see, a user or group of users could belong to multiple roles because they perform multiple duties, or wear multiple hats, within an organization. Approaching security in this manner is much more appealing to system administrators because an understanding of COM and components is not required. An administrator simply adds or removes the Windows NT user and group accounts that belong to MTS role(s) using the MTS Explorer.

The first level of MTS security is at the package level using declarative security. As you may infer, declarative security is based on roles. Although this level of security is in-between having no MTS security and having security at the interface level, this is often the best choice.

> **Using declarative security, each component in a package must authenticate the validity of each user with a set of predefined roles.**

The most flexible type of MTS security is programmatic security. Programmatic security is also based on roles. However, it relies on access verification through hard-code. By adding specific code to the component the programmer can add greater security control. Simply, programmatic security is good for fine tuning MTS security. You know that declarative security can be used to allow a user access down to a specific interface, but suppose you want to put in other restrictions.

Natasha is the chief accountant of the Grog Company. Using declarative security, you can create a role that allows her to have full access to the company's salary list. Robert is a clerk in the accounting office. He needs to be able to access the same salary information except for upper management. You can use declarative security so Robert can access the component. However, here declarative security falls short: it either lets Robert use the component that is responsible for displaying all salaries or lets him see nothing at all.

Using programmatic security solves this problem. You can still use declarative security to allow Robert and Natasha to access the component responsible for listing employee salaries. However, you can program specific restrictions into the component. In this example, you can program a restriction for upper level management and senior accountants to have full access while general accounting employees can only see salary information for regular employees. If Robert is later promoted, all the administrator needs to do is change his role.

> **MTS security is very flexible. It even allows you to combine declarative and programmatic security together.**

MTS security resides on a layer above COM security. Because of this, MTS utilizes two areas from COM security and extends its own security model. MTS will validate each user through COM's security authentication. Additionally, MTS will use COM's activation security. However, from this point on, COM security becomes inadequate..

Before an MTS package can be accessed, the user must first be authenticated through Windows NT. Once a login authentication for the user has been achieved through Windows NT security, the user must be validated through COM before it can enter MTS. Once validated through COM, MTS adds its own security layer. This is where declarative security and programmatic security come in. When using declarative security, the access control for MTS authenticates through the use of roles. On the other hand, when using programmatic security, the programmer is essentially customizing the access control for MTS through code.

Roles cannot be shared across server packages and their scope is limited to the server package they are defined in. You should consider this limitation when organizing your components into packages, and attempt to minimize the number of server packages you have for an application. Synchronizing roles and role membership for multiple packages can be difficult and problematic.

Where MTS Security is Not Supported

The Activation tab for package security gives you two options: Server Packages, and Library Packages.

Server packages run in their own processes on the local computer as opposed to operating in the same process as the client (Library packages). Server packages will support role-based security.

On the other hand, **Library packages** operate in the same address space as the calling client. This type of setup can result in security problems. Roles need to be validated before the process is executed but, because a calling client can be from anywhere, role checking is not available. As a result, Library packages cannot be secured using role-based security.

The only exception to this restriction is when a Library package is loaded into the process of another Server package. If you try to create a role in a Library package, MTS will give you a warning message before allowing you to proceed. Roles and their membership can still be viewed and modified. However, any changes will not take affect because MTS just turns off all security for Library packages.

> *It's also important to mention that security is not supported with MTS running on Windows 95/98. Windows 95/98 lack support for a Security Accounts Management (SAM) database and several other security features provided by Windows NT.*

Creating a Role

Creating a new role is the easiest operation to perform in the MTS Explorer. Right-click on the Roles folder under your package and select New | Role from the pop-up menu. You can also select New | Role from the Action menu or click the New button on the toolbar. When the New Role dialog window is displayed, enter the name for your new role (in this example Managers) and click OK when finished:

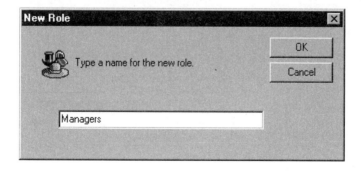

To add Windows NT User and/or Group accounts to our new role, first expand the tree to view the Users folder under the new Managers role. Right-click the Users folder and select New | User from the pop-up menu; select New | User from the Action menu or click the New button on the toolbar. The MTS Explorer will then display the Add Users and Groups to Role dialog that will let you add Windows NT User and/or Group account(s) to the Managers role:

When a new role is created, behind the scenes, MTS creates a GUID value to identify the role (called a RoleID) and adds a new registry key with the name of the `RoleID` under:

```
HKEY_LOCAL_MACHINE\
SOFTWARE\Microsoft\
Transaction Server\
Packages\{PackageID}\
Roles\:
```

A registry key in the format DOMAIN_NAME\ACCOUNT_NAME is also created for each User or Group account added to the role.

One recommended approach to administering security in MTS is to create a Windows NT group for each role and assign just this new group to the role it represents. An administrator can then change role membership just by adding and removing users from groups using a single application (such as User Manager or User Manager for Domains) that they are already familiar with. Administrators can just think of roles as another resource, like shares or printers, that are easier to manage by using local groups than with many individual user accounts.

Any time you make any security changes, you must shut down all the server packages affected before your changes are reflected by MTS. Shutting down a server package will kill the process associated with the package and cause it to be recreated to service the next client's request.

Understanding MTS Declarative Security

Let's look at declarative security in a bit more detail. You recently learned that MTS replaces COM's access control with its own. Let's look at this process through declarative security.

One thing to keep in mind is that security authentication takes time, so authentication can slow an application down. MTS eliminates this performance degradation by only having security at the front lines. This is accomplished through the use of roles.

MTS impersonates a client when it tries to access a component. Before the client can have access, MTS verifies the user with what is known as an **access control list**. An access control list is simply a compilation of information that specifies users and/or user groups with their permission rights to a component. Additionally, MTS checks the client's SID in case there is a level of programmatic security as well. If the user has proper permissions to the component, MTS allows user access and impersonation via MTS is withdrawn.

Declarative Security allows you to define authorization permissions for roles without writing a line of code. MTS currently supports declarative security at three different levels:

- ❑ Package
- ❑ Component
- ❑ Interface

Package Level Declarative Security

With package level declarative security enabled, you can control whether a user is granted access to the components within the Server package (process). Access is granted if either the caller's user account, or a group account that the user belongs, to is mapped to at least one role in the package.

In the following example, the client application is calling methods on MTS components in a server package using the JCox user account. This account is mapped to the Managers role. With only package level security, user account JCox is allowed access to all components in the package:

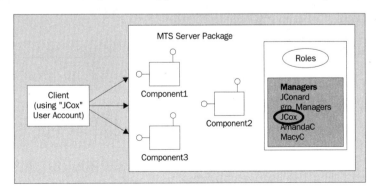

Package level declarative security can be extended with component or interface level declarative security to further restrict which roles have access to a component or it's interfaces. However, both lower levels require package level declarative security to be enabled. Package level declarative security, just like DCOM's current security model, only blocks against calls into the process. Process security alone is not sufficient for most distributed applications.

Component Level Declarative Security

If package level security is enabled, MTS can also enforce declarative security at the component level. Users are granted permissions to components by mapping roles to components. Role mappings can be viewed, added and deleted from the Role Membership folder under each component listed in MTS Explorer. If the caller has access to a component, they also have access to all of the component's interfaces.

In this example, the application can call methods on Component1 because the JCox user account is a member of the Managers role:

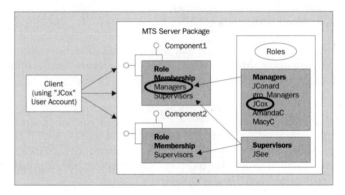

Component level security is enabled by default. It can be disabled by selecting the Enable Authorization Checking checkbox on the Security tab when viewing your component's properties.

Interface Level Declarative Security

If both package level and component level declarative security are enabled, MTS can also enforce declarative security on the interfaces implemented by a component. Just like with component level security, users are granted access to interfaces by mapping roles to the interfaces. Role mappings can be viewed, added and deleted from the Role Membership folder under each interface listed in MTS Explorer.

In the next example, the client application has the ability to call methods of the IManager interface because the JCox user account is a member of the Managers role:

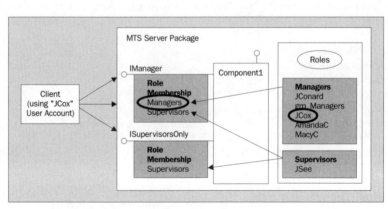

Remember, a role that is mapped to a component has access to all of the component's interfaces. This is important when a user account belongs to multiple roles.

Declarative security at the interface level is a very powerful security mechanism, and this is yet another reason to define multiple interfaces. You can define a separate interface for each role that will be accessing your component. Alternatively, you can define a separate interface for each type of operation that can be performed by the component, and restrict security on just these interfaces. Consider our earlier example of the Everyone, Managers and Human Resources roles working with employee information:

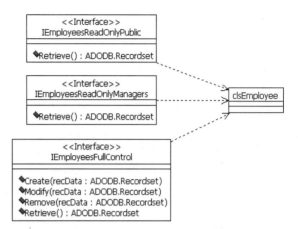

The Everyone role will be mapped to the IEmployeesReadOnlyPublic interface, the Managers role will be mapped to the IEmployeesReadOnlyManagers interface and the Human Resources role will be mapped to the IEmployeesFullControl interface. All of these interfaces will be implemented by the clsEmployees component. The alternative to this approach would be creating a separate component for each of these roles. However, since transactional attributes for components are set at the component level, a better design would move the IEmployeesFullControl interface to another component.

Components should always be broken up into interfaces, like in this example, based on the sets of behavior they provide, a concept that's foreign to us VB developers. This is even more evident now with MTS providing declarative security at the interface level, and yet another reason to stop relying on VB's implementation of the hidden, default interface.

Security Checking Process

When a method is called on an MTS object, MTS first looks through all of the roles for the caller's SID or the SID of any group the caller belongs to. Once MTS has a list of roles for the caller, it is ready to perform authorization checking, starting at the package level and working down to the component and interface levels.

- ❑ If package level security (authorization checking) is enabled, the direct caller must belong to at least one role, otherwise access is denied.
- ❑ Provided that the caller does belong to a role, MTS checks whether component level declarative security is enabled. If it is, MTS will only allow access if a role in the caller's role list is mapped to the component.
- ❑ However, when the caller has access to a component, they also have access to all of the component's interfaces. To support interface security, you should not assign any role memberships to the component. Instead, map the roles to the interfaces you want to allow access to. If none of the caller's roles are allowed access by the component, but at least one role is allowed access to an interface then MTS will allow the caller to call methods only on that interface.

Package level security must be enabled for any authorization checking to be performed. Likewise component level security must be enabled for interface level security to work.

The diagram opposite illustrates how these 3 levels of security work together as a call is made on an MTS object:

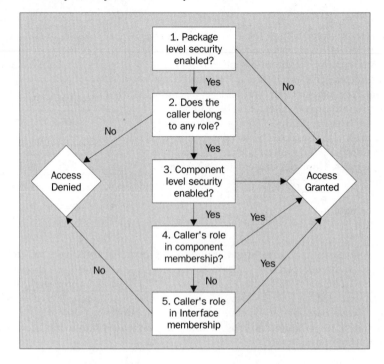

Any time a client is denied access when calling a method on an MTS object, MTS returns the infamous Permission Denied error (error number 70) and logs a warning entry in the Windows NT Application Event Log on the machine MTS is running on. This event log entry audits the name of the caller and the package, component and interface that denied access to the caller.

MTS uses the interception scheme provided by the context wrapper to perform security checks during the preprocessing of method calls. There are two benefits to this approach:

❑ **MTS can perform security checks at lower levels than DCOM could previously** – As I mentioned before, DCOM only provided security on the process the components were executing in, the MTS equivalent of package level security.

❑ **MTS prevents an unauthorized client from using an object reference obtained from an authorized client** – It's bad for a client to share references to MTS objects because of possible concurrency problems. However, if you ignore this advice and try to share an MTS object with a client or process that is not authorized, MTS will deny access to the unauthorized client. This is just a side benefit of security checks being performed every time a method is invoked on an MTS object.

With authorization checks performed by the MTS Executive as part of the Context Wrapper's preprocessing routines, a client could actually obtain a reference to an object's interface or even create an instance of a component that they are not authorized to use. It's also another reason to make sure you use the SafeRef function when passing around your Me reference. If you don't, the client or another MTS object will call methods directly on your object's interfaces, bypassing the Context Wrapper and authorization checking.

Remember, MTS is not a replacement for DCOM. It is layered on top of DCOM, so MTS must integrate with DCOM's existing security model. Users must be able to get past DCOM's security checking in order to reach MTS's security checking. To accomplish this, MTS turns off DCOM's launch security by granting launch (authorization) permissions for each component to all users. DLL in-process components don't normally have to provide any security, but because MTS hosts our components in a surrogate process (MTX.EXE), security is specified for each component. When a component is loaded into the MTS surrogate process everyone has permissions to create instances and obtain interface pointers. However, when a method is called, MTS performs its own authorization checking and allows or denies access. If your components execute within MTS, let MTS manage DCOM's security for your components, otherwise you could cause a security nightmare.

Declarative security in MTS is only provided at the process (package), component, and interface levels, however, with the release of COM+ declarative security will be extended to the method level. Although this might sound very appealing at first, if not used properly, administrating role membership for a handful of methods could be a support nightmare. Instead, define your security for groups of methods using interface level security and implement multiple interfaces in your components as we described earlier. This technique can be implemented today, and will be much easier to support and troubleshoot security issues.

When Security Checks are Performed

The security checking process we have just discussed is performed on the process calling into an MTS server process. MTS does not perform security checks when one component calls another within the same process. This also contributes to faster performance with intra-process calls. However, because components within a process trust each other, you must protect your distributed applications from *unintended* security holes. Specifically, you should watch for security holes when a component uses other components in the same package. To illustrate the possible security hole, consider the following scenario:

The client application, executing under the JCox user account, creates an instance of Component1 and calls a method. MTS finds the caller's user account in the Managers role and locates the Managers role in the Role Membership list for Component1. It then determines if the caller is authorized to perform the method call and finally executes the method. Component1 creates an instance of Component2 and calls a method on the new instance:

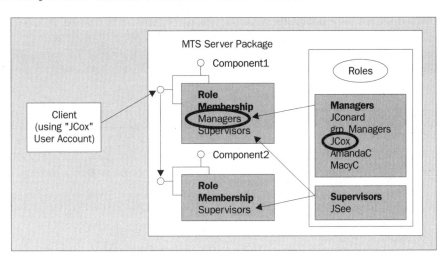

You would expect the call to fail because the user account JCox is not in the `Supervisors` role. However, since both `Component1` and `Component2` execute in the same process, security checks are not performed and the method call completes successfully. But what if `Component1` returns this new instance of `Component2` to the client, and the client invokes a method on the returned reference? This time, the call will fail because the client is executing in a separate process.

> **The deciding factor that determines whether security checks are performed or not is whether the client is in the same process as the object. Well-designed components and a thoroughly-planned security strategy will reduce your distributed application's vulnerability to this or any other potential security holes.**

Since security checks are always performed when a process boundary is crossed, security checking would also occur when an MTS object in one server package calls an MTS object in another server package. We will discuss this type of scenario in the Data Security section later in this chapter.

Implementing Declarative Security

Declarative Security can be implemented in a simple 3-step process:

1. **Define roles for each package and assign them to the components and interfaces role memberships** – Defining roles is nothing more than understanding the different categories of users that will use the MTS components. If you have a well designed distributed application, implementing your security design will be very simple. It's worth spending extra time up front planning your security strategy, otherwise the first step of implementing declarative security can be very time consuming and error prone.

2. **Enable security** – You must enable authorization checking for your Server packages or security checks will not be performed. Remember, component level declarative security is enabled by default. For users to access a component, you must either map the appropriate roles to the component or the component's interfaces, or disable authorization checking for the component altogether. This step should occur during the final stages of development

3. **Map Windows NT user and group accounts to roles** – Once authorization permissions have been established, a non-COM savvy administrator can simply map Windows NT user and group accounts to roles you defined in Step 1. Or, better yet, if there is a corresponding Windows NT group account for each role, an administrator can just add user accounts to that group using the User Manager for Domains, a tool they are most likely already familiar with.

Enabling MTS Security

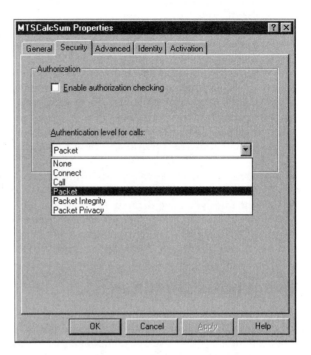

Up to this point, we've investigated what MTS declarative security is. But how do you turn MTS declarative security on? Simply right-click on your package in MTS Explorer and select Properties from the pop-up menu. On the Security tab, you will find a checkbox to Enable authorization checking. Selecting this box actually turns on declarative security for the selected package. Note that newly created packages have authorization checking disabled.

The authentication level for a Server package can also be changed from the package's Security tab. The drop-down combo box labeled Authentication level for calls gives the following options:

❑   None – Selecting None will override the checkbox enabling authorization checking, and cause it to be grayed out.

❑   Connect – Connect authentication only checks the caller's identity once, during the first call to a package.

❑   Call – Selecting Call will check security every time a request is made to access a package.

❑   Packet – With authorization level checking enabled, Packet authentication becomes the default. The caller's identity is verified on every packet of every method call received by the server. The caller's identity is encrypted when transmitted between the client and the MTS component. This means a user cannot gain access by impersonating another user.

For very secure systems, you have the option of using Packet Integrity or Packet Privacy:

❑   Packet Integrity – Packet Integrity verifies whether network packets have been tampered with along the way. When using Packet Integrity, the sender's identity and the sender's signature are encrypted.

❑   Packet Privacy – The most secure level for authentication is Packet Privacy. The senders identity, the sender's signature, and all data for the packet is encrypted.

> **One thing to keep in mind is that using a high level of security causes degradation in performance – very high security can be obtained, but at a cost.**

By default, MTS uses packet-level authentication. This level is recommended for most situations. MTS verifies that each data packet was sent by the expected caller, but packet-level authentication doesn't have the overhead of the Packet Integrity or Packet Privacy levels because only the caller's identity is encrypted.

If you require data integrity checks to ensure that packets are not modified, or you require each data packet to be encrypted, you should change the authentication level to Packet Integrity or Packet Privacy. On the other hand, if your not worried about a hacker "sniffing" data packets and trying to impersonate another user, adjusting the authentication level to Call or Connect will provide slight performance gains. As with any other package configuration option, after the authentication level has been changed you must shutdown and restart the server package for the change to take affect.

The best part about declarative security is the amount of code required in your MTS components – none. With declarative security, MTS is responsible for implementing all authorization checking based on the roles you have defined, the mapping of those roles to components and interfaces, and the enabling of security at the package and/or component level. For this reason, declarative security is very easy to implement, support, maintain and change. However, sometimes your MTS components may need more control over security. That's where Programmatic Security comes in.

Programmatic Security

Programmatic security allows us to supplement and extend declarative security by implementing code in our MTS components. This is enabled through the components source code. Chapter 3 introduced the `ObjectContext` component, which has two methods available for implementing MTS security: `IsSecurityEnabled` and `IsCallerInRole`. As you will see, they both can and should compliment each other. Additionally, you can use the `SecurityProperty` object that comes in handy for auditing purposes.

The IsCallerInRole Method

The `IsCallerInRole` function allows a component to have more control over security by checking whether or not the direct caller is in a particular role. When used in combination with declarative security, the `IsCallerInRole` function can extend simplistic authorization checking to providing different behavior based on the direct caller's role.

`IsCallerInRole` takes a single parameter of a specified role name. It's Boolean, and returns a value of `True` if the current user account (or a group account that the current user belongs to) is a member of the role. If the specified role doesn't exist, MTS will raise an `mtsErrCtxRoleNotFound` error. To help you diagnose the problem, a warning event is logged in the Windows NT Application Log, indicating the name of the requested role. It is important to understand that this method applies to the direct caller of the method that is currently being executed.

The following is a code snippet checks between two different roles and grants access accordingly:

```
Private Sub ValidateSalaryUsers()

  Dim objContext As ObjectContext
  Set objContext = GetObjectContext

  On Error GoTo Error_NotValidated

  If objContext.IsCallerInRole("Senior_Accountant") Then
    View_Complete_Salary_List
  End If

  If objContext.IsCallerInRole("General_Accountant") Then
    View_Partial_Salary_List
  Else
    objContext.SetAbort
    Set objContext = Nothing
  End If

  Exit Sub

Error_NotValidated:

  objContext.SetAbort
  Set objContext = Nothing
  Err.Raise vbObjectError + 9876

End Sub
```

The `IsCallerInRole` function can be called by a component residing in a Library package, if the Library package is loaded in the process of an MTS Server package (a secured process). In this scenario, instead of checking the direct caller against a role(s) defined in the library package, the `IsCallerInRole` function should specify a role defined in the Server package in which the component is loaded. If you want to implement programmatic security for components in this scenario, define your roles in both the Library package and the Server package. This way, if the package type (activation setting) is ever changed for the Library package, the clients will gracefully be denied access instead of the components generating an `mtsErrCtxRoleNotFound` error.

On the other hand, if the `IsCallerInRole` function is called by a component running inside a Library package loaded in any process MTS hasn't created (an unsecured process), it will always return `True`. As a result, the direct caller will always appear to the component as if they belong to the specified role, effectively opening up a security hole. To avoid this problem, you should always call the `IsCallerInRole` function together with the `IsSecurityEnabled` function, as we'll see in the next example.

The IsSecurityEnabled Method

The method `IsSecurityEnabled` is also Boolean and returns a value of `True` if the component's security is enabled. If `IsSecurityEnabled` is called by a component in a Server package, it will always return `True`, indicating that the package is secure. `IsSecurityEnabled` also returns `True` when it is called from a Library package that's been loaded in the process of a Server package. However, when a component in a Library package has been loaded into any other process that's not created by MTS, `IsSecurityEnabled` will return `False`.

As we said earlier, it's a good idea to use this method with `IsCallerInRole`. `IsCallerInRole` will return a value of `True` if a Library package running in process calls it. This can cause unanticipated results because the components cannot be secured. However, because the components from an in process server are not secured, `IsSecurityEnabled` will return a value of `False`. Using programmatic security, you can circumvent problems by taking alternate action in the event security is disabled.

The following code snippet uses the two methods `IsSecurityEnabled` and `IsCallerInRole`:

```
Private Sub VerifyRole()

  On Error GoTo VerifyCallerInRole_Error

  Dim objContext As ObjectContext
  Set objContext = GetObjectContext

  If objContertext.IsSecurityEnabled = False Then Exit Sub

  'Because the objContext is a local variable, the object references will
  'automatically be released when the variable goes out of scope.
  'Because of this, it is not necessary to explicitly release the
  'object by setting it to nothing.

  If objContext.IsCallerInRole("Senior_Accountant") Then
    RollVerified
  End If

  Exit Sub

VerifyCallerInRole_Error:

  Exit Sub

End Sub
```

The SecurityProperty Object

The **SecurityProperty** object is typically used for auditing purposes using programmatic security. It is used for determining the creator or the caller of the current object. Essentially, the user's name can be retrieved to identify various situations.

In addition to the role-based programmatic security we've just discussed, MTS can also provide the Windows NT user account names for both the original and direct object's creator, and the object's caller. After all, the MTS executive must have this information to be able to find all the roles that the caller belongs to. The `SecurityProperty` class, returned from the `Security` property of the ObjectContext object, provides access to this information through the following four methods:

- ❑ `GetDirectCallerName`
- ❑ `GetDirectCreatorName`
- ❑ `GetOriginalCallerName`
- ❑ `GetOriginalCreatorName`

The GetDirectCallerName Method

This method will retrieve the Windows NT user account associated with the external process that is calling the current executing method:

```
Public Function GetCaller() As String

    Dim objContext As ObjectContext
    Set objContext = GetObjectContext

    GetCaller = objContext.Security.GetDirectCallerName

End Function
```

The GetDirectCreatorName Method

This method is similar to the method GetDirectCallerName, except that this method retrieves the user name associated with the external process responsible for directly creating the object:

```
Public Function GetCreator() As String

    Dim objContext As ObjectContext
    Set objContext = GetObjectContext

    GetCreator = objContext.Security.GetDirectCreatorName

End Function
```

The GetOriginalCallerName Method

The GetOriginalCallerName method returns the Windows NT user account for the first caller in the call stack:

```
Public Function GetOriginalCaller() As String

    Dim objContext As ObjectContext
    Set objContext = GetObjectContext

    GetOriginalCaller = objContext.Security.GetOriginalCallerName

End Function
```

The GetOriginalCreatorName Method

This method is similar to GetOriginalCallerName, except that it retrieves the associated user name of the indirect creator, or the creator of the object at the root of the call stack:

```
Public Function GetOriginalCreator() As String

    Dim objContext As ObjectContext
    Set objContext = GetObjectContext

    GetOriginalCreator = objContext.Security.GetOriginalCreatorName

End Function
```

The information returned from these methods can be used to implement a fine-grained security check without the depending on roles. It can also be used for auditing and logging purposes. User accounts returned from these functions are returned in the Domain\User format.

As with `IsCallerInRole`, whenever you use the methods of the `SecurityProperty` class, you should first verify that security is enabled using `IsSecurityEnabled`:

```
' Check if security is enabled using the Object Context
If GetObjectContext.IsSecurityEnabled = True Then

  'log the direct caller's name to the Windows NT Event Log

  App.LogEvent "DirectCallerName: " & _
             GetObjectContext.Security.GetDirectCallerName

End If
```

Remember, if `IsSecurityEnabled` returns `True`, it does not necessarily mean that authorization checking is enabled on the package or the component. It means that the component is executing in a secured process. To be specific, a return value of `True` simply means that the component resides in a Server package or a Library package that happens to be loaded in the same process as a Server package. If you happen to call any of the methods of the `SecurityProperty` class and security is not enabled, (`IsSecurityEnabled` returns `False`), MTS will raise an `mtsErrCtxNoSecurity` error.

Don't worry if you're confused about the difference between the direct and original caller and creator, we'll discuss them in more depth later in this chapter. For now, just remember that MTS provides an easy way to implement Windows NT user account-based programmatic security through the `SecurityProperty` component, as well as role-based programmatic security through the `IsCallerInRole` function.

Resource Security

Protecting MTS objects from being called by unauthorized users is only the first step in securing a distributed application. Most MTS objects access some type of resource, such as a database system, a file system, or other MTS objects. The next step involves authorizing these types of MTS objects to access resources on behalf of the client. We're not going to focus on implementing security with various resources in this section. Instead, we'll concentrate on understanding the flow of security from MTS objects to resources.

Each MTS Server package must be configured to perform all execution using a Windows NT user account or an **identity**. All of the MTS objects that execute within the same process share the same identity. This includes instances of components within the Server package, as well as instances of components in a Library package when the Library package is loaded in the same process as a Server package. When resources are accessed by MTS objects, the identity of the process hosting the objects is used to access resources, not the identity of the caller.

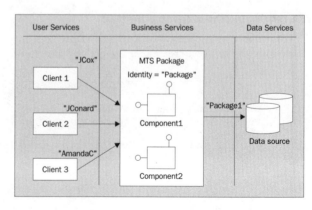

Basically, we're authenticating user requests at the component level (Application Security) and then using a shared user account (the package's identity) for all components in a server package to access resources (Resource Security). We're using either of the role-based security models provided by MTS (and DCOM and Windows NT) instead of various security models provided by the resource(s). This approach, using the package's security credentials to access resources, has several advantages:

❑ **Reduced Administration** – Instead of assigning and maintaining security permissions for each user or group account to access each resource, we only need to provide permissions for the identity of our Server package to access each resource. Once the initial permissions are established, performing security administration simply involves changing the mappings of user and group accounts to roles, or changing the role membership lists for components and/or interfaces. An administrator does not need to have a thorough understanding of each resource's security model, or a working knowledge of each resource's separate tool for managing security. Additionally, managing security at the application level is much more natural than managing security on tables, stored procedures, or views within a database. The reduced administration is especially evident if your MTS components access several resources or different types of resources.

❑ **Connection Pooling** – MTS can utilize pool managers called Resource Dispensers to pool connections to resources. Currently Microsoft provides Resource Dispensers to pool ODBC Connections and OLE DB Sessions (ADO connections). When a new connection is requested, an existing connection from the pool can only be used if they both share the same connection information (User ID, Password, etc.). If components use the security credentials of the caller when they try to connect to a resource, they will almost always receive a new connection instead of an existing one from the pool. This is because the connection information would most likely be different from any existing connections in the pool. Pooling of expensive connections to resources can dramatically improve the scalability and performance of a distributed application.

❑ **Anonymous Users** – Clients can effectively perform identity switching by routing their requests for resource(s) through components. The need for identity switching commonly occurs when requests come from ASP pages as the Anonymous User (IUSR_MACHINENAME user account). Resources can grant permissions to the user account used for a package's identity instead of granting permissions to the Anonymous User. A component can access the resources using the package's user account instead of the anonymous user's. Granted, you are opening up a security hole by allowing access to potentially unauthorized users. However, this approach is better than the alternative of providing permissions for the anonymous user to access the resource(s) directly. On the other hand, identity switching is usually much more of a danger than a benefit for the same reasons. You should consider the implications of identity switching when designing MTS components and implementing MTS security.

MTS Identity Settings

MTS provides two possible settings for the package identity:

❑ **Interactive User** – Interactive User is the default setting for the package identity. It causes the package to use the identity of the user that is currently logged-on. If no user is logged-on to the system when the client accesses a component in the server package, MTS will fail to create the server process. With different users logging-on to the system, your components will have different permissions. For these reasons, in a production environment, you should use a specific Windows NT user account for a package's identity by selecting the This User option. However, the Interactive User setting is helpful within a development or testing environment, because it will allow components to display windows and message boxes that the logged in user can respond to.

❑ **This User** – The This User setting for a package's identity allows you specify which user account MTS will assign as the identity for the package's server process. The user account must have the Log on as a Batch Job user right.

Setting Package Identity

You can specify the package identity from the Identity tab in your package's Properties window:

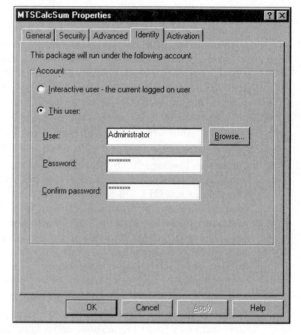

Any user account specified for a package's identity should have the following settings:

❑ User Cannot Change Password
❑ Password Never Expires
❑ Member of the Users group
❑ Log on as a Batch Job user right

It is recommended that a separate group is used for managing the Windows NT user accounts assigned to packages. Then, any resource permissions can be assigned to the group instead of individual user accounts, effectively granting permissions to all packages that use any of the accounts in the group as their package identity. Using a naming convention also makes it much easier to distinguish user accounts used for package identities from other Windows NT user accounts.

When the identity for a package is changed, MTS updates the RunAs registry value under a component's AppID key for each component in the package. This is actually the same registry value used by DCOM.

If you rename, delete or change the password of a user account that is used for the identity of a server package, you must manually update the package's identity to reflect the changes.

Direct and Original Caller

As we discussed earlier, MTS objects within the same process must trust one another, because MTS will not perform security checks between MTS objects in the same process. However, when a process boundary is crossed, MTS performs security checks against the identity of the calling process. This applies when a client application calls into an MTS server process, as well as when calls are made between MTS objects executing in separate server processes (Server packages). To understand how MTS performs security checking between MTS objects in separate processes, consider the following scenario.

A client application (`ClientApp.Exe`), executing under the JCox user account, invokes a method on a new instance of `Component1`. `Component1` belongs to an MTS server package named `MTS Server Package 1`. Since a process boundary was crossed when the method call was made, MTS performs the required security checks. The JCox user account is found in a required role, so access is granted to the caller and the method call is executed by the context wrapper.

To complete the requested work, `Component1` creates an instance of `Component2`, which resides in a separate server package named `MTS Server Package 2`. `Component1` then calls a method on this new object. Again a process boundary is crossed, and MTS must perform the required security checks. But instead of checking if the identity of the original caller (`ClientApp.Exe`) is in any of the required roles, MTS always checks if the identity of the direct caller (`MTS Server Package 1`) is in any of the required roles. The method call on the instance of `Component2` is executed because the identity for `Component1`'s server package, (`MTSPackage1`) belongs to the required `MTS Packages` role in `Component2`'s server package.

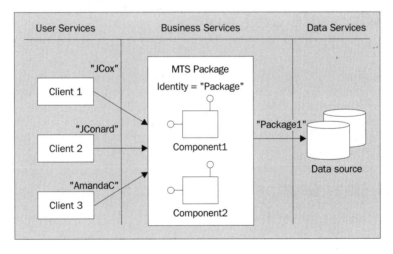

The direct caller and the original caller will be the same if the call stack is only one level deep. When a MTS component needs to make cross-process calls to another MTS component, you need to make sure that the calling process (package) is executing under an identity that has sufficient privileges to invoke methods on the second component. Both role-base programmatic security and declarative security implemented by MTS perform security checks only against the direct caller.

This point-to-point security model is not complicated. However, with it comes a responsibility to design your components carefully so that you don't accidentally open a security hole, allowing a user to access a resource indirectly through an MTS component.

Administration Security

The final step in establishing a secure, distributed application utilizing MTS, is defining which users or groups can view or modify the configuration of the MTS environment. The System package, a server package installed by MTS and used by MTS, defines two roles that are used for establishing MTS administration privileges:

❑ **Reader** – Users mapped to the Reader role can view everything about the MTS environment using MTS Explorer or the MTS Administration Library, but they cannot install, create, change, or delete any objects, shut down server processes, or export packages.

❑ **Administrator** – Users mapped to the Administrator role have full control of the MTS Environment and configuration.

By default, the System package does not have any users mapped to either role and security on the System package is disabled. As a result, any user can modify the configuration of the MTS environment. In a production environment, you should map valid Windows NT user accounts to the appropriate roles and enable security after MTS is installed.

> *Be careful when enabling security on the System package. If security is enabled and no users are assigned to the Administrator role, all users will be permanently locked out from using MTS Explorer or the MTS Administration Library.*

Creating Accounts and Roles

Now it's time to put what we've covered in this chapter into practice.

Because MTS security is built on the foundation of Windows NT security, the first step is to create NT user accounts (and groups) that can be assigned to MTS roles. The first exercise will show you how to create a user from the User Manager in Windows NT. In the second exercise, you will create a group account to manage several users. The third exercise is your chance to create a role for the package MTSCalcSum and then assign a user to it. After you have had practice creating roles and assigning users to them, you will learn about the System package and secure it.

Creating NT User Groups and Accounts

User groups are created to make administration easier.

> *This exercise is designed to show you how to create user groups and accounts so you can use them with MTS roles. Working with NT user and group security is a book of its own and is beyond the scope of this chapter.*

Select Programs | Administrative Tools | User Manager from the Windows Start menu. The User Manager displays two panes. The top pane represents NT user accounts, and the bottom represents group accounts. Notice that Username icons have the face of a person while Groups have multiple faces as an icon:

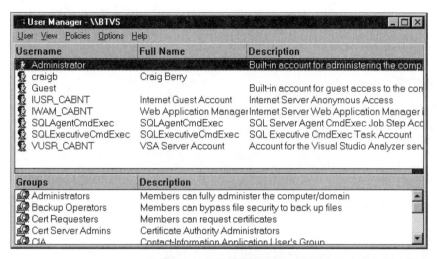

If you double-click a user account, the User Properties dialog appears. This allows you to easily manage the user's account. The user name cannot be changed here. However, you can rename the user and still keep all access privileges through the main menu in the User Manager. Additionally, renaming does not affect the SID for the current user:

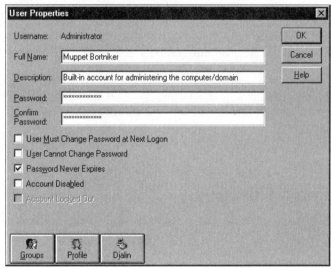

Notice the password is displayed with asterisk symbols. This feature keeps unauthorized people from being able to see the password – including the Administrator. When an Administrator receives a call from a user who forgot their password, all that can be done is to create a new one.

When a new user account is created, the checkbox User Must Change Password at Next Logon is enabled by default. Users will be prompted to change their password the first time they log in.

At the bottom there are three icons that allow you to set up other user properties including adding the user to groups.

Let's go ahead and create some users so we can later add them to MTS roles. From the User Manager menu, select User and then New User...

As you can see, the New User dialog is identical to the User Properties dialog. Type in Albert for the Username, Albert Einstein for the Full Name, and MTS User for the Description:

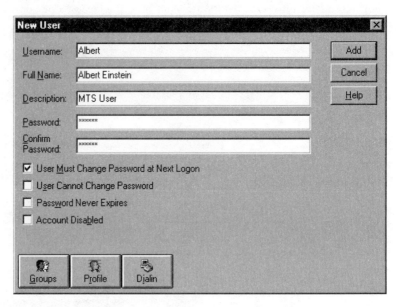

For test purposes only, type in albert (all in lower case) in the text box labeled Password, and Confirm Password. For security reasons, whenever you type in a password, it will show as asterisks. When creating an NT password, keep in mind that it is case sensitive.

The User Must Change Password at Next Logon is selected as a default. To make things easy for this exercise, disable it by deselecting the check box. Keep in mind that, under normal circumstances, leaving this default is considered a good security policy. It also makes the user feel better knowing that they have a choice in passwords.

Select OK. Now go back and create user accounts for Thomas Edison and Marie Curie.

Creating NT Groups

The next step is to create a user group, so we can easily manage multiple users in MTS roles.

From the User Manager, highlight the user Marie. Select User and then select New Local Group... from the main menu.

From the New Local Group dialog, type MTS Users in the text box labeled Group Name, and type General Users for the Description.

Because you highlighted Marie before creating the new group, Marie was added automatically:

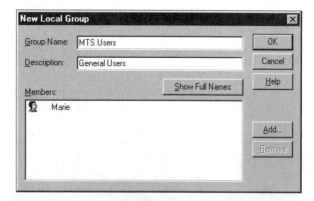

Before selecting OK, click the command button labeled Add... . Select the users Albert and Thomas from the Add Users and Groups dialog. Now you can click OK.

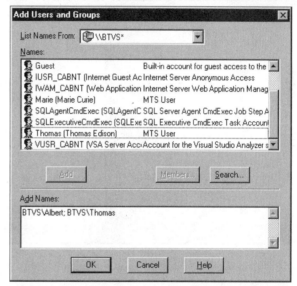

Locate the group MTS Users from the User Manager, and double-click its icon to see the users in this group:

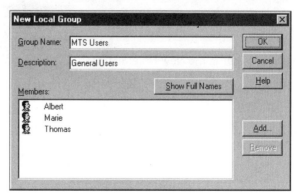

Creating MTS Roles

Now that you have created some user accounts and a group, let's create a role for the package MTSCalcSum that you created earlier.

From the Packages Installed folder in MTS Explorer, open the package MTSCalcSum and double-click the folder Roles. Because you have not defined any roles, this folder will be empty:

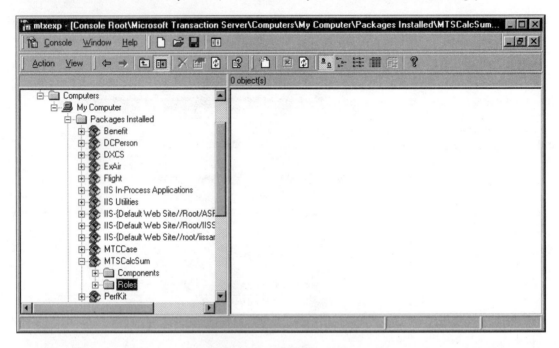

Select <u>N</u>ew from the <u>A</u>ction menu, and then select Role.

Type Administrator in the New Role dialog:

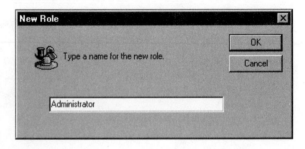

OK, you have just created an MTS role. Now go back and create another role called General. Be aware that before these roles can be of any use, you first must assign a user account or user group to it:

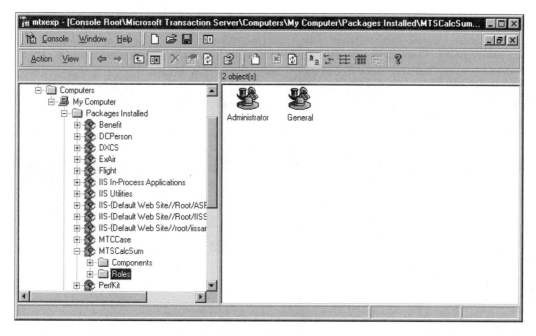

From the left pane, expand the role Administrator. Highlight the Users folder and click your right mouse button. Select New and then select User.

When the Add User and Groups to Role dialog first appears, it will only show Group accounts. Click the command button labeled Show Users. This will display all user accounts after displaying all available groups:

With users displayed, scroll down and locate and highlight the user Administrator. Click the command button Add. Next, scroll down through the users, locate your user account and highlight it. Again, click the Add. When you have added the appropriate names, select OK.

> *Administrator is being used for learning purposes only. In real situations, Administrator accounts should be disguised with a different name. Why? Because an account named Administrator (that has administrative privileges) is a weakness to your systems security. Anyone wanting to breach your system will first look for the Administrator account.*

You should have two icons: one representing the user account Administrator and another for your own user account. Note that there is little you can do with these icons other than right-click them and select Delete to remove them:

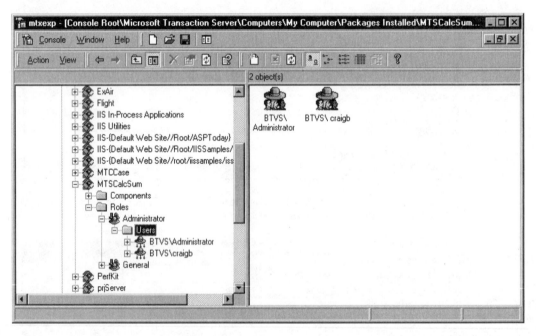

We'll now add several users to the General role, but instead of adding each user individually, we can make use of a group.

The beauty of using a group is the ease of administration. For example, you just added yourself to the Administrator role. If you were to leave the company, the new administrator would have to remove your user account from the User Manager as well as delete you from the Administrator role. Remember that this is only one package. What if you added yourself to every package? Suppose you have 100 or more packages? You'd have an administrative nightmare.

Using group accounts in roles, all the administrator has to do is remove a user from NT groups. Because the group is a representation (it has its own SID) of all the users in a group, you don't need to make any changes to the packages. In addition, if another user was added to a group account that is used in a role, the new user is automatically reflected.

Open the role you created called General and then highlight the Users folder. Right-click Users and select New and then User as you have done before. This time from the Add Users and Groups to Role dialog, add the group MTS Users.

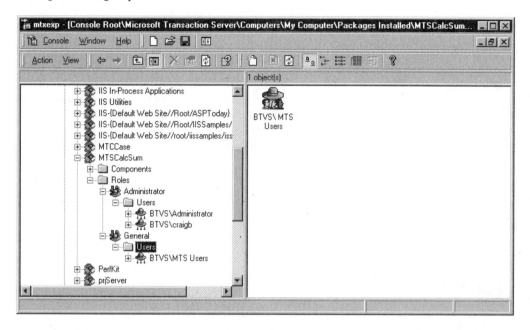

Let's go over what has just been done. First you created two roles on the package level. Bear in mind that roles set on the package level are carried out through all the components in the package. If this project involved more components and interfaces, you could have also created roles for a specific component and interface access. Recall our earlier example, where the chief accountant can access a view of all the salaries in the company and the general clerk could only view a partial salary list. This was solved through programmatic programming. However, the developer could have used a component with different interfaces: one designed to access full views and another to access only partial views. With this scenario, the MTS administrator would again assign either specific users and/or groups to the appropriate components and or interface.

After you created two roles, you added users and groups to them. If you think about what you've done with users and groups in this exercise, you may realize that the users represented in the Administrator role have the same privileges as the users represented in the General role. Obviously this is not good practice, however, MTSCalcSum is a very small and limited project where you either can have access and the project runs, or you are denied access where the project fails to run. Nevertheless, I hope you've achieved a good idea of how you should implement role security to your own MTS packages.

There is still one thing left for you to do before declarative security will work with your roles, user group, and user accounts. You still need to enable authorization checking for the package.

> *A challenge for you: continue to the next section, The System Package. In this exercise, you will learn to enable authorization checking using the System Package. It is crucial that you follow the instructions carefully because you can lock yourself out of MTS Explorer permanently! After you learn the required techniques, come back and enable authorization checking for* MTSCalcSum *by yourself.*

The System Package

If you open the folder `Packages Installed` through MTS, you will find a package labeled System. The System package is a special in that it is designed to control administrative access to the MTS Explorer. It is actually a part of the MTS Explorer and it cannot be deleted.

By default, the System package grants read privileges to any user who has access to the machine where MTS is located. This is because the Reader role contains the group called `Everyone`, and it means that anyone who can log in to the machine can learn the contents of the packages installed. More troubling, anyone who may have been added to the Administrator role has full access to your packages and components. You should therefore be careful about arbitrarily adding users to the Administrator role. Any person who can gain access to your MTS server with Administrator privileges can create havoc with your packages and components. You can even be locked out of your own MTS Explorer!

But there is hope. You can configure your roles to allow only your trusted users to administer packages and components, and keep casual users from looking in and learning about the makeup of your system. Let's go though the process.

> **Caution. Pay close attention to the following steps. If done incorrectly, you can lock yourself out of MTS Explorer. If this occurs, the only fix is to uninstall MTS and then reinstall without saving any previous configurations!**

Start the MTS Explorer and open the System package. Next, open the Roles folder. You should see two roles: Administrator and Reader. The Administrator role grants full access while the Reader role only provides read access:

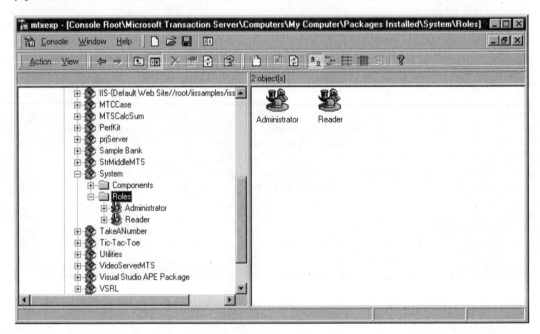

From the left-pane, expand the Administrator role and highlight the User folder. Right-click your mouse button, and select <u>N</u>ew and then User from the pop-up menu. This will bring you to the Add Users and Groups to Role dialog. Add the Administrator user account (not the group Administrators) and then add your own user account:

You now should have two user accounts: one for Administrator and the other your own personal user account:

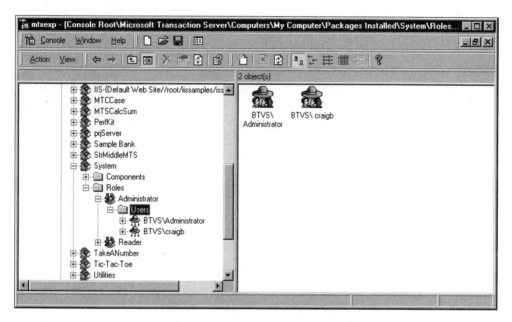

Look carefully at the screen shot below. If the User icon says Administrator you are all set. However, if you accidentally selected the group, it will be labeled as Administrators (note the s).

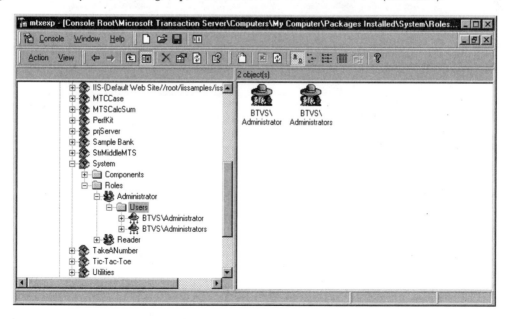

In the right-pane, the icon on the left (labeled **Administrator**) is the user account.

Now that you have double-checked everything let's enable declarative security by opening the System Properties dialog.

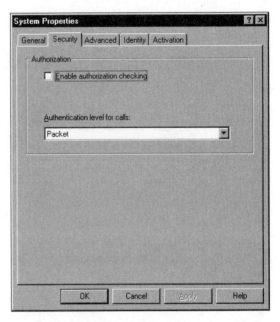

Highlight the **System** package and right-click your mouse. From the pop-up menu, select **Properties**. When the properties dialog appears for the **System** package, select the **Security** tab:

Upon selecting **Enable authorization checking**, a warning message box pops up. This is your last chance to be sure that you have the system role correctly configured without the potential of being permanently locked out of MTS Explorer. When you are ready, select **Yes**.

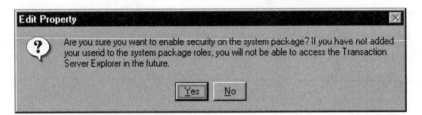

Close your applications and restart your system. Log back into the system using `Albert`. (Don't forget `Albert`'s password is `albert`, all in lower case letters.)

> Note, passwords are case sensitive, user names are not.

Now try opening the MTS Explorer. You should receive an error message stating that you do not have permission to perform the requested action. You have verified that MTS declarative security is working.

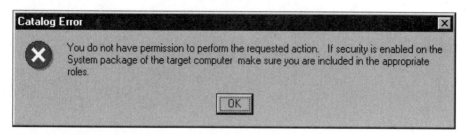

Close your applications and log back into the system as yourself or Administrator. Try accessing the MTS Explorer. If you followed all the steps correctly, you will have no problem getting back into MTS Explorer.

Now that you have successfully secured MTS Explorer, go back and enable declarative security for the package MTSCalcSum.

Package Identity

Before ending this chapter, I want to discuss package identity. In a way, you are already familiar with package identity. Earlier you learned that in the MTS security model, user IDs are hidden from server resources through roles. Roles are based at the package level. The package identity simply allows you set a user identity for all the components in a package. The default value is set to Interactive User, which means that any user who is logged on to the Windows NT server account can access it. However there are many instances where using a Windows NT user account is advantageous as opposed to using Interactive User.

Suppose you have a package that is responsible for updating employee salaries in a SQL Server database. Instead of having to create an account at the database for every user that accesses employee salaries, you can configure database access for one single user account and then set the package identity for the user account. The benefits of scalability and ease of administration should be apparent.

From the MTS Explorer, highlight the package you want to assign a user identity and right-click your mouse. Select Properties from the pop-up menu. Then select This user from the Identity tab, and enter the domain name\user name. You can also select Browse to locate the user account:

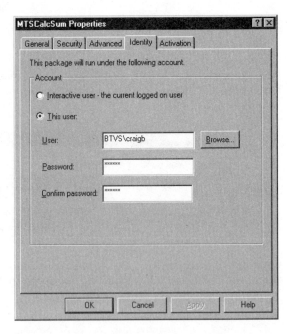

You must provide the current password for the selected user account. MTS will validate it when you enter it. However, there is one possible problem and you need to be aware of its consequences. If you change the password for the account, you must also update it though MTS Explorer. Failure to do so will result in the package not being able to run. To complicate matters, if you do not update the password but change the user account instead, MTS will not validate the password for the new user you just entered. Now you have an invalid password and MTS accepts it. However, when you try to access your packages, you will receive a run-time error.

Securing Our PasswordPersist Components

In the last chapter, we installed our components for PasswordPersist in MTS and created a VB client to test these components. Now we'll look at security and see who should and should not have access to the components.

Obviously, we need the IIS default user to have access to the system, since we know that the main client will be the Internet client we'll develop later on in the book. But what about any other user? Remember, this is an Internet site, so it has to be running on a server somewhere by some kind of organization or company. It's doubtful that we would want just anybody in the company to use the components – we would probably want only a selection of personnel to have access to the system. Therefore, we'll add a role that has the IIS default user as the only member of the role, and then we'll add some programmatic security to our components.

After this role is in place, we'll run our VB client, and see that we won't have access to our system anymore. We'll add our account to the role and verify that our VB client now has access to the component.

Adding A New Role

Let's add a role to our component package called PPAllowedUser. Follow the steps we went through earlier in the chapter to add this role to the PasswordPersist package:

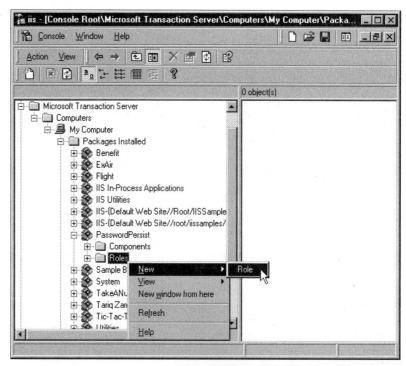

Once the role has been created, we need to configure the components to use the role for declarative security. To do this, double-click the first component of the PasswordPersist package to reveal two sub-folders. Highlight the Role Membership folder then right-click with the mouse and select New | Role. This brings up the Select Roles dialog which allows you to add the roles you have defined in the Roles folder for the package to this particular component. You should see the PPAllowedUsers role we just created:

Select the PPAllowedUsers role and press OK. You should now see the role has been added to the component:

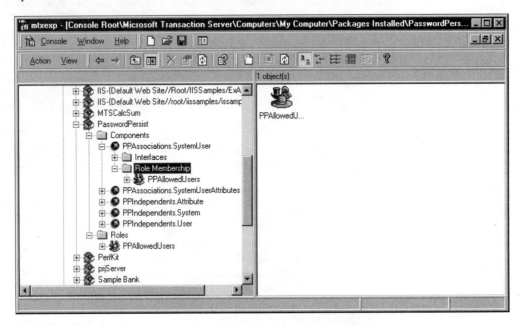

Repeat this for all the components in the PasswordPersist package.

Before we can use the role we need to add the valid users for our components. To do this, right-click on the Users folder under the PPAllowedUser role, and select New User. Click the Show Users button on the following screen and select the default IIS user:

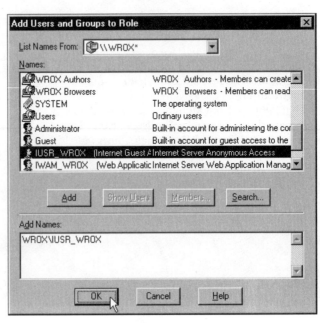

Press OK when you're done.

Adding Programmatic Security

Now let's add the programmatic security to our components. The first thing we need to do is add some constants to our module files (called `PPILib` in PPIndependents, and `PPALib` in PPAssociations):

```
Public Const NOT_AUTHORIZED As Long = vbObjectError + 1000
Public Const SECURITY_NOT_ENABLED As Long = vbObjectError + 1001
Public Const NOT_AUTHORIZED_DESC As String = _
                "You are not authorized to use this system."
Public Const SECURITY_NOT_ENABLED_DESC As String = _
                "This component is not secure."
```

We'll see how they are used in a moment. Now let's take a look at the `GetByID` function in the `User` class – I'll emphasize where the changes have occurred:

```
Public Function GetByID(ByVal UserID As Variant, _
                    ByRef UserName As Variant, _
                    ByRef Password As Variant, ByRef EMail As Variant)
                    As Variant

  On Error GoTo Error_GetByID

  Dim objConn As ADODB.Connection
  Dim objRS As ADODB.Recordset
  Dim strSQL As String

  GetByID = False

  If mobjContext.IsSecurityEnabled = True Then

    If mobjContext.IsCallerInRole("PPAllowedUser") = True Then

      Set objConn = CreateObject("ADODB.Connection")
      Set objRS = CreateObject("ADODB")

      objConn.Open DB_CONN

      strSQL = "SELECT UserName, UserPassword, UserEMail " & _
               "FROM PPUser " & _
               "WHERE UserID = " & CStr(UserID)

      objRS.Open strSQL, objConn, adOpenStatic

      If Not objRS Is Nothing Then

        If objRS.EOF = False Then
          UserName = Trim$("" & objRS("UserName"))
          Password = Trim$("" & objRS("UserPassword"))
          EMail = Trim$("" & objRS("UserEMail"))
          GetByID = True
        End If

        objRS.Close
        Set objRS = Nothing
      End If

      objConn.Close
      Set objConn = Nothing
```

```
    Else
          Err.Raise NOT_AUTHORIZED, "User_GetByID", NOT_AUTHORIZED_DESC
      End If

    Else
      Err.Raise SECURITY_NOT_ENABLED, "User_GetByID", _
              SECURITY_NOT_ENABLED_DESC
    End If

    mobjContext.SetComplete

    Exit Function

Error_GetByID:

    GetByID = False

    If Not objRS Is Nothing Then
      Set objRS = Nothing
    End If

    If Not objConn Is Nothing Then
      Set objConn = Nothing
    End If

    mobjContext.SetAbort
    Err.Raise Err.Number, Err.Source, Err.Description

    End Function
```

The first thing we add is a check to make sure we're running under MTS through a call to
IsSecurityEnabled. If for some reason the components are out of MTS's environment, we throw
an error using our SECURITY_NOT_ENABLED constant along with the
SECURITY_NOT_ENABLED_DESC error description.

If we are running in MTS, we then check to make sure that the caller is in the PPAllowedUser role
via a call to IsCallerInRole. If the client isn't in the role, we raise an error using the
NOT_AUTHORIZED error code and the NOT_AUTHORIZED error description.

The last piece of code we added is in the error handling – we raise any error that we got back to the
client. As we'll see in a moment, the VB client is going to get an interesting surprise. Make the above
changes to all the main returns for both PPIndependant and PPAssociations.

Running the VB Client

Since we haven't added ourselves to the PPAllowedUser role, let's run the VB client and see what
happens. When we try to log in with a U/P and press the **Log In** button, the following message box
appears:

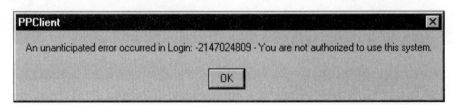

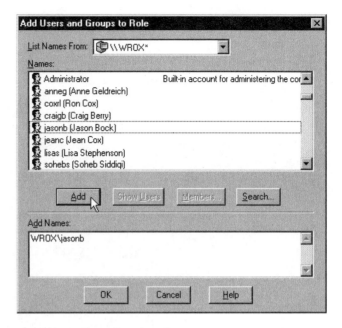

To eliminate this lock-out, go back to the role definition in MTS and add yourself to the list.

Now when you press the Log In button, everything should work as before.

Summary

This chapter demonstrates why security is important to any computer and network, and introduced fundamental concepts that will allow you to implement security for your own system. In particular, you took a tour of three security models – Windows NT, COM, and MTS – and you have seen how these models build upon one another.

You learned:

- ❑ The differences between declarative security and programmatic security. How programmatic security can be used for fine tuning MTS security, and how declarative security and programmatic security can be used together.
- ❑ How to use `IObjectContext` methods `IsSecurityEnabled` and `IsCallerInRole` when implementing programmatic security, and how to audit user names with the `SecurityProperty` object.
- ❑ How to create Windows NT user accounts and group accounts.
- ❑ How to create roles and add users to access MTS packages.
- ❑ How to secure MTS Explorer itself, and add users to the Administrators role.

Now that you can create and secure your own MTS applications, it's time to fine-tune your system to enhance their performance. In Chapter 10, Administration, we'll do just that. But first, we'll take a look at what to do when things go wrong...

Debugging MTS Components

Unfortunately errors do and will happen. Although the best way to avoid the need for debugging is to write perfect components, this is never going to happen. We therefore need to be familiar with the range of tools on offer to us, so that we can quickly and easily work out what the problem is.

Unfortunately for us, debugging errors in an MTS component has never been particularily easy. In fact, before the release of Visual Studio and Service Pack 4, it was positively infuriating at best. Now, however, the situation has improved somewhat. We can use the Visual Basic debug environment, but it still has limitations. In this chapter, you're going to learn how to go about tracking down those elusive problems in your MTS components.

After reading this chapter you should know:

- ❑ How to handle errors properly in your MTS components
- ❑ How to debug MTS components with Visual Basic 6
- ❑ How to track what's going on in a compiled DLL
- ❑ How to debug a DLL with the VC++ debugger

MTS and Errors

Although MTS maintains internal consistency and integrity checking to ensure all components are working properly, MTS components can still fail. MTS objects cannot generate exceptions outside the object. So, when a component fails, any unhandled errors will result in the termination of the current process, without raising an error to the calling client. This immediate termination of the process due to a failing MTS component should be regarded as an undesirable safety feature.

Why is this a safety feature? Because terminating the process reduces the chance that an error may go undetected. Undetected errors can lead to corrupt data and even system failures.

And why is it undesirable? Regardless of this safety feature, it's preferable that you design your MTS components to handle errors gracefully. By this, I mean that MTS components should be designed to trap errors in order to call `ObjectContext.SetAbort`, as opposed to having MTS terminate the process for you. By calling the method `SetAbort`, transactional work that may have already been completed can be rolled back.

Error Handling

Handling errors can be difficult in any application. However, proper error handling is critical when it comes to MTS components. Debugging MTS components can be difficult, but the best way to eliminate debugging problems is to create quality error handlers.

Putting an error handler at the beginning of each and every function and then making sure that the last item of your error handler makes a call to `ObjectContext.SetAbort` is the most commendable practice any developer can follow:

```
Public Function Example()

   On Error GoTo OopsErrorEncountered

   'Declarations
   'Work is done here

   mobjContext.SetComplete 'If all goes well
   Exit Function

OopsErrorEncountered:   'If things go astray

   mobjContext.SetAbort   'Roll back MTS Transaction
   Err.Raise Err.Number, Err.Source, Err.Description

End Function
```

Debugging MTS Components

Prior to Visual Basic 6.0, debugging MTS components written in Visual Basic was a challenging task. Did I say challenging? Perhaps arduous is a better word. The problem with earlier versions of Visual Basic was that you could not run code outside of MTS and still have it return valid information from the Object Context. As a result, any calls to Object Context methods, such as `SetComplete` or `SetAbort`, would result in a run time error

There are still some limitations with Visual Basic's debugger. For example, you can only debug a single client component with a single MTS component. In other words, you can't debug problems that involve multiple components using the Visual Basic 6.0 debugger. Furthermore, MTS components that are being debugged in the Visual Basic IDE run as a library package. As a result, you can't debug MTS component security or multi-threading problems. With these limitations, it may be necessary for the MTS developer to look elsewhere for help. If the programmer is fortunate enough to have a copy of VC++ or Visual Studio, they can compile and execute MTS components using the Visual C++ IDE. Additionally, the Visual C++ IDE will allow you set break points as well as step through Visual Basic code

Debugging MTS components with Visual Basic 6 is not supported under Windows 9x.

As a word of advice, always start with Visual Basic's debugger for VB MTS components. Use Visual C++ as a second choice, and only if you can't solve the problem using VB's debugger.

Debugging with Visual Basic 6

Although debugging MTS components with Visual Basic has its limits, it's still the best place to start. Two new features are available in Visual Basic 6 that greatly enhance MTS component debugging by producing a simulated MTS run time environment. One major enhancement that was not available in previous versions of Visual Basic is the ability debug your MTS components while a component runs in MTS.

The second debugging enhancement in Visual Basic 6 is the ability to debug MTS components without having to install components through the MTS Explorer. No doubt, this is a quick and easy way to debug MTS components. Again, you'll still have limitations with the MTS run-time environment in particular, when working with component security.

Preparing to Debug MTS Components

Before debugging your MTS components in Visual Basic's IDE, you need to be aware of a few requirements:

- ❑ In order to acquire enhanced debugging features for Visual Basic 6.0, you must run Visual Basic's IDE under Windows NT 4.0 with Service Pack 4 (or later). Service Pack 4 is our hero, as it upgrades MTS 2.0 to Service Pack 1. This service pack for MTS is responsible for VB6's enhanced MTS debugging features.
- ❑ You must make sure the MTS component's MTSTransactionMode property is set to a value *other than* 0 - NotAnMTSObject.
- ❑ The MTS component you wish to debug needs to be compiled as a DLL.
- ❑ Make sure that the component version compatibility is set to Binary Compatibility. Be aware that when you compile your component, Visual Basic will set the version compatibility to Project Compatibility by default.
- ❑ Visual Basic does not register changes for components installed in MTS Explorer. If you change the configuration of a component that's registered through the MTS Explorer, you'll need to refresh the registry through the MTS Explorer or remove the component and then re-install it.

Building the Test Project

For our example, we're going to make a request for an ADO recordset from an MTS component. As we want our MTS component to be stateless, we'll make this a disconnected recordset.

The ADO disconnected recordset is the perfect mechanism to allow us to show that things don't always work in the debugger as they do when the application is compiled. Also, one of the most common functions of an MTS component is to get and update data for the client component. It's very important that you have an understanding of the ADO, and how it works with MTS. Thus, using ADO in our example will both illustrate our point and give you some valuable code that you can use in your projects. You'll only need a basic understanding of the ADO to understand these examples.

The Server Component

Begin by creating a new ActiveX DLL project. Name the project `prjMTSTest`. You should have one class; name it `clsMTSTest`. In the **Properties** window of the class, set the **MTSTransactionMode** property to **3 - UsesTransaction**. Open the **References** dialog and add references for the Microsoft Transaction Server Type Library and the Microsoft ActiveX Data Objects 2.x Library. We are now ready to start adding code.

We want to see how the Context object looks under the debug environment, so we'll want a reference to the Object Context. To do this, we'll declare a Context object variable and implement the Object Control interface.

We'll also need to get an ADO Connection object, so we'll need a `Private` variable for that. Finally, we'll set up a constant to point to a database. Putting this together will give us the following declarations in our `clsMTSTest` class:

```
Option Explicit

Implements ObjectControl

Private mobjADOConnection As ADODB.Connection
Private mobjContext As ObjectContext

Private Const mcstrDatabasePath As String = "C:\Program Files\Microsoft " & _
                                    "Visual Studio\VB98\NWind.mdb"
```

Change the constant to point at the location for your NorthWind database.

Implement the Object Control interface as follows:

```
Private Sub ObjectControl_Activate()

    Set mobjContext = GetObjectContext

End Sub
```

You may be wondering why we're initialising the Context object variable but not the ADO Connection variable. The Object Context will be around from the moment we create the MTS component: we're only getting a reference to it with our `mobjContext` variable. Our ADO Connection object, though, doesn't exist until we initialize it. If we initialize it as soon as the component is created, it may be some time before that Connection object is actually used. The number of connections that can be made to the database is limited, so Connection objects are a valuable resource that you want to quickly use and then get rid of. Therefore, we don't want to initialise our ADO Connection object until we're ready to use it.

```
Private Function ObjectControl_CanBePooled() As Boolean

    ObjectControl_CanBePooled = False

End Function
```

Finally, we want to do the deactivation. We should destroy our ADO connection as soon as we're done using it, but just in case we forget, we include a line of code to set the ADO connection to `Nothing`. If it's already nothing, this won't hurt anything. It's better to be cautious than take a chance that something is overlooked:

```
Private Sub ObjectControl_Deactivate()

    Set mobjADOConnection = Nothing
    Set mobjContext = Nothing

End Sub
```

We'll want to see how MTS works with and without a Context object. When there is a Context object, we want to use the `CreateInstance` method of the Context object to create our objects. MTS will then create the new object within the Context object our component is running under. This is the way MTS is supposed to work. If we have a Context object, and we use the `New` keyword, the object may not be created under the Context object our component is running under. This could create many problems.

If for some reason something has gone wrong and we don't have a Context object, we would like our component to still function, so we can see how an MTS component works without a Context object. Thus, we want the ability to create objects with the `New` keyword when there's no Context object. To do this, we'll create a function called `CreateInstance` that will allow us to create objects under MTS. This function will use the `CreateInstance` method when we have a Context object, and the `New` keyword when we don't. We will need to pass in a ID for the component we want to build. The ID for a recordset is `ADODB.Recordset`, and for a Connection object it is `ADODB.Connection`. These will be the only two objects we'll be creating in our MTS component. Add the following code to your project:

```
Private Function CreateInstance(ProgID As String) As Object

  On Error GoTo CreateInstanceError

  If Not mobjContext Is Nothing Then
    Set CreateInstance = mobjContext.CreateInstance(ProgID)
  Else

    Select Case ProgID

      Case "ADODB.Connection"
          Set CreateInstance = New ADODB.Connection

      Case "ADODB.Recordset"
          Set CreateInstance = New ADODB.Recordset

    End Select

  End If

  Exit Function

CreateInstanceError:

  Err.Raise Err.Number, Err.Source & " CreateInstance", Err.Description

End Function
```

We now want to add three functions: one to open an ADO connection, one to close an ADO connection and finally one to get a reference to the ADO connection. Let's begin with the function to get an ADO function, which I'll call SetADOConnection. We'll need parameters for the userID and the password, as we need to make a connection to the database. We will also make an optional parameter for the connection string in case we want to use something other than the default:

```
Private Sub SetADOConnection(ByVal v_strUserID As String, _
                             ByVal v_strPassword As String, _
                             Optional ByVal v_strConnectionString As String _
                             = "Empty")
```

The IsMissing function, which is used to tell if an Optional parameter is passed in, only works with variants. As we have made our v_strConnectionString a string, IsMissing will not work. Therefore, we've set a default value of Empty for v_strConnectionString so we can know when a value has actuallybeen passed in. We will begin by putting in our error handler:

```
On Error GoTo SetADOConnectionError
```

Next, we want to use our CreateInstance function to create our ADO connection:

```
Set mobjADOConnection = CreateInstance("ADODB.Connection")
```

Then we want to set the properties of our Connection object:

```
With mobjADOConnection
    .CursorLocation = adUseServer
    If v_strConnectionString = "Empty" Then
        .ConnectionString = "Provider=Microsoft.Jet.OLEDB.4.0;" & _
                            "Persist Security Info=False;" & _
                            "Data Source=" & mcstrDataBasePath

    Else
        .ConnectionString = v_strConnectionString
    End If
```

Finally, we will open the ADO connection:

```
    .Open
End With

Exit Sub
```

ADO has its own collection of errors, so we'll loop through this to get any errors in this collection:

```
SetADOConnectionError:

Dim lngErrorCounter As Long
Dim strErrors As String

strErrors = Err.Number & ": " & Err.Description

If mobjADOConnection.Errors.Count > 0 Then
```

```
        For lngErrorCounter = 0 To mobjADOConnection.Errors.Count - 1
            strErrors = strErrors & _
            mobjADOConnection.Errors(lngErrorCounter).Number & _
            ": " & mobjADOConnection.Errors(lngErrorCounter).Description & _
            vbCrLf
        Next lngErrorCounter

    End If

    Err.Raise Err.Number, "SetADOConnection", strErrors

End Sub
```

Now, we'll create a function to get the ADO connection. First, we'll make sure the function has been set before we actually return a connection:

```
Private Function GetADOConnection() As ADODB.Connection

    If mobjADOConnection Is Nothing Then
        Err.Raise 2001, "GetADOConnection", _
            "Trying to Get Connection prior to setting it"
    Else
        Set GetADOConnection = mobjADOConnection

    End If

End Function
```

Finally, we'll make a function that allows us to close the connection. As an error would be raised if the connection is already closed for whatever reason, we'll check to see if the connection is open before closing it:

```
Private Sub CloseADOConnection()

    With GetADOConnection
        If .State = adStateOpen Then
            .Close
        End If

    End With
End Sub
```

Now that we have everything set up to get a connection, we can retrieve a disconnected recordset. Let's create a function called `GetRecordset`, which will return a customer recordset from the `Northwind` Access database:

```
Public Function GetRecordset() As ADODB.Recordset
```

We'll need a String variable to store the connection string, and a recordset variable to build the disconnected recordset:

```
    Dim strADOConnection As String
    Dim recCustomers As ADODB.Recordset
```

Now we'll set the connection string:

```
On Error GoTo GetRecordsetError

strADOConnection = "Provider=Microsoft.Jet.OLEDB.4.0;" & _
                   "Data Source=C:\Program Files\Microsoft Visual " & _
                   "Studio\VB98\Nwind.mdb;Persist Security Info=False"
```

Again change this to point to your local copy of the database.

Next, we'll set the ADO connection, and set all of the properties of the recordset:

```
SetADOConnection "", "", strADOConnection
Set recCustomers = New ADODB.Recordset
recCustomers.CursorLocation = adUseClient
recCustomers.CursorType = adOpenStatic
recCustomers.LockType = adLockPessimistic
recCustomers.Source = "Customers"
Set recCustomers.ActiveConnection = GetADOConnection
```

We'll open the recordset, and disconnect it by setting the active connection to `Nothing`:

```
recCustomers.Open
Set recCustomers.ActiveConnection = Nothing
```

Finally, we'll return the recordset and create an error handler:

```
Set GetRecordset = recCustomers

CloseADOConnection
Exit Function

GetRecordsetError:

CloseADOConnection
Err.Raise Err.Number, Err.Source & " GetRecordset", Err.Description

End Function
```

The final part of our component will be a sub that changes the value of one of the fields of the recordset:

```
Public Sub ChangeRecordset(ByVal v_recCustomer As ADODB.Recordset)

v_recCustomer.Fields("ContactTitle") = "NewValue"

End Sub
```

We've passed the parameter `v_recCustomer` by value, as we want to test if the recordset is really going to be passed in by value or by reference.

> If a variable is passed by reference, any changes to the parameter
> `v_recCustomer` will also change the variable passed in on the client. If we
> pass it in by value, any changes made on the client will not affect the values
> of the recordset on the client.

This completes our middle tier
component. Make a copy of
`prjMTSTest.dll` and then set
the **Binary Compatiability** of the
project to the newly created
DLL:

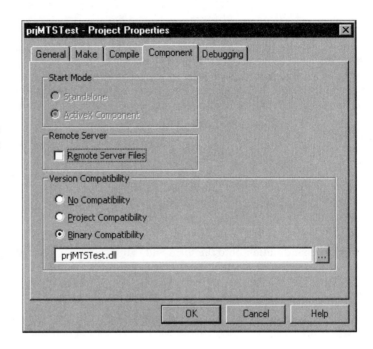

Finally, save the project.

The Client Component

Now we need to build a client component that will test this server component. Add a Standard EXE
project. Call this new project `prjClientTest`, and the form `frmClientTest`. Your Project
Explorer should look as follows:

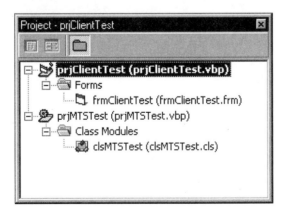

Set prjClientTest to be the start up project and make sure you also reference the ADO Library in the client project.

Open up the code window for frmClientTest and put this in the declarations:

```
Option Explicit

Private WithEvents mrecCustomer As ADODB.Recordset
```

We have created a recordset WithEvents so we can use the events associated with the recordset. The event we are interested in is the WillChangeField event. If we pass this recordset in by value, and the component changes a field on the recordset, the WillChangeField event should not be raised to the client. If the recordset is passed in by reference, and we try to change the recordset in the component, the WillChangeField event should not be raised:

```
Private Sub mrecCustomer_WillChangeField(ByVal cFields As Long, _
                            ByVal Fields As Variant, _
                            adStatus As ADODB.EventStatusEnum, _
                            ByVal pRecordset As ADODB.Recordset)

    Beep

End Sub
```

Add a command button onto the form and call it cmdTest. Add the following code to the Click event of the button:

```
Private Sub cmdTest_Click()

    Dim objTest As prjMTSTest.clsMTSTest
    Dim strReturnValue As String

    Set objTest = New prjMTSTest.clsMTSTest
    Set mrecCustomer = New ADODB.Recordset

    mrecCustomer.CursorLocation = adUseClient
    mrecCustomer.CursorType = adOpenStatic

    Set mrecCustomer = objTest.GetRecordset
    objTest.ChangeRecordset mrecCustomer

    Set objTest = Nothing
    MsgBox "Finished!"

End Sub
```

Place a breakpoint in the `cmdTest_Click` event:

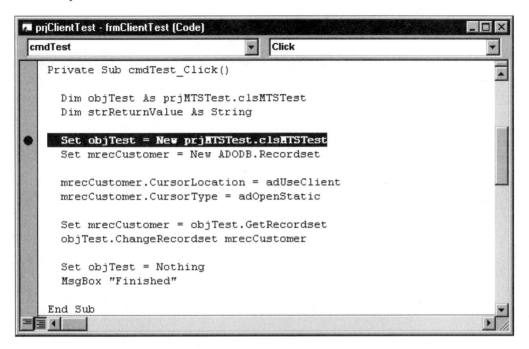

```
prjClientTest - frmClientTest (Code)

cmdTest                                    Click

    Private Sub cmdTest_Click()

        Dim objTest As prjMTSTest.clsMTSTest
        Dim strReturnValue As String

        Set objTest = New prjMTSTest.clsMTSTest
        Set mrecCustomer = New ADODB.Recordset

        mrecCustomer.CursorLocation = adUseClient
        mrecCustomer.CursorType = adOpenStatic

        Set mrecCustomer = objTest.GetRecordset
        objTest.ChangeRecordset mrecCustomer

        Set objTest = Nothing
        MsgBox "Finished"

    End Sub
```

The Visual Basic Debugger

Run the project. You should get the following warning:

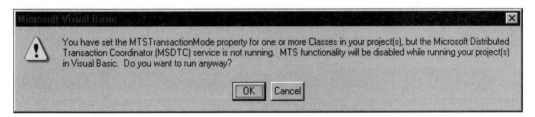

Microsoft Visual Basic

⚠ You have set the MTSTransactionMode property for one or more Classes in your project(s), but the Microsoft Distributed Transaction Coordinator (MSDTC) service is not running. MTS functionality will be disabled while running your project(s) in Visual Basic. Do you want to run anyway?

[OK] [Cancel]

Select **OK** (we're not going to be using MS DTC) and then press the **Test** button. When you get to the break point, step through the code using *F8*. Even though we didn't set up the package in MTS, this project runs. You should notice a few very strange things happen. To begin with, you should not have entered into any of the Object Control events. You won't enter the server component until you reach the `Set mrecCustomer = objTest.GetRecordset` line of code.

Step through the code until you get to the `SetADOConnection` function. Put the cursor over the `mobjContext` variable in the `If Not mobjContext Is Nothing Then` line of code. You should see the following:

This is why we didn't get the Object Control events, there's no Context object. We've now found out something interesting about the Visual Basic debugger: if you don't register the component in MTS, you don't have a reference to the Context object.

Keep stepping through the code until you reach the point where the client calls the `ChangeRecordset` routine of the component. In theory, when we call the `ChangeRecordset` routine and it changes the value of the field, the `WillChangeField` event of the recordset on the client should not be raised. Step through the code and you'll discover that the `WillChangeField` event is raised. This means that the parameter has not been passed by value, but actually by reference.

The reason this happens is not important: it has to do with the properties of the ADO recordset. What is important to realize is that very strange things happen in the debug environment which will probably not happen with the final, compiled DLL. In this case, a by value parameter became by reference and we didn't get a Context object for our MTS component. If you were not careful, you may think the problem is with your code, and not with the debugger. This in turn could result in hours of wasted testing and rewriting of your code.

This teaches us that we need to rely on several methods of debugging to test our MTS components. The Visual Basic IDE is great for finding errors caused by typos or improper logic (setting the wrong path to the database, not initialising an object, etc.). Yet, it's not our definitive test. Things may behave very differently in the compiled component compared to the Visual Basic IDE.

VB Debugging While Running a Component in MTS

You can debug your MTS component while it is installed in MTS Explorer. This can help speed things up by not having to first delete the component from the MTS Explorer, debug it and then re-install it back into its MTS package. However, you need to understand that if you make changes while your component is in Visual Basic's IDE, it's possible to get mismatches between the MTS configuration and the configuration currently in Visual Basic. This is because Visual Basic does not register changes for components installed in MTS Explorer.

Let's move our `prjMTSTest` project into a package and see how the debugger works under MTS.

Create a new empty package called DebugTest and install our component into it:

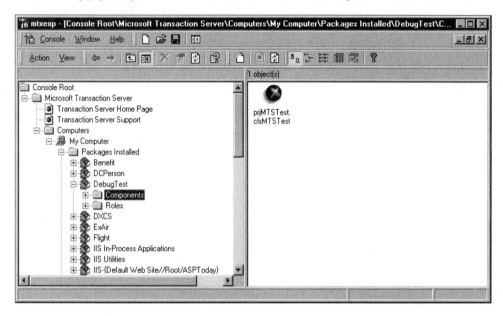

Now run your project again. You'll notice that nothing has changed: we're still referencing the ADO recordset by reference and we're still not getting a Context object. What is wrong here?

The answer to this question is simple: we're running the client and server components together. When we do this, we will never get a Context object, nor will our by value ADO objects be by value. To fix this problem, all you have to do is run the two projects in **separate** instances of Visual Basic.

Remove the client project from the group and run just the `prjMTSTest` component project. Open another instance of the Visual Basic IDE, open the `prjClientTest` project, and put the break point in the `cmdTest Click` event again. Run the client, click the command button and step through the code. This time you'll find that your ADO recordset is actually passed in by value (the `WillChangeField` event on the client will not be raised when you change the field). You may not actually enter the Object Control events, but when you go into the `CreateInstance` function, you can check and see that `mobjContext` is no longer `Nothing`.

You can play around with the code here. You'll notice one very interesting thing. Now that the parameter is behaving properly (i.e. it's now by value), Visual Basic still allows you to change the values of the parameter in the sub. These changes, though, are not passed back to the client.

By the way, if you are wondering why we are so concerned with using by reference parameters versus using by value parameters, remember that the communication between the client and server is over the network. This means that every change you make to a by reference parameter on the server needs to be passed back to the client. This is not very efficient and limits the scalability of your MTS component.

VB Debugging MTS Components without Registering in MTS Explorer

A nice feature that Visual Basic 6.0 provides is the ability to debug MTS components without having to register then with MTS Explorer. In other words, your component does not need to be installed into the MTS Explorer. This can be a real time saver when you're first developing your MTS components. Additionally, you don't have to worry about mismatched configurations that often occur between the MTS Explorer and the current configuration in Visual Basic's IDE.

Be sure that your MTS ActiveX DLLs are not registered with the MTS Explorer. If they are, go into the MTS Explorer and delete them from the package.

Open Visual Basic and load your MTS project. Check that Binary Compatibility has been selected from the Component tab in the Project Properties dialog.

From Visual Basic's design environment, go to the Properties window. You'll need to set the MTSTransactionMode property for each class in your ActiveX DLL to any setting except NotAnMTSObject.

Set appropriate break points. Then select Run from the main menu bar and select Start With Full Compile.

Now run your client application, and step through your code.

Considerations for Debugging with Visual Basic

There are some additional limitations of debugging a component within the Visual Basic environment.

Limitations of Class Events

Ideally, you want to avoid placing any code within either the `Class_Initialize` or `Class_Terminate` events. This is because the VB run time will call `Class_Initialize` before the object and its context have been activated within MTS,therefore any operations performed in this event handler will fail. Likewise, you should avoid coding for the `Terminate` event as the object will be deactivated and the context lost before the event is fired.

If you set a breakpoint in the `Terminate` event then the debugger will stop as it will attempt to access a deactivated object.

If you need to implement code during the start-up and shut-down of your objects then place it in the `Activate` and `Deactivate` events of Object Control. However, you should still avoid placing a breakpoint in these routines because of the way the run time activates objects.

The Debugger may Reactivate Objects

If you're stepping through your code, Visual Basic may reactivate deactivated objects because of the way it finds out information about objects. For example, if you call a method on an MTS object that within the method's implementation calls `SetComplete`, then MTS will free the object from memory. However, in returning from the method call, the debugger will actually reactivate the object. This happens because there's a call to `QueryInterface` on the `IProvideClassInfo` interface. The Context Wrapper intercepts this call and activates a new instance to furnish the request. Thus, when you return from the method call in the debugger, you will actually have a reference to an uninitialised object.

Setting Watches on MTS Objects

You should not watch any of the object variables, such as the Context object, that are returned from MTS. This is because Visual Basic makes method calls on watched objects to return information on them. However, whenever the debugger breaks, the MTS run time also pauses its operation - so that the run time environmemt might run more effectively. Consequently, because the MTS environment is paused, when VB tries to make a method call on a watched MTS object, the call might fail. Should you attempt to watch an MTS-wrapped object, you may get inconsistent state detected and the process will be terminated.

Component Failure Stops Visual Basic

Finally, because an MTS component being debugged runs in the same process space as the instance of Visual Basic, a component failure will also cause Visual Basic to stop running.

In addition, if MTS detects an inconsistent state internally then the MTS run time environment will automatically shut down the run time process. If this happens, you'll be notified and an event will be logged in the system event log.

Debugging a Compiled DLL

We can now see that even when things work perfectly in the Visual Basic IDE, we still need to test the final compiled component to make sure that everything works the same as it does in the IDE. There are other reasons we wouldn't use the Visual Basic IDE. After all of the tests have been completed in the test environment, it's good practice to run a series of tests on the production server. It's unlikely that the production server would have Visual Basic on it, so you'll have to use a compiled version of the component. There are basically three ways to test a compiled component:

- ❑ Write information to a text file
- ❑ Write information to a database
- ❑ Write information to the NT event log

It's unlikely you will put testing information into the event log, so for testing purposes, you probably want functions to write to a database or a text file.

If a database is available (such as SQL Server 7) and it is legally available (has the proper licensing), it's usually the best option for testing. Test information can be placed into the database, specialized applications can be written to analyze the data, and these applications can be run from anywhere on the network. This allows everyone from management to development to see the results of the tests. It's possible that something could go wrong and your component may not be able to write to the database. In that case, you should write to a text file, so the information on why this happened is not lost.

Writing to the event log is a good choice for when the final application is rolled out. The event log can keep track of errors, or provide information on how your component is functioning. The major problem with the event log is that someone needs to look into the log to find an error. As this may be forgotten, or not done at all, it's advisable to have an additional function that sends an alert to a system administrator. This can be accomplished by creating a function that will email the system administrator, or send a message through the internet to the system administrator's beeper. Building these components goes beyond the level of this text, but we will show you how to make a function to write to the event log.

We're going to expand our existing class so that it has the ability to write to a database, a text file and the event log. We'll begin by creating a database that will allow us to log information from our MTS component.

The Log Database

We need to create two tables. One table, called `ApplicationLog`, will be used for logging general information, and a second table, called `ErrorLog`, will be used for logging errors.

Create a database called `Log` with the two tables, `ApplicationLog` and `ErrorLog`. Set both tables up as follows:

Field Name	Data Type	Size
DateLogged	Date/Time	–
Message	Text	100
Level	Number	Integer
MethodProperty	Text	15
Class	Text	15
Application	Text	15

Let's now code our component, starting with the declarations.

Writing to the Database

We'll add an enumerated type to our component for the different types of error levels we may have. The standard levels for the event log are **Informational**, **Warning** and **Error** and we'll use these for our enumerated type. We will also make `Private` constants for all of the field names, and change the database constant (in our case it's set to `C:\Log.mdb` – remember to put the appropriate path or name for your database):

```
Option Explicit

Implements ObjectControl

Private mobjADOConnection As ADODB.Connection
Private mobjContext As ObjectContext
```

```
Public Enum eErrorLevels
  Informational = 4
  Warning = 2
  Error = 1
End Enum

Private Const mcstrDatabasePath As String = "C:\Log.mdb"
Private Const mcstrDateField As String = "DateLogged"
Private Const mcstrMessageField As String = "Message"
Private Const mcstrLevelField As String = "Level"
Private Const mcstrMethodPropertyField As String = "MethodProperty"
Private Const mcstrClassField As String = "Class"
Private Const mcstrApplicationField As String = "Application"
```

Now, let's add a function called `WriteToDatabase` to log information to the database. We need to pass in as parameters the name of the application that has requested this log, the name of the class (module, form, etc.) that has made the log, the name of the method or property that has made the log, the actual message, and the level of error:

```
Public Function WriteToDatabase(ByVal v_strAppName As String, _
                      ByVal v_strClass As String, _
                      ByVal v_strMethodProperty As String, _
                      ByVal v_strMessage As String, _
                      ByVal v_eLevel As eErrorLevels) As String
```

We'll need a local Recordset object to get a reference to the table we want in the logging database. And don't forget our usual error handler:

```
Dim recLog As ADODB.Recordset

On Error GoTo WriteToDatabaseError
```

We'll call our `SetADOConnection` function, but we won't need to pass the path in, as we'll use the default path:

```
SetADOConnection "", ""
```

Next, we need to set the properties of the ADO recordset:

```
Set recLog = New ADODB.Recordset
recLog.CursorLocation = adUseServer
recLog.CursorType = adOpenDynamic
recLog.LockType = adLockPessimistic
```

If the level is informational, we will put a log in the `ApplicationLog` table. Otherwise, the log is an error and will go into the `ErrorLog` table:

```
If v_eLevel = Informational Then
  recLog.Source = "ApplicationLog"
Else
  recLog.Source = "ErrorLog"
End If
```

We then set the active connection of the recordset, and open the recordset. Once it is open, we can start an `AddNew`:

```
Set recLog.ActiveConnection = GetADOConnection
recLog.Open
recLog.AddNew
```

Next we set all of the fields to the values that have been passed in. In a final production version, you would probably want to make sure the parameters have actual values passed in:

```
recLog.Fields(mcstrApplicationField) = v_strAppName
recLog.Fields(mcstrClassField) = v_strClass
recLog.Fields(mcstrDateField) = Now
recLog.Fields(mcstrLevelField) = v_eLevel
recLog.Fields(mcstrMessageField) = v_strMessage
recLog.Fields(mcstrMethodPropertyField) = v_strMethodProperty
```

Finally we update and set up our exit to our function:

```
recLog.Update

ExitWriteToDatabase:

CloseADOConnection
Exit Function
```

In our error handler, we set the return value of our function to a string showing the errors. This information can then be written to a text file. You could also write to a text file in the error handler:

```
WriteToDatabaseError:

WriteToDatabase = "Error Description: " & Err.Description & vbCrLf & _
                  "Error Number: " & Err.Number & vbCrLf & _
                  "Error Source: " & Err.Source
```

Finally, we want to clear the error and go to the exit routine:

```
Err.Clear
GoTo ExitWriteToDatabase

End Function
```

Writing to a Text File

Now, we'll create our function to write to a text file with the same parameters as our database function:

```
Public Function WriteToTextFile(ByVal v_strAppName As String, _
                                ByVal v_strClass As String, _
                                ByVal v_strMethodProperty As String, _
                                ByVal v_strMessage As String, _
                                ByVal v_eLevel As eErrorLevels) As String
```

Our text file will have fields of a uniform length, to make it easier to read the text with an application. To do this, we'll create string fields for each of the parameters. Plus, we'll need a file number for the log file we are about to open:

```
Dim intFileNumber As Integer
Dim strAppName As String * 15
Dim strClass As String * 15
Dim strMethodProperty As String * 15
Dim strMessage As String * 100
Dim strLevel As String * 5
```

Notice that we have made the fields the same size as they are in the database. We'll now set the local strings equal to the parameters that were passed in:

```
strLevel = v_eLevel
strAppName = v_strAppName
strClass = v_strClass
strMethodProperty = v_strMethodProperty
strMessage = v_strMessage
```

Now we can just use the standard text file methods. We get a file number using `FreeFile` and if the error level is informational, we'll write to a log file, otherwise we'll write to an error file:

```
intFileNumber = FreeFile
If v_eLevel = Informational Then
   Open "C:\" & v_strAppName & "Log.txt" For Append As #intFileNumber
   Write #intFileNumber, intFileNumber & Chr(34) & _
                        strAppName & Chr(34) & _
                        strClass & Chr(34) & _
                        strMethodProperty & Chr(34) & _
                        strMessage
Else
   strLevel = Str(v_eLevel)
   Open "C:\" & v_strAppName & "ErrLog.txt" For Append As #intFileNumber
   Write #intFileNumber, intFileNumber & Chr(34) & _
                        strAppName & Chr(34) & _
                        strClass & Chr(34) & _
                        strMethodProperty & Chr(34) & _
                        strMessage & Chr(34) & _
                        strLevel
End If

Close #intFileNumber

End Function
```

We have not put any error handling in this function, but for a final production version you should add an error handler. In this case, it's likely you would raise an error back to the calling application.

Writing to the Event Log

You can write to the Windows NT **Event log** using the `App` object that comes with Visual Basic. The `App` object has a function called `LogEvent`. You can also set the `App.Title` that will be written into the event log. Once again, we'll use the same parameters:

```
Public Function WriteToEventLog(ByVal v_strAppName As String, _
                                ByVal v_strClass As String, _
                                ByVal v_strMethodProperty As String, _
                                ByVal v_strMessage As String, _
                                ByVal v_eLevel As eErrorLevels) As String
```

If `App.LogMode` is `vbLogAuto` or `vbLogToNT` then we are logging to the event log in NT. If we're in Windows 9x, we'll simply log to a text file by calling the `WriteToTextFile` method we just created:

```
If App.LogMode = vbLogAuto Or vbLogToNT Then
   App.Title = v_strAppName
   App.LogEvent v_strMessage & "(" & v_strClass & "/" & v_strAppName & ")", _
             v_eLevel
Else
   If WriteToDatabase(v_strAppName, v_strClass, v_strMethodProperty, _
                   v_strMessage, v_eLevel) <> "" Then
      WriteToTextFile v_strAppName, v_strClass, v_strMethodProperty, _
                   v_strMessage, v_eLevel
   End If
End If

End Sub
```

Next, we'll modify some of our previous functions to peform some writes.

CreateInstance

We'd like to know when our application is not able to get the Context object, so we'll write to the event log when our MTS component can't get the object:

```
Private Function CreateInstance(ProgID As String) As Object

   On Error GoTo CreateInstanceError

   If Not mobjContext Is Nothing Then
      Set CreateInstance = mobjContext.CreateInstance(ProgID)
   Else
      WriteToEventLog App.EXEName, "LogFile", "CreateInstance", _
                   "Can not get reference to Context", Warning

      Select Case ProgID

         Case "ADODB.Connection"
            Set CreateInstance = New ADODB.Connection

         Case "ADODB.Recordset"
            Set CreateInstance = New ADODB.Recordset

      End Select

   End If

   Exit Function

CreateInstanceError:

   Err.Raise Err.Number, Err.Source & " CreateInstance", Err.Description

End Function
```

SetADOConnection

If we have an error getting the Connection object, we'll want to write this to a text file, as it's a critical error. We can't write to the database as there's something wrong with our connection to it. If we had the email or beeper function, it's likely we would use it in the error handler of this function:

```
Private Sub SetADOConnection(ByVal v_strUserID As String, _
                             ByVal v_strPassword As String, _
                             Optional ByVal v_strConnectionString _
                                             As String = "Empty")

   On Error GoTo SetADOConnectionError

   Set mobjADOConnection = CreateInstance("ADODB.Connection")

   With mobjADOConnection
      .CursorLocation = adUseServer
      If v_strConnectionString = "Empty" Then
         .ConnectionString = "Provider=Microsoft.Jet.OLEDB.4.0;" & _
                             "Persist Security Info=False;" & _
                             "Data Source=" & mcstrDatabasePath
      Else
         .ConnectionString = v_strConnectionString
      End If
      .Open
   End With

   Exit Sub

SetADOConnectionError:

   Dim lngErrorCounter As Long
   Dim strErrors As String

   strErrors = Err.Number & ": " & Err.Description

   If mobjADOConnection.Errors.Count > 0 Then

      For lngErrorCounter = 0 To mobjADOConnection.Errors.Count - 1
         strErrors = strErrors & _
         mobjADOConnection.Errors(lngErrorCounter).Number & _
         ": " & mobjADOConnection.Errors(lngErrorCounter).Description & _
         vbCrLf
      Next lngErrorCounter

   End If

   WriteToTextFile App.EXEName, "LogFile", "SetADOConnection", _
                   "Connection Failed", Informational

End Sub
```

Now save and recompile the project.

Testing with the Client

Go to frmClientTest and add another command button called cmdTest2. In the Click event for cmdTest2 add the following code:

```
Private Sub cmdTest2_Click()

   Dim objLog As prjMTSTest.clsMTSTest
   Dim strReturnValue As String

   Set objLog = New prjMTSTest.clsMTSTest

   objLog.WriteToEventLog "Test", "frmClientTest", "FormLoad", _
                      "This is a test", Informational

   objLog.WriteToEventLog "Test", "frmClientTest", "FormLoad", _
                      "This is a test", Error

   objLog.WriteToEventLog "Test", "frmClientTest", "FormLoad", _
                      "This is a test", Warning

   If strReturnValue <> "" Then
      objLog.WriteToTextFile "Test", "frmClientTest", "FormLoad", _
                          strReturnValue, Informational
   End If

   Set objLog = Nothing
   MsgBox "Finished!"

End Sub
```

You'll notice something rather interesting about this code. Our MTS object is created and held open until the end of the sub. This means we're holding our server component for a long time, and also maintaining state across many calls. This will not scale, and is not how we should build our components. A better way to code this would be the following:

```
Private Sub cmdTest2_Click()

   Dim objLog As prjMTSTest.clsMTSTest
   Dim strReturnValue As String

   Set objLog = New prjMTSTest.clsMTSTest
   objLog.WriteToEventLog "Test", "frmClientTest", "FormLoad", _
                      "This is a test", Informational
   Set objLog = Nothing

   Set objLog = New prjMTSTest.clsMTSTest
   objLog.WriteToEventLog "Test", "frmClientTest", "FormLoad", _
                      "This is a test", Error
   Set objLog = Nothing

   Set objLog = New prjMTSTest.clsMTSTest
   objLog.WriteToEventLog "Test", "frmClientTest", "FormLoad", _
                      "This is a test", Warning
   Set objLog = Nothing

   If strReturnValue <> "" Then
     objLog.WriteToTextFile "Test", "frmClientTest", "FormLoad", _
                          strReturnValue, Informational
   End If
   Set objLog = Nothing

   MsgBox "Finished!"

End Sub
```

This is still not too readable, though. It would be best to make a log object for each situation. So we would have `objLogText`, `objLogDatabase`, etc. If you are concerned about the work to create the MTS component, remember MTS will not completely destroy the object when you set it to `Nothing`. It will keep a copy around for the next call, so you're not losing any performance by doing this.

As a final comment, you may find that the Event log will not work when you debug your component, but when you compile the component, it will work fine. Once again, things do not always work the same in the debugger as in the compiled component.

The Event Viewer

The **Event Viewer** provides a list of system events in date and time order. Three types of logs can be viewed: Application, Security, and System.

- ❑   The **Application log** contains application events including those logged through Visual Basic. In other words, if you use Visual Basic's `App` object to direct error messages to the application log, you can view these error messages here.
- ❑   The **System log** receives events generated by Windows NT system components. An example would be if the MS DTC services failed to start. Every time I try to start MS DTC and it failed, an event was sent to the System log.
- ❑   The **Security log** is for security generated events. Some events are system generated, but other security related events can be configured to generate messages to the security log. As an example, you can set security events to be logged through the Audit Policy dialog found in the User Manager. The screen shot of the Audit Policy dialog shows the types of security events that can be selected:

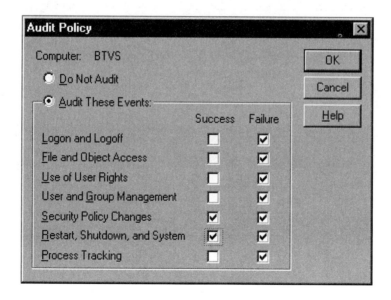

You can open the Event Viewer by selecting the link found in Administrative Tools from the Programs menu or you can run `eventvwr.exe`.

From the Event Viewer you can select the Log menu to choose which log you wish to view and select the type of event you wish to view:

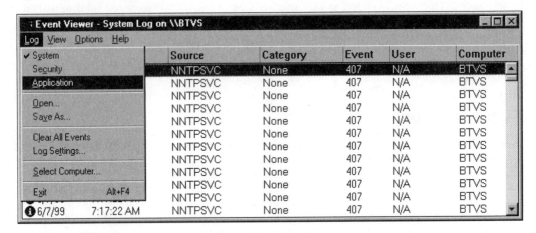

As we touched on before, in addition to the 3 types of log, there are three levels of log entry that can be recorded:

❑ **Informational** - represented by a blue icon with the letter i in the center. Information messages inform about major events that don't occur very often.

❑ **Error** - represented by a red icon with the word Stop in the center. This indicates that a significant error has occurred.

❑ **Warning** - represented by a yellow icon with a ! in the center. A warning message means that a problem is occurring that may develop into a more serious problem.

In our client project we logged a version of each the above levels. If you ran the project you should see each of the entries in the Application log:

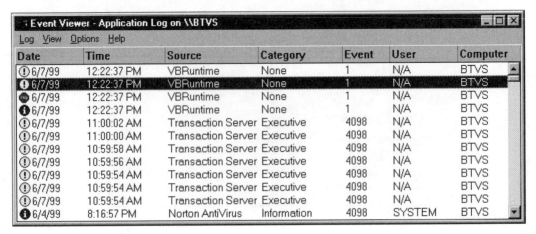

You can see that the log view is good for showing general messages and their severity. However, this is often not enough to figure out what actually has happened. By highlighting a particular message and double-clicking with your left mouse button, a detailed explanation of the event message appears. If you open one of the events we logged ourselves you can see how the information we passed into the `App` objects `WriteToEventLog` method has been recorded:

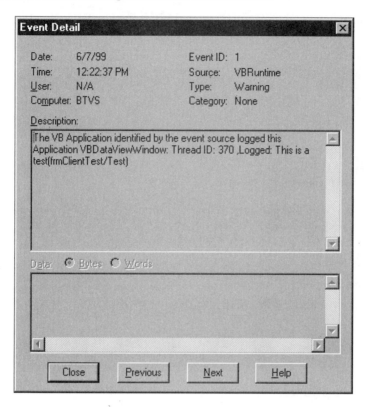

Debugging with Visual C++

There may be times when none of the above methods have really helped you to track down the problem. In that case, there is another alterative. As previously mentioned, Visual C++ can be of valuable help in debugging your VB MTS components where debugging problems involve multiple MTS components, MTS component security, or multi-threading problems, all of which Visual Basic's IDE can't handle.

> **Visual C++ will only let you debug a compiled VB component.**

The following is a step-by-step procedure for debugging Visual Basic MTS components using Visual C++.

From Visual Basic, open the Project Properties dialog for the component you want to debug. Click the Compile tab and select the following properties:

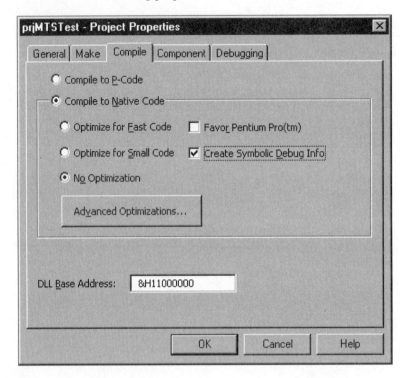

- ❑ Compile to <u>N</u>ative Code
- ❑ N<u>o</u> Optimization
- ❑ Create Symbolic <u>D</u>ebug Info

The Compile to <u>N</u>ative Code option simply compiles your code into the low-level native code that the computer's processor executes. Using native code allows the use of standard code debugging tools such as the Visual C++ debugger.

Using Create Symbolic Debug Info generates a .pdb file for the DLL (or EXE). This .pdb file includes symbolic information that allows code view styles of debugging such as the C++ debugger.

Compile your component, and save your project and the component to be debugged. Then exit Visual Basic and open the MTS Explorer.

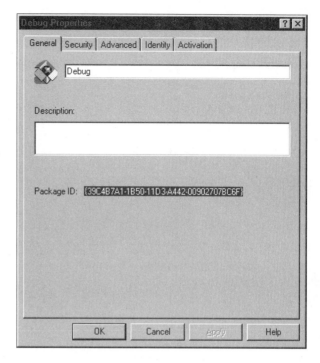

From the MTS Explorer, locate the package where your component is installed and open its Properties dialog. Copy the PackageID GUID to your clipboard:

For now, minimize MTS Explorer and open Visual C++. From File on the main menu bar, open the DLL that you want to debug:

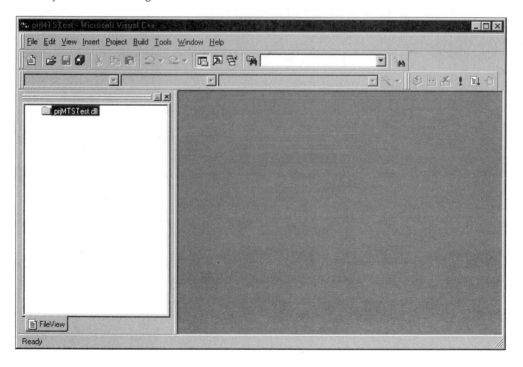

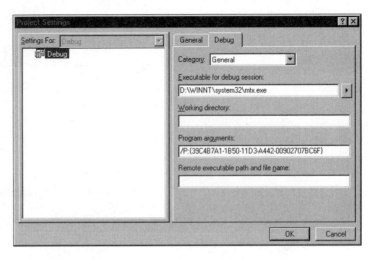

From Visual C++, open the
Project menu and then click
Settings. Select the tab
labeled Debug from the
dialog box:

Notice from the screen shot above, the entry for Executable for debug session – Make sure the
default path points to mtx.exe:

```
C:\WINNT\System32\mtx.exe
```

Still from the Project Properties Debug tab, go to the Program arguments text box and paste in the
Package ID from the clipboard. Put a / followed by P: directly in front of the Package ID. Click OK
when done.

Make sure that there is no space between the PackageID and the colon.

Open the .cls file for the particular component that you want to debug, and set any breakpoints
that you feel are necessary:

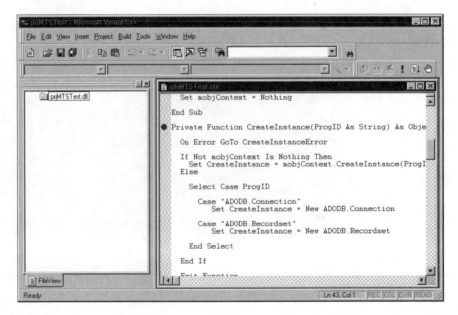

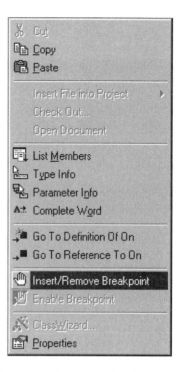

To set a breakpoint in the VC++ IDE you need to right-click on the line of code and select Insert/Remove Breakpoint from the pop-up menu:

You can display variable information in the VC++ debug environment. Select Tools from the main menu bar and select Options. Then select the Debug tab and check the Display Unicode Settings checkbox, located below the Memory window frame on the right:

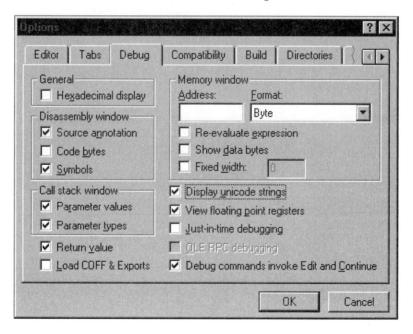

Maximize the MTS Explorer and highlight MyComputer. Right-click to bring up the pop-up menu and select Shutdown Server Process:

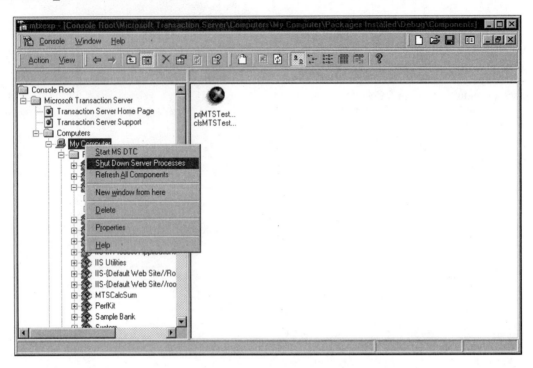

After the server processes have been shutdown, you can close MTS Explorer.

OK, it's time to go back to Visual C++ and debug your project. From the main menu in C++, select Build and then select Start Debug and Go.

Now start your client application.

Before re-deploying your component, be sure to go back to Visual Basic and return to the Compile tab from the project properties. Clear the checkbox for Create Symbolic Debug Info. Also, don't forget to select Binary Compatibility from the Components tab of the Projects Properties dialog.

Visual Studio Analyzer

As of MTS 1.5, you can generate MTS events that can be tracked using the Visual Studio Analyzer Tool that comes with the Enterprise Edition of Visual Studio. A full exploration of this tool probably deserves a book in it's own right, so I'm not going to go into using this tool. I'll provide you with a list of the events that can be generated so you can evaluate for yourself if it's worth exploring this tool in greater detail.

This tool does allow you to analyse a distributed application and can track more that just MTS events, such as COM, ODBC, SQL Server etc.

Most of these are fairly self-explanatory:

Event	Description
Begin Session	MTS is ready to start generating events
Disable Commit	`DisableCommit` has been called
Enable Commit	`EnableCommit` has been called
Set Complete	`SetComplete` has been called
Transaction Aborted	Transcation has been aborted
Transaction Prepared	Transasction is ready to be committed but hasn't actually been so yet
Object Activate	MTS has activated the object using IObjectControl
Object Create	Object regsiterd as MTS component has been created using `CreateInstance`
Object Deactivate	MTS has deactivated the object using IObject Control
Object Release	MTS has released the object
Package Activation	MTS Package has been activated
Package Shutdown	MTS package has been shutdown
Resource Allocate	A resource has been asigned from the pool
Resourece Create	A new resource has been created
Resoure Destroy	A resource has been destroyed
Resource Recycle	A resourece has been placed into the pool

When Things Go Wrong in MTS

In an earlier chapter, you had the opportunity to watch the ball spin in MTS Explorer when an instance of the object was created and then watch the ball stop when the instance was terminated. As cute as this may seem, this is an easy and reliable way of determining if your components are working through MTS. Remember that MTS-specific components can still operate outside of MTS. Viewing a graphic representation of your component objects being created and destroyed lets you verify that your package(s) and component(s) are being recognized through MTS.

Here's a real life example that can happen to anyone. You create a new package and install your components accordingly. You run your application and it seems to work but the balls representing your components in MTS fail to spin. You double-check your steps and everything seems correct. So why does MTS fail to work with this application? Like a bolt out of the blue, your realize that you didn't set MTS properties for the component. You open the Transaction tab and see that you have the component set to NotAnMTS Object.

Clearly, a spinning ball quickly and effectively lets the administrator/developer know if MTS is doing its job. But MTS does not stop here. You can obtain detailed information about the status of a component by selecting Status View from the View menu. The next screen shot shows a list of all the packages installed. Additionally, the package ID, the type of activation, and a running status are presented after the package name. Note that DebugTest is running:

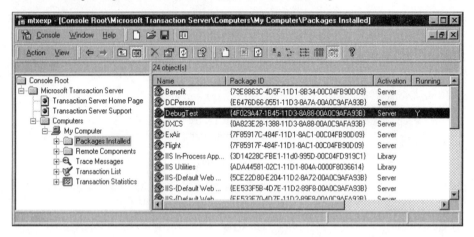

If you fail to find out why MTS doesn't seem to be working, MTS may not have installed properly. If you have C++ or Visual Studio, you can use the utility OLE/COM Object Viewer to create an instance of an MTS component.

OLE/COM Viewer

The OLE/COM Object Viewer can be accessed by running `oleview.exe`. As soon as you open the OLE/COM Object Viewer, select View from the main menu and then select Expert Mode.

Because there's no find utility, you'll have to locate your MTS component by expanding the appropriate folder and scanning for it. In the left-pane, under the folder Object Classes, is another folder Grouped by Component Category. If you have an idea of how your component may be grouped (such as automation object, control, etc.) you can look for the component's name under a category folder. It's probably quicker to find your component by simply looking for its name under the sub folder All Objects:

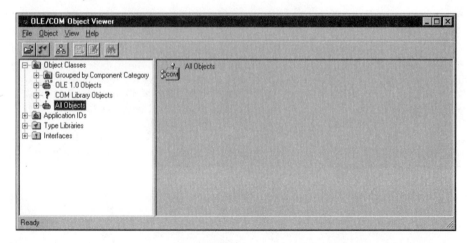

Select your component in the left-pane, and in the right-pane you'll see various information relating to how it runs. As this should be an MTS component, you'll find that under the Registry tab in the right-pane, the LocalServer32 key is pointing at `mtx.exe`:

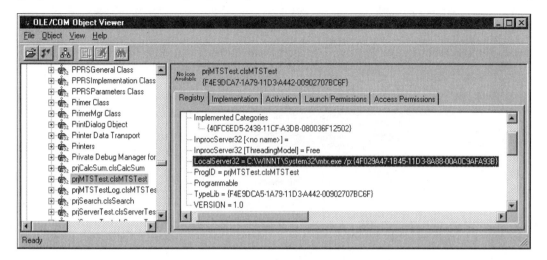

You can use this tool to instantiate an instance of the object. To do this, either select Object from the menu bar, or right-click the object in the left-pane, and then select Create Instance. If the instance was created successfully, you won't receive any error messages and you should see the object expanded in the left-pane to show all it's interfaces:

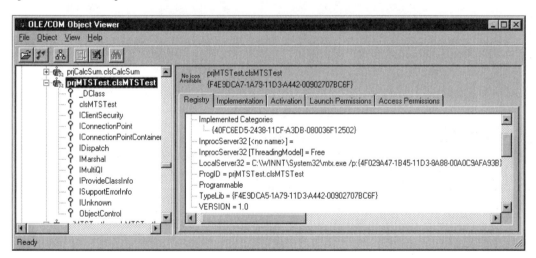

Additionally, upon creating an instance of the component, the Create Instance from the menu will gray itself out. Using the OLE/COM Viewer only lets you create one instance. At this point Release Instance has become active.

Now that you have created an instance of your component, go back to MTS Explorer and look in the appropriate package to see if the ball is rotating. Then make sure that you go back to the OLE/COM Object Viewer and release the object instance by selecting Release Instance from the Object or pop-up menu.

Verifying DCOM

Although DCOM is automatically configured to run with Windows NT, it's worth mentioning that you can turn DCOM on and off through the utility `dcomcnfg.exe`. If you're having problems verifying that MTS components are communicating, check to ensure that DCOM is enabled.

To do this, simply enter `dcomcnfg` at a command prompt. When the dialog appears, verify that the Enable Distributed COM on this computer check box has been ticked on the Default Properties tab:

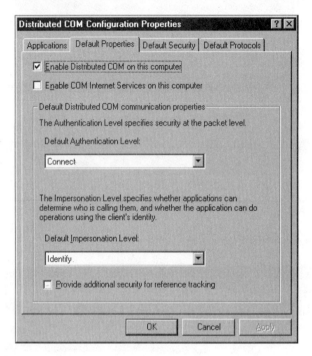

Error Messages

The vast majority of COM interfaces return a special 32-bit code from all of their methods called HRESULT. Although this code is basically just a mechanism to return status information, it is actually the method by which COM returns errors to the caller of the method.

COM objects cannot transmit errors to their clients using standard exception mechanisms, because these execeptions can't cross process boundaries and different languages handle exceptions differently.

An HRESULT is simply a 32-bit number containing structured error code in 4 parts:

- ❑ **Severity** uses a single bit. It returns a value indicating how successful the method call was. A value representing S_OK or S_FALSE indicates if the call was successful. If an error occurred, it returns a value indicating the type of error (e.g. E_POINTER indicates that the function has been given an invalid pointer).
- ❑ **Reserved** are selected bits that may be used in the future but currently need to remain set to zero values.

❑ **Facility** provides information to the client as to where the error occurred.

❑ **Code** is used to describe the error that occurred. COM defines its own error codes that range from 0x000 through 0x01FF. Additionally, COM allows the range of 0x2000 through 0xFFFF which COM uses for `FACILITY_ITF`. Here the application developer can define `HRESULT`s .

COM Error Messages

Message	Description
`FACILITY_NULL`	This is used for general status codes that do not belong to specific code groups.
`FACILITY_RPC`	Remote Procedure Call error. This error usually does not provide specific information about the RPC error.
`FACILITY_DISPATCH`	Results in `IDispatch` related codes.
`FACILITY_STORAGE`	Code results for errors regarding storage.
`FACILITY_ITF`	The ITF stands for interface and is used for most result codes that are related to COM interfaces.
`FACILITY_WIN32`	This is used for mapping error codes to an `HRESULT` that occur in the Win32 API.
`FACILITY_WINDOWS`	Error codes that can occur form Microsoft-defined interfaces.
`FACILITY_CONTROL`	This represents OLE Control related errors.

MTS Error Messages

MTS has an important role by constantly monitoring its internal integrity. If an error occurs internally in MTS, MTS immediately terminates the process. This immediate termination is referred to as **failfast**. Failfast is necessary with MTS to prevent errors from being committed. Suppose you have a transaction occurring and an MTS consistency check indicates that something is corrupt. The problem is MTS can only tell that corruption has occurred but not how much. Because MTS components run in the same process, it is likely an error has or will spread throughout the entire process. As a result of failfast, MTS immediately shuts down the problem process.

When an internal error is detected, it is possible that MTS will convert the HRESULT status codes into its own MTS error code before returning the error to the calling party. The following are common MTS errors.

Visual Basic has a minor flaw that sometimes masks the HRESULT value. When this happens, Visual Basic returns a generic raised error instead.

Error	Description
S_OK	The call was successful.
E_INVALIDARG	Arguments that have been passed are invalid.
E_UNEXPECTED	The error that occurred was unexpected.
CONTEXT_E_NONCONTEXT	The context for the current object is non-existent.
CONTEXT_E_ROLENOTFOUND	A role that is specified in IsCallerInRole does not exist.
E_OUTOFMEMORY	The object cannot be instantiated due to not enough memory.
	Note: COM often uses E_OUTOFMEMORY as a catchall error. In other words, if you receive this error, it does not necessarily mean that you have run out of memory.
REGDB_E_CLASSNOTREG	The specified component is not recognized as a COM component.
DISP_E_CLASSNOTREG	Arguments that have been passed contain a locked array.
DISP_E_BADVARTYPE	Arguments that have been passed do not contain valid variant types.

Decoding Error Messages

If you have access to Visual Studio or Visual C++, you can use the **Error Lookup** (ERRLOOK.EXE) tool to help you decipher those cryptic looking error messages:

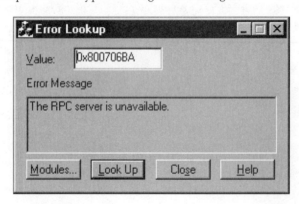

MTS Error Constants

Visual Basic abstracts us from the details of HRESULTs by interpreting these HRESULTs for us. It notifies our components when an HRESULT other than S_OK is returned by branching to the error handler that we defined with the On Error Goto statement. This error catching behaviour provided by VB eliminates the need for us to inspect the HRESULT returned from each method call personally. When VB catches an error, before it branches to our error hander, the VB run time instantiates a Err object. VB converts the HRESULT to a Long integer and places it in the Err object's Number property. In our error handler we can inspect the Err object's Number property, as well as the Source and Description properties, to determine how to handle an error. For example, the following code sample traps the error number -2147164156 if an error occurs when we call the GetObjectContext function:

```
Private Sub ObjectControl_Activate()

' Turn on our Error Handler
  On Error Goto ActivateError

Set mobjContext = GetObjectContext

' Turn off our error handler
  On Error Goto 0
  Exit Sub

ActivateError:
' An error occurred, try to trap and handle it gracefully

  Select Case Err.Number
    Case -2147164156
    ' This object's ObjectContext is not available
      App.LogEvent "The ObjectContext is not available!", _
        vbLogEventTypeError

    Case Else
      'An Unhandled Error Occured
      '...log the Error's Number, Description, and Source
      App.LogEvent vbCrLf & "An error occured in ObjectControl_Activate:" _
        & vbCrLf & "Number: " & Err.Number _
        & vbCrLf & "Description: " & Err.Description _
        & vbCrLf & "Source: " & Err.Source, vbLogEventTypeError

  End Select

End Sub
```

The Microsoft Transaction Server Type Library defines an Error_Constants enum that defines trappable MTS error codes. These are the error codes defined in the Error_Constants enum:

Constant	Description
mtsErrCtxAborted	The object's transaction aborted
mtsErrCtxAborting	The object's transaction is aborting
mtsErrCtxActivityTimeout	The object's activity timed out

Table Continued on Following Page.

Constant	Description
`mtsErrCtxNoContext`	The object's context is unavailable
`mtsErrCtxNoSecurity`	Security is not enabled for the object because it is loaded in an unsecure process
`mtsErrCtxNotRegistered`	The object being created is not registered properly
`mtsErrCtxOldReference`	The object is no longer valid
`mtsErrCtxRoleNotFound`	The role specified in the IsCallerInRole function was not found in the object's package.
`mtsErrCtxTMNotAvailable`	The transaction manager is unavailable
`mtsErrCtxWrongThread`	The call occured on the wrong thread

We can use these error constants instead of their long value when we interpret the `Err` object's `Number` property. For example, the following code sample revises our previous example to use the `mtsErrCtxNoContext` constant instead of the number `-2147164156` when trapping an error that the Object Context is not available:

```
Private Sub ObjectControl_Activate()

' Turn on our Error Handler
  On Error Goto ActivateError

  Set mobjContext = GetObjectContext

' Turn off our error handler
  On Error Goto 0
  Exit Sub

ActivateError:
' An error occurred, try to trap and handle it gracefully

  Select Case Err.Number
    Case mtsErrCtxNoContext
      ' This object's ObjectContext is not available
      App.LogEvent "The ObjectContext is not available!", _
        vbLogEventTypeError

    Case Else
      'An Unhandled Error Occured
      '...log the Error's Number, Description, and Source
      App.LogEvent vbCrLf & "An error occured in ObjectControl_Activate:" _
        & vbCrLf & "Number: " & Err.Number _
        & vbCrLf & "Description: " & Err.Description _
        & vbCrLf & "Source: " & Err.Source, vbLogEventTypeError

  End Select

End Sub
```

Summary

No doubt proper error handling is the first step to eliminating problems with your MTS components. However, as much as we hate to admit it, we all write buggy components. We therefore looked at a variety of mechanisms that we can use to answer the question, "Why isn't it working?"

We started off looking at methods we're famiilar with for debugging, and then covered more obtuse methods such as writing to the Event log, and even how to use VC++.

Now that we know how to track errors down in our components, let's take a look at how we can administer them to make them run better and avoid some troublesome problems.

10

Administration

You've reached the point where you can build your own MTS applications. However, having MTS applications that work is only one side of the coin. The other side involves how well your application will perform. Even when you've debugged each component in your MTS application, you still need to pay attention to its effects on the operating system it was designed to run on. This chapter introduces a variety of tools and techniques to help you administer and monitor MTS and the Windows NT operating system in order to achieve maximum performance.

After completing this chapter you should be able to answer the following questions:

- ❏ How do I configure MTS monitoring settings?
- ❏ Is there a way of stopping all MTS processes from the command prompt?
- ❏ Can I start and stop MS DTC processes from MTS Explorer?
- ❏ Why do the computer icons in MTS Explorer sometimes change color?
- ❏ I'm tired of manually configuring MTS Explorer, can't I automate these tasks?
- ❏ Why should I learn to use Windows NT administrative tools?
- ❏ Is Windows NT Task Manager a good choice for quickly checking CPU and memory resources?
- ❏ How do I use Windows NT Performance Monitor?

Performance Tuning

There's no doubt that monitoring system performance is a necessary step, not only during the development stage, but also through continued normal operations. Monitoring is not just a technique to see that everything is running smoothly, it's a tool to help you fine tune your system to maximize its performance. What's more, good monitoring skills are based on techniques that can help you debug problems.

You'll soon learn about Windows NT monitoring features that can help you tune and debug performance problems including MTS components. However, let's first concentrate on the excellent monitoring capabilities found in MTS Explorer.

Configuring MTS Monitoring

You can configure MTS monitoring settings from MTS Explorer using the Advanced property settings . The Advanced tab is available by highlighting the computer you wish to configure and right-clicking your mouse button. Select Properties from the pop-up menu, and then select the tab labeled Advanced:

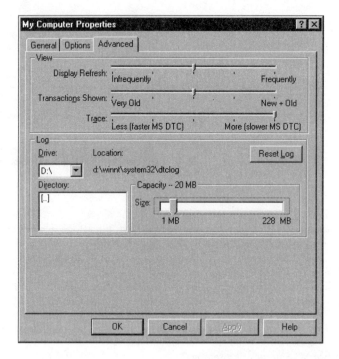

You'll see three horizontal slide bars. The first slide, labeled Display Refresh, is used for changing the rate MTS displays information in its transaction window. The setting on the extreme left (Infrequently) is equivalent to 20 seconds, and the one on the extreme right (Frequently) is equivalent to 1 second. A setting of 1 second will provide the most current information.

The second slide bar represents Transactions Shown. This has to do with the amount of time a transaction has to be active before information about it will be displayed. The setting to the extreme left (Very Old) is equivalent to 5 minutes. This means you can display transactions only after they've been active for a minimum of 5 minutes. A setting to the extreme right (New + Old) represents 1 second. With this setting, information will be displayed for transactions that have been active for 1 second or more.

The third slide control is used to set the level of trace messages from MS DTC to the Trace Messages window in MTS Explorer. Setting the slide to Less (faster MS DTC) essentially turns all trace messages off. Setting it to More (slower MS DTC) results in receiving all types of trace messages, including traces for information, warnings, and errors.

> **Set the slide bar to the middle position for Trace Messages. With this setting, only error and warning traces will be received.**

Directly under the slide bars, you'll find a frame containing the settings for log information. The first item is a command button labeled Reset Log. Clicking this will purge all of your MTS log files.

The slide bar labeled Capacity allows you to specify the amount of space allocated for storing MTS log files. The Capacity is dynamic in that it reflects the maximum free space you have available on the drive selected. However, a setting at the extreme left will always represent 1 MB, which is the minimum amount of space required.

To the left of Capacity are the drive letter and directory path settings: you can use these settings to specify where MTS log files will be written to.

MTS Processes – Stopping & Restarting

You can stop MTS processes from the command line using the utility `MtxStop.exe`

> **Caution: Stopping all server processes can have negative results if you have other MTS applications running.**

You can also stop all server process from MTS Explorer by highlighting My Computer, selecting the Action menu and then selecting Shut Down Server Processes.

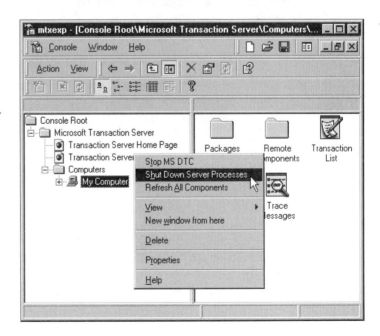

Restarting MTS server processes is just as easy as shutting them down. From the MTS Explorer, all you need to do is expand one of the folders or packages. Alternatively, if the MTS Explorer is closed, simply reopen it.

MS DTC Administration

In Chapter 2, you learned how to start and stop services through the MTS Explorer, and to monitor MS DTC services. Let's briefly review how this is done.

You can start and stop MS DTC services on any machine that's been added to MTS Explorer. Simply highlight the name of the computer (such as My Computer), select Action from the menu, and then select either Start MS DTC or Stop MS DTC depending on the situation.

For each computer configured through MTS Explorer, the running status of MS DTC processes can easily be verified by noting the color of the computer icons. If an icon has a greenish color, it indicates that MS DTC services are running on that particular machine. Conversely, if an icon has a dull gray color, it means that MS DTC services are not running on that particular machine. When MS DTC are first starting, you may be lucky enough to briefly notice the computer icon turn yellow before turning green.

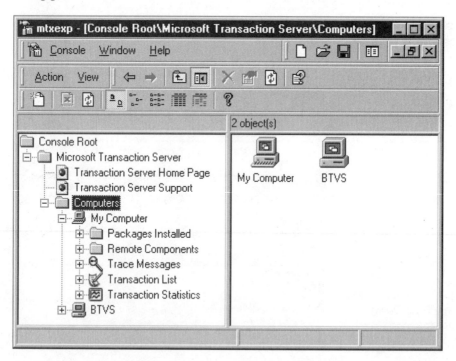

You may find it easier to distinguish the status of MS DTC by displaying large icons. Large icons only appear in the right pane. Select View from the menu, and then select Large Icon View.

As an alternative to distinguishing colors, you can also check MS DTC process status by selecting Status from the View menu while highlighting the Computers folder. The status for each machine installed in MTS Explorer will be displayed in the right-pane.

Automating MTS Administration

Throughout this book, I've shown you how to perform MTS administration using MTS Explorer to add and remove components and packages, as well as add roles to your MTS components and packages. Through the use of Visual Basic and scriptable MTS administration objects, you can automate these same tasks. As a matter of fact, you can use scriptable MTS administration objects to automate any task in the MTS Explorer.

> **Scriptable MTS administration objects can be accessed by adding project references for MTS 2.0 Admin Type Library to your Visual Basic project.**

Before we can start writing administration scripts, you need to understand the scriptable administration objects that are available for automating MTS. First, we need to clarify some terms.

Let's start by defining what a **catalog** is. In simple terms, a catalog is a data store: think of an MTS catalog as a source of information. More specifically, a MTS catalog is a data store that maintains the configuration information for components, packages, and roles. When you use MTS Explorer to create, delete or modify components, packages, or roles, you are actually administering the catalog.

Now that you've an idea of what a catalog is, let's extend this concept and learn what a collection is. Look at the diagram below of the hierarchy in MTS Explorer. Each folder represents a collection (of information) that is stored in the catalog:

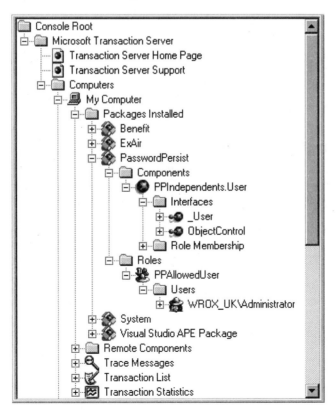

There are three types of catalog objects:

- ❏ The Catalog object
- ❏ The CatalogCollection object
- ❏ The CatalogObject object

These objects provide the core functionality to scriptable MTS administration. You can use them to add, remove, and modify objects, so, with these three core objects, you can configure MTS programmatically.

There are also four utility objects. These objects allow you to perform very specific tasks, such as installing components, exporting packages, and even associating a role with a user or class of users.

Catalog Objects

Let's take a look at each of these objects in more detail.

The Catalog Object

The **Catalog object** is the starting point that enables you to connect to an MTS catalog and access its collections. You should realize that the MTS catalog can be any MTS machine on the network. This means that you can use the Catalog object to connect to any MTS machine attached to the network.

The two most common methods the Catalog object supports are:

Method	Description
GetCollection()	Retrieves a collection on the catalog. Note that this method does not read objects from the catalog, it only retrieves.
Connect()	Returns a root collection from a remote catalog. In other words, this method is used for connecting to a remote catalog.

The CatalogCollection Object

Now that we can connect to a catalog and access a collection, we need a way to manipulate items in the collection. By using the **CatalogCollection object**, you can enumerate, add, delete, and modify MTS objects in the collection such as roles, packages, components, interfaces and methods.

The CatalogCollection object is capable of doing a lot of work, and as a result there are numerous methods it can support. The following methods are the most commonly used:

Method	Description
GetCollection()	Retrieves a collection that is related to a specific object.
Name()	Retrieves the name of a collection.
Add()	Adds an object to the collection.
Remove()	Removes an object from a collection.

Method	Description
Populate()	Fills a CatalogCollection object with the most recent information from the MTS catalog data source.
GetUtilInterface()	Retrieves the utility interface for the collection. GetUtilInterface is responsible for determining which utility object to make available, and is based on the items in the CatalogCollection
SaveChanges()	In order to make any changes to the collection into the MTS catalog permanent; they must be committed (saved).

The CatalogObject Object

The **CatalogObject object** is used to retrieve and set MTS object properties. This object represents an individual member of the CatalogCollection. For example, if the CatalogCollection contains a collection of components, the CatalogObject would represent a single component.

The following methods are commonly used with the CatalogObject object:

Method	Description
Name()	Retrieves the name of an object.
Value()	Gets and sets a property value.

Utility Objects

There are four utility objects, each of which must be accessed through the GetUtilInterface method of a CatalogCollection object.

PackageUtil

The **PackageUtil object** is used for importing pre-built packages and for exporting packages. It uses the following methods:

Method	Description
InstallPackage()	Imports pre-built packages.
ExportPackage()	Export packages.

ComponentUtil

The **ComponentUtil object** is used when you want to install a component from a DLL, or import a component that's already registered as an in-process server into a package. Its methods include:

Method	Description
InstallComponent()	Used to install a component from a DLL into a package.
ImportComponent()	Used to import a component that is already registered as an in-process server by supplying the component's CLSID.
ImportComponentByName()	Used to import a component that is already registered as an in-process server by supplying the component's ProgID.

RemoteComponentUtil

Similar to the ComponentUtil object, you can use the **RemoteComponentUtil** to install components from remote MTS computers to the local machine. The RemoteComponentUtil can be used with the following methods:

Method	Description
InstallRemoteComponent()	By supplying the package ProgID and CLSID, you can install components to the local machine from a package located on a remote MTS machine.
InstallRemoteComponentByName()	By supplying the package name and ProgID, you can install components to the local machine from a package located on a remote MTS machine.

RoleAssociationUtil

The **RoleAssociationUtil object** is used to associate a role with a component or a component's interface. Two methods are available with the RoleAssociationUtil object:

Method	Description
AssociateRole()	Used to associate a role with a component or a component's interface by providing a role ID.
AssociateRoleByName()	Used to associate a role with a component or a component's interface by providing a role name.

Using MTS Administration Objects

Now that you've been introduced to scriptable MTS administration objects, let's put them to good use. You're going to create an executable program that uses the MTS 2.0 Admin Type Library to create a new package called `Look Mom No Hands!` and install the component `svrCalculator.dll` that you worked with in earlier chapters.

Start Visual Basic and select **Standard EXE** from the **New Project** box.

Select <u>P</u>roject from the main menu and Refere<u>n</u>ces from the drop down menu. Locate and add MTS 2.0 Admin Type Library. As we mentioned earlier, this is necessary in order to use scriptable MTS administration objects with Visual Basic:

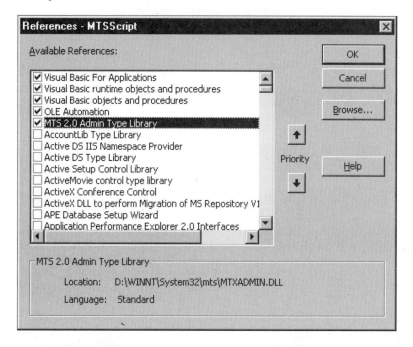

Name your project `MTSScript`, and name the form `Demo`, setting the caption to DEMO Create Package & Install Component.

Add a command button to the form, name it `cmdRunScript` and set the caption to Run MTS Admin Script.

Open the code window by double-clicking the form and enter the following code:

```
Option Explicit

Private Sub cmdRunScript_Click( )

   Dim objCatalog As Object
   Dim objPackage As Object
   Dim objMkNewPackage As Object
   Dim objPutCompInPackage As Object
   Dim objUtility As Object
   Dim strNewPackageID As String

   On Error GoTo AdminScriptingError

   'create an instance of the Catalog object
   Set objCatalog = CreateObject("MTSAdmin.Catalog.1")

   'get Packages collection from CatalogCollection
   Set objPackage = objCatalog.GetCollection("Packages")

   'adds a new package
   Set objMkNewPackage = objPackage.Add

   strNewPackageID = objMkNewPackage.Key
   'set the name of the package
   objMkNewPackage.Value("Name") = "Look Mom No Hands!"
   objPackage.SaveChanges  'Commit changes

   'use GetCollection method to access the collection ComponentsInPackage
   Set objPutCompInPackage = objPackage.GetCollection("ComponentsInPackage", _
                   strNewPackageID)

   'GetUtilInterface calls ComponentUtil in order to call InstallComponent
   Set objUtility = objPutCompInPackage.GetUtilInterface
   'note path & name of component
   objUtility.InstallComponent "C:\Wrox\VB MTS\svrCalculator.dll", "", ""

   Exit Sub

AdminScriptingError:

   MsgBox "Sorry, MTS Scripting Failed Reff Error# " + Str$(Err.Number)

End Sub
```

You will need to specify the correct path to your copy of `svrCalcualtor.dll`.

Save your work and run your application.

Open MTS Explorer and expand the **Packages** folder. Notice that the package **Look Mom No Hands!** has been added.

> **Note that if you run your application while MTS Explorer is running, you'll not see your package installed! All you need to do is highlight the `Packages Installed` folder and then click your right mouse button. From the pop-up menu, select Refresh.**

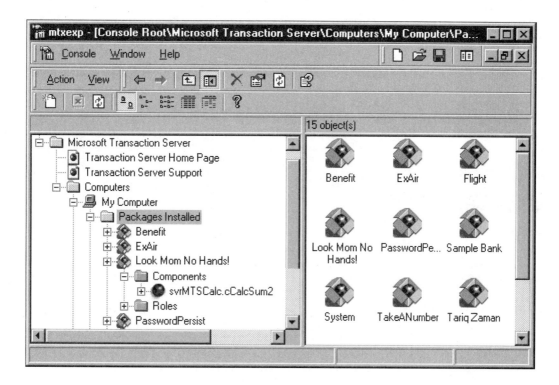

Windows NT System Performance

As an application developer, you may be asking why you should you concern yourself with Windows NT performance. After all, isn't that the job of the network administrator? Up to a point, you're right: once your application has been distributed, it should be the Windows NT administrator's job to make sure the system where your application is installed is running properly.

But let's try looking at Windows NT system performance in another way. When you're developing applications, how do you know if your application will meet the hardware specifications of the future users of your application? It's quite possible that your development machine has more horsepower than the machine where your application will be installed. Your application may run fine on your super charged 500 MHz Pentium III with 256 MB of RAM, but how will your application act on a lesser machine?

As a developer, it's important to think about the user. Will your application support the user's hardware? Did you even consider the user's hardware before you started building the application? What if your application is not properly destroying object instances? Your system will start to eat up valuable resources, but how will you know? During testing, your application may appear to run fine.

So, once you have your components debugged and everything appears to be running properly, you should test your application to match similar specifications to the user's hardware. In other words, paying attention to system performance is the second part of application development.

Windows NT offers two useful tools for monitoring your Windows NT system: **Task Manager** and **Performance Monitor**. Although these tools don't offer specific diagnosis for MTS components, they're important in overall system performance. And that doesn't mean that these tools won't aid in solving specific MTS problems. On the contrary, with a little deduction, and some luck, you can indeed isolate MTS problems.

A paradox! A system that is being measured can affect the measurement. It takes system resources to run diagnostic tools, and having too many diagnostic tools running will effect the outcome of the measurements you receive. A good rule of thumb is to turn monitoring off as soon as you have retrieved the information you want to see.

Task Manager

The Task Manager is handy for quickly spotting problems. Its drawback is that it doesn't log information to a file. However, for a straightforward check on system performance, Task Manager is accurate and reliable. In addition, you can use it to start application processes, as well as terminate system services that may be causing problems.

The Task Manager can be started by:

❑ Clicking the right mouse button on the Task Bar at the bottom of your desktop, and then selecting Task Manager... from the pop-up menu

❑ Pressing *CTRL + ALT + DELETE* and then selecting Task Manager

❑ Pressing *CTRL + SHIFT + ESC*

❑ For those of you who like to run applications from the command prompt, you can type in `Taskmgr.exe`

The Task Manager has three tabs: Applications, Processes, and Performance. Regardless of which tab is being viewed, the Task Manager displays a status bar at the bottom, which provides information such as:

❑ The total number of processes that are running

❑ CPU Usage in percentage form

❑ Virtual Memory being utilized by the system (Mem Usage).

The Applications tab simply shows the applications that are running, and provides no more information (other than the status bar). The information we need is displayed by the Performance and Processes tabs.

The Performance Tab

The Performance tab gives you a quick, graphical view of the current CPU and memory usage, and the CPU and memory usage history:

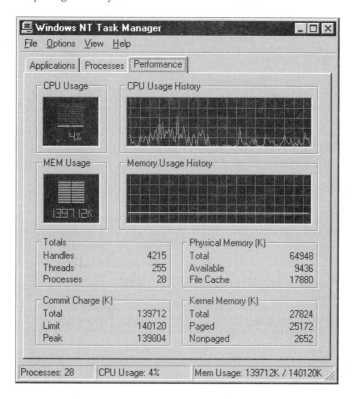

In this screen shot, you can see from the current CPU Usage graph that the system is almost idle. Looking at the CPU Usage History graph, you can see that there was enough activity to briefly peg CPU resources. Notice that I said briefly peg CPU resources. If CPU usage consistently remains around 95 – 100%, you can start to suspect that something may be wrong. Chances are, if CPU usage is sustained at a very high level, so is memory usage.

Just because CPU usage is high, it doesn't necessarily mean you have a problem. However, it's the first thing to consider when looking for potential problems.

The graph in the screen shot shows that very little memory is being utilized. However, if you find that memory usage is very high, you need to try and find out what's using it up. Perhaps your MTS application is not properly destroying object instances, thus eating up all your resources. Perhaps your application is running properly, but your system can't handle heavy usage without physically increasing memory.

Let's pretend that CPU Usage and MEM Usage are pegged out at 100%. The performance monitor has quickly indicated that something's wrong. If you change over to the Processes tab, you can see what processes are executing and view useful information about them.

The Processes Tab

The next screen shot shows the Processes tab. You can see from the status bar that there are 28 processes running. In this case, each process is followed with the amount of CPU usage and the amount of memory usage:

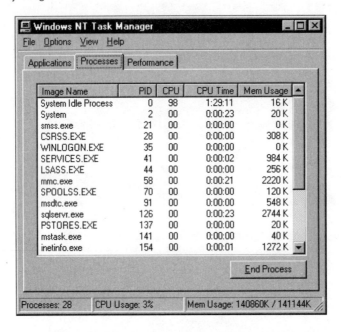

For example, SQL-Server (`sqlservr.exe`) is running and is using the most amount of memory. But what if `sqlservr.exe` was utilizing all system resources, both in CPU usage and in memory usage. It would appear that you may have found the process that's causing the problem.

The first thing to try is ending the process in question. Highlighting the process name and then clicking the End Process button located at the lower right corner will terminate it. Then check your resources. Hopefully they have returned to normal levels.

In many cases, the application that was causing a problem simply needed to be restarted. You can restart an application through the menu in Task Manager, regardless of which tab you are working with. Select File and then select New Task (Run...). From the Create New Task dialog, enter the path or select Browse to locate the application you wish to restart:

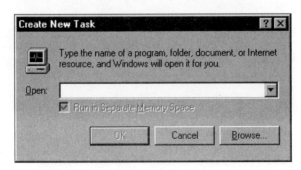

Customizing the Processes Tab

The amount of information that is displayed with the Processes tab can be customized by selecting View from the menu bar, and then selecting Select Columns...

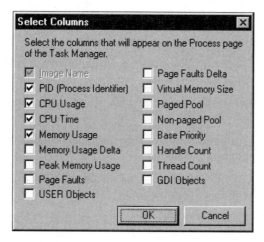

Although **Peak Memory Usage, User Objects,** and **GDI Objects** are seen in the **Select Columns** dialog, they are non-functional.

Starting from the left, you see that Image Name is selected but grayed out. This is the minimum amount of information that can be displayed. However, you can display all the information available in the Select Columns dialog (other than the non-functional items).

Column	Description
PID (Process Identifier)	The numerical ID that is automatically assigned when the process starts and is maintained while it's running.
CPU Usage	The amount of time in percentages when threads for a process utilize the processor (since the last update).
CPU Time	The total amount of time since the process started running.
Memory Usage	The amount of memory that is being utilized by the process.
Memory Usage Delta	The change in memory since the last update.
Peak Memory Usage	Non-Functional
Page Faults	Page faults occur when data has to access the disk because the information is not in memory. This value is accumulative since the process has been running.
User Objects	Non-Functional
Page Faults Delta	The change in page faults since the last update.

Table Continued on Following Page

Column	Description
Virtual Memory Size	The amount of the paging file (in kilobytes) that the process is using.
Paged Pool	Paged Pool indicates the amount of user memory (in kilobytes) that the process is using.
Non-paged Pool	Indicates the amount of system memory (in kilobytes) that the process is using.
Base Priority	This is the order in which threads are scheduled for the processor.
Handle Count	An integer representing the amount of object handles in the process's object table.
Thread Count	An integer representing the amount of threads that are running in a process.
GDI Objects	Non-Functional

Performance Monitor

The **Performance Monitor** is more robust than the Windows NT Task Manager, as you can monitor several types of processes at the same time, as well as setting alerts and error logging. Problems are often hidden among other activities. While using the Task Manager is practical for a quick reference (particularly when monitoring CPU and Memory usage), in most situations you need to rely on other tools that can provide you with a detailed report over a greater amount of time.

As an example, I was once working with a system that dropped in performance. Coincidentally, I had added a new MTS application. I say coincidentally, because it turned out that the new application was only related to the problems and was not the actual problem. But how do you find out what's wrong? Is it a new MTS application or is it something else?

Analyzing the graph and log files produced by Performance Monitor, I was able to see that CPU levels were moderately high; yet CPU levels were not sustained. However, memory utilization showed to be considerably high over a long duration. Additionally, the log showed that there was a lot of reading and writing going on with my hard drive. Knowing that my system performed properly before adding my MTS application, and seeing that both memory and disk activity was high, I concluded that I needed more memory in my server. The MTS application was fine, but it drew more memory resources than the server could provide. Problem solved!

Using Performance Monitor

Windows NT Performance Monitor can be displayed by opening the Programs menu and then selecting Administrative Tools followed by Performance Monitor. You can also run perfmon.exe from the command line.

> Note that when you first open the performance monitor, it appears empty. You need to add the items you wish to monitor. After you have configured the chart (see below) you can save your settings.

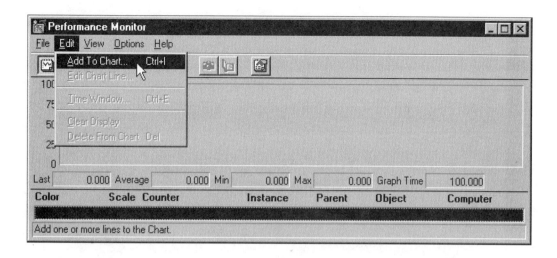

In addition to providing important information for Windows NT OS performance, the Performance Monitor offers some excellent options for SQL Server.

From the main menu, select Edit and then Add to Chart...

Each object counter you want to monitor is represented by a color that is automatically designated, simply by selecting the Object and Counter from the appropriate boxes. You can also assign a color of your choice for a particular item, provided the color is not already being used.

Additionally, you can change the Scale, Width and Style options. Scale is used to change the size at which the information is displayed. It's typically best to use the default, because the scale numbers on the value bar aren't changed. The Width and Style options allow you to change respectively the thickness and appearance of the line representation on the graph. Note that Style can only be modified from a solid line to another style when Width is set to the minimum thickness:

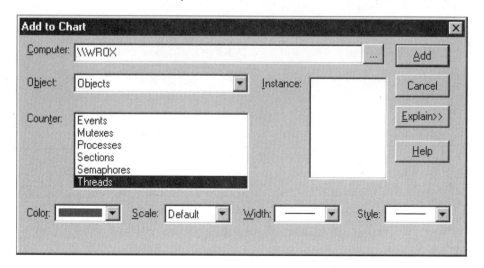

The Object drop down list shows the items (called counters) that you can monitor. Currently, MTS doesn't provide any of its own performance counters. However, monitoring items such as CPU, memory, and disk utilization can give you clues to potential MTS problems. Furthermore, many MTS performance problems may come from database accessing. Microsoft SQL Server provides numerous counters that can be used to solve MS SQL bottlenecks:

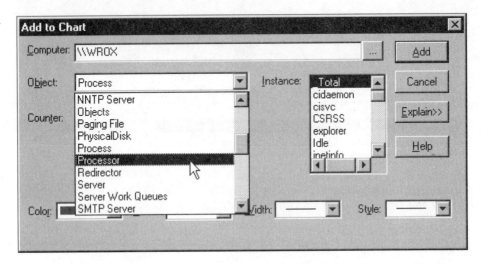

Selecting Processor Time displays a graphical representation of the percentage of processor time that's being utilized by the system. Pages/sec indicates the number of virtual memory swaps that occur per second. Cache Faults/sec represent the number of times per second the system is unable to retrieve data from cache.

In the following screen shot, Pages/sec pegged the scale for a while, and sharp increases in both %Processor Time and Cache Faults/sec occurred for a short duration. The key point to notice here is that all three counters only peaked briefly. If any one peaks and remains at high levels, then we should start to suspect something is wrong:

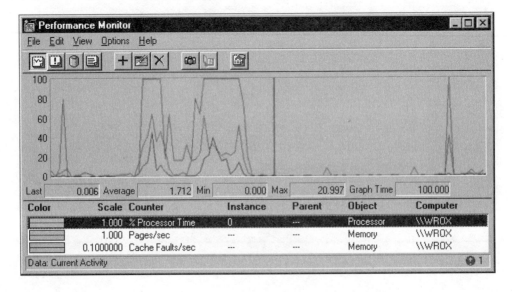

As a general rule of thumb, if the **%Process Time** counter results in a sustained reading of 90 or above, it's likely that a processor bottleneck is occurring. If **Pages/sec** maintains a count of 60 or higher, then your system probably needs more memory. High readings for **Cache Faults/sec** also indicate that more memory is needed.

In the previous screen shot, the thick vertical line down the middle separates the graph in time: the information displayed to the right of the vertical line is the older information, everything to the left is new. This vertical line moves across the graph from left to right.

If you need to monitor several items at once, the graph view can become too cluttered to read. You can change views from graph to histogram by selecting Options from the menu and then selecting Chart:

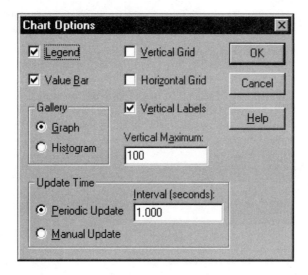

From the frame labeled Gallery in the Chart dialog you can choose between displaying the data as a graph or histogram. The Chart Options dialog also allows you to add vertical and horizontal gridlines to the display, and to set the Vertical Maximum. The standard is a value of 100, but if you're monitoring a process that utilizes very little, it's often practical to lower the vertical settings. The vertical maximum can exceed the value of 100, although system counts never go above 100.

The Update Time is set by default to every 1.000 seconds. You can create a snap shot by changing the radial button labeled Periodic Update to Manual Update. In order to refresh a snap shot, you need to select the Options menu from the Performance Monitor menu and select Update Now.

In the screen shot showing the chart above, an alert icon followed by a number '1' is displayed at the far bottom right corner. This indicates that an alert was triggered at some time.

Setting Alerts

You can use alerts to monitor numerous items simultaneously. By setting a maximum or minimum count, you can have the event recorded. You can also create a network alert to message you or someone else.

The alert view is displayed by selecting View and then Alert from the menu. To create an alert, select Add To Alert from the Edit menu.

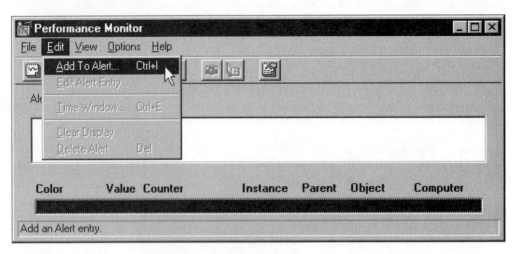

The Add to Alert dialog is similar to the Add to Chart dialog, where you can select the computer you want to monitor, the object to monitor, and the color of the icon to distinguish alert messages.

The frame labeled Alert If lets you specify that an alert should be issued when a count falls Over or Under the number specified in the text box:

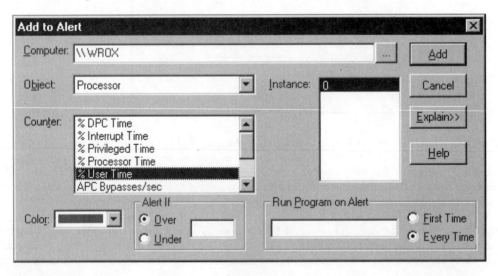

Run Program on Alert allows you to run an application in the event an alert is triggered. You can enter the path of a program you want executed. If you select the button labeled First Time, the program you choose to execute will only run the first time an alert is triggered. In other words, if the same alarm is triggered twice, the second alarm will not cause the program to execute. However, if you select the Every Time button, the program will execute every time the alarm is triggered.

The alert log uses round color icons (in front of the date) in the alert log to represent the items selected for monitoring. These colors are selected in the Add To Alert dialog and don't correspond with items selected for the performance chart.

You can also set alert options to automatically switch to the Alert View and/or enter a Log event in Application Log:

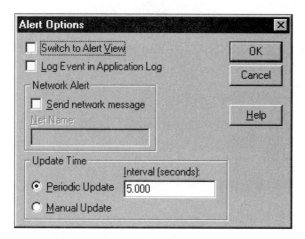

Finally, because an administrator rarely has time to constantly monitor system processes, an alert message can be sent to a specified network name if an alert is triggered. Although this may not help directly with MTS, this may come in handy for monitoring performance for SQL Server, IIS, and Active Server Pages.

Testing the PasswordPersist System

We have been building our `PasswordPersist` application steadily through the previous chapters. In this chapter, we'll come up with a test to make sure that `PasswordPersist` is working as expected. There are many third-party tools that you can use to perform rigorous regression testing on your applications; we won't try to duplicate that level in this example. However, when we're done, we will have a test plan that will verify if our system is working as expected. If at any time during the test you get results that do not match what this test plan gives, you know that something isn't set up right and that the current release should not go into production mode.

Before we begin the test, we need to have the following applications up and running:

❑   The VB client
❑   The Access database to view client changes

Adding a New User

The first thing we need to do is add a new user to the system. Therefore, add the user Joe Taylor with a password of jt27, and press the Add User button. If the addition was successful, the VB client should look like this:

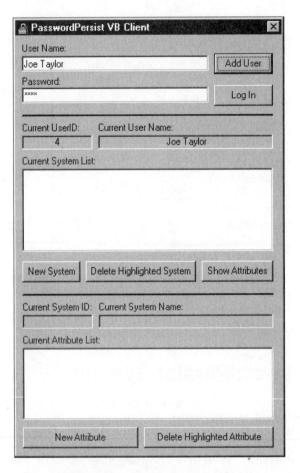

And the Access database will have the following entries:

UserID	UserName	UserPassword	UserEMail
1	Joe	JoesPW	joe@somewhere.com
3	Jason Bock	highgear	
4	Joe Taylor	jt27	
(AutoNumber)			

Record: 3 of 3

Adding Two Systems

With Joe Taylor added to the system, let's add two systems for Joe. Press the New System button, and enter Big Bank in the input box. Repeat this process and add the Stock Checker system. If everything is OK, you should have two new systems for Joe Taylor:

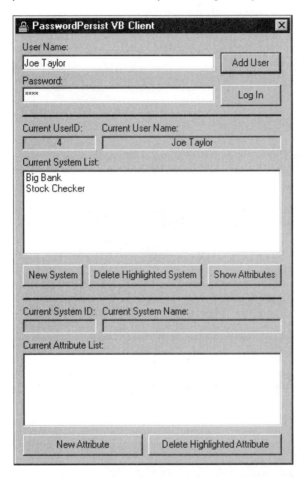

Check the PPSystem table to verify that these systems exist:

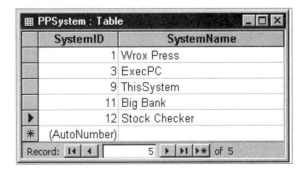

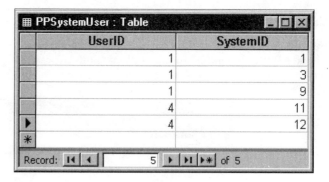

Also, check the `PPSystemUser` table to see that the correct association records have been made:

Add Three Attributes

Let's add three attributes to the Big Bank system. Highlight this system in the Current System List list box, and press the Show Attributes button. There should be no attributes to show at this stage. Now press the New Attribute button, and add the following information:

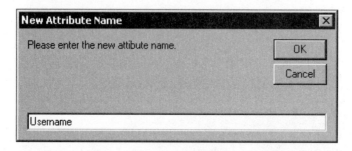

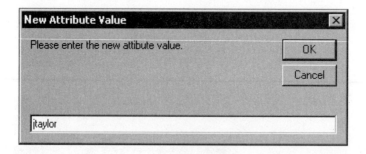

You should now have the Username – jtaylor entry in the Current Attribute List list box. Also, the `PPAttributes` table should have this entry present:

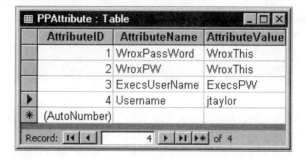

The `PPSystemUserAttribute` table should also have the appropriate association:

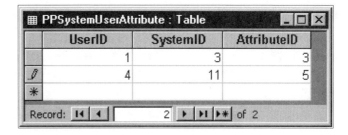

UserID	SystemID	AttributeID
1	3	3
4	11	5

Once this attribute is added, add the following two attributes:

- ❑ Name: Password Value: 32kjtvx
- ❑ Name: Location Value: Milwaukee

When all of the attributes have been added, the VB client should look like this:

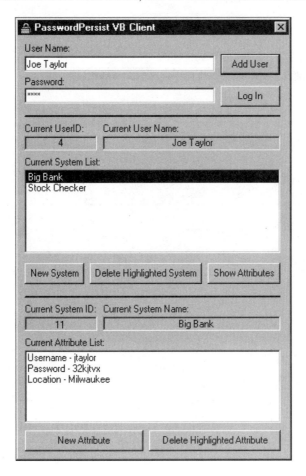

Verify that the Access database has the correct additions on the `PPAttributes` and `PPSystemUserAttributes` tables.

Add a New Attribute to the Stock Checker System

Now we'll add one attribute to the Stock Checker system. Select Stock Checker from the Current System List list box, and press the Show Attributes button. No attributes should show up in this list box. Now press the New Attribute button, and add the attribute name Company to check and value XYZ. This new attribute should now be in the list:

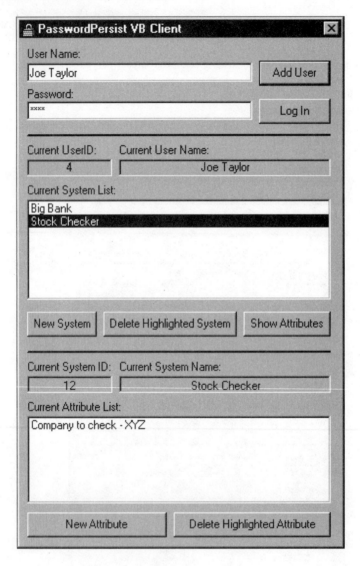

Deleting the Stock Checker System

To test out the deletion of a system, make sure that the Stock Checker system is highlighted, and press the Delete Highlighted System button. Select Yes from the Delete System message box, and verify that the system is deleted:

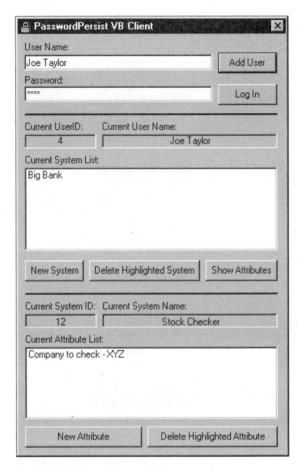

Wait! The attribute information for this system is still in the list box! This is a VB client error and not an MTS/database error. If you check the PPSystemUser table, you'll notice that the association to the Stock Checker is not there anymore:

UserID	SystemID
1	1
1	3
1	9
4	11

Record: 14 | 4 | 5 | ▶ | ▶I | ▶* | of 5

Nor is there any information in our `PPSysterUserAttribute` table:

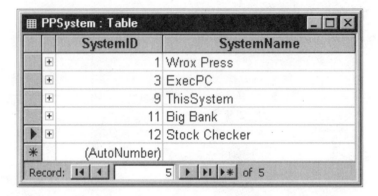

Also, note that the Stock Checker system is still in the `PPSystem` table:

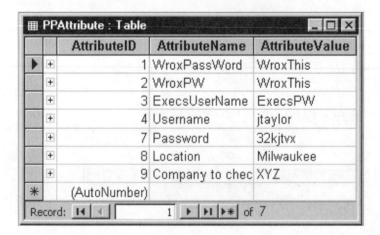

Furthermore, our attribute hasn't been deleted from the `PPAttribute` table either:

Therefore, we need to clear out the attribute information in our user interface. This can be done by adding three lines of code to our `DeleteSystem` method in `frmMain`:

```
Private Sub DeleteSystem()

  On Error GoTo Error_DeleteSystem

  Dim blnRet As Boolean
  Dim lngRet As Long
  Dim objSystemUser As PPAssociations.SystemUser
  Dim vntSystems(0) As Variant

  If lstSystems.SelCount > 0 Then
    lngRet = MsgBox("Are you sure you want to delete " & _
                    lstSystems.List(lstSystems.ListIndex) & _
                    " from the current system list?", vbYesNo + _
                    vbQuestion, "Delete System")
    If lngRet = vbYes Then
      vntSystems(0) = lstSystems.ItemData(lstSystems.ListIndex)
      Set objSystemUser = CreateObject("PPAssociations.SystemUser")
      blnRet = objSystemUser.DeleteSystems(lblCurrentUserID.Caption, _
                                vntSystems)

      If blnRet = True Then
        If lstSystems.ItemData(lstSystems.ListIndex) = _
                          lblCurrentSystemID.Caption Then
          ClearAttributes
        End If

        lstSystems.RemoveItem lstSystems.ListIndex
      End If

      Set objSystemUser = Nothing
    End If

  Else
    MsgBox "Please select a system to delete.", _
           vbOKOnly + vbInformation, _
           "Delete System"
  End If

  Exit Sub

Error_DeleteSystem:

  MsgBox "An unanticipated error occurred in DeleteSystem: " & _
         Err.Number & " - " & Err.Description

End Sub
```

If the system's attributes are currently listed, we make a call to `ClearAttributes` to remove any information from the UI.

Add Another User

This is the same as the first step, so repeat the same process, except add the following user information:

- ❑ User Name: Jane Taylor
- ❑ Password: ljtmpw

Verify that the correct information was added to the `PPUser` table.

Add a New System

Now let's "add" a new system for Jane. Press the New System button, and add the Big Bank system (sound familiar?). If everything worked out OK, you shouldn't have a new Big Bank system in the `PPSystem` table:

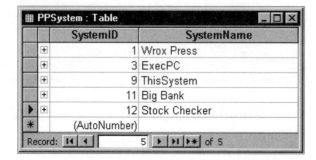

	SystemID	SystemName
+	1	Wrox Press
+	3	ExecPC
+	9	ThisSystem
+	11	Big Bank
+	12	Stock Checker
*	(AutoNumber)	

Record: 5 of 5

You should also have a record in the `PPSystemUser` table that reuses this system:

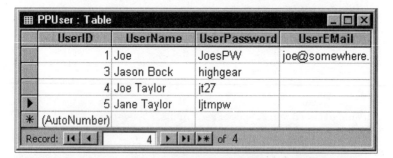

PPUser : Table

UserID	UserName	UserPassword	UserEMail
1	Joe	JoesPW	joe@somewhere.
3	Jason Bock	highgear	
4	Joe Taylor	jt27	
5	Jane Taylor	ljtmpw	
(AutoNumber)			

Record: 4 of 4

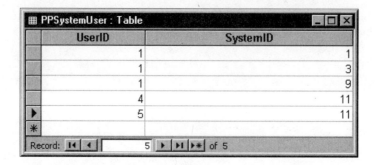

PPSystemUser : Table

UserID	SystemID
1	1
1	3
1	9
4	11
5	11

Record: 5 of 5

Add Two New Attributes

For the last step in our test, let's add two new attributes for Jane's **Big Bank** system. This is just like the third step, so refer to that section to see how the following attributes should be added:

- ❑ Name: Username Value: jtaylor
- ❑ Name: Password Value: 59xpa27

Verify that the `PPAttributes` did not duplicate the first attribute entered and that the proper associations are in the `PPSystemUserAttributes` table.

A Quick Summary on the Testing Procedure

In developing this test procedure, we were able to find a bug in our UI. We also now have a repeatable process to verify that new versions of the system can repeat the same test with the same results. Granted, if changes are made to the system such that the test needs to be changed, we will have to revisit the regression test. But by having a test plan in place, we've decreased the chances of errors showing up for our users.

Creating an Installation Script for PasswordPersist

Now that we have tested our components and VB client, we should create an installation script to make the addition of our MTS package easier for administrators. We'll need our script to do the following things:

- ❑ Recreate the `PasswordPersist` package
- ❑ Import all of the components and verify that certain attributes are in place (like transaction support)
- ❑ Create the `PPAllowedUser` role and add the necessary users

I'll go through each function that the script needs in detail, and then I'll tie it all together at the end of this section.

Enter the following routines into Notepad, or other simple text processor, and save as `PPInstall.vbs`.

The RecreatePackage Function

The first function we need is `RecreatePackage`. This function will search to see if the given package currently exists in MTS. If it does, it deletes it. Then, it adds the package back into place – this gives us a clean, empty package. Here's the code to do this:

```
Function RecreatePackage(PackageName)

  On Error Resume Next

  Dim lngC
  Dim objCatalog
  Dim objNewPackage
  Dim objPackages
  Dim objUtil
```

```
        Set objCatalog = CreateObject("MTSAdmin.Catalog.1")

        If Err Then Exit Function

        Set objPackages = objCatalog.GetCollection("Packages")

        If Err Then Exit Function

        objPackages.Populate

        For lngC = 0 To (objPackages.Count - 1)
          If objPackages.Item(lngC).Value("Name") = PackageName Then
            '  Get rid of the package.
            Set objUtil = objPackages.GetUtilInterface
            objUtil.ShutdownPackage objPackages.Item(lngC).Value("ID")
            objPackages.Remove (lngC)
            Exit For
          End If

        Next

        If Err Then Exit Function

        objPackages.SaveChanges

        Set objNewPackage = objPackages.Add
        objNewPackage.Value("Name") = PackageName

        If Err Then Exit Function

        objPackages.SaveChanges

        RecreatePackage = objNewPackage.Value("ID")

        Set objNewPackage = Nothing
        Set objPackages = Nothing
        Set objCatalog = Nothing

    End Function
```

The first thing we do is create a `Catalog` object (`objCatalog`), and get a `Packages` collection (`objPackages`) from `objCatalog` via the `GetCollection` method. Once `objPackages` is populated, we search the collection to see if the given package already exists. If it does, we create a `PackageUtil` object (`objUtil`) and call the `ShutdownPackage` method on `objUtil` to make sure the components in the package are stopped. Then we remove the package.

Once we know that we don't have the package in MTS anymore, we add it, making sure to call `SaveChanges` when we're done. If everything went as planned we return the package's `ID` value. The callee can use the `VarType` function to determine if the recreation was successful or not (we'll see how this is done at the end of this section).

The ImportComponent Function

With the package created, we can proceed to import components into the package. This is what the `ImportComponent` function is used for:

```
Function ImportComponent(PackageID, ComponentProgID, TransactionType, _
                         SecurityEnabled)

  On Error Resume Next

  Dim lngC
  Dim objCatalog
  Dim objComponent
  Dim objComponents
  Dim objComponentUtil
  Dim objPackage
  Dim objPackages

  ImportComponent = False

  Set objCatalog = CreateObject("MTSAdmin.Catalog.1")

  If Err Then Exit Function

  Set objPackages = objCatalog.GetCollection("Packages")

  If Err Then Exit Function

  objPackages.Populate

  For Each objPackage In objPackages
    If objPackage.Key = PackageID Then
      '  We now have the correct reference.
      Exit For
    End If
  Next

  If objPackage Is Nothing Then Exit Function

  Set objComponents = objPackages.GetCollection("ComponentsInPackage", _
                                                objPackage.Key)
  Set objComponentUtil = objComponents.GetUtilInterface

  objComponentUtil.ImportComponentByName(ComponentProgID)

  If Err Then Exit Function

  objComponents.Populate

  For Each objComponent In objComponents
    If objComponent.Value("ProgID") = ComponentProgID Then
      objComponent.Value("Transaction") = TransactionType
      objComponent.Value("SecurityEnabled") = SecurityEnabled
      Exit For
    End If
  Next
```

```
    If Err Then Exit Function

    objComponents.SaveChanges

    If Err Then Exit Function

    Set objCatalog = Nothing
    Set objComponent = Nothing
    Set objComponents = Nothing
    Set objComponentUtil = Nothing
    Set objPackage = Nothing
    Set objPackages = Nothing

    ImportComponent = True

End Function
```

This function starts out the same as `RecreatePackage`. However, once we have our `Packages` collection, we use the `For Each...Next` syntax to find the correct package via the `Key` property. If we find it, we then get `ComponentsInPackage` (`objComponents`) and obtain a `ComponentUtil` object (`objComponetUtil`). We then import the given component via the `ImportComponentByName` method. If the import is successful, the changes are immediately saved. Now we call `Populate` on `objComponents` and find the correct component. Once we do, we make sure that the `Transaction` and `SecurityEnabled` values are set to the given arguments. Finally, we make a call to `SaveChanges`. The callee can check to see if the function was successful or not by seeing if the return value is `True` or `False`.

The CreateRole Function

We can use this function to add any new roles to our package:

```
Public Function CreateRole(PackageID, NewRoleName)

    On Error Resume Next

    Dim lngC
    Dim objCatalog
    Dim objNewRole
    Dim objRoles
    Dim objPackage
    Dim objPackages

    Set objCatalog = CreateObject("MTSAdmin.Catalog.1")

    If Err Then Exit Function

    Set objPackages = objCatalog.GetCollection("Packages")

    If Err Then Exit Function

    objPackages.Populate

    For Each objPackage In objPackages
        If objPackage.Key = PackageID Then
            ' We now have the correct reference.
            Exit For
        End If

    Next
```

```
        If objPackage Is Nothing Then Exit Function

        Set objRoles = objPackages.GetCollection("RolesInPackage", _
                                          objPackage.Key)

        If Err Then Exit Function

        objRoles.Populate

        Set objNewRole = objRoles.Add

        objNewRole.Value("Name") = NewRoleName

        If Err Then Exit Function

        objRoles.SaveChanges

        If Err Then Exit Function

        CreateRole = objNewRole.Value("ID")

        Set objCatalog = Nothing
        Set objNewRole = Nothing
        Set objRoles = Nothing
        Set objPackage = Nothing
        Set objPackages = Nothing

    End Function
```

We're running into a pattern here: get the package collection from the catalog, and get the right package from that collection. This time, we obtain the `RolesInPackage` collection (`objRoles`) and add the new package. As we did in the `RecreatePackage` function, we return the new role's `ID` value so that the callee can determine if the new role was added or not.

The AddUserToRole Function

Finally, we have the `AddUserToRole` function:

```
    Function AddUserToRole(PackageID, RoleID, UserName)

    On Error Resume Next

    Dim lngC
    Dim objCatalog
    Dim objNewRole
    Dim objRoles
    Dim objRole
    Dim objPackage
    Dim objPackages
    Dim objUser
    Dim objUsers

    AddUserToRole = False

    Set objCatalog = CreateObject("MTSAdmin.Catalog.1")

    If Err Then Exit Function

    Set objPackages = objCatalog.GetCollection("Packages")
```

```
    If Err Then Exit Function

    objPackages.Populate

    For Each objPackage In objPackages
      If objPackage.Key = PackageID Then
        Exit For
      End If

    Next

    If objPackage Is Nothing Then Exit Function

    Set objRoles = objPackages.GetCollection("RolesInPackage", _
                                             objPackage.Key)

    If Err Then Exit Function

    objRoles.Populate

    For Each objRole in objRoles

      If objRole.Key = RoleID Then
        Exit For
      End If

    Next

    If objRole Is Nothing Then Exit Function

    Set objUsers = objRoles.GetCollection("UsersInRole", objRole.Key)

    If Err Then Exit Function

    objUsers.Populate

    Set objUser = objUsers.Add

    objUser.Value("User") = UserName

    If Err Then Exit Function

    objUsers.SaveChanges

    If Err Then Exit Function

    If UserName = objUser.Name Then
      AddUserToRole = True
    End If

    Set objCatalog = Nothing
    Set objNewRole = Nothing
    Set objRole = Nothing
    Set objRoles = Nothing
    Set objPackage = Nothing
    Set objPackages = Nothing
    Set objUser = Nothing
    Set objUsers = Nothing

  End Function
```

The same story applies here: get the catalog, get the correct package, and then get the correct role from the package collection. Once we have the correct role, we get a `UsersInRole` collection (`objUsers`) and `Add` a new user, which is now stored in objUser. We change the name of this new user to the given user name, and subsequentially call `SaveChanges`. The function will return a `True` or `False` to the callee.

Installing our PasswordPersist Components

Now that we have all of our functions defined in our script file, the last thing we need to do is tie them together:

```
Option Explicit

'Stop

On Error Resume Next

Dim blnRet
Dim strPackageID
Dim strRoleID

strPackageID = RecreatePackage("PasswordPersist")

If VarType(strPackageID) = 0 Then
  MsgBox "Package PasswordPersist was not created."

Else
  ' Now install each component.
  blnRet = ImportComponent(strPackageID, "PPIndependents.User", _
                     "Required", "Y")
  If blnRet = False Then
    MsgBox "Component PPIndependents.User was not added to " & _
          "PasswordPersist."
  End If

  blnRet = ImportComponent(strPackageID, "PPIndependents.System", _
                     "Required", "Y")
  If blnRet = False Then
    MsgBox "Component PPIndependents.System was not added to " & _
          "PasswordPersist."
  End If

  blnRet = ImportComponent(strPackageID, "PPIndependents.Attribute", _
                     "Required", "Y")
  If blnRet = False Then
    MsgBox "Component PPIndependents.Attribute was not added to " & _
          "PasswordPersist."
  End If

  blnRet = ImportComponent(strPackageID, "PPAssociations.SystemUser", _
                     "Required", "Y")
  If blnRet = False Then
    MsgBox "Component PPAssociations.User was not added to " & _
          "PasswordPersist."
  End If
```

```
        blnRet = ImportComponent(strPackageID, _
                    "PPAssociations.SystemUserAttributes", "Required", "Y")
        If blnRet = False Then
          MsgBox "Component PPAssociations.SystemUserAttributes was not " & _
                 "added to PasswordPersist."
        End If

        '  Add a role
        strRoleID = CreateRole(strPackageID, "PPAllowedUser")

        If VarType(strRoleID) = 0 Then
          MsgBox "Role PPAllowedUser was not added to PasswordPersist."

        Else
          '  Now add users to the role.
          blnRet = AddUserToRole(strPackageID, strRoleID, "ServerName\UserName")
          If blnRet = False Then
            MsgBox "User WROX\Mattb was not added to PPAllowedUser"
          End If

          blnRet = AddUserToRole(strPackageID, strRoleID, _
                            "ServerName\IUSR_ServerName")
          If blnRet = False Then
            MsgBox "User ServerName\IUSR_ServerName was not added to PPAllowedUser"
          End If

        End If

      End If

MsgBox "Installation is complete."
```

You'll need to specify the correct user settings for your setup.

We call `RecreatePackage` to make our `PasswordPersist` component. When that's done, we add our five components to `PasswordPersist` via `ImportComponent` calls. Then, we add our `PPAllowedUser` role via `CreateRole` and add our two users through `AddUserToRole`. If at any time during the installation process something doesn't work right, the script will create a message box informing the user of the error. Hopefully, the only message box you should see is this one:

Try running the script, and then run the VB client to verify that the installation worked as expected.

Summary

By completing this chapter, you've learned that having a working MTS application is only part of the picture. In order to achieve maximum performance from MTS, you must also make sure your MTS application performs properly with the operating system and hardware it resides on.

You have seen how to:

❑ Configure MTS monitoring settings, such as refresh rates, the amount of transactions shown, and the amount of trace messages provided by MS DTC.

❑ Start and stop MTS processes though MTS Explorer and through Windows NT command prompt.

❑ Use scriptable MTS administration objects with Visual Basic to automate MTS administration tasks, such as adding and removing components and packages as well as adding roles.

❑ Use Windows NT Task Manager for quickly spotting problems.

❑ Use Windows NT Performance Monitor, which has the capability to monitor several types of system processes as well as create alerts and write system information to log files.

In the next chapter, we'll move towards the back end of the distributed environment and take a look at accessing data sources from MTS components, with particular reference to Microsoft SQL Server.

Data Services and MTS

This chapter focuses on issues relating to the data tier in an n-tier application. Even though most of the examples in this chapter relate directly to SQL Server, much of the information applies equally to other relational database management systems (RDBMS), such as Oracle. In addition, this chapter compares and contrasts transaction management at the application server using MTS, and at the database server using SQL Server's integrated implementation of Microsoft Distributed Transaction Coordinator (MS DTC).

I'm not going to tell you how to use SQL Server: it's important for you to learn how to operate the database you choose for the data tier in your application, whatever database system that might be. What I am going to do is present you with database theory to help you better understand and handle your MTS transactions.

After all, transactions in an n-tier structure typically involve the data tier. It's at the data tier that durable data is placed when MTS commits a transaction. It just so happens that MTS and SQL Server (as well as other RDBMS products, including Oracle) work seamlessly together.

But don't skip over this chapter if you're not currently implementing an RDBMS in your application: there's still a lot of interesting and practical information for you to learn and incorporate into your own n-tier projects. In the next chapter, you'll be able to build upon concepts presented here and incorporate them with the Internet.

After completing this chapter, you should be able to answer the following questions:

- ❑ What is Universal Data Access (UDA)?
- ❑ Is OLE DB the same thing as UDA?
- ❑ Why should I use SQL transactions in my applications?
- ❑ What is MS DTC and how does it work?
- ❑ Should I use stored procedures?
- ❑ How can I encapsulate a stored procedure in an MTS component?
- ❑ How does SQL Server handle security?

Univeral Data Access

> Microsoft's Universal Data Access (UDA) is a key component in the Windows
> DNA architecture and is Microsoft's strategy for providing a common way to
> access both relational and non-relational data across an Enterprise system.

UDA is reliant upon **OLE DB**. You can think of OLE DB as a generic binder, because it is OLE DB
that actually enables UDA.

> **OLE DB is a low-level (system) interface that implements database
> transparency in such a manner that client applications don't need to know
> what kind of database they are accessing.**

Unlike DCOM on non-Windows platforms, Universal Data Access is not a novel concept. It's here
today, and it works now. OLE DB is touted to access *any* data source. Relational or non-relational,
from Microsoft Exchange Folders to HTML, OLE DB provides the standard set of COM interfaces
that make any data source look the same regardless of its format or storage method.

> *It's comparable to COM servers communicating regardless of how they are implemented because of
> their support for the standard interface* Iunknown.

This is how OLE DB supplies abstraction from the implementation details of the data source. These
are all features of COM, and they're now being applied at the data access level to provide the same
benefits they do at the binary component level. In other words, these benefits are provided through
interfaces, the same technology found in both Universal Data Access and in COM. This explains the
name OLE DB, which more appropriately should have been named COM DB.

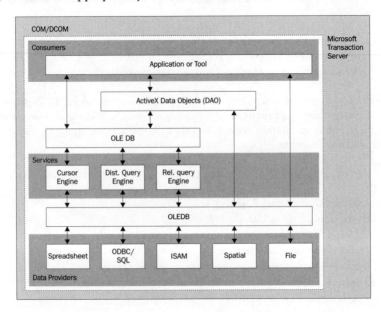

The architecture for UDA comprises three basic elements:

- ❑ OLE DB Providers
- ❑ OLE DB Consumers
- ❑ OLE DB Services

Data Providers

> **Data providers, or OLE DB Providers, are components that represent data sources.**

OLE DB Providers expose all types of data through the same standard OLE DB interfaces for consumers to access in a standard way. The OLE DB Provider provides abstraction from all of the details about the data source, such as the storage mechanism and indexing. Just as in component development, this allows the implementation of data retrieval and data manipulation to change, due to new algorithms, bug fixes, etc., without affecting the consumers of the data.

> *You may be wondering what the difference is between OLE DB and ODBC. In simple terms, OLE DB is designed to access all types of data while ODBC is designed only for accessing relational data.*

However, it's important to remember that OLE DB is not a replacement for ODBC. Instead, OLE DB builds on the foundation of ODBC as a wide-spread and accepted data access technology, as we'll see in the next section.

Consumers

> **A Consumer, or OLE DB Consumer, is any application or component that uses OLE DB data through OLE DB or ADO.**

In other words, when referring to OLE DB Consumers, we are really referring to ADO, or an application accessing data through ADO or OLE DB. Examples of OLE DB consumers include applications or components written in languages like Visual Basic, Visual C++, or Java. OLE DB Consumers even include development tools themselves. In fact VB 6.0 is actually an example of an OLE DB Consumer because of its Data Link and Data Environment Designers.

ADO can be described as a high level interface used to access all types of data. So how does ADO differ from OLE DB? First, remember that OLE DB is a system (or low-level) interface as opposed to a (application level) high level interface provided by ADO. Simply, ADO is an easy-to-use application level interface that leads us to OLE DB. Try picturing ADO as a level above OLE DB, thus ADO acquires the benefits from the UDA infrastructure.

Services

OLE DB Services are probably the most important piece of the OLE DB architecture. Yet, OLE DB Services are nothing more than components that consume and produce OLE DB data. These components act as another layer between the OLE DB Consumer, such as ADO, and the OLE DB Provider.

Data and Transactions

Most business applications require some sort of data manipulation using a database. For example, a sales application will require data to be added and modified for customers. Information is added to a database any time there's a new customer. Existing customer information, such as addresses, often change, requiring changes to the database. Along with this is the need to track sales activity, purchases from vendors, inventories, and so forth. All of this means on-going changes to your data files.

In addition to having data manipulation, most business applications will require several concurrent user connections. Applications that require both the manipulation of data and high concurrent user volume are referred to as **Online Transaction Processing** (**OLTP**) applications.

> *Typically, OLTP applications are written to use a relational database such as SQL Server or Oracle. OLTP applications can also be written for other data sources, such as to files and message queues.*

Things can start to get more confusing when it becomes necessary (or appropriate) to spread the data across multiple databases. In the previous example, it would not necessarily be unusual to find customer and invoicing information residing on one database server and inventory and warehouse management information on a different server.

In Chapter 4, you learned about transactions and the ACID requirements each transaction must have. Recall that a transaction is an action or series of actions that transform a system from one consistent state to another. Using (MTS) transactions makes it easier to manage data integrity by guaranteeing that resources are not updated (committed) unless all items in the transaction have completed successfully.

Not only do the ACID guidelines remain true when working with an RDBMS data source, ACID transactions are *critical*. Transactions can be implemented from within the data source and use its internal management systems to help avoid data degradation. When initiating and managing transactions through MTS, the ability of MTS to maintain data validity is a must.

SQL Server

Microsoft SQL Server is a high performance and scalable relational database management system. It can utilize multi-processor technology without the need for complex server reconfigurations. This ability to execute a single transaction across multiple processors not only adds to SQL Server's scalability, it can greatly enhance performance and throughput.

MS Distributed Transaction Coordinator (MS DTC) seamlessly integrates with MTS. By utilizing MS DTC to manage Microsoft's two-phase commit protocol, SQL Server can process distributed transactions while maintaining the rules provided in the ACID specifications. MS DTC is automatically used to process distributed transactions initiated by SQL Server. This is a very powerful feature that allows an application developer to concentrate on developing business logic as opposed to being concerned with how to deal with transaction management.

> *Fun Fact: According to the Transaction Processing Council, MS SQL Server Enterprise running on a DELL Power Edge computer can process over 23,460 transactions per minute based on Benchmark C specifications.*

Why Not SQL Server?

SQL Server is being used as the primary example during this chapter, but don't get the idea that it's your only option. You have other RDBMS choices available. MS DTC, both the SQL Server component and as a component of MTS, works with any XA compliant server, such as Oracle. You can even support distributed transactions with a single transaction spanning multiple platforms.

Of course, the underlying database, or databases, may not be your decision. You may find yourself building applications to support legacy databases or be restricted by organizational standards.

Distributed Transactions

A distributed transaction is one that spans two or more data sources, referred to as resource managers. Simply put for our usage, a distributed transaction spans multiple database servers. To ensure proper commit or rollback of the transaction, it must be coordinated by a transaction manager. MS DTC, either as part of SQL Server or as a component of MTS, acts as that transaction manager.

> *For your information, SQL Server also treats transactions between two databases on the same server as distributed transactions. These are handled locally, with no need to explicitly identify the transactions as distributed. The client or client application will see these transactions as local transactions.*

Client-Server Transactions

In the classic two-tier (client-server) model, writing a transaction to a single database such as SQL Server is relatively easy. For example, you can execute a series of transactions using ANSI SQL (standard SQL), Transact SQL (Microsoft's personal flavor of SQL) or you can use various database APIs, such as ODBC, ADO, and OLE-DB, to manage a database through an open connection.

Because SQL Server has its own transaction manager, SQL Server is able to commit, abort and rollback transaction data as necessary. SQL Server's transaction manager utilizes key words such as BEGIN, COMMIT, and ROLLBACK TRANSACTION to identify and manage transactions. In other words, for transactions in a client-server environment, SQL Server is responsible for ensuring that each of the ACID properties is enforced.

The following code is an example of Transact SQL. Although it contains multiple SQL statements, it is only one transaction. The transaction is explicitly framed by BEGIN TRANSACTION and either COMMIT TRANSACTION or ROLLBACK TRANSACTION. In this example, if both SQL statements complete, both are committed. However, if one statement fails, all work in this transaction is reversed (rollback). Simply, everything is returned to the original state as if nothing happened.

```
BEGIN TRANSACTION

INSERT NewCustomer (CusNo, LastName,AdType )
VALUES ('M01', 'Muppett', 05)

IF @@error ! = 0
BEGIN
      ROLLBACK TRANSACTION
      RETURN
END

UPDATE MailingListTotals
      SET CustomerTotals = CustomerTotals + 1
      WHERE AdType = 05

IF @@error !=0
BEGIN
      ROLLBACK TRANSACTION
      RETURN
End

COMMIT TRANSACTION
```

Let's look at this code a little closer. The first line is BEGIN TRANSACTION. This tells the transaction manager in SQL Server that this is the beginning of a transaction. Following BEGIN TRANSACTION is a SQL statement that adds a new customer to the database. In the event something goes wrong, the statement ROLLBACK TRANSACTION tells the transaction manager to reverse the course of action. Otherwise, the transaction will continue with the next SQL statement (if any).

In this example, the second SQL statement performs an update to the table MailingListTotals. Once again, the work is verified. If an error occurred, all work performed for this transaction will be returned to the original state as if nothing happened. If the work performed was successful, the transaction will continue with the next item to be processed.

This step-by-step process of 'do work' and 'verify work' will continue until the transaction ends. There are two ways that the transaction manager knows whether a transaction has completed. First, when a rollback occurs, the transaction is considered complete. Once an error occurs, all statements in the transaction are aborted and everything is returned to the previous original state.

The second (and preferred) method occurs when the transaction comes to the final statement, COMMIT TRANSACTION. This tells the transaction manager that everything completed successfully and that all changes in the database are to be committed.

One thing to note is that this is *not* a distributed transaction. Even though multiple tables are modified, it's only affecting one database on one data source.

> @@ *that precedes some types of name denotes an SQL Server global variable. For example,*
> @@*error is a global variable that contains the status of an error.*

Triggers

When discussing transactions, some mention should be made of **triggers**.

> **Triggers are specialized procedures created, maintained, and invoked at the table-level.**

Triggers are tied to data inserts, updates, or deletes - when the event occurs, the trigger fires (executes). Triggers are used as a way of supporting business rules at the database level. For example, in a sales database, there may be a trigger that blocks you from deleting a customer (rolls back the attempt) if the customer has an outstanding balance.

Why is this important to you? You may be involved only in implementing the middle and client tiers of an application. A database specialist may be brought in to implement the RDBMS, or you may be dealing with an existing database. You may find that some actions you attempt as MTS transactions fail, not because of a problem inherent in the transaction, but because it violates a condition being monitored by a trigger.

Stored Procedures

Another concept you should be aware of are **stored procedures**.

> **Stored procedures are database objects, each tied to a particular database, which contain executable SQL Statements.**

They are precompiled by the server and typically run more efficiently than *ad hoc* queries or transactions.

Sometimes you may find it better to make use of stored procedures available on the database server, rather than implementing all of the code relating to your transactions through MTS objects and the client front-end. Keep in mind that one of the advantages of multi-tier applications is that you're able to use the components in each tier in the most efficient way.

At some time, you may encounter references to **remote stored procedures**. This is simply a stored procedure stored on a server other than your local database server. When remote stored procedures are executed, they run on the remote server. Execution of remote stored procedures is automatically coordinated through MS DTC.

We'll be taking a look at stored procedures in more detail later in the chapter.

MS DTC

A major feature that Microsoft introduced into MTS is a **Transaction Manager** (TM) which works together with a **two-phase commit** protocol designed to handle distributed transactions. This transaction manager is the **Microsoft Distributed Transactions Coordinator (MS DTC)** and the COM based two-phase commit protocol is called **OLE Transactions**.

What makes OLE Transactions preferred over the other industry standard, **X/Open protocol**, is that OLE Transactions is object-based and can support multi-threaded applications, while X/Open is not object-based and it can only handle single-threaded applications. Because OLE Transactions is COM based, Microsoft intends to add enhanced transaction features in future releases.

In the world of business, it's not uncommon to need to work with more than one database at a time. You saw when working with standard client-server database systems that data integrity was fairly easy to guarantee. However, X/Open protocol support is important in that it provides support for additional data sources that may not be accessible through OLE Transactions.

It's critical to guarantee a successful commit or abort and rollback of a distributed transaction (a transaction across multiple databases) and still guarantee that the ACID rules are maintained and coordinated. How does MTS coordinate distributed transactions? By using an integral part of SQL Server and MTS: the MS DTC. The MS DTC monitors and manages each transaction and is responsible of coordinating, creating, and destroying transactions.

Don't become confused with the MS DTC that is viewed through MTS Explorer and through the MS DTC Administrative Console that comes with SQL Server. Although MS DTC is installed with both applications, the MS DTC component is *one and the same*.

Keep in mind that the DTC is equally important to SQL server and MTS. MTS can reside on its own machine, completely separate from the database machine, and MTS uses the DTC to coordinate its transactions. If only one MTS installation is used, then the MTS machine automatically becomes the transaction coordinator. Additionally, each SQL Server must have DTC installed so it can monitor its own transactions and report-back to the commit coordinator.

In this example, the DTC that is part of MTS is the commit coordinator:

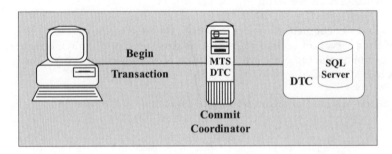

The following two screen shots show corresponding views of both MS DTC as seen from MTS Explorer and from MS DTC Administration Console:

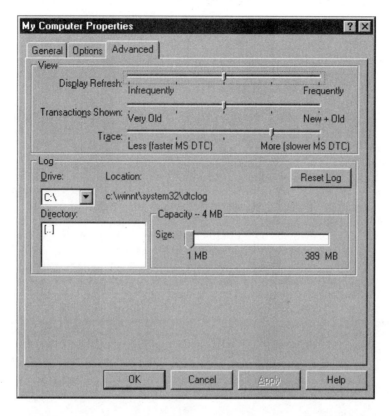

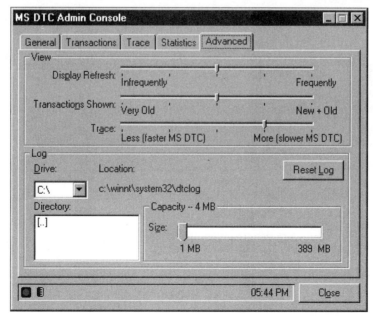

MS DTC Admin Console can be accessed by executing `dac.exe` *from the command line, or through the SQL Server group from the* Start *button.*

MS DTC in Action

We're going to write a Transact-SQL statement that will run though MS DTC. Because you may not have multiple database servers to experiment with, we will simulate a distributed transaction by using MS DTC, but we'll only write to one database.

To save a lot of work creating a database for this project, we're going to use the `pubs` database that comes as a sample and is installed by default when you install SQL Server 7.0. We need to create two new tables in the `pubs` database: `MTSBooks` and `MTSOutOfPrint`.

In Chapter 2, you should have created a custom snap-in for the MMC that includes SQL Server. If you did, simply open your snap-in in the MMC and expand the Microsoft SQL Servers node. Otherwise, you can start the SQL Server Enterprise Manager from the Start menu.

There are several mechanisms that we could use to create tables in SQL Server. As we'll be building a stored procedure later, we shall create them using SQL statements.

From the Tools menu, select the SQL Server Query Analyzer tool. When it has loaded, add the following statement to the top-pane:

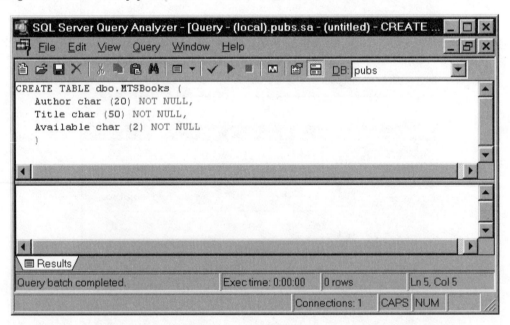

Make sure you have selected the pubs database from the combo box in the upper-right of the tool, and then execute the statement using the green arrow icon, or press *F5*.

The statement for creating a table is really rather simple. You start off by defining the name of the new table followed by an opening parenthesis:

```
CREATE TABLE dbo.MTSBooks (
```

Then you simply describe the fields you want to create by providing a name, data type and giving an indication as to whether or not the field can contain null values:

```
Author char (20) NOT NULL,
```

You can do many other things when creating tables with SQL statements, such as creating indexes etc., but for our purposes this is sufficient.

If you go back to the MMC, expand the Databases folder for your server and then expand the pubs folder you should see your newly created MTSBooks table under the Tables folder:

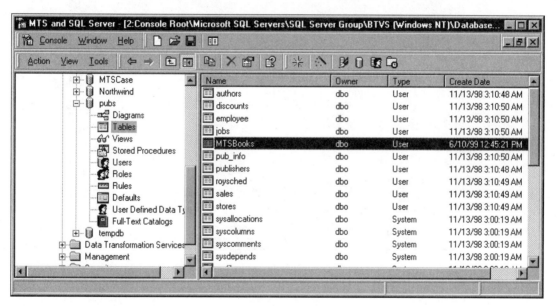

If you double-click the entry, you'll see the fields you've defined:

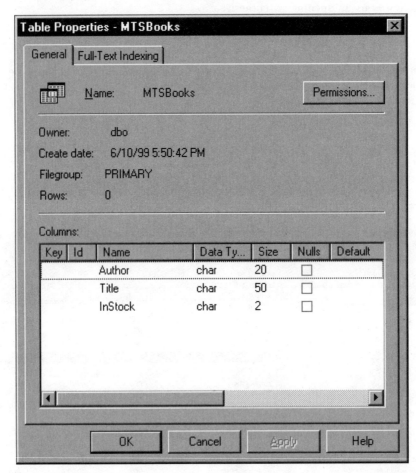

To clear the top-pane in the Query Analyzer, click the X from the tool bar or type *Ctrl+Shift+Del*. Next, to create the MTSOutOfPrint table, enter the following statement and execute it.

```
CREATE TABLE dbo.MTSOutOfPrint (
        BookID char (5) NOT NULL,
        InStock char (2) NOT NULL,
        OutOfPrint char (2) NOT NULL
        )
```

Now that we've created both tables, we want to create the transaction.

Type the transact-SQL as shown in the top-pane of Query Analyzer:

```
BEGIN DISTRIBUTED TRANSACTION

INSERT MTSBooks (Author, Title, Available)
VALUES ("Matthew Bortniker","Professional VB6 MTS Programming","Y")

IF @@error!=0
BEGIN
     ROLLBACK TRANSACTION
     RETURN
END

INSERT MTSOutOfPrint (BookID, InStock, OutOfPrint)
VALUES ("ac12","N","Y")

IF @@error!=0
BEGIN
     ROLLBACK TRANSACTION
     RETURN
END

COMMIT TRANSACTION
```

Notice that this transaction starts with `BEGIN DISTRIBUTED TRANSACTION`. You may recall from the previous Transact SQL statement that it started with `BEGIN TRANSACTION`. By using the keyword `DISTRIBUTED`, we are invoking MS DTC.

> *Remember it's not a true distributed transaction. Even though multiple tables are modified and we're using MS DTC, it is only affecting one database on one data source.*

Before we can execute the transaction, we need to make sure that MS DTC is actually running. The easiest way to do this from the MMC is to open the **Microsoft Transaction Server** node and right-click on the **My Compute** icon. If MS DTC is running, there will be an option to S**t**op MS DTC on the pop-up menu: if it's not running, the option will be to **S**tart MS DTC.

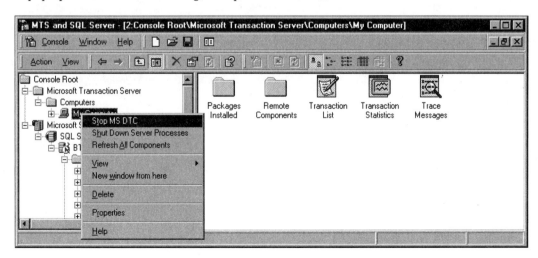

Now swap back to the **Query Analyzer** and execute the transaction.

Go back to the MTS Explorer on the MMC and look at Transaction Statistics. Although items were updated in two different tables, both are treated as one transaction. Either both successfully completed and committed, or both transactions are rolled back and aborted:

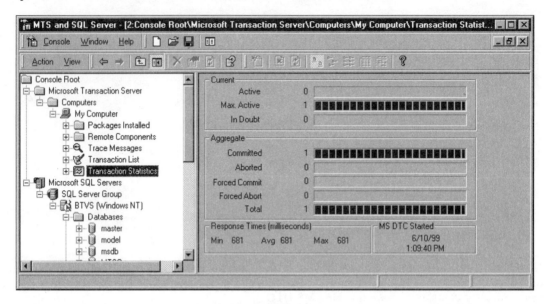

Although this transaction was not an MTS transaction, you can still monitor it from MTS Explorer because MTS and MS DTC are tightly integrated together.

MS DTC – Under the Hood

You now have a general idea how MS DTC works, but let's look under the hood and see what is actually occurring behind the scenes.

When an application wants to issue a transaction, it must first contact the MS DTC by calling an API referred to as `DtcGetTransactionManager`. A reference for `ITransactionDispenser` is returned, thus establishing a connection between the application and MS DTC.

The interface `ITransactionDispenser` contains the method `BeginTransaction`. Invoking this method causes MS DTC to create a new transactional object containing two methods: `Commit` and `Abort`. A reference to this transactional object is returned to the application through the interface `ITransaction`.

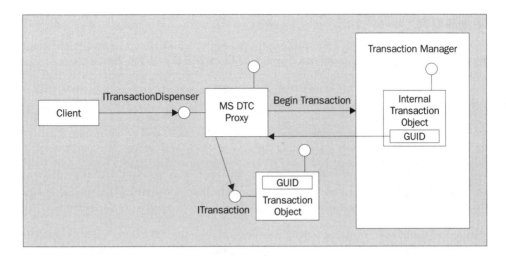

After a reference for `ITransaction` is received, a connection to a resource manager(s) needs to be established. ODBC is often used to connect to various databases such as SQL Server and Oracle. The ODBC driver takes on the task as a **resource manager proxy**. It's here that the ODBC driver makes a connection to the database. Now the ODBC resource manager proxy sends the transaction to the database resource manager via the function `SQLSetConnectAttr`.

What's actually happening here is that the resource manager proxy asks the resource manager for the particular database to use its local DTC, so it can be involved as part of a two-phase commit. Now the transaction can either commit or abort.

> *You aren't limited to controlled SQL Server transactions through the ODBC driver. You also have the option of using OLE DB methods to have a server connection join a transaction started by the application.*

MS DTC and SQL Server

When a distributed transaction is initiated at the server, the MS DTC component installed with the server takes sole responsibility for acting as transaction manager. It will handle managing the two-phase commit across all of the servers involved.

If a `COMMIT TRANSACTION` statement is issued during a distributed transaction, SQL Server will automatically call MS DTC's `TransactionCommit` method. DTC will have each server involved in the transaction confirm whether or not it's ready to commit the transaction. If each of the servers return `True`, DTC issues a commit to the servers. If any one of the servers return `False`, an abort is issued and the transaction is rolled back.

It's important to remember that whether acting as part of MTS or acting at the server, you're still dealing with the same MS DTC component with the same capabilities. The difference is where transaction management is taking place: either at the *application server* or at the *database server*. If MTS is installed on the same server as SQL Server, there will be a single MS DTC service running which will be used by both.

MTS and MS DTC

One question that may be nagging you at this point is simply, which do you use? Should you be managing all of your database transactions through MTS or MS DTC? The best answer to this is, unfortunately, the most vague – it depends on the situation. What you will most likely find is that the solution you implement (even if you don't plan it this way) uses both. In fact, that may easily be your best solution.

There are going to be many situations where optimum performance will come from initiating the distributed transaction at the server and letting the server's MS DTC act as transaction manager. There will be other situations where you'll get better performance having MTS cause the servers to join the transaction, especially when dealing with widely divergent data sources. One of the best ways to tell is to prototype your solution and test different performance scenarios. Even when using MTS to control SQL Server databases, it will require and use MS DTC on each of the servers.

One advantage of using MTS is that it supports connection pooling. Database server connections are typically at a premium when supporting most applications, especially when implemented using a standard client-server model. With connection pooling, the connection with the database server is made through MTS rather than a connection being made by the client. MTS connects to the server at the beginning of the transaction and releases the connection at the end of the transaction. This means that fewer database connections are required, even when supporting a large number of client end-users.

Either way, there's a strong case of managing client access through MTS, whether or not MTS is directly managing the distributed transactions. In addition, using MTS let's you take advantage of connection pooling and MTS security to support the application.

Using Stored Procedures

Stored Procedures are interesting creatures, as programmers either like to use them or they don't. Both sides of the debate of whether to use stored procedures are valid.

The argument for using stored procedures is that they lead to better performance. When a stored procedure is executed, it is parsed at the SQL server as opposed to executing from the client. Usually, a database server has more horsepower than the machine that hosts the client. Additionally, executing a stored procedure eliminates a transaction from traveling from the client to the database server and back to the client before processing.

The argument against using stored procedures is equally sound: using stored procedures encapsulates business logic, thus exposing the applications functionality. Additionally, maintenance overhead can be high. For example, suppose you have multiple database servers and you need to add or change an existing stored procedure - you'll need to make adjustments on each server.

If you're one of those who don't like to use stored procedures because they add another level of difficulty in managing business rules, let me show you a compromise where you can encapsulate stored procedures inside your business rules. Using such a method allows for efficient server-side processing while keeping business rules hidden (encapsulated).

In this exercise, you're going to update two different tables in a database using a stored procedure that is encapsulated into your MTS component

Creating the Stored Procedure

You'll be working with security, so be sure you're logged in to SQL Server as the Administrator.

To save a lot of work by creating a database for this project, we're going to use the pubs database and the two tables we created in the previous exercise. So, open the **SQL Server's Query Analyzer** tool again and select the database pubs.

Creating a stored procedure is easy. The basic syntax is as follows:

```
CREATE PROCEDURE ProcedureName AS SQLStatement
```

You can also shorten the keyword PROCEDURE to PROC:

```
CREATE PROC ProcedureName AS SQLStatement
```

We are going to create a stored procedure called spMTSBookInfo. Type in the following code in the top-pane of **Query Analyzer**:

```
CREATE PROCEDURE spMTSBookInfo

@Author char (20),
@Title char (50),
@Available char (2),
@BookID char (5),
@OutOfPrint char (2)

AS

BEGIN DISTRIBUTED TRANSACTION

INSERT MTSBooks (Author, Title, Available)
VALUES (@Author, @Title, @Available)

IF @@error!=0
BEGIN
      ROLLBACK TRANSACTION
      RETURN
END

INSERT MTSOutOfPrint (BookID, InStock, OutOfPrint)
VALUES (@BookID, @Available, @OutOfPrint)

IF @@error!=0
BEGIN
      ROLLBACK TRANSACTION
      RETURN
END

COMMIT TRANSACTION
```

As you can see, it's very similar to the transaction we defined earlier, except that this time, we defined parameters that can passed in rather then hard coding the values into the stored procedure. You define parameters in a stored procedure by preceding them with an ampersand, and placing them after the name of the stored procedure but before the AS keyword:

```
CREATE PROCEDURE spMTSBookInfo

@Author char (20),
@Title char (50),
@InStock char (2),
@BookID char (5),
@Available char (2)
@OutOfPrint char (2)

AS
```

Execute the stored procedure so that SQL Server compiles it and adds it to the list of stored procedures for the pubs database:

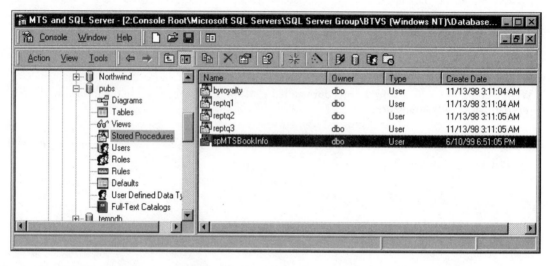

Let's test the stored procedure you just created. In the top-pane of **Query Analyzer,** type in the following and execute it:

```
EXECUTE MTSBookInfo "Sussman and Homer", "Pro MTS MSMQ", "Y", "1460", "N"
```

This will let us know if our stored procedure worked. You can verify that the data was added to the two tables MTSBooks and MTSOutOfPrint by executing the following two SQL statements in the top-pane of **Query Analyzer:**

```
SELECT * FROM MTSBooks
SELECT * FROM MTSOutOfPrint
```

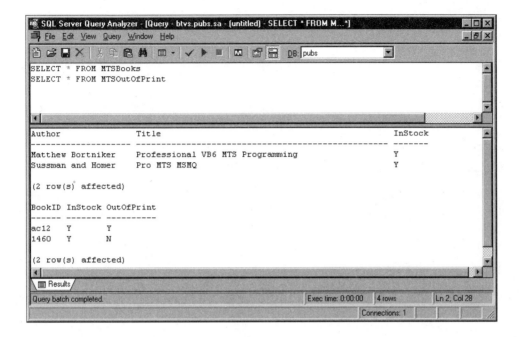

Now that we have created our stored procedure, we can start building our MTS component.

Building the MTS Component

Create a new ActiveX DLL project in Visual Basic and name it `prjSvrStoredProc`. Remove the default class and add a new class based on our MTSTemplate. Call it `clsStoredProc`.

Before you start entering code, add references to the **Microsoft Transaction Server Type Library** and the **Microsoft ActiveX Data Objects 2.x Library**. Then change the MTSTransactionMode property to **2 - Requires Transaction**.

Under the **General Declarations**, add an ADO Connection object variable:

```
Option Explicit

Implements ObjectControl

Private mobjContext As ObjectContext
Private mcnADO As ADODB.Connection
```

Also add an extra line to the `Deactivate` event of Object Control to make sure this variable is destroyed:

```
Private Sub ObjectControl_Deactivate()

    Set mcnADO = Nothing
    Set mobjContext = Nothing

End Sub
```

Create a routine called `InsertMTSBookInfo` and enter the following code:

```
Public Sub InsertMTSBookInfo(Author As String, Title As String, _
                             Available As String, BookID As String, _
                             InStock As String, OutOfPrint As String)

On Error GoTo RaiseError

Dim strConnect As String
Dim strCommand As String
Dim StoredProc As ADODB.Command

strConnect = "Provider=MSDASQL.1;Persist Security Info=False;" & _
             "User ID=sa;Data Source=StoredProc;Initial Catalog=pubs"

Set mcnADO = New ADODB.Connection
mcnADO.ConnectionString = strConnect
mcnADO.Open


strCommand = "spMTSBookInfo '" & Author & "', '" & Title & "', '" & _
             Available & "', '" & BookID & "', " & InStock & _
             "', '" & OutOfPrint & "'"

Set StoredProc = New ADODB.Command
Set StoredProc.ActiveConnection = mcnADO
StoredProc.CommandText = strCommand

StoredProc.Execute

mobjContext.SetComplete
mcnADO.close
Set mcnADO = Nothing
Exit Sub

RaiseError:

mobjContext.SetAbort
mcnADO.Close
Set mcnADO = Nothing
Err.Raise Err.Number, Err.Source, Err.Description

End Sub
```

You will need to set the connection string up as appropriate for you.

Save your work and create the `prjSvrStoredProc.dll`. You then need to place it in an MTS package:

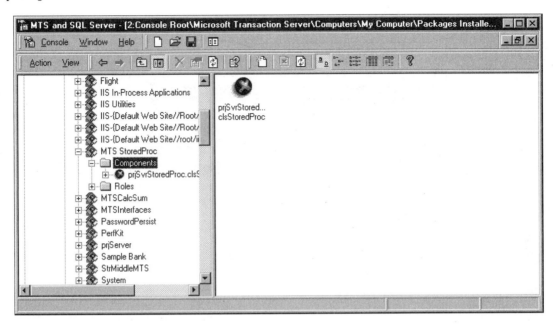

The next step is to build the client.

Building the Client

Create a new Standard EXE project in VB and name it `prjSPClient`.

Before doing anything else, let's make sure we set a reference to our DLL:

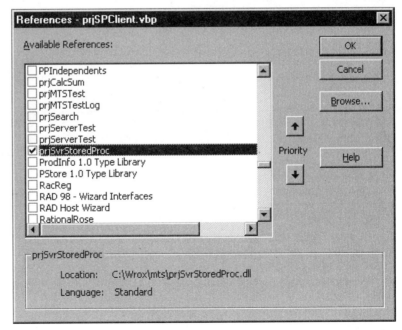

Name the form `frmSPClient` and set the caption to **MTS & MS DTC DEMO**. Next, add a command button, two frames, three text boxes, and three check boxes to the form.

- ❑ Name the command button `cmdInsert` and enter the caption as **Insert MTS Book info**.
- ❑ Name the text boxes `txtAuthor`, `txtTitle`, and `txtBookID`.
- ❑ Name the check boxes `chkAvailable`, `chkInStock`, and `chkOutOfPrint`

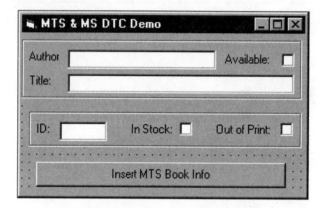

Open the code window and enter the following under **General Declarations**:

```
Option Explicit

Private objInsertMTSBookInfo As prjSvrStoredProc.clsStoredProc
```

Next, add the following code under `cmdInsert_Click`:

```
Private Sub cmdInsert_Click()

    Dim strAvailable As String
    Dim strInStock As String
    Dim strOutOfPrint As String

    If chkAvailable.Value Then
        strAvailable = "Y"
    Else
        strAvailable = "N"
    End If

    If chkInStock.Value Then
        strInStock = "Y"
    Else
        strInStock = "N"
    End If

    If chkOutOfPrint.Value Then
        strOutOfPrint = "Y"
    Else
        strOutOfPrint = "N"
    End If
```

```
    Set objInsertMTSBookInfo = CreateObject("prjSvrStoredProc.clsStoredProc")

    objInsertMTSBookInfo.InsertMTSBookInfo txtAuthor, txtTitle, strAvailable, _
                                       txtBookID, strInStock, strOutOfPrint

    Set objInsertMTSBookInfo = Nothing

    MsgBox "Insert Complete!"

  End Sub
```

When you've entered all the code for the client, be sure to save your work. Before trying to execute this application, open the Transaction Statistics window in MTS Explorer and place it at a convenient location for viewing. Now run the client application:

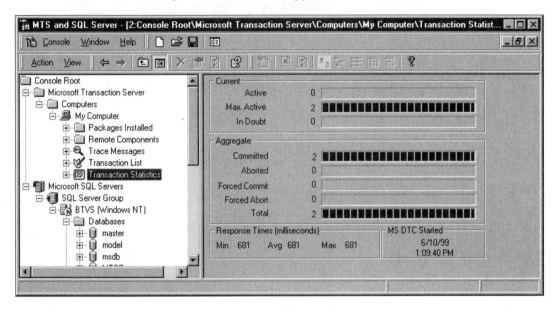

Every time you successfully execute the client, committed (and aborted) transactions are added to the statistics.

You can also view transactions from the MS DTC Admin Console by selecting the Statistics tab:

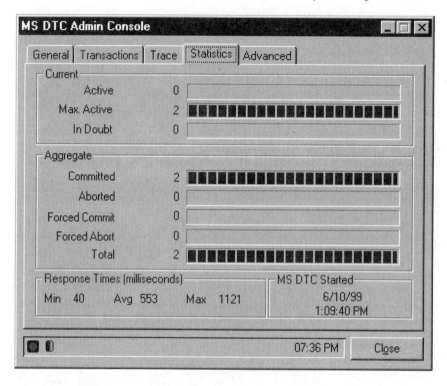

Database Security

In traditional client-server applications, the client application connects directly to the database. One of the administrative chores is to configure users and their privileges: in other words, database security requires that users be setup for specific use.

When using MTS with SQL Server, this burdensome administration can and should be eliminated. MTS components should not rely on the user's name and password in order to connect to the SQL database. Instead, access to SQL Server should be configured to allow MTS components to connect by providing the role(s) assigned to the package.

Recall how roles are used to isolate components from actual users: they define a single user or group of users that can access a component's package. Roles not only eliminate the extra user administration that's required in traditional client-server applications, using roles also ensures that database connections can be pooled.

If each connection to the database requires validation of the user with the user's password, each database connection is treated as a unique connection. This is because each database connection is first validated through the user's security identifier (SID). Since each database connection is unique, database pooling is eliminated. As a result, system resources are tied up and scalability is drastically degraded.

The beauty of SQL Server is it that it tightly integrates with Windows NT security. Between Windows NT and SQL Server, there exists a hierarchical security system. Here users, user groups, roles, and permissions can be granted across various layers.

SQL Server 7.0 can also be configured to use its own SQL Server authentication, where a user and password are separate and independent of Windows NT. Thus, SQL Server authentication relies on a non-trusted connection between the client and SQL server. Additionally, you can configure SQL Server to use a combination of both security methods.

Because MTS security is based on roles that build upon the Windows NT security model, the logical decision is to stay with Windows NT authentication. When a connection from Windows NT to SQL Server is initiated, a trusted relationship is established between the SQL Server and the client.

How does MTS fit into this picture? MTS is simply treated like any other client. Keep in mind that MTS security is also really just an extension of Windows NT security. MTS relies on roles, and roles isolate packages and components from actual users. This makes administration easier to deal with because a role can contain a Windows NT user group. Simply adding and deleting users from a user group at the Windows NT Server side is easy.

Adding Security to SQL Server

Going back to SQL Server, instead of having to add Windows NT accounts for each user, you can create a single login for the NT user group. Let's go through this process step by step.

> *Later in this exercise, you'll be generating error messages from the client that you just built. For ease of use, be sure to execute this application from the Visual Basic IDE and not from an executable file.*

The first thing to do is create a user login for the Windows NT user group MTS Users. Recall from Chapter 8 that you created this user group within Windows NT User Manager.

Open either SQL Server Manager or the node in MMC and expand the folder called Security. Locate and highlight the icon labeled Logins. Right-click your mouse and from the pop-up menu select New Login.

From the SQL Server Login Properties dialog, select the General tab. The first item at the top is a text box labeled Name: type in MTS USERS.

Continue to the next frame labeled Authentication. Select the option button for Windows NT authentication. Directly under this option button is a list box labeled Domain: locate and select the domain where SQL Server resides from the list box.

> *If you're using Windows NT Workstation with SQL server installed locally, the domain name will be the name of your local machine.*

After selecting the domain, notice that the domain name has also been inserted into the Name: text box at the top followed with a backslash.

Once again, we're going to use the sample `pubs` database that comes with the installation of SQL Server 7.0. Towards the bottom of the dialog is a frame labeled Defaults. From the dropdown list labeled <u>D</u>atabase, locate and select `pubs`. Leave the <u>L</u>anguage set at <Default>. It is important to understand that selecting `pubs` as your default has nothing to do with whether access is granted to this database. All this does is allow the database `pubs` to be authenticated first:

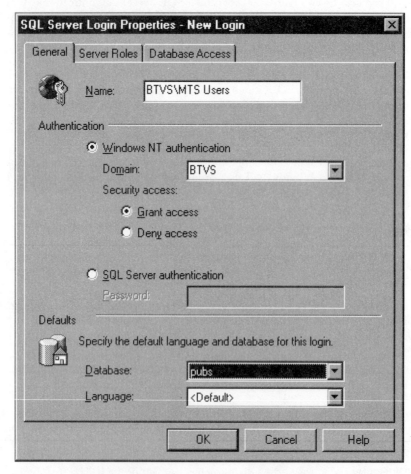

We're not going to assign any server roles so we'll skip the Server Roles tab. Briefly, server roles are used to administer users accessing the SQL Server. They're designed to grant server-wide security permissions to a particular login. For example, we just created a user group called MTS Users. This is designed to allow users in that user group to retrieve an SQL query. However, if you wanted all the users in this group to be able to create databases as well, you can assign the group to the SQL Server roll of Database Creators. As you can see, Server roles are not the same as MTS roles.

Let's go on to the last tab labeled Database Access. Regardless of whether you have access granted in the General tab, unless the database is selected at the Database Access tab, you will not be granted access.

Select `pubs`. Note that in the User column, MTS USERS has been entered.

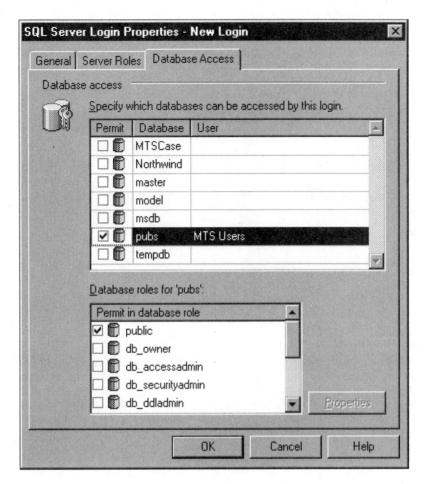

OK, you're now configured to allow users in the user group MTS Users to access the database pubs in SQL Server 7.0.

Testing Security Settings

Now that you've successfully configured database access for the pubs database, let's have some fun with it. In this next exercise, you're going to setup MTS security at the package level for the MTS StoredProc package. Then you will login as one of the users in the MTS role. Next, you'll try logging in as a user who is not in the MTS role.

When does the fun start? In the final exercise, you'll be able to see where security is taking place. First, you'll be stopped at the MTS package. Then you'll try again, but this time you will be denied access to SQL Server.

You should be fairly familiar with Window NT User Manager from the exercises in earlier chapters, and an expert with MTS Explorer, so I won't go into great detail when working with these.

Setting up the Users

Before starting this exercise, it's important to make sure the user group for MTS Users exists.

Open Windows NT User Manager and locate the user group MTS Users. Of course, if you no longer have this group, now is the time to recreate it.

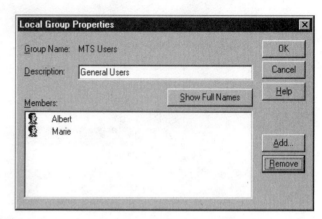

Originally, we had three members: Albert, Marie, and Thomas. Remove Thomas by highlighting his name and then clicking the Remove button. Then click OK:

Setting the MTS Security Settings

Open MTS Explorer and locate the package you created earlier in this chapter called MTS StoredProc.

For safety reasons, create an Administrator role. You will use this in case something goes wrong and you need access back into the package. Add the user Administrator to the Administrator role - be careful not to select the group Administrators by mistake.

Next, create a role called MTS Users. This will be the primary role where our fictitious users Albert and Marie will be granted access to the package. Add the MTS Users group to the role:

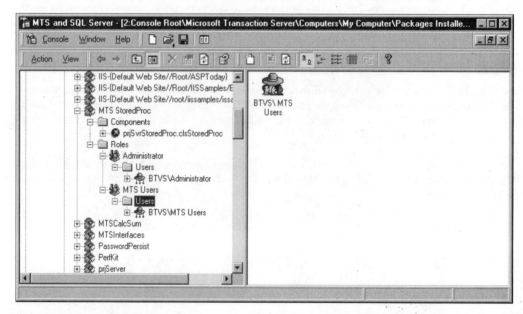

Bring up the properties dialog for the MTS StoredProc package and switch to the Identity tab. Make sure that the option button Interactive user – the current logged on user is selected:

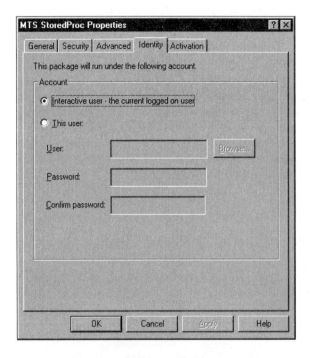

Next, select the Security tab and select the check box Enable authorization checking. This will activate declarative security for this package:

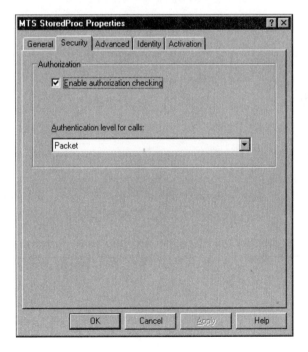

The first experiment is to verify that security is working properly. This means making sure security permissions are validated starting with Windows NT, through MTS, and finally to the SQL Server. To do this, simply execute the client prjSPClient. You should still be logged in as Administrator.

If all goes well, then you know that security down the line is active. First, you would not be logged in to Windows NT without being authenticated. Second, MTS would not allow you to access the package. Thus, the application would fail since it relies on calling MTS components. Finally, you would not be able to retrieve any data from SQL server if the administrator role in MTS didn't have permission to access the pubs database.

> *By default, Administrator is granted full permissions to access SQL Server when using Windows NT authentication.*

Now let's see security stop us at the MTS package and then at the SQL Server.

Security at the MTS Package Level

I had you take the user id Thomas out of the user group. Log off your machine, and then log in again as Thomas. Now try executing the client prjSPClient. What happened? You should have received an error stating that permission has been denied when you tried to run the client application.

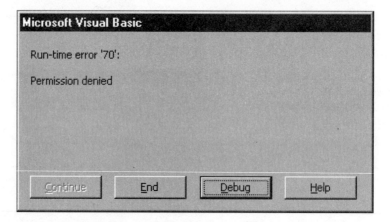

The simple fact that you successfully logged into NT tells you that you passed the first level of security. However, when trying to execute the client, you immediately receive the message Permission denied. This is telling you that you don't have permission to access the MTS package.

> *Knowing that this type of Run-time error occurs when permission is denied offers you the opportunity to set up an appropriate error handler.*

Security at the SQL Server Level

Now let's try another experiment. Open up SQL Server Enterprise Manager and open the Security folder as you did earlier in this chapter. In the left-pane, you'll see the login that you created for YourDomainName\MTS USERS. Highlight this login and click your right mouse button. From the pop-up menu, select Properties.

You should recognize the SQL Server Login Properties dialog, as this is where you earlier granted access to the user group `MTS Users` for the database `pubs`. This time you're going to take away access privileges so no one in the group MTS Users can access `pubs`, or for that matter, any other database.

Select the option button labeled Deny access. It's not necessary to return to the tab for Database Access as you have just denied access to all databases in SQL Server.

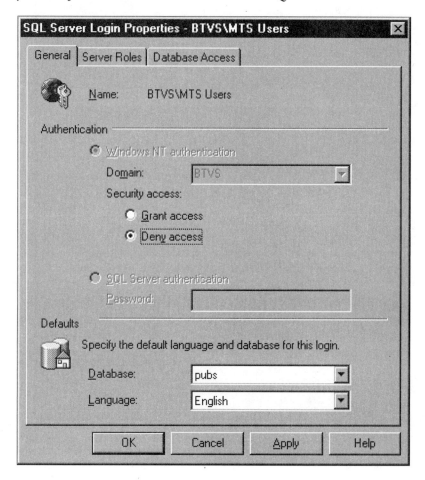

But suppose a user needs to be able to access other databases? If you stop access from the General tab, you prevent access to all databases. In this case, you could simply deselect the database(s) that you want to deny access from the Database Access tab and leave the setting at the General tab set to Grant access.

Log off your computer and log in as either Albert or Marie (as both are in the group MTS USERS) and try executing the client. What happens? The application does in fact open so we have successfully accessed the MTS package MTS StoredProc. But there is no data. Try clicking the command button. You should have generated an error. Why? Because MTS can't access SQL Server.

Let's try one more experiment. Log back in as Administrator, go back to the General tab for SQL Server Login Properties and make sure that Grant access is selected. Now change over to the Database Access tab. We're not going to use the other sample database called Northwind, but for demonstration purposes, select it. Now de-select the pubs database.

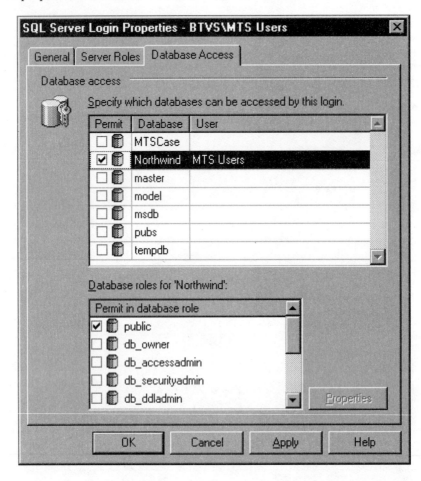

Log off your computer and log in as either Albert or Marie and try executing the client. You will receive the same run time error.

Now as one final experiment, log back in as Administrator and try executing the client. Why did the client work? The client works for the Administrator because you only denied access for the group MTS Users. If you had denied access to Administrator as well, you not only would have received the same error, you would not be able to get back into SQL Server Manager. You would have locked yourself out – and so ends this lesson!

Upsizing PasswordPersist to Use SQL-Server 7

Now let's move our test database that we developed in Access for `PasswordPersist` over to SQL-Server 7, and modify our components so they can use the new database.

Using the Upsizing Wizard

To get our Access database into SQL-Server, we could use a multitude of approaches. Two that immediately come to my mind are:

❑ Write the SQL scripts to create tables, foreign key relationships, etc.
❑ Use a database modeling tool to create the database

However, the easiest approach by far is to use the **Upsizing Wizard**, so this is what we'll do to get our tables into SQL-Server.

The Upsizing Wizard comes with Access 2000 or you can download it from the Microsoft website.

The first thing we'll need to do is create a SQL-Server database that the Upsizing Wizard will create the `PasswordPersist` schema in. Open up the SQL Server Enterprise Manager, and right-click on the Databases node to select a New Database...

This will bring up the Database Properties dialog box:

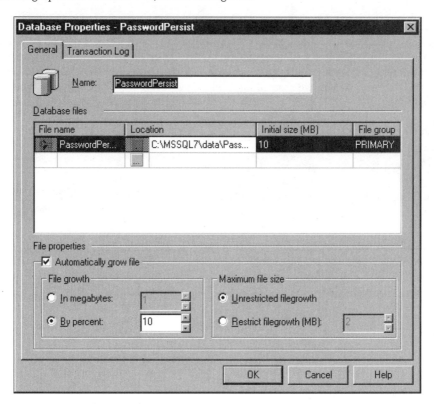

Name the new database PasswordPersist, and change the Initial size to 10 MB (which should be more than enough to suit our needs). Once you press OK, the `PasswordPersist` database should be listed under the Databases node:

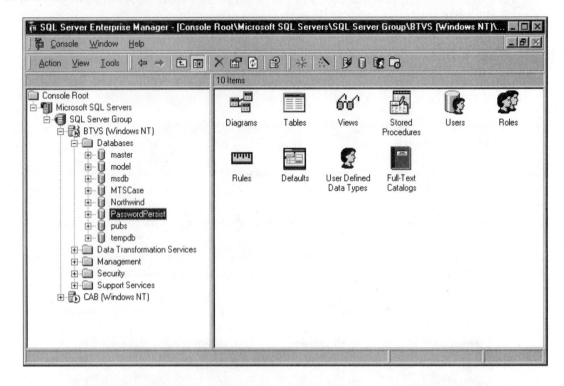

We'll also need to create a data source for this database that the Upsizing Wizard can use. We saw how to do this in Chapter 6, where we created an Access DSN using the Control Panel. The only differences this time are:

- ❑ Use the SQL Server ODBC driver
- ❑ Name the data source PPSQLServerDB
- ❑ Use `PasswordPersist` as the default database from the correct server

Now that the database is in place, we can use the Wizard. Make sure the `PasswordPersist` database is open in Access and launch the wizard:

From Access 97, it is found under the Add-Ins menu option of the Tools menu: from Access 2000, it's under the Database Utilities option.

The first screen in the Wizard will ask you if you want to use an existing database or a new one:

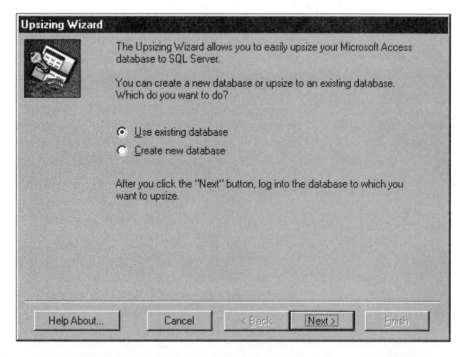

Choose the existing database option. This will prompt you to select the proper DSN:

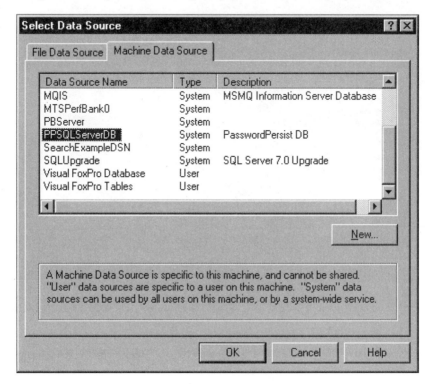

Choose the **PPSQLServerDB** DSN. Once that's done, you'll be given the choice to select which tables should be included in the process:

If you're asked about login information, just leave it as system administrator.

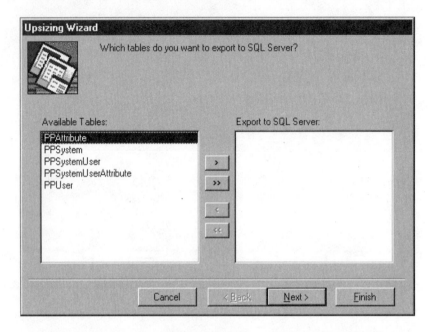

Select all of the tables from our Access database. The next screen in the Wizard looks like this:

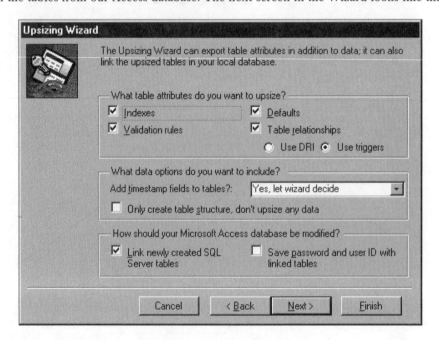

Make sure that you have all of the options selected correctly. Finally, you're given the option to create an upsizing report:

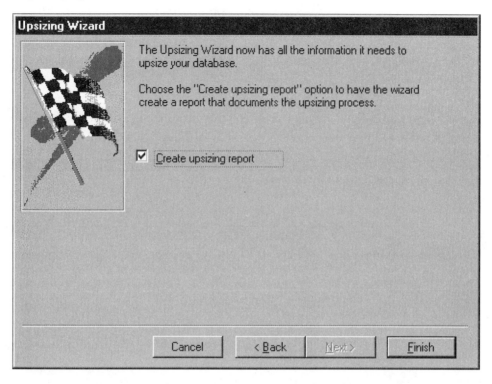

I'd recommend that you do, just in case anything goes wrong. During the upgrading process, you'll see a status screen:

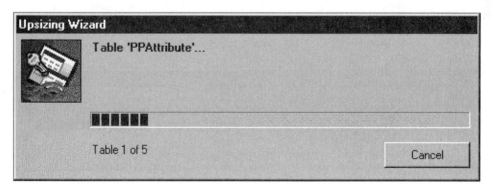

And once the wizard is done, you should see the following confirmation:

Finally, you should go back to **SQL Server Enterprise Manager** just to confirm that the structures are there. Here's a screen shot of the `PasswordPersist` database in SQL Server with the new tables:

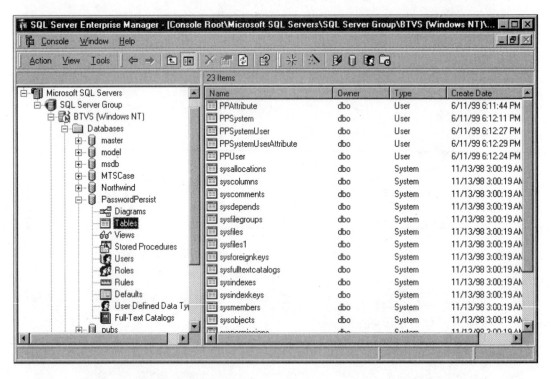

Using the SQL-Server Database From the Components

Now that we have our SQL-Server database in place, we should modify our components to use this database. However, this modification is extremely easy - only two lines of code need to be changed in both projects:

```
Public Const DB_CONN As String = "PPSQLServerDB"
Public Const DUPLICATE_RECORD As Long = 2601
```

That's it! We change our data source and we use SQL-Server's duplicate error number instead of Access's. All that's left to do is compile the components and run the test procedure we saw earlier to confirm that the SQL-Server database is running smoothly.

> *By the way, I found the error code by setting* DUPLICATE_RECORD *to 0 and running the components. I also logged the real error number via the App objects* LogEvent *method. When the duplicate error was raised, I looked in the Event Log and found the real error number. I did try to search through* **SQL-Server's Books Online**, *but I found my brute-force method worked quicker than searching through a plethora of error codes.*

Summary

This chapter has taken you through the data-tier, introducing general database techniques and methods by working with MS SQL Server 7.0.

You began the chapter with a short introduction to SQL Server and then relaxed with a brief review about transactions. You looked at examples of a Transact SQL transaction and a transaction executed through ADO, and learned how these methods for executing transactions are used in a typical client-server environment.

We then moved on to MS DTC, and took a detailed look at how it works. You had the chance to execute a distributed transaction using MS DTC.

Next, you learned how to enhance overall database performance. With a hands on project, you encapsulated stored procedures in an MTS component.

Your tour then continued with a lesson in SQL Server database security.

Finally, you used the Upsizing Wizard to convert your PasswordPersist database from Access to SQL Server.

So what's next? In the following chapter, we'll look at using MTS and the Internet.

12

MTS and the Internet

In the last chapter we were concerned with how MTS interacted with the Data tier. Now we are going to go to the complete other end of the spectrum and discover how MTS interacts with web-based technologies at the front-end.

This chapter is an introduction to Internet technologies that can be used to incorporate MTS transactions. We will cover the Internet, Active Server Pages (ASP), and finally how to integrate MTS transactions into Active Server Pages. In order to understand how to incorporate MTS with ASP, we'll put MTS to the side for a short while and learn about Active Server Pages themselves.

> *Note that it's beyond the scope of this book to cover HTML, VBScript or ASP programming in depth. We're introducing certain key items to help you better understand the concepts necessary to incorporate MTS into your Internet applications, as well as providing explanations to the code examples that you will work with in this chapter.*

After completing this chapter, you should be able to answer the following questions:

- ❑ What is Internet Information Server?
- ❑ What are Active Server Pages?
- ❑ Why should you avoid using VBScript for client scripts?
- ❑ Why use VBScript for server scripts?
- ❑ How does MTS work with ASP?
- ❑ What are ASP intrinsic objects?
- ❑ How do I make Active Server Pages transactional?
- ❑ What is a Web Administrator Manager object?
- ❑ Can I run my web applications in a separate memory location?

Internet Information Server (IIS)

Web sites today are nothing like they were a few years ago. They've evolved from static HTML into dazzling pages incorporating multimedia and user interaction. Furthermore, web sites are capable of delivering dynamically generated web pages to the user, to provide unique, customized information based specifically on that user's identity. In order for a web site to accomplish such complicated tasks, a web server needs to be able to integrate with software components and databases, including older legacy systems. This can be accomplished with Microsoft Internet Information Server (IIS), through the use of special extensions (DLLs) referred to as **Internet Server Application Programming Interface (ISAPI)**.

Internet Information Server (IIS) is no doubt the core to Microsoft's Internet strategy. IIS is tightly integrated with Windows NT Server security. In addition, IIS includes a new technology referred to as Active Server Pages (ASP), which integrates itself tightly with MTS. Active Server Pages can be coded as transactional, thus giving ASP the same benefits as any other MTS transactional component.

Perhaps best of all, like MTS, it's free. Internet Information Server can be downloaded from Microsoft's web site or installed from the Windows NT 4 Option Pack.

Internet Information Server can be managed from Microsoft Management Console (MMC) by adding in a snap-in, as previously done with MTS Explorer. In fact, you may find that saving a MMC configuration that combines MTS, IIS, and SQL Server managers in one view is a practical administrative method. A configuration that displays all three snap-ins into one view can allow you to manage various tasks without jumping around from one manager to another.

Additionally, you can run a separate window for each snap-in by selecting Window from the menu bar and then selecting New Window.

Active Server Pages

Web severs relay information to a user's web browser through **HyperText Markup Language (HTML)**. HTML is static in the sense that it doesn't change. Look at any page in this book that you're reading. You see print, perhaps a diagram, and it's static: every time you look at this page, it will appear the same as before. If changes to this page were needed, it would be a difficult process to say the least. HTML pages are similar in the sense that, once a page is coded in HTML and placed on the web server, that code doesn't change.

Suppose you wanted to display a current list of items in stock to a potential customer via a web browser. The information is constantly changing, and you want to be able to dynamically display new information as it changes. How would you do it? You could take the customer's request through a web browser and retrieve the information from a database using ADO. But how do you display this information into a document that the user's browser understands?

Microsoft's solution is through the use of **Active Server Pages**. You can use ADO to retrieve a recordset and then use an Active Server Page to generate a dynamic HTML page. An Active Server Page is a text file, closely related to an HTML file. The major difference is that ASP files can contain script that must be executed at the server before the page is sent to the client, whereas HTML scripts are only executed at the client. Where HTML files use a file extension of htm or html, an ASP file uses asp for its extension. The asp extension tells the web server that any existing server scripts need to be parsed at the server.

This is accomplished through the use of a **Web Application Manager (WAM)** object that communicates with the application and various DLL extensions (such as ISAPIs) every time an HTTP request is received. A WAM object is an in-process COM object (`WAM.DLL`). When a request is received from a browser client, a WAM object is responsible for screening the ASP for server script code. You'll learn more about the Web Application Manager later in this chapter.

For now, understand that Active Server Pages can contain HTML and both client and server script. When an HTTP request for an ASP is received at the web server, the server script is executed and a file is generated and placed into memory. This file is the response information that will be returned to the requesting client browser, and essentially contains static HTML (or XML) and client side script.

> It's important to understand that any HTML or client scripting is automatically returned to the client browser for execution. Server script is never returned to the client.

Client scripting allows for several types of enhanced interaction with the user. Through client script, one can generate responses to events such as a mouse-click or data entry from an input box. For example, suppose you have a web site that sells books about MTS. Using client script, you can validate a web page form to ensure that all pertinent information about the customer and payment information is supplied before sending the information to the server.

However, with every positive, there seems to be a negative. Because client scripting is returned to the browser for processing, problems can occur when the client is unable to process the request. The major reason for potential problems is browser incompatibility. Recall that **Browser-Neutral** applications are designed to work with any browser. These applications are based on standard HTML, so don't support any enhanced features such as ActiveX controls or scripting languages. **Browser-Enhanced** applications are usually browser specific, and only work with certain architectures. For example, while Netscape's browser can only use JavaScript and its own version of DHTML, Microsoft's browsers can also take advantage of VBScript and MS enhanced DHTML. There are even differences between Netscape's JavaScript and Microsoft's version of JavaScript (JScript).

Unless you're operating an intranet where you can enforce the use of a particular browser, Browser-Enhanced applications that rely on client scripts are not of much use. Active Server Pages solve numerous problems of browser incompatibly, by making use of server side scripting. As long as the scripting is done at the server, the client browser doesn't care what scripting language is used.

Active Server Pages use VBScript as the default language. Browsers such as Internet Explorer and Netscape use JavaScript (JScript) as their default language.

VBScript – Server Script Language of Choice

It's important to understand that ASP is not a scripting language.

> **ASP is an environment that permits script language code to be executed.**

This is accomplished through the use of COM script engines. Active Server Pages can use a variety of scripting languages including Perl, although ASP only has built in support for **Visual Basic Script (VBScript)** and JavaScript (JScript). In the case of Perl and other scripting languages, it will be necessary to seek out third party vendors.

Visual Basic programmers will probably prefer to use VBScript as their language of choice for server side scripting. As a matter of fact, VBScript is the default for Active Server Pages. If you use JScript or another scripting language, you must specify the language with a language tag.

Perhaps one of the best reasons to use VBScript (especially if you are a Visual Basic programmer), is that you can quickly and easily learn to use it. VBScript is closely related to Visual Basic, but you shouldn't let this be the only influencing factor in your decision. Another excellent reason for using VBScript is that it provides better integration with Active Server Pages as opposed to other scripting languages. For example, VBScript offers better error handling and reporting than other script languages. VBScript also provides better support for ActiveX Server components. I would even say that ASP was designed with VBScript in mind.

So why does ASP support JScript? JavaScript is a very popular scripting language among web developers. Many web and application developers are C++ programmers, and this allows for C++ users to quickly become comfortable with ASP. Furthermore, most non-Microsoft Internet programming is done with Java and JavaScript.

Working with VBScript

As previously mentioned, VBScript is a close relative of Visual Basic. Nevertheless, there are differences that may take some time getting used to. For example, VBScript only uses variants for variables.

Let's take a look at some short scripts designed to return the date to the user. I recommend that you follow along in the book as opposed to entering this code. After going over a few different scripts, you'll have the opportunity to try a hands-on project.

> Note, because Netscape does not support VBScript, you'll need to use Internet Explorer when working with the client scripts presented in this section.

Client VBScript

The following VBScript will return the date from the client machine and display it in an HTML web page.

```
<HTML>
<B>Display a Message Box</B><BR>
<B><I>This Script is Executed at the Client</I></B>
<BR>
<BR>

<SCRIPT LANGUAGE ="VBScript">
Dim dtm
dtm="The date is: " & Date
MsgBox (dtm)
</SCRIPT>
</HTML>
```

If you were to execute this code, a Visual Basic message box would pop up from the browser window displaying the date. Clicking OK would close it. The only way to make it appear again is to either refresh the page or exit the page and then call it up again:

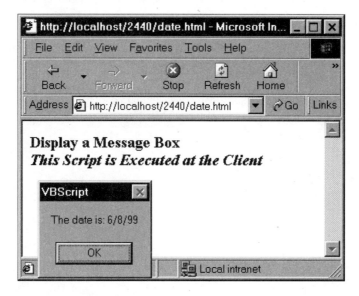

Looks simple doesn't it? Nevertheless, let's review this script. The first few lines are standard HTML statements that all browsers are capable of reading, and simply format the text lines that are displayed on the HTML page:

```
<HTML>
<B>Display a Message Box</B><BR>
<B><I>This Script is Executed at the Client</I></B>
<BR>
<BR>
```

The following statement is used to mark the beginning of the script and to specify the script language. This is necessary in our example, as the default language in HTML is JScript:

```
<SCRIPT LANGUAGE ="VBScript">
```

The script routine makes use of simple Visual Basic statements (recall that VBScript is essentially Visual Basic with minor nuances of its own). For example, notice that the variable dt is a variant. VBScript does not specify variable data types. In other words, all variables are typed as a variant:

```
Dim dtm
dtm="The date is: " & Date
MsgBox (dtm)
```

The last two tags are used to tell the browser where the script routine and the HTML page end:

```
</SCRIPT>
</HTML>
```

Server VBScript

Now we'll look at another script that returns the date. However, this time VBScript will be used in an Active Server Page in order to return the date from the server as opposed to having the date returned from the client machine.

In the previous example you created a client side script and made use of a message box. However, when using code that executes on the server, there are certain restrictions. For example, you can't use message boxes or input boxes, as server scripts don't provide a user interface. Suppose you were able to create a message box in a server script: how would the user see it? Because the scripts are executed at the server, the user would have to travel to the server just to click an OK response! With this in mind, let's alter our code to generate a dynamic HTML page, where VBScript is executed at the server.

Take a look at the following ASP page:

```
<HTML>
<B>VBScript - Display Date</B>
<BR>
<BR>

<SCRIPT LANGUAGE ="VBScript" RUNAT="Server">
Dim dtm
dtm="The date is: " & Date
Response.Write dtm
</SCRIPT>
</HTML>
```

This simple script displays a web page with a static text string and concatenates the date that is retrieved from the server:

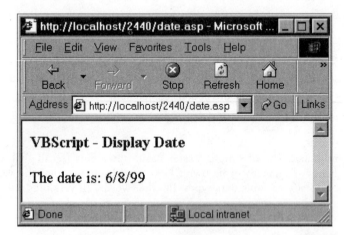

You may notice that there are no provisions for using a message box in this code. But did you notice the key item in the script that makes it execute at the server as opposed to executing at the client machine?

The first four lines are standard HTML code:

```
<HTML>
<B>VBScript - Display Date</B>
<BR>
<BR>
```

The next line tells ASP which script language you wish to use. Now, pay close attention to the command RUNAT="Server". This tells ASP that the script is to be run at the server. Remember an ASP can also contain client script:

```
<SCRIPT LANGUAGE ="VBScript" RUNAT="Server">
```

The following three lines makes up the script routine. Here we have declared the variable dtm, which will concatenate the string The date is: and the current date, by executing the Date function at the server side.

```
Dim dtm
dtm="The date is: " & Date
Response.Write dtm
```

It's important to understand that this routine can only be executed because it comes between the start <SCRIPT> and the end </SCRIPT> tags.

You could also retrieve the date in the following way:

```
<HTML>
<B>Display Date</B>
<BR>
<BR>

The date is: <%=date%>
</HTML>
```

You don't have to tell the Active Server Page that you are using VBScript because it's the default for server scripting. Using script statements between the delimiters <%   %> allows more flexibility when designing web pages. In this example, the text The date is: is actually an HTML statement and not a text string in VBScript.

As you can see, either method works fine. However, when you want to execute a long script, using the previous method where you can enter a block of script statements may be easier to manage. This will appear more obvious in the exercise later in the chapter.

ASP Intrinsic Objects

Before you go on to create any Active Server Pages, let's look at some of the framework for ASP. This provides five built-in objects:

❑ Request
❑ Response
❑ Server
❑ Application
❑ Session

Whenever an ASP receives an HTTP request, a **Request object** is created. The Request object is used to store information about the client browser making the request. Perhaps the most common use for this object is to retrieve data entered into an HTML form by the user. For example, the Request object could be used to return order information, such as customer and payment details, that has been supplied by a user.

The **Response object** can be used to return information to the user. For example, if the user has supplied order information from an HTML form using the Request object, you can return a confirmation or failure message back to the user using the Response object.

The Response object is also commonly used to return **cookies** to the client. Cookies are blocks of data that a web server can store on a client machine. They are often used to identify users and provide information to the web server for administrative purposes. Despite privacy concerns about the use of cookies, they can benefit the user, as we'll see when we look at the Session object in a moment.

Interaction between the server and the client is achieved through methods and functions provided by the **Server object**. Perhaps one of the most commonly used methods with the Server object, is CreateObject. CreateObject is used the same way as in MTS components that are developed with Visual Basic. In other words, CreateObject is used to instantiate COM components on the server.

The **Application object** is created by a group of files on the web server that make up a virtual root directory, and is designed to share information between all users. When the first request comes for one of these files, an Application object is created. This Application object is capable of sharing data among all users.

The **Session object** is capable of storing information about a particular user's session. Generally speaking, a session is a sequence of interactions that occur between the client and the server. The first time a user makes a request to the web application, a Session object is created for that specific user. Only one Session object per user can be created.

State among Session object variables will persist until the session ends. As soon as the user exits the web application, the session is considered over and the Session object will terminate.

So how can `Session` objects be put to good use? Information such as user preferences can be stored in cookies and locally stored by the web server to the client machine. Such information can include user settings, passwords, and other data that is relevant to the specific user. This client information can then be retrieved by the web server during a different session. So, when a new session is started, cookie information can be placed into session variables that can be used throughout the current session.

Before we learn about how MTS can work with ASP, let's get our feet wet and create a simple ASP.

ASP comes with the Microsoft web servers IIS and Personal Web Server (a scaled down version of IIS). You'll need to have one of these installed in order to run the following exercises.

Creating a Simple ASP

To create Active Server Pages, you can either use one of a variety of development tools (such as MS InterDev and MS Front Page), or you can use a simple text editor such as MS Notepad. The only requirement for creating Active Server Pages is that the file you create can be saved in ASCII format using the extension `.asp`.

To demonstrate how easily you can create Active Server Pages, we're going to use MS Notepad for all our coding. Open Notepad and enter the following:

```
<HTML>
<HEAD>
<TITLE>Welcome To My Active Server Page!</TITLE>
</HEAD>
<B>ASP Server Scripts - <I>VBScript</I></B>

<%RANDOMIZE%>

<BR>
<P>Your Lucky Lottery Number for <% =Date %> <U>is</U>
   <%= Int(10000 * Rnd) %></P>
<BR>
<P>Thank you for visiting Lucky Lottery Number Picker </P>
<BR>
<BR>

<SCRIPT LANGUAGE ="VBscript" RUNAT="Server">
Dim dtm
dtm="The date is: "  & Date
Response.Write dtm
</SCRIPT>

</HTML>
```

Now you need to publish your page to the server. If you're working on a test machine where IIS or Personal Web Server is installed, you can save your file directly to a folder on the web server.

Save the file you just created as `lottery.asp`. In the screen shot below, `lottery.asp` is saved to the folder `webpub`. Be sure to set **Save as type** for **All Files**.

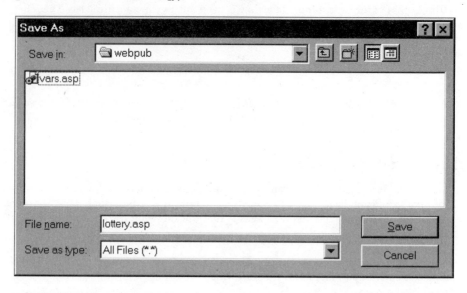

Because this Active Server Page only utilizes server script, you can view it with the browser of your choice. The following is the syntax necessary to view your page:

```
http://your server name/folder name/asp page name
```

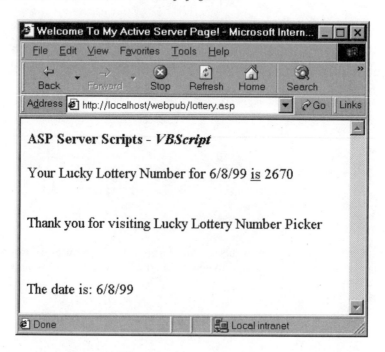

When working with Active Server Pages, you may find it quicker and easier to open the pages through MMC. It also helps if you are having trouble identifying the correct path.

Open MMC with the IIS snap-in. Expand the folder where your Active Server Pages reside. Locate the page you just created named `lottery.asp` and highlight it. Next, click your right mouse button and select **Browse** from the pop-up menu:

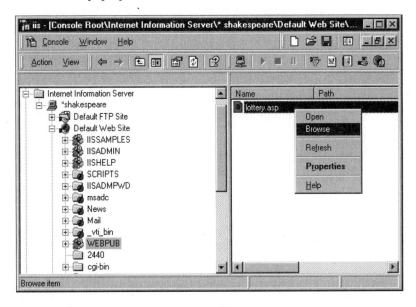

You may be interested to know that when viewing the source code for an ASP from a browser, actual server script code is not available. It's more than hidden, it's not there! This is because server script is never sent to the browser. Instead of being able to view business logic, only the results are displayed:

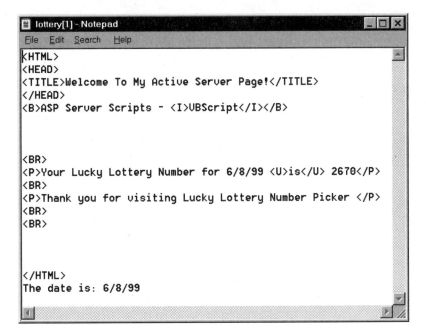

Notice that the date and a number is displayed instead of showing actual server script code.

Using ASP and SQL Server

In this next example, you'll create a dynamic HTML listing by retrieving information directly from SQL Server. In this project, you'll be bypassing MTS, and going directly to SQL Server. But don't despair – MTS is coming. After completing this exercise, you'll have the foundation needed to incorporate MTS into your project.

This project requires SQL Server and either IIS or Personal Web Server to be installed.

To save time creating a database on SQL Server, we'll use the pubs database that's provided as a sample when SQL Server 7.0 is installed. Open Notepad and enter the following code:

```
<HTML>
<HEAD>
<TITLE>Database Access</TITLE>
</HEAD>

<BODY>
<CENTER>

<H1>Connecting to SQL Server</H1>
<H2>Using ADO & VBScript in an Active Server Page</H2>

<%

Dim ADOConnection
Dim ConnectString

'note: change the server name to the name of your server. Also, if you are using
'ODBC, change Data Source to the name you have configured

ConnectString = " Server=YourSvrNm; Data Source=YourDSNnm;" & _
                " Driver=SQL Server; Database=pubs; UID=sa;Password;"

Set ADOConnection = Server.CreateObject("ADODB.Connection")
Set RecordsetEmployee = Server.CreateObject("ADODB.Recordset")
ADOConnection.Open ConnectString
Set RecordsetEmployee = _
    ADOConnection.Execute("SELECT fname,lname,hire_date FROM employee")

%>

<TABLE ALIGN=CENTER CELLPADDING=5 BORDER=0 WIDTH=300>
  <TR>
    <TD VALIGN=TOP>First Name</TD>
    <TD ALIGN=CENTER>Last Name</TD>
    <TD ALIGN=CENTER>Hire Date</TD>
  </TR>
```

```
<% Do While Not RecordsetEmployee.EOF %>
  <TR>
    <TD ALIGN=CENTER>
      <%=RecordsetEmployee("fname")%>
    </TD>
    <TD ALIGN=CENTER>
      <%=RecordsetEmployee("lname")%>
    </TD>
    <TD ALIGN=CENTER>
      <%=RecordsetEmployee("hire_date")%>
    </TD>
  </TR>

  <% RecordsetEmployee.MoveNext %>
<%Loop%>
</TABLE>

</CENTER>
</BODY>

</HTML>
```

I'll explain the code you just entered shortly. For now, name and save your file as ADO.asp. Store your Active Server Page into a folder on your web server (such as the webpub directory) as shown in the previous example. If you're using ODBC, you'll also need to set up a Data Source Name (DSN) using the ODBC Administrator from the Control Panel. Now, view your file using your favorite browser:

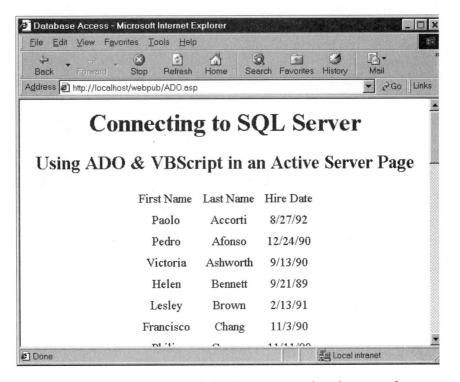

Impressive, isn't it? Let's take a look at the code for this project and see how it works.

The first eight lines are standard HTML. Here we are simply making two header statements:

```
<HTML>
<HEAD>
<TITLE>Database Access</TITLE>
</HEAD>

<BODY>
<CENTER>

<H1>Connecting to SQL Server</H1>
<H2>Using ADO & VBScript in an Active Server Page</H2>
```

The next block of code is isolated between the brackets `<% %>`, to indicate that it is server script. The code between the brackets is nothing unusual. You're simply creating a connection string and using ADO to connect to the database:

```
Dim ADOConnection
Dim ConnectString

Connectstring = " Server=YourSvrNm; Data Source=YourDSNnm;" & _
                " Driver=SQL Server; Database=pubs; UID=sa; Password;"

Set ADOConnection = Server.CreateObject("ADODB.Connection")
Set RecordsetEmployee = Server.CreateObject("ADODB.Recordset")
ADOConnection.Open ConnectString
```

When a connection is established, the SQL statement `SELECT fname,lname,hire_date FROM employee` is executed. The result is placed into `RecordsetEmployee`, which serves as a recordset:

```
Set RecordsetEmployee = _
    ADOConnection.Execute("SELECT fname,lname,hire_date FROM employee")
```

The next block of code is a little tricky, as it is a combination of server script that cycles though the recordset and HTML that is used to format how the recordset is displayed to the user.

The first line below is server script, and it introduces a `Do While...Loop` that will cycle through the recordset `RecordsetEmployee`. This is followed by an HTML `<TR>` tag, that is used to start a new table row. Data is added to the table between the `<TD>` and `</TD>` tags. Think of the `<TD>` tag as a cell where data is placed. The data is centered in this cell by having `ALIGN=CENTER` inside the table data tag. Notice that server script is placed between the lines that contain `<TD ALIGN=CENTER>` and `</TD>`. These script statements are used to output the desired column information from the recordset.

The last two lines are used to advance to the next record in the recordset, and the loop returns back to the top of the `Do While...Loop`:

```
<% Do While Not RecordsetEmployee.EOF %>
  <TR>
    <TD ALIGN=CENTER>
      <%=RecordsetEmployee("fname")%>
    </TD>
    <TD ALIGN=CENTER>
      <%=RecordsetEmployee("lname")%>
```

```
    </TD>
    <TD ALIGN=CENTER>
      <%=RecordsetEmployee("hire_date")%>
    </TD>
  </TR>

  <% RecordsetEmployee.MoveNext %>
<%Loop%>
```

The remaining statements are HTML used to format the table's columns. For example CELL PADDING is the amount of space between the edges of the cell and the cell's contents. BORDER is used to declare the border width. Because we specified BORDER=0, the border is not shown. Finally, WIDTH is used to declare the width of the table in pixels:

```
<TABLE ALIGN=CENTER CELLPADDING=5 BORDER=0 WIDTH=300>
  <TR>
    <TD VALIGN=TOP>First Name</TD>
    <TD ALIGN=CENTER>Last Name</TD>
    <TD ALIGN=CENTER>Hire Date</TD>
  </TR>
```

Now that you've covered the basics of Active Server Pages and VBScript, let's go on and learn how to incorporate MTS into your web pages.

MTS and ASP

Thanks to the integration between MTS and IIS, you can include transactional scripts within Active Server Pages. Each ASP is capable of creating one transaction every time a transactional ASP is called. In other words, whenever a transactional ASP is executed, a new transaction is created.

Any objects that may be created within an ASP will be included within the transaction. If any part of the transaction fails, then the entire transaction is rolled back. Furthermore, if the transaction requires the use of more than one component in order for it to complete, you need to call all components from the same Active Server Page. In simpler terms, you cannot have a single transaction span multiple ASP scripts. This is to ensure that the transaction remains atomic.

Creating Transactional Active Server Pages

In order for an ASP to become transactional, the first script line on the page must start with:

```
<%@ Transaction = parameter %>
```

Transaction parameters can be any of the following:

Requires_New	This parameter requires a new transaction.
Required	Using Required starts a new transaction.
Supported	Using this parameter does not start a new transaction but will support an existing one.
Not_Supported	This parameter states that an ASP is not to be included in a transaction. Non-transactional scripts do not need to use this statement as Not_Supported is the default for all ASP scripts.

> **Failing to put <%@ Transaction = parameter %> in the first line of an ASP script will result in a script error.**

If these values remind you of transaction properties that you set in MTS components, you're right – these values have the same effect.

One thing to be aware of is that transactional scripts lack an explicit indicator to show when the transaction has ended. Recall in a Transact-SQL statement that the end of the transaction is indicated with the statement COMMIT TRANSACTION. As you'll soon see, transactional scripts simply end when the script comes to an end in the current ASP.

Like MTS components designed with Visual Basic, Active Server Pages can use the ObjectContext object. Two methods are available that can be used in Active Server Pages: SetComplete and SetAbort. Interestingly, SetComplete is often not necessary in server script, because the transaction is automatically considered complete when the ASP completes the script (as long as SetAbort is not called):

```
<%@ TRANSACTION = Required %>

<%
Set objInventory = Server.CreateObject("MTSbooks.Inventory")

'Running a check to verify items are in stock
strQuanCheck = objInventory.InvQuanCheck(intMTSQuantity)

If strQuanCheck = "OutOfStock" Then
  ObjectContext.SetAbort

' Note that Response.Write is being used to let the user know that the
' transaction failed.
  Response.Write("This transaction cannot complete - Temporarily OUT OF STOCK")

Else
  ObjectContext.SetComplete
  Response.Write("This transaction can complete")

End If
%>
```

Unfortunately there's not an explicit way of determining whether a transaction actually completes or aborts within an ASP script. In the previous code example, you can see that the only indication of whether the transaction completed or failed was a written response when SetAbort occurred due to the value of strQuanCheck being set to OutOfStock.

A handy way of providing information to the user regarding the status of a transaction is through the use of two events, OnTransactionCommit and OnTransactionAbort. With these events, you can supply conditional logic in order to provide information to the user reflecting when a transaction commits or aborts:

```
<%@ TRANSACTION = Required %>

<%
Sub OnTransactionCommit( )
  Response.Write("Your Order for Prof MTS App Dev w/VB6 has been placed.")
End Sub
```

```
Sub OnTransactionAbort( )
  Response.Write("There was a problem completing your transaction")
End Sub
%>
```

It's important to understand that these events don't occur until after `SetComplete` or `SetAbort` occurs. If a transaction is successful, a response from the `OnTransactionCommit` event cannot occur until the entire server script has been successfully processed and `SetComplete` has been called.

Now that you've worked with a variety of ASP scripts and have learned how to make an Active Server Page transactional, let's move on to the next exercise and use MTS with an ASP.

Using MTS with ASP

One of the first exercises you tried in this book used a simple calculator (using COM) that added two numbers so the owners of the Grog Company could give themselves bonuses. We've come a long way since then. As one of your last hands-on exercises, you will upgrade the bonus calculator and incorporate it into an Active Server Page and MTS.

You'll be creating three items for this project. First you'll create the MTS component. Next you'll create an HTML page to pass information from the user to the third item that you'll build, the ASP.

Creating the MTS component

We'll start with our MTS component. Create a new ActiveX DLL project in VB and name it `ASPCalc` and the class `clsNewBonusCalc`. Locate the window that displays the class properties for `clsNewBonusCalc` and set **MTSTransactionMode** to **2 – RequiresTransaction**.

Next add project references for:

❑ Microsoft ActiveX Data Objects 2.0 Library (or higher)
❑ Microsoft Transaction Server Type Library

Then open the class window and enter the following code:

```
Option Explicit

Implements ObjectControl

Private mobjContext As ObjectContext

Public Function BonusAmt(curSal As Single, sngPercent As Single) As Single

  BonusAmt = ((curSal * sngPercent) + curSal)

End Function

Private Sub ObjectControl_Activate()

  Set mobjContext = GetObjectContext

End Sub
```

```
Private Function ObjectControl_CanBePooled() As Boolean

   ObjectControl_CanBePooled = True

End Function
```

```
Private Sub ObjectControl_Deactivate()

   Set mobjContext = Nothing

End Sub
```

After entering your code, save your work and create `ASPCalc.dll`.

Next you need to register your component with MTS. Open MTS Explorer, create a new package named `ASP Project`, and install the component `ASPCalc.dll` into the package.

> *Although you created your component specifying MTSTransactionMode to be set for RequiresTransaction, double check the transactional mode for your package (ASP Project) to ensure it is set for RequiresTransaction.*

Creating the HTML Form

Open Notepad and enter the following HTML code:

```
<HTML>
<HEAD>
<TITLE>Bonus Calculator</TITLE>
</HEAD>

<BODY>
<CENTER>

<H1>Welcome to the Bonus Calculator</H1>
<H2>This Project uses HTML, ASP & MTS!</H2>

<FORM ACTION="Bonus.asp" METHOD=POST>
<BR>Current Salary: <INPUT TYPE="TEXT" NAME="CurSal" VALUE="" SIZE=40>
<BR>Percent (use decimals): <INPUT TYPE="TEXT" NAME="Percent" VALUE="" SIZE=33>
<P><INPUT TYPE="SUBMIT" NAME="" VALUE="Total Payable">
<INPUT TYPE="RESET" NAME="" VALUE="Clear Values">
</FORM>

</CENTER>
</BODY>
</HTML>
```

Save the file as `Bonus.html`. Make sure you store this file on the web server, such as in the `webpub` directory we used earlier. Note that this file uses an extension of `html` and not `asp`. When this page is called, all code will be executed at the client browser.

Creating the Active Server Page

Create a new document using Notepad and enter the following code:

```
<%@ TRANSACTION = Required %>

<HTML>
<HEAD>
<TITLE>Bonus Calculator </TITLE>
</HEAD>

<CENTER>
<BODY>

<H1>Welcome to the Bonus Calculator</H1>
<H2>This Project uses HTML, ASP & MTS!</H2>

<%
CurSal=Request.form("CurSal")
Percent =Request.form("Percent")
%>

Current Salary: <% = FormatCurrency(CurSal) %><BR>
Bonus Percent : <% = Percent %><P>

<%
Set Bonus=Server.CreateObject("ASPCalc.clsNewBonusCalc")
ASPAmt=Bonus.BonusAmt(CSng(CurSal),CSng(Percent))
Response.Write("Your Paycheck with Bonus will be : "+ FormatCurrency(ASPAmt))
%>

<BR>
<BR>
<BR>

<%
Sub OnTransactionCommit()
  Response.Write("This request processed successfully!")
End Sub

Sub OnTransactionAbort()
  Response.Write("There was a problem with your request")
End Sub
%>


</BODY>
</CENTER>
</HTML>
```

Name the file `Bonus.asp` and store it in the same folder as `Bonus.html`. Again, notice that this file is using the extension `asp` indicating that it's an Active Server Page, and server script will be executed at the server as opposed to the user's browser.

Running the Application

OK, it's time to test the application. You need to launch the HTML file `Bonus.html` from you web browser. Looking over your handy work, you should see that there are two input boxes where you can enter information.

Enter a large number in the input box labeled Current Salary and a decimal number in the input box labeled Percent.

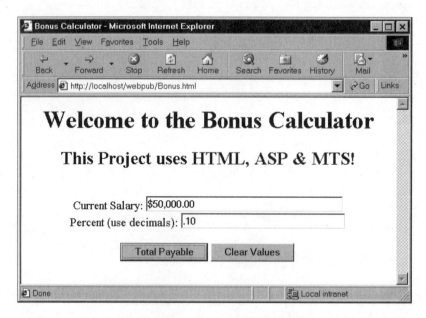

Now select the Total Payable button:

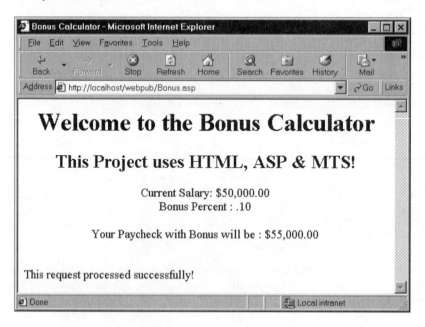

Cool, isn't it? Be sure to pay attention to the last statement displayed on the form. Hopefully is says **This request processed successfully!** This statement was generated from the following code in the Active Server Page:

```
<%
Sub OnTransactionCommit()
  Response.Write("This request processed successfully!")
End Sub

Sub OnTransactionAbort()
  Response.Write("There was a problem with your request")
End Sub
%>
```

In case you're still unsure whether everything went the way it should, you can open MTS Explorer and look at the transaction statistics:

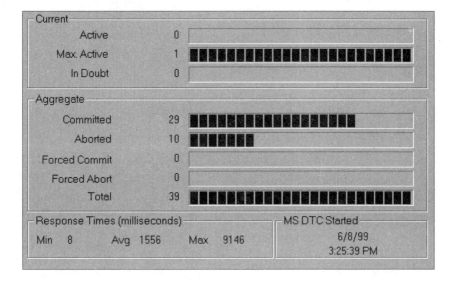

Running MTS and IIS in Separate Processes

Although you can run MTS components in the same process as ASP pages, any failure that causes MTS to terminate can also bring down Internet Information Server. IIS version 4.0 introduces a new feature that aids in crash prevention.

You now can configure IIS so that each application can run in a separate process by using MTS. This is a practical feature that offers protection to other applications running on the same system. In the event an ASP application fails, only the application's process terminates and not IIS itself. Furthermore, running ASP applications in different processes allows for easy administration and maintenance, since you have the ability to shut down a specific process without affecting other applications.

Managing MTS and IIS - WAM

Before we actually isolate our Active Server Pages, you need to understand how IIS applications are managed through Web Application Manager (WAM) components. WAM has the job of loading all associated application Internet Server Application Programming Interface (ISAPI) DLLs as well as the ASP runtime environment. Recall that ISAPI DLLs are special extensions to IIS. Active Server Pages are also ISAPIs. It is WAMs responsibility to communicate with these DLLs every time an HTTP request is made.

> **You should understand that WAMs are MTS components.**

MTS is responsible for managing each web application process, regardless of whether the application is running in process or resides in its own process. Thus every application will have its own instance of a WAM object. As you'll see shortly, whenever you use IIS to configure an application to run in a separate process, MTS automatically creates a new MTS package and installs a WAM component.

> *When you install MTS and IIS 4.0, they become tightly integrated with each other. As a matter of fact, you can't install IIS 4.0 by itself – installing IIS 4.0 automatically installs MTS as well. As a result, all ASP applications will run with packages in MTS.*

If you open MTS Explorer and then open the Components folder for IIS In- Process Applications, you'll see a number of installed components showing a reference to WAM. For example, one component will be labeled IISWAM.1_ROOT. By default, applications are automatically configured to run in the same process as IIS:

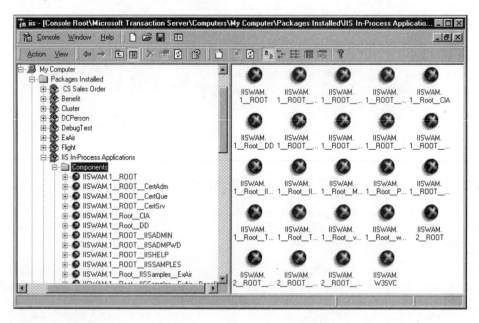

To isolate Active Server Pages into another process, you need to create a virtual directory on the web server and then place your web files into this folder. You can use MMC for this.

Isolating ASP

Open IIS through MMC. Locate and highlight the web server and click your right mouse button. In this example the web server is named `Default Web Site`. From the pop-up menu select <u>N</u>ew and then select Virtual Directory:

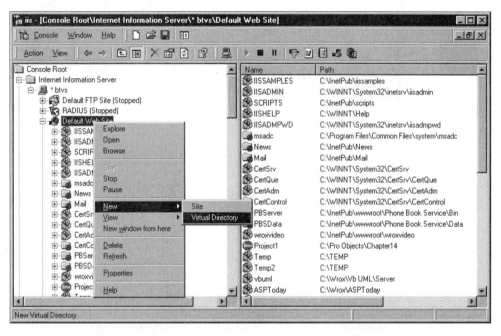

From the New Virtual Directory Wizard, type in an alias for accessing the virtual directory you want to create. In this example, the alias is MyVirtualDirecory:

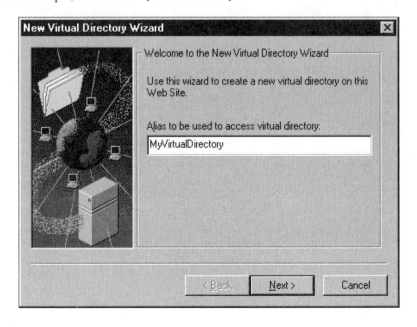

Next, you need to enter the physical path for the directory where you are going to store your Active Server Pages.

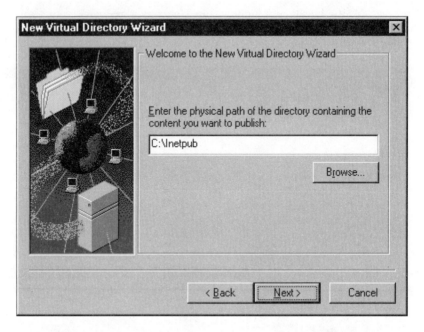

The next dialog allows you to set access permissions to the virtual directory:

You can now see the new virtual directory named `MyVirtualDirectory`:

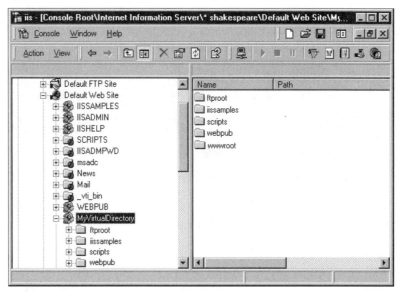

If your virtual directory doesn't contain copies of the Active Server Pages you created earlier, copy and place them into this folder now.

To test this directory and verify the path, expand `MyVirtualDirectory` and open the directory `webpub`. In the right pane, locate and highlight the `.asp` file you created earlier. In this example, I selected `Lottery3.asp`. Click your right mouse button and from the pop-up menu select Browse. This will open your web browser and display the selected page:

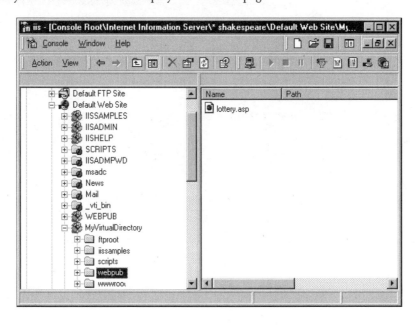

Notice the URL address in the next screen shot. It's using:

```
http://localhost/MyVirtualDirecory/...
```

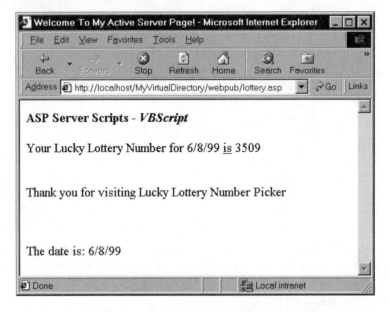

Now that you've created a virtual directory, you need to modify its default properties.

Highlight the virtual directory you just created. Click your right mouse button and select Properties from the pop-up menu. This will bring up a Properties dialog. Select the tab labeled Virtual Directory, and locate the frame labeled Application Settings. Select the check box labeled Run in separate memory space, then click OK:

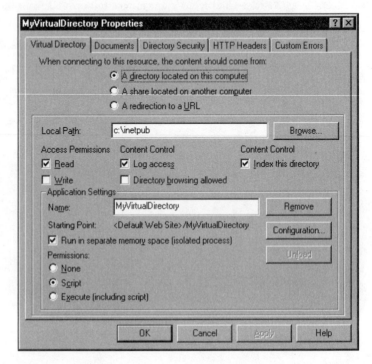

Selecting Run in separate memory space will separate the execution of ASP scripts from IIS.

Incidentally, when configuring an ASP application to run out of process, MTS will remove the application from the package names IIS In Process Applications and create a new package under Packages Installed in MTS Explorer that is set to run in its own memory location. Because MTS has to provide a separate process for the application, running applications in separate memory spaces results in a slight cost of memory resources.

Furthermore, because the new package runs in its own memory space, it must be started separately as a new process. Of course there's a catch here; IIS and MTS do not have permissions for starting new processes. Luckily, MTS and IIS have a way of getting around this problem.

When you install IIS, a user account that provides the necessary permissions for starting new processes is created. This account is called IWAM_NameOfMachine (reflecting the name of the machine where IIS is actually installed) and grants MTS and IIS the necessary permissions for starting a new process. You can view the user account IWAM_NameOfMachine by opening Windows NT User Manager:

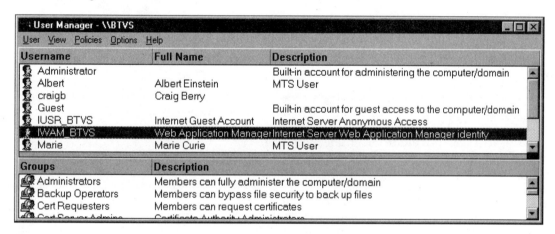

If you look at the Group Memberships assigned to IWAM_NameOfMachine, you'll see that Guests and MTS Trusted Impersonators are added by default:

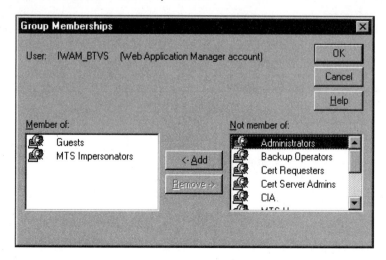

Exploring a little further, you should find that your user account is a member of the group MTS Trusted Impersonators:

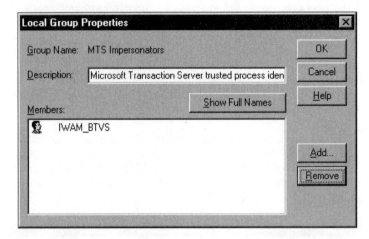

RDS

One of the major disadvantages of using Active Server Pages is the time consuming process of retrieving and re-posting new data after it's been manipulated. **Remote Data Services (RDS)**, formally known as **Advanced Data Connector**, was designed to provide an alternative to web applications like Active Server Pages, that utilize server-side processing.

RDS is based on a client-side architecture. It's capable of delivering a disconnected (stateless) recordset from the server and sending it to a web browser. This means that large amounts of data, such as recordsets retrieved from a database, can be cached at the client machine. Performance is increased, because multiple records can be pulled from cached information without having to send out a new request to the server and have the information re-post at the client's browser. Additionally, multiple records can be manipulated while still on the client machine and then sent for processing as one batch, again providing the user with immediate responses.

RDS does have a few drawbacks. These may eventually be worked out, but in the meantime, using RDS may not be a sound option except for in-house (intranet) use. One major drawback is that RDS does not work with Netscape. Currently, only IIS 3.0 and higher and Internet Explorer 4.0 and higher are capable of supporting Remote Data Services. Obviously this is a major drawback for users who may want to access your web site but prefer to use a browser other than Microsoft's. It's estimated that Netscape holds approximately 40 percent of the web browser market: that's a lot of potential users you're eliminating if your site doesn't provide an alternative for non-Internet Explorer users!

Another drawback with RDS involves security issues. Internet Explorer treats MTS components as potentially dangerous items that can damage the client's machine. As a result, Internet Explorer does not, by default, allow these components to run on the client's machine. Without making some special security arrangements, RDS will not work. We'll talk more about RDS security shortly.

How does RDS work? When a user enters a request for database information through a client web browser, client-side RDS components send a request to the web server. RDS components located at the server process the client's database request, and then direct it to the database management system (DBMS). The DBMS processes the data request and sends the results back to the RDS components at the server. Now, RDS converts the data from the DBMS into an ADO Recordset object, which is returned to the client browser where the request originated. The recordset can also be cached into the client's memory and displayed through a datagrid, listbox, textbox, or other visual control.

What makes this process more efficient than an Active Server Page is that the user at the client browser can make multiple changes, such as adding new records and editing existing records, before submitting the work to be recorded via batches. To make things even more efficient, RDS sends only the altered records and any new records back to the web server for processing in one batch, leaving out the records that are unaltered:

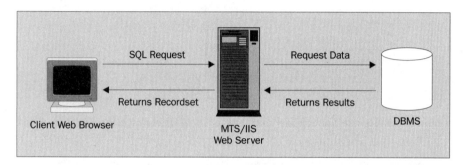

Active Server Pages don't exhibit multiple batches: only one record can be manipulated at a time. This means that the altered data must be sent back to be updated at the database and a new recordset must be returned back to the client web browser. You can imagine how inefficient and time consuming this process can be.

RDS Security Issues

Under normal circumstances, Internet Explorer (by default) will not allow executable components that originate from a web server and execute at the client's machine. The reason for this is simple: it would be very easy for a malicious person to transfer programs that can damage the client's machine. Unfortunately, honest and non-threatening components must be treated as a potential danger to the client.

In this section, I'm going to describe how to get around the security problem so that RDS will work. Then I am going to tell you why running RDS is still dangerous.

The first thing you must do is to make a few entries into the Windows registry where your application's MTS components reside. For example, you must add an entry to the Windows registry for each MTS component in order to tell the client browser that the MTS component can safely be initialized.

To make safe for initialization:

```
\HKEY_LOCAL_MACHINE\SOFTWARE\Classes\CLSID\{YourComponent CLSID} \
Implemented Categories\{7DD95801-9882-11CF-9FA9-00AA006C42C4}
```

You also need to add an entry to the registry to tell the client browser that MTS methods are safe to call:

```
\HKEY_LOCAL_MACHINE\SOFTWARE\Classes\CLSID\{YourComponent CLSID} \
Implemented Categories\{7DD95802-9882-11CF-9FA9-00AA006C42C4}
```

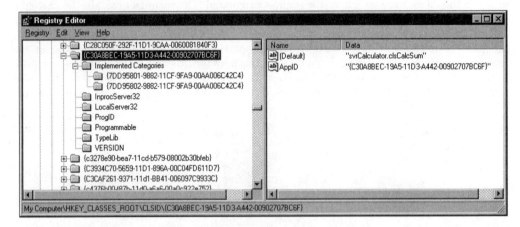

The third requirement is another registry entry for each MTS component, so IIS can have permission to launch them:

```
\HKEY_LOCAL_MACHINE\SYSTEM\CurrentControlSet\Services\W3SVC\Parameters\
ADCLaunch\YourComponent ProgID
```

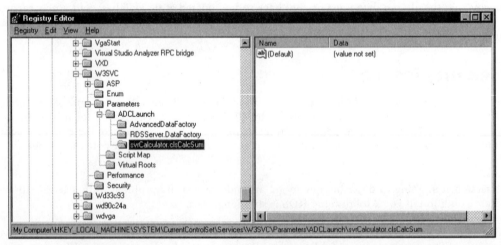

There's still one more barrier before a user with Internet Explorer can make use of a web site that uses RDS. In order for the user to access the site, the user must change Internet Explorer's default security configurations to allow Internet Explorer to download unsigned ActiveX controls.

Now that you have an idea of how to change security, let's think about what you're actually doing. Basically, you're telling Internet Explorer that it should trust your components because you say they're safe. But who is telling Internet Explorer it's safe to run MTS components on the client's machine? It's the web server. Unfortunately, unless a user is sure of the web site being visited, one really can't be sure what applications are being sent to the client machine – and this must be taken as a serious danger.

ASP Design in PasswordPersist

So far throughout the book, we have developed our components for the `PasswordPersist` application, and set them up in MTS. We now need to work on the front-end of the system. In this section, we'll go over the ASP design, and how the front-end will flow from one page to another. The primary purpose of this section is to show you how an Internet front-end will converse with our objects in MTS, so I'll try to keep the ASP conversation as general as possible.

> **There are two books available on ASP design and development from Wrox that are very good. They're called Beginning Active Server Pages and Professional Active Server Pages 2.0. If you're interesting in all of the ins and outs of ASP, these are excellent references.**

Who Starts the Transaction?

As we stated before, each object will use a pre-existing transaction if one exists. However, if there isn't a transaction, our objects won't be transactional. Therefore, we need to have a transaction created before we tell our objects to save their data. In ASP, this is pretty straightforward. All we need is the following code in our ASP:

```
<%@TRANSACTION = Requires_New %>
```

We can set this value to `Required`, `Supported`, or `Not_Supported` if we wish. However, for our needs, we need a new transaction when our objects are saving their data.

Web Page Flows and Descriptions

Generally, a user will come into the login page to access the system. If the given U/P is correct, they can now access the system list, where they can maintain their systems along with the attributes associated with them. Let's concentrate on the login and system pages in more detail (the attribute pages are virtually identical to the system pages). I won't get into every nook and cranny with the ASP code, but I will cover them in enough detail for you to get a fundamental understanding of what's going on.

Login/New User

This is the first screen that the user sees:

The ASP code for the login screen looks like this:

```asp
<%@ LANGUAGE="VBSCRIPT" TRANSACTION = Requires_New %>

<%
  Response.Expires = 0
  Response.Buffer = True

  On Error Resume Next

  Dim lngC
  Dim lngRet

' Clear out the user ID.
  Session("UserID") = 0
  Session("UserName") = ""
  Session("UserPassword") = ""

  Response.Write "<HTML><HEAD><TITLE>PasswordPersist - " & _
                 "Login</TITLE></HEAD>"
  Response.Write "<CENTER><H3>User Login</H3></CENTER>"
%>

<SCRIPT LANGUAGE="VBScript">
<!--

  Sub cmdPost_OnClick()

    On Error Resume Next
    frmMain.Submit()

  End Sub

-->
</SCRIPT>

<%
  Response.Write "<FORM Action=LoginResults.asp Name=frmMain " & _
                 "ID=frmMain Method=Post OnSubmit=" & _
                 """javascript:return false""">"
  Response.Write "UserName:<BR>"
  Response.Write "<INPUT TYPE=TEXT NAME=txtUserName " & _
                 "ID=txtUserName SIZE=30><BR>"
  Response.Write "Password:<BR>"
  Response.Write "<INPUT TYPE=PASSWORD NAME=txtPassword " & _
                 "ID=txtPassword SIZE=30><BR>"
  Response.Write "Add New User"
  Response.Write " <INPUT TYPE=CHECKBOX NAME=chkAdd ID=chkAdd>"
  Response.Write "<BR><BR>"

  Response.Write "<INPUT TYPE=BUTTON NAME=cmdPost ID=cmdPost "& _
                 "VALUE=""Login"">"
  Response.Write "</FORM></HTML>"

  Response.AddHeader "Cache-Control", "Private"
  Response.AddHeader "Pragma", "No-Cache"
%>
```

Save this as `Login.asp`. Now let's take a look at the code that will be run when the user presses the **Login** button – the `LoginResults.asp` page:

```
<%@LANGUAGE="VBSCRIPT" TRANSACTION = Requires_New %>

<%

On Error Resume Next

Response.Write "<HTML><HEAD><TITLE>PasswordPersist - " & _
               "Login Results</TITLE></HEAD>"
Response.Write "<CENTER><H3>User Login Results</H3></CENTER>"

' Get the username and password and check the given value.
Dim blnRet
Dim lngUserID
Dim objPPUser
Dim strName
Dim strPassword
Dim blnExit

strName = Trim(Request.Form("txtUserName"))
strPassword = Trim(Request.Form("txtPassword"))

Set objPPUser = Server.CreateObject("PPIndependents.User")

If Request.Form("chkAdd") Then

  If Not objPPUser Is Nothing Then
      blnRet = objPPUser.GetByVals(lngUserID, strName, strPassword)
      If blnRet = True Then
          Response.Write "<P>This U/P already exists in the" & _
                         " system!</P>"
          Set objPPUser = Nothing
          blnExit = True
       Else
          lngUserID = objPPUser.Save(strName, strPassword, "")
      End If
  End If
End If

If Not objPPUser Is Nothing Then
  blnRet = objPPUser.GetByVals(lngUserID, strName, strPassword)
  Set objPPUser = Nothing
  If blnRet = True Then
  ' We have a valid user.
    Session("UserID") = lngUserID
    Session("UserName") = strName
    Session("UserPassword") = strPassword
    Response.Write "<P>Welcome, " & strName & "!</P>"
    Response.Write "<P><A HREF=""SystemList.asp"">" & _
                   "System List Page</A></P>"
  Else
  ' This isn't a valid user.
    Response.Write "<P>The given username/password does " & _
                   "not exist in the system.</P>"
    Response.Write "<P><A HREF=""Login.asp"">Login Page</A></P>"
  End If
```

```
    Else

      If Not blnExit Then
        Response.Write "<P>The system objects are currently " & _
                     "unavailable - please try again.</P>"
      End If
      Response.Write "<P><A HREF=""Login.asp"">Login Page</A></P>"

    End If

    Response.Write "</HTML>"

    Response.AddHeader "Cache-Control", "Private"
    Response.AddHeader "Pragma", "No-Cache"
    %>
```

We grab the U/P given out of the `Request` object, and use the `User` object's `GetByVals` method to validate the U/P combination. If there's a match, we'll give the user a friendly introduction:

However, if the U/P was not in our database, we would not let the user into the system. Note that we're storing the user information into the `Session` collection. We can use this to make sure that a user has logged in whenever they go to another page in the system. If the `UserID` is equal to 0, we'll redirect them back to the login page.

System Maintenance

After a successful login, we can now get to the system list page by clicking the link on the previous page:

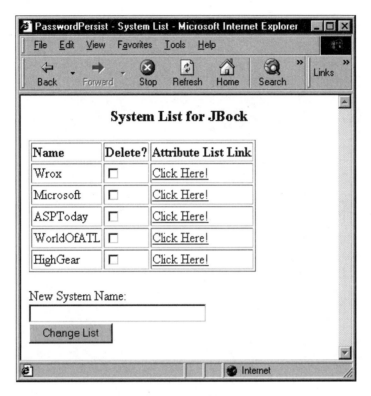

Here's the ASP code that generated the `SystemList.asp` page:

```
<%@ LANGUAGE="VBSCRIPT" TRANSACTION = Requires_New %>

<%
  Response.Expires = 0
  Response.Buffer = True

  On Error Resume Next

  If Session("UserID") = 0 Then
    ' Redirect to the login page.
    Response.Redirect "Login.asp"
  Else
    Dim blnRet
    Dim lngC
    Dim lngCSystems
    Dim lngSystems
    Dim objPPSystem
    Dim objPPSystems
    Dim strSystemName
```

```
Response.Write "<HTML><HEAD><TITLE>PasswordPersist - " & _
               "System List</TITLE></HEAD>"
Response.Write "<CENTER><H3>System List for " & _
               Session("UserName") & "</H3></CENTER>"
%>

<SCRIPT LANGUAGE="VBScript">
<!--
  Sub cmdPost_OnClick()

  On Error Resume Next
  frmMain.Submit()

  End Sub
-->
</SCRIPT>

<%
  Set objPPSystems = _
          Server.CreateObject("PPAssociations.SystemUser")

  If Not objPPSystems Is Nothing Then
    Err.Clear
    blnRet = objPPSystems.GetSystems(Session("UserID"), _
             lngSystems)

    If Err Then
      Response.Write "<P>GetSystems" & Err.Number & " - " & _
                     Err.Description & ".</P>"
      Err.Clear
    End If

    If blnRet = True Then
    ' Get each system name.
      Set objPPSystem = _
          Server.CreateObject("PPIndependents.System")
      Response.Write "<FORM Action=SystemListResults.asp" & _
                     "Name=frmMain ID=frmMain Method=Post" & _
                     "OnSubmit=""javascript:return false"">"
      Response.Write "<TABLE BORDER=1>"
      Response.Write "<TR ALIGN=Center> <TH>Name</TH> <TH>" & _
                     "Delete?</TH><TH>Attribute List" & _
                     "Link</TH></TR>"
      For lngC = LBound(lngSystems) To UBound(lngSystems)
        blnRet = objPPSystem.GetByID(lngSystems(lngC), _
                                     strSystemName)

        If Err Then
          Response.Write "<P>GetByID" & Err.Number & " - " & _
                         Err.Description & ".</P>"
          Err.Clear
        End If
```

```
        If blnRet = True Then
          lngCSystems = lngCSystems + 1
          Response.Write "<TR><TD>" & Trim(strSystemName) & _
                         "</TD>" & "<TD>" & _
                         "<INPUT TYPE=checkbox NAME=" & _
                         "chkSystem" & CStr(lngCSystems) & _
                         " ID=chkSystem" & CStr(lngCSystems) & _
                         ">" & "<INPUT TYPE=hidden " & _
                         "NAME=txtSystem" & CStr(lngCSystems) & _
                         " ID=txtSystem" & CStr(lngCSystems) & _
                         " Value=""" & CStr(lngSystems(lngC)) & _
                         """"></TD>" & "<TD><A " & _
                         "HREF=""AttributeList.asp?SystemID=" & _
                         CStr(lngSystems(lngC)) & _
                         "&SystemName=" & strSystemName & _
                         """>Click Here!</A></TD></TR>"
        End If

      Next

      Set objPPSystem = Nothing
      Response.Write "</TABLE><BR>"
      Response.Write "<INPUT Type=Hidden Name=" & _
                     "txtTotalSystemCount ID=" & _
                     "txtTotalSystemCount Value=""" & _
                     CStr(lngCSystems) & """>"

    Else
    ' No systems currently exist.
      Response.Write "<BR>"
      Response.Write "<FORM Action=SystemListResults.asp " & _
                     "Name=frmMain ID=frmMain Method=Post" & _
                     "OnSubmit=""javascript:return false"">"
    End If

    Response.Write "New System Name:<BR>"
    Response.Write "<INPUT TYPE=TEXT NAME=" & _
                   "txtNewSystemName ID=txtNewSystemName " & _
                   "SIZE=30><BR>"
    Response.Write "<INPUT Type=Button Name=cmdPost " & _
                   "ID=cmdPost Value=""Change List"">"
    Response.Write "</FORM>"

  Else
    Response.Write "<P>The system objects are currently " & _
                   "unavailable - please try again.</P>"
  End If

  Response.Write "</HTML>"
End If

Response.AddHeader "Cache-Control", "Private"
Response.AddHeader "Pragma", "No-Cache"
%>
```

We first make sure that the user is logged into the system. If they are, we look up all the systems associated with the user via the `SystemUser` object. If there are any there, we then lookup the names via the `System` object. We also use hidden fields in our form so we can store the system IDs on the page. When the form is submitted, we can see if any of the check boxes have been checked via the `Request`'s `Form` collection, as the `SystemListResults.asp` code shows:

```
<%@LANGUAGE="VBSCRIPT" TRANSACTION = Requires_New %>

<%

Response.Expires = 0
Response.Buffer = True

On Error Resume Next

If Session("UserID") = 0 Then
  ' Redirect to the login page.
  Response.Redirect "Login.asp"
Else
  Response.Write "<HTML><HEAD><TITLE>PasswordPersist - " & _
              "System List Results</TITLE></HEAD>"
  Response.Write "<CENTER><H3>System List Results for " & _
              Session("UserName") & "</H3></CENTER>"

  Dim blnOK
  Dim blnRet
  Dim lngC
  Dim lngSystems()
  Dim lngSystemID
  Dim objPPSystem
  Dim objPPSystems

  blnOK = True

  ' Find all of the systems that need
  ' to be deleted.
  For lngC = 1 to Request.Form("txtTotalSystemCount")
    If Request.Form("chkSystem" & lngC) = "on" Then
      If blnRet = False Then
        blnRet = True
        Redim lngSystems(0)
      Else
        Redim Preserve lngSystems(UBound(lngSystems) + 1)
      End If
      lngSystems(UBound(lngSystems)) = _
              Request.Form("txtSystem", lngC)
    End If
  Next

  If blnRet = True Then
    ' There are systems to delete.
    Set objPPSystems = _
      Server.CreateObject("PPAssociations.SystemUser")
```

```
      If Not objPPSystems Is Nothing Then
           blnRet = objPPSystems.DeleteSystems(Session("UserID"), _
                                        lngSystems)
           Set objPPSystems = Nothing
        Else
           Response.Write "<P>The system objects are currently " & _
                        "unavailable - please try again.</P>"
           blnOK = False
        End If
     End If

     If Trim(Request.Form("txtNewSystemName")) <> "" Then
        ' Now add the new system.
        Erase lngSystems

        Set objPPSystem = _
             Server.CreateObject("PPIndependents.System")

        If Not objPPSystem Is Nothing Then
           blnRet = objPPSystem.GetByVal(lngSystemID, _
                     Trim(Request.Form("txtNewSystemName")))

           Set objPPSystem = Nothing

           If lngSystemID = 0 Then
             ' We need to add it.
             Set objPPSystem = _
               Server.CreateObject("PPIndependents.System")
               lngSystemID = _
               objPPSystem.Save(Trim(Request.Form("txtNewSystemName")))
             Set objPPSystem = Nothing
           End If

           If lngSystemID <> 0 Then
             Redim lngSystems(0)
             lngSystems(0) = lngSystemID

             Set objPPSystems = _
               Server.CreateObject("PPAssociations.SystemUser")

             blnRet = objPPSystems.SaveSystems(Session("UserID"), _
                  lngSystems)

             Set objPPSystems = Nothing
           End If

        Else
           Response.Write "<P>The system objects are currently " & _
                        "unavailable - please try again.</P>"
           blnOK = False
        End If
     End If
```

```
      If blnOK = True Then
         Response.Redirect "SystemList.asp"
      Else
         Response.Write "</HTML>"
      End If

   End If

   Response.AddHeader "Cache-Control", "Private"
   Response.AddHeader "Pragma", "No-Cache"

%>
```

One interesting thing to note right away is that there's little HTML generated code on this page. In fact, this page's primary function is to parse the form's contents, save the information, and load the system page again! If there were an error (for example, not being able to load the objects) then we would let the users know.

The first thing we do is determine which systems we should delete by inspecting the contents of the Form collection. Once we get all of the system IDs into an array, we call the DeleteSystems method on the SystemUser object. Then, if the user entered a new system, we save that information. Note that we check to see if that system is already in the database. If it is, we "reuse" that system for this user.

This is a great example of how MTS can really aid in your component development. We've logically grouped our services together into small components and we really didn't have to worry about the transactional aspects of the entire call flow. Granted, in each method we were very aware of its success or failure, but we left it up to MTS to determine if the whole transaction should commit or rollback.

Let's see how this works – I'll delete the **Microsoft** and **WorldOfATL** systems from my list and add a new system called **ExecPC**:

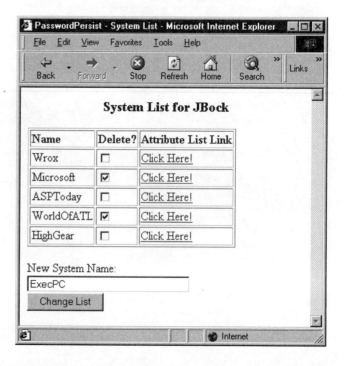

In this case, there's already an ExecPC record on the System table, so we won't add a new record to the System table. Once the Change List button is pressed, we should see the following results:

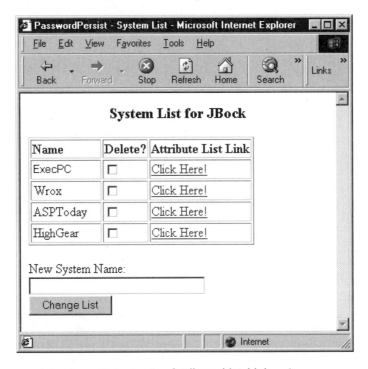

By clicking on one of the hyperlinks in the Attribute List Link column, you are able to access the attributes for a given system:

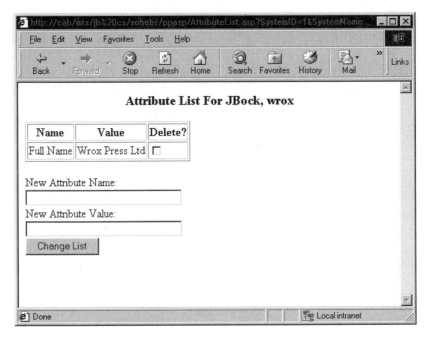

Here's the code for the `AttributeList.asp` file:

```
<%@ LANGUAGE="VBSCRIPT" TRANSACTION = Requires_New %>

<%

Response.Expires = 0
Response.Buffer = True

On Error Resume Next

If Session("UserID") = 0 Then
' Redirect to the login page.
  Response.Redirect "Login.asp"

Else

  Dim blnRet
  Dim lngC
  Dim lngCAttribs
  Dim lngAttribs
  Dim objPPAttrib
  Dim objPPAttribs
  Dim strAttribName
  Dim strAttribValue

  Response.Write "<HTML><HEAD><TITLE>PasswordPersist - Attribute" & _
              "List</TITLE></HEAD>"
  Response.Write "<CENTER><H3>Attribute List For " & _
              Session("UserName") & ", " & _
              Request.QueryString("SystemName") & "</H3></CENTER>"
%>

<SCRIPT LANGUAGE="VBScript">
<!--

Sub cmdPost_OnClick()

  On Error Resume Next

  frmMain.Submit()

End Sub

-->
</SCRIPT>

<%
Set objPPAttribs = _
    Server.CreateObject("PPAssociations.SystemUserAttributes")

If Not objPPAttribs Is Nothing Then
  Err.Clear
  blnRet = objPPAttribs.GetAttributes(Session("UserID"), _
          Request.QueryString("SystemID"), lngAttribs)
  If Err Then
    Response.Write "<P>GetAttributes" & Err.Number & " - " & _
                Err.Description & ".</P>"
    Err.Clear
  End If
```

```
Session("SystemID") = Request.QueryString("SystemID")
Session("SystemName") = Request.QueryString("SystemName")

If blnRet = True Then
' Get each attribute name.
  Set objPPAttrib = Server.CreateObject("PPIndependents.Attribute")
  Response.Write "<FORM Action=AttributeListResults.asp " & _
              "Name=frmMain ID=frmMain Method=Post " &_
              "OnSubmit=""javascript:return false"">"
  Response.Write "<TABLE BORDER=1>"
  Response.Write "<TR ALIGN=Center><TH>Name</TH><TH>Value</TH>" & _
              "<TH>Delete?</TH></TR>"
  For lngC = LBound(lngAttribs) To UBound(lngAttribs)
      blnRet = objPPAttrib.GetByID(lngAttribs(lngC), _
                                 strAttribName, strAttribValue)

      If Err Then
          Response.Write "<P>GetByID" & Err.Number & " - " & _
                      Err.Description & ".</P>"

          Err.Clear
      End If

      If blnRet = True Then
          lngCAttribs = lngCAttribs + 1
          Response.Write "<TR><TD>" & Trim(strAttribName) & _
          "</TD><TD>" & Trim(strAttribValue) & "</TD>" & _
          "<TD><INPUT TYPE=checkbox NAME=chkAttrib" & _
          CStr(lngCAttribs) & " ID=chkAttrib" & _
          CStr(lngCAttribs) & ">" & _
          "<INPUT TYPE=hidden NAME=txtAttrib" & CStr(lngCAttribs) & _
          " ID=txtAttrib" & CStr(lngCAttribs) & " Value=""" & _
          CStr(lngAttribs(lngC)) & """></TD></TR>"
      End If
  Next

  Set objPPSystem = Nothing
  Response.Write "</TABLE><BR>"
  Response.Write "<INPUT Type=Hidden Name=txtTotalAttribCount " & _
              "ID=txtTotalAttribCount Value=""" & _
              CStr(lngCAttribs) & """>"
Else

' No systems currently exist.
  Response.Write "<BR>"
  Response.Write "<FORM Action=AttributeListResults.asp " & _
              "Name=frmMain ID=frmMain Method=Post " & _
              "OnSubmit=""javascript:return false"">"
End If

Response.Write "New Attribute Name:<BR>"
Response.Write "<INPUT TYPE=TEXT NAME=txtNewAttribName " & _
            "ID=txtNewAttrbiuteName SIZE=30><BR>"
Response.Write "New Attribute Value:<BR>"
Response.Write "<INPUT TYPE=TEXT NAME=txtNewAttribValue " & _
            "ID=txtNewAttrbiuteValue SIZE=30><BR>"
Response.Write "<INPUT Type=Button Name=cmdPost ID=cmdPost " & _
            "Value=""Change List"">"

Response.Write "<BR><BR>"
Response.Write "<A HREF=""SystemList.asp"">Back to System List </A>"
Response.Write "</FORM>"
```

```
    Else

      Response.Write "<P>The system objects are currently " & _
                     "unavailable - please try again.</P>"
    End If

    Response.Write "</HTML>"

  End If

  Response.AddHeader "Cache-Control", "Private"
  Response.AddHeader "Pragma", "No-Cache"
%>
```

The code here works in almost an identical way to the System pages, so I won't bother to explain what's going on here or in the following `AttributeListResults.asp` page:

```
<%@LANGUAGE="VBSCRIPT" TRANSACTION = Requires_New %>

<%

Response.Expires = 0
Response.Buffer = True

On Error Resume Next

If Session("UserID") = 0 Then
' Redirect to the login page.
  Response.Redirect "Login.asp"

Else

  Response.Write "<HTML><HEAD><TITLE>PasswordPersist - " & _
                 "Attribute List Results</TITLE></HEAD>"
  Response.Write "<CENTER><H3>Attribute List Results For " & _
                 Session("UserName") & ", " & _
                 Request.QueryString("AttribName") & "</H3></CENTER>"

  Dim blnOK
  Dim blnRet
  Dim lngC
  Dim lngAttribs()
  Dim lngAttribID
  Dim objPPAttrib
  Dim objPPAttribs

  blnOK = True

' Find all of the attributes that need to be deleted.
  For lngC = 1 to Request.Form("txtTotalAttribCount")
    If Request.Form("chkAttrib" & lngC) = "on" Then
      If blnRet = False Then
        blnRet = True
        Redim lngAttribs(0)
      Else
        Redim Preserve lngAttribs(UBound(lngAttribs) + 1)
      End If
        lngAttribs(UBound(lngAttribs)) = _
                   Request.Form("txtAttrib" & lngC)
    End If
```

```
    Next

  If blnRet = True Then
' There are attrbitues to delete.
    Set objPPAttribs = _
       Server.CreateObject("PPAssociations.SystemUserAttributes")

    If Not objPPAttribs Is Nothing Then
       blnRet = objPPAttribs.DeleteAttributes(Session("UserID"), _
                                              Session("SystemID"), _
                                              lngAttribs)
       Set objPPAttribs = Nothing
    Else
       Response.Write "<P>The system objects are currently " & _
                      "unavailable - please try again.</P>"
       blnOK = False
    End If
  End If

  If Trim(Request.Form("txtNewAttribName")) <> "" Then
' Now add the new attribute.
    Erase lngAttribs

    Set objPPAttrib = Server.CreateObject("PPIndependents.Attribute")

    If Not objPPAttrib Is Nothing Then
       blnRet = objPPAttrib.GetByVals(lngAttribID, _
               Trim(Request.Form("txtNewAttribName")), _
               Trim(Request.Form("txtNewAttribValue")))
       Set objPPAttrib = Nothing

       If lngAttribID = 0 Then
' We need to add it.
         Set objPPAttrib = _
             Server.CreateObject("PPIndependents.Attribute")
         lngAttribID = _
           objPPAttrib.Save(Trim(Request.Form("txtNewAttribName")), _
           Trim(Request.Form("txtNewAttribValue")))
         Set objPPAttrib = Nothing
       End If

       If lngAttribID <> 0 Then
         Redim lngAttribs(0)
         lngAttribs(0) = lngAttribID

         Set objPPAttribs = _
             Server.CreateObject("PPAssociations.SystemUserAttributes")
         blnRet = objPPAttribs.SaveAttributes(Session("UserID"), _
                 Session("SystemID"), lngAttribs)
         Set objPPAttribs = Nothing
       End If

    Else

       Response.Write "<P>The system objects are currently " & _
                      "unavailable - please try again.</P>"
       blnOK = False

    End If
  End If
```

```
      If blnOK = True Then
          Response.Redirect "AttributeList.asp?SystemID=" & _
                             Session("SystemID") & "&SystemName=" & _
                             Session("SystemName")
      Else
          Response.Write "</HTML>"
      End If

  End If

  Response.AddHeader "Cache-Control", "Private"
  Response.AddHeader "Pragma", "No-Cache"

  %>
```

Using SSL for Added Security

Some readers may have balked at my use of passing a password over the Internet without any security, and that's a good point. As the pages stand right now, the password isn't encrypted and could easily be picked up by a hacker. Considering that our system is holding a lot of sensitive information for our customers, this isn't good. One way to encrypt the pages is to use the **Secure Sockets Layer**, or SSL, protocol. I won't cover this in detail here (the *Professional Active Server Pages 2.0* book does a great job of it already), but by using this protocol, we can use the encryption and decryption services already provided by IIS and SSL enabled clients.

Future Enhancements

As with any system, it's never right the first time. There are bugs in the implementation, requirements were missed, or enhancements are needed. I'll cover two enhancements that I think should be added in the next iteration of development.

Forgot Your Password?

Even though we allow clients to store U/P's on our system, they still need to remember the one that lets them into *PasswordPersist*! Just like anything in life, information can be forgotten, so we should give registered users the ability to retrieve their U/P if they forgot it. One easy way would be to ask the client for their e-mail address. If that address exists in the PPUser table, the corresponding user information would be sent to the user via an e-mail message. One way to do this is to use **Collaboration Data Objects**, or CDO. There's a lot of code snippets on many web sites (namely Microsoft's) that demonstrate how this could be done, so it's possible that this feature could get added into the first release.

Is This Service Free?

One glaring hole that could be easily exploited right now is unlimited storage for a user. If a client wanted to add 10,000 attributes for a system, there's nothing to prevent them from doing this (other than running out of room on the database). Therefore, we might want to allocate a cost per systems associated for a user as well as the number attributes associated per system. Implementing this may be tricky, but not impossible. We would probably need a credit card number to charge to per month for system usage, but this type of analysis is beyond the scope of the discussion at hand.

Summary

This chapter was more like a bonus chapter, as you spent more time learning about HTML, VBScript, and Active Server Pages than actually working with MTS. This was a necessary and, hopefully, fun experience for you.

To recap, we have covered:

- ❑ What Internet Information Server (IIS) is
- ❑ Why VBScript is an excellent choice for writing your server script code. You also had a chance to write and work with some script examples.
- ❑ How to create Active Server Pages and ASP intrinsic objects.
- ❑ How to make Active Server Pages transactional. We developed a hands-on project that could send user information from a web browser, call an ASP that uses server script to access MTS components, and then have the Active Server Page generate a response back to the web browser.
- ❑ How to protect your system from fatal crashes by running your applications in separate processes.

We also put the finishing touches to the `PasswordPersist` application by creating an ASP front-end so that it can finally be deployed for the intention that it was built for.

That pretty much wraps it up for our discussion of the key topic of this book. However, before I go I'm going to hold your attention a bit longer by talking about how MTS fits in with the next generation of COM: COM+.

The Future of MTS = COM+

Well, here we are, after twelve detailed chapters of telling you how MTS works and how you can use it to create efficient, flexible and scalable enterprise applications, I'm now going to tell you some bad news; MTS, as we know it today, does *not* exist under Windows 2000. The good news is that MTS now plays a pivotal role in achieving Microsoft's goal of making Windows 2000 the *best* application server platform around, period. It's just not called MTS anymore.

This is a book on MTS not Windows 2000, so all I want to give you here is a taster for the sort of things we can expect from this latest platform from Microsoft.

By the end of the chapter you will be able to answer the following questions:

- ❑ What is COM+ and how does relates to MTS?
- ❑ What new services does COM+ provide?
- ❑ What services does COM+ extend and improve upon?
- ❑ How does COM+ change the basics of COM?
- ❑ How does COM+ fit in with the Windows DNA model?

COM+

To achieve their goal of the best application server platform, Microsoft have internally merged the COM team with the MTS team, with the hopes of achieving tighter integration between their **component model** and the **services** that they provide for these components. This new team is the COM+ team, and their end product in Windows 2000 is the **COM+ run time**:

> **COM+ is the unification of COM, DCOM, MTS and MSMQ into one tightly integrated run time.**

Like MTS, COM+ provides an infrastructure of run time services, which now includes additional services such as Object Pooling, an In Memory Database and Dynamic Load Balancing. Components can easily take advantage of these by simply changing **declarative attributes** that are external to the implementation of the component.

In this chapter, we'll discuss the additional services included with COM+, understand how COM+ affects distributed application development and examine the changes to the COM+ programming model from an MTS developer's perspective.

By the end of this chapter, you'll have an idea of what COM+ is, and hopefully you'll be prepared to move your existing MTS components over to COM+ when it's released.

> *The information presented in this chapter is based on the beta releases of COM+ and some details may well change in the final build of Windows 2000.*

What is Actually in COM+?

When Microsoft first announced COM+ in September 1997, it was described as mainly being a powerful new run time library that would make it easier to develop COM-based components from any language. This COM+ run time would allow developers to work with COM coclasses just like they use a language's own native classes. In other words, there would not be a distinction between using or creating a COM component and a standard class.

This would require the COM+ run time to work closely with the development tools. The COM+ run time would also provide system implementations for the repetitive code that has to be written for every component, such as self-registration and unregistration, class factories, reference counting, IDispatch and IUnknown implementation, connection points (events) and persistence. Additionally, there would be a common set of data types supported by all COM+ objects no matter what language the components were developed in.

Again, the goal of the original COM+ was to make component development easier from any language. These features don't seem as important to us as VB developers because this is the way VB behaves. We only have to adjust a few property settings and worry about the logic of a component. We don't need to know about the required plumbing to make a VB class module a COM coclass, or defining the interface and generating the required GUIDs. However, developers in other languages, such as Visual C++, would like component development to be as easy in their languages as it is in Visual Basic.

Well, unfortunately for Visual C++ and Visual J++ developers, the version of COM+ that will be released with Windows 2000 will be different than this original description. Microsoft still promises to ship a version of the COM+ run time providing this functionality, but it's now been postponed until the second release of COM+.

> *This lack of functionality has actually pleased a lot of people. If Microsoft had changed C++ and Java to natively supported COM by the use of attributes, it would have meant the introduction of a Microsoft specific variant of C++ and Java.*

The first release of COM+ is much more than simply another run time layered on top of COM, like MTS. COM+ is a combined version of the COM, DCOM, MTS and MSMQ programming models. This unified architecture, also known as **Windows Component Services**, makes it significantly easier to develop components because the distinction between MTS and COM will be eliminated:

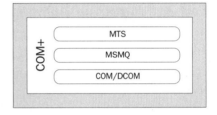

If you recall from our discussion about the architecture of MTS in Chapter 3, there are several issues developers must worry about when developing MTS components. This is because MTS is currently implemented as a separate layer and must coexist with COM.

For example, when creating an instance of an MTS component from another MTS object, instead of using the standard `CreateObject` function, or `New` keyword, you must use the `CreateInstance` function of the Context object. Otherwise the creation request will go through COM's Service Control Manager (SCM) instead of through the MTS Executive and, as a result, the new MTS object will reside in a different activity. This scenario can introduce a number of problems, including the fact that the new MTS object will not be able to participate in the creator's transaction.

Or consider the requirement of calling `SafeRef` on your `Me` reference when passing it to another object or to the client, to ensure that the caller only gets a reference to the Context Wrapper rather than the actual object. These issues cause unnecessary confusion and problems for MTS component developers.

The unified COM+ programming model will eliminate the difference between developing or using COM components and MTS components. No longer will there be a COM way of doing things and a separate MTS way.

You'll be able to create instances of all components using the `CreateObject` function, regardless whether the creator is another MTS object or the base client. Every component will have a Context Wrapper. Because the Context Wrapper is now part of COM+ and COM+ is therefore aware of it, you'll no longer have to worry about method calls by-passing the interception mechanism.

All of the programming techniques used with MTS components that deal with the lack of COM and MTS integration will be eliminated with COM+, as the MTS Executive is integrated into the COM run time libraries. In addition, this unified programming model will also eliminate the frequently asked question of, "Should I use MTS or not?"

Unified and Improved Administration

The unification of COM, DCOM, MTS and MSMQ also applies to administration. COM+ provides a single administration environment, called the **Component Services Explorer** that allows you to manage your components, packages, run time services and role-based security:

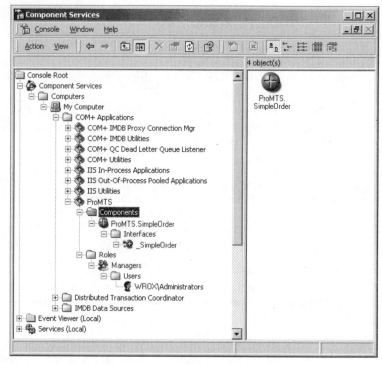

This administration interface has a very similar structure to the existing MTS Explorer. You'll find that after a couple of hours playing with the various pages and options, COM+ is actually pretty easy to work with if you have an MTS background. The only real difference you'll notice, and should be aware of, is that Microsoft has changed many of the names in COM+, so no surprise there. What was an MTS package is now called a **COM+ Application**. The services that MTS provided, such as distributed transactions and security, are now called **COM+ Services**. The MTS catalog is now the **COM+ Catalog**.

The Component Services Explorer utilizes the COM+ Catalog administration library, which physically stores configuration information in a new resource manager called the **Registration Database** (RegDB). For backward compatibility with older, non-configured components, the HKEY_CLASSES_ROOT key in the system registry is still used.

> *In fact, in an attempt to try and reinforce the multi-user aspects of NT, developers are recommended not to access data in* HKEY_CLASSES_ROOT, *instead you are directed to use the keys under* HKEY_CURRENT_USER\Software\Classes. *My experience of the current build of Windows 2000 is that very few developers have taken this advice although this perhaps merely reflects the fact that most of the applications that I have installed know nothing about Windows 2000 and hence still use the old registry hives. However, as a developer you should be aware that there will be* three *places for COM information in the foreseeable future:* HKEY_CLASSES_ROOT, HKEY_CURRENT_USER *and the COM+ Catalog.*

Components that are managed from the Component Services Explorer are known as **configured components**. Configured components execute in the new **COM+ Surrogate** (what was the MTS Executive) and can take advantage of the COM+ services. Older legacy COM components that are not managed using the Component Services Explorer are known as **unconfigured components**. So don't worry, you'll still be able to utilize your existing COM components and take advantage of your current investments in COM, even though features of MTS have been merged into the COM run time libraries. However, it's also important to remember that only configured components will be able to take advantage of the new features of COM+.

> *Remember the terms component and class can be pretty much used interchangeably. Most recent Microsoft documentation uses the term class.*

Simplified Development

The bottom line is that with several 'automatic' run time services, a simplified and proven programming model, and improved component management tools and configuration storage, developing and administrating components is easier than it has ever been. Just as Visual Basic revolutionized Windows development, COM+ is revolutionizing component development.

All the tedious and sophisticated work of distributed transaction management and enlistment, security authentication and authorization, load balancing, etc. will be handled for you. All you have to do is focus on creating software components that solve business problems instead of worrying about these complex infrastructure issues. This doesn't mean you won't have to write any code, but instead it means that the amount of code required to develop components is dramatically reduced.

One of the best parts about COM+ is that as MTS component developers, you have a head start. The MTS programming model is so similar to COM+ that your existing MTS components are also COM+ components. These can easily be configured to execute in the new COM+ surrogate without any code changes. If you're developing new components for COM+, they must meet the same requirements as they would for MTS.

So in summary, COM+ provides three things:

- ❑ A unified programming model
- ❑ Unified Administration and Registration
- ❑ An infrastructure of run time services

Let's start with a brief overview of what new services COM+ has to offer.

COM+ Services

COM+ encompasses more than just the merging of the COM, DCOM, MTS and MSMQ programming models and administration. COM+ also picks up where MTS left off, by continuing to provide an infrastructure of robust and flexible services, leaving developers to focus on business problems and their solutions. In addition to supporting MTS's declarative transactions, role-based security and improved component management, COM+ adds the following services:

- ❑ Load Balancing
- ❑ Object Pooling
- ❑ Security
- ❑ Compensating Resource Managers
- ❑ Queued Components
- ❑ Loosely Couple Events (LCE) – Publish/Subscribe Events
- ❑ In-Memory Database (IMDB)

Most of these services are invoked automatically by the COM+ run time during a component's activation or the pre-processing and post-processing of a method call. Other COM+ services are invoked manually in other ways. COM+ services can also be combined together or composed to provide the desired functionality for a component. In several cases, the use of one COM+ service will require the use of other COM+ services. For example, when used together, Dynamic Load Balancing and Object Pooling can greatly improve the scalability and performance of COM+ components.

As with MTS components, COM+ components use declarative attributes to indicate which services they will utilize. These attributes, and other metadata for each component, are stored in a **component library**, which supplements the information available in the component's type library. When components are configured to execute in the COM+ environment using the Component Services Explorer, these attributes are loaded into the new registration database called RegDB. These attributes in a component's library are only default values, and can be overridden using the Component Services Explorer. During the pre-processing and post-processing of method calls, the COM+ run time then checks these attributes from RegDB and invokes the required services.

Don't worry, COM+ will continue to support the features of MTS that we've grown to love. In fact, COM+ enhances many MTS features, including:

❑ Declarative Transactions
❑ Role-based Security

Let's discuss each of these COM+ services individually in more detail, and learn how we can use them for our COM+ components.

Load Balancing

One of the most common requirements of a distributed application is the ability to scale to support additional users as business needs grow and expand. Software development is usually much more expensive in terms of time and money than hardware. Therefore, the most common solution to meet the demanding needs of a growing business is to buy bigger, faster (more expensive) hardware, in an attempt to increase performance and scalability.

However, anyone who has worked with multiple processor systems knows that a quad processor server doesn't yield the performance that four separate servers do, and yet they almost cost the same. A better approach to scaling a distributed application is to replicate components across multiple servers, and balance the processing load of client requests among them. This concept of distributing the workload among all the available machines is known as **load balancing**.

> *Load balancing can be thought of as like a grocery store line. Customers wait in line to pay a cashier for products. If the line becomes to long, another cashier opens their checkout lane to balance the load of customers' requests.*

Consider the scenario of a small company that created some interactive, on-line auctioning software using Active Server Pages and COM+ components. In the first few hours that the web site goes live it has over 5,000 concurrent users. System administrators realize that the two dual processor Pentium III application servers hosting these COM+ components won't be able to support much more of an increase in activity. So, they quickly grab the beta and test servers to balance the processing load across the group of servers. But how do administrators or developers manage which server a client is directed to? That's where the two general types of load balancing come in: **static load balancing** and **dynamic load balancing**.

Static Load Balancing

With static load balancing, each component is statically linked to a server by the server's name or IP address, and all instances of the component are created on the specified server. This server name or IP address can be hard coded within an application's call to the `CreateObject` function, or it can be stored in the component's `RemoteServerName` registry key.

This very simplistic and primitive approach to load balancing always instantiates the component on the machine it is configured for, regardless of the processing load or availability of a server. As a result, static load balancing requires a fair amount of administration to configure and maintain every client's registry. It's also necessary to distribute new builds of an application whenever an additional server is added, an existing server is renamed or removed, or load-balancing performance needs to be improved. The lofty decisions of how many clients should access which particular server is usually left up to the unaware or unknowledgeable administrator.

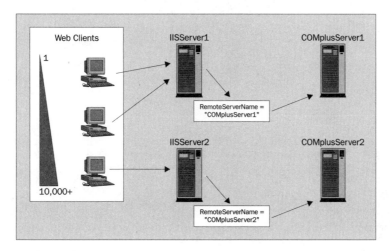

Additionally, since static load balancing is configured at the component level, it doesn't take into account the number of component instances. Consider the on-line auctions scenario we just discussed. With Active Server Pages executing on an IIS Server creating and making calls to COM+ objects on the behalf of thousands of clients, one client (IIS Server) could potentially be holding references to thousands of instances of the same COM+ component all located on the same machine.

Static load balancing also does not provide any fault tolerance against server failures. If a server is unavailable, all requests to create instances of component(s) on that server will return the famous 429 error, ActiveX Component can't create Object. Still, static load balancing is much better than no load balancing at all when it comes to fault tolerance. If a server is unavailable, clients configured to create instances of component(s) on other servers will not be interrupted.

However, overall static load balancing is much too primitive and simplistic for today's distributed applications. COM+ needs some way to dynamically route client's component instantiation requests to different servers, based on server availability and processing load. COM+ solves this need with its support for dynamic load balancing.

Dynamic Load Balancing

Dynamic load balancing takes a more strategic approach to balancing processing load and managing server failure with a group of middle-tier servers. With dynamic load balancing, a centralized list is maintained of performance statistics for each available and configured server. Components are then intelligently instantiated on the server performing the least amount of processing. The use of dynamic load balancing results in a more scalable distributed application.

Because the list of available servers is centrally located on one or more application server(s), dynamic load balancing doesn't require nearly as much administration as static load balancing. Administrators are not required to configure client machines to reference a new or renamed application server. If an additional server comes on-line, or an existing server is renamed or removed, only the centralized list of available servers needs to be adjusted.

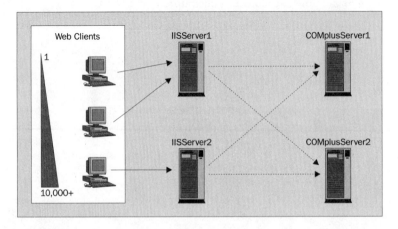

As I mentioned, dynamic load balancing also takes a more strategic approach to managing server failure. Static load balancing requires an administrator to reconfigure *all* components on *every* client machine when the assigned server is unavailable. Dynamic load balancing will automatically only route COM+ component instantiation requests to an available server. Servers that aren't available, or have failed, are not even considered as candidates to service client component instantiation requests.

With reduced administration and increased fault-tolerance, dynamic load balancing sounds like the perfect solution to increasing scalability by balancing processing load across multiple machines. However, it requires a significant amount of sophisticated code and logic to route instantiation requests to the least busy server. Dynamic load balancing trades the increased administration of static load balancing for a lot more code. But don't worry, COM+ has provided help.

COM+ Dynamic Load Balancing

According to Microsoft, intrinsic support for dynamic load balancing has been one of the most requested additions to DCOM and MTS. COM+ provides a dynamic load balancing service that is completely transparent to the COM+ components, and requires no additional code or changes to existing code. Also, implementing the COM+ dynamic load balancing service requires no extra client configuration, and allows centralized administration from any application server using the Component Services Explorer. It sounds too good to be true, doesn't it?

Behind the scenes, Microsoft has implemented a sophisticated and well-planned architecture to provide this transparent and simplified load balancing service for COM+ components. This is true with all of the COM+ services. The better you understand this behind the scenes architecture, the more effectively you'll be able to utilize the dynamic load balancing service to achieve maximum scalability.

Application Cluster

With COM+'s implementation of dynamic load balancing, a maximum of 8 servers capable of servicing component instantiation requests are grouped together to define an **Application Cluster**. COM+ Applications are assigned and automatically replicated across each server in the Application Cluster. An Application Cluster provides a level of abstraction from the physical architecture, by making multiple servers appear to the client as a single application server. As we've seen with the Context Wrapper, abstraction from physical implementation always provides a great deal of flexibility, and the same is true with the abstraction provided by an Application Cluster.

Router

All component instantiation requests are directed to the server in the Application Cluster that acts as the **Load Balancing Router**. The Load Balancing Router is like an Object Request Broker (ORB), and is the center of the COM+ dynamic load balancing architecture. The Router works with the **Load Balancing Analyzer**, sometimes called the **Load Balancing Engine**, which is responsible for collecting run time performance information about the servers in the Application Cluster.

So what happens when the Router receives an instantiation request for a COM+ component that's configured to support dynamic load balancing? The Router's local SCM transparently redirects or reroutes the instantiation request to the most available server in the Application Cluster. The Load Balancing Router then steps out of the way and is no longer involved with this instantiation request. Finally, the chosen application server services the instantiation request, and returns a reference to the new object directly back to the client. All method calls are made directly to the COM+ object and don't pass through the Load Balancing Router.

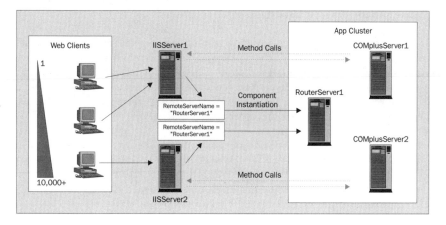

The Dynamic Load Balancing architecture implemented by COM+ is fairly simplistic. However, the complex functionality of COM+ dynamic load balancing is implemented by the Load Balancing Analyzer. This continuously executes an intelligent response time algorithm to determine the most responsive server in the Application Cluster. The response time algorithm is calculated by timing each method call through each interface on every instance of a given machine.

If you don't like this default response time algorithm, you can replace it with your own load balancing algorithm, simply by developing a COM+ component that implements a handful of standard interfaces. However, the default response time algorithm should be adequate for most situations.

Remember, this complex algorithm executes continuously in the background. So when the Router receives an instantiation request, the application server that will service the request has already been determined. COM+ doesn't wait until it receives an instantiation request to determine the most responsive server. Instead the most responsive server is determined before an instantiation request is ever made. As a result, the response time to service an instantiation request is greatly minimized.

Object Pooling/Object Recycling

Pooling, or recycling, of expensive resources is not a new concept to component developers. MTS provides thread pooling and integration with the ODBC Driver manager and OLE DB Services, which provide the very important data source connection pooling. COM+ extends resource pooling to COM+ component instances by introducing an **Object Pooling** run-time service.

> **Object Pooling, more appropriately called Object Recycling, is the process of reusing existing component instances instead of instantiating new ones.**

Suppose a client application requests a new instance of a component. The specified component supports pooling, and an instance is available in a pool of object references. Then, the client application will immediately receive a reference to an existing object from the pool, instead of a reference to a new object. After an object is deactivated, instead of being destroyed, it remains loaded in memory and is placed back into the pool. The pool of COM+ objects can also be replenished by the COM+ run time as needed. This process of reusing component instances reduces the amount of time it takes for the COM+ run time to provide the client with an object. It can ultimately result in higher performance and increased scalability in some situations.

Object recycling is similar to the common situation of renting videos from your local video store, using books from the local library or any other borrowing/renting real-life situation. Video stores, for example, maintain several copies of the latest movies to rent to customers. Think of a video store as the pool and a video as like a COM+ object. You see a preview for an exciting movie, so you drive to the video store and the salesperson (pool manager) checks out the video (object) to you. At that time you remove the video (object) from the video store (pool).

The next day, you return to the video store and check in (deactivate) the video. The salesperson (pool manager) then places the copy you returned (deactivated object) back onto the shelf for another customer to rent (activate). The state of the video changed through this rental process from *not rented* to *rented* and then back to the *not rented* state, just as an object is deactivated, activated and then deactivated again as it is pooled, used and placed back in the pool.

Renting videos from a video store instead of purchasing them can be much more cost effective, just as using an existing component instance from a pool can be much more cost effective (in terms of performance) than creating a new object.

However, before you rush into implementing object pooling for your COM+ components, you need to decide if your COM+ components can really benefit from Object Pooling. There are two general types of components that are likely to benefit:

❑ **Components that are expensive to create or destroy**

Object Pooling is most commonly used for objects that take a long time to initialize or terminate. A good candidate for Object Pooling would be an object that loads configuration information (such as business rules) from a file or another data source when it is created, and then uses that information for its entire lifetime. It would only have to load the information once, and it could then service method calls for potentially thousands of different clients before being destroyed. If Object Pooling was not utilized for this type of component, each individual client would have their own instance created, and the configuration information would be loaded many times.

Without Object Pooling, creating and destroying large numbers of objects can severely degrade performance and scalability. In addition, the more generic these expensive components are, the more likely they will benefit from Object Pooling. A component that only performs specific tasks won't be utilized by as many applications or other components as a component that performs very general tasks.

❑ **Components that control a limited amount of valuable resources**

Pooling can also be beneficial for components that access a limited resource such as a database, mainframe or dial-up networking connection. This is because COM+ provides the ability to control the maximum size of a component's object pool. If you're limited to 10 mainframe connections, you can configure the object pool to be limited to only 10 instances of the component that controls access to the mainframe connections.

This decision of whether or not to implement Object Pooling for a particular component should not be taken lightly. In several situations Object Pooling can actually degrade overall system performance and scalability.

Most COM+ objects don't fall into the categories we just discussed. They perform very little or no work when they are created or destroyed, and don't control access to limited resources. In the case of your typical COM+ components, the resources (memory, CPU cycles, etc.) required to maintain the Object Pool outweigh the benefits of reusing an existing object to avoid the creation or destruction overhead of a new one. Maintaining a pool of COM+ objects that don't really benefit from Object Pooling would be wasting resources that could be utilized by other components or services. Therefore, the overall system performance and scalability is degraded.

Additionally, COM+ already provides or participates in providing pooling of the most common expensive resources (such as threads and ODBC and OLE DB/ADO data source connections) through the use of system-supplied COM+ Resource Dispensers. Considering these facts, in my opinion, Object Pooling isn't as significant to the scalability of distributed applications as some of the other COM+ run time services. Dynamic Load Balancing, Queued Components and the In Memory Database (IMDB) are much more important.

In COM+ you configure object pooling on the activation tab of the component:

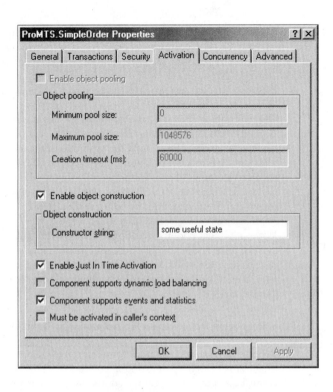

Security

Under MTS 2.0 you could apply security to packages (to specify the authentication level and whether role-based authorization is used) and components (to indicate if role-based authorization is used). Under COM+ you will find security tabs on the properties of not only applications and components, but also on the property tabs of interfaces and methods:

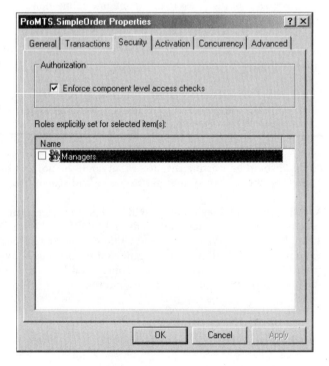

As with MTS 2.0 the authorization checks are made against Roles defined in the Application.

Security Tab for:	Description
Application	Specifies the authentication and impersonation levels that will be used – specifies if authorization checks are made and the granularity of those checks (either at the process-level, or both at the process- and component-levels).
Component	Specifies if access checks are made at the component-level and the roles that can access the component.
Interface	Determines the roles that can access the methods on this interface. The tab lists the roles that have been given permission to access the component and allows you to give permission to other roles defined for the Application.
Method	Determines the roles that can access the particular method. The tab lists the roles that have been given permission to access the component and the interface; it also allows you to give permission to other roles defined for the Application.

As the previous table implies, you define roles for the Application and then progressively add roles that can access a specified component, specified interfaces on the component, and specified methods on the interfaces. You cannot take permissions away (so the roles that can access a component will be able to access any interfaces and any methods on those interfaces), so you should make careful choices of which roles to give which permissions.

As with MTS 2.0, you can configure COM+ Applications to run under a specific Identity, which indicates the account under which the surrogate process, `DllHost.exe`, will run. This, of course, only applies to Server (not Library) Applications.

Checking Security

Checking security is done under COM+ using the `SecurityCallContext` object accessed using `GetSecurityCallContext` method. In this code we do a simple check to ensure that the caller of the method is in the role `Managers`, because only managers are allowed to perform the task of submitting payroll:

```
Sub DoPayroll()

  Dim objCallContext As SecurityCallContext

' Get the security call context
  Set objCallContext = GetSecurityCallContext

' Perform the role check

  If objCallContext.IsCallerInRole("Managers") = True Then
' ****Do something here****
  End If

End Sub
```

As with MTS, under COM+ we also need to check if security is enabled before performing security checks. The preferred way to do this is also via a method of the `SecurityCallContext` object:

```
Dim secCallContext As SecurityCallContext

Set secCallContext = GetSecurityCallContext

If secCallContext.IsSecurityEnabled() = True Then
' Security is enabled!
End If
```

Security Callers Objects

In the payroll code above, it is possible that the method call could have taken a path involving callers with different identities, especially if the call was made remotely across one or more machines via DCOM and passed on using delegation. COM+ uses the **Security Callers object**, which represents a chain of callers.

This Collection object provides access for each caller in the chain (via the usual COM collection mechanisms, e.g. the `Item` method) and for each one provides access to a **Security Identity object** which provides access to the following named items:

Item	Description	Data Type	Index
SID	The unique Windows 2000 security identifier of the caller.	V_ARRAY	"SID"
Account Name	The account name that the caller of the method is using.	V_BSTR	"AccountName"
Authentication Service	The authentication service being used by the caller. Includes values such as NTLMSSP, Kerberos, or SSL.	V_I4	"AuthenticationService"
Impersonation Level	Indicates how much authority the caller has been given when acting on a client's behalf.	V_I4	"ImpersonationLevel"
Authentication Level	The authentication level used by the caller. Indicates the amount of protection given during the call.	V_I4	"AuthenticationLevel"

These new COM+ objects provide information to enable applications to implement a more sophisticated security system if required. This is very important when using Kerberos security provider, which enables delegation of client credentials across multiple machines.

Compensating Resource Managers

All of the COM+ services we've discussed until now are designed to enhance the scalability and performance of component-based applications. However, COM+ also provides a new feature called the **Compensating Resource Manager (CRM)** that provides an infrastructure that enhances COM+'s support for transaction processing. Compensating Resource Managers provide an easy way to allow a non-transactional resource to participate in transactions managed by the Microsoft Distributed Transaction Coordinator (MS DTC).

CRMs are a simpler alternative to developing a complex COM+ Resource Manager and Resource Dispenser pair, while still using the MS DTC to coordinate transactions. For example, CRMs could be developed to provide transactional access for resources such as file systems, memory or the Windows 2000 registry. Transactional COM+ components can then access these resources through the CRM 's interface(s) and all operations performed by the CRM would be protected by an MS DTC Transaction.

Additionally, because the MS DTC is utilized as the transaction coordinator for both the COM+ Resource Managers/Dispensers and Compensating Resource Managers, a single transaction can be composed of operations against resources using either architecture. This feature makes Compensating Resource Managers an attractive solution to providing transactional access to resources.

Suppose we utilize Active Server Pages and COM+ components to develop a collaborative web site that allows users to upload and download files. This is a typical requirement for Internet and intranet sites. The lists of files that are available for download must dynamically adjust to display the files that have been uploaded by other users. So we implement the simple approach of storing the physical file on our IIS server and store the URL to the file in our SQL Server database. For each file on our web server that is available for download, there's a corresponding record in our SQL Server database's `Files` table.

When the `FileListing.asp` page is requested, it calls a COM+ component that retrieves all of the records from the `Files` table. The user can then simply click on a link to download the appropriate file from the web server.

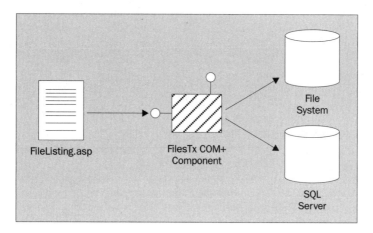

But we're also going to allow managers to delete files through the web-based interface. To delete a file that is currently available for download, we must delete both the physical file on the IIS server and the corresponding record in the `Files` table, otherwise our database and file system would become out of sync. Both of these operations must complete successfully, or else neither should complete. If the record in the `Files` table is deleted and the physical file is not deleted, we would have unneeded files on the web server taking up precious disk space. If the physical file is deleted and the record is not deleted from the `Files` table, we would have irritated users trying to download files that don't exist. What we really need to do is perform both of these operations as a single atomic unit of work – a single transaction.

However, simply creating a COM+ component that performs these operations and configuring the component's transactional support to Requires a Transaction won't ensure that all of these operations are performed in a single transaction. Yes, the operations performed against the SQL Server database will be performed in a transaction. The SQL Server OLE DB Provider (assuming we're using ADO or OLE DB for our Data Source access) is a Resource Dispenser that automatically enlists the transaction with MS DTC, and SQL Server is a Resource Manager that works with MS DTC to commit or rollback the transaction. But there is no Resource Dispenser and Resource Manager pair for file manipulation.

An easy solution is to develop a generic Compensating Resource Manager for the file system, and code a COM+ component to utilize this CRM for all file access and manipulation. Because both the Resource Dispensers/Managers and the CRMs rely upon MS DTC to coordinate the commitment and rollback of transactions, operations against resources that utilize either architecture can be composed as a single transaction:

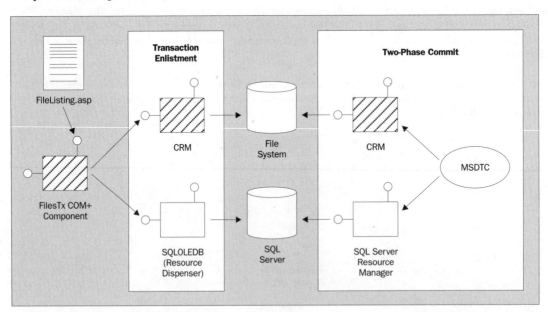

You've seen what a Compensating Resource Manager is and how it enhances COM+'s support for transaction processing. Now let's discuss the architecture of CRMs and examine the details of how they work.

Compensating Resource Manager Architecture

A CRM is implemented as a pair of simple COM+ components called the **CRM Worker** and **CRM Compensator**. Both of these components utilize the **CRMClerk** component defined in the COM+ Services Type Library. CRMClerk is a generic component on top of MS DTC. It implements most of the complex functionality required for CRMs to participate in MS DTC transactions. This component layer allows developers to concentrate on the custom aspects of providing transactional access to resources. They can simply develop these two COM+ components that call methods on an instance of CRMClerk at the appropriate times:

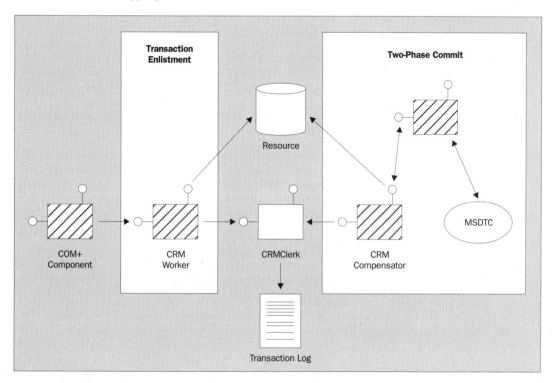

CRM Worker

The CRM Worker is responsible for accessing and manipulating resources when COM+ transactional components invoke methods provided by the CRM Worker's interfaces. You can think of the CRM Worker as simply a component layer on top of a resource.

Developing a CRM Worker is simple, however, there are a few requirements the CRM Worker must meet so it can enlist in an MS DTC transaction. All of these requirements involve calling methods on an instance of the CRMClerk component, which handles the more complex functionality to perform operations inside an MS DTC transaction:

❑   Register the CRM Compensator with the CRMClerk
❑   Perform write-ahead logging before attempting to perform any operations
❑   Vote on the outcome of the transaction

The CRM infrastructure provides a durable transaction log that can be used by the CRM Worker and the CRM Compensator. As methods are invoked on the CRM Worker that effect the CRM's underlying resource, the CRM Worker should perform write-ahead logging before it actually carries out any operation that would change the state of the resource. In the case of transaction or system failure, the CRM Compensator can then work with the transaction log to rollback or finish committing the operations performed within the transaction.

The CRMClerk component provides the following methods for working with the CRM transaction log:

Method	Description
WriteLogRecordVariants()	This function is used to write the actual log entry. Since it accepts a single parameter of the type variant, you can pass it an array, collection, ADO Recordset or any other data type or object. However, it is important to remember that the log entry is not created in the durable CRM transaction log when this method is called.
ForceLog()	This is used to ensure that the previous log entries are durable in the CRM transaction log. After this function is called, any log entries created with the WriteLogRecordVariants that have not been written to the durable log will be persisted, even if a transaction or system failure was to occur.
ForgetLogRecord()	This function is used to delete any log entries that were created with the WriteLogRecordVariants function, but are not yet persisted to the durable CRM transaction log.

All operations performed against a resource through a CRM Worker should change the state of the resource from one constant state to another. A CRM Worker should not change the state of a resource based on its current state, because it would be difficult to perform recovery in the event of a transaction or system failure.

The CRM Worker also has the ability to vote on the outcome of the transaction by calling methods on an instance of the CRMClerk component, in much the same way as a transactional COM+ component votes on the outcome of a transaction through the Context object. However, with the case of a CRM Worker, the CRM infrastructure will automatically assume that all operations have completed successfully. If an unrecoverable error occurs when the CRM Worker is servicing a client's method call, the CRM Worker should call the ForceTransactionToAbort function of the CRMClerk. By calling this function, the CRM Worker will force the entire MS DTC transaction to abort. As a result, all operations performed against all resources involved in the transaction will be rolled back.

CRM Compensator

The CRM Compensator is responsible for voting on the outcome of the transaction, and for committing or aborting the operations performed against the resource by the CRM Worker. In the case where a transaction is aborted for any reason, the CRM Compensator must perform a compensating action that counteracts or undoes the effects of the normal actions performed by the CRM Worker.

When a transaction completes, the CRM infrastructure creates an instance of the CRM Compensator that was registered by the Worker, and MS DTC starts the two-phase commit protocol. The CRM infrastructure then invokes methods on the CRM Compensator through the ICrmCompensatorVariants interface (defined in the COM+ Services Library), to notify the CRM Compensator about the prepare, commit and abort phases in the MS DTC transaction. Behind the scenes, the COM+ run time is acting as an interception layer for the Compensator. It traps the MS DTC events and invokes the corresponding method(s) on the Compensator's implementation through the ICrmCompensatorVariants interface.

Deployment of CRMs

Once you have developed the CRM Worker and CRM Compensator components, they must be installed and configured in a COM+ Application. Typically, a COM+ Library Application is more beneficial than a Server Application for hosting the CRM Worker and CRM Compensator. A Library Application will load into the process of the creator, resulting in a higher performance.

The CRM Worker should then be configured to **Requires a Transaction** and the Compensator's transaction attribute should be set to **Not Supported**. If the CRM Worker is not configured to require a transaction, then it will be unable to participate in an MS DTC Transaction and an error will be recorded in the Windows 2000 Event Log when a client tries to call methods on an instance of the CRM Worker:

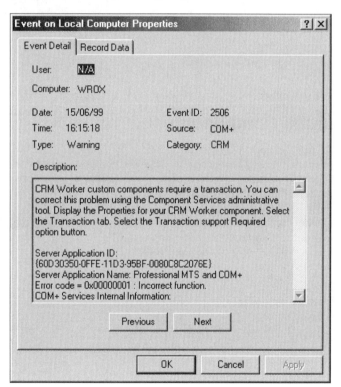

Before COM+ components can utilize a Compensating Resource Manager, the component's Server Package must be configured to enable CRMs, using the Component Services Explorer. Components can then perform operations against resources within a protected transaction by calling methods implemented by the CRM Worker:

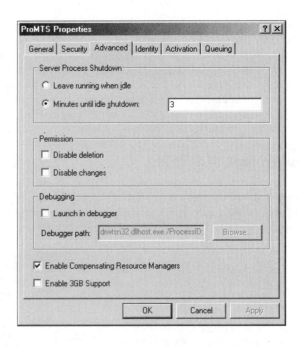

Queued Components

COM+ now provides an integration of MSMQ (Microsoft Message Queue Server) into the COM+ run time. This enables method calls of a component to be invoked asynchronously via a message queue. This queue is later read by a server process and forwarded to the target component to be processed.

Queuing attributes are applied on two pages within the component services snap-in. The first is the Queuing tab on the Properties page for an Application:

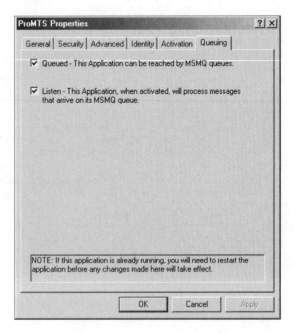

The other is the Advanced tab on the Properties page for a component:

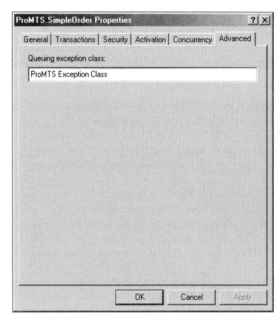

On the Application's Queuing page there are two check box options. The first specifies whether the Application will use queued components. Selecting this option enables the second. This second option indicates that the Application is a **Listener**, that is, it will respond to component requests via messages. When you do this COM+ will create a queue for the Application (using the Application name). Now, when a client makes a request to a queued component it is made via a message in this queue. The client is fully aware that the Application may not exist, but it does not matter because the queue will record all method calls made to the component. The component and client, of course, will have to be written in such a way to take this into account, in particular, methods should only have [in] parameters. [out] parameters are not permitted due to the asynchronous nature of the call.

Recorder, Listener, Player

There are essentially three main entities used with queued components: a **Recorder**, that takes queued component requests and puts them into a message, a **Listener**, which polls the queue for a message and a **Player**, that 'plays' the message to create and use a component. Messaging is regarded as *reliable*, and so once a message is put into a queue the client can assume that the message will be delivered. Queued components can be used in a disconnected case, where the transaction on the client side is not distributed across to the server side; indeed, the message is only sent once the client transaction is committed.

If the message cannot be sent for some reason (the queuing system fails or a server is down) the system tries to re-send the message. COM+ generates a **Loosely Coupled Event** (LCE – described next) to indicate that there is a problem and to allow the message to be modified. On the third re-try the message is moved to a dead letter queue where it will sit until the administrator of the system decides what to do with the message.

Although COM+ implements a lot to allow you to use queued components, the client code also needs to be written to use them so that the Recorder will be used. This occurs through a new system moniker called Queue, which creates the Recorder based on the CLSID. Whenever the client makes calls to the component these are recorded in the message. There may be more than one method call to the component, perhaps representing several property set calls followed by some method call to process those properties.

To process the message the server needs to be run, and needs a listener thread. This is applied by checking the **Listener** check box on the Application's properties, which ensures that it polls its message queue. Any messages in the queue are read and then passed to the Player, which creates the component and makes the property and method calls in the order in which the Recorder recorded them.

On the server side there are a few considerations that you need to take into account, other than specifying that the Application uses queued components. The interface methods *must* only use [in] parameters (reflecting the fact that the methods are called asynchronously, and hence the client cannot expect a response except to know if the initial queue request worked). In addition, you should use IDispatch-based interfaces and, in general, only use the interface marked as [default].

The Component Services Explorer also has queuing properties on the **Advanced** tab of a component's **Properties** page: the name of an exception class. This class is activated by the Player before sending a message to the dead letter queue and it is used to playback the message so that the exception component can perform some handling based on the message. This exception class should implement the IPlaybackControl interface.

Unlike many of the other COM+ attributes a queued component can be identified as using queued component-friendly interfaces in IDL. This is done by applying the QUEUEABLE attribute (actually a macro that applies a [custom()] attribute) to these interfaces.

Loosely Coupled Events (LCE)

COM+ introduces a new asynchronous publish/subscribe event system. Unlike the existing connection point system used in COM, LCE is designed more for broadcasting information in a distributed system and provides a level of indirection between the component that raises an event and the components that receive the event.

LCE consists of three main components:

❑ Publishers
❑ Event Classes
❑ Subscribers

Publishers

Publishers are pretty much like the components we write today, that use the Raise method to generate an event, except they don't use the raise keyword. Instead, they generate events using an **Event Class** when interesting things happen, that is, they publish information:

```
Dim objSomething As Object

Set objSomething = CreateObject("Interesting.New")

objSomething.NewsFlash 1, "COM+ to be launched in October"

Set objSomething = Nothing
```

Any publisher can create these event classes and publish events by calling their methods.

Event Classes

An event class is a component developed by an application that wants to generate COM+ events. Its interface describes a list of events that can be raised by a **publisher** and received by zero or more **subscribers**.

The interface we used in the sample code above could be defined like this:

```
Interface INewsFeed

    {
      HRESULT NewFlash( [in] long lChannel, [in] BSTR sHeadline );
    };
```

Parameter can only be marked as [in] due to the asynchronous nature of LCE.

Event classes are registered in the COM+ catalog so are persistent.

Subscribers

Subscribers register their interest in events by adding subscription information to the COM+ catalog. These subscriptions are listed in the COM+ Explorer.

A typical subscription has the following attributes:

❑ The name of the event class
❑ The IID of the event class interfaces
❑ The method name from the event interface
❑ A filter – can be used to pass on only pertinent events to the subscriber by checking values of method properties, etc.

The following diagram shows the basic structure of LCE in COM+:

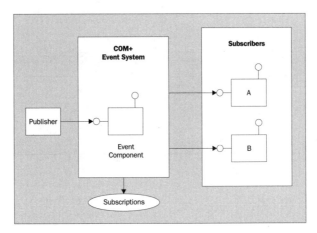

As part of the MSMQ integration in COM+, LCE also supports the concepts of queued/disconnected events. These are useful when, for whatever reason, the publisher or subscribers are disconnected from a system for a period of time.

If the publisher is disconnected, then the queue is between the Publisher and Event Class. If the subscriber is disconnected, the queue is between the COM+ Event system (event class) and the subscriber.

In-Memory Database (IMDB)

IMDB is a technology that is designed for components that need to achieve very fast read access of data by pre-loading database tables into memory. Implemented as an OLEDB provider (MSIMDB), IMDB can cache tables based upon administrator configuration, which as well as enabling high speed access, dispenses with the need to perform slow, out of process, calls to a backend DBMS.

As VB programmers we can just access the IMDB provider using ADO:

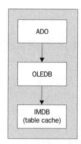

IMDB saves us from having to write our own caching systems, which in general, are not simple, as they involve dealing with complex concurrency (locking) and update issues. IMDB takes care of all of this and is a fully transactional OLEDB data source, which means we can perform updates via IMDB. However, writing to data sources via IMDB is slower than going directly against OLEDB provider due to the extra level of indirection.

IMDB under Windows 2000 is implemented as a service that you enable from the My Computer Properties tab:

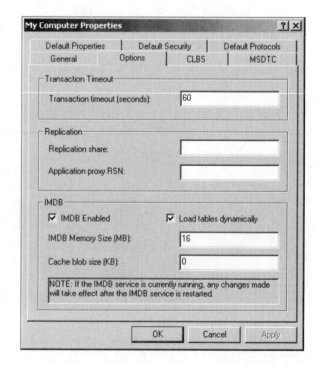

You specify the size of the cache, which the service owns, and whether or not tables are loaded when the service starts, or if the load is delayed until the first client accesses a table.

The cache is allocated as shared memory, which enables each client to access it directly in-process, results in blisteringly quick performance, in some cases, 100 times quicker than non-IMDB access.

Configuring IMDB

You configure IMDB database sources and the tables in the Component Services Explorer, under the IMDB data sources key:

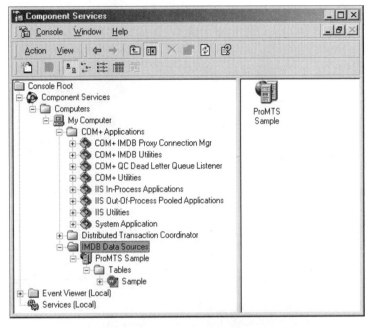

Each data source has the usual set of properties, as you would expect:

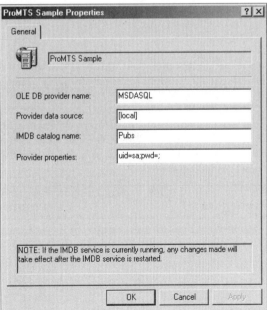

Just as you can specify individual tables to be cached, you can also specify whether or not BLOBs (Binary Large Objects) are pre-loaded or if their loading is delayed:

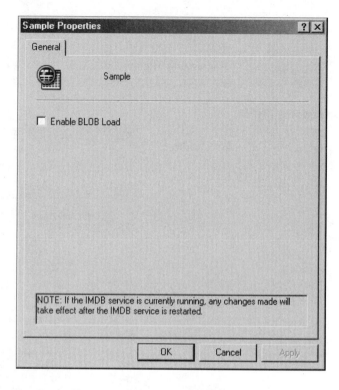

The Transaction Shared Property Manager – TSPM

One of the much-discussed missing features of MTS 2.0 was the ability to perform transactional operations against the Shared Property Manager. This feature, had it been implemented, would have enabled developers to use it more like a temporary database table, providing developers with a more flexible method sharing of state within a package. Of course, what developers really wanted was IMDB.

As we've already discussed, IMDB is one choice that is now available to us, but COM+ also introduces a **Transaction Shared Property Manager (TSPM)**.

TSPM in COM+ is implemented using IMDB. What it essentially does is provide a SPM type interface to a number of in-memory database tables, via an interface that is already pretty familiar to us as MTS developers. This saves you as a developer from having to invent such as system. The TSPM provides a number of interfaces that will immediately be recognisable due to their non-transactional ancestors:

Interface	Description
ITxPropertyGroupManager	Used to create property groups.
ITxPropertyGroup	Used to create and access properties within a group.

Interface	Description
ITxProperty	Provides access to shared properties. These properties govern the types of access available, the concurrency model, and indicate the number of properties available under the TxPropertyGroup.

As TSPM is implemented using IMDB, which uses shared memory, shared property groups and properties can now be accessed **across processes**, and not just packages. This opens up whole new dimensions for state sharing between packages within an enterprise.

Here are a couple of obvious but key points to note about TSPM and its difference from SPM:

❑ The creation and deletion of property groups requires a transaction
❑ Getting and setting property values does not require a transaction
❑ IMDB uses the temporary tables PropertyGroupNames and PropertyGroupProperties to store the TSPM information
❑ You must know the name of a property group to be able to use it, due to the way the IMDB security model works.

To finish off, here is some code showing how the TSPM can be used:

```
' Create the TxPropertyGroup manager
Dim objManager As New TSPM.TransactedPropertyGroupManager

' Specify the isolation level (default value)
objManager.isolationlevel = READ_COMMITTED

' Create a new TxPropertyGroup

Dim blnFExists As Boolean
Dim objGroup As TSPM.TxPropertyGroup

Set objGroup = objManager.CreatePropertyGroup("ProMTSGroup", blnFExists,_
                                              False, False, 0, "", False)

' Create a new property
Dim objProp As TSPM.TxProperty
set objProp = objGroup.CreateProperty("Authors", fExists)

' Set value of TSPM.TxProperty
objProp = "Matt and James"
```

COM+ Concepts

Now that we've taken a quick look at some of the new COM+ services, let's take a closer look at how these changes have affected the basics of the COM run time.

Activation

Whenever you create a COM+ object, the COM+ run time will compare the context of the client with that of the configured object being created to see if it is compatible. The object's context will indicate the COM+ services that it uses, which the COM+ run time will apply through interception, much as the MTS Executive does, for example to perform security checks.

An apartment can have one or more contexts. When a COM+ object is accessed from outside of its context (for example from another apartment or from another context that has different transactional or synchronization attributes) a proxy will be used. However, because the proxy really does represent the object (and hence have the requirements of COM+ services) the proxy too is context relative, and represents the difference between the contexts of the client and the object. This way, the proxy adds only as much of the context as is needed.

This does mean that when you have more than one client context, proxies must be marshalled if you want to use your object in those different contexts. This is not too much of a problem, since as a seasoned COM developer you will be used to marshalling object references between apartments; in COM+ the apartment is just one of the context attributes. This is shown in the figure opposite:

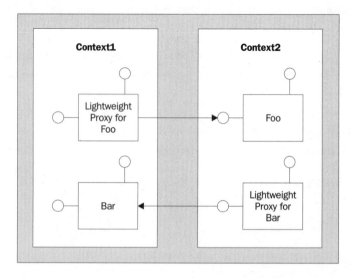

When the proxy has been created with the correct context, COM+ can apply its services through interception as discussed.

Apartments

Apartments still exist in COM+ but they are not the primary utility in call-synchronization. As with COM, COM+ has MTAs and STAs, where the STAs ensure that the code will only ever be executed by the same thread. However, certain components that simply require call-serialization can now be moved from an STA into an MTA, and the serialization performed using the COM+ synchronization attributes. This wins on the performance front, as cross-apartment marshalling is a lot more expensive than cross-context marshalling.

STAs must remain in COM+, because sections of the Windows operating system, and probably your own code, have thread affinity, and so can only be accessed by the same thread. In particular, all UI COM *must* execute in an STA. However, it is now possible to configure STA components to run in an MTA, and have COM+ enforce synchronization that should result in higher performance.

TNA – Thread-Neutral Apartment

COM+ also adds the much-discussed **Thread Neutral Apartment (TNA)**. As the name suggests, this apartment does not have native threads, because threads live in STAs or MTAs. Like those other apartment types, objects can use the `ThreadingModel` registry key to specify that they want to live in a TNA, and, like classic COM, an object can only be accessed from a thread within the apartment it lives.

To perform this feat, a thread from an STA or MTA temporarily joins the TNA for the purpose of accessing the object. Because the TNA is thread neutral, when a thread runs code in the TNA there is no thread context switch. However, there may be a context switch, which will involve marshalling across the context boundary, but this marshalling is lightweight compared to thread context switches. Contrast this with the Free Threading Model, which means that an object is context neutral, requires no context switches and hence runs under the context of the client.

Since a TNA allows quicker access to an object's code, it is the preferred apartment type in COM+. However, since there are no native threads in an TNA you still need to create threads to execute the code! This is the reason why the other two apartments still exist. When creating a thread (or rather determining what apartment type a thread should join) your choice will depend on whether the thread will be used to service UI code or not, and you should not be persuaded by synchronization issues.

Although apartments do still have synchronization requirements, and by supplying a `ThreadingModel` value an object indicates the synchronization it supports, this is no longer the main way to ensure concurrency. Instead, COM provides a **synchronization attribute**, which indicates the synchronization that is applied through the more generalized concept of an activity.

Windows DNA under Windows 2000

Don't forget that COM+ is only one piece in the Windows DNA puzzle. The long-term goal of Windows DNA is to have three groups of technologies:

- ❑ **Forms+** at the Presentation tier
- ❑ **COM+** at the Middle tier
- ❑ **Storage+** at the Data Services tier

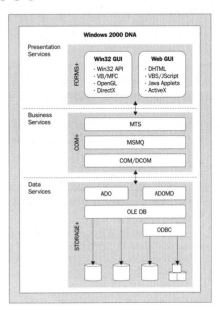

Forms+ will likely represent a merging of the Win32 user interfaces with web user interfaces. Web GUIs are very eye-pleasing, but they lack the sophistication of Win32 applications. Web user interfaces are usually developed with typeless scripting languages that provide little debugging support and a slew of problems related to browser incompatibility. In addition, because of the many technologies commonly used together to create a web GUI, they usually take much longer to develop. However, they are usually easier to deploy.

On the other hand, Win32 GUIs must be fully compiled, rebuilt and distributed whenever a bug fix or enhancement is made, but they are usually much faster and easier to develop. Large deployments of EXE-based applications and their dependencies are usually a nightmare. Hopefully, Forms+ will neatly merge the best attributes of both Win32 and DHTML user interfaces to create a single, simplified programming model that eliminates the guesswork required when choosing between user interface technologies. To reach this ultimate goal, a lot of work will also have to be done by Microsoft with both the development and deployment tools. Internet Explorer 5.0, with its Document Object Model (DOM) and its support for XML, might possibly be where Forms+ is headed.

Storage+ is Microsoft's long-range solution to data storage and retrieval. The aim is to unify all the storage technologies, and eventually create a single storage engine capable of storing and searching everything from Microsoft Office documents and email messages to objects such as music clips and digital photos. Storage+ will most likely be very similar to OLE DB (this is one of Microsoft's successful data access technologies based on COM that's delivering on the promise of Universal Data Access). Only time will tell, because Microsoft currently isn't.

It's likely that we won't hear much information or see any beta releases of the full-blown Forms+ or Storage+ until a second release of COM+. For now, at least Microsoft recognizes that attention needs to be applied to the Presentation and Data Services tiers, as well as the Business Services tier. We'll probably see some type of help for these key areas in the near future.

Summary

We started this chapter by discussing how COM+ encompasses and extends the functionality that we know today as MTS.

We discussed the new services that COM+ has introduced to provide more functionality and power to our enterprise applications.

We then took a look at how base COM has changed, with the introduction of the context as a primary feature in the COM run time with the demoting of the apartment to a 'context container'.

And finally, we discussed how COM+ is really the glue that holds together DNA.

Note: For the latest information about COM and COM+ don't forget to check the Wrox Press COMdeveloper website:

`http://www.comdeveloper.com`

A Simple Sales Order Application Case Study

By Donald Xie

This case study aims to demonstrate the techniques used to develop MTS components in Visual Basic 6. It is an n-tiered Microsoft Windows application that consists of a group of components spread out across 4 logical tiers. Having said that we're not going to go hell for leather and develop a highly complex application. Rather we're going to concentrate on developing transactional and non-transactional MTS components so that we can get an idea of where they fit into a application such as this. The basic purpose of the application is to allow the user to maintain customers and sales orders based on the sample Northwind database.

The Presentation Tier

The user will be able to look up, add, edit, and delete customers, as well as query and add sales orders.

We will provide three Visual Basic forms:

- ❑ Customer-Data entry - the user can create a new customer by entering the customer's ID and Name. Existing customer records can also be retrieved from the database, modified or deleted.
- ❑ Sales-Order entry - the user can use this form to create a new sales order. The user will also be able to retrieve an existing sales order.
- ❑ Item-Entry - the user will be able to add products to an order.

Case Study

The User-Centric Business Objects Tier

Our application will provide a collection of User-Centric objects that encapsulate the properties and behaviors of the Customer, Sales-Order, Sales-Order Items, and Products. All objects are packaged into one ActiveX DLL, `UCObjects`. They are responsible for communicating with the Data-Centric objects to provide data access capabilities to the UI application. This DLL will be deployed to the workstation where the user interface program is installed.

The Data-Centric Business Objects Tier

The Data-Centric business objects are responsible for reading data from the database and updating the tables in the database. They will be packaged into three ActiveX DLLs:

- ❑ `DCCustomer`
- ❑ `DCProduct`
- ❑ `DCSalesOrder`

These will provide access to Customer, Product, and Sales-Order data respectively. These DLLs will be hosted in MTS and can be deployed on different servers where MTS is installed.

For the User-Centric objects `Customer` and `SalesOrder`, we develop two Data-Centric objects – one for transactional operations that update the table in the database, such as adding or deleting records, the other for non-transactional operations, such as retrieving data from the database. The `Product` object provides read-only access to product data. Therefore we will only develop one non-transactional Data-Centric object to access the database. The `SalesOrderItem` does not communicate with Data-Centric objects directly as all sales order operations are managed between the `SalesOrder` objects.

> *All transactional MTS components have a postfix letter T, and all non-transactional MTS components have a postfix letter N in their names.*

When we update customer data, a single component transaction will be created. When we update sales order data, we will create transactions that span two components: `SalesOrderT` and `SalesOrderItemT`.

The Data Tier

The sample database NorthWind that comes with SQL Server 7 provides the access to the sample data. In this case study, we will be using four tables: `Customers`, `Products`, `Orders`, and `Order Details`. However, only a subset of fields from each table will be used. This frees us from being buried in details and allows us to concentrate on the issues related to developing MTS components. It also simplifies the user interface of our application.

We'll begin by creating the business objects that we need. We'll use UML class diagrams to illustrate the properties and methods of each object and their relationships.

Business Objects – The Customer Objects

Let's start with objects that deal with the Customer records. Collectively, the User-Centric and Data-Centric Customer objects provide us with the functionality to query, add, edit, and delete customer records in the database.

The User-Centric Customer Class

This class provides an interface that encapsulates the attributes and behavior of the Customer object to the user interface program:

```
                    <<Class Module>>
                       Customer
-----------------------------------------------------
mstr ID : String
mstrName : String
mcstrClassName : String = "UCObjects.Customer"
mcstrObjectError : String = vbObjectError + &H1100
mblnIsNew : Boolean
mrecCustomers : ADODB.Recordset
-----------------------------------------------------
<<Let>> ID(ByVal Value : String)
<<Get>> ID() : String
<<Let>> Name(ByVal Value : String)
<<Get>> Name() : String
<<Let>> IsNew(ByVal Value : Boolean)
<<Get>> IsNew() : Boolean
Read(Optional ID : String = "")
Save()
Delete()
Populate(Optional CustomerRS : ADODB.Recordset = Nothing)
Serialize() : String
Class_Initialize()
Class_Terminate()
<<Event>> Changed()
Clear()
<<Let>> CustomerList()
<<Get>> CustomerList()
```

Attributes and Properties

In our simple application, a customer has two attributes: ID and Name:

❑   The ID attribute is a string that uniquely identifies a customer

❑   The Name attribute is a string that represents the customer's business name

A common practice in object-oriented design and implementation is to store these values privately and provide access to them through a public interface.

In this class, we'll create two private data members, mstrID and mstrName, to store the values of customer ID and Name, respectively. As we can see in the diagram, they are both of type String.

For each private data member, we'll provide a pair of functions: one for retrieving its value and one for modifying it. In Visual Basic, these functions are implemented as Property Get and Property Let routines.

Case Study

Let's leave the rest of the class for a moment, and take a look at how the attributes and properties are represented in Visual Basic. If, like me, you would prefer to enter the code to get a better feeling about how things are put together, it's time to start dancing with your fingers. If you do not have the time to enter the code yourself, you can skip the following code section and jump straight into the discussion.

Fire up the Visual Basic IDE and create an ActiveX DLL named UCObjects. Now change the name of the class module from Class1 to Customer, and enter the following code:

```
Option Explicit

Private mstrID As String
Private mstrName As String

'Returns the Customer's name.
Public Property Get Name() As String

    Let Name = mstrName

End Property

'Assign a name to a customer.
Public Property Let Name(ByVal Value As String)

    Let mstrName = Value

End Property

'Returns a Customer ID.
Public Property Get ID() As String

    Let ID = mstrID

End Property

'Assign an ID to a customer
Public Property Let ID(ByVal Value As String)

    Let mstrID = Value

End Property
```

In the user interface clients, we can read and assign values to them:

```
Dim TheCustomer As UCObjects.Customer
Dim CustomerID As String
Dim CustomerName As String

Set TheCustomer = New UCObjects.Customer
TheCustomer.ID = "AROUT"
TheCustomer.Name = "Around the Horn"

CustomerID = TheCustomer.ID
CustomerName = TheCustomer.Name
```

The next task is to retrieve the values stored in the database. In the Customer class, we can implement a method that pulls the data out of the database and populates mstrID and mstrName with their corresponding values. However, we want to encapsulate database access to the Data-Centric objects to achieve better scalability. Connection pooling provides scalable database access, and MTS provides scalable object management, such as JIT activation and ASAP deactivation.

Data Access Methods

One of the techniques to pass data obtained in the Data-Centric objects to the User-Centric objects is to use disconnected ADO recordsets. We will look into how this is done in the Data-Centric objects in a moment. For now, assume that we have a Data-Centric Customer object, CustomerN, in an ActiveX DLL, DCCustomer. This provides a method, GetByID, which accepts a customer ID and returns a recordset. We can use it to get the recordset in our User-Centric Customer class:

```
Dim CustomerObject As DCCustomer.CustomerN
Dim CustomerRS As ADODB.Recordset

Set CustomerObject = CreateObject("DCCustomer.CustomerN")
Set CustomerRS = CustomerObject.GetByID("AROUT")

With CustomerRS
  ID = .Fields("CustomerID").Value
  Name = .Fields("CompanyName").Value
End With
```

Recall that we defined a Read method in the class diagram above.

We can implement the above routine in this method. Add this code to the Customer class in UCObjects:

```
Option Explicit

Private Const mcstrClassName As String = "UCObjects.Customer"
Private Const mcstrObjectError As String = vbObjectError + &H1100
Private mobjCustomerN As DCCustomer.CustomerN
Private mrecCustomers As ADODB.Recordset

Public Sub Read(Optional ID As String = "")

  On Error GoTo ErrHandler

  Dim recCust As ADODB.Recordset
  Set recCust = mobjCustomerN.GetByID(ID)
  Populate recCust

  If mrecCustomers Is Nothing Then
    Set mrecCustomers = recCust.Clone(adLockReadOnly)
  End If

FuncExit:

  On Error Resume Next

  If Not recCust Is Nothing Then
    If recCust.State = adStateOpen Then
      recCust.Close
    End If
    Set recCust = Nothing
  End If

  Exit Sub

ErrHandler:

  Err.Raise mcstrObjectError + 1, mcstrClassName, Err.Description
  Resume FuncExit

End Sub
```

```
Private Sub Populate(Optional CustomerRS As ADODB.Recordset = Nothing)

  On Error GoTo ErrHandler

  If Not CustomerRS Is Nothing Then

    With CustomerRS
      If Not (.BOF And .EOF) Then
        ID = .Fields("CustomerID").Value
        Name = .Fields("CompanyName").Value
      End If
    End With

  Else
    ID = ""
    Name = ""
  End If

  RaiseEvent Changed

FuncExit:

  Exit Sub

ErrHandler:

  Err.Raise mcstrObjectError + 11, mcstrClassName, Err.Description
  Resume FuncExit

End Sub
```

Firstly, we define two constants, `mcstrClassName` and `mcstrObjectError`, that specify the name of our class and the base offset of error numbers that might be raised by this class. They are used to return useful error information to the client, that is, the UI components of our application. Next, we define a `mobjCustomerN` object that caches the reference to an instance of the Data-Centric customer object `CustomerN`. It should be initialized in the `Class_Initialize` event and destroyed in the `Class_Terminate` event, both of which we will see shortly.

The `Read` method accepts an optional string as the ID of the customer we are querying. Why optional? In this case, we want to be able to find a customer by its ID, so there doesn't seem to be a need to make it optional. However, we often want to retrieve a list of all customers so that the user can select one of them by its business name. To do this we'll provide another property that allows the user interface to get a complete list of customers. Add the following code:

```
Private mrecCustomers As ADODB.Recordset
```

```
Public Property Get CustomerList() As ADODB.Recordset

    Set CustomerList = mrecCustomers

End Property
```

```
Public Property Set CustomerList(vdata As ADODB.Recordset)

    Set mrecCustomers = vdata

End Property
```

As you'll see in a minute, the Data-Centric Customer object will retrieve either one customer or all customers. When we pass the `GetByID` method a customer ID, it will read the record of this particular customer. If we don't give it an ID, it will return all customers in the database.

In the `Read` method, we define an ADO recordset. This will be used to accept the disconnected recordset returned by the `GetByID` method of the `CustomerN` object. After we get the recordset, we call another method, `Populate`, to assign the data members with the value for the customer. This method is specified as `Private` because we do not want our clients to be able to call it directly.

This method is pretty simple. If we give it a recordset, it will assign the data members with the customer's data. Otherwise, it simply clears the data members. Again, we will see why clearing the data members is useful in a moment.

The `Populate` method next raises an event, `Changed`, to inform its clients that its internal state has been changed. The client objects can then update their own state accordingly.

You will need to add this line in the **General Declarations** section of the `Customer` class:

```
Public Event Changed()
```

Updating the Customer Records

The next two methods of this class, `Save` and `Delete`, are responsible for updating the customer data.

The `Save` method, as its name suggests, will save the potentially modified customer data to the database. This will be used if the user has created a new customer record and needs to save it, or if an existing customer's record has been modified.

Here comes a problem: how do we know whether or not we have a new customer? We could query the database to find out whether the customer's ID is already in the database. If it is, we should update the associated business name, otherwise, we should create a new record. This approach is reliable, because it reduces the chance of user error. The disadvantage is that we need to access the database twice: first to query the existing records and then to save the new one.

Alternatively, we could track changes to the data members internally. If the customer's ID has not changed since the last call to the `Read` method, we can assume that a record should be updated. Otherwise we have a new customer and need to create a new record. However, this method fails when the user enters a different customer ID for an existing customer. We will get an error saying that we are trying to create a new customer record with the identical name as an existing customer.

To keep our application simple, the approach we take in this case study is to rely on the user telling us whether they're creating a new customer. Although this makes the implementation easier, keep in mind that it's far from ideal. The user can, and will, make mistakes. For instance, she might think that she's creating a new customer, but assign an ID that belongs to an existing customer.

So we need to provide a method for the users, or the client objects, to tell us that we should save a new customer. A private data member and property combination will do the job.

Case Study

Add the following code to the `Customer` class:

```
Private mblnIsNew As Boolean

Public Property Get IsNew() As Boolean

   Let IsNew = mblnIsNew

End Property

Public Property Let IsNew(ByVal Value As Boolean)

   Let mblnIsNew = Value

   If Value Then
     Populate
   End If

End Property
```

If `IsNew` is `True`, we clear the object state and are ready to accept new values. The `Save` method will then be able to check this value and decide whether it should add a new record or modify an existing one. This is implemented as follows:

```
Private mobjCustomerT As DCCustomer.CustomerT

Public Sub Save()

   On Error GoTo ErrHandler

   Dim CustomerData As String

   CustomerData = Serialize
   mobjCustomerT.Save CustomerData
   IsNew = False

FuncExit:

   Exit Sub

ErrHandler:

   Err.Raise mcstrObjectError + 2, mcstrClassName, Err.Description
   Resume FuncExit

End Sub
```

`mobjCustomerT` is a reference to the transactional Data-Centric Customer object. There are several ways of passing the data to `mobjCustomerT`. We could pass each attribute as a parameter to the `mobjCustomerT.Save` method. We could create a disconnected ADO recordset that is populated with the customer's attributes, and pass it. We could also use a PropertyBag in a similar way. Each mechanism has its own advantageous and drawbacks. In this instance we shall use the PropertyBag object.

In a nutshell, we will store the value of the customer's ID and Name to a PropertyBag object using its `WriteProperty` method. We will then use the PropertyBag's `Content` property to obtain a serialized byte array and pass it to the `Save` method of the Data-Centric object. The Data-Centric object will decompose, or deserialize, this byte array, and extract the ID and Name value. The `Serialize` method is implemented in the User-Centric `Customer` class as shown below. We'll explain the `Deserialize` method when we discuss the Data-Centric object:

```
Private Function Serialize() As String

    On Error GoTo ErrHandler

    Dim PropBag As PropertyBag
    Set PropBag = New PropertyBag

    With PropBag
       .WriteProperty "IsNew", IsNew
       .WriteProperty "ID", ID
       .WriteProperty "Name", Name
       Serialize = .Contents
    End With

FuncExit:

    On Error Resume Next

    If Not PropBag Is Nothing Then
       Set PropBag = Nothing
    End If

    Exit Function

ErrHandler:

    Err.Raise mcstrObjectError + 12, mcstrClassName, Err.Description
    Resume FuncExit

End Function
```

Here we instantiate a PropertyBag object, `PropBag`, then invoke its `WriteProperty` method to save the customer data. The `WriteProperty` method accepts two compulsory parameters and one optional parameter:

```
PropBag.WriteProperty PropertyName, PropertyValue, [DefaultValue]
```

`PropertyName` is a string that gives the name of the property, and `PropertyValue` is its value. If we specify the optional `DefaultValue`, the property will only be saved if this value is different from `PropertyValue`. We won't use it here as there is no reasonable default value for the properties.

After we assign all properties, we return the byte array returned from the `PropBag.Contents` function. The `Save` method then passes the byte array to the `mobjCustomerT.Save` method.

Finally, we set `IsNew` to `False`, to indicate that this is no longer a new customer.

Case Study

The `Delete` method is pretty straightforward – it simply calls the corresponding `Delete` method of `mobjCustomerT`, and gets it to delete the customer record from the database:

```
Public Sub Delete()

  On Error GoTo ErrHandler
  mobjCustomerT.Delete ID
  Populate

FuncExit:

  Exit Sub

ErrHandler:

  Err.Raise mcstrObjectError + 3, mcstrClassName, Err.Description
  Resume FuncExit

End Sub
```

After it calls `mobjCustomerT.Delete` and passes the customer's ID, it clears the data members by calling the `Populate` method without passing it a recordset.

To finish, let's have a quick look at the `Initialize` and `Terminate` events.

The Initialize and Terminate events

Add the following to the `Customer` class:

```
Private Sub Class_Initialize()

  On Error GoTo ErrHandler

  Set mobjCustomerN = CreateObject("DCCustomer.CustomerN")
  Set mobjCustomerT = CreateObject("DCCustomer.CustomerT")
  IsNew = False

FuncExit:

  Exit Sub

ErrHandler:

  Err.Raise mcstrObjectError, mcstrClassName, Err.Description
  Resume FuncExit

End Sub

Private Sub Class_Terminate()

  On Error Resume Next
  Set mobjCustomerN = Nothing
  Set mobjCustomerT = Nothing

End Sub
```

The `Class_Initialize` event handler creates two Data-Centric objects. It follows the principle of acquiring references to MTS components as early as possible. MTS will only instantiate them when the first method call is issued, so there is no performance or resource penalties here.

This concludes the User-Centric Customer class. You should now have a very good idea as to what to expect from the Data-Centric Customer classes.

The Data-Centric Customer Classes

As their names suggest, the Data-Centric classes work closely with the database to provide data access capabilities to their clients. In a typical n-tiered application, the User-Centric classes have exclusive control over the Data-Centric classes.

In our application, the User-Centric `Customer` class uses the two Data-Centric classes `CustomerN` and `CustomerT` to retrieve data from and update the database. These two Data-Centric classes are ideal candidates for MTS components.

The CustomerN Class

`CustomerN` is a class that performs non-database update operations that are typically non-transactional. Recall that MTS manages not only transactions, but also object activation and deactivation. We have decided that `CustomerN` should be hosted in MTS to take advantage of its object management features:

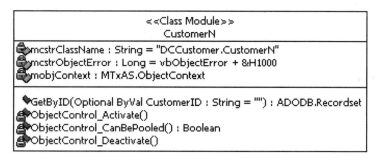

From our discussion of the User-Centric `Customer` class, we know that we will need a `GetByID` method in `CustomerN` to retrieve one or more customer records. This is the only Public method defined in `CustomerN`. Since it is hosted in MTS, we should implement its ObjectControl interface to let MTS control its activation and deactivation.

It is coding time again. Let's create a new ActiveX DLL in Visual Basic, and name the project `DCCustomer`, a short hand for Data-Centric Customer component. As good component development practice, we need to assign a human friendly description to it. We can do this by opening the Project Properties dialog and entering a brief phrase in the Project Description box, for example VBMTSCS Customer Data Components. When you need to reference this component in your other projects, you can find it by this description.

Now change the name of the class module from `Class1` to `CustomerN`. `CustomerN` itself does not actually require a transaction for retrieving data. However, it might become part of a transaction if its client starts one and invokes the `GetByID` method. Therefore, we should add a reference to the Microsoft Transaction Server Type Library, and set `CustomerN`'s MTSTransactionMode to 3 - Uses Transaction. We should also add a reference to Microsoft ActiveX Data Objects Library, since we will use ADO to perform database access.

Now enter the following code to the class:

```
Option Explicit

Implements ObjectControl

Private Const mcstrClassName As String = "DCCustomer.CustomerN"
Private Const mcstrObjectError As Long = vbObjectError + &H1000

Private mobjContext As ObjectContext
```

As usual, we define two private class data members, `mcstrClassName` and `mcstrObjectError`, which will be used to report errors that might arise in this class. The last data member, `mobjContext` will hold a reference to the MTS Object Context.

Since `CustomerN` implements the `ObjectControl` interface, it must provide all methods defined in this interface. You should be familiar with what's going on here by now:

```
Private Sub ObjectControl_Activate()

  On Error GoTo ErrHandler

  Set mobjContext = GetObjectContext

FuncExit:

  Exit Sub

ErrHandler:

  Err.Raise mcstrObjectError, mcstrClassName, Err.Description
  Resume FuncExit

End Sub

Private Function ObjectControl_CanBePooled() As Boolean

  On Error Resume Next
  ObjectControl_CanBePooled = False

End Function

Private Sub ObjectControl_Deactivate()

  On Error Resume Next
  Set mobjContext = Nothing

End Sub
```

The GetByID Method – Connecting to the Database

Now we have done everything for MTS to manage the `CustomerN` objects, we can turn our attention to providing the functionality we need in the application. Enter the following code in the class:

```
Public Function GetByID(Optional ByVal CustomerID As String = "") _
        As ADODB.Recordset

  On Error GoTo ErrHandler

  Dim cnCust As ADODB.Connection
  Dim recCust As ADODB.Recordset
  Dim strSQLQuery As String

  Set cnCust = New ADODB.Connection

  With cnCust
    .CursorLocation = adUseClient
    .Open ConnString
  End With

  strSQLQuery = "SELECT CustomerID, CompanyName FROM Customers"

  If CustomerID <> "" Then
      strSQLQuery = strSQLQuery & " WHERE CustomerID = '" & CustomerID & "'"
  End If

  Set recCust = cnCust.Execute(strSQLQuery)
  Set recCust.ActiveConnection = Nothing
  cnCust.Close

  Set GetByID = recCust
  mobjContext.SetComplete

FuncExit:

  On Error Resume Next

  If Not recCust Is Nothing Then
      Set recCust = Nothing
  End If

  Exit Function

ErrHandler:

  If Not recCust Is Nothing Then
      If recCust.State = adStateOpen Then
        recCust.Close
      End If
      Set recCust = Nothing
  End If

  Err.Raise mcstrObjectError + 1, mcstrClassName, Err.Description
  mobjContext.SetAbort
  Resume FuncExit

End Function
```

This function accepts a customer ID as its optional parameter and returns a disconnected ADO recordset containing the customer record(s). If the customer ID exists in the database, the recordset will contain the required data of that customer. Otherwise, the recordset will be empty. If a customer ID is not given, the recordset will contain all customer records in the database.

You must implement proper error handling in MTS components. It's good practice to raise a custom error with your own error number and description, and include a list of possible error numbers and their meanings in the component's documentation. Developers writing User-Centric object code can then catch errors raised in your components and decide how to handle them in the User-Centric objects. In this application, we'll simply raise an error with a customer error number and pass the description of the original error. We'll also assign the source property of the error with the name of this class.

In the function body, we create a new instance of the ADO connection:

```
Set cnCust = New ADODB.Connection
```

Note the use of the New keyword. When an object is created with New, it's not bound to the context of the current object. This is fine for creating ADO objects, since ADO components are not registered with MTS and they don't use the Object Context.

Before getting data out of the database, we need to establish a connection. Since we will return a disconnected recordset we should use a client side cursor, so we set the ADO connection's CursorLocation to the constant adUseClient, defined in ADO. We can then call the ADO connection object's Open method to open the connection.

The Open method takes at least one parameter: the connection string. The connection string should specify the location and the name of the database server and its driver. For security reasons, we should also specify the user name and password for the connection. For example, the following is a connection string to a SQL Server database:

```
Data Source=<SQLServerName>; Provider=SQLOLEDB; User ID=sa; Password=; _
            Initial Catalog=Northwind"
```

The Data Source property is the name of your SQL Server, which is the same as the machine name where SQL Server is located. The Provider property specifies the database driver. Here, we're using the OLE DB Provider for SQL Server. For convenience, we use the database administrator's user name, sa, and an empty password. In a production environment, you should always connect as a dedicated user to ensure that the security policy is properly followed. The Initial Catalog property is the name of the database in a SQL Server. In this case, it points to the sample Northwind database shipped with SQL Server.

You could hard code the server name into your connection string, but with a price: you then need to recompile your components every time the SQL Server is moved. A better option is to store the SQL Server name into the registry, and read in this value when you construct the connection string. In this application, you will need to store the name of the SQL Server in registry under the key:

```
HKEY_CURRENT_USER\Software\VB and VBA Program Settings\VBMTSCS\Data
```

And in a string value

```
Source = SQLServerName
```

Where SQLServerName is the name of your particular server.

We can call the GetSetting function to retrieve this name:

```
SQLServerName = GetSetting("VBMTSCS", "Data", "Source")
```

And build the connection string using this value:

```
ConnString = "Data Source=" & SQLServerName & _
             "; Provider=SQLOLEDB; User ID=sa; Password=; " & _
             "Initial Catalog=Northwind"
```

Since this connection string will be used by all our components, it would be easier if we can put this into a common module and include it into each component that needs to connect to the database.

Add a module to the DCCustomer project and name it Common. You can then enter the following code to this module:

```
Option Explicit

Public Function ConnString() As String

  ConnString = "Data Source = " & GetSetting("VBMTSCS", "Data", "Source") & _
               "; Provider=SQLOLEDB; User ID=sa; Password=; " & _
               "Initial Catalog=Northwind"

End Function
```

We can then use it to open an ADO connection to the database, as we do in CustomerN:

```
With cnCust
  .CursorLocation = adUseClient
  .Open ConnString
End With
```

Reading Customer Records from the Database

Once connected to the database, we can perform a SQL query to read customer records. We build the SQL query with these statements:

```
strSQLQuery = "SELECT CustomerID, CompanyName FROM Customers"

If CustomerID <> "" Then
  strSQLQuery = strSQLQuery & " WHERE CustomerID = '" & CustomerID & "'"
End If
```

Case Study

If no `CustomerID` is given, we just get all customer records. If a `CustomerID` is specified, we will build a SQL `SELECT` statement to read only that customer's record using the `WHERE` clause. In a production quality application, we should use a stored procedure rather than a dynamically built SQL statement. Stored procedures are optimized and provide better performance than plain SQL statements. However, in this application we'll opt to keep it simple by hard coding a SQL statement.

Once we have built the SQL query, we can run it to get the data. The ADO Connection object's `Execute` method does exactly that: it runs the query and returns an ADO recordset:

```
Set recCust = cnCust.Execute(SQLQuery)
```

We can then disconnect this recordset from the database by setting its `ActiveConnection` property to `Nothing`:

```
Set recCust.ActiveConnection = Nothing
```

Connections to databases are expensive, so we close the connection as soon as we have done with it using the ADO Connection object's `Close` method:

```
cnCust.Close
```

If everything runs smoothly we've done what we set out to do, so we want to tell MTS that the function is completed successfully. The Object Context's `SetComplete` method does that work for us. If something goes wrong in the process, the error handler is called. Since it is unlikely that the ADO recordset we created in this function contains any useful information, we can close it and release it from the memory.

```
If Not recCust Is Nothing Then
  If recCust.State = adStateOpen Then
     recCust.Close
  End If
  Set recCust = Nothing
End If
```

We then raise an error to the client object and call the Object Context's `SetAbort` method to inform MTS that this function is completed with error. MTS will then deactivate this object.

That's the `CustomerN` class – it's quite straightforward. The `CustomerT` class, however, is a bit more complicated.

The CustomerT Class

The `CustomerT` class performs operations that update the database. It adds new customer records and updates existing ones. It is also responsible for deleting records from the database.

```
                    <<Class Module>>
                      CustomerT
─────────────────────────────────────────────────
 mcstrClassName : String = "DCCustomer.CustomerT"
 mcstrObjectError : Long = vbObjectError + &H1010
─────────────────────────────────────────────────
 Save(ByVal CustomerData : String)
 Delete(ByVal CustomerID : String)
 Deserialize(Data : String, IsNew : Boolean, ID : String, Name : String)
 ObjectControl_Activate()
 ObjectControl_CanBePooled() : Boolean
 ObjectControl_Deactivate()
```

Add a new class module to the `DCCustomer` project and rename it `CustomerT`. Since database update operations are transactional, we will set its MTSTransactionMode to 2 – RequiresTransaction.

Now add the following code to the class:

```vb
Option Explicit

Implements ObjectControl

Private Const mcstrClassName As String = "DCCustomer.CustomerT"
Private Const mcstrObjectError As Long = vbObjectError + &H1010

Private mobjContext As ObjectContext

Private Sub ObjectControl_Activate()

  On Error GoTo ErrHandler
  Set mobjContext = GetObjectContext

FuncExit:

  Exit Sub

ErrHandler:

  Err.Raise mcstrObjectError, mcstrClassName, Err.Description
  Resume FuncExit

End Sub

Private Function ObjectControl_CanBePooled() As Boolean

  On Error Resume Next
  ObjectControl_CanBePooled = False

End Function

Private Sub ObjectControl_Deactivate()

  On Error Resume Next
  Set mobjContext = Nothing

End Sub
```

Case Study

It's almost identical to the corresponding code in the `CustomerN` class, except that the class name and customer error offset are different. It implements the MTS `ObjectControl` interface and its methods, as we will do for all MTS components.

Saving and Updating Customer Records

The first application specific function is the `Save` function, which either adds a new customer record or updates an existing one. Recall that our User-Centric `Customer` class invokes this function and passes a byte array that serializes the Customer object data.

```
mobjCustomerT.Save CustomerData
```

The `Save` function will accept the byte array as a Visual Basic String. It will then decompose, or deserialize, that string to extract customer data. Once it has the data, it can run appropriate SQL statements to write it to the database. First, add the following to the class module:

```
Public Sub Save(ByVal CustomerData As String)

  On Error GoTo ErrHandler

  Dim blnIsNew As Boolean
  Dim strCustomerID As String
  Dim strCustomerName As String
  Dim cnCust As ADODB.Connection
  Dim strSQLQuery As String

  Deserialize CustomerData, blnIsNew, strCustomerID, strCustomerName

  If blnIsNew Then
      strSQLQuery = "INSERT INTO Customers (CustomerID, CompanyName) " & _
                    "VALUES ('" & strCustomerID & "', '" _
                    & strCustomerName & "')"
  Else
      strSQLQuery = "UPDATE Customers " & _
                    "SET CompanyName = '" & strCustomerName & "' " & _
                    "WHERE CustomerID = '" & strCustomerID & "'"
  End If

  Set cnCust = New ADODB.Connection
  With cnCust
    .Open ConnString
    .Execute strSQLQuery, , adExecuteNoRecords
    .Close
  End With

  mobjContext.SetComplete

FuncExit:

  Exit Sub

ErrHandler:

  Err.Raise mcstrObjectError + 1, mcstrClassName, Err.Description
  mobjContext.SetAbort
  Resume FuncExit

End Sub
```

```
Private Sub Deserialize(Data As String, IsNew As Boolean, ID As String, _
                    Name As String)

    On Error GoTo ErrHandler

    Dim PropBag As PropertyBag
    Dim ByteArr() As Byte

    ByteArr = Data
    Set PropBag = New PropertyBag

    With PropBag
      .Contents = ByteArr
      IsNew = .ReadProperty("IsNew")
      ID = .ReadProperty("ID")
      Name = .ReadProperty("Name")
    End With

FuncExit:

    Set PropBag = Nothing
    Exit Sub

ErrHandler:

    Err.Raise mcstrObjectError + 11, mcstrClassName, Err.Description
    mobjContext.SetAbort
    Resume FuncExit

End Sub
```

When the `Save` function gets the customer data string, it calls the `Deserialize` method to extract the customer attributes. This method first converts the string to a byte array, `ByteArr`. It then creates a new PropertyBag object, `PropBag`, and assigns `ByteArr` to its `Contents` property. The `PropBag` object knows that the byte array contains three properties: `IsNew`, `ID`, and `Name`. Therefore, we can read them out to the corresponding variables passed in by reference.

```
With PropBag
  .Contents = ByteArr
  IsNew = .ReadProperty("IsNew")
  ID = .ReadProperty("ID")
  Name = .ReadProperty("Name")
End With
```

As you can see, the PropertyBag object is smart enough to figure out the contents of a byte array that contains serialized properties. This makes it very easy to pack a number of values in the source object, send it over the network, and unpack it at the destination object.

The `IsNew` property is critical to help the `CustomerT` object to decide whether it should create a new customer record or update an existing record in the database. If this is a new customer, we can build a SQL INSERT statement to add a record. Otherwise, we build a SQL UPDATE statement to modify a record:

```
If blnIsNew Then
    strSQLQuery = "INSERT INTO Customers (CustomerID, CompanyName) " & _
                  "VALUES ('" & strCustomerID & "', '" _
                  & strCustomerName & "')"
Else
    strSQLQuery = "UPDATE Customers " & _
                  "SET CompanyName = '" & strCustomerName & "' " & _
                  "WHERE CustomerID = '" & strCustomerID & "'"
End If
```

With all the information handy, updating the database is very easy:

```
Set cnCust = New ADODB.Connection
With cnCust
  .Open ConnString
  .Execute strSQLQuery, , adExecuteNoRecords
  .Close
End With
```

Here, we create an ADO connection and call its `Open` method to connect to the database. It uses the connection string built by the `ConnString` function in the `Common` module. We then execute the query using the ADO connection's `Execute` method, as we did in the `GetByID` method in `CustomerN`. There is a difference though. We pass an optional parameter, (`adExecuteNoRecords`) to the `Execute` method, to indicate that we don't expect to have any records returned as a result of the query. This provides better performance, as ADO does not need to return anything from the database to the `CustomerT` object, thus saving a network round trip.

After the query has been executed, we can close the connection and invoke the Object Context's `SetComplete` method to inform MTS that we are home safe-and-sound. If there's an error, we catch it and abort the transaction by calling the `SetAbort` method of the Object Control.

Wait a minute, I hear you say. What happens in the `Deserialize` method? What if it had an error? This could happen if the byte array is corrupted during its travel from the User-Centric `Customer` object to the `CustomerN` object. Well, the method will raise its own error, which will in turn be caught in the `Save` function and the transaction is aborted. But why does the `Deserialize` method call `SetAbort`?

As we have seen, it is not strictly necessary to call `ObjectContext.SetAbort` in the `Deserialize` method, as the `Save` method will do it anyway. However, it's useful to inform MTS that there is an error during a transaction and the transaction should be aborted as soon as the error is caught. This helps MTS to release the transaction as early as possible. While it might only save us a fraction of a second, we should look at the big picture. Our application is designed to be highly scalable and might well be used by thousands of users. A fraction of a second here and a fraction of a second there can add up to huge savings. Maintaining transactions is expensive in terms of resource usage. Each transaction consumes memory and CPU time, so releasing it as soon as possible is paramount to provide optimum, or at least acceptable, response of the application.

But there is more. Why shouldn't we call `SetComplete` in `Deserialize` when it is successful? The answer is that `Deserialize` is a part of the `Save` operation. Even if `Deserialize` is completed, the `Save` operation is not. If the `Deserialize` method calls `SetComplete`, the transaction will be committed immediately, although there is nothing to be committed yet.

So the rules of thumb are:

- Call `SetAbort` as soon as possible
- Call `SetComplete` only after all actions in a transaction are completed
- Never call `SetComplete` in private methods

The last rule is really a result of the second rule. Since private methods are always called by other methods, they are always a part of a transaction. They should never tell MTS that the transaction is completed, as they don't have a clue whether the transaction is indeed completed or not.

Deleting Customer Records

The `Delete` method is relatively easy. Add the following code snippet to the `CustomerT` class:

```
Public Sub Delete(ByVal CustomerID As String)

  On Error GoTo ErrHandler

  Dim cnCust As ADODB.Connection
  Dim strSQLQuery As String

  strSQLQuery = "DELETE Customers " & _
                "WHERE CustomerID = '" & CustomerID & "'"

  Set cnCust = New ADODB.Connection
  With cnCust
    .Open ConnString
    .Execute strSQLQuery, , adExecuteNoRecords
    .Close
  End With

  mobjContext.SetComplete

FuncExit:

  Exit Sub

ErrHandler:

  Err.Raise mcstrObjectError + 2, mcstrClassName, Err.Description
  mobjContext.SetAbort
  Resume FuncExit

End Sub
```

We start by building a SQL `DELETE` query. Next, we establish a connection to the database, and execute the SQL `DELETE` query to remove the customer record from it (if the record exists). Once the query is executed, we close the connection. At last, we call the Object Context's `SetComplete` method to inform MTS that we're done.

Simple? It is! However, we need to finish our work properly. We need to do a few things before we claim that we have created the `Customer` business objects.

Case Study

Testing and Deploying Components

First, compile the project and fix any typo and syntax errors. Eventually, we will fix all syntactical errors and the project will compile. As you know, compiling a project successfully does not mean that the component will do what it's supposed to do. We must ensure that it performs all tasks as advertised. In a production environment, we should create at least one test harness project for every component we have created. In the test harness project, we test all operations so that they are all performed according to our specification.

Don't leave this testing process until you are developing your UI components. It's a lot easier if you test it earlier in the process. Testing it along with your UI components increases the complexity, as you will be encountering errors from both the Data-Centric and the User-Centric components. In this application, we can afford to leave this out to simplify our code.

> **Just remember, test components as thoroughly as possible before using them in a production environment.**

Once it works as expected, we should set its version compatibility option to Binary Compatibility and compile it. Setting binary compatibility ensures that we never change its public interface inadvertently. If we do, the Visual Basic compiler will generate a warning. We can set the version compatibility option in the Component tag in the Project Property form.

In the same tag, we should also change another important setting – the Remote Server property. In a distributed environment, the Data-Centric components are usually deployed on a server while the user interface components are installed on the user's workstation. Checking the Remote Server Files check box tells the Visual Basic compiler that this component may be deployed remotely to its clients. The compiler will generate .vbr and .tlb files in addition to the .dll file for the ActiveX DLL components. We'll see how those additional files are used when we discuss the deployment issues. For now, recompile the project with the new settings. If it compiles at the first try, it should compile without problem after the setting changes.

Now it's ready to be deployed. Since we'll be using it to provide data access to our User-Centric objects, we should add a reference to it in the UCObjects project. In the Project References form, find the component VBMTSCS Customer Data Components and select it. The Customer class, as well as all other classes in UCObjects, can use the CustomerN and CustomerT classes to perform the tasks. You can now compile UCObjects to see if there are any syntax errors.

Our next task is simpler – we will build the Product classes that provide read-only access to the Product data in the database.

Business Objects – The Product Objects

In this application, we need to retrieve product names and prices when creating sales orders. We will not provide product data maintenance capability here, as the implementation will be very similar to the approach used with the Customer objects.

The User-Centric Product Class

This class encapsulates the attributes of products used and the ability to read product data from the database:

```
                    <<Class Module>>
                        Product
  mcstrClassName : String = "UCObjects.Product"
  mcstrObjectError : String = vbObjectError + &H1110
  mlngID : Long
  mstrName : String
  mcurPrice : Currency
  mrecProducts : ADODB.Recordset

  <<Get>> ID() : Long
  <<Get>> Name() : String
  <<Get>> Price() : Currency
  Read(Optional ID : Long = 0)
  Populate(ProductRS : ADODB.Recordset)
  Class_Initialize()
  Class_Terminate()
  <<Get>> ProductList()
```

A Product object has three attributes: ID, Name, and Price. We also define the two standard private constant data members, mcstrClassName and mcstrObjectError, to assist in error handling.

Reopen the UCObjects project and add a class module to it. Rename the new class module Product.

Since the Product class is read-only (that is, no database update is to take place), we define three read-only properties to provide access to its attributes to the client objects. Other than that, this class is very similar to the Customer class and uses techniques that we've already discussed. Therefore, we'll go through the code quickly:

```
Option Explicit
```

```
    Private Const mcstrClassName As String = "UIObjects.Product"
    Private Const mcstrObjectError As String = vbObjectError + &H1110

    Private mlngID As Long
    Private mstrName As String
    Private mcurPrice As Currency

    Private mobjProductN As DCProduct.ProductN
    Private mrecProducts As ADODB.Recordset
```

```
'Retrieve the ID of a product (a read-only property automatically assigned by the
'database)
Public Property Get ID() As Long

  Let ID = mlngID

End Property
```

```
'Retrieve product name.
Public Property Get Name() As String

  Let Name = mstrName

End Property
```

```
'Retrieve the product price.
Public Property Get Price() As Currency

  Let Price = mcurPrice

End Property
```

```
'Retriece a complete list of products
Public Property Get ProductList() As ADODB.Recordset

  Set ProductList = mrecProducts

End Property
```

```
Public Sub Read(Optional ID As Long = 0)

  On Error GoTo ErrHandler

  Dim recProd As ADODB.Recordset
  Set recProd = mobjProductN.GetByID(ID)
  Populate recProd

    If mrecProducts Is Nothing Then
      Set mrecProducts = recProd.Clone(adLockReadOnly)
    End If

FuncExit:

  On Error Resume Next

  If Not recProd Is Nothing Then
    If recProd.State = adStateOpen Then
      recProd.Close
    End If
    Set recProd = Nothing
  End If

  Exit Sub

ErrHandler:

  Err.Raise mcstrObjectError + 1, mcstrClassName, Err.Description
  Resume FuncExit

End Sub
```

```
Private Sub Populate(ProductRS As ADODB.Recordset)

    On Error GoTo ErrHandler

    With ProductRS
        If Not (.BOF And .EOF) Then
            mlngID = .Fields("ProductID").Value
            mstrName = .Fields("ProductName").Value
            mcurPrice = .Fields("UnitPrice").Value
        End If
    End With

FuncExit:

    Exit Sub

ErrHandler:

    Err.Raise mcstrObjectError + 11, mcstrClassName, Err.Description
    Resume FuncExit

End Sub

Private Sub Class_Initialize()

    On Error GoTo ErrHandler
    Set mobjProductN = CreateObject("DCProduct.ProductN")

FuncExit:

    Exit Sub

ErrHandler:

    Err.Raise mcstrObjectError, mcstrClassName, Err.Description
    Resume FuncExit

End Sub

Private Sub Class_Terminate()

    On Error Resume Next
    Set mobjProductN = Nothing

End Sub
```

When the class is initialized, it gets hold of a reference to the Data-Centric ProductN object. A client object can read in a product by calling the Read method. Like the Read method in the Customer class, it's capable of returning either one or all of the products in the database. The Read method simply calls the GetByID method of the ProductN object to get an ADO recordset containing the qualified products, and then calls the private Populate method to assign the product data to the corresponding attributes. The client objects can access the attributes using the provided public properties.

We can now move to the Data-Centric Product class.

The Data-Centric Product Class

There is only one Data-Centric Product class, namely `ProductN`.

<<Class Module>>
ProductN
◈ mcstrClassName : String = "DCProduct.ProductN"
◈ mcstrObjectError : Long = vbObjectError + &H1020
◆ GetByID(Optional ByVal ProductID : Long = 0) : ADODB.Recordset
◈ ObjectControl_Activate()
◈ ObjectControl_CanBePooled() : Boolean
◈ ObjectControl_Deactivate()

Perhaps not surprisingly, this looks almost identical to the `CustomerN` class that we've already discussed – it should, since it offers similar functionality to `CustomerN`. Let's take a look at the underlying code.

Create an ActiveX DLL project in Visual Basic and name it `DCProduct`. As it will be hosted in MTS and uses ADO to retrieve data, we should add references to the **Microsoft Transaction Server Type Library** and **Microsoft ActiveX Data Objects Library**. Following the standard, we should provide a description of this project to make it easy for client objects to use. **VBMTSCS Product Data Components** sounds good, so we will use that. We can also check the **Remote Server Files** box on the **Component** tab. Leave the version compatibility setting to **Project Compatibility** for the time being – we've not had a binary compatible server yet.

We need to add the `Common` module created with the `DCCustomer` project into this project so that we can reuse its `ConnString` function to build connection strings.

Next, change the name of the class module from `Class1` to `ProductN`. Set its **Instancing** property to **5 – MultiUse** and its **MTSTransactionMode** to **3 – UsesTransaction**. Now, enter the following code to the class:

```
Option Explicit

Implements ObjectControl

Private Const mcstrClassName As String = "DCProduct.ProductN"
Private Const mcstrObjectError As Long = vbObjectError + &H1020

Private mobjContext As ObjectContext

'Get a Product record by its ID.
Public Function GetByID(Optional ByVal ProductID As Long = 0) As ADODB.Recordset

   On Error GoTo ErrHandler

   Dim cnProd As ADODB.Connection
   Dim recProd As ADODB.Recordset
   Dim strSQLQuery As String

   Set cnProd = New ADODB.Connection
   With cnProd
      .CursorLocation = adUseClient
      .Open ConnString
   End With
```

```
    strSQLQuery = "SELECT ProductID, ProductName, UnitPrice FROM Products"

    If ProductID <> 0 Then
        strSQLQuery = strSQLQuery & " WHERE ProductID = " & ProductID
    End If

    Set recProd = cnProd.Execute(strSQLQuery)
    Set recProd.ActiveConnection = Nothing
    cnProd.Close

    Set GetByID = recProd
    mobjContext.SetComplete

FuncExit:

    On Error Resume Next

    If Not recProd Is Nothing Then
        Set recProd = Nothing
    End If

    Exit Function

ErrHandler:

    If Not recProd Is Nothing Then
        If recProd.State = adStateOpen Then
            recProd.Close
        End If
        Set recProd = Nothing
    End If

    Err.Raise mcstrObjectError + 1, mcstrClassName, Err.Description
    mobjContext.SetAbort
    Resume FuncExit

End Function


Private Sub ObjectControl_Activate()

    On Error GoTo ErrHandler
    Set mobjContext = GetObjectContext

FuncExit:

    Exit Sub

ErrHandler:

    Err.Raise mcstrObjectError, mcstrClassName, Err.Description
    Resume FuncExit

End Sub

Private Function ObjectControl_CanBePooled() As Boolean

    On Error Resume Next
    ObjectControl_CanBePooled = False

End Function
```

```
Private Sub ObjectControl_Deactivate()

  On Error Resume Next
  Set mobjContext = Nothing

End Sub
```

Look familiar? It is indeed a near carbon copy of the CustomerN class. I'll not waste your time by going through this code again. Just note that the GetByID does the real work to retrieve product data in our application.

Before we go on to look at the SalesOrder objects, let me briefly introduce the modeling of class relationships in UML.

Class Relationship Modeling - Associations

The relationship between the Data-Centric and the User-Centric Product classes is illustrated in the following class diagram:

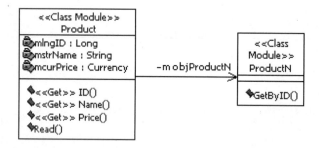

The directed line from the User-Centric Product class to the Data-Centric ProductN class denotes an **association** between them. The line is *directed* because the Product class uses the ProductN class, but not visa versa.

The word mobjProductN near the arrowhead indicates that this association is implemented by defining a reference, mobjProductN, in the Product class to the ProductN class. If we look at the Product class in UCObjects, we'll see that this corresponds to its private data member mobjProductN. The dash prefix denotes that it is a private association, that is, the client objects of a Product object cannot use this association to access the ProductN object. In fact, they cannot use this association directly.

The relationships between the `Customer` classes are similar, as shown in the following class diagram:

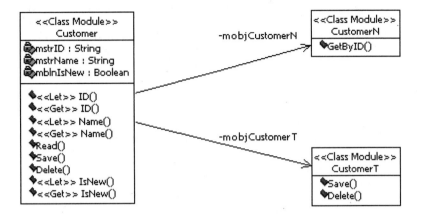

The User-Centric `Customer` class associates to the Data-Centric `CustomerN` and `CustomerT` classes. These associations are implemented using two private data members: `mobjCustomerN` and `mobjCustomerT`.

The other middle-tier business object is the `SalesOrder` object. Relationships among various `SalesOrder` classes are a bit more complicated. First, take a look at the diagram:

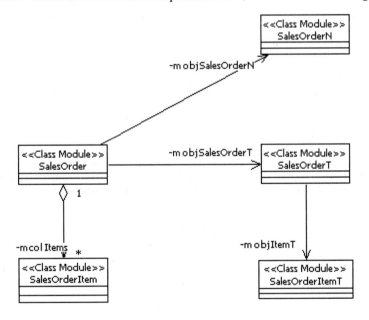

The top half of the diagram should be familiar – it's virtually the same as the `Product` and `Customer` diagrams. Before we go any further, let's examine how these classes are related.

Case Study

In a typical ordering system, a customer can order a list of products. The system usually creates one sales order that includes all of the products ordered by the customer. We say that there is a **one-to-many** relationship between a sales order and its items. That is, one sales order can have many items.

An implied condition is that every sales item must belong to an order. In general, it doesn't make sense if we have an order item on its own, without a customer order. So an item is a part of an order. This whole-part relationship is modeled as an **aggregate** in UML:

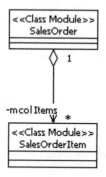

An aggregate is represented as a line with a diamond at one end and an arrowhead at the other. The diamond is attached to the parent class (the class that represents the whole). The arrowhead is attached to the child class.

The number of instances of each class in a relationship is recorded as its multiplicity. In this relationship, every one sales order may have zero or more items. This aggregate relationship is implemented by a private `SalesOrder` data member, `mcolItems`, that contains a collection of `SalesOrderItem` objects. We will see this when we examine the code for the `SalesOrder` class.

Should the `SalesOrderItem` class associate to some Data-Centric classes? It could, if each order item can be updated individually. However, since an order item never exists without a sales order, it is logical to let the `SalesOrder` object manage the updating of its items. Therefore, the `SalesOrderItem` class is not associated with any Data-Centric classes.

On the other hand, one principle of object-oriented design is that each class only models one well-defined object. While it is possible to access sales items in the Data-Centric `SalesOrder` classes, this is not a desired solution. It should delegate the responsibility of managing order item data access to a dedicated Data-Centric `SalesOrderItem` class, as shown in the diagram:

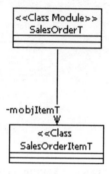

When we add a new sales order, the `SalesOrderT` object saves the order header and then uses the `SalesOrderItemT` object to save all order items.

Why do we not define a `SalesOrderItemN` class, and use it in the `SalesOrderN` class to retrieve item data? In the pure object-oriented sense, this is how it should be done. In practice, however, it is unnecessary and expensive. SQL is capable of retrieving a sales order and all its items using one statement, in one execution. We don't have to use this capability, but in that case, we would have to execute multiple SQL queries and create multiple network roundtrips to pass the queries and the results. It's not a good idea to go down that path.

Now that we've seen the relationships on each of our business objects, how do they fit together? The following class diagram shows all the business objects and their relationships:

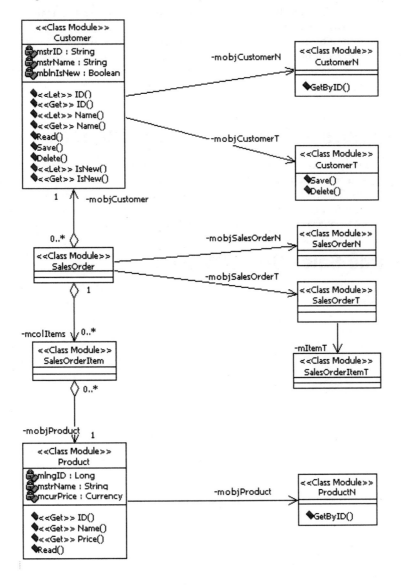

The relationships that we've not explained are between the User-Centric `Customer` class and the `SalesOrder` class, and between the `SalesOrderItem` class and the `Product` class. A customer can have none or many sales orders. This is implemented with the `mobjCustomer` data member in the `SalesOrder` class. If we were going to generate a customer sales report, we would also implement a `mobjOrders` data member in the `Customer` class. We will not implement this report, so there is no need to do so.

The relationship between the `SalesOrderItem` class and the `Product` class is also a one-to-many relationship. Many order items can order the same product. Again, we could define a data member in either of the two classes to implement this relationship as required. In this class, implementing it with the `mobjProduct` data member in the `SalesOrderItem` class is sufficient.

From this class diagram, we see that the `SalesOrder` business objects are by far the most complicated of the three. Don't panic – if you've followed the study so far, you now have a very good understanding of developing business objects using MTS, so we've already done most of the hard work. We just need to work out how the `SalesOrder` class and the `SalesOrderItem` class interact with each other to provide the functionality required in this application. In the next section, we'll see how this can be achieved.

Business Objects – The SalesOrder Objects

By now, we should be very familiar with the role of the business objects. They encapsulate the business rules and data access functionality to provide UI objects with rich object-oriented data management capabilities. The `SalesOrder` objects are no exception – they enable the User-Centric objects to query, add, and delete sales orders. While they only have limited functionality in this application, it should be very easy to extend them to provide full data manipulation features.

The User-Centric Sales Order Classes

As we have already discussed, our application will have two User-Centric SalesOrder classes, namely `SalesOrder` and `SalesOrderItem`. A `SalesOrder` object has a collection of `SalesOrderItem` objects, and no `SalesOrderItem` object can exist without a `SalesOrder` object:

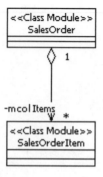

The SalesOrder Class

First, let's look at the `SalesOrder` class.

```
                    <<Class Module>>
                       SalesOrder
  mcstrClassName : String = "UCObjects.SalesOrderItem"
  mcstrObjectError : String = vbObjectError + &H1120
  mlngID : Long
  mdtmDate : Date

     <<Get>> ID() : Long
     <<Get>> OrderDate() : Date
     <<Get>> Customer() : UCObjects.Customer
     Read(OrderID : Long)
     Save()
     Delete()
     Populate(OrderRS : ADODB.Recordset)
     Serialize() : String
     <<Let>> CustomerID(Value : String)
     <<Get>> Items() : Collection
     AddItem(ProductID : Long, Quantity : Integer)
     Class_Initialize()
     Class_Terminate()
     <<Event>> Changed()
```

It has two attributes, order ID and order date, that are represented as private data members `mlngID` and `mdtmDate` respectively. As usual, we provide two read-only properties to access them. Since an order ID will be assigned by the database automatically and the order date will be recorded when a sales order is created, we never need to explicitly assign values to them.

Recall from our previous discussion about class diagrams that the `SalesOrder` class also holds references to a `Customer` object and a collection of `SalesOrderItem` objects. These two references are represented with two private data members, as we will see in the class code.

If you have not already done so, open the `UCObjects` project and add a class module, `SalesOrder`. Its **Instancing** property is again **5 – MultiUse**. Now enter the following code into the class:

```
Option Explicit

Public Event Changed()

Private Const mcstrClassName As String = "UIObjects.SalesOrderItem"
Private Const mcstrObjectError As String = vbObjectError + &H1120

Private mlngID As Long
Private mdtmDate As Date

Private mobjCustomer As UCObjects.Customer
Private mcolItems As Collection

Private mobjSalesOrderN As DCSalesOrder.SalesOrderN
Private mobjSalesOrderT As DCSalesOrder.SalesOrderT
```

```
'The SalesOrder ID. It is automatically generated by the database and is
'read-only to the clients.
Public Property Get ID() As Long

  Let ID = mlngID

End Property
```

```
'Sales order date. This is assigned when an order is saved to the database and
'is read-only to the clients.
Public Property Get OrderDate() As Date

  Let OrderDate = mdtmDate

End Property
```

```
'Retrieve the Customer object associated with a Sales Order.
Public Property Get Customer() As UCObjects.Customer

  Set Customer = mobjCustomer

End Property
```

```
Public Property Get Items() As Collection

  Set Items = mcolItems

End Property
```

This code is pretty straightforward. Like the `Customer` class, it will raise an event `Changed` when its state is changed. We define two constants, `mcstrClassName` and `mcstrObjectError`, to hold the name and error number offset of the class. We then define four private data members, `mlngID`, `mdtmDate`, `mobjCustomer`, and `mcolItems`, to hold the order data. We also need references to the Data-Centric SalesOrder objects so that we can read data from the database and write data to it. All four class data members can be read by the client objects through their corresponding properties.

Reading Sales Order Data

Since we will allow the client objects to read sales order data, we should provide a `Read` method:

```
Public Sub Read(OrderID As Long)

  On Error GoTo ErrHandler

  Dim recSO As ADODB.Recordset

  Set recSO = mobjSalesOrderN.GetByID(OrderID)
  Populate recSO

FuncExit:

  If Not recSO Is Nothing Then
    If recSO.State = adStateOpen Then
       recSO.Close
    End If
    Set recSO = Nothing
  End If
  Exit Sub
```

```
ErrHandler:

    Err.Raise mcstrObjectError + 1, mcstrClassName, Err.Description
    Resume FuncExit

End Sub
```

The Read method just calls the GetByID method of the Data-Centric SalesOrderN object to retrieve an ADO recordset. This will contain the data of a sales order with the given order ID. It then invokes a private Populate method to populate its data members with the recordset:

```
Private Sub Populate(OrderRS As ADODB.Recordset)

    On Error GoTo ErrHandler

    Dim recItem As ADODB.Recordset
    Dim objItem As SalesOrderItem
    Dim intItemIndex As Integer

    If Not (OrderRS.BOF And OrderRS.EOF) Then

        With OrderRS
            mlngID = .Fields("OrderID").Value
            CustomerID = .Fields("CustomerID").Value
            mdtmDate = .Fields("OrderDate").Value
            Set recItem = .Fields("recItems").Value
        End With

      ' Clear the Items collection
        For intItemIndex = 1 To mcolItems.Count
            mcolItems.Remove 1
        Next

        With recItem
            While Not .EOF
                Set objItem = New SalesOrderItem
                objItem.ProductID = .Fields("ProductID").Value
                objItem.Quantity = .Fields("Quantity")
                mcolItems.Add objItem
                .MoveNext
            Wend
        End With

    Else

        mlngID = 0
        Customer.Clear
        mdtmDate = Now

        For intItemIndex = 1 To mcolItems.Count
            mcolItems.Remove 1
        Next

    End If

    RaiseEvent Changed

FuncExit:

    Exit Sub
```

Case Study

```
ErrHandler:

  Err.Raise mcstrObjectError + 11, mcstrClassName, Err.Description
  Resume FuncExit

End Sub
```

```
Public Property Let CustomerID(Value As String)

  mobjCustomer.Read Value

End Property
```

In this class, we are using the data-shaping feature of ADO to retrieve a sales order record and all its item records. I won't go into the details of data shaping here. If you are not familiar with it, you can read the ADO documentation on the MSDN CD shipped with Visual Basic or Visual Studio.

> *Alternatively, you can pick up a copy of ADO 2.0 Programmer's Reference from Wrox for a detailed explanation of this subject.*

We'll see how we create a shaped recordset in the Data-Centric `SalesOrderN` class in a moment. The code in the `Populate` method demonstrates how we extract data out of a shaped recordset.

We can get the order ID, date and customer ID as we do normally with a non-shaped recordset. The line:

```
CustomerID = .Fields("CustomerID").Value
```

invokes the `Property Let CustomerID` routine, which calls the `Read` method of the `mobjCustomer` object to populate it.

The `OrderRS` recordset is a shaped recordset that embeds a child recordset containing all items associated with the order. It is stored in the `recItems` field. To access it, we define an ADO recordset and assign a reference to this field.

```
Dim recItem As ADODB.Recordset

With OrderRS
' Other code

  Set recItem = .Fields("recItems").Value
End With
```

We can then go through each record in this recordset and create a list of `SalesOrderItem` objects from it:

```
Dim objItem As SalesOrderItem

With recItem
   While Not .EOF
     Set objItem = New SalesOrderItem
     objItem.ProductID = .Fields("ProductID").Value
     objItem.Quantity = .Fields("Quantity")
     mcolItems.Add objItem
     .MoveNext
   Wend
End With
```

We will see the `SalesOrderItem` class in a moment, but its usage here should be easy to guess: we can assign the product ID and order quantity to its `ProductID` and `Quantity` properties.

If the `OrderRS` is empty (that is, there is no sales order record with the given ID in the database) the `Populate` method will clear the contents of the data members.

Once we have populated the object, we raise the `Changed` event to notify the client objects.

Saving Sales Orders to the Database

The `Save` method saves a new sales order and its items to the database. Again, we'll use a `PropertyBag` object to serialize the order data and send the resulting byte array to the Data-Centric `SalesOrderT` object, which will add the record to the database:

```
Public Sub Save()

  On Error GoTo ErrHandler

  Dim strOrderData As String

  strOrderData = Serialize
  mlngID = mobjSalesOrderT.Save(strOrderData)

' Update object properties
  Read ID

FuncExit:

  Exit Sub

ErrHandler:

  Err.Raise mcstrObjectError + 2, mcstrClassName, Err.Description
  Resume FuncExit

End Sub
```

The `Save` method serializes its data, sends it to `mobjSalesOrderT`, and assigns the returned new order ID to its `mlngID` data member. The `Serialize` method is more complicated, as it needs to serialize not only the order header data, but all items as well.

```
Private Function Serialize() As String

  On Error GoTo ErrHandler

  Dim PropBag As PropertyBag
  Dim intItemIndex As Integer
  Dim objOrderItem As SalesOrderItem

  Set PropBag = New PropertyBag

  With PropBag
    .WriteProperty "CustomerID", Customer.ID
    .WriteProperty "ItemCount", mcolItems.Count

    For intItemIndex = 1 To mcolItems.Count
        Set objOrderItem = mcolItems.Item(intItemIndex)
        .WriteProperty "Item" & CStr(intItemIndex), objOrderItem.Serialize
    Next
```

```
        Serialize = .Contents
    End With

FuncExit:

  On Error Resume Next

  If Not PropBag Is Nothing Then
     Set PropBag = Nothing
  End If

  Exit Function

ErrHandler:

  Err.Raise mcstrObjectError + 12, mcstrClassName, Err.Description
  Resume FuncExit

End Function
```

The trick is that it does not actually serialize the items itself - it delegates this responsibility to the SalesOrderItem objects. Each SalesOrderItem object in the mcolItems collection will serialize itself and return the resulting byte array to the SalesOrder's Serialize method. The latter then adds the serialized item data to the PropertyBag.

The Data-Centric SalesOrderT class follows this process. It extracts the serialized item data and asks the SalesOrderItemT class to deserialize the data.

Adding and Deleting Sales Orders

We will allow the client objects of our SalesOrder class to delete an order, therefore we need to provide a Delete method:

```
Public Sub Delete()

  On Error GoTo ErrHandler

  mobjSalesOrderT.Delete ID
  Read 0

FuncExit:

  Exit Sub

ErrHandler:

  Err.Raise mcstrObjectError + 3, mcstrClassName, Err.Description
  Resume FuncExit

End Sub
```

It invokes the Delete method of the mobjSalesOrderT object, and calls the Read method with a parameter value zero to clear the data members.

The last method in the SalesOrder class is the AddItem method. Since we will allow the client objects to add items to a new sales order, we need to add the new items to the mcolItems collection.

```
Public Sub AddItem(ProductID As Long, Quantity As Integer)

  On Error GoTo ErrHandler

  Dim objOrderItem As SalesOrderItem
  Set objOrderItem = New SalesOrderItem

  With objOrderItem
    .ProductID = ProductID
    .Quantity = Quantity
  End With

  mcolItems.Add objOrderItem
  RaiseEvent Changed

FuncExit:

  Set objOrderItem = Nothing
  Exit Sub

ErrHandler:

  Err.Raise mcstrObjectError + 4, mcstrClassName, Err.Description
  Resume FuncExit

End Sub
```

When this method is called, it creates a new `SalesOrderItem` object, populates it, and adds it to the `mcolItems` collection. It then raises the `Changed` event to notify its client objects, and releases the reference to the new item.

Finally, we come to the `Initialize` and `Terminate` events:

```
Private Sub Class_Initialize()

  On Error GoTo ErrHandler

  Set mobjSalesOrderN = CreateObject("DCSalesOrder.SalesOrderN")
  Set mobjSalesOrderT = CreateObject("DCSalesOrder.SalesOrderT")
  Set mcolItems = New Collection
  Set mobjCustomer = New UCObjects.Customer

FuncExit:

  Exit Sub

ErrHandler:

  Err.Raise mcstrObjectError, mcstrClassName, Err.Description
  Resume FuncExit

End Sub

Private Sub Class_Terminate()

  On Error Resume Next

  Set mobjSalesOrderN = Nothing
  Set mobjSalesOrderT = Nothing
  Set mcolItems = Nothing
  Set mobjCustomer = Nothing

End Sub
```

Case Study

The `Initialize` event handling code is standard: it gets references to the Data-Centric `SalesOrder` objects, and creates a new `Customer` object and a new collection for storing the sales item data. The `Terminate` event does the reverse: it releases the references and destroys the `mobjCustomer` and `mcolItems` objects.

The SalesOrderItem Class

Now we'll look at the `SalesOrderItem` class:

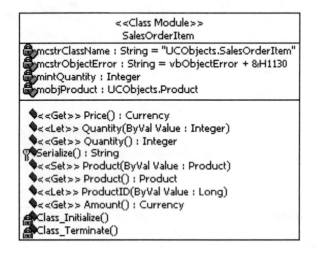

```
                    <<Class Module>>
                     SalesOrderItem
  mcstrClassName : String = "UCObjects.SalesOrderItem"
  mcstrObjectError : String = vbObjectError + &H1130
  mintQuantity : Integer
  mobjProduct : UCObjects.Product

    <<Get>> Price() : Currency
    <<Let>> Quantity(ByVal Value : Integer)
    <<Get>> Quantity() : Integer
  Serialize() : String
    <<Set>> Product(ByVal Value : Product)
    <<Get>> Product() : Product
    <<Let>> ProductID(ByVal Value : Long)
    <<Get>> Amount() : Currency
  Class_Initialize()
  Class_Terminate()
```

From the class diagram for all business objects, we know that each `SalesOrderItem` object has data member `mobjProduct` that stores a reference to a `Product` object. (This member is not shown here, since it is illustrated with the relationship between the `SalesOrderItem` and `Product` classes.)

To keep our application simple, we assume the business rule that we must always use the price set for each product. The user cannot change the product price when entering orders, so there is no need to create a data member for storing the price. The user can select a product and enter the order quantity.

Add another class module to `UCObjects` and name it `SalesOrderItem`:

```
Option Explicit

Private Const mcstrClassName As String = "UCObjects.SalesOrderItem"
Private Const mcstrObjectError As String = vbObjectError + &H1130

Private mintQuantity As Integer
Private mobjProduct As Product

Public Property Let ProductID(ByVal Value As Long)

  mobjProduct.Read Value

End Property
```

```
'Retrieve the price of an item.
Public Property Get Price() As Currency

   Let Price = Product.Price

End Property

'Assign the order quantity for an item.
Public Property Let Quantity(ByVal Value As Integer)

   Let mintQuantity = Value

End Property

'Retrieve quantity ordered for a product.
Public Property Get Quantity() As Integer

   Let Quantity = mintQuantity

End Property

Public Property Get Amount() As Currency

   Let Amount = Price * Quantity

End Property

Public Property Get Product() As Product

   Set Product = mobjProduct

End Property

Public Property Set Product(ByVal Value As Product)

   Set mobjProduct = Value

End Property

Friend Function Serialize() As String

   On Error GoTo ErrHandler

   Dim PropBag As PropertyBag
   Set PropBag = New PropertyBag

   With PropBag
     .WriteProperty "ProductID", Product.ID
     .WriteProperty "Price", Price
     .WriteProperty "Quantity", Quantity
     Serialize = .Contents
   End With

FuncExit:

   On Error Resume Next

   If Not PropBag Is Nothing Then
      Set PropBag = Nothing
   End If

   Exit Function
```

```
ErrHandler:

    Err.Raise mcstrObjectError + 11, mcstrClassName, Err.Description
    Resume FuncExit

End Function
```

```
Private Sub Class_Initialize()

    Set mobjProduct = New Product

End Sub
```

```
Private Sub Class_Terminate()

    On Error Resume Next
    Set mobjProduct = Nothing

End Sub
```

Since the user can select a product when entering an item, we define a pair of `Get/Set Product` properties to allow the client objects to read and write to the `mobjProduct` object. In addition, we also define a `Property Let ProductID` that will populate the `mobjProduct` object. The client object can simply pass a product ID to us rather than having to create a `Product` object.

We enforce the business rule of not allowing changes to product price by defining a read-only `Price` property that always returns the price of the `mobjProduct` object. The `Quantity` property is read-and-write, so the user can specify the order quantity. The `Amount` property returns the sub-amount of the item. At the moment, it only returns the product of `Price` and `Quantity`, but we could easily embed some business rule (such as a sales tax rule) here.

Recall that the `SalesOrder` class delegates the task of serializing order items to the `SalesOrderItem` class. Our `Serialize` method looks after this job. It packs three properties, `ProductID`, `Price` and `Quantity`, into a PropertyBag object and returns the serialized byte array, mapped as a string.

Finally, the `Class_Initialize` and `Class_Terminate` event handlers respectively create and destroy the `mobjProduct` object.

The Data-Centric Sales Order Classes

According to the business object class diagram, we will develop three Data-Centric sales order classes: `SalesOrderN`, `SalesOrderT` and `SalesOrderItemT`.

The SalesOrderN Class

The first class we'll create is the `SalesOrderN` class:

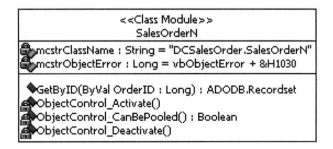

Create a new ActiveX DLL project and name it `DCSalesOrder`. We will need to add references to the **Microsoft Transaction Server Type Library** and **Microsoft ActiveX Data Object Library**, and give the project a meaningful name such as **VBMTSCS Sales Order Data Components**. Don't forget to check the **Remote Server Files** option.

Change the name of the class module to `SalesOrderN` and set its **Instancing** property to **5 – MultiUse**. `SalesOrderN` will be hosted in MTS, although it does not need to run in a transaction. Therefore, we should also set its **MTSTransactionMode** to **3 – UsesTransaction** so it can run with or without a transaction.

Enter the following code into the class:

```
Option Explicit

Implements ObjectControl

Private Const mcstrClassName As String = "DCSalesOrder.SalesOrderN"
Private Const mcstrObjectError As Long = vbObjectError + &H1030

Private mobjContext As ObjectContext

Private Sub ObjectControl_Activate()

  On Error GoTo ErrHandler
  Set mobjContext = GetObjectContext

FuncExit:

  Exit Sub

ErrHandler:
```

```
        Err.Raise mcstrObjectError, mcstrClassName, Err.Description
        Resume FuncExit

End Sub

Private Function ObjectControl_CanBePooled() As Boolean

    On Error Resume Next
    ObjectControl_CanBePooled = False

End Function

Private Sub ObjectControl_Deactivate()

    On Error Resume Next
    Set mobjContext = Nothing

End Sub
```

This should be very familiar now – after we've developed a few MTS components, we find that there's a pattern for writing them. We always implement the MTS Object Control interface and define a pair of constants to specify the class name and error number offset.

Shaped ADO Recordsets

The `GetByID` method is where the action is, as far as we are concerned:

```
Public Function GetByID(ByVal OrderID As Long) As ADODB.Recordset

    On Error GoTo ErrHandler

    Dim cnSO As ADODB.Connection
    Dim recSO As ADODB.Recordset
    Dim strSQLQuery As String

    strSQLQuery = "SHAPE " & _
              "{" & _
              "    SELECT OrderID, CustomerID, OrderDate " & _
              "    FROM Orders WHERE OrderID = " & OrderID & _
              "} " & _
              "APPEND " & _
              "(" & _
              "   {" & _
              "       SELECT OrderID, ProductID, UnitPrice, Quantity " & _
              "       FROM [Order Details]" & _
              "   } " & _
              "   \ AS rsItems " & _
              "   RELATE OrderID TO OrderID" & _
              ")"

    Set cnSO = New ADODB.Connection

    With cnSO
        .CursorLocation = adUseClient
        .Open ShapedConnString
    End With
```

```
      Set recSO = cnSO.Execute(strSQLQuery)
      Set recSO.ActiveConnection = Nothing
      cnSO.Close
      Set GetByID = recSO

      mobjContext.SetComplete

FuncExit:

   On Error Resume Next

   If Not recSO Is Nothing Then
      Set recSO = Nothing
   End If

   Exit Function

ErrHandler:

   If Not recSO Is Nothing Then
      If recSO.State = adStateOpen Then
         recSO.Close
      End If
      Set recSO = Nothing
   End If

   Err.Raise mcstrObjectError + 1, mcstrClassName, Err.Description
   mobjContext.SetAbort
   Resume FuncExit

End Function
```

We've promised that this method will return a shaped ADO recordset that contains an order and its items. To achieve this, we need to do two things that differ from what we've done with non-shaped ADO recordsets.

First, we need to build a shaped command where we usually give SQL statements. The ADO shaped command has the following syntax:

```
SHAPE
{
    SQL Statements for retrieving parent records
}
APPEND
(
    {
        SQL Statement for retrieving child records
    }
    AS      ChildRecordsetName
    RELATE ParentColumnName TO ChildColumnName
)
```

Note that this is not the formal shape command grammar and it does not cover all options – you should read the ADO documentation for that. However, this simplified syntax is adequate for our `SalesOrderN` *class.*

The SQL statement for retrieving the parent record is:

```
SELECT OrderID, CustomerUD, OrderDate
FROM    Orders
WHERE   OrderID = AnOrderID
```

The SQL statement for retrieving the child records is:

```
SELECT OrderID, ProductID, UnitPrice, Quantity
FROM    [Order Details]
WHERE   OrderID = AnOrderID
```

We can plug the parent SQL statement straight into the SHAPE command. The child SQL statement needs a little modification. We no longer need the WHERE clause to filter the records – the RELATE ... TO... option filters the records according to the retrieved parent records. The OrderID column in the Order Details table is a foreign key linked to the OrderID field in the Orders table. Therefore, we insert these field names into the RELATE ... TO ... part of the shaped command. The completed shape command is:

```
SHAPE
{
    SELECT OrderID, CustomerID, OrderDate
    FROM    Orders
    WHERE OrderID = AnOrderID
}
APPEND
(
    {
        SELECT OrderID, ProductID, UnitPrice, Quantity
        FROM    [Order Details]
    }
    AS rsItems
    RELATE OrderID TO OrderID
)
```

To put this into the context of the GetByID method, we build the following shaped command string:

```
strSQLQuery = "SHAPE " & _
        "{" & _
        "    SELECT OrderID, CustomerID, OrderDate " & _
        "    FROM Orders WHERE OrderID = " & OrderID & _
        "} " & _
        "APPEND " & _
        "( " & _
        "    { " & _
        "        SELECT OrderID, ProductID, UnitPrice, Quantity " & _
        "        FROM [Order Details]" & _
        "    } " & _
        "    AS recItems " & _
        "    RELATE OrderID TO OrderID" & _
        ")"
```

Next, we need to specify a different data provider, as the normal OLE DB Provider for SQL Server (SQLOLEDB) does not understand the ADO shaped command. We need to use the MSDataShape provider, which parses ADO shaped commands and generates SQL statements that normal OLE DB Providers do understand. It then uses the specified OLE DB Provider to query the database. This separation of functionality means that we can use the ADO data shaping with any OLE DB compliant database drivers.

The connection string with data shaping for our SalesOrderN class is:

```
Provider=MSDataShape; Data Provider=SQLOLEDB;
Data Source=<SQLServerName>;
User ID=sa; Password=; Initial Catalog=Northwind"
```

Compare this to a normal connection string

```
Provider=SQLOLEDB; Data Source=<SQLServerName>;
User ID=sa; Password=; Initial Catalog=Northwind"
```

The only difference is that we now specify MSDataShape as the Provider and SQLOLEDB as the Data Provider which provides database access.

Remember, we saved the name of the SQL Server in the registry? We need to provide a routine that will read the registry and build the connection string for us, just like the ConnString function in the Common module.

Add the Common module created with the DCCustomer project into this project and enter the following code for building the connection string for data shaping:

```
Public Function ShapedConnString() As String

    ShapedConnString = "Provider=MSDataShape; " & _
                    "Data Provider=SQLOLEDB; " & _
                    "Data Source=" & _
                    GetSetting("VBMTSCS", "Data", "Source") & _
                    "; User ID=sa; Password=; Initial Catalog=Northwind"

End Function
```

Apart from these two differences, our GetByID method is identical to the GetByID methods in other Data-Centric classes.

The SalesOrderT and SalesOrderItemsT Classes

The other two Data-Centric sales order classes are the `SalesOrderT` and `SalesOrderItemT` classes:

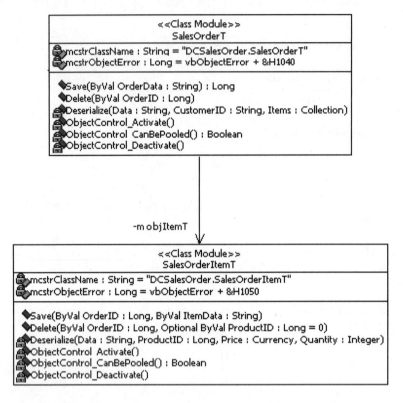

Add two class modules to the `DCSalesOrder` project and name them `SalesOrderT` and `SalesOrderItemT`. We should set their Instancing property to 5 –MultiUse and their MTSTransactionMode to 2 – RequiresTransaction.

Now enter the following code into the `SalesOrderT` class:

```
Option Explicit

Implements ObjectControl

Private Const mcstrClassName As String = "DCSalesOrder.SalesOrderT"
Private Const mcstrObjectError As Long = vbObjectError + &H1040

Private mobjContext As ObjectContext
Private mobjItemT As DCSalesOrder.SalesOrderItemT
```

```
Private Sub ObjectControl_Activate()

  On Error GoTo ErrHandler

  Set mobjContext = GetObjectContext
  Set mobjItemT = mobjContext.CreateInstance("DCSalesOrder.SalesOrderItemT")

FuncExit:

  Exit Sub

ErrHandler:

  Err.Raise mcstrObjectError, mcstrClassName, Err.Description
  Resume FuncExit

End Sub

Private Function ObjectControl_CanBePooled() As Boolean

  On Error Resume Next
  ObjectControl_CanBePooled = False

End Function

Private Sub ObjectControl_Deactivate()

  On Error Resume Next
  Set mobjItemT = Nothing
  Set mobjContext = Nothing

End Sub
```

It is common for MTS components to create other MTS objects – here we use the MTS Object Context's `CreateInstance` method. The conventional Visual Basic or COM `CreateObject` creates an instance of the child MTS component in a separate context, so it does not deliver what we need here. Instead, by creating child MTS objects using the `CreateInstance` method, the child objects are run as a part of the parent object's transaction. Either the parent or the child object can call the object context's `SetAbort` method to abort the whole transaction. We will see how the parent and child objects work together in a transaction in a moment.

Enter this into the `SalesOrderItemT` class:

```
Option Explicit

Implements ObjectControl

Private Const mcstrClassName As String = "DCSalesOrder.SalesOrderItemT"
Private Const mcstrObjectError As Long = vbObjectError + &H1050

Private mobjContext As ObjectContext

Private Sub ObjectControl_Activate()

  On Error GoTo ErrHandler
  Set mobjContext = GetObjectContext

FuncExit:

  Exit Sub
```

```
ErrHandler:

    Err.Raise mcstrObjectError, mcstrClassName, Err.Description
    Resume FuncExit

End Sub
```

```
Private Function ObjectControl_CanBePooled() As Boolean

    On Error Resume Next
    ObjectControl_CanBePooled = False

End Function
```

```
Private Sub ObjectControl_Deactivate()

    On Error Resume Next
    Set mobjContext = Nothing

End Sub
```

This code is all standard, so I won't explain it further. Let's move on to the Save operation.

Saving Data Using SQL Stored Procedures

First, enter the Save and Deserialize functions into the SalesOrderT class:

```
Public Function Save(ByVal OrderData As String) As Long

    On Error GoTo ErrHandler

    Dim cnSO As ADODB.Connection
    Dim cmSO As ADODB.Command
    Dim strSQLQuery As String
    Dim lngOrderID As Long
    Dim strCustomerID As String
    Dim colItems As Collection
    Dim intItemIndex As Integer
    Dim strItemData As String

    Set colItems = New Collection
    Deserialize OrderData, strCustomerID, colItems

' Create header
    Set cnSO = New ADODB.Connection
    cnSO.Open ConnString

    Set cmSO = New ADODB.Command
      With cmSO
        Set .ActiveConnection = cnSO
        .CommandType = adCmdStoredProc
        .CommandText = "spAddOrder"
        .Parameters.Append .CreateParameter("OrderID", adInteger, _
                                    adParamReturnValue, 4)
        .Parameters.Append .CreateParameter("CustomerID", adChar, adParamInput, _
                                    5, strCustomerID)
        .Execute
    End With

    lngOrderID = cmSO("OrderID").Value
```

```
' Create lines
For intItemIndex = 1 To colItems.Count
    strItemData = colItems.Item(intItemIndex)
    mobjItemT.Save lngOrderID, strItemData
Next

Save = lngOrderID
mobjContext.SetComplete

FuncExit:

On Error Resume Next
Set colItems = Nothing
Set cmSO = Nothing
cnSO.Close
Exit Function

ErrHandler:

Err.Raise mcstrObjectError + 2, mcstrClassName, Err.Description
mobjContext.SetAbort
Resume FuncExit

End Function
```

```
Private Sub Deserialize(Data As String, CustomerID As String, Items As Collection)

On Error GoTo ErrHandler

Dim PropBag As PropertyBag
Dim ByteArr() As Byte
Dim intItemCount As Integer
Dim intItemIndex As Integer

ByteArr = Data
Set PropBag = New PropertyBag

With PropBag
  .Contents = ByteArr
  CustomerID = .ReadProperty("CustomerID")
  intItemCount = .ReadProperty("ItemCount")

  For intItemIndex = 1 To intItemCount
    Items.Add .ReadProperty("Item" & CStr(intItemIndex))
  Next

End With

FuncExit:

Set PropBag = Nothing
Exit Sub

ErrHandler:

Err.Raise mcstrObjectError + 11, mcstrClassName, Err.Description
mobjContext.SetAbort
Resume FuncExit

End Sub
```

The `Save` method creates a new collection and passes it, along with other order data variables, to the `Deserialize` method. The `Deserialize` method unpacks the byte array passed in from the client object. It first assigns the `CustomerID` variable with a property `CustomerID` in the PropertyBag. It then finds out the number of order items in this order and populates the `Items` collection with the order item data.

Remember that the data for each order item is itself a serialized byte array. We simply add this byte array to the collection. They will later be further deserialized by the `SalesOrderItemT` class.

When the `Deserialize` method returns, the `CustomerID` variable stores the customer ID of the order. This is all we need to add an order record to the database. We could have used the same technique as in the `Save` method in the `CustomerT` class, where we simply call a SQL `INSERT` query. However, things are a little more complicated here. When a new order record is added to the database, it will be assigned a unique `OrderID`. This ID must be sent to the database when we save the items for this order. There are several methods of obtaining the ID of our newly created sales order. One of them is using a combination of a SQL Server stored procedure and an ADO Command object to pull the ID out of the database.

The stored procedure looks like this:

```
CREATE PROCEDURE spAddOrder
(
    @CustomerID char(5)
)
AS

    INSERT INTO Orders (CustomerID, OrderDate)
    VALUES         (@CustomerID, GetDate())
    RETURN         @@IDENTITY
```

The name of this stored procedure is `spAddOrder`. It takes one parameter, `CustomerID`, which is a string of 5 characters. By convention, parameter names are prefixed with an @ symbol.

The keyword `AS` starts the body of the stored procedure. First, we execute a SQL `INSERT` query to save the order record. The `GetDate` function is a function built into the SQL Server to get the current date and time – it's handy when you want to time-stamp a record. After the `INSERT` query is executed, we use the SQL Server variable `@@IDENTITY` to retrieve the ID of the new order and return it. We will see how this can be picked up in an ADO command shortly.

To create a stored procedure in SQL Server, fire up the SQL Server Enterprise Manager and expand the SQL Server tree until you find the `Northwind` database. Under the `Northwind` database, there is a Stored Procedure node – you can click on it to see a list of existing stored procedures. You can then double-click any stored procedure to open it in an editor.

Now we want to add a stored procedure, so right click the Stored Procedures node and select New Stored Procedure. When the stored procedure editor comes up, enter the code for `spAddOrder` that we've just discussed. You can click the Check Syntax button to check whether there are any syntax errors. When you're done, click the OK button to save it.

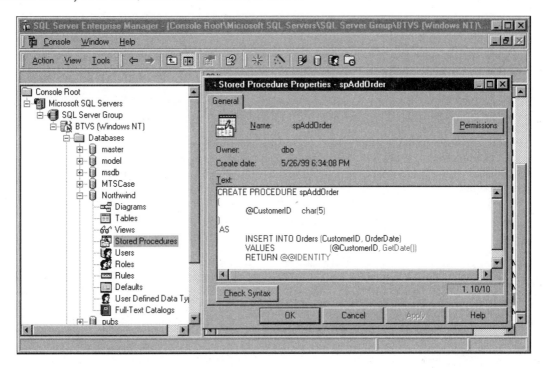

Now we have the stored procedure, we can use the ADO command object to interact with it. Here are the relevant code fragments, extracted from the `SalesOrderT.Save` method:

```
Dim cnSO As ADODB.Connection
Dim cmSO As ADODB.Command
...
Dim lngOrderID As Long
..
Set cnSO = New ADODB.Connection
cnSO.Open ConnString

Set cmSO = New ADODB.Command
With cmSO
   Set .ActiveConnection = cnSO
   .CommandType = adCmdStoredProc
   .CommandText = "spAddOrder"
   .Parameters.Append .CreateParameter("OrderID", adInteger, _
                                       adParamReturnValue, 4)
   .Parameters.Append .CreateParameter("CustomerID", adChar, adParamInput, _
                                  5, strCustomerID)
   .Execute
End With
lngOrderID = cmSO("OrderID").Value
```

Case Study

First, we need to open a connection using the ADO `Connection` object's `Open` method. Then we create a new ADO `Command` object, `cmSO`, and attach it to the connection. Its `CommandType` property should be set to `adCmdStoredProc` to indicate that we'll be using a stored procedure. The `CommandText` property specifies the name of the stored procedure.

The stored procedure `spAddOrder` accepts a customer ID and returns the Order ID.

```
CREATE PROCEDURE spAddOrder
(
    @CustomerID char(5)
)
AS
  ...
    RETURN @@IDENTITY
```

The ADO Command object records both parameters and returns values in its `Parameters` collection. We will refer them both as parameters. We can create a parameter using the ADO Command object's `CreateParameter` method, which has the following syntax:

```
CreateParameter(ParameterName, ParameterDataType, ParameterType,
                ParameterDataSize, [OptionalParameterValue])
```

For an input parameter, such as customer ID, we set `ParameterType` to `adParamInput` and provide its value as the `OptionalParameterValue`. For a return value, such as order ID, we need to set its `ParameterType` to `adParamReturnValue`. We don't need to assign it a value, as it will be filled with the return value from the stored procedure. The `CreateParameter` method returns a `Parameter` object which should be added into the ADO Command object's `Parameters` collection.

```
Dim Param As ADODB.Parameter
Set Param = CreateParameter("CustomerID", adChar, _
                            adParamInput, 5, strCustomerID)
cmSO.Parameters.Append Param
```

Once we have specified all the information required by the ADO command object, we call its `Execute` method to run it. When it is returned, the order ID can be accessed with the following statement:

```
OrderID = cmSO("OrderID").Value
```

Where `OrderID` is the name of the return-value parameter.

Well, we're ready to save the items in this order. Note that the transaction will not complete until all items are saved. If there's an error when saving the items, the whole transaction will be rolled back, which means that the order record will not be actually saved after all:

```
For intItemIndex = 1 To Items.Count
   strItemData = Items.Item(intItemIndex)
   mobjItemT.Save lngOrderID, strItemData
Next
```

The Save method will then go through each item in the Items collection and ask the Save method of the SalesOrderItemT class to save them. It passes the order ID and a byte array containing serialized data for an item. Let's see how the Save method is implemented in the SalesOrderItemT class:

```
Public Sub Save(ByVal OrderID As Long, ByVal ItemData As String)

    On Error GoTo ErrHandler

    Dim lngProductID As Long
    Dim curPrice As Currency
    Dim intQuantity As Integer
    Dim cnSO As ADODB.Connection
    Dim strSQLQuery As String

    Deserialize ItemData, lngProductID, curPrice, intQuantity
    strSQLQuery = "INSERT INTO [Order Details] " & _
                "(OrderID, ProductID, UnitPrice, Quantity) " & _
                "VALUES " & _
                "(" & CStr(OrderID) & ", " & CStr(lngProductID) & ", " & _
                CStr(curPrice) & ", " & CStr(intQuantity) & ")"

    Set cnSO = New ADODB.Connection

    With cnSO
        .Open ConnString
        .Execute strSQLQuery, , adExecuteNoRecords
        .Close
    End With

    mobjContext.SetComplete

FuncExit:

    Exit Sub

ErrHandler:

    Err.Raise mcstrObjectError + 1, mcstrClassName, Err.Description
    mobjContext.SetAbort
    Resume FuncExit

End Sub
```

```
Private Sub Deserialize(Data As String, ProductID As Long, _
                    Price As Currency, Quantity As Integer)

    On Error GoTo ErrHandler

    Dim PropBag As PropertyBag
    Dim ByteArr() As Byte

    ByteArr = Data
    Set PropBag = New PropertyBag

    With PropBag
        .Contents = ByteArr
        ProductID = .ReadProperty("ProductID")
        Price = .ReadProperty("Price")
        Quantity = .ReadProperty("Quantity")
    End With
```

```
      FuncExit:

        Set PropBag = Nothing
        Exit Sub

      ErrHandler:

        Err.Raise mcstrObjectError + 11, mcstrClassName, Err.Description
        mobjContext.SetAbort
        Resume FuncExit

      End Sub
```

Perhaps not surprisingly, the Save method in this class is actually quite simple. It calls the Deserialize method to unpack the item data and executes a SQL INSERT query to save the record. It then calls the SetComplete method to finish off.

But should it call the SetComplete method? Does that contradict with our No. 2 rule of thumb that states:

❏   Call SetComplete only after all actions in a transaction are completed

Yes it surely does, but it is required. That rule applies to transactions that don't span across different MTS components. For transactions that do, it turns out that each participating object should call SetComplete as soon as it's completed its task successfully. It's like a voting scheme – MTS will only commit the whole transaction when all participating components vote for it. If any one of them votes against committing the transaction, the transaction will not be committed.

We should really update our rules of thumb:

❏   Call SetAbort as soon as possible
❏   Call SetComplete in each participating object when it has completed its part of the transaction
❏   Never call SetComplete in private methods

That's about it for the Save method. After all items are saved, the Save method in SalesOrderT calls its own SetComplete and MTS will happily commit the transaction for us.

Deleting Data

The Delete method is the reverse of the Save method. Enter the following code to the SalesOrderT class:

```
Public Sub Delete(ByVal OrderID As Long)

    On Error GoTo ErrHandler

    Dim cnSO As ADODB.Connection
    Dim strSQLQuery As String

    mobjItemT.Delete OrderID

    strSQLQuery = "DELETE Orders WHERE OrderID = " & OrderID

    Set cnSO = New ADODB.Connection
```

```
    With cnSO
        .Open ConnString
        .Execute strSQLQuery, , adExecuteNoRecords
        .Close
    End With

    mobjContext.SetComplete

FuncExit:

    Exit Sub

ErrHandler:

    Err.Raise mcstrObjectError + 2, mcstrClassName, Err.Description
    mobjContext.SetAbort
    Resume FuncExit

End Sub
```

When we add a new order, we first save the header and then all the items, since we need to save the order ID in each item. There is another reason for this: `OrderID` in the `Order Details` table is a foreign key to an order record in the `Orders` table. That means the order record must exist before any item records can be created.

When we delete an order, we need to delete all items that belong to the order first. Otherwise, SQL Server will not allow us the delete the order, since that would break the referential integrity defined in the database.

Again, the `SalesOrderT` class delegates the task of deleting items to the `SalesOrderItemT` class by calling its `Delete` method. Enter the following code to the `SalesOrderItemT` class:

```
Public Sub Delete(ByVal OrderID As Long, Optional ByVal ProductID As Long = 0)

    On Error GoTo ErrHandler

    Dim cnSO As ADODB.Connection
    Dim strSQLQuery As String

    strSQLQuery = "DELETE [Order Details] " & _
                  "WHERE OrderID = " & OrderID

    If ProductID <> 0 Then
        strSQLQuery = strSQLQuery & " AND ProductID = " & ProductID
    End If

    Set cnSO = New ADODB.Connection

    With cnSO
        .Open ConnString
        .Execute strSQLQuery, , adExecuteNoRecords
        .Close
    End With
```

```
    mobjContext.SetComplete

FuncExit:

   Exit Sub

ErrHandler:

   Err.Raise mcstrObjectError + 2, mcstrClassName, Err.Description
   mobjContext.SetAbort
   Resume FuncExit

End Sub
```

It is designed to be capable of deleting one item or all items in an order. Since our application does not allow for editing orders, we will only delete all items with a given OrderID. A SQL DELETE query does the job just fine here. A call to SetComplete is necessary to notify MTS that the SalesOrderItemT object has performed its operation successful.

Once all items have been deleted, the Delete method in SalesOrderT deletes the order header from the Orders table using another SQL DELETE query. It then calls the SetComplete and asks MTS to commit the transaction.

That's it for the business objects. We can now turn our attention to the user interface.

The User Interface

We'll minimize the functionality of the user interface of this application, so that it won't distract us from concentrating on MTS component development. It consists of three forms: OrderEntry, OrderItemEntry, and CustomerEntry.

Create a new Visual Basic Standard EXE project and name it SimpleOrder. Add a reference to our User-Centric component, UCObjects. Change the name of Form1 to OrderEntry, and then add two more forms into the project and name them CustomerEntry and OrderItemEntry. The OrderEntry form should be the start up form of the project.

The `CustomerEntry` and `OrderEntry` forms use the User-Centric objects `Customer` and `SalesOrder`, as illustrated in the following class diagram:

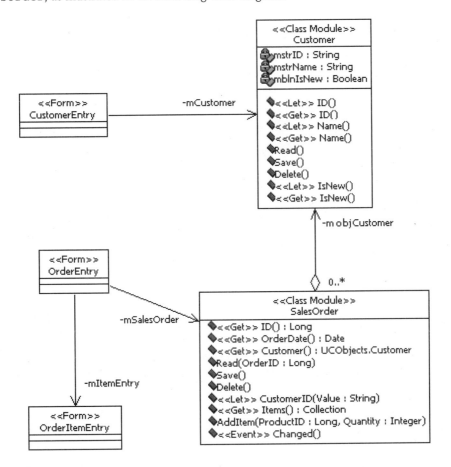

The Customer Entry Form

The user can use the Customer Entry Form to maintain customer records:

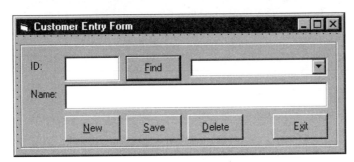

Create the form as shown in this screen shot by adding the following controls to the `CustomerEntry` form:

Case Study

Control	Name	Caption/Text
Frame	Frame1	
Label	Label1	ID:
Label	Label2	Name:
Text Box	txtID	
Text Box	txtName	
Combo Box	cboCustomer	Combo1
Command Button	cmdFind	&Find
Command Button	cmdNew	&New
Command Button	cmdSave	&Save
Command Button	cmdDelete	&Delete
Command Button	cmdExit	E&xit

This form lets the user find and display a customer's name in two ways. First, you can enter a customer ID in the text box, and click the Find button. Alternatively, you can select a name from the drop down combo box. You can then edit the customer name and click the Save button to update the record. You can also delete a customer by clicking the Delete button. To create a new customer, first click the New button to clear the text boxes. Then enter a customer ID and name and click the Save button to save it.

The CustomerEntry form code is listed below:

```
Option Explicit

Private WithEvents mobjCustomer As UCObjects.Customer

Private Sub cboCustomers_Click()

    mobjCustomer.CustomerList.AbsolutePosition = (cboCustomers.ListIndex + 1)
    txtID = mobjCustomer.CustomerList("CustomerID")
    txtName = mobjCustomer.CustomerList("CompanyName")

End Sub

Private Sub cmdDelete_Click()

  Dim lngRes As Long

  lngRes = MsgBox("Are you sure you want to delete " & txtName & _
                "?", vbYesNo + vbQuestion)
```

```
        If vbYes Then
          With mobjCustomer
              .ID = UCase(txtID.Text)
              .Delete
          End With
          cboCustomers.Text = ""
          LoadCombo True
        End If

End Sub

Private Sub cmdExit_Click()

    Unload Me

End Sub

Private Sub cmdFind_Click()

    mobjCustomer.Read UCase(txtID.Text)
    PopulateControls

End Sub

Private Sub cmdNew_Click()

    mobjCustomer.IsNew = True
    cboCustomers.Text = ""

End Sub

Private Sub cmdSave_Click()

    Dim strTempName As String
    Dim strTempID As String

    With mobjCustomer
      .ID = UCase(txtID.Text)
      .Name = txtName.Text
      .Save
      strTempName = .Name
      strTempID = .ID
    End With

    LoadCombo True
    cboCustomers.Text = strTempName
    txtName = strTempName
    txtID = strTempID

    MsgBox "Customer saved.", vbInformation

End Sub

Private Sub Form_Load()

    'Set mobjCustomer = New UCObjects.Customer

    LoadCombo False

End Sub
```

```
Private Sub Form_QueryUnload(Cancel As Integer, UnloadMode As Integer)

    Set mobjCustomer = Nothing

End Sub

Private Sub PopulateControls()

    txtID.Text = mobjCustomer.ID
    txtName.Text = mobjCustomer.Name

End Sub

Private Sub mobjCustomer_Changed()

    PopulateControls

End Sub

Private Sub LoadCombo(Refresh As Boolean)

    Dim intCounter As Integer

    If Refresh Then
        cboCustomers.Clear
        Set mobjCustomer.CustomerList = Nothing
    End If

    mobjCustomer.Read
    mobjCustomer.CustomerList.MoveFirst

    For intCounter = 1 To mobjCustomer.CustomerList.RecordCount

        cboCustomers.AddItem mobjCustomer.CustomerList("CompanyName")
        mobjCustomer.CustomerList.MoveNext

    Next

    cboCustomers.ListIndex = 0

End Sub
```

The `Form_Load` event handler creates an instance of the `UCObject`'s `Customer` class. `mobjCustomer` is declared as `WithEvents` so that every time the object state changes, it will invoke the `PopulateControls` method to update the form display. `LoadCombo` populates the combo box when the form is loaded, and updates it as records are added or removed.

Note that the **New** buttons `Click` event sets the `IsNew` property of the `Customer` object. If the user does not click it before creating a new customer, the customer record will not be saved.

The Order Item Entry Form

This form is used by the Order Entry form to add items to new orders:

Add the following controls and code to the `OrderItemEntry` form:

Control	Name	Caption/Text
Frame	Frame1	
Label	Label1	ID:
Label	Label2	Quantity:
Label	Label3	Name:
Label	Label4	Price:
Text Box	txtProductID	
Text Box	txtQuantity	
Text Box	lblPrice	
Combo Box	cboProducts	Combo1
Command Button	cmdOK	OK
Command Button	cmdCancel	Cancel

```
Option Explicit

Public Event Completed(ShouldAddItem As Boolean, ProductID As Long, _
                    Quantity As Integer)

Private mblnShouldAddItem As Boolean
Private mobjProducts As UCObjects.Product

Private Property Get ProductID() As Long

   ProductID = CLng(txtProductID.Text)

End Property
```

```
Private Property Get Quantity() As Integer

   Quantity = CInt(txtQuantity.Text)

End Property

Private Property Get ShouldAddItem() As Boolean

   ShouldAddItem = mblnShouldAddItem

End Property

Private Sub cmdCancel_Click()

   RaiseEvent Completed(False, ProductID, Quantity)
   Unload Me

End Sub

Private Sub cboProducts_Click()

   mobjProducts.ProductList.AbsolutePosition = (cboProducts.ListIndex + 1)
   txtProductID = mobjProducts.ProductList("ProductID")
   lblPrice = mobjProducts.ProductList("UnitPrice")

End Sub

Private Sub Form_Load()

   txtQuantity.Text = 1
   Set mobjProducts = New Product
   LoadCombo

End Sub

Private Sub Form_QueryUnload(Cancel As Integer, UnloadMode As Integer)

   Set mobjProducts = Nothing

End Sub

Private Sub cmdOK_Click()

   RaiseEvent Completed(True, ProductID, Quantity)
   Unload Me

End Sub

Private Sub LoadCombo()

   Dim intCounter As Integer

   mobjProducts.Read
   mobjProducts.ProductList.MoveFirst

   For intCounter = 1 To mobjProducts.ProductList.RecordCount
       cboProducts.AddItem mobjProducts.ProductList("ProductName")
       mobjProducts.ProductList.MoveNext
   Next

   cboProducts.ListIndex = 0

End Sub
```

When the form loads, it puts a default value of 1 into the Quantity text box. It also displays the ID and price of the first item in the product list. The user can either select a product from the combo box or directly type a product ID into the ID text box. They can also change the quantity ordered. Clicking the OK button will then get the chosen product ID and quantity values, and raise an event. The `OrderEntry` form will pick up this event and add the item to a new order.

If the user clicks the Cancel button, the event will still be raised, but with its `ShouldAddItem` parameter set to `False`.

Ideally, we should handle the possible errors a bit better. For instance, if you enter a letter into either of the two text boxes, the program will crash – not a very pleasant experience to the users. You might like to implement error handling yourself.

The Order Entry Form

This is the entry point of the project.

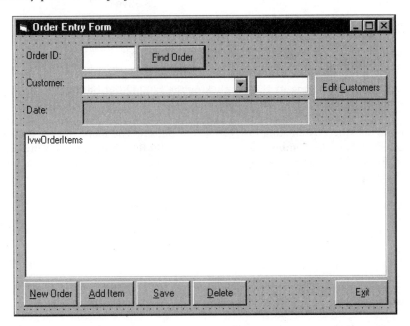

It has the following controls. You must add the Microsoft Windows Common Controls 6.0 component to your toolbox in order to use the ListView control.

Control	Name	Caption/Text
Label	Label1	OrderID:
Label	Label2	Customer:
Label	Label 3	Date:
Label	lblDate	

Table Continued on Following Page

Case Study

Control	Name	Caption/Text
Text Box	txtOrderID	
Text Box	txtCustomerID	
Combo Box	cboCustomer	Combo1
ListView	lvwOrderItems	
Command Button	cmdFind	&Find Order
Command Button	cmdEditCustomer	Edit &Customer
Command Button	cmdNew	&New Order
Command Button	cmdAddItem	&Add Item
Command Button	cmdSave	&Save
Command Button	cmdDelete	&Delete
Command Button	cmdExit	E&xit

A user can query an order by entering its ID and clicking the <u>F</u>ind Order button. Once an order is found, it can be removed by clicking the <u>D</u>elete button.

A new sales order can be added by clicking the <u>N</u>ew Order button. The name of the customer placing the order can be selected from the combo box. Clicking the <u>A</u>dd Item button then brings up the OrderItemEntry form, which can be used to add one item at a time to the order. When the order list is complete, it can be saved by clicking the <u>S</u>ave button.

Finally, a user can call up the Customer Entry form to maintain customers.

The code for the form is as follows:

```
Option Explicit

Private WithEvents mobjOrder As UCObjects.SalesOrder
Private mobjCustomer As UCObjects.Customer

Private WithEvents mfrmItemEntry As OrderItemEntry

Private Sub cmdAddItem_Click()

   mobjOrder.CustomerID = txtCustomerID.Text

   If Not mfrmItemEntry Is Nothing Then
      Set mfrmItemEntry = Nothing
   End If

   Set mfrmItemEntry = New OrderItemEntry
   mfrmItemEntry.Show vbModal

End Sub
```

```vb
Private Sub cmdDelete_Click()

   mobjOrder.Delete

End Sub

Private Sub cmdEditCustomer_Click()

   Dim CustomerEntryForm As CustomerEntry
   Set CustomerEntryForm = New CustomerEntry

   CustomerEntryForm.Show vbModal
   Set CustomerEntryForm = Nothing

   LoadCombo True

End Sub

Private Sub cmdExit_Click()

   Unload Me

End Sub

Private Sub cmdFind_Click()

   mobjOrder.Read CLng(txtOrderID.Text)
   If mobjOrder.ID = 0 Then MsgBox "No Order found for this ID", _
                             vbExclamation

End Sub

Private Sub cmdNew_Click()

   mobjOrder.Read 0
   cboCustomer.ListIndex = 0

End Sub

Private Sub cmdSave_Click()

   With mobjOrder
      .CustomerID = txtCustomerID.Text
      .Save
   End With

End Sub

Private Sub Form_Load()

   Set mobjOrder = New UCObjects.SalesOrder

   With lvwOrderItems
      .ColumnHeaders.Add Text:="Product", Width:=lvwOrderItems.Width / 2 - 240
      .ColumnHeaders.Add Text:="Price", Width:=lvwOrderItems.Width / 6
      .ColumnHeaders.Add Text:="Quantity", Width:=lvwOrderItems.Width / 6
      .ColumnHeaders.Add Text:="Amount", Width:=lvwOrderItems.Width / 6
      .View = lvwReport
   End With
```

```
      Set mobjCustomer = New UCObjects.Customer
      LoadCombo False

      cmdNew_Click

End Sub

Private Sub Form_QueryUnload(Cancel As Integer, UnloadMode As Integer)

   Set mobjOrder = Nothing
   Set mobjCustomer = Nothing

End Sub

Private Sub Populate()

   Dim objOrderItem As UCObjects.SalesOrderItem
   Dim ViewItem As ListItem

   With mobjOrder
      txtOrderID.Text = .ID
      txtCustomerID.Text = .Customer.ID
      lblDate.Caption = .OrderDate

      lvwOrderItems.ListItems.Clear

      For Each objOrderItem In .Items
         Set ViewItem = _
            lvwOrderItems.ListItems.Add(Text:=objOrderItem.Product.Name)
         ViewItem.SubItems(1) = objOrderItem.Price
         ViewItem.SubItems(2) = objOrderItem.Quantity
         ViewItem.SubItems(3) = objOrderItem.Amount
      Next

   End With

End Sub

Private Sub mfrmItemEntry_Completed(ShouldAddItem As Boolean, _
                        ProductID As Long, Quantity As Integer)

   If ShouldAddItem Then
      mobjOrder.AddItem ProductID, Quantity
   End If

End Sub

Private Sub mobjOrder_Changed()

   Populate

End Sub

Private Sub cboCustomer_Click()

   mobjCustomer.CustomerList.AbsolutePosition = (cboCustomer.ListIndex + 1)
   txtCustomerID = mobjCustomer.CustomerList("CustomerID")

End Sub
```

```
      Private Sub LoadCombo(Refresh As Boolean)

        Dim intCounter As Integer

        If Refresh Then
           cboCustomer.Clear
           Set mobjCustomer.CustomerList = Nothing
        End If

        mobjCustomer.Read
        mobjCustomer.CustomerList.MoveFirst

        For intCounter = 1 To mobjCustomer.CustomerList.RecordCount
           cboCustomer.AddItem mobjCustomer.CustomerList("CompanyName")
           mobjCustomer.CustomerList.MoveNext
        Next

        cboCustomer.ListIndex = 0

      End Sub
```

The Order Entry Form defines two private references declared as WithEvents, so that we can process the events raised in them: one to a User-Centric SalesOrder object, and another to an OrderItemEntry form. When the form loads, we instantiate the mobjOrder object and set up the ListView control to display order items.

Clicking the <u>F</u>ind Order button calls the mobjOrder.Read event to read in the order specified in the text box, and when mobjOrder is filled with the order data, it raises a Changed event. The event handler in this form simply calls the Populate method to refresh the controls. Clicking the Delete button deletes the order using the mobjOrder.Delete method. It will also raise a Changed event that clears the form display.

When the user clicks the New button, the mobjOrder.Read method is invoked to try find an order with ID 0. Since there is no such an order, it clears the mobjOrder properties and the form.

Clicking the <u>A</u>dd Item button creates a new instance of the OrderEntryForm and uses it to accept data entry. When the user enters the item data and clicks either OK or Cancel, its Completed event is fired and the new item is added to mobjOrder.

We have now gone through the creation of a simple yet functional n-tiered application. The primary use of such applications is to create an enterprise solution that can be deployed in a distributed operation environment. In the final section, we'll see how we can deploy the components of this application across machines in a network.

Component Deployment

Our `Simple Order` application is a typical 3-tiered application. The data tier is a SQL Server database that can be installed on a database server. The presentaton tier is a combination of Visual Basic forms and User-Centric business objects. It can be installed on workstations across the network. The middle-tier consists of three Data-Centric business objects that can be deployed on one or more servers running MTS. The figure below shows a possible configuration:

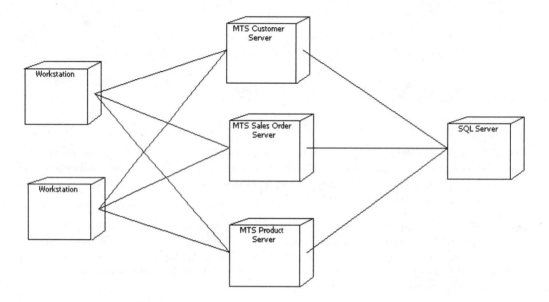

MTS Deployment

Although our components will work as standard COM servers we really ought to take advantage of the work we did to make the components compatible with MTS. Moving them to MTS should be simplicity itself for you by now. Simply place the Data-Centric components within one or more packages:

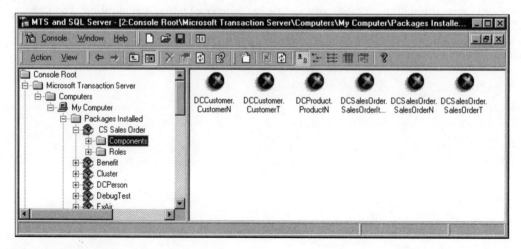

The only real issue is whether to place all three Data-Centric components on the same server or spread them across more than one machine. If you want to spread the load about you will need to install them as Remote Components.

Packaging for Deployment

One of the many methods of deploying the components is to use the Package and Deployment Wizard (PDW). First, we can use it to create setup packages for all Data-Centric components – DCCustomer, DCProduct, DCSalesOrder. Since they all use the Microsoft Transaction Server Type Library and the Microsoft ActiveX Data Objects Library, the PDW will include those libraries in the setup packages. You can normally remove the MTS Type Library from it – these components will be deployed on servers where MTS has already been installed and the MTS Type Library should be on those servers already. The ADO Library may be needed if the servers don't have Microsoft Data Access Components installed.

The next package is the UCObjects component. When you use PDW to create a setup package for UCObjects, PDW will add all the Data-Centric component DLLs, since the UCObjects project has references to them. Unless the Data-Centric components will be run on the workstations (which is very unlikely), you should remove them from the setup package, because you don't want to install the Data-Centric components on the workstations. What you want to do is to install the Data-Centric type libraries on the workstations, and use DCOM to invoke the DLLs on the MTS machines.

This seemingly difficult task is made easy by Visual Basic. Remember that we have checked the Remote Server Files option in the Project Properties form of each Data-Centric project? The Visual Basic compiler will create a remote server file (such as DCCustomer.vbr) and a type library file (such as DCCustomer.tlb) for each project when the project is compiled. These files contain the information required call the components remotely. In the PDW, you should add these files into the setup package for any components that will use them. In our application, we need to add them to the UCObjects' setup package. Don't forget to remove the DLLs – you don't want to install them on the workstations.

PWD recognizes that they're remote server files, so it will ask you to name the machines where the Data-Centric component DLL will be installed. If you know the machines when creating the setup package, enter a machine name for each VBR file. If you intend to configure the servers dynamically, leave the machine names blank.

When you install UCObjects onto a workstation, it will create registry entries that point to the machines where the Data-Centric components are installed. If you don't specify a machine name in PDW, the setup will ask you during the installation. You must enter the machine name, otherwise the UCObjects won't be able to find them.

When creating the user interface project setup package, you have two options. You can either distribute UCObjects.dll with it, or distribute them separately. If you decide to distribute them separately, you should remove UCObjects.dll from the setup package. If you decide to distribute them together, you must add the remote server files to the setup package, just like you do with UCObjects setup package. You don't need to create a setup package for the UCObjects anymore.

Summary

In this case study, we have demonstrated some of the important issues enterprise developers face when designing and implementing n-tiered distributed applications using Visual Basic.

We created an application consisting of:

❑ A Presentation tier that lets the user query and edit customer records and sales orders
❑ A User-Centric Business Objects Tier, responsible for communicating with the Data-Centric objects to provide data access capabilities to the application
❑ A Data-Centric Business Objects Tier, consisting of objects responsible for reading data from the database and updating the tables in the database
❑ A Data Tier provided by the sample SQL Server 7 database NorthWind.

Now you can go on to expand and modify this application to suit your own needs.

Microsoft Transaction Server Type Library Reference

Objects

Name	Description
ObjectContext	Provides access to the current object's context
SecurityProperty	Used to determine the current object's caller or creator

ObjectContext

Methods

Name	Returns	Description
CreateInstance	Variant	Creates an object using current object's context. This method uses a programmatic identifier in order to create the MTS object.
DisableCommit		Indicates that the object is not yet finished its work and any attempt to commit the transaction will force an abort. This method is used for objects that need to maintain state.

Table Continued on Following Page

Name	Returns	Description
EnableCommit		Indicates that the object is not yet finished its work, but would allow the transaction to commit. Using this method allows for a transaction to commit yet keep internal state to the component while additional work is being done.
IsCallerInRole	Boolean	Returns TRUE if the caller's UserID is included in the identified role.
IsInTransaction	Boolean	Returns TRUE if this object context has an active transaction. You can use this method as a safety feature to ensure that an object designed to run in a transaction actually does.
IsSecurityEnabled	Boolean	Returns TRUE if security is enabled.
SetAbort		Indicates that the object has completed its work and the transaction must be aborted.
SetComplete		Indicates that the object has completed its work and can be deactivated. If the object is part of a transaction, SetComplete indicates that the transaction should be committed.

Properties

Name	Returns	Description	Type
Count	Integer	Returns the number of named properties.	Read only
Item	Variant	Gets a named property	Read only
Security	SecurityProperty	Returns the security object	Read only

SecurityProperty

Methods

Name	Returns	Description
GetDirectCallerName	String	Returns the name of the direct caller
GetDirectCreatorName	String	Returns the name of the direct creator
GetOriginalCallerName	String	Returns the name of the original caller
GetOriginalCreatorName	String	Returns the name of the original creator

Constants

Error_Constants

Name	Value	Description
mtsErrCtxAborted	-2147164158	The transaction was aborted
mtsErrCtxAborting	-2147164157	The transaction is aborting
mtsErrCtxActivityTimeout	-2147164154	The activity timed out
mtsErrCtxNoContext	-2147164156	There is no object context
mtsErrCtxNoSecurity	-2147164147	There is no security context
mtsErrCtxNotRegistered	-2147164155	The context is not registered
mtsErrCtxOldReference	-2147164153	The context has an old reference
mtsErrCtxRoleNotFound	-2147164148	The role was not found
mtsErrCtxTMNotAvailable	-2147164145	The Transaction Monitor is not available
mtsErrCtxWrongThread	-2147164146	Execution on wrong thread

XactAttributeEnum

Name	Value	Description
adXactAbortRetaining	262144	Performs retaining aborts, so calling Rollback automatically starts a new transaction
adXactCommitRetaining	131072	Performs retaining commits, thus calling CommitTrans automatically starts a new transaction. Provider dependant.

Index

A

Index

Index

Index

Index

Index

Index

Index

wrox

PROGRAMMER TO PROGRAMMER™

Wrox writes books for you. Any suggestions, or ideas about how you want information given in your ideal book will be studied by our team. Your comments are always valued at Wrox.

Free phone in USA 800-USE-WROX
Fax (312) 397 8990

UK Tel. (0121) 687 4100   Fax (0121) 687 4101

Professional Visual Basic 6 MTS Programming - Registration Card

Name _____

Address _____

_____

_____

_____

City_____ State/Region _____

Country_____ Postcode/Zip _____

E-mail _____

Occupation _____

How did you hear about this book? _____

☐ Book review (name) _____

☐ Advertisement (name) _____

☐ Recommendation _____

☐ Catalog _____

☐ Other _____

Where did you buy this book? _____

☐ Bookstore (name)_____ City _____

☐ Computer Store (name)_____

☐ Mail Order _____

☐ Other _____

What influenced you in the
purchase of this book?

☐ Cover Design

☐ Contents

☐ Other (please specify) _____

How did you rate the overall
contents of this book?

☐ Excellent   ☐ Good

☐ Average   ☐ Poor

What did you find most useful about this book? _____

_____

What did you find least useful about this book? _____

_____

Please add any additional comments. _____

_____

What other subjects will you buy a computer
book on soon? _____

What is the best computer book you have used this year?

_____

Note: This information will only be used to keep you updated about new Wrox Press titles and will not be used for any other purpose or passed to any other third party.

wrox

PROGRAMMER TO PROGRAMMER™

NB. If you post the bounce back card below in the UK, please send it to:

Wrox Press Ltd., Arden House, 1102 Warwick Road,
Acocks Green, Birmingham B27 6BH. UK.

——— *Computer Book Publishers* ———